Specialty Gardens

Specialty Gardens

BY THEODORE JAMES, JR.
PHOTOGRAPHS BY HARRY HARALAMBOU

Stewart, Tabori & Chang
New York

Published in 1992 by
Stewart, Tabori & Chang, Inc.
575 Broadway, New York, New York 10012

Library of Congress Cataloging-in-Publication Data

James, Theodore.
    Specialty gardens / by Theodore James, Jr. :
photographs by Harry Haralambou.
        p. cm.
    Includes bibliographical references and index.
    ISBN 1-55670-190-X
    1. Gardens.   2. Gardens—Styles.
    3. Gardens—Pictorial works.
    I. Title.
    SB465.J28 1992
    712—dc20   91-33252
                                          CIP

Distributed in the U.S. by Workman Publishing,
708 Broadway,
New York, New York 10003

Distributed in Canada by Canadian Manda Group,
P.O. Box 920 Station U,
Toronto, Ontario M8Z 5P9

Distributed in all other territories by
Little, Brown and Company, International Division,
34 Beacon Street,
Boston, Massachusetts 02108

Printed in Japan
10 9 8 7 6 5 4 3 2 1

Half-title page: *Old Westbury Gardens, Westbury, New York.*

Frontispiece: *Quinta da Aveleda, northern Portugal.*

Title page: *Recently introduced Siloam Ethyl Smith is a particular favorite of Ethyl Buccola, who specializes in day lilies and has hundreds of varieties of this very popular and carefree plant in her garden in East Quogue, New York.*

Dedication page: *At Saling Hall in Essex, England, Hugh Johnson installed fuchsia lychnis and white nicotiana in the perennial border in the walled garden. The belfry of St. James church rises in the background.*

Table of Contents: *At Keukenhof Gardens, near Lisse, Holland, Jeanne d'Arc Dutch crocus are interplanted with brilliant Red Riding Hood Greigii tulips, a classic but daring combination.*

For

Christine Pappas,

with

affection

and

admiration

Contents

Introduction

There comes a time in every gardener's experience when he or she begins to specialize in one or several different types of gardens. Some turn to roses, others to alpine or rock gardens, perennial borders, water gardens, shade gardens, rhododendron or azalea gardens, dwarf conifers, or combinations thereof. Who knows what exactly will excite a gardener enough so that he or she will begin to specialize in one or another type of garden?

I recall having a long conversation a number of years ago with the late great photographer Edward Steichen and his wife, Joanna. We had all been invited to a party in honor of a friend's new book. Although I knew Steichen's work, I had never met him, but I had read somewhere that he had

taken up hybridizing delphiniums as a diversion. Rather than say something fatuous and probably superfluous about his art, I engaged him in conversation by mentioning that I knew of his interest in delphiniums. Apparently I struck the right note, for he talked of his new interest for at least half an hour. Mercifully, I knew enough about delphiniums and was sincerely interested enough in learning more to carry on an intelligent conversation with him. I recall asking him what it was about delphiniums that drove him to plant an entire acre of them. He shrugged his shoulders and said, "Well, they are very beautiful, but so are roses and other flowers. To tell you the truth, I don't really know exactly why, I just like them."

Similarly, Francis H. Cabot, whose extraordinary garden in Cold Spring, New York, is now more than thirty years old, became interested in alpine plants after he saw some in a friend's garden.

There is neither rhyme nor reason to the kinds of gardens and plants specialty gardeners select.

So then, here are scores of specialty gardens from many different parts of the world. Some are grand, some are small. Some are world famous, some are unknown. Some are ancient, and some are spanking new. Some are traditional, some are eccentric. All betray, however, a special interest in a special kind of garden. Even more than that, they all reveal the imagination, dedication, and devotion of their makers.

Perhaps one of these will interest you, then preoccupy you, and then even addict and possess you. But not to worry, for gardening is a healthy, relatively inexpensive, and rewarding pastime. And always remember, you are never closer to God than when on your knees cultivating, weeding, nurturing, and enjoying your very own garden.

—Theodore James, Jr.

ONE

Water Gardens

Water has been integral to garden design in all civilizations, serving to refresh, beautify, cool, impress, animate, and add gentle sound. It has also served both religious and philosophic pursuits and has enhanced tranquility, hedonism, recreation, and meditation. Today, whether it takes the form of a simple fish pool, a small cataract, or a grandiose pond with fountains, water continues to be a part of distinguished gardens throughout the world.

Western civilization's earliest literature contains references to water gardens. In the *Odyssey,* Homer describes a "sanctuary of nymphs" at Ithaca, where a "basin of streams gush down from rocks". Pliny describes the elaborate waterworks at his garden in Tuscany and at Tivoli. The remains of Hadrian's villa include an extensive system of streams, canals, pools, and fountains.

Although little remains of the Islamic gardens of the Middle East, it is known that the Paradise Gardens included canals that intersected a geometric garden. Pools with lotus flowers floating on the surface were also a feature. The existing Moorish gardens of Spain, particularly those at the Alhambra, reveal a preoccupation with the aesthetic use of water as do the Moorish-influenced gardens in Portugal.

Marco Polo's record of his travels includes a reference to "the Chinese gift for managing water, of making lakes with islands strung together with high semicircular bridges giving back perfect circles in reflection." The Japanese, too, have very often used water in their gardens.

Water played an integral role in garden design during the Renaissance, baroque, and rococo periods, as well as in the various garden styles which subsequently evolved: French formal, Italian romantic, and English informal. To this day, in contemporary gardens everywhere, water continues to offer its tranquil beauty to the surroundings.

The grandiose aquatechnics at Versailles, the seemingly endless waterworks at the Boboli Gardens in Italy, and the vast, parklike creations of Capability Brown in England are all impressive sights, but perhaps it is at Annevoie in Belgium that water has been used most effectively in a European garden.

Annevoie is set in the lush valley of the meandering Meuse River not far from the ancient city of Namur. The forestland of the Ardennes lies nearby. Before one enters the grounds there is little to indicate the magic that lies within, for the gardens are to the rear and side of the Louis XV château, out of view.

Towering, wrought-iron entrance gates open to the first series of fountains, and throughout the gardens can be heard the gentle gurgling, the raucous gushing, the splattering and splashing of the fountains, cascades, geysers, and waterfalls of this aquatic fantasy.

The gardens are unique, a harmonious blend of the French formal, Italian romantic, and English informal garden styles, unified by an extraordinary waterworks that remains largely true to its original plan devised in the eighteenth century by Charles-Alexis de Montpellier. The château and gardens are still owned by the family; scion Jean de Montpellier currently resides there.

The story of Annevoie's water gardens begins in 1758, after Charles-Alexis, an avid amateur gardener, had returned from travels in France and Italy with ambitious plans for his new water gardens and an addition to the château. He had seen Versailles, the formal and vast playground of the Sun King, Louis XIV, and his heirs. He had also seen the Villa d'Este at Tivoli, with its secret gardens, intimate schemes, and gushing fountains operated by gravity. And he had seen the now-defunct gardens at Marly-le-Roi, designed

Preceding pages: A gently undulating waterfall in one of the intimate water gardens at Annevoie, in Belgium, contributes to the ubiquitous sound of water.

by the Bourbons' court architect, the famed André Le Nôtre. De Montpellier sat down with his father and seven sisters and brothers and set forth his proposals, over which they concluded he had gone hopelessly mad. De Montpellier's prophetic comment was, "The next generation will be grateful." Today the gardens and château, which are open to the public, support the maintenance of the estate.

The fountain system at Tivoli inspired de Montpellier's scheme for Annevoie. First an eleven-hundred-foot-long reservoir—now called the Grand Canal—was dug at the top of the hill overlooking the château. Conduits were fashioned from oak bored with red-hot iron pokers at the family's foundry, and through them water from four nearby woodland brooks and springs was channeled into the reservoir. Then the waterworks were laid out with descending levels of fountains, cascades, grottos, and pools fed by four canals. Gravity created the pressure that caused the water to spew up from the fountains; pumps were not relied on. Unlike Versailles, where lack of pressure keeps most fountains from running at all, at Annevoie the water never stops, its rapid flow preventing it from freezing during the winter. De Montpellier's garden was the first of its kind in northern Europe and remains one of the few water gardens in the world operated by gravitational pressure.

The first garden at Annevoie is small and formal in the French manner and incorporates a series of descending fan fountains, so called because the water spout is designed to create a silver fan of water. Bordered by a 130-year-old hornbeam hedge, parterres of tulips and hyacinths bloom in spring, followed by tuberous begonias, heliotrope, and other annuals in summer.

An entrance in the hedge leads to a series of intimate enclosures, romantic retreats in the Italian manner, containing simple fountains, pools, and antique statuary. Paths through leafy bowers, arbors, and hornbeam hedges connect the enclosures. One contains a statue of a boar set in a pool, modeled after that in the main square of Florence. Another, approached by a path along a latticed wall, contains a "fountain of love" with a small spray emerging from a moss bed. An artichoke fountain and a gently undulating cascade lie at the end of one arbor. There is also a charming grotto peopled with statues of dwarfs.

After this captivating introduction to the water garden, Le Miroir, a large reflecting pool, pure French in inspiration and planted with water lilies, unfolds. Scores of waterfowl—mallards, mandarin ducks, and others—splash and cavort in it. *Pêcheur* martins, the electric-blue members of the swallow family, dart above the trout-stocked waters. Two groups of gilded-lead dolphin fountains, green with a lovely patina, fill the pool. A mysterious grotto containing a statue of Neptune is also in view.

A stroll past the château leads to the triumphant finale of this green and silver garden symphony: a two-tiered cataract spills with a roar into an octagonal pool with a tower flume, then into Le Paon, a fan fountain whose pool leads to another waterfall. The leaves and branches of ancient purple and green beech, pine, Atlas cedar, and larch form a canopy overhead.

Totally different in concept, the erotic and exotic gardens at the Reales Alcázares and Alhambra in Spain reflect the Moorish preoccupation with all that is sensuous. And once again, water is of primary concern, unifying, embellishing, pacifying, and provoking.

By 1492, when the Spanish Christians expelled the last significant bastion of Moors from Granada, Moorish culture had long since lapsed into magnificent decadence. The palaces had become outrageously ornate, with stucco work unequaled before or since embellishing the *artesonados* (ceilings of carved panels). In their wake, the Moors left to Spain, and particularly to Andalusia in the south, an array of delicately filigreed architecture

Opposite: *At the Reales Alcázares in Seville, Spain, the wall frescoes of the elaborate facade of the palace are graced with a pool guarded by Mercury, the messenger god of ancient Rome.*

Following pages: *Lions spout water into a pool at Maria Luisa Park in Seville, Spain, creating a cool oasis during the torpid summers.*

and, perhaps their liveliest legacy, the water gardens of Seville and Granada.

The Moors designed their gardens in Spain not only to appeal visually, but also to catch visitors' ears, arouse their taste buds, and coax them into touching all that surrounded them. Today these gardens are still filled with the music of gently gurgling or boisterously splashing water issuing from fountains set amid placid reflecting pools.

Lovely Seville, which lies in the shadow of the Moorish-style Giralda Tower, certainly embodies the sensuous legacy left by the Moors. Its sumptuous grace has inspired scores of composers and artists. The operas *Carmen, The Barber of Seville, Don Giovanni,* and *The Marriage of Figaro,* among many others, are all set in Seville. Velasquez was a native son and both Murillo and Zurbaran studied here. No doubt, they all visited, enjoyed, and quite probably were inspired by the gardens of the Reales Alcázares, in the heart of old Seville.

The Reales Alcázares was extensively remodeled by Spain's Christian kings after their victory over the Moors. Nonetheless, the Moorish architecture is still evident, and many of the Moorish water gardens live on. Upon entering the Reales Alcázares, one first encounters the Pool of Mercury, a large water basin dominated by Diego de Pesquera's sixteenth-century bronze statue of the Roman messenger god. Orange and gold carp splash about, and hungry swallows, as blue as gentian, skim the water's surface. Cascades of magenta bougainvillaea droop from the rustling cypress trees.

From the pool, an imposing double staircase leads down to a series of poetic "secret" gardens. The first, the Garden of the Dance, consists of a series of tile-floored compartments with fountains and benches covered in dazzling green, blue, yellow, and white polychromatic tiles. A nymph and a satyr dance on nearby pedestals. An allée of ancient *Magnolia grandiflora* trees, Canary date palms, brilliant red hibiscus, white oleander, and cypress and orange trees offers welcome shade. White trumpet flowers dangle from

vines on walls encrusted with green moss and rust-colored lichens.

Beyond the labyrinth of secret gardens, an impressive mudejar (Moorish-Christian) arch leads to the Moorish-style bedroom pavilion and the garden of Carlos V, constructed in 1540. Despite the sweet scents of nearby lime, lemon, and orange trees, the aroma of lavender, jasmine, artemisia, lantana, and eucalyptus, and the bright colors of the tiled folly, the place has a melancholy atmosphere. A smaller Moorish building, with a cedar-wood dome and a fountain and pool in front, faces the main pavilion. Beyond

At the legendary gardens of the Alhambra Palace in Granada, Spain, a somber reflecting pool sets off the delicate filigreed details of the walls of the Moorish-style pavilion.

Cooling fountains enhance every courtyard of the extravagant Alhambra.

lie the Garden of the Alaides, with its fountain of Neptune, and a vast, informal, English-style park that was installed during the last century.

Seville's great Maria Luisa Park, like Paris's Bois de Boulogne and New York's Central Park, is the city's great greensward. Situated on the banks of the Guadalquivir River, it was once a part of the San Telmo Palace and was given to the city by Princess Maria Luisa in 1893. In 1929, at the time of the Ibero-American Exhibition, it was redesigned as a sunken garden with pools and fountains fashioned of elaborate tile work, reflecting the Moorish style seen at the Reales Alcázares. Miles of woodland paths meander through a veritable arboretum of exotic trees from all over the world; the cooling sounds of the ubiquitous fountains enhance a visitor's experience.

At the Alhambra Palace in Granada the fusion of Moorish architectural detail and garden waterworks reached its apotheosis. Erected during the fourteenth century by Sultan Yusuf I and his son, Muhammad V, the fortress contains some of the world's most memorable courtyards. The tranquil Court of Myrtle Trees, with its reflecting pool, and the later Granadian-Arabic Court of the Lions, with its fountain of twelve lions spewing water, are familiar and dear to architects and gardeners alike.

But the landscaping at the adjoining Generalife is perhaps the most remarkable in all of Spain. Although the Moorish sultans conducted their business at the

Alhambra, the gardens at the Generalife served strictly for rest and relaxation, a place to indulge in undisturbed hedonism.

Once in the gardens, the sound of splashing water beckons one to the Cypress Walk, an avenue of fountains and reflecting pools accented by somber, velvety cypress trees. Swallows and iridescent dragonflies dart about above the water's surface, where water lilies nod in the sun. The pools are edged with tree roses: scarlet Christian Dior, pale pink Queen Elizabeth, snow white Iceberg, and pastel Peace. Towering hedges of cypress clipped into Moorish-style archways enclose the refuge and lead from one garden to the next. *Magnolia grandiflora* and oleander exude their fragrances along the way.

Running beside this two-hundred-foot walk are scores of gardens enclosed by myrtle and cypress hedges and planted with aromatic feverfew, pink and red roses, and scarlet carnations, the last a symbol of Andalusia. Cataracts of deep purple wisteria and radiant orange trumpet vine plunge from the trees.

The climax of the display is the Courtyard of the Pool, a fountain garden at the pavilion. It is here, according to legend, that the sultans sat behind intricately decorated screens and reviewed their riches. "This is the area where the sultan sat and threw a piece of fruit down to the harem girl he wanted for the night," reads a sign on the wall.

The waters are clamorous, as scores of small, hidden fountain jets spew silver sprays into the pool. Day lilies of pastel

Above: *A detail of the tile work that decorates the "water tank" at the Palace of the Marquez de Fronteira, near Lisbon, Portugal. The tile work ranks among the most extravagant in the world.*

Left: *The lavish use of blue and white tiles around the "water tank" at the Fronteira Palace adds a luxuriant dimension to the cool garden setting.*

Following pages: *Outside of Lisbon, Portugal, at the Quinta da Bacalhoa, a "water tank"—a typical feature of seventeenth-century Portuguese gardens —reflects the surroundings, cools the air, and provides a place for swimming and boating.*

and flamboyant shades contrast with snow white calla lilies.

Beyond the pavilion are the upper gardens, reached by climbing an unusual Moorish stairway. Circular landings, each with its own tiny spraying fountain, separate three short flights of stairs. Water races down raised channels on either side of the steps, in effect transforming the banisters into miniature waterfalls.

To leave the gardens the visitor follows a shadowed terrace walk that offers a spectacular overview of the landscape. Here the sculpted cedar and myrtle plantings take on a primeval quality. Only when past the garden gates and back out in the blistering heat of Granada does one realize that for a brief hour or so one has visited another place, another time, a long-departed civilization.

The private gardens of Portugal are unlike any others in Europe, for although the designs derive from French, Italian, Moorish, and even informal English garden concepts, they possess an exuberant quality of fantasy seen only there. The French- or Italian-inspired parterre gardens, with their precisely trimmed box and topiary, are adapted to the Portuguese taste by the addition of a profusion of fountains and large reflecting pools called "water tanks" and the awesome tile decorations that in many gardens make every wall a sensuous orgy of blue and white glazed terra cotta.

About fifteen minutes from the heart of Lisbon are the gardens of the

Palace of the Marquez de Fronteira. Built around 1670 as a hunting pavilion, the palace has been owned and lived in by the same family ever since. The basis of the garden is a series of parterres designed in the Italian style. All are quite attractive, but it is the adjoining marble King's Gallery, a two-storied open veranda, that is nothing less than astonishing. Its design reveals Italian mannerist influence, as well as classical Portuguese, and it is covered with thousands of blue and white tiles. The kings of Portugal sit in a series of niches garnished with fruit swags and gaze down on the placid tile-lined water tank. At both ends of the structure, grand staircases, embellished with jardinieres and statuary, lead to small, intimate pavilions at either end of the upper story. Everywhere can be seen nature's living patina of brick red lichens and soft, jade green moss.

In the nearby province of Estremadura there lies a rural area renowned not only for the peerless grapes from which Lancer's wine is made, but for the finest olive oil in Portugal. Here narrow, twisting roads pass through gently undulating, semiarid, rock-strewn Mediterranean terrain. Spanking white limestone farmhouses dot the landscape. Forests of pine and eucalyptus alternate with seas of the shimmering gray-green foliage of vast olive and cork oak groves, some of which are more than two thousand years old. Beneath, evergreen rock rose and dust-laden lavender, rosemary, and thyme compete for what little moisture is available.

This is the setting for the Quinta da Bacalhoa, which means "farm of the codfish," one of the earliest surviving private palaces of Portugal. The palace was built at the end of the fifteenth century in the Italian Renaissance style, with touches of Moorish influence, but the upper level of gardens is in the French parterre style. A Moorish-inspired ornamental Portuguese water tank graces the lower level.

A path wanders past shrub rose plantings, tile planters containing pendulous white geraniums, and a mandarin orange grove. It leads to a graceful, arcaded summerhouse, which faces the characteristic water tank. This tank also serves for swimming and rowboating and acts as an irrigation reservoir. The pool mirrors the trees and sky and is lined with gray- and silver-foliaged rosemary, santolina, lavender, and artemisia. Clumps of pale pink *Licoris* accent the sea of silver.

In the northern part of Portugal is the world-renowned winery Quinta da Aveleda. Antonio Guardes, a highly knowledgeable gardener, currently presides

over the quinta, which has been in his family for generations. It was originally built in the late seventeenth century and remodeled during the nineteenth. The garden here is English inspired, informal, and romantic, and unexpected encounters with small water installations offer surprises at every turn.

Upon entering, one leisurely ambles through a wooded planting of azaleas and hydrangeas and soon arrives at a pond with several islands. Ducks splash about, and frogs leap in panic from their place in the sun into the moss green waters. One of the islands sports a beguiling, rustic summerhouse, accessible by a wooden bridge. Another supports a granite window from the palace where Prince Henry the Navigator was born. It was moved to the premises when the palace was razed.

This enchanting walk continues, passing over bridges and through a moss

At Barnsley House, in Gloucestershire, England, Rosemary Verey created an intimate water garden in front of the Greek-style temple that she and her late husband moved onto the property.

garden with its dribbling fountain to a formal lawn enhanced by an exotic oriental cage, which several Portuguese ringdoves call home.

Although the vast National Trust gardens of England almost all incorporate water in their landscapes, it is the smaller, private gardens that offer the intimate experience water affords. Rosemary Verey's Barnsley House, in Gloucestershire, has a fine old pavilion, a small temple in the Tuscan style that was built in 1740 and moved to the premises piece by piece in 1964. It is certainly one of the focal points at the estate. Set before it is a small pond that gently gurgles and serves as a bed for water lilies, Japanese iris, and other aquatic cultivars.

At Hugh Johnson's Saling Hall, in Essex, beyond the traditional walled garden to the rear of the manor house, a boscage with a mysterious, deeply shaded water garden has been installed. Here bog plants such as ostrich fern (*Lysichiton;* known in the United States as skunk cabbage), hosta, and Japanese iris thrive. Nearby, a large pond, called a "moat" in Britain, comes to life, for it is the home of a very imperious, dignified swan and scores of waterfowl. Toward the back of the grounds in what was a large hollow, a Japanese water garden has been installed.

Alive with the call of the European thrush and the chattering of sparrows, the garden at Saling Hall is more natural than precise. The traditional teakwood benches scattered about invite one to sit and enjoy

the garden's beauty and peace and the bells of adjacent St. James's Church tolling the quarter-hour. "The mood of the walled garden is always, I hope, cheerful, spruce, and on parade," Johnson says of his creation. "My intention is that the water garden is just as positively melancholy and romantic. It is a great deal to ask of plants. I can't tell whether they manage it or not—my mind's eye has got there already."

Below: *Although the emphasis of the gardens at Saling Hall in Essex, England, is on the tree collection, a Japanese-style water garden provides seclusion amid the more open areas of the grounds.*

Opposite: *The tranquil reservoir in the middle of The Hague, in Holland, is planted with azaleas, Japanese maples, and iris.*

Right: *In the glen at Anne's Grove, near Limerick, County Cork, Ireland, a stream was diverted more than a hundred years ago to offer a setting for the now towering rare specimens of trees planted on the estate.*

Opposite: *At Fernhill, Sally Walker's estate near Dublin, Ireland, a waterfall and bridge provide an ideal setting for several sculptures. Every summer an exhibition of contemporary Irish sculpture is displayed on the grounds for visitors to enjoy.*

Preceding pages: *One of the many small water gardens at the Botanic Gardens in Singapore is beautifully enhanced by the undulating hedges that flank the water parterres.*

Certainly one of the most beautiful botanical gardens on earth is the 132-year-old Botanic Gardens in Singapore. During the eighteenth and nineteenth centuries, Southeast Asia was colonized extensively by the imperialistic powers of Europe. During that time, the British occupied Singapore and were initially motivated to exploit commercially the jungles of the area and the tropical plants that grew there. Rubber, coffee, palm oil, tamarind, cloves, nutmeg, cinnamon, mahogany, teak, rattan cane, and exotic fruit such as mangoes, rambutan, duku, langsat, starfruits, and durian were all available. And so, in order to study the plants for commercial use, the Botanic Gardens, inspired by England's famed Royal Botanic Gardens at Kew, were established in 1859. Today the forty-seven-hectare garden, which contains two

thousand different species of plants, is very much as it was when originally laid out.

The garden was also designed to act as an oasis in the steaming city. And so, much of the design involved water. There are two large lakes, a waterfall garden lush with ferns, begonias, and gingers, a marsh garden, an honest-to-God jungle, a small, intimate water garden, lotus ponds, and a large, formal water garden.

Among the more exotic plants in the gardens are the Monkey Pot (*Lecythis ollaria*), which sports bizarre-looking woody fruit, and a palm collection that ranks among the world's finest. Palms range in size from the squatty Mexican Fan Palm (*Washingtonia robusta*) to the towering Livistonas.

Most unusual is the double coconut (*Lodoicea maldivica*), which produces a pair of eighteen-inch-long fruits that are joined together in Siamese twin fashion. This coconut is the largest and heaviest seed in the plant kingdom and has inspired much legend and lore. Early mariners first came upon these giant coconuts floating in the sea. Legends evolved regarding their source, one of which was that these gargantuan seeds fell from a giant tree that grew in the navel of the Indian Ocean and was unreachable because of violent storms.

A collection of rubber trees from throughout Southeast Asia has been installed in the park in recognition of the prosperity the exportation of rubber brought to Singapore in the nineteenth century. Included in the collection is the Para rubber (*Hevea brasiliensis*). Seedlings of this cultivar were brought from Brazil to Singapore in 1877 and became the basis for Singapore's rubber industry.

Designed by Irish landscape architect William Robinson, the gardens at Mount Usher, in Ashford, County Wicklow, Ireland, are not centered on the house, but on the stream that runs through the property. Plantings of rhododendrons, azaleas, eucalyptus, and rare conifers and palm trees line the stream on which cataracts and a series of gently gurgling weirs were built.

The gardens of Ireland almost all incorporate water in their schemes. Near Dublin, Sally Walker's Fernhill contains a waterfall that was installed in the rock garden. Each summer, thirty or so sculptors are invited to display their work in the garden, so the small bridge that crosses the cataract is almost always decorated by an amusing work of art.

At Anne's Grove, near Limerick, in County Cork, the home of Mr. and Mrs. Patrick Grove Annesley, there is a "wild" water garden, set on the floor of a small ravine. It was installed by an ancestor, Richard Grove Annesley, in 1900. The river Awbeg, immortalized by Edmund Spenser in *The Faerie Queene*, gently meanders through the valley. Annesley had the river diverted and installed a number of weirs and rapids. He planted tall Lawson cypress, water-loving poplar, and willow along the banks of the river. Here thrive immense clumps of gunnera and native American skunk cabbage (*Lysichiton americanum*), in addition to moisture-loving plants such as Japanese iris, bergenia, and brilliant yellow, candelabralike *Primula florindae*.

The use of water in garden design continues, both here and abroad, on large estates and at intimate houses. Several years ago,

At Powerscourt, in Enniskerry, County Wicklow, Ireland, one of the country's grandest estates, the classic eighteenth-century-style formal gardens were installed when the house was built between 1731 and 1740. A century later, the elaborate reflecting pond and fountain flanked by winged Pegasi were added, along with the intricate, immense wrought-iron gates. The fountain's soaring geyser of water dominates the landscape.

Right: Bill and Pat Milford's water garden at their residence in Southold, New York, sports a pink tropical water lily called Missus George H. Pring.

Opposite: At her estate in Southampton, New York, Charlotte Ford recently excavated a large potato field on her property and installed a pond that is graced with an elegant bridge and gazebo. The Atlantic Ocean is just beyond the dunes in the distance.

at her house in Southampton, New York, Charlotte Ford looked out on a vast potato field stretching a considerable distance to the dunes that meet the Atlantic Ocean to the south. Although the swimming pool could be seen from most of the windows in the house, Ford opted to excavate the potato field and install a large pond within view of the house. Two years later, the pond was complete. A gazebo was built on a small island reached by a bridge, and plantings of water lilies, Japanese iris, and other aquatic plants were installed in the water, with day lilies, grasses, purple liatris, and splashes of annual color lining the banks. This placid vista contrasts sharply with the pounding ocean surf.

Bulb Gardens

Many gardeners who delight in the early spectacle of crocuses, tulips, daffodils, hyacinths, and the scores of "minor" bulbs available plant specialty gardens of spring bulbs. Bulbs are easily grown and are almost pest and disease free. Many varieties multiply freely, becoming more and more beautiful with each passing year. In terms of investment of time, labor, and expense, the rewards of a spring bulb garden are bountiful beyond expectation. And, after the spring bulb season has passed, these specialty gardeners often turn to the summer parade of bulbs, the lovely lilies, gladioli, dahlias, and lesser-known species.

The history of flowering bulbs can be traced to the ancient Minoan civilization, which thrived on the island of Crete around four thousand years ago.

The Minoans discovered that the stigmas of one of the seventy or so species of crocus that grew on the island could be dried and ground into a powder known today as saffron. It was used as a spice, dye, scent, and miracle drug.

Of all the flowering bulbs, however, it is the tulip that has had the most colorful history. Prior to 1554 tulips had not been seen in Europe. That year, Austrian Emperor Ferdinand I sent Ogier Ghiselin de Busbecque from Flanders, which at the time was subject to Austria, as his emissary to Constantinople to negotiate peace with Sultan Suleiman the Magnificent. De Busbecque's mission was a success and, more to the point, his keen interest in botany led to the introduction of the tulip into Europe. While traveling from Adrianople, now Edirne, to Constantinople, now Istanbul, de Busbecque saw "an abundance of flowers everywhere—narcissus, hyacinth and those which the Turks call tulipam—much to our astonishment because it was almost midwinter, a season unfriendly to flowers."

Although the Turkish word for tulip is "lale," de Busbecque's interpreter probably described the flower as looking like a "thoulypen," the Turkish word for turban. De Busbecque probably heard "tulipam," which ultimately was shortened to "tulip." The Fleming bought some bulbs, "which

Below: Designed by architect Sir Edwin Lutyens and landscape designer Gertrude Jekyll, the plantings in the classic rose garden at Folly Farm, Berkshire, England, include pink Fairy roses, lavender, and plantings of regal lilies (Lilium regale).

Preceding pages: The shapes and colors of bright orange fritillaria and yellow daffodils provide a successful contrast in a planting at Keukenhof Gardens, near Lisse, Holland.

cost me not a little." Upon arriving in Vienna, he planted them in the imperial gardens. They multiplied and word of their existence and beauty spread. Soon wealthy merchants in Holland coveted these new, prestigious flowers.

Although images of tulips, particularly those which today are called lily-flowering, already appeared on Turkish fabrics, it was not until 1561 that an accurate botanical drawing of a tulip appeared in Europe. Swiss botanist Konrad Gesner included one in a garden manual he published. Linnaeus, the renowned plant classifier, later named all garden tulips after him, *Tulipa gesnerana*.

In 1593, Carolus Clusius, a Flemish botanist who had been imperial gardener in Vienna, returned to Holland to chair the botany department at the University of Leiden. He brought with him a supply of tulip bulbs and planted them in his garden. Word spread and soon Clusius was besieged with extravagant offers for his prized specimens. One night, while he slept, someone entered his garden and stole almost all of the tulips. A period document relates that the thief "wasted no time in increasing them by sowing seeds, and by this means the seventeen provinces [of Holland] were well stocked."

The romance of the tulip does not end here. New, rare varieties of tulips occur when cultivated varieties "break," often unpredictably, producing new colors and markings. It has only been recently that scientists have concluded these "breaks" are caused by a combination of natural mutations and a virus that spreads among the tulip bulbs. These flamboyantly striped and wildly colored tulips were most prized among the rich of early-seventeenth-century Europe.

In 1624, one bulb of Semper Augustus, a red-and-white tulip with a base of a blue tinge, sold at auction for twelve hundred dollars. The next year the owner sold two propagated from the first for three thousand dollars. Shortly, three bulbs commanded thirty thousand dollars. "Tulip mania" ensued, as all gardeners, rich and poor alike, realized that new varieties, which might lead to untold riches, could appear from any bulb in anybody's garden. By 1634, the mania had turned to madness, as bulb speculating tempted many. What was being traded, however, was not bulbs, but bulb futures, often bulbs that had not even bloomed yet. Men frantically mortgaged their houses or hocked the family jewels to raise money for tulip speculation. A brewer traded his brewery for one coveted bulb, and a miller swapped his mill for another. Meanwhile, a botany professor at the University of Leiden, Evrard Forstius, was so incensed by the exploitation that he beat to death with his walking stick any tulip he encountered.

Then in the spring of 1637, three years after the start of the madness, the tulip market collapsed. A financial panic ensued. Fortunes were lost, and some investors were driven to suicide. The government banned further tulip speculation, and the Dutch turned to hybridizing and growing bulbs commercially as they do to-

Clumps of daffodils were planted for a cheerful springtime display on the grounds at Glenfoechan House, an elegant country inn near Oban, Scotland.

day. Two centuries later, around 1850, Alexandre Dumas, the French novelist, wrote of tulip mania in his romance *The Black Tulip.*

By the end of the eighteenth century, tulips had become a primary planting on the great estates of Europe and in America. George Washington and Thomas Jefferson installed major plantings at Mount Vernon and Monticello. American botanist John Bartram, a colleague and friend of Benjamin Franklin and King George III's official botanist for North America, was perhaps the first to import the bulbs to the North American continent. Bartram, whose extensive correspondence with English botanist Peter Collinson has survived, received a supply of bulbs from Collinson in 1735. In 1739, Collinson sent some double tulips, and in 1740, "twenty varieties of crocus, some narcissus and ornithogalum." In 1763, Bartram received "thousands of bulbs" from his English friend. Today Bartram's house is preserved as a museum and his Philadelphia garden, the United States's oldest surviving botanical garden, dating from 1728, is being restored.

By 1750, William Logan, son of William Penn's secretary James Logan, had planted hyacinths and tulips imported from England in his garden at Stenton, Pennsylvania, and in 1770 Daniel Wister, of Germantown, Pennsylvania, was growing "beds of tulips and 'named' hyacinths" at his estate, Grublethorpe. Wister's plantings were the first of their kind in North America.

According to the Netherlands Flowerbulb Information Center, the first Dutchman to come to America specifically to sell flowering bulbs was J. B. van der Schoot. He traveled throughout the United States for six months in 1840, selling Dutch bulbs to the people of New York City, Philadelphia, Baltimore, Washington, Albany, and Buffalo. His descendants are still in the bulb business under the name of W. R. van der Schoot Company.

Before 1850, wild cultivars of daffodils were the only daffodil bulbs available. But then hybridization began, primarily in England. In 1899, King Alfred was introduced, to this day the most popular of all daffodil varieties. During the 1920s hybridization accelerated and Carbineer, Carleton, Trevithian, and Mrs. R. O. Backhouse, varieties that are still popular, were introduced.

Perhaps the most elaborate specialty garden in the world is the spring bulb garden at Keukenhof Gardens, near Lisse, Holland. The parklike garden, which contains a large lake, small streams, fountains, and waterfalls, is located in the heart of the bulb-growing district. It is the showcase of Holland's bulb industry, a seventy-acre extravaganza, a kind of horticultural Disneyland. More than seven million tulips, daffodils, hyacinths, and minor bulbs are planted each fall for the spring display, all set amid hundreds of gloriously flowering trees and shrubs.

Each year, almost one hundred bulb

*J*ust beyond the grounds of Keukenhof, fields of tulips brightly carpet the landscape during the spring.

Below: In a planting at Keukenhof, scores of Anemone blanda provide a lovely contrast to miniature daffodils.

Opposite: In Peconic, New York, the author installed a drift of Muscari 'Blue Spike', its loose blossom texture contrasts nicely with the more formal texture of white Muscari botryoides 'Album'.

Preceding pages: In Holland, at the peak of tulip season, spectacular bands of color reach as far as the eye can see. Many tulips are grown for their bulbs rather than their flowers. The flowers are mowed from the plants soon after they open to allow the bulbs to grow to harvesting size.

growers participate, drawing locations within the park by lot and then designing and finally planting their schemes. Keukenhof has become a mecca for horticulture enthusiasts, with close to one million people from all corners of the world visiting during the short blooming season.

The idea for a vast parklike garden originated in 1949. A group of prominent Dutch bulb growers decided to plan a series of displays both in parklike, natural surroundings and in smaller, contained gardens in home settings. Until then, visitors had made pilgrimages to Holland to see some forty-one thousand acres of patchwork carpets of brilliantly colored bulb fields. It is a spectacular sight, for in some areas, save for a distant view of a church spire, the lush color patterns stretch uninterrupted for almost as far as the eye can see. These tulips and other

flowering bulbs are grown to develop the bulbs rather than the flowers, however, so their spectacular beauty is on display for only a short time. All blossoms are mowed from their stalks soon after they open.

When the bulb growers looked for a site for their garden, they luckily found some land near Lisse. In the fifteenth century, the property belonged to Countess Jacoba van Beieren, who used the grounds for hunting and for growing vegetables. Thus the name Keukenhof, which means kitchen (*keuken*) garden (*hof*).

Today the grounds are open for seven or eight weeks, for the entire sequence of bulb bloom. Vast, sweeping plantings of tulips border the central lake on the grounds. A great promenade, a half-mile long, is lined with bed after bed of more than five hundred varieties of tulips and other bulbs. In one area, there is a veritable river of deep blue grape hyacinths, lined with dignified, brilliant red Emperor tulips and nodding King Alfred daffodils.

But Keukenhof is not just dazzling, gargantuan plantings of bulbs. Throughout the park there are intimate walks past small bulb gardens tucked in here and there, all on a human scale, that offer inspiration to the home gardener. Because weather is a factor in the success of any garden, a five-thousand-square-meter greenhouse has also been installed at Keukenhof, in case the elements delay or damage the vast outdoor displays. A permanent flower show is on view, as well as an indoor spring garden where more than five hundred different varieties of

Above and right:
At Virginia House,
near Richmond, Virginia,
and at Brodick Castle on
the island of Arran, off
the coast of Scotland,
pink tulips are used to
complement and set off
the plantings.

Opposite: At Virginia
House, a planting of pink-
and-white Angelique peony
tulips that is underplanted
with pale blue forget me
nots and set off by pale
pink English daisies looks
like a pastel-colored cloud,
over which a statue of a
child is gazing.

thousands of daffodils in the meadow in front of their eighteenth-century house. Each spring, garden lovers from miles around visit the bountiful display. Alice Levien of Cutchogue, New York, succumbed to bulb fever a number of years ago and each fall installs more and more in her lovely shade garden. Although interspersed with flowering trees and shrubs and early-blooming perennials, bulbs are the backbone of the garden. She has combined many varieties and colors of bulbs in her landscape; however, her use of pink hyacinths overplanted with a carpet of white early-blooming Arabis is breathtakingly beautiful.

Mien Ruys, the doyenne of Dutch landscape architects, has an aversion to hybridized daffodils and tulips. She feels they are too stiff and artificial-looking and has planted, instead, cultivars that are native to the wild in her naturalized plantings. Included among them is a whimsical delight, a collection of loosely growing species daffodils planted in a lawn area. Their blossoms gently nod in the breeze while several droll sculptures of grazing sheep appear to be nibbling at the foliage.

Although alpine gardens are a specialty unto themselves, many rock gardeners install large numbers of the early blooming minor bulbs to provide foliage contrast to the spreading, mat-like foliage of the traditional perennial plants. Like tiny sparkling jewels, electric-blue scilla, pale blue puschkinia, bell-shaped snowdrops, primrose-flowering winter aconite, species crocus, and *Iris reticulata* and *danfordiae* are often present in rock gardens. Most of these bulbs are native to

The naturalized planting of daffodils in front of the residence of Mrs. William Terry in Orient, New York, never fails to attract the attention of passing motorists.

Alice Levien, of
Cutchogue, New York,
opted to interplant old-
fashioned lemon lilies with
phlox, creating a colorful
midsummer garden.

Opposite: *Though she is Dutch, Mien Ruys has an aversion to using tulips, hyacinths, and hybridized daffodils in her garden, as she believes they are too artificial-looking. Instead, she installed miniature species daffodils in a naturalized planting at her home in the countryside.*

Preceding pages: *Moved by the beauty of photographs of the tulip beds at Keukenhof, Alfred Smith of Peconic, New York, installed a miniature version of the Dutch garden on his property. There are more than three thousand tulip bulbs in his planting.*

the mountainous areas of the world, so they appear to be right at home when tucked into the nooks and crannies of the rockscape.

Many who are first inspired by spring-blooming bulbs find their special interest carries on into the summer. Summer-blooming bulbs, although rarely featured alone, add interesting foliage and flower-shape contrast to annual and perennial borders.

Harking back to the days of tulip mania in Holland, the addictive charm of the tulip still leaves its mark on gardeners. Alfred Smith, of Peconic, New York, got somewhat carried away with tulips a number of years ago. As if in a daze, he scoured catalogue after catalogue for tulip varieties. After several weeks of making his selections, he found that his list numbered more than fifty varieties and close to three thousand tulips. He realized that if he planted them in a row, allowing the six-inch planting spacing required for tulips, he would have to dig a ditch about a quarter mile long. Undaunted, he ordered them all anyway and installed massive beds in front of his house. It took him weeks to dig, fortify the soil, and plant the bulbs, all the while ruing the day he had ever seen a tulip. However, when spring finally rolled around, he did have one of the most impressive displays of tulips ever seen outside of a public garden.

Dwarf Conifer Gardens

For the gardener who is limited by space, dwarf conifers are an ideal choice for specialization. Dwarf conifers are highly suitable for smaller gardens, as their
growth remains within bounds for many years. As a
rule, the ultimate height of most specimens is seven
or eight feet, although some grow to ten or twelve
feet, but usually only after fifty years or so. And
heights vary from twelve feet down to less than one
foot. These little trees come in many shapes: some
are minuscule columnars, bushy cones, or ball-like
shrubs; others are pyramidical or flat-topped; and
some have round, umbrellalike tops and low, round
or humped cushions. Some bushes are regular, others
irregular; some are neat and compact, others twisted
and tangled like an unruly head of hair. They also

differ greatly in color and are available in every shade of green, as well as glaucous gray and blue. Some are monochromatic, some variegated. There are yellow and gold varieties and some with pure white or brilliant red shoots. And during the winter not only do they retain their leaves, but many change color.

Today many garden centers and nurseries stock dwarf conifers, but their popularity is a fairly recent occurrence. *Dwarf and Slow Growing Conifers*, the first book on dwarf conifers, was written in 1923 by Murray Hornibrook, and only recently have other books appeared on the subject. Thirty years ago, dwarf conifers were unavailable in the general nursery or garden center in the United States. And even today, although more and more varieties are becoming available, a gardener— and not just a specialty gardener seeking unusual varieties—must still search high and wide for some specimens.

Although new to Western gardeners, dwarf conifers have been used in Japanese gardens for thousands of years. With their acute sense of proportion, Japanese garden designers realized long ago that a 150-foot-high blue spruce was quite out of place in a small, enclosed garden. They used dwarf conifers to enhance their temple courtyards and intimate gardens, either installed in the earth or as pot plants.

In England around the middle of the

Below: A bird's-eye view of Ed Rezek's dwarf conifer garden in Malverne, New York, reveals the delicate contrasts of texture and color he has achieved by careful planning and selection.

Preceding pages: Rezek's garden contains several hundred rare specimens, including this meticulously pruned Chamaecyparis pisifera squarrosa intermedia shaped into a series of globes.

Right: *Through careful pruning and maintenance, a dwarf Mugho pine in Rezek's bonsai collection is now almost fifty years old.*

nineteenth century, there was a short-lived trend among some gardeners to plant dwarf conifers. They were used in lawn plantings, often just stuck in the middle of a vast greensward, and were status symbols for parvenus rather than enhancements to the beauty of the landscape.

Perhaps the most notable, and one of the oldest, among the few dwarf conifer specialty gardens in the United States is that of Edward Rezek. A retired postman, Rezek lives on a quiet, tree-shaded street in a Long Island suburb about five miles east of the New York City line.

Traces of Rezek's touch are evident all along his street, as he has shared his plants with his neighbors. Here and there a dwarf Alberta spruce or a dwarf Hinoki cypress strikes a quirky note among the routine azaleas, yews, and junipers.

Standing in front of Rezek's house, one realizes that the landscape is decidedly unusual in this neighborhood, as it would be in almost any. There are no rhododendrons, azaleas, yews, or junipers in sight. Instead, there are a *Sequoiadendron giganteum* 'Pendulum' and a fifty-five-year-old *Picea abies* 'Nidiformis'. The *Picea* was originally grown as bonsai, but it outgrew its pot, so Rezek installed it in the ground. There are some *Juniperus sabina* 'Variegata' and a golden taxus grafted atop a *Taxus cuspidata*.

Flanking the house is a forty-five-foot-high columnar maple tree that towers above the chimney and resembles a telephone pole covered with ivy. "Acer saccharum 'Monumentale'," says the sixty-four-year-old, speaking Latin. "Kids ask what it is and I tell them it's Jack's beanstalk. It has no lateral branches, just these little stubs. I got it in 1962 from Henry Hohman, the great horticulturist who lived in Maryland."

In reality, the weird sugar maple is sort of a lark for Rezek, an introduction to the serious world of dwarf conifers that lies beyond. For in the fifty-by-eighty-foot garden in back of his house, Ed Rezek has created an enchanting, diverse, and wondrous paradise.

His lifelong love affair with plants began when he was a child, for his parents gardened extensively. His introduction to the world of dwarf conifers, however, came in 1945, just after World War II, when Rezek was sent to China with the United

Left: *Rezek trained a dwarf moss cypress (*Chamaecyparis squarrosa intermedia*) into a spiral topiary, a form that works well with the natural shapes of the rest of his collection.*

Right: *One of Rezek's finest specimens is a dwarf Canadian hemlock (*Tsuga canadensis *'Hussii'), which has been trained and pruned to offer a layered effect. This form is typical of those seen in Chinese and Japanese gardens.*

 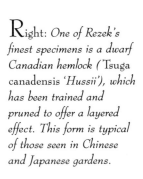

For color contrast, Rezek planted a Japanese red maple as a backdrop for his phantasmagoria of dwarf conifers. The Atlas cedar in the background has been trained to resemble a cascading waterfall.

States Marine Corps and was among the first Westerners ever allowed to visit the gardens at the Forbidden City in Beijing. There he saw examples of *penjing,* the Chinese art of miniature landscaping, in which nature is recreated in a concentrated way using stones and dwarf trees as the raw material. Penjing is an art form far older than Japanese bonsai, having been practiced in the imperial Chinese court more than twelve hundred years ago.

Penjing made a lasting impression on Rezek. In 1950 he bought his own home and decided to landscape the bleak, plantless area around the house. He avidly read scores of horticultural magazines and books on landscaping. The scale of gardens discussed then, and far too often today, however, was just too grand for his limited property. He then recalled the dwarf conifers he had seen in China. Realizing that he didn't have room on his property for large plants, he decided to install "a lot of little gems," and so his extraordinary garden was born. He started to research dwarf conifers, pouring through the pages of what little was available at the time. Then, after deciding to go ahead with his plans, he discovered that there were no dwarf conifers available in local nurseries. Undaunted, he contacted English and Dutch horticultural sources

Above: *The edge of the pond at the Brooklyn Botanical Gardens in Brooklyn, New York, is planted with spring-flowering trees and carefully pruned dwarf conifers.*

Right: *At the Brooklyn Botanical Gardens, a tranquil Japanese garden combines dwarf conifers with classic flowering cherry trees.*

and learned that there was one source in the United States, Kingsville Nursery in Maryland, that offered a selection of dwarf conifers. A large part of his original collection was purchased there.

Like all master gardeners, Rezek's eyes beam and his face glows when he unfolds the secrets of his garden. While strolling along the side of his house, he proudly points out such rare specimens as a table top pine (*Pinus densiflora* 'Umbraculifera'); a thirty-five-year-old Sargent's weeping hemlock (*Tsuga canadensis* 'Sargentii'); and an exquisitely delicate, pale red Japanese maple (*Acer*

palmatum), among other treasures. This is only a sampling, however, of the wonders that lie ahead. Entered through a brick archway, Rezek's secluded fantasy land is a staggering collection of more than two hundred dwarf conifers that are set off by a trickling waterfall, a goldfish pond, and a collection of oriental garden ornaments. These are crowned by a verdant canopy, formed by a lofty umbrella-shaped Young's weeping birch (*Betula pendula* 'Youngii'), and framed by a tall hedge.

There is an extraordinary example of espalier, a weeping Atlantic cedar (*Cedrus atlantica* 'Pendula'), that has been trained

The yellows, blues, and dozens of shades of green in Rezek's garden reveal just how varied the colors of dwarf conifers can be.

into the shape of a waterfall. From the upper horizontal framework, a blue-green cascade resembling icicles tumbles gently to the ground.

The range of foliage coloration in the garden is virtually endless: the soft blue of *Picea glauca* 'Furi Ogon', the golden tones of *Taxus cuspidata* 'Aurescens', and the rich, nearly black-green foliage and reddish-brown bark of about one hundred varieties of Hinoki cypress (*Chamaecyparis obtusa*), which Rezek confesses he is most serious about in terms of his own personal hybridization experiments. He has grown many of these plants from seed. "A Hinoki is supposed to be sterile," he says, "but every once in a while, nature relents and you'll find some seed. Even then, it's chancy, because only five percent will germinate and most revert back to the large-growing cypresses. But if you're lucky, you'll get some new dwarfs."

Here and there for accents are the delicate reds and elegant foliage of various Japanese maple cultivars. Leaf textures teem, ranging from feathery *Pinus densiflora* 'Pendula' to the stocky needles of dwarf Scotch pines. Shapes vary from the diminutive globe-shaped moss cypress to supine hemlocks and pancake-shaped junipers. Rezek's efforts over the past thirty-five years have produced bird's nest spruces pruned to one third their normal size and conifers sheared into spirals, one variety grafted upon another and trained into convoluted tangles of bark.

Many of the specimens in Rezek's garden are highly personal and have come to him through exciting discoveries. His Sanders Blue Dwarf Alberta spruce, for

The Farell Duran collection of bonsai outside of Barcelona, Spain, is installed amid an extraordinary collection of cactus that the owner has gathered from the four corners of the world. Although it would seem to be an unlikely combination of plants, the effect is startling and yet harmonious.

Right: *In order to create an illusion of depth, Rezek installed an archway, flanked by an oriental statue, which leads the eye to a specimen dwarf conifer (Cryptomeria japonica 'Globosa') and a small tender palm tree, which he winters in his greenhouse.*

Opposite: *At strategic points in Rezek's garden, oriental statues offer focal points that create the illusion of space, making the garden seem much larger than it is.*

example, was found in 1983 as a mutant on a standard Alberta spruce. Sent to Rezek by a collector in Oregon, it is the most diminutive Alberta spruce so far discovered.

His *Cedrus deodara* 'Pygmy' is a descendant of a specimen originally obtained by James Nobel in the early 1940s from a California nursery. The tree was found growing in a seedling bed. Growing only a quarter inch a year, it is of an intense blue hue. The late William Goteli of South Orange, New Jersey, whose entire collection of dwarf conifers was donated to and planted at the National Arboretum in Washington, procured a specimen from Nobel and in 1960 sent Rezek a cutting of it.

The oldest specimen in the collection is a century-old *Chamaecyparis pisifera* 'Compressa', a gift from Washington State horticulturist Jon Spann. Spann had brought it from Groningen, Sweden, in 1892. The first dwarf conifer Rezek installed in his garden, back in 1952, when it stood a mere twelve inches high, was a dwarf Alberta spruce; it is now twelve feet high.

In addition to obtaining cultivars from other collectors, Rezek has hybridized several varieties which are registered at the National and Arnold arboretums. These include a Hinoki cypress, Rezek's Dwarf, and two *Chamaecyparis obtusa*, Jamie and Little Chris, both named after his grandchildren. He is in touch with dwarf conifer collectors in New Zealand, Australia, England, Holland,

Germany, and Czechoslovakia, and his correspondence includes news of new mutations, mutant seedlings, and the continuing science of hybridization. As for what we might expect in terms of new dwarf varieties in the near future, he says that new varieties deriving from the Japanese white pine are on the not too distant horizon.

Rezek suggests that before taking up a grafting knife, potential dwarf conifer gardeners should do their homework. A few helpful books are *Conifers* by D. M. Van Gelderen and J. R. P. Van Hoey Smith (Timber Press), *Ornamental Coni-*

fers by Charles R. Harrison (Macmillan), and *Manual of Dwarf Conifers* by Humphrey J. Welch (Theophrastus).

Rezek dreams of discovering a blue Hinoki cypress. To date, none have been found, but Splitrock has some blue in it, so among connoisseurs there are high hopes of eventually finding one. Rezek has been hybridizing Hinoki cypresses for almost twenty years now, chiefly in anticipation of creating a blue variety. "The only problem," he says, "is that life is too short. A collector needs three lifetimes to do what he wants in plant development."

In sharp contrast to Rezek's intimate dwarf conifer paradise is the garden of the late Alfonso A. Ossorio, for this garden is unmistakably done in the grand manner of another era. Set on a fifty-seven-acre estate in East Hampton, New York, known as The Creeks, the late artist and his longtime companion, Edward F. Dragon, turned what was an extravagant Victorian garden into a unique conifer sculpture garden that showcased more than a hundred of the artist's brightly painted sculptures. A recent American Conifer Society bulletin called The Creeks "the eighth wonder of the horticultural world" and "the most outstanding private conifer collection in the United States, a living work of art."

More than five hundred species of conifers dot the grounds in a mélange of shapes, including globular, weeping, vertical, and spreading varieties in foliage colors of gold, blue, and many shades of green. "Even in the dead of winter, when other estates have that hangdog look, this place stays bright and cheerful with the brilliance of the evergreens," Dragon said in an interview that appeared in the *New York Times*. Dragon, who inherited the estate, has put it up for sale, so there is no knowing at this point what will happen to the collection.

The late artist Alfonso Ossorio installed one of the largest dwarf conifer gardens in the world at The Creeks, his fifty-seven acre estate in East Hampton, New York. The garden was designed to set off his collection of sculpture and to offer interest during the winter.

Rose Gardens

The earliest records of the rose are found in the realm of geology. Fossils more than a million years old have revealed that roses are among the most ancient plants. There is evidence, although inconclusive, that they were grown and admired in gardens in China, the Middle East, and northern Africa more than five thousand years ago.

Since the time of the ancients, roses have been appreciated in many civilizations. Dating from 1500 B.C., the first authenticated record of a representation of a rose is at Knossos, in Crete, in a Minoan fresco. Roses were painted on the tomb of Tuthmosis IV (1420–1411 B.C.) in Egypt. Frescoes and textiles dating from 300 B.C., discovered in Egyptian tombs, also bear representations of roses.

The Greeks were perhaps the first to recognize the medicinal properties of roses, as well as appreciating their beauty. In 300 B.C., Theophrastus, a Greek philosopher and naturalist, mentioned the health properties of roses in his *History of Plants*. In fact, the Greeks even had a word for the health properties of roses, "triantifillia," which means thirty petals. And the first replica of a rose was on a coin of Rhodes, minted in 325 B.C.

The rose was the symbol of Aphrodite, the goddess of love. Anacreon, an Ionian poet, wrote of the origin of the rose. When, as legend had it, the seas were formed and Venus was born off the coast of Cyprus, the earth, eager to show that it could equal the gods in the creation of beauty, produced the rose.

As far as we know, Homer was the first poet to write of the rose. In both *The Iliad* and *The Odyssey*, he wrote that Aurora, the goddess of the dawn, "has fingers of roses, and perfumes the air with their scent." Sappho wrote of her beloved roses in "Ode to the Rose":

> *Would Jove a Queen of Flowers ordain,*
> *The Rose, the Queen of Flowers,*
> *should reign.*

The expression "bed of roses" derives from the ancient Greeks, referring to Sybaris, a Greek colony in southern Italy whose citizens enjoyed the luxury of sleeping on mattresses stuffed with rose petals.

The ancient Romans knew roses well and even grew them commercially in both

Rome and Egypt. They used them not only medicinally, but for enhancing ceremony and in hedonistic pursuits. Pliny, in his *Natural History* (A.D. 77), mentioned twelve different kinds of roses and thirty-two remedies obtainable from them. The expression "sub rosa," which literally means "under the rose" or "in strict confidence," derives from this period. It is alleged to refer to the Roman habit of carving roses on the ceilings of dining rooms to remind those gathered beneath not to repeat all they heard.

Cleopatra used the rose so extensively in Egyptian ceremonies and to enhance her personal sensuality that it eventually supplanted the lotus in popularity. When she received Mark Antony, she made an extravagant gesture—either as a demonstration of her wealth or as a flamboyant indication of her licentiousness. Rose petals were strewn on the floor of her chamber to a depth of eighteen inches and covered with a very fine net. Later, Mark Antony reciprocated by receiving her in a room filled with rose petals to a depth of five feet!

The ways in which various Roman emperors used roses serve as testimony to their decadence. One reposed on soft cushions of transparent material filled with rose petals. Another overwhelmed guests at his orgies with avalanches of roses showered from a balcony above them. At one of Nero's saturnalias, the fountains were filled with rose water and roses and rose leaves were scattered on the ground and the cushions on which the

Above: *The pergola at La Roseraie, Helga and David Dawn's exuberant rose garden in Southampton, New York, is covered with the fragrant, bright red climber Danse du Feu, a French cultivar rarely seen in American gardens.*

Right: *Even in death, the fallen rose petals at La Roseraie possess an ethereal beauty. Lavender Lassi climbs on both sides of the trellis. The red cultivar to the left is Norwich Pink.*

guests lay. Garlands of roses were placed on the debauchees' brows and rose wreaths around their necks. At the grand climax of the revelry, a rose pudding was served for dessert. Another time Nero's largess ended in tragedy, for he filled a lavish party room with so many rose petals that five of the guests were asphyxiated.

The rose cast its spell on Christians as it had on pagans. It became, for example, the symbol of the Virgin Mary. In Christian narratives, one version of the creation of the briar rose is that it emerged from the crown of thorns worn by Christ at his crucifixion, the roses forming from his blood.

Men saw the thorns on Jesus' brow
But angels saw the roses.

During the Middle Ages, the rose persisted as a symbol of beauty and love. Artisans created the beautiful stained-glass windows at Chartres, Reims, Amiens, and

At Folly Farm, in Berkshire, England, one of the few surviving Lutyens-Jekyll gardens, a magical rose garden was installed in a corner of the grounds.

elsewhere, their patterns derived from the many-petaled rose. More importantly, however, the rose became a major medicinal plant. At least one resident of each Christian monastery was required to have knowledge of the curative powers of plants, including the rose.

Also during the Middle Ages, the rose became a symbol of the crown of England. King Edward I (1272–1307) was the first English sovereign to choose it as his badge, and it has been prominent in English heraldry ever since. The Order of the Rose originated sometime during the Age of Chivalry, when rose leaves or petals were embroidered on knights' clothing.

This represented gentleness allied with courage and the promise of beauty's reward for valor. The civil war between the houses of York and Lancaster is known as the War of the Roses (1455–58), for a white rose represented York, a red one Lancaster.

During the sixteenth century, the first authoritative printed information on roses began to appear in Europe, and fairly accurate descriptions of both native and imported species became available. But the rose continued to be revered primarily for its medicinal use and for the health-giving properties of rose hips, which we now know are an excellent source of vitamin C.

The box-lined parterre rose garden at the David and Alice van Buuren Museum near Brussels, Belgium, is planted with Queen Elizabeth, Peace, and Red Masterpiece, among other varieties of roses.

It was during this period that Queen Elizabeth I chose a white rose as her symbol. One was embroidered on the banner that flew wherever the queen slept. Some say it represented her somewhat dubious virginity. It was also during this century that attar of roses first began to be used in perfumes, rose petals in potpourris, and rose water in the bath. These were all used to enhance personal scent and, more to the point, to mask unpleasant odors.

The rose continued to appear in the literature of the era. Shakespeare wrote of "rosy-fingered dawn" and declared that "a rose by any other name would smell as sweet." In *Hamlet* (Act III, Scene IV), he wrote:

> *Such an act*
> *That blurs the grace and blush of*
> *   modesty,*
> *Calls virtue hypocrite, takes off the rose*
> *From the fair forehead of an innocent*
> *   love*
> *And sets a blister there.*

And in *Romeo and Juliet* (Act II, Scene II):

> *This bud of love, by summer's ripening*
> *   breath,*
> *May prove a beauteous flower when*
> *   next we meet.*

In France, both Madame de Pompadour and Marie Antoinette collected roses in their gardens, the latter at the Petit Trianon at Versailles. It was Empress Josephine's passion for the rose, however,

that helped make it the preeminent ornamental flower of the nineteenth century and is at least partially responsible for its modern-day popularity. In fact, Josephine so loved roses that she carried one in her hand whenever possible, and it became her trademark. History reveals, however, that Josephine carried roses not just to enjoy their beauty and fragrance, but for a practical reason: her teeth were notoriously poor and she cleverly used roses as camouflage.

Josephine began her collection in 1804 at Malmaison, her country estate near Paris. By 1814, she had collected all species and varieties known at the time. There were 167 gallicas, 27 centifolias, 3 mosses, 9 damasks, 22 Chinas, 4 spinosissimas, 8 albas, 3 foetidas, and 1 musk. A contemporary was prompted to write, "Here was such a gathering together of roses as had never been seen before." When Napoleon's armies were on the march, one of their assignments was to bring back rosebushes for the empress.

The innovative design of Josephine's garden set the tone for today's rose garden. Paths led visitors to bed after bed of different varieties. This style later came to be called "gardenesque," as opposed to the "picturesque" style then in vogue. Today this same rose garden form—that is, a planting of roses only—is preferred by many gardeners for aesthetic reasons and because it facilitates maintenance.

Josephine's garden also included structures such as archways, pergolas, and pillars, to be used primarily as support for

Opposite: *The Pecks enhanced a planting of Blaze and Iceberg roses with a carpet of lavender and a white picket fence.*

Above: *The lush blossoms of the roses add an additional dimension to the planting at Old Westbury Gardens.*

Left: *The pink hybrid perpetual Paul Neyron is one of many highly fragrant old-fashioned roses in Skip Wachsberger's rose garden in Orient, New York.*

Above: *A planting of old-fashioned pink climbing roses, white and purple delphiniums, and white peonies at Old Westbury Gardens, Westbury, New York, is reminiscent of Gertrude Jekyll's muted color schemes.*

the many rambling roses in the collection. They are still basic features in important rose gardens and contemporary garden design throughout the world.

Roses also have a place in American history. Captain John Smith, who founded Jamestown, Virginia, in 1607, noted that the Indians he encountered in the James River Valley had planted wild roses to beautify their camps. According to Edward Winslow, "an abundance of roses, white, red and damask, single but very sweete indeed" was planted at Plymouth by the Pilgrims in 1621.

Throughout history, the rose and its aura of romance have often been favorite subjects of artists. In fact, if one rearranges the letters of the word rose, they spell Eros, who was the Greek god of love. Roses have appeared on the stone facades of Romanesque and Gothic cathedrals and in Renaissance frescoes, medi-

seum of roses. Almost every type of old-fashioned and modern rose, even Austin's recently introduced English rose, is included in their collection of more than four hundred varieties, totaling more than fifteen hundred individual rosebushes. There are hybrid teas, polyanthas, floribundas, hybrid perpetuals, mosses, climbers, scores of varieties of old-fashioned damasks, and others.

Twenty years ago, the house was situated on a flat piece of land comprised of a neglected landscape and a potato field that looked out over a wetland tidal basin. With the help of landscape architect James Huntley, the property was graded and beds set for the roses, which were then surrounded by windbreaks of Japanese pine and California privet.

The Dawns started by collecting hybrid teas and a few floribundas. Their in-terest soon became a passion, however, and they began traveling abroad to visit the important rose gardens of the world. They traveled to France to view the schemes at the Bois de Boulogne in Paris and secured permission to visit the Sangerhausen Rosarium in then East Germany, where more than six thousand varieties of roses grow. And they visited collections of old-fashioned roses wherever they could find them. But it was when they visited Empress Josephine's garden at Malmaison that their ambitions were truly fired.

"I am trying to collect as many of the old roses as the empress did," David Dawn says. "She accumulated some two hundred and fifty varieties. We have around a hundred and twenty-five [old-fashioned roses], but we're still going strong."

When the Dawns returned home

Below: *Wachsberger planted more than two hundred varieties of old-fashioned roses in his "wild" garden, including the soft yellow rugosa hybrid Agnes, the apricot hybrid musk Bishop Darlington, and the bright red hybrid perpetual Hugh Dickson.*

Following pages: Prosperity, an old-fashioned hybrid musk rose, sports clusters of highly fragrant pink blossoms.

they started scouting for the rarer cultivars not available in the United States.

The gardens at Roseraie are spacious, but not overwhelming. To vary the monotony of the flat landscape with dramatic vertical thrusts, large trellises support hardy climbers. A colossal pergola, more than fifty feet long and ten feet high, forms a backdrop for the spreading greensward leading from the house. The climbing roses are so lush in foliage and bloom that the superstructure is barely visible, creating the effect of a floating phantasmagoria of color.

At Folly Farm, to the west of London in Berkshire, the best preserved of the extant gardens of Gertrude Jekyll (pronounced Gee'-kull) and Sir Edwin Lutyens (pronounced Lut'-chens), there is a grand sunken rose garden, featuring an octagonal central pool. Lutyens designed the architectural scheme and Jekyll the plantings. A towering ten-foot-high yew hedge encloses the space and four fan staircases embellish the corners. On these are placed Lutyens's famed benches. The whole design is held together with swirling brick and stone paths. Lutyens's love of geometric shapes and symmetry, apparent throughout all his gardens, is well demonstrated here.

Jekyll's scheme of complementary pastel plantings, a subtle palette of under-

stated rose colorations, is almost perfectly executed. On each side of the garden is a different rose variety: blush pink Queen Elizabeth grandiflora, pink Congratulations, ivory and blush pink Peace, and yellow Korresiai. Miniature pink Fairy roses grow alongside all four staircases. English lavender and white *Lilium regale* are planted on the central island of the pool and, for a startling accent, crimson Stephen Langdon roses surround the pool, lightly scenting the air. On the staircases, which are encrusted with moss and lichens, alpine strawberries, ferns, sedum, and mounds of juniper crawl over the bare stone. It is a fine place to pause, to sit on one of Lutyens's benches, and to savor the scents of the lavender and roses.

To the side of the manor house there is a series of captivating, small walled gardens, one of which is a jewel of a small rose garden. Planted with pastel pink floribunda roses and edged with dwarf purple campanula, it is a nearly perfect intimate hideaway garden.

The secluded gardens at the David and Alice van Buuren Museum, an art deco house dating from the late 1920s, can be found in the upscale Brussels suburb of Uccle.

The rose garden here is intimate and private, although planted in the traditional parterre manner introduced at Empress Josephine's Malmaison. Beyond a small rose garden with a reflecting pool, located to the left of the entrance, is the formal rose garden. Designed by Jules Buyssens in 1922, the garden is composed of a series of box-lined parterres, each planted with a different variety: Queen Elizabeth, Brandy, Peace, Red Masterpiece, and more. Set amid arbors and sharply contrasting wall plantings of blue campanulas, the formal rose garden leads to the great lawn, a sweeping greensward set off by majestic Atlantic cedars and willows.

Moving away from the formality of most traditional rose gardens, more and more gardeners, particularly in Great Britain, are experimenting by combining select roses with perennials in borders.

In the United States, radical experimentation is going on. Artist Robert Dash scatters undisciplined shrub roses here and there among the plantings at his extraordinary gardens in Sagaponack, New York. Skip Wachsberger is a great admirer of the old-fashioned rose. He has installed dozens of varieties in the very natural, somewhat wild-looking garden of native plants and perennials at his eighteenth-century house in Orient, New York.

The rules of gardening were made to be broken. Innovative gardeners continue to create new settings for the rose, which always has been, is now, and probably always will be the most popular flower in the world.

Alpine, Wall, and Crack Gardens

Because they are so well suited to today's life-styles, alpine, or rock, gardens are becoming increasingly popular with contemporary gardeners. First, they can be adapted to small properties. A rockery can range in size from a vast expanse to a vest-pocket planting. Second, they are easy to maintain. A few hours of weeding and deadheading every other week or so is all it takes to keep a rock garden tidy. Third, most plants that thrive in rockeries are drought resistant, requiring watering only under the driest conditions, and most are pest and disease free as well.

Many alpine plants and miniature bulbs suitable for planting in rock gardens are among the first plants to bloom in the spring, offering color early in the growing season. And, with proper planning and plant selection, color can be assured throughout the year; many alpine plants offer evergreen foliage of red, silver, purple, green, blue, or yellow. Finally, the charm of a lilliputian mountain habitat and of low-growing, unusual-looking plants—many varieties of which are rarely seen in the average garden—is irresistible to gardeners and nongardeners alike.

Rock gardens are usually planted with dwarf plants, conifers, and minor or miniature bulbs that adapt well to growing on or near rocky or gravelly surfaces, where relatively little moisture is available.

Most suitable plants detest overly wet conditions and generally will not survive if thus installed.

Some varieties of upland plants do not thrive in the crevices of large rocks but in scree, the gravelly debris that breaks off rocks as a result of freezing and thawing. This gravel gathers on mountainsides, hosting numerous types of plants. Many rock gardeners are including this feature in their rockery designs. Sometimes rock gardens are referred to as "scree beds."

The first recorded use of rocks in garden design was in Japan fifteen hun-

Below: *The alpine garden at the Royal Botanic Garden, Edinburgh, Scotland, is considered by many to be the most beautiful in the world. This section of the garden is planted with azaleas and heather.*

Preceding pages: *A gentle waterfall, which leads to a pond below, was installed in Mr. and Mrs. Francis H. Cabot's stunning rock garden at Stone Crop in Cold Spring, New York.*

Right: *One of the daz-zling showstoppers in any rock garden is the electric-blue* Gentiana acaulis; *the plant is somewhat temperamental, however, often thriving but not blooming. Francis H. Cabot advises to plant a number of them in different areas of the garden to get one to bloom.*

Following page: *Verney Naylor's captivating island rock garden in Dublin, Ireland, is planted not only with bulbs and alpine plants, but with dwarf conifers, such as* Juniperus communis *'Hibernica'.*

dred years ago, and stones have since been an important feature in Japanese gardens. The use of rocks in Western gardens, however, is a relatively recent innovation, first occurring in England during the eighteenth century. During this era, rock gardens were created to serve two purposes: to recreate the oriental garden and to educate people about geology.

At first, during the late eighteenth century, rock gardens were constructed with material that was blatantly artificial and out of context with the surrounding environment. Lava rock, sea shells, colored gravel, buhrstone, and crystalline spar comprised the backbone of the garden. This trend continued well into the nineteenth century, when the use of more natural materials—either manufactured or real stone, suggesting outcroppings of sandstone—came into vogue.

The rock garden as we know it today probably developed as a result of the exploration of the world's mountain areas, which began in the early nineteenth century. Botanists found that the wild flora of the higher elevations of the Alps, Himalayas, Andes, and Rockies was far more intense in color and more concentrated in growth habit than plants native to lower elevations. These sparkling little gems of the plant world were exported home and subsequently hybridized. Rock gardening soon became a popular pursuit of gardeners, as well as a major area of horticulture to be explored.

Avid gardeners installed outdoor rock gardens or, in some cases, indoor rock gardens in unheated greenhouses called alpine houses. These early rockeries boasted large numbers of ferns. Around 1880, in keeping with the alpine garden style in

Above: *In Ireland, rockeries are lushly planted, emphasizing overall color and foliage, with rock texture barely visible. At Helen and Val Dillon's Dublin, Ireland, home, a geometrical crack garden is enhanced with a winsome statue and set off by a low planting of boxwood.*

vogue on the Continent, soil pockets were introduced into rock gardens throughout England and the United States. It was also during this period and up until World War I that some gardeners tried to recreate the look of the mountains in their gardens, turning once again to crystalline spar, now to imitate the ice-covered slopes of the mountain peaks. After World War

I, the natural rock garden became fashionable, and it is to this day.

Today, with the renewed popularity of rock gardens, there has been a renaissance of interest in the alpine house. Unlike greenhouses and stove houses, alpine houses are provided with a refrigeration system, to keep temperatures cool for the plants during the summer.

Above: *Marggy Kerr
planted her medieval crack
garden in East Hampton,
New York, with herbs and
cultivars authentic to the
period. The classic pattern
of bricks that she employed
derives from the brickwork
in Bruges, Belgium.*

Left: *A starting cactus
container garden at the
Farell Duran residence near
Barcelona, Spain, is cer-
tainly one of the most
unusual rock gardens in
the world.*

outcroppings, and it is not until one reaches the summit that the dramatic view down the hillside and out onto the surrounding countryside of the spectacular Hudson River Valley is revealed.

Among the many alpine flowering plants installed is the *Gentiana acaulis,* which blooms profusely, tucked into rock crevices. This plant is known by gardeners to be an extremely difficult plant to bring to flower, but Cabot advises to try by planting a number of them in different areas of a garden. Stone Crop also contains several alpine houses, a series of striking wall gardens, and a number of raised alpine and trough gardens.

The Leonard J. Buck Garden in Far Hills, New Jersey, is the site of an extraordinary series of rock and ledge gardens that are open to the public. Buck, a rich international businessman and engineer, bought the fifteen-acre property during the 1920s. Located in Somerset County —an area that gives meaning to New Jersey's tag line, "The Garden State"—this lovely sylvan valley is now the site of the garden. As a disciple of Irish landscape designer William Robinson, he opted for a naturalistic garden, utilizing the dramatic landscape by planting cultivars that grew in this type of environment. In 1930, he hired the noted Swiss landscape architect Zenon Schreiber to oversee the project and within ten years had accomplished most of what he had set out to do.

Strolling along a series of woodland paths, one passes spectacular rock outcroppings and in and out of wooded

areas planted with rhododendrons, dogwood, azalea, pieris, heather, and kalmia. A stream leads into the Lower Pond, to Moggy Brook, and then to the Upper Pond. Many native plants as well as alpine plants from all over the world are installed throughout. The garden was donated to the county in 1976.

At Virginia Felbusch's garden in San Francisco, California, the traditional rock

Above: *With the help of designer Dennis Shaw, Virginia Felbusch transformed the steep slope in her backyard in San Francisco, California, into a series of terraces and planted them with succulents, perennials, and shrubs.*

Opposite: *Some of the brilliantly colored succulents in Felbusch's garden.*

garden prototype has been flamboyantly adapted to a highly individualistic concept. When she bought the property, Felbusch was faced with a steep slope of bare earth which looked up to her neighbor's house. With the help of designer Dennis Shaw, she solved the problems of privacy, erosion, and stark landscape by installing a series of terraces profusely planted with brilliantly colored succulents and some bulbs, shrubs, and perennial plants for foliage contrast. The result is a nearly maintenance-free phantasmagoria of bizarre colorations, shapes, and textures. Among the succulents are eight varieties of aloe, and many aeoniums, agaves, echeverias, ice plants, and sedums.

Even when the available landscape cannot be adapted to a rock garden, many gardeners are so taken with the charm of alpine plants that they install miniature landscapes in raised beds and ancient troughs. At the Royal Botanic Garden, Edinburgh, a series of stone troughs are planted with tender, miniature varieties of alpine plants that thrive neither in the natural rock garden nor in the nearby alpine house. They are protected from searing sun with slatting and from heavy rains with protective cover. Hundreds of varieties of plants can be found here, but most interesting are the saxifrages, with their tiny, low cushions of foliage, and the drabas, compact domes of greenery from which bright

Above: *Installed in an ancient water trough, this landscape-in-miniature is one of many at Dower House, Northamptonshire, England, the residence of the late Sir David and Lady Scott.*

Opposite: *A wall garden at Yew Tree Cottage in Ampney-St.-Mary's, England, is a good example of the English penchant for installing plants in every available nook and cranny.*

A *waterfall of deep
fuchsia aubrieta at the
Logan Botanic Garden,
one of the finest wall
gardens in Scotland.*

One of Jonathan and Daphne Shackleton's trough gardens at Beech Park, near Dublin, Ireland, contains pale blue Veronica armena *as well as a* Juniperus communis *'Hibernica', which provides an interesting vertical accent.*

yellow flowers protrude in spring. All over Britain, stone troughs have been rescued from farms by eager gardeners.

Lady Scott, also known as Valerie Finnis, the horticultural photographer, has an extensive collection of trough gardens at the Dower House, Northamptonshire, England. Each trough is planted to resemble an alpine landscape in miniature, containing many rare plants, gravel screes, and attractive rocks. Most

contain collections of saxifrages, the alpine plant that thrives in the British Isles but is hardy only along North America's Pacific coast. These small, silvery-gray-green domed cushions or small rosettes of foliage sport charming blossoms in many colors on one- to two-inch stems. Interplanted among the saxifrages are sempervivum, commonly called "hens and chicks," various sedums, and a host of other alpine plants.

On a smaller scale, but equally as charming, is the garden created by Barbara Shuker and her daughter Penelope Pollit. The two have created an exquisite cottage garden with an emphasis on alpines at their home, Yew Tree Cottage, in Ampney-St.-Mary, a tiny Gloucestershire village dotted with thatched-roof houses. Throughout the garden are placed troughs planted with sedums, sempervivums, and miniature alpines.

Both of these private English gardens, along with perhaps a thousand others, are open to the public at specified times of the year under the National Gardens Scheme Charitable Trust. A catalog of participating garden owners, informally called "The Yellow Book," is available in the United States through the British Travel Bookstore, 40 West Fifty-seventh Street, New York, New York 10019.

At Beech Park, near Dublin, Ireland, Jonathan and Daphne Shackleton continue to maintain the garden started by Jonathan's late father, David, in 1950. Since the property is flat, with no natural outcroppings of stone, miniature alpine

Spanking white candytuft
(Iberis) and magenta
aubrieta are combined with
miniature species daffo-
dils and pale blue Scilla
tubergeniana in the
author's rock garden in
Peconic, New York.

At Quinta da Aveleda, in northern Portugal, an elaborately embellished staircase is enhanced by potted fibrous begonias and variegated geraniums.

The crack garden is a recent innovation that seems to have started in England. Tough, low-growing alpine plants are perfectly suited to this environment. Rather than install large, uninterrupted patio areas of slate, brick, or other paving materials, gardeners plant tiny alpine plants such as creeping thymes, chamomile, miniature bulbs, and a host of others in the cracks between stones or, in some cases, in areas left unpaved to accommodate the plants. The effect is lovely, with the plants softening the harsh paved areas with varicolored foliage and bright blossoms.

One word of warning to would-be alpine garden enthusiasts. I installed one on my property and have found that after five years, I would like to enlarge it. My addiction to the charm and romance of rockery plants has brought out a previously unrecognized acquisitive nature. Somehow I cannot resist adding this or that plant from the Andes, Himalayas, Alps, or tundra areas to my collection. Mercifully, the addiction is not expensive, as most plants suitable for rockeries cost only about three or four dollars apiece.

A *deeply shaded area at Quinta da Aveleda has been turned into a crack garden and planted with moss and annual impatiens for a touch of color.*

Wild Flowers and Grasses

Wild flowers and ornamental grasses are enjoying an unprecedented popularity today. Boxes of wild flower seeds, customized for various geographical locations throughout the United States and abroad, are sold in just about every garden center. The instructions imply that one simply sprinkles the seeds around and a meadow or shaded wild flower garden will instantly appear. Unfortunately, it is not that simple. Before planting can be undertaken, all weeds must be removed from the area, a process that can take months. And then, after planting, the seedlings must be carefully nurtured. If one properly prepares and tends a wild flower garden—or one of ornamental grasses, whether planted in meadows or in an intimate water garden—the effect can be magnificent.

122

Opposite: Landscape designer Elizabeth Lear installed a magnificent wild flower meadow garden on artists David and Lucille Berrill Paulsen's grounds in Water Mill, New York. The brightly spotted landscape perfectly complements the

Designer Elizabeth Lear, of Southampton, New York, has installed several meadow gardens on the South Fork of Long Island. One such, for artists David and Lucille Berrill Paulsen in Water Mill, is a spectacular wild meadow garden surrounding the house. … nth-century … moved from

… the success … len rested in … natural environ … f the build … ary scheme … anticize the … len's profile … a that all of … s the under … landscape … o impose an … cape.

… I wanted to … ank which … ill side, al … ing allowed … from the … ortunity to … ubtle eleva … appears to … ard under … intentional … area feels like it was carved out of the field and planted minimally with evergreens," Lear adds.

In the garden she planted more than thirty varieties of wild flowers. "The meadow season begins in spring with the beauty of a pink Kwanzan cherry orchard (aligned to the house) underplanted with blues: *Nemophila menziesii, Dianthus deltoides,* and *Linum perenne lewisii.* The early midsummer season is heightened with an outrageous display of red, white, and blue *Centaurea cyanus, Chrysanthemum leucanthemum,* and *Papaver rhoeas.* In the late summer season masses of yellows, pinks, and oranges blend together for a grand finale of *Coreopsis lanceolata* and *tinctoria,* fescues, cosmos, *Achillea, Monarda, Rudbeckia hirta, Lythrum, Buddleia, Alcea, Physostegia,* delphinium, larkspur, and asters."

Lear's planting concept was to layer the garden high, medium, and low, thus creating large waves of bloom delicately intermixed with fescues.

"I mixed higher percentages of cosmos, black-eyed Susan, red Flanders poppy, bachelor button, oxeye daisy, California poppy, [and] Plains coreopsis to articulate the drifts of bloom. Perennials were planted in groups of eight to twelve in the higher areas.

"I would characterize the garden's continued performance as a painterly explosion in nature. Although its composition was intentional and designed, the scheme appears totally natural, as if cultivation of the previous potato fields just ceased and the field reverted to its natural form.

"The owners are landscape painters and gardeners, thus they encouraged my revolutionary approach to create a controlled mess," Lear adds.

Above: *In the Paulsen meadow garden, Lear planted fields of white oxeye daisies and accented them with blue salvia.*

Right: *Later in the season, the Paulsen meadow garden sports a carpet of wild daisies. Wouldn't it be nice to sit amid the flowers and eat fresh, wild strawberries while fashioning a daisy chain out of the seemingly endless supply of blossoms?*

Large drifts of red
Flanders poppies set off
sweeps of yellow Plains
coreopsis and oxeye
daisies in the Paulsen
meadow garden.

Below: *In a wild flower display at Mr. and Mrs. Mel Atlas's home in Bridgehampton, New York, Lear incorporated perennial balloon-flower (*Platycodon*), annual nicotiana, and lilies with wild foxglove (*Digitalis*), black-eyed Susan (*Rudbeckia hirta*), and daisies.*

Following pages: *In Scotland and Ireland, bluebells are seen all along the roadside during the late spring days.*

Wild flowers of many varieties are used both in North America and in Europe to produce gardens with a natural look. In Scotland and Ireland, bluebells provide carpets of blue beneath shade plantings. Often, the charming miniature species daffodils are naturalized in tandem with the bluebells. One particularly effective planting of bluebells is installed beneath towering eucalyptus trees at Mount Usher, County Wicklow, Ireland. And in the United States, the native Virginia bluebells (*Mertensia virginica*) provide a similar blanket of blue.

The extravagant *Trillium grandiflorum*, native to the United States, has for several centuries been a great favorite in European gardens, having been exported from Virginia during the early days of colonization. Substantial plantings of them are installed at the Royal Botanic Garden, Edinburgh, Scotland, as well as in many private gardens both in Europe and in North America.

From the earliest days of civilization, and even before, grasses have been essential to man's survival. It was the food grasses—corn, wheat, millet, rice, oats, barley, and sugar cane—that changed the human condition from nomadic to agricultural. The first settlements were created by those

early farmers who stayed in one place in order to grow food for themselves and for livestock. Trade and thus human civilization resulted directly from the cultivation of these food grasses.

The first paper, the ancient Egyptian papyrus, was made from a soft rush grass called *Juncus effusus*. It is still used today in Japan for weaving tatami, the traditional floor covering. Bamboo has been used for construction and to make fences, fishing rods, and water pipes since the beginning of civilization. Most bamboos are native to Asia; however, some are native to the Western Hemisphere as well.

In plantings, ornamental grasses offer interesting textures and colors and a low-maintenance profile, so they are being used more and more in contemporary gardens. Since they are pest and disease free, they do not require spraying. Because their stems are strong, staking is unnecessary. They do not sport blossoms, so deadheading is not necessary. And most are drought resistant, so they do not require watering during dry summer months. Available in a vast array of colors, including gold, gray, green, blue, yellow, and fiery red, and ranging in size from dense, ground-level clumps to soaring twenty-foot-high reeds, they are versatile, adapting to many different settings: lawns,

Bluebells have been naturalized beneath a grove of eucalyptus trees at Mount Usher, County Wicklow, Ireland. In the distance, the famous deciduous azaleas of the estate beckon.

A planting of the extravagant, North American cultivar Trillium grandiflorum at the Royal Botanic Garden, Edinburgh, Scotland.

Landscape designer Connie Cross installed a seaside garden of grass, native Rosa rugosa, and Sedum 'Autumn Gold' at the entrance to the public beach on Peconic Bay in Peconic, New York. Later in the season, Rosa rugosa sports brilliant red rose hips, which can be made into a delicious tea or jelly.

shady wooded areas, beach properties, and wetland bogs. In addition, they add texture and interest to perennial borders and flower beds.

Landscape designer Connie Cross has installed a number of gardens featuring grasses on Long Island. Particularly effective is a small planting on the beach in Cutchogue, New York, which includes autumn sedum, delicate pink Fairy rose, and some lovely colored grasses. In the fall, the pale pink blossoms of the sedum turn to a deep rust color, and the grasses contrast richly with these blossoms.

Left: *Native horsetail (*Equisetum hyemale*) offers vertical accents in the lily pool planting at William Shank's white garden in Amagansett, New York.*

Opposite: *At the Muso–de Tracia residence in Southold, New York, Cross installed a planting of* Miscanthus sinensis *'Gracillimus'. Considered by many to be the most elegant of ornamental grasses, it is a frequent subject of Japanese artists.*

Parterre, Espalier, and Topiary

Throughout history, human beings have imposed themselves on nature, attempting to "civilize" it. Parterre, topiary, and espalier are three examples of such attempts. Early Egyptian wall paintings, as well as Greek and Roman mosaics, reveal that people have pruned, trimmed, and trained plants since the beginning of civilization.

A popular form of garden from the Middle Ages to the early nineteenth century, the parterre garden is a series of geometric shapes, usually formed by trimmed hedges, and often containing plantings of flowers. The frescoes and paintings of the great masters of Renaissance Italy reveal a penchant for parterre gardens during this period. But it was not until the seventeenth century, when the parterre style

of gardens spread throughout Europe, that it became the dominant style in garden design. During this era, a number of parterre styles evolved.

Parterre gardens were popularized primarily by the French. A family named Mollet pioneered in this area with *Parterres de broderie,* or embroidered parterres. Planted with flowing, plantlike designs, embroidered parterres were generally made of boxwood set against a background of earth, sometimes edged with grass. The style was favored by the Bourbon kings, and the royal gardens at the Tuileries were originally done in this style. The royalty and nobility of other countries imitated the French, particularly the Polish royal family in the eighteenth century at their residences at Bialystok, Nieborow, and Wilanow.

By the middle of the eighteenth century, embroidered parterres were out of style in France, and severe geometric designs fashioned out of flowers and grass or pebbles had become popular in parterre design. A contemporary example of this style can be seen near Richmond, Virginia, at Redesdale, owned by Mr. and Mrs. Charles Reed, Jr. Here white and yellow pansies are set amid borders of sky blue forget-me-nots. After the French Revolution, perhaps because of aristocratic associations, parterre gardens were no longer in fashion in France.

Across the Channel, the English had invented their own style of parterres. These were designs of cut grass lined with paths with statues as focal points. With the advent of the Italian romantic and English naturalistic garden styles during the mid- to late-nineteenth century, parterre gardens fell out of favor and, although gardeners have made sporadic attempts to reintroduce them, they have never regained their former popularity.

The baroque parterre gardens at the Royal Palace of Het Loo in Appledorn, Holland, have recently been restored and are unique in Europe. Unlike other baroque royal gardens—many of which now employ nineteenth-century spacing and plantings—the design, plant selection, and spacing at Het Loo are all true to their seventeenth-century conception. Originally built between 1685 and 1692 as a hunting seat for William III, prince of Orange, stadholder of the Netherlands, and king of England, the palace was designed by architect Jacob Roman according to a plan made by the Academie d'Architecture in Paris. The interior and garden design were executed by Daniel Maros, a French Huguenot who had fled to Holland in 1685.

Some additions and changes were made to the original gardens during the eighteenth century. They were destroyed, however, when Louis Bonaparte, who had been named king of Holland by his brother Napoleon, used Het Loo as a summer residence during the years 1807–09. As parterre gardens were no longer in fashion, Louis Bonaparte redesigned Het Loo's grounds in the English manner and ordered the magnificent baroque creation filled in with soil. All of the waterways,

Left: *Baroque parterres at the Royal Palace of Het Loo in Appeldorn, Holland, carpet the intimate Queen's Garden. Orange trees, laurel, and tropical plants from the Cape of Good Hope line the long pergola, which is covered with hornbeam.*

Pages 136–137: *The parterre garden at the elegant Palace of the Marquez de Fronteira near Lisbon, Portugal, is accented with delicate Italianate statuary. The parterres set off the two grand staircases that lead to the King's Gallery, a lavish, blue-and-white tile-embellished terrace where Portugal's former rulers forever keep watch over the garden.*

Preceding pages: *At Redesdale, near Richmond, Virginia, parterres of white and yellow pansies bordered with sky blue forget-me-nots are set amid geometric-patterned brick paths. The garden is reminiscent of the French style of parterres in vogue after box-lined parterres went out of fashion in the middle of the eighteenth century.*

paths, ponds, sculptures, and parterres vanished beneath the tons of earth and were replaced by a more natural and romantic landscape. Oak trees were planted and informal borders installed; nothing remained of the original scheme.

Het Loo was owned by the royal family of Holland until 1975, when Queen Juliana relinquished further use of the palace by the royal family. Shortly thereafter, it was designated a national museum, and the original baroque gardens were restored with the removal of the eighteenth-, nineteenth-, and twentieth-century additions. The restoration commenced under the guidance of Willemien de Geer, a landscape designer. During the initial excavating, waterways, planting borders, wall foundations, and mosaics on the bottom of what were once waterways and ponds were unearthed. Each discovery created enormous excitement in Holland as well as further support of the restoration in Parliament.

Many seventeenth- and eighteenth-century engravings, drawings, and written accounts of the palace and gardens were extant, including *A Description of the King's Royal Palace and Gardens at Loo*, written in London in 1699 by Walter Harris, M.D., the "physician in ordinary to His Majesty," King William III. Waterways, paths, ponds, and walls were reconstructed first. Fountains were then recreated, and some of the original statues that had remained on the grounds were positioned in their original locations. Other Het Loo sculptures were found in different parts of Holland and returned to the site.

The parterres were then blocked out. First the entire scheme was laid out on a quarter-inch scale in nearby fields. Once the designers were satisfied with the design, each planting was measured to full scale and cut out of paper, which was then placed on the palace grounds in the appropriate place. Small stakes were driven into the ground surrounding the paper. It was then removed, plastic bender board was attached to the stakes, and *voilà* . . . parterres!

Once the geometric patterns had been installed, planting began. The search went on throughout Holland for specimens of flowering plants, fruit trees, and shrubbery that had existed during the seventeenth century. De Geer again referred to Harris's descriptions of the flower

Among the legacies that the British left to Singapore are their propensity for mirth, the ubiquitous English sparrow, the tea biscuit, and the Victorian ribbon parterre at the Botanic Gardens.

This parterre at the Het Loo Palace is a perfect restoration of the original baroque parterre installed during the seventeenth century.

plantings. Although invaluable, they were not as full as his extensive descriptions of the design and architectural details of the gardens. He had written: "In the spring there is a variety of the finest tulips, hyacinths, ranunculi, anemone, auricula, narcissi, etc. In the summer there are double poppies of all colors, Gilliflowers [Dianthus], Larks-heel, etc. In the autumn, the Sunflower, Indian Cresses, Pass-rose or Stock-rose, Marygolds, etc."

De Geer also researched seventeenth-century watercolors for additional clues. The precise horticultural drawings of Maria Sibylla Merian (Dutch, 1647–1717) and those of her contemporaries Pieter Withoos, Sister Alida Withoos, and Herman Henstenburgh provided additional information. Old books on medicine and horticulture in the archives at the University of Utrecht were poured over for further clues.

The baroque taste in flowers was by no means subtle, as floral still lifes by the Flemish and Dutch masters of the period indicate. Flamboyant striped tulips, similar in mien to the Rembrandt and parrot tulip varieties today, gigantic double cabbage roses, and startling double peonies were in fashion. Double red poppies, bright orange fritillaria, purple iris, yucca, and lilies were also popular. The brighter the colors and the larger the bloom, the more desirable the flower, according to seventeenth-century dictates. And one can see them all at Het Loo, as well as many other cultivars extant during the seventeenth century in Holland.

The cultivars at Het Loo include *Rosa gallica* 'Versicolor', *Rosa hugonis*, Tuscany rose, *Ranunculus aconitifolius*, *Geranium pratense*, dog-tooth violet

The secret "Garden of the Heart" at the David and Alice van Buuren Museum near Brussels, Belgium, invites visitors to pause and reflect on past, present, and future loves.

(*Erythronium dens-canis*), lily of Peru (*Scilla peruviana*), *Sternbergia lutea, Bulbocodium vernum,* autumn or saffron crocus (*Colchicum autumnale*), *Crocus sativus* and *vernus,* paper-whites (*Narcissus tazetta*), cyclamen, *Fritillaria imperialis* and *meleagris,* and *Leucojum vernum.* Also *Iris* × *germanica* in blue, white, and rose, *Camellia japonica,* king's-spear (*Asphodeline lutea*), common absinthe (*Artemisia absinthium*), and tarragon (*Artemisia dracunculus*), artists' acanthus (*Acanthus mollis*; prized for its ornamental properties and recurrent in Western art), maltese cross (*Lychnis chalcedonica*), widow's-tears (*Tradescantia*

virginiana), marguerite (*Chrysanthemum leucanthemum*), English daisy (*Bellis perennis*), garden wolfsbane or garden monkshood (*Aconitum napellus*), various campanulas, *Gentiana asclepiadea,* and columbine (*Aquilegia vulgaris*). Note that many of the flowers grown during the seventeenth century are still popular in gardens today.

From the entrance to the Het Loo garden—an elevated terrace at the rear of the palace—the entire sweep of the parterres looks like a gigantic, magical Persian carpet. To the west of the palace is the King's Garden, with a small mall originally used as a bowling green. This

The maze at the David and Alice van Buuren Museum was installed in 1968, and although the hedges are now only a little more than twenty years old, they are now tall enough for children to become hopelessly lost in the labyrinth of yew-lined paths.

Below: One of the horticultural oddities of the world, a tunnel created from cypress in the parterre garden at the Mateus vineyards in northern Portugal forms a nearly pitch-black vault, a perfect rendezvous for illicit encounters.

Opposite: At Quinta da Bacalhoa, near Lisbon, Portugal, the symmetric, boxwood parterre garden borders a walnut and mandarin orange grove.

garden is planted with blue and orange flowers that coordinate with the decor of the king's bedroom in the west wing, which overlooks the garden. The box-bordered parterres in the middle of this garden are vibrantly alive with color, incorporating blues and oranges with yellows and reds. The outer parterres are more subtle. The flowers utilized are orange *Fritillaria imperialis* in spring and nasturtium, delphinium, iris, and marigolds during summer and fall. Pyramidical junipers add vertical accents.

To the east of the palace is the Queen's Garden, intimate, subtle, and somewhat more feminine and refined than the King's Garden. It is enclosed by a long pergola covered with hornbeam. While the King's Garden has a mall, the Queen's has two fountains and small parterres. Around the parterres are orange trees, laurel, and tropical plants from the Cape of Good Hope. During the seventeenth century, these were grown in the nearby orangeries during winter. Hardy fruit trees, varieties extant during the seventeenth century, are espaliered against the south walls. Included in the planting are Present

Above: *A lush, precisely clipped arcade of beech, flanked by classic urns on pedestals, leads visitors into the box and lilac parterre garden at Birr Castle, Birr, County Offaly, Ireland. Visitors are overwhelmed by the intoxicatingly scented, rare lilacs when they are in bloom.*

Right: *In a restoration of a medieval parterre garden that is situated along a canal in Bruges, Belgium, Baron van der Elst combined topiary and grass parterres with a period herb garden. When the cacophonous bells toll in the tower of the nearby cathedral, a thrilling and unforgettable magic spell is cast over the garden, literally chilling the spine.*

of England, Price Mauritskers, and Princess Noble apples, as well as Tros de Orange apricot, orange pear, green mirabelle plum, perzik nectarine, and mulberry.

The restoration continues at Het Loo and, according to de Geer, the tasks ahead include yearly propagation of old varieties of tulips and narcissus until there are sufficient numbers to execute the entire bulb plantings. The search continues for more perennial plants of the period as well as for some of the missing statuary. The garden is expected to be totally restored to its seventeenth-century glory by 1995. "We've been literally digging into

history and will continue to do so until we have finished," de Geer says.

There is a captivating, small parterre garden at the David and Alice van Buuren Museum, near Brussels, Belgium. Designed by landscape architect René Pechère and installed in 1970 by the late Alice van Buuren, the Garden of the Heart is perfectly symmetrical and measures only eighteen yards square. With its heart-shaped, box-lined parterres planted with ruby red fibrous begonias set amid the fan-shaped paving of small gray Belgian blocks, it is a place in which to linger.

Above: *The collection of topiary included in Longwood Gardens at Kennett Square, Pennsylvania, has been trained, trimmed, and clipped into geometric forms, suggesting giant chess pieces playing on a chessboard of green grass.*

Opposite: *Towering topiary columns frame the entrance to one of the gardens at Beloiel, Belgium's Versailles. Prince Antoine de Ligne continues to maintain and expand the elaborate parklike gardens of the palace.*

An arbor at the far end and a white bench complete the scene in this peaceful garden, created especially for meditation.

Near Lisbon, Portugal, at the Palace of the Marquez de Fronteira, an Italian parterre garden—so identified because of its rounded corners, which are typical of the Italian school of parterre design—has a splendid planting of precisely trimmed boxwood that is accented with yew topiary and transversed with gravel paths. Fountains graced with captivating, childlike figures and subtly erotic statuary stand at the path crossings. The surrounding walls are covered with tile renderings of the planets, seasons, and signs of the zodiac.

Almost as magnificent is the marble-floored terrace at the side of the palace. Here the walls are totally covered with a series of tile paintings depicting the arts, interspersed with niches containing statues of the Greek gods after whom the planets are named. As many of the tile paintings in the garden depict astrological subjects, the current owner, the Marquez de Fronteira, wondered if there was any hidden meaning to the garden's theme.

"Some researchers are studying the cosmological aspects of the garden, trying to find a relationship to science," Fronteira says. "They have concluded that the garden is . . . some kind of zodiacal puzzle which has yet to be solved. The twelve horsemen rendered in tile on the water tank are divided into groups of four. These could represent the months of the year and the seasons. The parterre garden is divided into sixteen large parterres with

three hundred sixty-five smaller parterres within, the number of days in the year. There could be some sort of relationship to the microcosm," he concludes.

In Portugal, there are also parterre gardens at Quinta da Balcalhoa, near Lisbon, and at Solar de Mateus, near Guimaraes. At Mateus, the garden's broad terrace is lined with allegorical marble statues and looks out over a series of parterres on two levels. Various flowering trees—oleander, magnolia, camellia, lagerstroemia, rhododendron, and spirea—and soft, colorful beds of annuals contrast with the sharp edges of the clipped green box in the parterres. But it is a tunnel of cedar, pruned and trained for at least a hundred years, that is the jewel of this garden. The mysterious, murky passageway, formed from the dense foliage of live trees, is an extraordinary oddity. It leads from the foot of the first parterre terrace down a hundred feet to the lower parterres and out to the vineyard beyond. From the outside it resembles a giant caterpillar with green skin the texture of a soft carpet. The tunnel of cedar is adjacent to another extraordinary tunnel, about a hundred feet long, fashioned out of cypress trees.

In Ireland, where "wild," naturalized gardens are favored, there are, nonetheless, several parterre gardens. The one at Powerscourt, in Enniskerry, County Wicklow, is done in the grand manner, formal, stark, with paved areas delineating the patterns. At Birr Castle in Birr, County Offaly, the home of the Count

Opposite: At Powerscourt, in Enniskerry, County Wicklow, Ireland, an outbuilding sports a profuse display of climbing, pale pink Clematis montana rubens. Their delicate blossoms provide a striking counterpoint to the traditional lace curtains that frame the windows.

and Countess Rosse, a more informal parterre garden of box is planted with scores of rare lilacs, in a rather innovative use of the parterre style. There is also an allée of columnar box here, in fact, according to the *Guinness Book of World Records,* the tallest on earth.

A particularly captivating parterre garden, which predates the classic examples of this form in France and England, is a medieval restoration parterre at the Museum of Baron Joseph van der Elst in Bruges, Belgium. A visit to this garden, situated behind the ancient house, adjacent to the canal, and across from the soaring bell tower of the Church of Our Lady, is a trip back in time. Paving stones covered with moss are set amid grass, and blocks of stone delineate the parterres in which grass and herbs grow. Examples of tiered topiary trees set off the garden.

At the Botanic Gardens in Singapore, there are two unusual gardens that are related to the parterre garden. One is a clock garden, a planting that duplicates a sundial. The other is a ribbon parterre garden, which incorporates flowering plants into flowing "ribbons" of color. This style was universally popular during the Victorian era.

Closely related to parterre gardens are mazes or labyrinths, which are currently enjoying renewed popularity in Europe and the United States. Their origins are lost in prehistory, as early pictorial maze art and ancient earthworks attest. The Egyptians, Aztecs, Incas, Minoans, and Mycenaeans all designed mazes. It was at Knossos, on Crete, during the Bronze Age that, according to legend, Theseus confronted the Minotaur. The Romans peppered Europe with mosaic labyrinths, and every culture since has created mazes.

The small maze adjacent to the Garden of the Heart at the van Buuren Museum was designed by René Pechère and installed in 1968. This labyrinth measures a mere twenty-two by fifty-five yards, hardly big enough, one might think, to present any difficulty in solving. A maze traditionally has a goal at its center; here, a giant Atlantic cedar in a far corner serves as the focus. The winding flagstone paths that lead to the cedar—and mislead to many dead ends—are flanked with a hedge of thirteen hundred yews. The labyrinth also shelters seven rooms, each of which contains a small *cire perdue* cast sculpture on a narrow blue stone pedestal. These are all the creation of André Willequet. Beneath each statue is a quotation from the Old Testament's Song of Songs. Small mazes can also be visited at the Botanic Gardens in Singapore and at Beloiel, Belgium's stateliest home.

The art of topiary—shaping trees and shrubs by clipping, pruning, and training—dates from at least the days of Pliny the Elder, who lived in the first century A.D. In his writings Pliny describes a hunt scene, fleets of ships, and other images all shaped out of cypress trees. It is also known that boxwood was shaped into various forms during the Roman era. By the

Opposite: A vigorously growing, snow-white Clematis montana *climbs the ancient stone walls of the stable at Beech Park, near Dublin, Ireland. Docile white doves seem to find the environment to their liking, as they make their home in a nearby dovecote.*

Middle Ages, plants were not just clipped and pruned but also trained to grow on wire frames, although the shapes were nonrepresentational. During the Italian Renaissance, however, a major topiary revival took place. A book dating from 1499, by Hypnerotomachia Poliphili, contains illustrations for various basic topiary forms including spherical, mushroom, and ring forms as well as more sophisticated renderings of human figures, urns, and other architectural motifs. Representations of these horticultural oddities can be seen in paintings of the era.

During the sixteenth and seventeenth centuries, the use of topiary in garden design reached a frenzied crescendo, prompting Sir Francis Bacon, in "Of Gardens," to advocate simplicity and the use of topiary to create only architectural forms. "I for my part," Bacon wrote, "do not like images cut out of juniper or other garden stuff—they be for children. Low hedges round like welts, with some pretty pyramids I like well, and in some places fair columns." By the eighteenth century the craze for topiary had run its course, and it became associated with all that was old-fashioned and in bad taste. It had increasingly become the realm of the parvenu tradesman, as parodied in Alexander Pope's lampoon "Catalogue of Greens," published in 1713.

Topiary in architectural shapes can be found in many of the classic gardens of the world. In Belgium, at Beloiel, the palace of the Prince de Ligne, towering columns topped with urns, all sheared from

R osemary Verey's classic knot garden at Barnsley House, in Gloucestershire, England, is the successful result of scholarly research in horticultural sources dating from the sixteenth and seventeenth centuries. A hedge of rosemary encloses two early knot designs planted with boxwood and wall germander.

hornbeam and beech, form an impressive arcade. Longwood Gardens, in Kennett Square, Pennsylvania, also has a fine collection of architectural topiary. And topiary adapts nicely to container growing. Many gardeners include one or two examples in their collections.

Topiary in representational shapes can be quite amusing, particularly if the collection is a large one. Near one of the entrances to the Botanic Gardens in Singapore is the topiary display. Neatly clipped shrubs of *Carmona retusa* are trained and sculpted on wire supports to recreate the decorative shapes of the world's animal kingdom. An elephant, a crocodile, a tail-wagging dog, and an eagle poised on the edge of flight are some of the creatures under the watchful eye of the topiary's keeper, a figure of a man in a hat smoking a pipe and carrying a thick walking stick. The menagerie serves as a reminder of the short-lived garden zoo, which lasted from 1875 to 1905.

Espalier, a method of training trees or other plants to grow on one plane, has been used in Europe since Roman times, primarily in the cultivation of fruit trees. It has also been used decoratively, however, to soften large blank spaces on walls or fences or as a focal point in a garden. There are many forms of espalier—fan, candelabrum, single cordon, double cordon, and so forth. Although not technically espalier, there are many related ways to train plants to grow on the exteriors of buildings, on walls, or on pergolas or gazebos.

Below: *In Sagaponack, New York, Robert Dash's laburnum walk is now more than four years old. The display of cascading yellow panicles becomes more and more spectacular with each passing year.*

In England, Scotland, and Ireland, where many gardens contain ancient walls, gardeners train either *Clematis montana* or *Clematis montana rubens* to grow on walls or buildings. These cultivars grow vigorously and sport spanking white or soft, pastel pink flowers in spring. At Powerscourt and at Beech Park, near Dublin, Ireland, plantings of these cultivars scale ancient walls and towers. At Birr Castle, a lovely pale purple wisteria has been trained above an open-topped gazebo made of four stone pillars with wrought-iron grillwork above.

Mary Bowe, the amiable proprietress of Marfield House, an elegant country inn in Gorey, County Wexford, trained ivy and roses to climb a trellis attached to the side of the house. And in Sagaponack, New York, Robert Dash recently added a spectacular laburnum wall to his extraordinarily original garden. A large pergola supports a series of trained laburnum trees, and when they are in bloom the panicles of sweet-smelling yellow blossoms cascade down from the roof and along the sides of the structure. It is an utterly breathtaking sight.

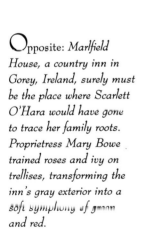

Opposite: *Marlfield House, a country inn in Gorey, Ireland, surely must be the place where Scarlett O'Hara would have gone to trace her family roots. Proprietress Mary Bowe trained roses and ivy on trellises, transforming the inn's gray exterior into a soft symphony of green and red.*

Perennial Borders

In the name of practicality, there are some obvious rules to follow in designing a perennial border. It is best to plant tall plants in the rear, medium-high plants in the middle, and low-growing plants in the front. This is only sensible, for low-growing plants would be hidden if taller plants were installed in front of them. And, for easy maintenance, it is best either to limit the width of the border or to ensure access to the deepest parts of it. With the exception of specimen plants, at least three of each variety and preferably five should be planted together. Beyond these guidelines, a perennial border is a very personal creation. There are probably no two on earth that are exactly the same.

The origins of the perennial border can be

traced to the seventeenth-century English countryside, where peasants planted borders of flowers around their cottages. It was not until the late nineteenth century, however, when the slowly emerging, informal English style of garden design fully replaced the formal French style in Europe, that the perennial border as we know it today came into its own.

Irish landscape designer William Robinson was certainly instrumental in the popularization of this natural form of gardening. He loathed the exotic, artificial ribbon bedding of annual plants and the patterned beds of screaming gold marigolds, fiery red salvia, electric-blue lobelia, and red or orange canna lilies that were ubiquitous in both private and public gardens during the Victorian era. In Newport, Rhode Island, a robber baron millionaire tossed a Persian rug on the

ground at his summer "cottage" and ordered his gardeners to duplicate it in annuals. Even today, the practice persists as clocks, the names of towns, and even the American flag are reproduced with bedding annuals.

Since they are tender, these annual plants must be started from seed in greenhouses during the late winter every year. The cannas have to be dug in the fall, stored over the winter, and replanted in the spring. It is said that Robinson so detested annuals that when commissioned to install one such bed in his native Ireland, he purposely opened all the vents in his employer's greenhouse one cold night so the plants would freeze to death.

Robinson's alternative was to install borders of herbaceous perennials, most of which are, or derive from, wild flowers of the fields. He logically suggested that they

Above: *One of the few remaining Gertrude Jekyll–designed perennial borders is at Folly Farm, in Berkshire, England. Note the way Jekyll blended pastel pink, blue, and white with deep red and cerise.*

Preceding pages: *The perennial borders at Beech Park, near Dublin, Ireland, offer a vast range of plants, textures, and colors. Bright yellow Himalayan poppies, rare, deep-red single peonies, and cultivars strategically planted for their foliage —such as green and yellow euphorbia—all add diversity to the scheme.*

be planted in a natural, informal manner. Later in his career, when he was in charge of the Royal Botanic Society's perennial gardens in London's Regent's Park, he wrote a number of books delineating his theory that flower gardens should be informal and should consist of plantings of hardy or perennial plants. His books were widely read by gardeners and the fashion for ribbon beds of annuals faded.

English garden designer Gertrude Jekyll, a friend and contemporary of Robinson, shared his ideas and transformed gardens throughout the world with her own innovative vision. She refined Robinson's concept of informal plantings by popularizing the planting of borders in large masses of color, arranged in informal drifts. The subtle use of color was paramount to her designs. Her schemes were

At Beech Park, brilliant red single peonies complement the rich copper red of the Japanese maple.

based on complementary colors and the gradation of warm and cold colors. She also created one-color borders, using shades and tinges of a given color to determine the sequence of plants. She was also the first to install an all-white flowering border, a planting she designed for her own garden in Surrey, England. Throughout her life she worked closely with the architect Sir Edwin Lutyens, whose garden bench designs are still reproduced all over the world. By the beginning of the twentieth century, Jekyll's informal, perennial border had replaced ribbon-bedding and the patterned bed in England, Scotland, and Ireland.

Perennials offer subtle colorations that enable the gardener to "paint" with plants. They are hardy, surviving winter cold and bringing their lovely colors and foliage to the garden every year. Most perennials are highly resistant to disease and infestation, thus reducing maintenance chores. And, unlike annuals, they do not have to be started from seed every year. All of these characteristics of perennials have contributed to the popularity of the perennial border.

Below: *Marie Donnelly's sunny summer garden in Southampton, New York, highlights old-fashioned lemon lilies, pale pink phlox, and purple liatris.*

Opposite: *Donnelly combined perennials with brilliantly colored annuals in her striking poolside garden.*

One of the few Lutyens-Jekyll gardens that remains true to its original plan is at Folly Farm, located in the Berkshire hills just west of London. The garden was designed before World War I. Here Jekyll's near-perfect perennial border and her "garden room" concept are magnificently on view. Fortunately, through the years the various owners of Folly Farm have cherished the garden, and it has thus remained closer to its original form than most of the more than one hundred gardens designed by Lutyens and Jekyll. Today it is regarded as one of the finest twentieth-century English gardens. The present owners have commissioned consultant Vernon Russell-Smith to "simplify without changing the feel" of the garden, and they work closely with him on all aspects of design. The perennial border includes bright blue *Delphinium* 'Blue Jay'; tall, pale lavender *Campanula lactiflora*; deep purple *Salvia* 'Victoria'; pink *Penstemon*; white *Lilium regale*; tall-growing pink *Sidalcea*; and the sky blue annual *Nemophila*. White and pink shrub roses are used as accents and silver-foliaged *Stachys* 'Silvercarpet' provides a low-growing carpet to set off the planting. An occasional group of salmon-colored *Dianthus* 'Doris' provides a subtle change of color for accent.

At Beech Park, near Dublin, Ireland, the extensive perennial borders are set in an area enclosed by towering ancient walls. Amid the rare peonies, New Zealand daisies, and other treasures are large plantings of the ethereal blue poppy, *Meconopsis grandis*. This showstopper is largely unfamiliar to North American gardeners, except to those who garden in the Pacific Northwest or British Columbia. The reason is that *Meconopsis* requires the temperate winter, cool summer, long growing season, and abundant moisture found in both these regions.

In Southampton, New York, Marie Donnelly installed two major perennial borders on her property. One surrounds

Hostas, rhododendrons, and even a stately Irish yew are used in the perennial borders at Beech Park. A sedate bench sits in a grassy area of the garden, which has been invaded by small, wild daisies.

Like its cousin in Egypt, this sphinxlike sculpture covered with ivy gazes eternally at Helen and Val Dillon's beautiful perennial border in Dublin, Ireland.

the swimming pool, the other encloses the lawn. Her personal planting style combines a wider range of colors than that in the traditional Jekyll border. Pale yellow day lilies (*Hemerocallis*), deep purple balloon flower (*Platycodon*), rich red bee balm (*Monarda didyma*), white spider flower (*Cleome*), and pink phlox are accented by bright red annual zinnias.

In Helen and Val Dillon's Dublin, Ireland, town house garden, two extensive perennial borders line the immaculate

Below: *At Beech Park, a planting of* Meconopsis grandis, *or blue poppy. Regrettably, this magnificent cultivar thrives only in areas with moist summer climates, like the British Isles and the Pacific Northwest. When traveling, I would drive a hundred miles out of my way to see a planting like this again.*

lawn that leads to a willowy wrought-iron arbor smothered with white clematis. Beneath the arbor, shade-loving perennials provide color accents. A wide range of perennial flowering plants accompany lush foliage plants such as the charming green-and-yellow *Euphorbia epithymoides,* silver-toned *Stachys,* and deep bronze-purple-leafed *Heuchera* 'Palace Purple', so-

named because the first plants were grown on the grounds of the queen's palace at Kew Gardens in London. This superb foliage plant, which adds such interest to a perennial border, was first grown in the United States in 1983 and finally is widely available. In fact, it was named Plant of the Year for 1991 by the American Perennial Plant Association.

Opposite:
Deep blue dwarf bellflowers (Campanula), *hostas, and delphiniums bring subtle, cool tones to the traditional Jekyll perennial border at Folly Farm.*

Shade Gardens

There are many plants that adapt well to shady conditions, but the three that have always fascinated gardeners are ferns, mosses, and, of late, hostas. All three are reasonably versatile and can be combined with shade-loving flowering plants such as tuberous begonias, caladiums, astilbe, and annual impatiens, and ground covers such as lamium, creeping euonymous, and lily of the valley to create lush, mysterious, romantic areas in any garden.

Ferns are among the oldest known plants; imprints of them have been found in fossils that are millions of years old. They were growing, reproducing, and decomposing through the eons long before dinosaurs roamed the earth. Fossil remains have helped scientists record the history of ferns and

ascertain how imposing and widespread they were.

Western civilization's earliest records of fern lore go back to the medieval period of its history. At that time, an aura of mystery, fear, and superstition surrounded ferns. It was known that in order to reproduce, plants needed flowers so that they could produce seeds. Ferns had no flowers, and there were no visible seeds. So how but through some bizarre twist of nature's wizardry could these plants not only survive but thrive and procreate? Eventually scientists discovered that ferns did, in fact, produce an extraordinary abundance of seeds. They were not like flower plants

with pods or trees with nuts, however; instead the seeds were dustlike reproductive organs called spores. But still superstition lingered. Humankind generally considered the spores supernatural, thus magical, and possessed of powers of good and evil.

Growing ferns in gardens first became popular more than two hundred years ago. A British surgeon named John Lindsay who had traveled to Jamaica sent word to England that he had succeeded in growing a number of different cultivars from spores. The news was passed on to the worlds of horticulture and science through the Linnaean Society of London.

Above: *In Cutchogue, New York, Alice Levien's collection of shade-loving plants includes a number of varieties of hosta, native ferns, and, for color, several evergreen azaleas in muted colors.*

Preceding pages: *At Folly Farm, in Berkshire, England, a lavish planting of shade-loving, blue-toned* Hosta sieboldii *surrounds a captivating statue. White Iceberg roses were installed at the top of the low brick wall for contrast.*

172

It wasn't long before nurserymen all over Europe were experimenting successfully with the method.

Horticultural enthusiasts, ever fascinated with the new and different, began installing stove houses, later called hothouses, to grow the tropical and subtropical plants that were brought back to Europe during this great era of horticultural exploration. Stove houses devoted to growing ferns were called ferneries, and several became world renowned. Although they no longer exist, there were famous ferneries at Birr Castle, Birr, County

Native ferns provide a soft underplanting for a stately, old purple rhododendron at Birr Castle, Birr, Ireland. Birr Castle was the sight of a world-renowned fernery in the nineteenth century.

Offaly, in Ireland, and at Tatton Park in Cheshire, England. During the late 1840s and early 1850s, a horticulturist named Thomas Moore wrote several handbooks on ferns that inspired the Victorian craze for ferns and tropical house plants, which lasted well into the present century.

Recently, in the United States and in Europe, there has been a renaissance of interest in ferns, primarily in those cultivars hardy enough to thrive in shade. A great many of the beautiful gardens of Europe and the United States, although not specifically shade gardens, do include shady nooks and crannies planted with ferns. Their lacy foliage contrasts perfectly with the lush foliage of hosta and other shade-loving plants.

Alice Levien installed a lovely fern and hosta garden in a shady nook on her property in Cutchogue, New York. And at Birr Castle, in what is perhaps a gesture by the current owners to honor the world-renowned fernery that existed there during the nineteenth century, a small fern garden has been installed in a shaded area.

Recently, what can only be called "hosta mania" has swept the United States, taken the British Isles by storm, and begun to engulf the Continent. Because hosta is easy to maintain, almost indestructible, and pest and disease resistant, and because it provides nearly instant gratification in terms of lush foliage and subtle flowers, it is the perfect plant for the busy contemporary gardener.

Hybridizers have been busily creating

Above: *In the shaded areas of the author's garden in Peconic, New York, native ferns have been naturalized. Other plantings have been installed around the ferns, allowing them to dominate these areas of the garden.*

Left: *At Stone Crop, in Cold Spring, New York, Francis H. Cabot enhanced his magnificent alpine garden by planting shady areas with many varieties of hosta.*

Above: *These bizarre-looking plants, called Gunnera, are often installed in tandem with native North American skunk cabbage, particularly in shady, boggy areas. At Brodick Castle on the island of Arran in Scotland, they appear unearthly, like a moonscape.*

Opposite: *In this mysterious grotto at Powerscourt, in Enniskerry, County Wicklow, Ireland, water gently cascades from level to level, providing the moisture needed by various mosses to grow on and between the surrounding rocks.*

scores of new varieties. Until recently, a limited selection of hostas was available, but now there are not only the usual cultivars that sport glossy green foliage and lavender flowers, but those with foliage of gold and green, white and green, green and blue, chartreuse, and many combinations thereof. Beyond the usual lavender or purple flowers, there are varieties with small lilylike blossoms of white. And some offer lovely fragrances. Hostas range in size from a mere two inches tall (*H.* 'Thumbnail') to more than four feet high with fourteen-inch-long leaves (*H.* 'Blue Angel').

Leaf texture ranges from smooth to puckered and leathery and from glossy to dull. Leaf shape varies widely: cupped-shaped, circular, heart-shaped, oval-shaped, straplike, and lance-shaped. Growth habit includes upright, vase-shaped, and mound-shaped. Hostas are easy to propagate, for at virtually any time in the growing season one can dig them, divide them, and replant. There is a hosta available for perhaps every conceivable landscape use.

Although hosta mania is a relatively new phenomenon in the United States, the great gardeners of the distant past in the Far East have known the value of the hosta's foliage in garden design for centuries. The plant was first introduced to the West from China around 1790, when two plants were brought to England; *Hosta plantaginea* and *Hosta ventricosa* are

Above: *At Arduaine, in western Scotland, fallen, bright red rhododendron blossoms add just the right touch of color to a shaded walk that has been planted with mosses, ferns, and oxalis.*

Right: *Created by King Leopold II, the construction of the Royal Greenhouses in Laeken, Belgium, began in 1874. They are home to this lovely moss garden of hushed colorations and subtle textures, as well as a score of other indoor gardens.*

More than forty
varieties of native
Japanese moss carpet the
ground at the eighth-
century Saiho-Ji Moss
Temple in Kyoto, Japan.

still widely grown. In 1830, the Dutch horticulturist Philipp Franz von Siebold, who had lived in Japan for several years, brought the dramatic, blue-leaved *Hosta sieboldii* to Europe from Japan. Until his death in 1856, he distributed plants throughout western Europe.

During the mid-nineteenth century, hosta, then called funkia, was introduced to the United States. These early, shiny-leafed, green varieties with the stalks of purple flowers became a standard, indeed clichéd, planting throughout the country. After considerable confusion about proper names in 1905, the International Botanical Congress, which decides such matters, renamed the plant hosta.

Hostas are not evergreen. Their foliage turns brown and dies after the first frost of autumn, only to rise again from the ground in the spring. The Japanese do not use the plant as part of the in-ground landscape, but grow them in pots placed here and there throughout the garden for accents or indoors as house plants. Hosta has long been standard in Japanese flower arrangements.

Although there are large and small hosta gardens everywhere these days, one of the most beautiful is a fountain planting of immense *Hosta sieboldii* installed at the restored Lutyens-Jekyll garden at Folly Farm in Berkshire, England.

Moss gardens have also enjoyed a recent renaissance in Europe and the United States. Apparently, the only period during horticultural history when moss gardens were generally popular was the Victorian era. Structures called moss houses were built on the large estates of England. These were garden buildings made of wood and filled with cut pine or laurel branches. Mosses were planted and grew in between the branches.

These days, one occasionally encounters a garden where moss is used in the landscape. At Powerscourt, in Enniskerry, County Wicklow, Ireland, most of which is a formal garden in the grand manner, there is a murky, mysterious grotto featuring a grotesque fountain and small waterfall. Moss has been successfully introduced here and adds an elegant, velvet green look to the folly. At Quinta da Aveleda, in northern Portugal, a dribbling fountain assures moisture for the moss planting beneath.

An extravagant moss garden has also been installed at the Royal Greenhouses at Laeken, outside of Brussels, Belgium. These are an elaborate series of greenhouses built by King Leopold II to house a collection of plants from the Congo. Today, the greenhouses are still owned by the royal family; however, for a few select days during the spring they are open to the public. One of the houses is called Diana's House, named after a statue of Diana within. An extravagant planting of moss surrounds the statue and comprises the path that leads to it.

Herb Gardens

Of the many different kinds of specialty gardens, the herb garden is the richest in history, legend, and lore. For thousands of years, volume upon volume has been written about the cultivation, properties, and uses of herbs. Although today herbs are used primarily in cooking, there has been a recent widespread renewal of interest in their use for medicinal purposes and for natural scenting in potpourris, sachets, and cosmetics.

Long before the advent of modern medicine, individual herbs, combinations of herbs, and herbal infusions were the only medicines known to mankind. Those who knew how to use herbs for healing were considered everything from miracle workers to evil wizards, possessing a unique relationship with the divinities. Although herbalists were considered by contemporaries to be akin to sorcerers, they also served a purpose in the history of horticulture as their writings on various herbs and their characteristics have been preserved.

Medicinal herbs were regularly cultivated in the Far East centuries before they were in the West. According to legend, Chinese medicine was founded by Shen Nung, an herbalist and expert in poisons who lived twenty-seven hundred years before Christ!

Through discoveries of herbs in the tombs of the pharaohs of Egypt, it is known that they were used medicinally and in ceremony by the Egyptians. The Greek scholar Theophrastus of Eresus, a pupil of both Plato and Aristotle, wrote of herbs in his *History of Plants,* the earliest extant botanical work and the greatest single influence on the study of plants for close to two thousand years. In this book Theophrastus described and classified trees, shrubs, half-shrubs, and herbs.

In addition to Theophrastus's work, herb lore and usage appears in the mythology and poetry of the ancient Greeks. The use of sweet bay laurel (*Laurus nobilis*) as a head wreath in ancient Greek and Roman mythology and ceremony appears to derive from the legend of Daphne and Apollo. Pursued by Apollo, Daphne in desperation called upon the gods to save her. They responded with a merciful act of metamorphosis and changed her into a laurel tree. Thus the sweet bay laurel became Apollo's favorite

tree, and the ancient Greeks came to believe that it was a gift of the gods. So a crown of laurel leaves was always placed upon the heads of victors of war, athletic competition, and poetry contests. Today, far less poetically, sweet bay leaves are used to flavor stew, meat loaf, and poultry stuffing.

Another Greek myth that is part of herb lore is that of Pluto and the young

Below: *A particularly lovely combination: velvety betony, or lamb's ears, and the soft bluish-purple flowers of lavender.*

Preceding pages: *Annual purple basil adds rich coloration to any herb garden and, for that matter, can even be used in a perennial or annual border for color contrast.*

nymph Menthe, after whom mint is named. When Pluto, god of the nether regions, became enthralled by Menthe, his jealous wife, Proserpine, turned her into mint, leaving her to grow in shade and moisture forever. The ancient Greeks, who were particularly fond of this refreshing herb, used mint almost daily in their diet. To this day mint continues to be enjoyed worldwide for its soothing taste.

A god might also be associated with an herb because he gave it to one of the heroes of Greek myth. For example, it is likely that rue was the "moly" that Hermes gave Ulysses so he might better withstand the enchantment of the siren Circe.

Thus it was thought that rue was favored by Hermes, and it was used to decorate his temple and honor him in ceremonies. These "favored" herbs were used in religious rituals and in sacred offerings to a particular god.

Incense may have first been used in the Western world in these ceremonies. The ancient Greeks believed that sweet-smelling smoke would rise to Olympia and bring them favor from the gods. For the same reason, sacrificial animals were burned with herbs. Perhaps after a ceremony, a sacrificial lamb—smothered with the needlelike leaves of rosemary—was consumed and enjoyed, thus sparking the complement that has persisted to this day.

Following the Greeks, the Romans continued to use herbs in religious ceremonies and healing. During the reign of Nero, however, a more practical use for herbs evolved, as mint, sweet calamus, and saffron were often strewn on the floors of theaters and baths. Claudius Galen (A.D. 130–200), whose writings on herbs continued to be referred to for the next thousand years, wrote descriptions of herbs and of their uses, as did Pliny in his *Natural History* (A.D. 77).

Early Christians at first forbade the cultivation of herbs because of their use in pagan ritual. In time, however, some herbs, such as rosemary and angelica, were once again considered special because a saint or apostle had blessed them or performed some miraculous deed with them. Rosemary has come to symbolize the Virgin Mary, as well as recalling the presence of God in the garden of Gethsemane, where it grew and blossomed amid the ancient, gnarled olive trees.

The Bible contains many references to myrrh, calamus, and other herbs as being suitable for incense and as additives in the holy oils used to anoint priests. Medicinally, hyssop was thought to cleanse the body and soul, ridding them of not only disease but sin as well. And it was generally used to protect the houses of good people from plagues. The traditional Passover feasts included a number of bitter herbs. And, as in ancient Greece, herbs were considered valuable enough to be used to pay taxes and tithes.

Charlemagne appears to have been instrumental in spreading the practice of cultivating herbs throughout Europe. Considering that he died in A.D. 814, presumably in the darkest of the Dark Ages, it is enlightening to learn that not only did he have an herb garden himself, but he encouraged botanical study by sponsoring gardens in France and other regions. One story tells of how Charlemagne summoned the learned monk Alcuin from Ireland to teach him all he knew of herbs and their uses. It is said that Alcuin asked Charlemagne, "What is an herb?" Charlemagne is said to have answered, "The friend of the physician and the praise of cooks." His answer still holds true today. The "Johnny Appleseed" of his day, Charlemagne commanded by royal edict that anise and fennel be grown near every dwelling in his empire. Thus the first secular herb gardens were born.

We can piece together information on English herb gardens of the Dark Ages from surviving herbals by the Druid priests and in the Anglo-Saxon "leech books"— one of which was known to Alfred the Great. From these sources we know that the Druidic Celtic priests used herbs for healing purposes. Herbs were thought to hold magic powers over humans when they recited elaborate incantations while planting, gathering, and administering them. In addition, it was thought that herbs, including primrose, club moss, verbena, mistletoe, and pulsatilla, all guarded mankind against evil.

On the dark side of Anglo-Saxon

Opposite: *At Maymont Park, near Richmond, Virginia, an ambitious parterre herb garden of lavender, boxwood, santolina, and other aromatic plants reveals the versatility of herb garden design.*

186

history, witch gardens, cleverly constructed to terrify people into belief in evil powers, were said to have been installed by witches. Witches not only feared those herbs associated with the devil, including mandrake, henbane, mugwort, belladonna, dill, vervain, betony, and St.-John's-wort, but supposedly used them to evoke spirits.

Beyond information in herbals, early Anglo-Saxon literature contains frequent references to betony, mugwort, yarrow, feverfew, pennyroyal, and sage. Herbs native to Mediterranean climates are also mentioned and were presumably brought to Britain by Rome's legions. These include lupine, nettles, coriander, rosemary, borage, iris, southernwood, onion, fennel, hyssop, rue, chervil, chives, and celandine, among others.

By the Middle Ages, Galen's herbal had been replaced by those written by monks and nuns. All monasteries and convents contained small gardens where medical herbs were grown. The Benedictines, in particular, not only grew herbs but studied them extensively. These small medieval gardens, close within the confines of monastery, castle, or palace walls, were the forerunners of the great seventeenth-century "physic gardens," in which herbs were collected from the known world. The monks and nuns became healers of the body as well as the soul and ministered with equal skill to rich and poor alike.

Of the later medieval cloister herb garden we know quite a lot, for many diagrams as well as actual gardens have survived. These are usually what come to mind when we think of traditionally designed herb gardens. They were geometric,

Left: The author's potpourri garden, in Peconic, New York, is planted with a great variety of aromatic herbs, such as hyssop, artemisia, pineapple sage, feverfew, and tansy. Flowering plants that dry particularly well are also included to add color to the various potpourris.

Opposite: For whatever reason, this tiger swallowtail butterfly finds the aroma and taste of the blossoms of Chinese chives delectable.

usually enclosed with box hedges and surrounded by a wall or by hedges.

Garden paths, which were planted with low-growing, sweet-smelling chamomile or sweet woodruff, separated the geometric areas. Most herb gardens had earthen or turf benches, built into the garden's surrounding walls, on which creeping thyme, chamomile, or low-growing mints—such as Corsican mint—were planted so that pleasant fragrances would emerge when someone sat upon them. The walls were often faced with brick, stone, or wattled fencing.

Birdbaths or sundials were sometimes used as a central focal point, and water—in the form of a central fountain or perhaps a tiny stream, bathing pool, dripping sluice, or dipping well—was also present. Flowers symbolic in Christian liturgy, such as irises, rose lilies, and violas, were grown along with the healing herbs.

Beyond their use in the healing arts and in cooking, herbs were also used for the practical purpose of scenting. Rue, hyssop, and meadowsweet were strewn on the dirty floors of castles and cottages. Sweet woodruff, lavender, and rosemary formed soft carpets in bed chambers. In England, rue—known to eliminate foul odors and vermin—was strewn in judges' chambers, a practice that continued late into the nineteenth century.

During the Renaissance interest in herbs spread from the monasteries into the secular world as herb gardens became a standard at country houses, both grand and humble. With the age of exploration,

Above: *Another view of the author's potpourri garden reveals a variety of leaf colors and textures. Artemisia, tansy, feverfew, rosemary, and pineapple sage provide contrast and complement one another.*

many new cultivars from distant lands took their places alongside native plants. At the University of Padua during the 1500s, the plants in the herb garden came not only from Europe but from the Far East and the New World as well.

The herb garden, which had originated as a purely practical place in which to grow medicinal or cooking herbs, slowly evolved into a refuge, a place of beauty during the Renaissance and baroque eras. Like those of the cloisters of the medieval period, the herb gardens of these eras were composed of elaborate geometric patterns; however, due to an increased awareness of the principles of humanism, herb gardens in Europe were designed to encourage people to use them and many innovations were introduced. Sir Francis Bacon wrote of herb gardens in his essay "Of Gardens" (1625). "Walls were turfed and planted with sweet herbs that crushed and trodden do perfume the aire most delightfully"; he further advised gardeners to "set whole alleys of them to have pleasure when you walk or tread." The overhead branches of parallel rows of trees were woven together, producing a "pleached" effect and creating long tunnels of greenery "by which you may go in shade into the garden"; "when the wind blowes sharpe you may walke as in a gallery." Summerhouses called "herbers," where people could sit and relax in the heat of the day, were often covered and enclosed with the sweetest of fragrant vines, which were called arch herbs. Fountains were also included for their cooling effect.

R*ight: Barbara Harrington of Southold, New York, cherishes this large rosemary plant, which she winters over indoors every year. Rosemary is for remembrance, according to William Shakespeare.*

Several different kinds of idiosyncratic specialty herb gardens also emerged during the Renaissance. Mazes—garden playthings, constructed for diversion and amusement—made their appearance. Winding paths were enclosed with shrubs and herbs such as southernwood, rosemary, lavender, rue, marjoram, and basil. As young and old alike paraded through the mazes, their clothes brushed against the herbs and released their scents.

Knot gardens also made their appearance during this time. These were creations of intricate patterns of herbs that were interlaced with one another to resemble a knotted rope. They were usually edged with rue, hyssop, box, santolina, thrift, and thyme. Sometimes they were designed in the shape of hearts filled with lavender, with colorful serpentine coils of forget-me-nots and marigolds surrounding the herb. At Barnsley House, in Gloucestershire, England, Rosemary Verey has installed a knot garden of box, and at Well-Sweep Herb Farm in Port Murray, New Jersey, a knot garden employing several different kinds of box and lavender is placed amid elaborate plantings of geometric herb parterres and herb-edged walks.

The sundial garden was also introduced during this era. Flowering plants that opened and closed at different times of the day were planted in circular beds to form either a clock or a sundial.

It also appears that during this period the concept of a potted herb garden emerged. Many people who were either unwilling or unable to cultivate gardens, but who, nonetheless, had to grow herbs for their households, resorted to growing herbs in pots on their doorsteps. This practice seems to have begun in France. Cultivars that were not hardy in that part of the world, but were necessary for medicinal or culinary purposes, could easily be wintered indoors and then placed back outside in the spring.

During the eighteenth century, innovations in the design of herb gardens occurred primarily in the New World. The English colonists had brought familiar herbs to America—mint, thyme, angelica, and many others. In fact, at Plymouth, by the Pilgrim Spring, a descendant of a mint planted during the first year of the settlement still grows. Germans, Scots, and Irish brought dill, savory, and calendulas to Pennsylvania. Native wild plants, such as goldenrod, sassafras, and bayberry, were added to herb gardens. With later immigration waves came cilantro and coriander from Mexico. The Chinese laborers who built the railroads brought coriander and planted it near their work camps.

The herb gardens at Mount Vernon and Monticello, two of the great eighteenth-century plantations in the United States, reveal that aesthetics and the pleasure garden concept yielded to the practical cultivation of herbs for their scent and medicinal and culinary use. Geometric patterns were still employed, but gardens were not enclosed with herbal hedges, and bowers and decorative garden struc-

Opposite: At Agecroft Hall, near Richmond, Virginia, various colored gravels have been laid down in the knot garden between the boxwood and other cultivars to provide pattern and contrast.

tures were not used. Paths were made from available materials: brick, gravel, wood chips, sand, or, simple grass.

With the advent of the Victorian era, herb garden styles both in the United States and abroad once again reverted to the pleasure garden concept, as elaborate square or triangular plots, delineated by straight paths, were added to already popular structured patterns.

Today there is renewed interest in herbs and herb gardens. Cooks install herb gardens containing perennial chive, tarragon, sorrel, oregano, mint, sage, thyme, annual marjoram, savory, dill, chervil, parsley, basil, caraway, mustard, and others. Those who opt to grow scented herbs for use in potpourris and sachets install potpourri gardens. Herbs such as pineapple sage, with its gentle pineapple scent, lavender, lemon verbena, lemon balm, the mints, tansy, feverfew, hyssop, sweet woodruff, and a wide variety of scented geraniums are all aromatic additives to potpourri and can be grown in such a garden. These herbs are usually combined with flowers that dry well and retain their color, such as chrysanthemums, calendula, bachelor's buttons, and roses.

Some gardeners specialize in one type of herb. Silver-foliaged herbs such as santolina, artemisia, and lavender are often grown by those interested in creating dried flower arrangements for the home. And those who have experimented with and enjoyed healthful herbal teas grow mint, chamomile, and other herbs suitable for infusion.

One of the most impressive herb gardens in the United States is that of Mr. and Mrs. Cyrus Hyde at their four-and-a-half-acre home, Well-Sweep Herb Farm. The garden, set beside the house, is laid out in a series of formal, geometric patterns interspersed with paths paved with weathered brick. The Hydes' garden contains ninety-two varieties of scented geraniums and more than thirty different lavender cultivars. There are so many varieties of basil planted that the Hydes have lost count of them. At least forty-five types of rosemary are grown. Some of these have been trained as tree-shaped standards set amid low hedges of germander that border and cross the bed.

One path, which leads to what was once the six-sided, louvered outhouse, is lined with velvet-foliaged betony, with an occasional red poppy planted for accent. As one wanders through the maze of paths and brushes against the foliage of the herbs, the heady scents of artemisia, southernwood, basil, and licorice verbena waft through the air. In other areas of the garden, lemon verbena, lavender, and pineapple sage, with its crimson blossoms, release their sweet, subtle aromas.

Cyrus Hyde's interest in herbs started in childhood, for his family always had a garden and raised much of the food for their table. A wagon house on their property was used for drying herbs. After he married and moved to his present residence, he started a small herb garden for his wife who, he notes, "happens to be a very good cook." Before long he began

Above: *When in bloom, chive plants offer interesting coloration in an herb garden. The blossoms are edible and can be added to salads for taste as well as color.*

Preceding pages: *At Well-Sweep Herb Farm in Port Murray, New Jersey, not only have topiary and espalier been installed, but a classic knot garden as well.*

drying and selling herbs, and the hobby blossomed into a fine business. Today Well-Sweep Herb Farm attracts visitors from all over the world. In addition to selling herbs, Hyde has installed an educational herb garden that contains many of the rare and unusual cultivars he has collected over the years.

Beyond the traditional herb garden—which today takes many forms derived from the medieval geometric herb garden, the Renaissance pleasure garden, and even the overdone Victorian bedding style—

silver- and blue-toned herbs such as artemisia, lavender, betony, southernwood, yarrow, silver sage, silver thyme, rue, germander, and santolina are often combined with perennials in borders and beds to provide foliage contrast. Oldfashioned pinks, heliotropes, foxgloves, and violets add gentle color touches and lovely scents to flower gardens. Many herbs, such as sweet woodruff, catnip, chamomile, pennyroyal, and speedwell, are now used as ground covers, emitting their subtle fragrances when walked upon. And, from a purely practical point of view, many

At Well-Sweep Herb Farm, herbs not only provide leaf texture, but also offer bloom. An uncommon variety of chive sports pink blossoms that blend nicely with purple-flowering hyssop.

gardeners install certain herbs to ward off insects. These include basil, bergamot, garlic, catnip, dill, horseradish, and lovage.

Every garden, from the contemporary "wild" to the traditional formal, can be enhanced by the use of herbs, whether for color, foliage contrast, or conversational reasons. And even the poor soul who has only a windowsill garden to cultivate can include herbs in his or her collection of plants, as many adapt well to pot culture.

Right: In Southold, New York, Bill and Pat Milford opted to enclose their informal kitchen herb garden with a traditional white picket fence. Old-fashioned flowering herbs such as yarrow and digitalis add dashes of color to the scheme.

Opposite: An extravagant planting of betony along a walk at Well-Sweep Herb Farm is unquestionably a showstopper. The small, louvered building that stands at the end of the path was once an outhouse but is now used to dry and store herbs.

Rhododendron and Azalea Gardens

The rhododendron group of plants, which botanically includes azaleas, is one of the largest in the plant world. About 850 species grow all over the world, and this number does not include subspecies, hybridized varieties, or clones, which number nearly ten thousand. "Rhodos," as they are called among collectors, grow in a vast array of forms, sizes, and colors. Some, mainly from arctic or high alpine environments, are dwarf in stature, rarely growing to more than a foot tall, while others, primarily from subtropical climes, grow to seventy or eighty feet. The range of blossom colors that these plants offer is even greater than that of roses. There are deep purples, brilliant scarlets, oranges, yellows, blues, whites, and even pale green varieties.

Their adaptability to various types of environments makes rhododendrons suitable plants for a wide variety of growing locales. In fact, it can almost be said that there is a rhododendron that will grow in almost any environment of which one can think. Most thrive in shade and therefore are often suitable for city planting, although some prefer full sun. All crave acidic soils, which most plants detest. With careful selection, the blooming season of rhododendrons can extend from early spring to late summer. The blossoms are sumptuous bursts of color, and most varieties sport evergreen foliage that remains attractive through the winters in northern climates. Enthusiasts, in a discreet effort not to detract from the glory of the rose, which is often called the "Queen of flowers," have designated the rhododendron the "King of flowers."

Most rhododendrons are native to the Northern Hemisphere. They can be found in the wild in the far northern reaches of the arctic tundra, in the icy swamps of the North, on hills and in valleys in temperate climates, on the peaks of the Himalayas, in the rain forests of Burma and Malaysia, and in the tropical jungles of Indonesia; only a few, however, are native to Australia. Their concentration is greatest in the wilds of western Yunnan, in China, where more than two hundred species have been discovered in a very small area. Botanical expeditions continue to search for as yet undiscovered

Below: *A colorful planting of white, pink, yellow, and red rhododendrons has reached glorious maturity in Paul Karish's garden in Amagansett, New York, which is more than thirty years old.*

Opposite: *Marjorie Dietz's collection of rhododendrons in East Hampton, New York, contains many cultivars that originated at the Sandwich, Massachusetts, estate of the late Charles Dexter, who was an important hybridizer of rhododendrons during the 1920s and 1930s.*

Preceding pages: *Friends have dubbed the author's garden in Peconic, New York, the "Gauguin Garden," for the color combinations are reminiscent of those used by the famous French artist.*

species of rhododendrons in China.

In Europe, new discoveries of rhododendrons have occurred, although rarely, on the mountain ranges of middle Europe as well as in the Russian Caucasus. They grow more abundantly in the eastern United States, the greatest concentration in the Appalachian Mountains, primarily in western North Carolina. Because of the cold winters in this area, native rhododendrons are hardy, a factor that was important in the hybridization of these plants during the eighteenth and nineteenth centuries. A few even grow in eastern Canada, but they are sparsely represented on the Pacific Coast of North America.

The word "rhododendron" comes from the Greek and literally translates as "rose tree," but we know that the rhododendrons of the ancient Greeks were oleanders and not the rhododendrons of today, which as far as we know were not cultivated in Europe until the eighteenth century. Nonetheless, we do know that during the Hellenic period of Western history one variety, the Pontic azalea (*Rhododendron luteum*), grew on the shores of the Black Sea. The first account in history of the rhododendron occurred around the year 400 B.C. An army of Greek soldiers retreating from a Persian defeat had camped along the Black Sea. Dazed from battle, they sought refreshment in honey made by bees from Pontic azalea blossom nectar. Shortly after, they were afflicted with severe stomach pains. Another report, written three centuries later, tells of a Roman army that camped at the same

location. The soldiers ate the same honey, became delirious, and, defenseless, were massacred by the enemy.

Medieval herbalists knew that honey made from the nectar of this rhododendron's blossoms was poisonous and also knew that some rhododendron leaves were toxic. They discovered, however, that small quantities of the leaf, prepared in various herbal teas and brews, somewhat eased the effects of crippling arthritis.

The Siberian snow rose (*Rhododendron chrysanthum*) arrived in western Europe during the Middle Ages and was planted in monastery gardens. Its leaves were used to make tea for medical experiments, and for the first time, a rhodo-dendron was used for decorative purposes in a garden.

The forefathers of modern-day rhododendrons were discovered during the era of European imperial expansion in the eighteenth and nineteenth centuries. While the imperialist powers expanded their economic base, their scientists, naturalists, botanists, anthropologists, archaeologists, and zoologists traipsed through jungles and climbed mountains seeking all manner of undiscovered treasures. During this era zoological parks and botanical gardens were first established. In 1656, the first "exotic" rhododendron reached Britain. It had been discovered in the Alps. Eighty years later, four species

M*r. and Mrs. Leslie Cheek of Richmond, Virginia, installed a white azalea garden to set off the fountain on the grounds of their home.*

discovered in North America were sent to England. By 1800 another seven species, these native to northern Asia, joined the cultivated rhododendron family.

In 1809, several other species arrived in Britain, most importantly the native American *Rhododendron catawbiense*, which lavishly colors North Carolina's Appalachian Mountains with its pink-lavender-mauve blossoms every spring. Hardy, attractive, and adaptable to temperate environments, this particular species was directly responsible for the rhododendron explosion that occurred around 1830. Michael Waterer, a British pioneer in rhododendron hybridization, recognized the versatility of *Rhododendron catawbiense* in 1810, a mere year after its introduction. He crossed this plant with *Rhododendron maximum*, another eastern United States native, and the modern-day rhododendrons were underway.

Scores of rare plants native to Japan grow in tandem with North American and European cultivars in Harold Epstein's ledge garden in Larchmont, New York.

The following year another important species arrived, this time from India. *Rhododendron arboreum*, a tree-form plant that was the first specimen to arrive in England from Southeast Asia, was carefully nurtured in warm greenhouses for fourteen years after its introduction, and then flowered, in resplendent scarlet! Imagine the excitement. The newspapers were full of information about the plant, and crowds of people came to see it.

The early hybridized plants were still too tender to thrive in most areas of the British Isles. Hybridizers got busy, however, and started to cross the plants with hardier species, the first being *Rhododendron catawbiense*. These hybrids eventually flowered, producing both pink and red blossoms. And although these first hybrids were not nearly as spectacular as later ones, to this day some of them are still growing in gardens in England.

Thus ground was broken for future development. Hybridizers began crossing all available tender rhododendrons with the hardier species and usually found that the lovely colors of the blossoms on the tender plants successfully transferred to the hardier stock. The British explored India further and moved on to Sikkim, Nepal, Bhutan, and the Tibetan areas of the Himalayas. In 1850, Sir Joseph Hooker sent back forty-five beautiful new species from Sikkim and soon after wrote a book, *Rhododendrons of the Sikkim Himalayas*, which was beautifully illustrated with exquisite botanical drawings of the new species.

Until 1860, the new hybrids were still quite tender, thriving only in the warmer climates of England and Scotland. As a result of attempts to cross and backcross, and the continuing introduction of newly discovered species, mostly from Asia, three hundred different varieties were in cultivation by 1900. Today there are thousands.

Deciduous azaleas made their bow in England in 1680, when Bishop Henry Compton planted seeds sent to him from Virginia by John Banister, a missionary in the colony. Banister rendered a botanical drawing of the plant and labeled it "Virginia rock rose with flowers and odor of honeysuckle." The Chinese azalea (*Rhododendron molle* or *Azalea sinensis*) arrived in England in 1823. Azaleas were used as greenhouse plants, however; their irregular growth patterns did not suit the formal garden style then fashionable.

The earliest hybrids, Mollis and Ghent, were developed from these greenhouse plants, primarily in Belgium. By 1870 the Knap Hill hybrids were introduced into England from Belgian and Chinese stock. Evergreen azaleas such as Kurume are native to Japan and have been hybridized there for more than three hundred years, with the Kaempferi and Gable hybrids more recent introductions.

Many public gardens in the United States include extensive plantings of rhododendrons and azaleas. Among the most notable are those at Winterthur, in Wilmington, Delaware; Longwood Gardens, in Kennett Square, Pennsylvania; the Leonard J. Buck Garden, in Far Hills, New Jersey; Old Westbury Gardens, in Westbury, New York; and Filoli in Woodside, California. These vast plantings are breathtakingly beautiful, but it is the smaller, private rhododendron and azalea gardens that almost always offer a more personal experience to the visitor. Several on New York's Long Island rendered in a naturalistic woodland style are particularly lovely. Paul Karish's garden in Amagansett, on the East End of Long Island, is a good example. Barely three acres in size, it is planted with hundreds of rare cultivars, all selected, nourished, and cherished by its owner. The garden is now thirty years old, and Karish acknowledges that he was inspired by the spectacular azalea and rhododendron gardens of England. Among his prized rhodos are Cynthia, a deep rose pink cultivar that dates from the mid-nineteenth century, and Mary Belle, with its peach-colored blossoms that turn almost yellow when fully opened. "And it doesn't get too big," says Karish. "It's ideal for a small garden."

Marjorie Deitz's rhododendron garden is located in East Hampton, New York, and although the property covers less than an acre, the serpentine paths that wind through the wooded garden create the illusion that it is much larger. The garden was started in 1957 and contains about a hundred different cultivars. Many originated on the Sandwich, Massachusetts, estate of the late Charles Dexter,

Opposite: One of Scotland's foremost rhododendron gardens, Arduaine, located in Argyll, is now owned and maintained by Edmund and Harry Wright At the lower end of the garden, the azalea and rhododendron planting at the small pond provides a dazzling display of light, water, and color.

who was an important hybridizer of rhododendrons during the 1920s and 1930s. They were given to Deitz by a subsequent owner of the estate. Since the fragrant *Rhododendron fortunei* was one of the parents of most of the Dexter hybrids, many of her plants, including Scintillation, are highly fragrant. Many hybrids developed by the American David Leach are also in the collection. During one recent spring, several pairs of dazzling orange-and-black Baltimore orioles, now called Eastern orioles, had nested in the oak trees towering above the plantings. Their frequent visits to the birdbaths fronting the brilliantly flowering rhodos were indeed a spectacle.

Many noncollectors of rhodos, such as Mr. and Mrs. Leslie Cheek of Richmond, Virginia, include extensive plantings of azaleas and rhododendrons in their spring gardens. Plantings of white and pink azaleas and rose-purple rhododendrons enclose the Cheeks' large lawn area.

Scotland and Ireland are the homes of some of the world's most extravagant public and private rhododendron gardens. As in the United States, private rhododendron gardens offer visitors the chance to view planting schemes through the doting eyes of the family that owns the property. Owners are often on hand to guide visitors through and explain the designs, so one goes away understanding why the garden is planted as it is.

Arduaine, in Argyll, on the west coast of Scotland, is in the heart of Campbell country. James Arthur Campbell, a tea

planter who purchased the rocky peninsula overlooking Arknish Bay in 1898, installed a now-famous rhododendron collection. To create a frost-free shelter, he first planted a great stand of larch. Once the trees had grown to reasonable size, he installed a collection of tender rhododendrons. Many were grown from seed, having arrived in Britain in the tea chests Campbell imported. In the mid-1960s, the estate was split up among heirs, and the garden all but reverted to the wild.

In 1971 two bachelor brothers from Essex, nurserymen Harry and Edmund Wright, purchased the peninsula with the intention of restoring and improving the garden. It is thanks to them that the rhododendrons of Arduaine have survived; the garden is now probably more beautiful than it ever was.

The entry to Arduaine is through wrought-iron gates and then an ascent up winding paths to the woodland garden. It is here, amid Campbell's now-mature larches, that the monumental rhododendrons grow and thrive. A far cry from the specimens found in clichéd foundation plantings in the United States, these plants, native to the foothills of the Himalayas, stand as tall as sixty feet, with brilliant red, purple, white, yellow, and pink blossom clusters the size of basketballs. *Rhododendron sinogrande*, with its massive convoluted branches and huge leaves, can be seen, as well as *Rhododendron giganteum*, which first flowered on the grounds of the estate in 1936.

Here also bamboo, hydrangea, pieris,

magnolia, eucalyptus, and holly all vie for attention. Forest peat moss and lichens cushion the footpaths, and fallen petals create a delicate tapestry of color on the ground. Bordering the paths are ferns and the delicate blossoms of native wild oxalis. After wending one's way first up and then down through the tranquility of this paradise, the waters of Jura Sound and the Firth of Lorne come into view. Down below are the herbaceous borders and the pond area with its percolating springs and brooks, a place to relax and meditate.

The Wrights have created a semiformal water garden from several springs and have surrounded it with water-loving plants such as the giant gunnera, American skunk cabbage, elephant ears, hosta, native candelabralike *Primula florindae*, bergenia, and many smaller azalea and rhododendron specimens. All of this is gently overhung by the narrow, pendulous branches of *Cupressus macrocarpa*, native to the Monterey peninsula in California. One feels slightly disoriented by the exotic ambience of this lovely garden.

When I visited Arduaine, I spoke with a visitor who told me that this was his seventh trip there. "The garden is a living thing and as such is always changing. The light, time of day, time of year, constantly

Above: *White azaleas line a section of one of the woodland paths at Mount Congreve. Miles of paths crisscross the property, offering extravaganzas of color in the spring.*

Preceding pages: *Ambrose Congreve installed tens of thousands of azaleas and rhododendrons at Mount Congreve, County Waterford, Ireland, one of the largest collections of these plants in the world.*

At Mount Usher in Ashford, County Wicklow, Ireland, one of the few surviving gardens designed by the great Irish landscape designer William Robinson, a quarter-mile azalea walk on the grounds is planted with hundreds of specimens, a breathtaking sight, indeed, when in bloom.

change its appearance. It is a different garden each time I visit," he said.

A short distance from Arduaine is Crarae Glen Gardens, also in the heart of Campbell family country. The hour drive from Arduaine follows the west side of Loch Fyne, and passes through some of the most dramatically rugged and beautiful scenery in western Scotland. The emerald green hills are dotted with Black Angus cattle, Shetland ponies, and thousands of sheep, wearing their traditional gray sweaters, as terriers nip at their heels. The chrome-yellow blossoms of celastine bushes sparkle along the roadside. Perched high upon the aeries are the ruins of an-

cient castles, and here and there along the route arc groups of monoliths, remains of Druidic religious rites.

Crarae Glen Gardens is set in a deeply shaded highland glen, with a burn gushing through a gorge and cascading down in waterfalls. On the adjacent paths, above the melodious calls of the chaffinches, robins, and thrushes, the din of the rushing water is ever present. Since the glen garden faces east and is not directly warmed by the North Atlantic Drift, some of the more tender plants that thrive at Arduaine do not survive here.

The garden—or perhaps, more correctly, the setting—is host, however, to

Paul Karish effectively
combined several intense
shades of red azaleas in
his garden.

scores of varieties of deep green conifers and masses of rhododendrons, elegant eucalyptus, and lighter green deciduous trees and shrubs, which create striking contrasts of texture and color. At its peak in April, when the immense, vividly colored, almost lurid blossoms of the rhododendrons burst into bloom, and in the fall, when the leaves of the deciduous trees assume their blazing autumn guise and the rowans, cotoneasters, and berberis their glowing berries, the garden is spectacular.

The property has been in the Campbell family since 1712. Currently, Sir Ilay and Lady Campbell are striving to preserve, maintain, and improve the gardens and have established a trust, The Friends of Crarae, to that end. It was Sir Ilay's grandfather, Sir George Campbell, who decided to beautify the glen with plantings of rare flowering cultivars, conifers, and deciduous trees. Visitors see and frequently meet the Campbells, as, being dedicated gardeners, they spend "an enormous amount of time in the garden," to quote Lady Campbell. In fact, the diminutive lady, who has a saucy wit, calls herself the "Scissor Lady." It is she who walks around deadheading the plantings. One visitor, upon seeing her on her hands and knees weeding, asked what her "employer" was like. "Well," she replied, "he's very nice, very fair, but he overworks me terribly."

The gardens at Mount Usher, in Ashford, County Wicklow, Ireland, date back to around 1870. Four generations of the Walpole family maintained them over the years, installing plants from all over the world. Robert Walpole sold the property in 1980, and today the twenty acres of gardens, which include more than five thousand different species of plants, are owned by Madeleine Jay.

Mount Usher is significant in that the Walpoles were dedicated disciples of Irish landscape architect William Robinson. Around 1880, Robinson started his rebellion against the then fashionable "formal" garden. He felt that trees and shrubs should be allowed to grow as they do in nature. He also believed that all gardens should have a natural rather than an architectural focus. So, at Mount Usher, the stream that winds through the property, rather than the house, is the focus of the garden's design. This garden is considered by many horticultural historians the most perfect example of the Robinsonian romantic paradise garden.

Beyond the impressive collections of eucalyptus and rare conifers is the resplendent Azalea Walk. Hundreds of deciduous azaleas, which have grown so tall that they reach to the foliage of the surrounding rare palms and conifers, are planted in color combinations that seem to work only with rhododendrons and azaleas: mixes of orange, yellow, gold, purple, brilliant reds, pink, salmon, and white. The effect is startling and unforgettable. The walk, which begins at the croquet court and stretches for about a thousand feet, is in full bloom around the end of May.

Mount Congreve, County Waterford, Ireland, is the home of Mr. and Mrs.

Although the Royal
Botanic Garden in
Edinburgh, Scotland, is
famed for its magnificent
alpine garden, the plantings
of azaleas and rhododen-
drons add glorious color in
the spring.

At the Crarae Glen Garden, in western Scotland, Sir Ilay and Lady Campbell maintain the rhododendron garden installed by his grandfather during the nineteenth century. Some of the rare specimens tower more than seventy feet high and are more than a hundred years old.

Ambrose Congreve and has been in the Congreve family since 1725. It was once the home of William Congreve, the Restoration dramatist, but today it is recognized throughout the world for its extraordinary garden, the lifetime creation of the now eighty-four-year-old Ambrose Congreve. Like many of the great gardens of Ireland, it is barely visible on the approach to the manor house. Even from the rear windows of the house, there is little indication of what lies beyond. But once past the gilded wrought-iron gates, one hundred acres of spectacular gardens unfold, including what is surely one of the world's most extensive and beautiful rhododendron and azalea gardens.

When the towering Mr. Congreve leads visitors through the gardens, he is accompanied by his German shepherds—Dick, Jack, and Harry. His energy and stride are those of a man one-quarter his age. It is easy to understand how one man, albeit with the help of an army of gardeners, was able to accomplish so much during the past thirty-five years.

At Mount Congreve, the cultivars are not planted singly or in groups of three, or five, but in great stands of twenty-five or fifty. One such planting of pale pink deciduous azaleas forms a fluffy cloud upon which one can imagine angels playing harps. If there is any place on earth that is like heaven, it surely must be here at Mount Congreve. A walking tour through the garden takes about four hours, with no retracing of steps. There is one planting of more than fifty *Rhododendron macabeanum,* which open their lovely yellow blossoms in April, and there are many large plantings of *Rhododendron sinogrande,* with its creamy white blossoms. The rhododendron beds are often twenty to thirty yards wide and are set off with wide beds of deciduous and evergreen azaleas. All of this is underplanted with endless blankets of blue *Scilla campanulata.*

The scale of the garden is hard to comprehend without a visit. For example, at Exbury in England, still one of the world's great rhododendron and azalea gardens, there are two giant pink tulip trees, *Magnolia campbellii,* native to the Himalayas. At Mount Congreve there are eighty in one riverside walk alone. More than five hundred different cultivars of *Camellia* are here, as are scores of varieties of Scotch broom, hundreds of rare Japanese maples, and hydrangea plantings that are hundreds of yards in length. There is a floribunda rose border at least five hundred feet long. Although not yet mature, hundreds of magnolias, Asiatic species and their hybrids, provide a breathtaking display in the spring. And what is to become of all of this in the future? Congreve has thought ahead, and arrangements have been made for the state eventually to assume ownership, thus assuring that one of the jewels in Ireland's crown will remain undimmed forever.

Opposite: Marjorie Dietz's rhododendrons are beautiful even when just in bud.

Collectors' Gardens

Some gardeners select one cultivar or one particular color as the theme for their gardens. In the British Isles, where the climate is ideal for their cultivation, quite a few gardeners specialize in primroses (*Primula*) in their spring gardens. In North America, perhaps the most popular highly specialized gardens are iris, chrysanthemum, and day lily gardens.

Surely the iris ranks as one of the world's favorite flowers, and many gardeners include large plantings of different varieties of irises in their gardens. There are many to choose from. In fact, with careful selection, one can have irises blooming in the garden from late winter through spring and summer and into the fall. There are the early-blooming bulbous *Iris reticulata* and *danfordiae*, North American *Iris*

cristata, the magnificent, flamboyant rhizomous bearded or German iris, Siberian iris, flag iris, spuria iris, Japanese iris, and so forth. Some grow in dry alpine environments, some in wet swampy areas; some like full sun, others shade. No wonder they are so popular, for there is probably an iris suitable for every possible growing condition.

Today's irises have evolved over the centuries; they come from many different parts of the world, and in most cases, from rather insignificant flowering plants. Because they are relatively easy to hybridize and are generally hardy, irises—sometimes called "the rainbow flowers" because of their wide range of colors—were among the first of all plants to be hybridized. And they have long been associated with royalty. The fleur-de-lis, the symbol of the Bourbons in France, is a representation of the iris.

More than 350 years ago the iris had already joined the list of preferred cultivars for the garden. John Gerard wrote of them:

There be many kinds of Iris or Flouer-de-Luce, whereof some are tall and great and some little, small and low. Some smell exceeding sweete in their roote, some have not anie smell at all; some flowers are without any smell and some with; some have one color, some have many colors mixed; Vertues attributed to some, others not remembered; some have tuberous or knobbie rootes, others bulbus or onion rootes, some have leaves like flags, others like grass and rushes.

At about the same time, Carolus Clusius described twenty-eight varieties of tall bearded iris and remarked, "A long expe-

Left: A lovely iris garden flanks the white stone driveway of Mr. and Mrs. Brownlee Currey's home in Southampton, New York.

Preceding pages: At Old Westbury Gardens in Westbury, New York, a planting of purple Siberian iris that edges the pool is a glorious sight when in bloom in June.

Ambrose Congreve's magnificent collection of bearded iris at Mount Congreve, County Waterford, Ireland.

rience has taught me that Iris grown from seed vary in a wonderful way." And today, even amateur hybridizers find an almost infinite variety of color and form resulting from their efforts.

In the mid-seventeenth century, a Dutchman, François Van Ravelingen, wrote an expanded version of the *Herbal* of Dodonaeus. In it he described nineteen variations of iris standards and eighteen of the falls of iris blossoms, as well as sev-

enty-four variations of nine other parts of the plant: flowers, stems, foliage, and roots. This is evidence that hybridization of iris was already well established by this time in Europe.

Hybridized iris were brought to America by early colonists, and by the nineteenth century, a dozen or more, such as Germanica, Florentina, Flavescens, Odoratissima, and Sambucina were known as "flags." When the American

somewhat recent. Today there are literally thousands of varieties available to the gardener.

At their home in Southampton, New York, Mr. and Mrs. Brownlee Currey installed a large planting of shrubs interspersed with both Siberian and bearded or German iris in blues, purples, yellows, and whites. The bed sits amid a sweeping greensward, which flanks the long driveway leading to the house, and is dazzling to behold when in bloom.

At Mount Congreve, County Waterford, Ireland, in addition to his massive plantings of azaleas, magnolias, camellias, and rhododendrons, Ambrose Congreve also has gardens planned to peak at different times of the season. The border of German iris here is well over a hundred feet long, planted with perhaps thirty or forty different cultivars. Since other gardens in other areas of the property peak at different times during the season, he is not disappointed with this garden's lack of color after the short iris season.

What would an autumn garden be without substantial plantings of chrysanthemums? Pretty dreary, to say the least. And so, chrysanthemums are yet another flower variety that seems to attract specialty gardeners. Native to the Far East, and closely related to the common daisy, they have been grown in China for more than two thousand years and in Japan for almost as long. More than a thousand years ago, the chrysanthemum was selected by the mikado as his personal emblem, and it is

Above: As the white rose Iceberg is cherished by rose lovers, so this stately, tall-growing, ruffled, pure white iris, White Raiment, grown in the author's garden in Peconic, New York, is beloved by iris cultivators.

Opposite: The author's iris collection includes descendants of older varieties no longer widely available.

Iris Society was founded in 1920, there was no written history of the development of the bearded or German iris. Through the efforts of the society—by searching through old manuscripts and catalogs of German, Belgian, French, British, and American origin—an account of the work of hybridizers between the years 1870 and 1920 was created. And so, the documentation of the garden iris is really

Above: *Ethyl Buccola's day lily garden in East Quogue, New York, displays the great variety of colors in which day lilies are now available. The buds of this plant are used in Chinese cuisine.*

Right: *Mrs. Ralph Parks, who lives outside of Philadelphia, Pennsylvania, specializes in chrysanthemums. Although she grows them mainly for competition, her garden is ablaze with color in the fall.*

known that chrysanthemum shows were already being held at that time. The flower became so revered that only the emperor and select members of the nobility were allowed to grow it. The flag of Japan, the "rising sun," is actually a representation of a chrysanthemum with sixteen petals.

By the eighteenth century, chrysanthemums were widely grown in Europe, and today their popularity continues undiminished. Those specializing in chrysanthemums, however, usually grow them for show competition, cutting, or indoor decoration rather than for garden display. Many varieties, both hardy and tender, that are not usually found in the average garden are often cultivated by these connoisseurs. Among these varieties are Charms, Cascades, Koreans, Pompoms, Reflexed Decoratives, Intermediate Decoratives, Incurved Decoratives, Spoons, and Rayonnante, to name a few.

Although she is primarily interested in growing chrysanthemums for show in her greenhouse, Mrs. Ralph Parks installed an extravagant planting of them around her house near Philadelphia, Pennsylvania.

Day lilies are another cultivar that attracts the highly specialized gardener, and with good reason, for these tough plants provide profuse bloom throughout the season in an ever-growing range of colors. They are virtually indestructible, pest and disease free, drought resistant, and quick growing. As recently as thirty years ago, only a handful of cultivars were available.

However, during the past few decades, hundreds of new cultivars have been introduced. Some even bloom at night, and many now have lovely scents. There are dwarf varieties and many new dazzling colors: red, lilac, deep purple, pale green, and so forth. The common day lily has been grown in China for centuries; the lily buds used in Chinese cuisine are, in fact, those of the day lily.

At her home in East Quogue, New York, Ethel Buccola's garden contains scores of day lily cultivars that provide color in her garden all during the season.

Among the most elegant specialty gardens are those planted according to color. In the United States, during the days of the robber barons, blue gardens, planted solely with blue-flowering plants, were considered the ultimate status symbol. This seems to have been a strictly American phenomenon, for lengthy inquiry at the Royal Horticultural Society in England revealed no record of blue gardens in the British Isles.

There was a famous blue garden at the Arthur Curtiss James estate in Newport, Rhode Island, one at the J. P. Morgan estate in Princeton, New Jersey, and one at Florham, the estate of Florence and Hamilton Twombley near Madison, New Jersey. Sadly, there do not seem to be any significant blue gardens anymore.

The white garden, however, which originated in England, is still appreciated today. The most renowned white garden in the world can be found at Sissinghurst,

The national flower of Singapore is the orchid. Hundreds of varieties of this highly prized plant are grown in the orchid enclosure at the Botanic Gardens in Singapore.

Following pages: *Belgian landscape architect Jacques Wirtz installed a subtle white garden at the Hôtel de Rosier in the heart of Antwerp, Belgium. The parterre plantings of white impatiens add just the right touch of color to the green of the surrounding plants.*

once the home of Vita Sackville-West and Harold Nicolson. Mr. and Mrs. William Shank have installed a particularly effective formal white garden at their home in Amagansett, New York. Until it was ravaged by a colony of raccoons during a recent winter, the garden contained a small water garden planted with white water lilies. A wide variety of silver, green, and variegated green-and-white foliage plants have been installed, in addition to plants that bear white blossoms. The visitor can see *Artemisia* 'Silver King' and 'Silver Mound', both green and variegated boxwood, and scores of white-blooming plants such as roses, native daisies, Montauk daisies, violets, azaleas, Japanese iris, native Queen Anne's lace, dianthus, nicotiana, astilbe, fothergilla, digitalis, California poppy, sweet alyssum, white-blooming creeping thyme, phlox, and peonies. White tropical plants such as bougainvillaea are also installed here and there in pots.

Another lovely white garden is located in the inner courtyard of the Hôtel de Rosier, a quiet, elegant hotel located in the heart of Antwerp, Belgium. Strolling down the narrow Rue de Rosier in the business district of this busy Flemish city, one would never guess that tucked away behind the facade of a rather stark, seventeenth-century mansion lies an enchanting, secluded white garden. Designed by Belgian landscape architect Jacques Wirtz, the garden is reached by a lime walk. In the center stands a pensive statue of François surrounded by the giant leaves of *Hosta sieboldiana*. Plantings of white digitalis, white *Lilium regale,* Iceberg roses, and edges of white hebe create the white theme. The gentle gurgling of a small fountain brings motion and sound to the hush of this near-secret garden.

Certainly one of the most esoteric specialty gardens in the world is the orchid enclosure at the Botanic Gardens in Singapore. The orchid is the national flower, and there are large plantings of them everywhere.

At the entrance to the enclosure, Singapore's national flower, the delicate mauve-colored orchid Vanda 'Miss Joaquim', introduces what lies ahead. Beyond, there are countless specimens of hybrids named for dignitaries who have visited the garden including *Dendrobium* 'Elizabeth', named for Queen Elizabeth II, and *Dendrobium* 'Tsutako Nakasone', named for the wife of the Japanese prime minister.

Perhaps the most fascinating specimen here is the Tiger or Giant Orchid (*Grammatophyllum speciosum*), an epiphyte native to Malaysia and the world's largest orchid plant. During its flowering season, the plant sports as many as sixty long spikes of tiger-spotted flowers all open at the same time. The parent plant originally grew near Penang and weighed over a ton. Half of it was sent to the Columbian Exposition in Chicago, where it stunned millions of visitors, and the other half was sent to the Botanic Gardens in Singapore, where it was grown on a rain tree.

Bibliography

Ackerson, Cornelius. *The Complete Book of Chrysanthemums*. New York: The American Garden Guild, Inc. and Doubleday & Co., Inc., 1957.

Aden, Paul, ed. *The Hosta Book*. Portland, O.R.: Timber Press, 1988.

Bailey, Liberty Hyde, and Ethel Zoe Bailey. *Hortus Third: A Concise Dictionary of Plants Cultivated in the United States and Canada*. Revised and expanded by the Staff of the Liberty Hyde Bailey Hortorium, Cornell Univ., Ithaca, N.Y. New York: Macmillan Publishing Company, 1976.

Bowers, Clement Gray. *Rhododendrons and Azaleas: Their Origins, Cultivation and Development*. 1936. Reprint. New York: The Macmillan Company, 1968.

Coate, Randall, Adrian Fisher, and Graham Burgess. *A Celebration of Mazes*. London: Minotaur Designs, 1986.

Foster, F. Gordon. *The Gardener's Fern Book*. Princeton: D. Van Nostrand Co., Inc., 1964.

Foster, H. Lincoln. *Rock Gardening: A Guide to Growing Alpines and Other Wildflowers in the American Garden*. Boston: Houghton Mifflin Co., 1968.

Galle, Fred C. *Azaleas*. Portland, O.R.: Timber Press, 1985.

Gordon, Jean. *The Pageant of the Rose*. Woodstock, V.T.: Red Rose Publications, 1953.

Hornibrook, Murray. *Dwarf and Slow-Growing Conifers*. 1921. Reprint. Little Compton, R.I.: Theophrastus, 1973.

Jones, David L. *Encyclopaedia of Ferns*. Portland, O.R.: Timber Press, 1987.

Randolph, L. F., ed. *Garden Irises*. American Iris Society, 1959.

Shepherd, Roy E. *History of the Rose*. New York: The Macmillan Company, 1954.

Warburton, Bee, ed. *The World of Irises*. Wichita, K.S.: American Iris Society, 1978.

Welch, H. J. *Dwarf Conifers: A Complete Guide*. Newton, M.A.: Charles T. Branford Company, 1966.

Wyman, Donald. *Wyman's Gardening Encyclopedia*. 2nd ed. New York: The Macmillan Company, 1960.

Acknowledgments

The author and photographer are particularly grateful to the following for their interest, encouragement, and assistance in our work: Leila Leathers, Ellen Kosciusko, Sue Blair, L. Herndon Werth, Stella Zenon, Marian S. James, Phillip and Katerina Haralambou, William P. Johns, Laszlo Kepessy, Betsy Baker, Ellen Tallmadge, William Turnbull, Pierre Bennerup, and Marietta Silvestre. Special thanks are due Tom Cooper, editor-in-chief of *Horticulture Magazine*, for his suggestions.

We would like to thank the following for graciously sharing their gardens and/or their knowledge and experience with us.

In the New York City area: Mr. and Mrs. Francis H. Cabot; Harold Epstein; Mr. & Mrs. Cyrus Hyde, Well-Sweep Farm, Port Murray, New Jersey; and the staffs at Wave Hill, the Brooklyn Botanical Garden, and the Leonard J. Buck Garden.

On Long Island: Ed Rezek, Charlotte Ford, Malcolm Whipple, Alice Levien, Connie Cross, Skip Wachsberger, Bill and Pat Milford, Marilyn Stahl, Alfred and Delfina Smith, Barbara Harrington, Mr. and Mrs. Brownlee Currey, Bill Conklin, Gerald and Earl White, Ethel Buccola, William Shank, Robert Dash, David and Helga Dawn, Norman and Lilliane Peck, David and Lucille Berrill Paulsen, Marie Donnelly, the late Alfonso Ossorio, Marggy Kerr, Paul Karish, Josephine Little, and Marjorie Dietz. Also landscape designers Elizabeth Lear, David Green, Lisa Stamm, Sarah Donley, Denise Puccinelli and Bernard Hughes, Suzanne Koch-Gosman, Diane Sjoholm, Carol Baumann, and Martha Stein and the staff at Old Westbury Gardens.

In the mid-Atlantic area: Mrs. Ralph Parks, Dr. and Mrs. John Hopkins, and the staffs at Longwood Gardens and at Winterthur.

In Virginia: Mr. and Mrs. Joseph Knox, Mr. and Mrs. Leslie Cheek, and Mr. and Mrs. Charles Reed, Jr. Also the staffs at Virginia House, Maymount, and Agecroft Hall and the Garden Club of Virginia, the Tourist Board of the Commonwealth of Virginia, and the Metro Richmond Convention and Visitor's Bureau.

In California: Sonny Garcia, Marcia Donahue, Virginia Felbusch, Beatrice Bowles, Robert J. Barry, and designer Dennis Shaw. Also the staffs at the Fullerton Arboretum and Filoli and the Doubletree Hotel in Santa Monica.

In Ireland: Mr. and Mrs. Ambrose Congreve, Helen and Val Dillon, Sally Walker, Jonathan and Daphne Shackleton, James Reynolds, Verney Naylor, Count and Countess of Rosse, Mr. and Mrs. Patrick Grove Annesley, and the staff at Powerscourt. Also the Irish Tourist Board; Aerlingus; Dooly's Hotel, Birr; Joe and Kay Flynn of Rathsallagh House, Dunlavin; Ray and Mary Bowe of Marlfield House, Gorey; Jane and William O'Callaghan of Longueville House, Mallow; and Peter and Moira Haden of Gregan's Castle, Ballyvaughan, for their kind hospitality.

In England: Vernon Russell-Smith, Rosemary Verey, the late Sir David and Lady Scott (Valerie Finnis), Mr. and Mrs. Hugh Johnson, Barbara Shuker, Folly Farm, the duke of Marlborough, Bedford Pace, and the British Tourist Authority.

In Scotland: Harry and Edmund Wright, Arduaine; Sir Ilay and Lady Campbell, Crarae Glen Garden; Dr. Ian Edwards, Royal Botanic Garden, Edinburgh; and the staffs at the Logan Botanic Garden and Brodick Castle. Also Glenfoechan House.

In Belgium: Jean de Montpellier, Annevoie; the royal family of Belgium; Monique't Kint; Madame de Belder; Prince Antoine de Ligne; Roger Nellens; Niki de St. Phalle; the late Jean Tinguely; Baron Joseph van der Elst; and the staff at the van Buuren Museum, Brussels. Also the Belgian Government Tourist Office and Sabena.

In Holland: Mrs. Sally Munnig-Schmidt, Baron de Vos van Steenwyk, Baroness van Heccheren van Brandtenburg, Baron van Zuylen van Nyeveld de Haar, Willem Hoeben, Carla Oldenburger-Ebbert, Renny Blaisse, Madame Mien Ruys, Serande Hora Siccama, Count and Countess van Limburg Stirum, and Willemien de Geer, consultant at the Het Loo restoration, Appeldorn. Also the Hotel des Indes, The Hague, KLM, Netherlands Flowerbulb Institute, Robert La Rue Associates, and Willem Schouten of the Netherlands Board of Tourism.

In Spain: Pere Farell Duran; the Ritz, Madrid; Spanish Government Tourist Bureau; and Iberia Air.

In Portugal: the marquez de Fronteira, Antonio Guardes of the Quinta da Aveleda, the Mateus Winery, the Portuguese Government Tourist Office, and TAP.

In Singapore: Ernest E. Alliott, landscape designer Mr. Jickky of Tropical Landscapes, landscape designer Richard Tan, the staff at the Botanic Gardens, the Mandai Orchid Gardens, the Shangri-La Hotel, the Marina Mandarine, the Goodwood Park Hotel, the Alkaff Mansion, Singapore Air, and the Singapore National Tourist Office.

In Hong Kong: our friend Samuel Chow, the Mandarin Oriental Hotel, the Regent, and the Hong Kong National Tourist Office.

In Japan: the distinguished landscape designer Kinsaku Nakane; Intercontinental Hotel, Yokohama; the New Otani Hotel, Tokyo; the Miyako Hotel, Kyoto; Japan Air Lines; and Japan National Tourist Office.

We would also like to thank our agent, Mrs. Carleton Cole, and our publisher, Andy Stewart, who saw the potential in our work. We also extend thanks to the highly professional staff at Stewart, Tabori & Chang: Leslie Stoker, editor-in-chief; Marc Watrel, our editor; and Julie Rauer, whose beautiful book design has so enhanced our work.

Index

Designed by Julie Rauer

The display type was set in Lys Calligraph
by Miller & Debel, Inc., Philadelphia, Pennsylvania.
The text was set in Bernhard Modern
by Graphic Arts Composition, Philadelphia, Pennsylvania.

The book was printed and bound by
Toppan Printing Company, Ltd.,
Tokyo, Japan.

EARTHQUAKES

GLENDOWER:
The frame and huge foundation of the earth
Shak'd like a coward....
I say the earth did shake when I was born....
The heavens were all on fire, the earth did tremble.
HOTSPUR:
Diseased Nature oftentimes breaks forth
In strange eruptions: oft the teeming earth
Is with a kind of colic pinch'd and vex'd
By the imprisoning of unruly wind
Within her womb; which, for enlargement striving,
Shakes the old beldam earth, and topples down
Steeples, and moss-grown towers. At your birth
Our granddam earth, having this distemperature,
In passion shook.

     Shakespeare, *Henry IV, Pt. 1*

EARTHQUAKES

G A Eiby

VNR VAN NOSTRAND REINHOLD COMPANY
New York Cincinnati Toronto London Melbourne

Printed in Hong Kong
D-83051
Published by Van Nostrand Reinhold Company
A division of Litton Educational Publishing, Inc.
135 West 50th Street, New York, NY 10020, U.S.A.

16 15 14 13 12 11 10 9 8 7 6 5 4 3 2 1

Library of Congress Cataloging in Publication Data

Eiby, G   A
    Earthquakes.

    Bibliography: p.
    1. Earthquakes. I. Title.
QE534.2.E36   551.2 2   80-10786
ISBN 0-442-25191-2

Contents

Preface

Earthquakes began as a series of notes answering questions raised by the volunteers who operate many of New Zealand's seismograph stations. They were combined with a series of radio talks to become a small book published by Frederick Muller in 1957, which ran to two editions in Britain and one in the U.S.A. Although intended for the man in the street who wanted to know 'something about earthquakes' it was also well received in academic and technical circles and by engineers and architects who wanted background information.

Since the original book was written there has been something of a revolution in seismological thought and practice, and a new book rather than a revision seemed to be called for. With a change in publisher, this has become possible.

Readers familiar with it will find vestiges of the original version — some chapter headings, some illustrations, and here and there a whole paragraph — and it is hoped that something of the style and flavour that pleased its readers still remains, but much is new in both content and presentation. The new concepts of plate tectonics, and of the role of dilatancy in the mechanism of earthquakes have had to be explained, lunar seismology has become a reality, and earthquake prediction appears at last to be an attainable goal. The new book is therefore larger than the old. All the original figures have been re-draughted, many new ones have been prepared, and there are additional photographs.

I must record my debt to all those seismologists, both of the present and of earlier generations, from whom I have learned. Chief among these is the late Mr R. C. Hayes, former Director of the Seismological Observatory in Wellington, who first introduced me to professional seismology, and whose long-neglected pioneering studies of the seismology of the south-west Pacific were belatedly recognized by the award to him in 1975 of the Royal Society of New Zealand's Hector Medal.

Thanks are also due to those colleagues who have pointed out errors and shortcomings of the earlier book, and offered criticisms of all or part of the new manuscript. Among these Mr M. A. Lowry, Dr M. J. Randall, Dr Warwick Smith, Dr John Latter, and Miss Diane Ware call for special mention. Their support and the encouragement of an even wider circle of colleagues and friends has added to the pleasure of the task.

G. A. Eiby

Acknowledgements

The author wishes to record his indebtedness and to express his thanks to the seismologists in many lands, the scientists working in related disciplines, the international agencies, the prospecting companies, and the instrument manufacturers who have helped in innumerable ways with the preparation of this book. His gratitude towards those who have provided illustrations or granted permission for their use is particularly deep. This help has been extended at various times over a period of more than twenty years, since the first edition of the book was planned. It is possible that the passage of time has resulted in the omission of some desirable acknowledgement. If this is so, I hope the person overlooked will accept this expression of intent as the equivalent of the deed.

Thanks are due to the following for the specific assistance listed:

To Dr R. D. Adams, former Superintendent of the Seismological Observatory of the Geophysics Division of the New Zealand Department of Scientific and Industrial Research, for all seismograms reproduced, except those in Figure 64, which are printed with the permission of Dr Frank Press, and the lunar seismograms in Figure 68, which were supplied by Dr Nafi Toksöz, both of the Massachusetts Institute of Technology. Mention must be made of the help of Mr Brian Ferris of the Observatory staff in finding seismograms with suitable characteristics.

To the Director of the Geological Survey, D.S.I.R. for permission to use photographs from the Survey files, to Mr Lensen of his staff for help in choosing them, and to the photographers S. N. Beatus (Plate 17), D. L. Homer (Plates 18, 38, 65, 84 and 86), and B. D. Scott (Plate 40), also to Mr I. A. Nairn, District Geologist, Rotorua, for Plate 35.

To the Alexander Turnbull Library, Wellington, for Plates 2, 42, 43, 45, 58 and 85.

To Dr T. Hisada of the Building Research Institute of the Japanese Ministry of Construction, for Plates 50, 61 and 70; and for his considerable help in collecting photographs from other Japanese colleagues, to whom I extend individual thanks: Drs K. Muto (Plate 49), S. Omote (Plate 33), and K. Kishida (Plate 66).

To Dr N. Ambraseys, Dept. of Civil Engineering, Imperial College, London for Plates 25, 26, 27 and 28.

To Mr John Hollings of Wellington for Plates 52, 53 and 68.

To Mr Ray Rodley of Nelson, for Plate 1, and to Mr Albert Jones for related help.

To Dr George Pararas-Carayannis, Director of the International Tsunami Information Centre, Honolulu, for Plates 31 and 32.

To Professor T. Matsuda of the International Institute of Seismology and Earthquake Engineering, Tokyo, for Plate 78.

To Dr George Plafker of the U.S. Geological Survey for Plates 57 and 78 and the information on which Figure 80 is based.

To Mr R. G. Enticknap of the Lincoln Laboratories, Massachusetts Institute of Technology, for Figures 65 and 66.

To the late Mr B. W. Spooner, formerly Chief Engineer of the N.Z. Ministry of Works, Wellington, for Plates 62 and 88.

To Professor A. Heim, of Zurich, Switzerland, for Plate 23.

To Professor R. Shepherd of the School of Engineering, University of Auckland, for Plates 46 and 60.

To Mr R. Stanton of the Christchurch Civil Defence Organisation, for Plates 51, 90 and 91.

To Dr Ersin Arioğlu, Yapi Merkezi, Istanbul, Turkey, for Plates 29 and 30.

To Profesor B. A. Bolt, Department of Geology and Geophysics, University of California, Berkeley, for Plates 55, 56 and 69.

To Dr Mattsson, UNESCO Field Science Office for Southeast Asia, Djakarta, Indonesia, for Plates 34, 36 and 37.

To Dr Nafi Toksöz of the Massachusetts Institute of Technology and the U.S. National Aeronautics and Space Administration for Plate 60.

To the late Professor Beno Gutenberg, to Professor C. F. Richter, and to the Princeton University Press for Figures 50 and 51, which have been taken from their *Seismicity of the Earth*.

To Dr M. Barazangi, of Cornell University, Ithaca, New York, and to the editors of the *Bulletin of the Seismological Society of America* for permission to reproduce Figure 52.

To Prakla-Seismos GMBH, Hannover, Germany, for Plates 10, 12 and 13.

To the Seismograph Service Corporation, Tulsa, Oklahoma, for Plates 10, 11 and 15.

To the Geotechnical Corporation, Dallas, Texas, U.S.A., for Plates 4 and 5.

To the W. F. Sprengnether Instrument Co. Inc., Saint Louis, Missouri, U.S.A. for Plates 6 and 7.

To the Cambridge Scientific Instrument Co., Cambridge, England, for Plate 8.

To Hilger and Watts, Ltd, London, England, for Plate 9.

To the Director, U.S. National Centre for Earthquake Research, Menlo Park, California, for Figure 70.

To the U.S. National Earthquake Information Centre, Rockville, Maryland, for Plates 63, 75 and 83.

To the publishers of *Life* magazine for permission to reproduce Plate 24 (Photograph by David Scherman).

To the Director of the Institute of Engineering Mechanics, Harbin, China for Plates 41, 47, 48, 54, 71, 88 and 89, 103, 104, and to Dr R. D. Adams for related help.

To Asahi Shimbun for permission to reproduce Plates 59, 64, 67, 87 and 92.

The picture of faulting in the Mino-Owari earthquake (Plate 22) is a detail from a Collotype by K. Ogawa.

All figures not otherwise acknowledged, and Plates 16, 19 and 21 are the work of the author.

Finally, the help of Messrs E. Thornley, S. N. Beatus, and J. Whalan of the Science Information Division of the N.Z. Department of Scientific and Industrial Research in copying seismograms and other material, and in preparing Figure 3 calls for special mention and thanks.

List of plates

List of figures

1 By way of introduction

THIRD AVOCATORE: I've an earthquake in me!
Ben Jonson, *Volpone*

The study of earthquakes is neither a matter of compiling ancient tales of desolation and destruction, nor one of exploiting recent human misfortune for journalistic sensation. Earthquakes are an important part of man's environment, and no part of the globe can claim to be completely immune from them. Seismologists will be found at work in every civilized country, and in many that are not. They are in the first place concerned with why and how earthquakes occur, but this is far from being the whole of seismology. No part of the globe is more inaccessible than that lying directly beneath our feet, but by studying the earthquake-waves that have passed through it, the scientist is able to build up a picture of its internal structure in considerable detail. The methods he devised for doing so have turned out to be of equal value in the search for oil and minerals. In countries where earthquakes are frequent, they pose social and economic questions of great importance, and present special problems to the architect and the engineer. Seismology, then, has something to offer both the practical man and the seeker for fundamental truths of nature.

Scientific seismology is among the younger sciences. It is less than a century since the first satisfactory records of ground movement were made, and a much shorter time from the beginnings of an effective world network of seismograph stations. Serious gaps remain even today, and there are only a few regions in which detailed study of the smaller shocks is possible. One of these regions is New Zealand and because the author is a New Zealander many of the examples discussed in this book will be New Zealand ones, but other countries have not been neglected. The wise reader will keep an atlas handy, preferably one that shows the height of the land and the depth of the sea clearly. There is a map of New Zealand, including most of the place-names used, to be found in the Appendix (Figure 81). Seismology is an international science, and the whole Earth is its field. It is all too easy to assume that one's tribal customs are universal laws.

Seismology is part of the larger science called geophysics, which overlaps and bridges the gap between the older sciences of geology and physics. In its widest sense, geology concerns itself with the complete study of the Earth, but today the term is more usually applied to the largely descriptive study of the nature and history of rocks and the fossils they contain, and the transformation of the Earth's surface at the hand of nature. Physics is concerned with matter in all its forms, and the way it behaves under the influence of heat, pressure, electricity, and other forces. Geophysics, then, takes as its province all those parts of geology that involve physical measurement and calculation, and those parts of physics that concern the Earth and its atmosphere.

Observatories, perhaps to a greater degree than other scientific institutions, tend to attract visitors; but at first many of them find the seismologist's headquarters a disappointment. Because the instruments are sensitive to vibration, only the most favoured callers are allowed to visit the instrument cellars. When they get there, they find that everything is hidden inside heavy draught covers, and that because the charts are made photographically the recorders must be kept in a dim red light, and it is not possible to see much happening. In the offices above, the staff are surrounded by piles of charts covered with wiggly lines. They seem to spend their time putting marks on the charts, making entries in ledgers, and preparing computer tapes. It hardly seems a fitting manner to treat so momentous an affair as an earthquake. It's not the instruments or the charts that are exciting, it's what they mean. After a talk with the staff, most visitors are satisfied.

In writing this book, I have kept in mind the kind of ordinary citizen who calls at the observatory. Most of them want to know more about an earthquake they have felt, about their local earthquake risks, or the earthquakes of the past. I have also had in mind those hundreds of volunteer observers who help us by reporting the times and intensities of the shocks they feel. These people should find the book an understandable account of what happens to their observations, and how they fit in with other types of earthquake research. I hope there will also be readers who have never felt and never expect to feel the slightest of seismic tremors. The nature and causes of earthquakes, the structure of the interior of the globe on which we live, and the behaviour of buildings when shaken are matters that should interest anyone endowed with normal human curiosity.

This is not a technical book, but I have done my best to see that the statements stand up to technical scrutiny. I have tried to distinguish opinion from fact, but the parts of the subject where the experts differ have not been avoided. To leave those out would be to deprive the reader of just the things that make men become seismologists.

2 On feeling an earthquake

The tott'ring China shook without a wind
Alexander Pope, *The Rape of the Lock*

Some people insist that they never feel earthquakes. It all depends: where they are, what they are doing, and what kind of earthquake. In some parts of the world tremors are frequent; in others they occur almost never. At their mildest, earthquakes can be taken for the passing of a truck or the effects of a gust of wind; at their most severe they can destroy buildings, roads and bridges, move hillsides, and cause the sea to rise in huge waves that sweep inland from the coast and complete the destruction that the shaking began.

As long ago as the eighteenth century, John Michell realized that the shaking in an earthquake was due to the passage of elastic waves through the Earth. If they could be traced back to their origin, it might be possible to find the cause of the disturbance. The obvious way to do this was to visit the region affected, examine the damage, and talk to the people who felt it, but nearly two centuries were to pass before there was a serious attempt to follow up Michell's ideas.

Modern seismology dates from the appearance in 1862 of two beautifully illustrated volumes bearing the title *The Great Neapolitan Earthquake of 1857: the first Principles of Observational Seismology*. They were the work of Robert Mallet, an Irish engineer, who had obtained the support of the Royal Society for his expedition to Italy. Mallet drew a map of the affected region, which he divided into four zones. In the first, whole towns had been destroyed; in the second, large buildings were thrown down and people killed; in the third, there was only minor damage and no casualties; and in the fourth, although the shock was felt, no damage was reported. Mallet's four categories constitute a primitive form of earthquake intensity scale.

A classification of this kind was certainly necessary. A year or two before his trip to Italy Mallet had received a letter. It came from a professional colleague in New Zealand and described the south-west Wairarapa earthquake of 1855:

The house . . . gave a very extraordinary shake, which seemed to continue, and was accompanied by a fearful noise. I at once jumped up, rushed, as well as the violent motion would permit me, into the front garden, the motion increasing in violence, accompanied by a roaring as if a large number of cannon were being fired near together, and by a great dust caused by the falling chimneys. The motion at first was a sharp jerk back and forwards in an N. E. and S. W. direction, increasing in extent and rapidity, until I got into the garden — say 25 seconds; it was then succeeded by a shorter and quicker motion at right angles, for nearly the same time, still increasing, but appearing to be perfectly in the plane of the horizon. This was followed by a continuation of both, a sort of vorticose motion, exactly like the motion felt in an ill-adjusted railway carriage on a badly-laid railway at a very high speed, where one is swayed rapidly from side to side. This was accompanied by a sensible elevatory impulse . . .

There is a great deal more, giving evidence of the observational and analytical powers of a writer whose refusal to panic seems exemplary.

Earthquake motions are complex, but they can be classified, and it is not difficult to make more subtle estimates of intensity than the four degrees of shaking mapped by Mallet. Much ingenuity has been expended in drawing up intensity scales. One of the earliest to come into wide use was that of Rossi and Forel, devised in Switzerland and Italy at the end of last century, and describing ten degrees of shaking. Most modern scales have twelve, which seems to be the greatest number of categories that can be adequately distinguished from one another. The scale in most common use in English-speaking countries today is the Modified Mercalli scale. It extends from MM I, a barely perceptible shock, to MM XII, a truly awesome state of destruction, and lists the effects in homely terms that even untrained observers have little difficulty in distinguishing from one another. (Details are set out in the Appendix, page 183.)

Recently there have been attempts to introduce an international scale, the one proposed being known as the MSK scale, after its sponsors Medvedev, Sponheuer and Karnık. The scale is a good one, but as soon as several tests of a single intensity are given, it becomes necessary to establish that they are truly equivalent. The observatory in Australia that gives as one of the degrees on its scale 'like a horse rubbing itself against the veranda post' would have little use for the description 'sets church bells ringing', which is common in scales used in Europe. Europeans in turn would find it difficult to decide whether the shock they had felt could have overthrown one of the stone lanterns that appear in Japanese scales, and the ideas of 'an ordinary well-constructed building' held in San Francisco are not the same as those held in rural Iran.

It must be emphasized that intensity scales have nothing to do with instruments. They provide a convenient way for an observer to summarize what happened to him and to his surroundings, so that it can be compared with the happenings in other places or in other earthquakes. It would be a mistake to think that they are just an historical curiosity. No observatory could afford to scatter instruments as widely as human observers and buildings, and the relationship of the position of the shock worked out by the seismologist in his observatory to its effects can be checked only by observations on the spot.

Plate 1: Felt intensity scales. The fall of these groceries from the shelves of a Nelson warehouse indicates an intensity of about MM VI.

Because the felt area of even a moderate earthquake can be a hundred kilometres across, and big ones can be felt for a thousand kilometres or more, field studies are usually supplemented by issuing postal questionnaires. They ask for the date and time of the shock, an estimate of the duration and direction of the movement, details of sounds heard, and particulars of objects moved and of any damage, so that the intensity can be rated. This task is usually left to the observatory staff, who can ensure that it is done in a consistent way. The accuracy of the information gathered is rather variable. In particular, few people have an accurate idea of the length of a second, and shocks lasting less than a minute are sometimes said to go on for ten minutes or more. The Jesuit missionary who described a shock as being 'as long as a *Paternoster* or a little longer' must be regarded as an exceptionally good observer.

Where shocks are frequent, it becomes worthwhile to organize permanent observers. New Zealand, for example, has a network of volunteers spaced about 40 to 50 km apart over the whole country, and in some of the islands of the South Pacific. These volunteers include postal officials, lighthouse keepers, park rangers and private citizens, and they report about two earthquakes a week to the Seismological Observatory in Wellington.

When the reports of a shock have been collected, the intensities are assessed and plotted on a map. Lines are then drawn in such a way as to enclose areas of the same intensity. These lines are known as *isoseismals*. Figure 1 shows such a map.

If the Earth was of exactly the same constitution in all places, we would expect the energy to spread out evenly in all directions from the origin of the earthquake (a region known as the *focus*), and that the most severely shaken spot would be at the *epicentre*, the point on the Earth's surface vertically above it. The isoseismals would be a set of concentric circles around the epicentre, with the intensity falling off gradually and evenly as we went away from it. Sometimes this is the case, and the position of the epicentre can also be confirmed by the direction in which objects have been moved, and by the pattern of cracks in the damaged buildings. More usually the existence of areas of weak ground and of peculiarities in the geological structure beneath the surface introduces complications.

On unconsolidated materials like loose gravels the intensity is increased, and we shall return to this topic when we deal with engineering seismology. The deeper geology often has the effect of making the isoseismals elliptical rather than circular. Sometimes this is because the structure influences the mechanism of the earthquake, so that more energy is sent out in some directions than in others, but it is more often because the elastic waves are more readily transmitted along the axis of the structural folds and faults than across them.

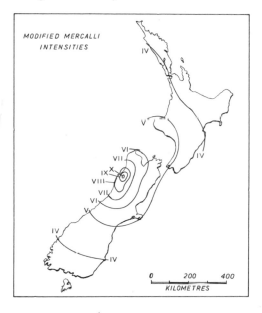

Fig. 1: An isoseismal map. These isoseismals show the distribution of felt intensity in the large shallow earthquake at Inangahua in May 1968.

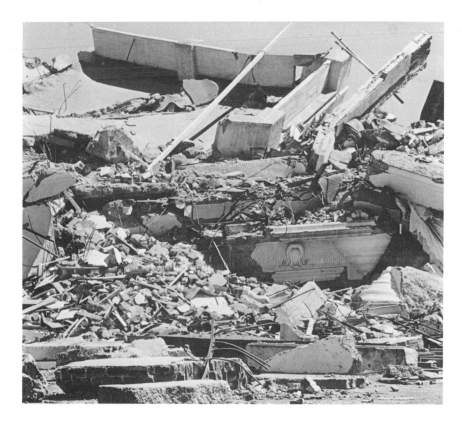

Plate 2: Felt intensity scales. Ruins of the nurses' home in Napier after the earthquake in 1931. Complete structural collapse indicates an intensity of at least MM X.

A major factor affecting the isoseismal pattern of an earthquake is the depth of its focus. A shallow shock may be felt heavily over a small area, but the effects do not extend very far. A deep shock gives a more moderate shaking to a much greater area. Figure 2 makes clear why this should be so. In the case of shallow shocks, estimates of focal depth based on isoseismals may sometimes be better than those made instrumentally, particularly when there are few close recording stations. The isoseismal patterns for very deep shocks, however, are usually very distorted for reasons we shall explain in a later chapter, and they may be so far displaced sideways that the epicentre lies right outside the felt area.

Earthquakes can be felt on ships at sea, as well as on dry land, but the effect is rather different. As a rule, there is just a single upward jolt, as if the ship had struck a submerged obstacle. This is a result of the fact that liquids can transmit only some of the waves that can travel through the solid Earth, and these waves are bent sharply upwards as they leave the Earth for the water at the ocean bottom. These different wave-types will be discussed later. Seismic sea-waves, which are discussed in Chapter 12, are not usually noticeable on the high seas, but in coastal waters or in harbours their effects can be serious.

Much useful information about earthquakes is still to be gathered from felt observations and inspection of damage, but for the accurate location of the origin and an understanding of the mechanism of the shock, instruments are clearly needed. For half a century after Mallet, therefore, the history of earthquake study became largely the story of the search for a suitable recorder, and the efforts to understand the records it produced.

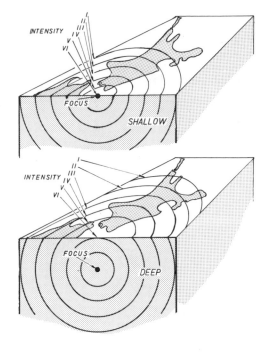

Fig. 2: Effect of focal depth on felt intensity. The two earthquakes shown have the same epicentre and the same maximum felt intensity, but the isoseismals of the deeper shock are more widely spaced and the whole felt area is larger.

3 Recording an earthquake

The moving finger writes; and having writ
Moves on:
    Fitzgerald, *Rubaiyat of Omar Khayyam*

Recording the motion of the ground during an earthquake is not an easy matter. The difficulty when everything fixed to the Earth is moving with it is to obtain some stationary point to start from. The method the seismologist adopts is to make use of *inertia*, the tendency a heavy body has to 'stay put'. A weight hanging from a flexible support tends to lag behind when the support is moved. If some method of recording the relative movement of the weight and the support is provided we have a primitive form of seismograph. The main defect of the arrangement is that once the support is moved, the weight will eventually follow, and it will tend to go on swinging after the support has come to rest. Quite a simple movement of the support becomes a most complicated movement of the weight, and it needs skill and experience to say exactly what the record indicates. When complicated movements are given to the support, it becomes almost impossible.

Science progresses by a combination of theory and experiment, and it will be easier to understand how a seismograph works if we perform a simple experiment ourselves. Get a piece of string about a metre long, and tie a small but reasonably heavy weight to one end. Hold on to the other end, and lift the weight just clear of the floor. Move your hand very slowly backwards and forwards. The weight will follow without any tendency to swing, so that there is no relative

Fig. 3: Response of a simple pendulum. Time-exposure photographs showing the three stages of the experiment described here: (a) Movement slower than natural period; (b) Movement coincides with natural period; (c) Movement faster than natural period.

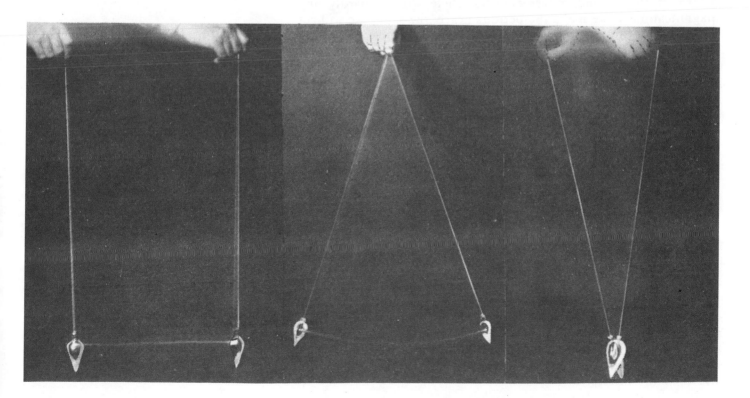

movement between the hand and the weight. If you increase the speed of the to-and-fro movement, the weight will begin to swing more and more vigorously. When you change the direction of movement of your hand about once a second, the swings of the weight will get very big, even if the movements of your hand are quite small. This occurs when the natural period of swing of the pendulum and the period of movement of your hand are the same. Under these conditions, you are obviously getting a big magnification of the movement of your hand, but when you stop, the pendulum will go on swinging, and give a spurious record. Stop the weight, and then try a sudden rapid to-and-fro movement of your hand. The weight remains almost stationary, whilst your hand moves relative to it. In this case we have just about reached the condition we need for recording the movement of the support in an earthquake. There are two disadvantages. There is very little magnification; and if we are going to measure the slower earthquake waves, we will need a pendulum which has a very long time of swing. Figure 3 shows photographs of an experiment of this kind, but the wise reader will repeat it for himself.

During an earthquake, buildings and other structures fixed to the Earth respond in a rather similar way, so the results are important. To sum up:

(1) When the period of movement of the support is much longer than the natural period of the pendulum, the weight just follows the support, and the magnification is zero. (2) When the period of the support movement is the same as the natural period of the pendulum, the magnification is very large. (3) When the period of the support movement is short compared with the natural period of the pendulum magnification is nearly one.

Let us try to apply these results to the design of a simple seismograph. The first problem is to choose a suitable period for the instrument. If we choose one that is long compared with that of the ground movements we want to record, we will get a very faithful record of the ground movement, but there will be hardly any magnification. If we make the periods nearly the same, we will get more magnification, but once the earthquake sets the instrument swinging, the later part of the record will depend more upon the instrument than upon the behaviour of the ground.

It becomes much easier to reach a useful compromise if we provide our pendulum with some form of *damping*. Damping is the drag that eventually brings any swinging object to rest, and usually results from air resistance and friction at the support. As our instrument must come to rest quickly, we shall have to increase the natural damping. This can be done by attaching a vane, which can either be arranged to increase the air resistance, or to trail in a bath of oil.

In more elaborate instruments, the vane is made of copper or aluminium and moves between the poles of a strong magnet. The eddy currents that are generated when it moves also have a damping effect, which cannot be upset by changes in temperature, air pressure, or humidity. The amount of damping is often arranged to be *critical*, that is to say, when the pendulum has been displaced, it will just return to the zero position without additional swings. Figure 4 shows how the magnification is affected by altering the amount of damping. A critically damped pendulum gives a fairly faithful picture of the ground movement over quite a wide range of periods, and by choosing the proper damping and pendulum period, it is possible to design a seismograph suitable for studying most of the problems in which we are interested.

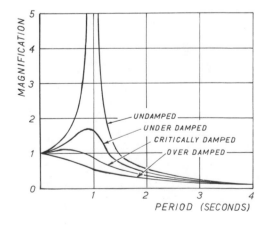

Fig. 4: Magnification of a seismograph. This graph shows how seismographs with a natural period of one second and different degrees of damping will amplify ground movements of differing periods.

Since faithful recording has to be obtained at the expense of magnification, a seismograph is usually provided with some mechanism for enlarging the pendulum movement before it is recorded. In early instruments, levers were used, and the permanent record was made by a stylus fixed on the end of the last lever, which scratched a mark on a drum covered with smoked paper. These records could be made permanent and clean to handle by fixing them in a solution of shellac in methylated spirit. Instruments of this kind are still used for recording strong earthquakes, but they are not very suitable for large magnifications. The friction at the point of the stylus is transmitted back to the weight by the levers, and interferes with its movement unless the weight is made very large. In Europe, seismographs were built with suspended weights as large as twenty tons (Plate 3). At least one of these is still in use, but they are naturally expensive to house and install. There are also mechanical difficulties in making the magnifying levers themselves both strong and light, and in avoiding backlash and 'lost motion' at the pivots.

More present-day instruments use photographic recording, either directly or indirectly. The direct method is to fix a small mirror to the pendulum, and to reflect a beam of light from it on to a sheet of light-sensitive paper wrapped about a recording drum. Every schoolboy who has played with a piece of mirror on a sunny day will know that a very small movement of the mirror produces a very large movement of the reflected light spot. In this way, the pendulum movement can be magnified and recorded without introducing any friction or interference from the levers. When the paper is developed, the movements of the spot will appear as black lines on a white background.

The indirect method is perhaps the most commonly used today, although direct types are far from being out of date. Instruments which use indirect recording are called electromagnetic seismographs. In these the pendulum carries a small pick-up coil, which can swing between the poles of a magnet mounted on the frame of the instrument. Whenever it moves, an electric current is generated, and this is fed to a galvanometer, a sensitive meter with a mirror instead of a pointer. The movements of the galvanometer mirror are then recorded on photographic paper just as those of the pendulum were in the direct method. At first sight, the extra instrument might seem to be an unnecessary complication, but it has a number of advantages. First, the part of the instrument which is sensitive to ground movement can be placed some distance from the recording drum, and is consequently less likely to be disturbed by the visits of the operator. Secondly, electric currents are very simple to control, and they can be amplified, reduced, or modifed in a great number of ways for special purposes. Electromagnetic seismographs have the further advantages that they can be operated in daylight, and that they are unaffected by ground tilt. When mechanical or direct recording seismographs are used, slow tilting of the ground causes the zero position of the spot to wander, and the lines on the chart become unevenly spaced. When the tilting is severe, the lines overlap and make the record difficult to read. In an electromagnetic instrument, the size of the current generated depends upon the speed at which the coil moves and not upon the distance it travels, so that these slow movements do not have any appreciable effect.

Until quite recently observatory seismologists tended to avoid electronic equipment. A simple galvanometer coupled directly to the seismometer would give enough magnification for most purposes.

Plate 3: Mechanical seismographs. The Omori seismograph is a classical horizontal pendulum with a mass of a few kilograms, a period of several seconds, and a magnification of about a hundred.

In the Wiechert instrument shown below, which can record both horizontal components, the mass is a great tank filled with 17 tons of iron ore. It has a period of about a second and a magnification of two thousand.

Valve amplifiers were erratic and unreliable devices, difficult to calibrate, and needing large amounts of electric power. The advent of the transistor and the printed circuit quickly changed all this. Seismometers have become smaller, as an amplifier needs less input power than a galvanometer, and can produce enough output to drive a pen or stylus against quite heavy paper friction. This has brought smoked paper records back into favour, as they produce a very fine even trace. They are particularly useful for portable equipment, for photographic processing under field conditions is never very satisfactory. In fixed observatories, recorders using a heated stylus marking a heat-sensitive paper, or writing with ink fed through a fine capillary tube are used to make records that are produced in daylight, and available for tsunami warning or press and radio information services without further processing. Power requirements are surprisingly small, and battery operation is feasible.

Another possibility is the use of a radio link to increase the separation between the seismometer and the recorder. Distances of several tens of kilometres are easily obtained, and operators need no longer be inconvenienced by the fact that the quietest sites are usually in the least accessible places. It is possible to link a whole network of seismometers to a single recording point, simplifying timing problems, and cutting down the number of operators required. Networks of this kind are in use in California, and in New Zealand, and are becoming increasingly common.

Before I describe some actual observatory seismographs, a more unassuming part of the equipment must be mentioned — the recording drum. A complete seismograph consists of two equally important parts — the seismometer, which is sensitive to ground movements, and the recorder which makes its indications permanent. The recorder may seem so simple as to be unworthy of discussion. It consists of a drum, 30 centimetres or so in diameter and the same in length, with a motor to turn it round, usually either twice or four times in an hour, and a screw arrangement to move it slowly sideways so that the successive traces do not overlap. The slow speed is very difficult to keep constant. Small irregularities in the gears are serious, and if the drum is not perfectly balanced it will run ahead at times and then wait for the motor to catch up. Since the seismologist often wants to measure the time of arrival of a wave with an accuracy of a tenth of a second, ordinary clockwork cannot be used for the motor. Clock escapements drive the hands in a series of jerks which may be a fifth or even half a second apart.

The steadiest drive is a synchronous motor driven by an electric current whose frequency is very carefully controlled. Sometimes the mains are used, but most stations today are equipped with very accurate electronic clocks for timing purposes, and from these an even more stable current can be derived and used to turn the drums.

When the recording is photographic there will also be a recording lamp. An arrangement of lenses concentrates its light upon the seismometer mirror and ensures that the reflected ray is focused on the surface of the drum as a tiny but sharply defined spot. If this spot is not clear and sharp the timing accuracy will suffer and very fast movements cannot be seen clearly.

Somewhere in the path of the light beam there is a shutter which is closed for an instant once a minute by an accurate clock, leaving a brief gap in the trace. In many instruments, instead of a shutter, a glass prism is used, and the trace is moved sideways instead of being blacked out. In this way none of the record is lost, but if the

Fig. 5: Common types of seismograph pendulum. A. Horizontal Pendulum (Omori, Milne-Shaw, Press-Ewing). B. Horizontal Pendulum with Zöllner Suspension (Galitzin). C. Inverted Pendulum (Wiechert 1 000 kg, 10 sec. period). D. Torsion Seismograph (Wood-Anderson). E. Vertical Pendulum (Galitzin, Press-Ewing). F. Vertical Seismograph (Benioff, Wilson-Lamison).

Recording arrangements are not shown. This diagram illustrates the principles involved, not the physical arrangement of the parts in the actual instruments.

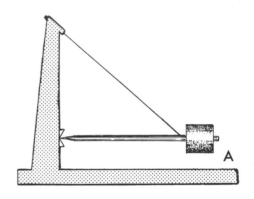

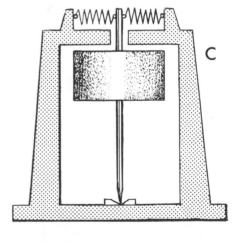

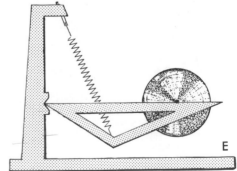

movements of the earthquake are large, the timing marks may be hard to see.

Many different kinds of pendulum have successfully been used as the basis of a seismograph, but not the simple pendulum we have been discussing so far. The reason is size. A pendulum designed to swing once a second is about a metre long, which is already a little large for convenience. It might be made to serve for local earthquakes, but if we wanted a simple pendulum to record the surface-waves from distant shocks, which have periods from 20 to 100 seconds or more, we should need the Eiffel tower to hang it from.

Figure 5 shows some of the arrangements that have been used to produce a more compact pendulum of the right period. The first four are sensitive to horizontal ground movements, and the last two to vertical ones. It will occur to some readers that arrangements like those shown at A, B and D will respond quite readily to movements at right angles to the plane of the paper, but that movements along the line joining the centre of the suspended weight to the hinges will have no effect on them at all. This is really an advantage, as it allows the seismologist to analyse the nature of an approaching wave, and to find what direction it is coming from. Seismographs often come in sets of three — two horizontal ones mounted at right angles (one usually north and south, and the other east and west, but not always), and a vertical one.

The elastic waves that an earthquake sets up have a very wide range of natural periods, and most observatories try to record those in the range between about a tenth of a second and a hundred seconds. It is possible to detect waves of even longer periods, but recording them is generally considered to be a special research project.

The limit to the magnification that we can use at any particular period is set by small movements of the ground called *microseisms*. They go on all the time, even when there are no earthquakes, and once a seismograph is sensitive enough to show them, an increase in the magnification only makes the recording more and more confused. The most common types of microseism have periods between two and six seconds, and it is therefore usual to install two sets of seismographs, one to cover the movements of shorter periods than the microseisms, and one for the longer periods. On a very quiet site short-period instruments can be operated with magnifications as great as a few hundred thousand, but the magnifications of long-period ones seldom go beyond a few thousand, and are often very much less. Strangely enough, it is the long-period instruments that are most useful for recording distant earthquakes. This is because short-period vibrations are more readily absorbed as they pass through the Earth, so that at great distances only the waves of longer periods are still strong enough to be detected.

At first, seismologists concentrated upon making their instruments as sensitive as possible, but less sensitive ones also have important uses. Engineers are particularly interested in the big waves close to the epicentres of destructive earthquakes. Even if these waves do not damage a sensitive instrument, they will give so confused a record that it is impossible to interpret it. Strong-motion instruments for engineering periods often have magnifications from one to about ten. A well-equipped observatory therefore has instruments with a very great range of periods and magnifications. At Wellington, for example, there are seventeen different samples of the ground movement being made continously.

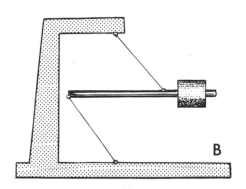

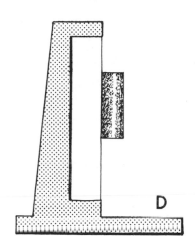

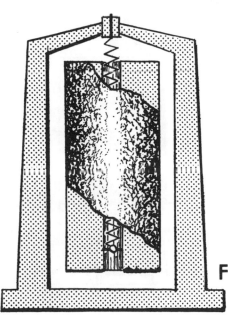

For the mechanically-inclined seismologist, seismographs exert all the fascination of a vintage car. The temptation to describe more than a representative selection of the more important must therefore be resisted.

When a station has only one instrument, it is usually a short-period vertical component. This will produce good records of local shocks, and of the first wave to arrive from more distant ones. Nowadays it will be an electromagnetic instrument, probably recording photographically, but possibly connected to an amplifier driving a pen-and-ink or heated stylus recorder.

In 1930, Dr Hugo Benioff produced the first seismometer to provide magnifications of a hundred thousand or more in the short-period range. The vertical instrument is shown in Figure 6 and Plate 4. A cylindrical mass of 100 kg is suspended from a framework about a metre in height by a spring that is housed in a hole passing along its axis. Flat metal guide-ribbons above and below the mass allow it to move freely up and down, but restrain it horizontally. Below the mass is the *transducer*, which converts its movements into electrical currents. It consists of a set of coils wound on soft-iron armatures that move with the mass, and a strong permanent magnet that is fixed to the frame. Relative movement between the two varies the magnetic flux through the coil, and generates the currents, which are fed to the galvanometer. Often there are two of these, one with a natural period of about a quarter of a second, and the other with a period of 90 seconds or more, coupled to separate coils, and recording on different drums.

In the horizontal instrument, the mass is divided into two parts, one placed on either side of the transducer (Plate 5). The guide ribbons provide sufficient restoring force to bring the mass back to the central position, so there is no central spring. The high sensitivity, simplicity and reliability of the Benioff instruments brought them into wide use, and they retain their popularity, but attempts were soon being made to retain their advantages in seismometers that were lighter and more compact.

Among the most successful of these is the one designed by Dr P. L. Willmore at Cambridge (Plate 9). In it, the transducer magnet also serves as the mass. It is supported on flat springs that can be disconnected if it is desired to record the horizontal movements, and induces currents in a coil fixed to the frame. The whole arrangement fits in a watertight cylindrical case 16 cm in diameter and 33 cm high, and its weight is less than 5 kg. It can easily be housed in a shallow concrete-lined pit, or even buried, greatly reducing the costs of housing and installation.

Both the Canadian and the New Zealand networks make extensive use of Willmore instruments, and they are in wide demand for field studies of volcanic tremor and aftershocks, but the earliest instrument to be really suitable for recording local earthquakes was a mechanical one, the Wood-Anderson torsion seismometer, developed in California in the late 1920s. The records of these intruments formed the basis of Professor Richter's magnitude scale (Chapter 11). The way they work can be seen in Figure 7.

The 'heavy' weight is a tiny cylinder of copper, only about 25 millimetres long, and not as thick as a piece of fencing wire. Since we do not ask it to drive anything, we can make it small and convenient. At the top end of the cylinder, a mirror is fixed, and the whole arrangement is carried on a thin tungsten wire about 20 cm long. Just above and below the weight, the wire passes through two small holes,

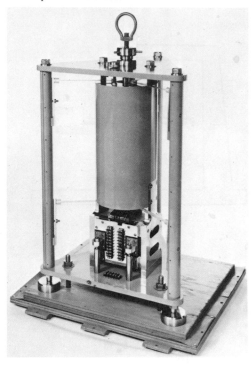

Plate 4: *Benioff variable-reluctance seismometer. This is the vertical component instrument shown diagrammatically in Figure 6. The coils of these instruments can be connected independently to short- and long-period galvanometers, but at stations of the World-Wide Standard Network only the short period is used.*

Fig. 6: *Benioff vertical seismometer. In this seismometer the magnet is fixed to the frame of the instrument, and the pick-up coils are carried by the moving mass. The cylindrical mass is constrained by tensioned guide-ribbons and supported by a spring passing through a central hole.*

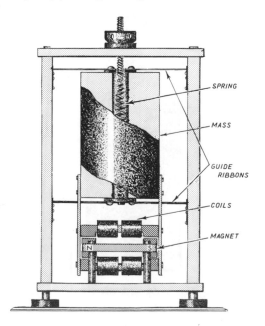

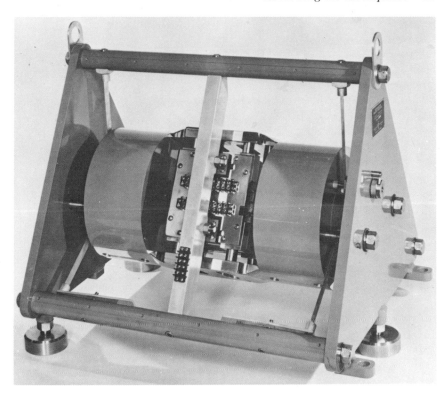

Fig. 7: Wood-Anderson torsion seismometer. This mechanical-optical instrument was the first really satisfactory seismograph for recording near earthquakes.

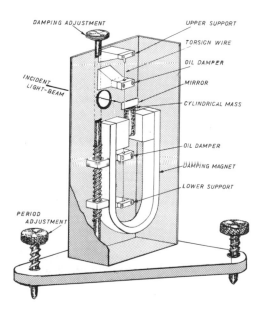

DAMPING ADJUSTMENT UPPER SUPPORT
TORSIGN WIRE
OIL DAMPER
INCIDENT LIGHT-BEAM MIRROR
CYLINDRICAL MASS
OIL DAMPER
DAMPING MAGNET
LOWER SUPPORT
PERIOD ADJUSTMENT

each holding a single drop of castor oil. This stops any tendency the wire might have to vibrate like the string of a violin, so that all the weight can do is to twist back and forth around the wire. On either side of the weight, the poles of a magnet provide eddy-current damping. This magnet is somewhat differently arranged in different models of the instrument, but it can always be moved up and down, and by arranging just the right length of the cylinder to come between the poles the damping can be adjusted to critical. This seismograph has a magnification of nearly three thousand, and a period of just over three-quarters of a second.

Historically, good short-period seismographs are comparative latecomers. This is partly because they are a little more difficult to design, and partly because the countries that had established schools of geophysics in the early part of the century were not the countries troubled by destructive earthquakes; but in 1889 a Japanese earthquake was recorded by von Rebeur-Paschwitz at Potsdam in Germany, on a pendulum intended for gravity studies, and the scientific uses of such records were at once realized. By 1900 several good horizontal pendulum instruments had been designed, and the British Association for the Advancement of Science had taken active steps towards setting up a world-wide network of earthquake recorders.

Some of the early instruments used photographic recording, but most of them produced a record on smoked paper. The Omori seismograph (Plate 3) is typical of these instruments, which did not develop greatly. Photographic intruments, on the other hand, were greatly improved, and the introduction of electromagnetic seismometers recording through a galvanometer made photographic recording the preferred method until the development of reliable amplifiers made a return to various forms of pen writing practicable.

Plate 6: A vertical pendulum. The boom of the vertical Press-Ewing instrument is a horizontal framework pivoted at the left. At the right is the mass, divided into two parts and supported by the diagonal spring. The framework also carries the perforated pillar carrying the pick-up coils. The magnets are fixed to the frame of the instrument and placed above the spring. The movement of the boom is conveyed to the pick-up coils by the perforated pillar just behind the centre of the mass. Like the horizontal instruments, the vertical Press-Ewings can be operated at periods of 15 to 30 seconds.

Plate 7: A horizontal pendulum. In this Press-Ewing long-period seismometer the mass is carried on the end of a pivoted boom and supported by wires connected to a rigid upright. The pick-up and calibration coils move between the poles of cylindrical magnets attached to the base and placed on either side of the mass. When in operation the instrument is protected from barometric changes by a strong airtight metal case, and from temperature changes by an outer cover of polystyrene. These instruments and their vertical counterpart are used in the World-Wide Standard Network and are usually operated at periods of either 15 or 30 seconds.

Plate 8: Galitzin seismograph. This is the classical form of the electromagnetic instrument. The boom is pivoted at the right, and the copper damping vane moves between the poles of the outer set of magnets at the left. The pick-up coil moves between those of the inner set.

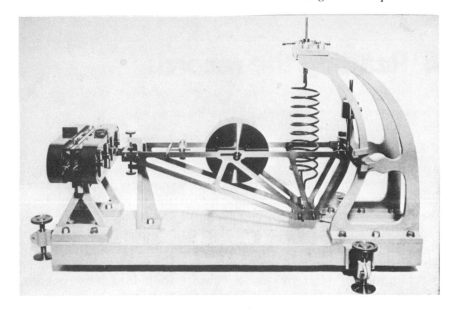

Plate 9: Willmore seismometer, with its cover removed. In this very compact instrument, widely used for recording near earthquakes, the magnet is suspended from leaf-springs and acts as the mass. The springs can be detached to allow its use as a horizontal component. The geophones used in seismic prospecting are similar in construction but smaller and lighter.

The first electromagnetic seismographs were produced in 1906 by the Russian Prince Boris Galitzin (Golitsyn in modern translitterations). A big attraction of the Galitzin instruments was that it was possible to make a homogeneous set in which the vertical instrument could be given the same period, damping, and magnification as the horizontal ones. Vertical seismographs have always been troublesome to design and operate. The only way to make the mass free to move up and down is to suspend it directly or indirectly from a spring, and springs do not behave conveniently. They change in length and elasticity when the temperature changes, and the metal of which they are made 'creeps' as it becomes fatigued. Special alloys and temperature-compensating devices have been used, but they add to the complexity, and the best seismographs have always been simple.

A classical Galitzin seismograph is shown in Plate 8. The mass is fixed to a boom, which takes the form of a triangular girder pivoted on flat springs at one end, and kept horizontal by the tension of a vertical coiled spring. The pick-up coil and a copper damping vane move between two sets of magnets mounted at the other end of the boom. By altering their position, the damping and sensitivity can be varied. They are usually operated with periods of twelve or twenty-four seconds, and magnifications of a few hundred.

The use of very long-period galvanometers in conjunction with Benioff seismometers led to a decline in the popularity of Galitzin-type instruments, but with the development of Press-Ewing seismometers at Lamont Observatory in the 1950s and their use in the American-sponsored world network of standardized stations, they have enjoyed a return to favour. The Press-Ewing instruments (Plates 6 and 7) are similar in principle and general mechanical arrangement to Galitzins, but special attention has been paid to their stability at long periods, and to the elimination of false resonances caused by the spring of the vertical component, and the pick-up coils are of a more efficient type. On suitable sites the pendulum can be made stable at periods as long as thirty seconds, and used to drive a galvanometer with a period of one hundred seconds or more.

4 Reading the records

The record of a distant earthquake (Figure 23) looks quite different from that of a near one (Figure 22). Can we use this difference to tell us the distance? If we can, it should be possible to locate the centre of the disturbance more accurately than we can by using isoseismals.

It is clear from the appearance of the records that the movement of the ground during the earthquake is a kind of wave. For a long time physicists have been interested in waves, and they have sorted out a great number of different kinds. There are about four or five possible ways in which the Earth could vibrate, and, if we are to understand the records, it is necessary to find out which types are actually involved.

Two kinds are of the greatest importance in earthquake study, and the seismologist has to refer to them so often that he has given them

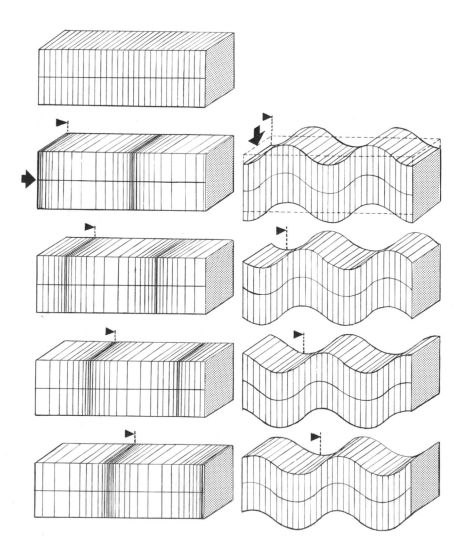

Fig. 8: Longitudinal and transverse waves. If the bar shown at the top left is given a sharp blow on its left-hand end a compressional wave will be sent along it towards the right. The particles move to and fro in the same direction as the wave is travelling and the wave is said to be longitudinal. A downwards blow, as shown on the right, starts a transverse wave like the one in a rope shaken at one end. Earthquakes send both kinds of wave through the Earth.

one-letter names, *P* and *S*. The letters really stand for 'primary' and 'secondary' in order of arrival; but it is easier to remember which is which if you think of them as 'push' and 'shake'. The physicist, who likes his names to give a mathematically exact description of what is happening, calls them 'longitudinal' and 'transverse' or 'compressional' and 'shear' respectively.

A longitudinal, or *P*-wave, is really a sound wave through the Earth, and is the fastest kind. As the wave passes, each particle of the rock moves to and fro in the same direction as the wave is travelling. The material therefore experiences a series of compressions and rarefactions. This is not the simplest kind of wave to picture, but Figure 8 will probably help. Imagine that the bar is given a sharp tap with a hammer at the left-hand end. Each particle hit by the hammer will move away for an instant and then spring back. When it moves away, it will transmit the force to its neighbour and cause a pulse to travel to the right. When the pulse gets to the other end, a ball resting against the rod would bounce away to show that it had arrived. In the transverse, or *S*-wave, the particles move at right angles to the direction in which the wave is travelling, exactly like they do in a rope which is fixed at one end and shaken at the other (Figure 8).

These waves do not travel at the same speed. The *P*-wave goes about eight kilometres in a second, and the *S*-wave only about four and a half kilometres. (Readers not yet used to the metric system may like to recall that a kilometre is about five eighths of a mile.)

This means that the *P*-wave always arrives first, and *S* lags behind. The farther the recorder is from the origin of the earthquake, the bigger the time interval between the arrival of the two waves. If we can identify them on the records and measure the time-interval between their arrivals we can work out how distant the origin was. The farther away an earthquake is, the deeper the waves will penetrate into the body of the Earth. The deeper they penetrate, the faster they travel, so a simple calculation based on the figures I have just quoted would not be accurate enough. Tables have been drawn up to show the amount of this change, or it can be shown in the form of a graph (Figure 9), so that in practice we can get the answer quite quickly.

If we have a three-component record, it is possible to work out the direction from which a wave has come, but several factors operate to make estimates of direction less reliable than estimates of distance. The more distant an earthquake is, the greater will be the effect that a small error in direction has upon the estimated position of the origin. It is therefore more usual to find earthquake origins by using distances from a number of stations that have recorded the shock. For this reason seismologists like to exchange readings with their colleagues in neighbouring countries as soon as possible.

Let us look at a practical case. We will forget for the present that the actual origin of the shock is at a focus some distance below the surface of the Earth, and concentrate upon the epicentre, the point on the surface vertically above it. This is convenient, because at some stage we will probably want to show our results on a map.

The Wellington record of a shock on 13th February, 1973 showed an earthquake with 17 seconds between the arrival of the *P* and the *S*. This indicates a distance of 149 km, so that the epicentre must lie somewhere on a circle with a radius of 149 km and its centre at Wellington (WEL). On the Tarata (TNZ) record the *S* - *P* interval was 14 seconds, making the radius of the corresponding circle 119

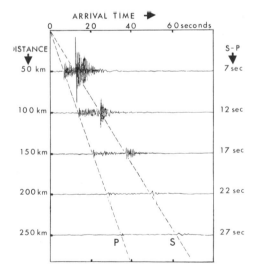

Fig. 9: Finding the distance. The time interval between the arrival of the longitudinal P-wave and the slower transverse S-wave increases with increasing distance from the origin of the shock.

km. If we draw these two circles on a map (Figure 10) we find that they cut in two points, and one of these must be the epicentre. One is near the coast, and the other some distance out to sea. Both these places have had earthquakes in the past, so we can't say that one answer is more likely than the other. We need a third station. The one at Taradale (TRZ) gave an interval of 16 seconds and a distance of 139 km. This lets us draw a third circle, which shows that the position near the coast is the correct one. The fact that the shock was felt quite strongly in the Wanganui district but not at all in the South Island makes it even more certain that we have the right answer.

We can use other stations to make absolutely sure, but if we do, we find that they don't all cut exactly in a single point, for the records are not perfect, and there are small local differences in the travel-times over different parts of the country. In spite of these difficulties a well-recorded shock can normally be located to within about five or ten kilometres, and by making lengthier calculations that allow for the regional variations important earthquakes can be located with even greater accuracy.

Instead of drawing circles most of the larger observatories now feed their readings to electronic computers in which details of the station positions and the travel-time tables have been stored. The computer goes about the job a little differently. First the seismologist has to guess roughly where the earthquake is, and tell the computer. It doesn't have to be a very good guess, but the computer has to start somewhere. From its tables it works out the times that *P* and *S* waves

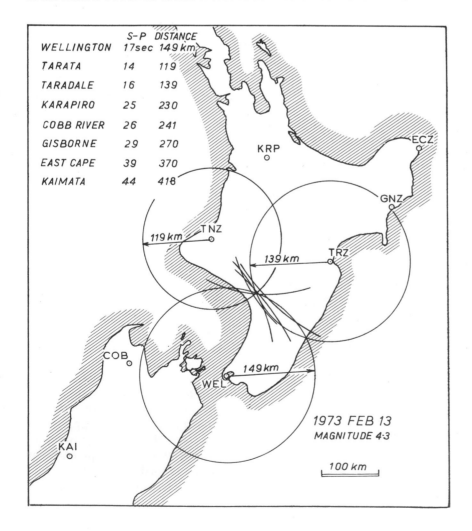

	S-P	DISTANCE
WELLINGTON	17sec	149 km
TARATA	14	119
TARADALE	16	139
KARAPIRO	25	230
COBB RIVER	26	241
GISBORNE	29	270
EAST CAPE	39	370
KAIMATA	44	418

1973 FEB 13
MAGNITUDE 4·3

100 km

Fig. 10: Locating an epicentre. The time between the arrival of P *and* S *at each station is used to find the distance of the origin. An arc with this distance as radius is then drawn round each station. The arcs intersect at the epicentre.*

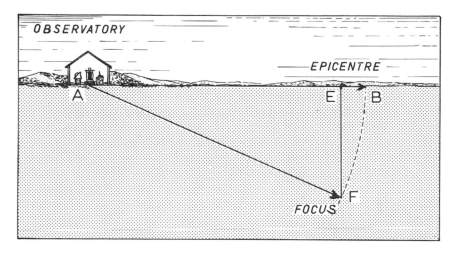

Fig. 11: Focus and epicentre. The epicentre is the point on the Earth's surface directly above the focus, where shock originates. The length A E from the recording station to the epicentre is known as the epicentral distance △. Distances found from S - P intervals are not △, but AF, the distance to the focus. For shallow shocks this does not matter, but if the shock is deep a circle drawn on a map with centre A and radius AF will be much too big, and go through the point B instead of through the epicentre.

from a shock in the position it was given should have arrived at the different recording stations, and compares them with the times of arrival that were actually recorded. If the trial position is too near the station, the calculated time will be too early; if it is too far away, it will be too late. The computer can now move the trial position a little in the direction indicated, and try again. This time the differences between the calculated arrival times and the real ones will be smaller, but the computer will go on moving the origin about until either it finds that further shifting gives bigger differences, or until the seismologist tells it that the fit is near enough. Three or four shifts are usually enough to give a satisfactory position, but there is one important kind of earthquake that seems never to give a good fit.

When we look at one of these problem shocks graphically, we find that the third circle does not go through either of the intersections of the other two. If we can be quite certain that the trouble does not lie in a poor record from one of the stations, or in something wrong with the timing, this is an indication that the focus of the earthquakes lies farther beneath the surface of the earth than usual; that is to say, we are dealing with a 'deep-focus' earthquake. The distances obtained from *S-P* intervals are of course distances between the focus and the recording station, not those between the station and the epicentre (Figure 11). It is not difficult to calculate the depth at which the focus must lie to make the circles meet in a point. Figure 12 shows the circles for a shock with an origin 160 kilometres below the central North Island, first assuming that it has a normal shallow focus, and then using tables worked out for the correct focal depth. The nearer a station is to the epicentre, the greater the effect changes in depth will have on the radius of the circle. To make good measurements of depth, we need a recording station as close to the epicentre as the shock is deep. This leads to the slightly surprising result that large depths are often more reliably known than small ones.

The records our seismographs produce give us a convenient method of locating the origin of an earthquake shock; and they tell us something about the way in which the ground at the recording station moved during the earthquake. This is important enough, but the geophysicist has found a use for earthquake waves which is of even greater interest to him. All of my country readers must at some time or other have tried to see how full the water tank is by thumping the outside, and listening to the way the sound changes when you thump above and below the water level. Town readers who have not will probably remember the proverb about empty vessels. The Earth is

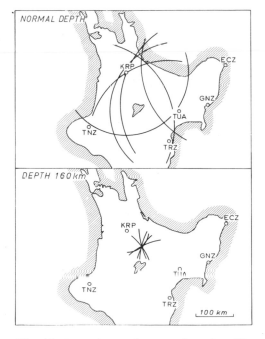

Fig. 12: Locating a deep earthquake. The arcs in the upper figure were drawn on the supposition that the earthquake was of normal focal depth. When appropriate corrections for depth are applied the satisfactory cut shown in the lower figure is obtained.

even harder to see inside than a water tank, and we have to look for equally indirect ways of working out what lies inside it. The principle used is almost the same, with earthquakes to do the thumping, and seismographs to listen. Since the *P*-wave is a sound wave, the analogy is quite a close one. An earthquake wave is the only thing we know of which can be sent to explore the very centre of the Earth.

Let us suppose that we have collected together all the records of a big earthquake. There will be a very big pile of them – perhaps five or six hundred, even if we don't count all three components at every recording station. Let us carefully measure each record, and find the time at which the first movement arrives. If we list the stations in order of their distance from the epicentre, we can see that there is a gradual change in the speed of the journey, and that it increases as the path lies deeper and deeper in the Earth. We should expect this to happen, because waves travel more rapidly in more rigid material, and the material deep in the Earth will be firmly packed together by the weight of the material on top of it.

This is a convenient place to note that when the seismologist deals with distances, he often states them in degrees, rather than in kilometres. This is like looking at the angle between two lines, one from the station and one from the epicentre, meeting at the centre of the Earth. There are 360° right round the Earth, and two points 180° apart are exactly opposite one another. A degree is about 111 km. There is a table in the Appendix to help you convert from one system to the other if you wish. The advantage of this system of measurement is that it reminds us that the Earth is a ball, and avoids any ambiguity between distances measured around the surface and through the middle.

But let us get back to our pile of records. As the distance between the station and the epicentre gets bigger, the size and clarity of the *P* movement gets rather worse, until at about 103°, the beginning of the record becomes indistinct. Something is happening to the wave in its

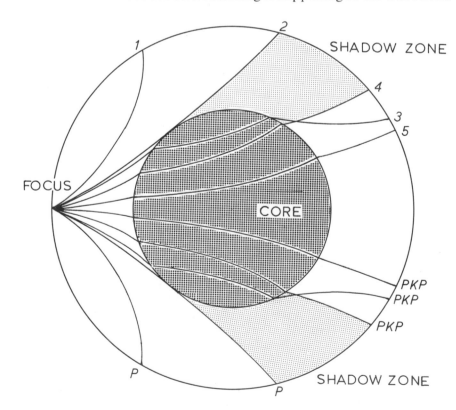

Fig. 13: The shadow zone. When **P**-*waves cross the boundary between the mantle and the core they are sharply bent. This creates a shadow zone for* **P** *at distances between 103° and 142° from the focus.*

travels. This something continues to happen until about 142°, when the movement again becomes sharp, but shows by its time of travel that it is not the same wave we started with. The region in between, where the wave is indistinct, is called the 'shadow zone for *P*' (Figure 13).

The reason the shadow zone exists is that at about half way to the centre the Earth's composition suddenly changes. The region above this boundary is known as the Earth's *mantle*, and the region below it is known as the *core*. Once a wave from an earthquake penetrates so deeply that it must pass through the core it is sharply bent, and emerges at a much greater distance that it otherwise would, creating the shadow zone. It was first observed by R. D. Oldham in 1906, and gave one of the earliest indications of the great part seismology would play in exploring the Earth's interior. With modern sensitive seismographs the core might have been harder to find, for the shadow zone is not one of complete darkness. In it are to be found waves that have taken rather less direct paths, but they are weaker than either the *P*-wave at 103°, or the wave through the core that re-appears at 142°, which can be very sharp and prominent. We shall discuss some of these other waves in due course.

The depth to the boundary between the mantle and the core is about 2 900 kilometres, and was first found by Professor Beno Gutenberg in 1913, using carefully measured travel-times. Although he believed that his estimate could be out by as much as fifty or a hundred kilometres, modern measurements have reduced it by less than twenty at the most. Because of his work the boundary is known as the *Gutenberg Discontinuity*.

Everyone is familiar with echoes. When a sound-wave meets an obstacle part of it is reflected, and we hear it as if there were another source behind the reflector. Sound-waves can also be *refracted,* or bent, whenever they pass from one medium to another in which their speed is different. Earthquake waves of both *P*- and *S*-type can also be both reflected and refracted, and we have already seen how the refraction of *P*-waves by the core creates a shadow zone. There are other boundaries inside the Earth at which reflection or refraction can occur, and waves can change type or meet a boundary more than once. As a result earthquake records become very complicated, but the complications are clues to the internal structure of the Earth.

Records of near earthquakes (within about 10° of the recording station) give information about layers near the surface, but first of all we shall look at the simpler construction of the deeper parts, which can be deduced from distant records.

The core is much denser than the mantle, and its surface reflects waves and sends them back like echoes. A reflected *P*-wave is called *PcP*, and a reflected *S*-wave *ScS*. The small *c* denotes a wave that reaches the core, but does not penetrate it. The time that the reflected wave takes to travel is naturally longer than that for the direct wave, for it has farther to go, and it appears as a distinct pulse on the records. But there is a complication here. When a wave is reflected or refracted at a boundary it can change type, from a *P*-wave to an *S*-wave or *vice-versa*. This means that instead of just two reflected waves there are four — *PcP, ScS, PcS* and *ScP*.

For *PcP* and *ScS*, in which there is no change of wave-type, the reflection takes place at the mid-point of the path, but when there is a change the two sections of the path are of unequal length, and the point of reflection is displaced to one side.

This means that *PcS* and *ScP* follow different paths, but have exactly the same time of travel (Figure 14).

In order to keep track of the different kinds of wave, the seismologist draws what is known as a *travel-time curve*. This is a graph which shows how long it will take a wave to travel by each of the possible routes, and there is a line on it for each separate kind of wave. Figure 14 shows the routes that the *P*- and *S*-waves and the core reflections take, and the corresponding travel-time for these phases. If the distance of the earthquake is read off along the horizontal line, the time at which the different pulses will arrive can be read off vertically.

A real seismogram shows many more phases than the half-dozen I have mentioned. In order to see what other kinds there are, I shall treat them in 'family groups'.

The first set are the surface reflections. There is a big difference in density between the air and the rocks of the Earth, and conditions are very favourable for reflecting a wave that comes up to the surface from the interior. If a *P*-wave is reflected at a point midway between the recording station and the epicentre, it gives rise to a wave called *PP*, and of course, there is an *SS*, following the same route. Once again, there can be a change of type on reflection, and there are also waves called *PS* and *SP*; but in this case, as with *PcS* and *ScP*, the point of reflection is not half way, though the waves again have the same travel-time. The paths of these phases are shown in Figure 15.

The number of possible internal reflections is not limited to one. Two reflections are quite common, and there is a whole series of this kind — *PPP*, *SSS*, *PPS*, *SPP*, *SSP*, *SPS*, and *PSP*. In the case of a very large earthquake, it is even possible to record *PPPP*, since the only limit to the complications is the amount of energy available. The energy is not of course divided equally between all the possible phases, and generally speaking, the simpler combinations are the most prominent in the records; but there are some striking exceptions, as the curved layers of the Earth can result in focusing effects for certain phases at some particular distances.

The next family of waves is the core refractions. We noticed earlier that beyond about 103° the direct *P*-wave cannot be recorded on account of the shadow effect of the core. Beyond this distance the first wave to appear on long-period instruments is often *PP*, which does not penetrate so deeply, and so is able to avoid the obstacle. Short-period ones often show a refracted wave arising from complexities within the core, but it is nothing like so prominent as *P* when it makes its re-appearance at 142°. Because it was deflected from its path, and disappeared altogether for nearly 40°, we give it a new name, and call it *PKP*. The *K* stands for *Kern*, the German word for core.

What are the other members of the family? If we look for an *S*-wave by the same route we find a surprise waiting, it seems to be much too early. In order to get through the core, it has had to change type and travel as a *P*. The core will not transmit transverse waves. We shall see why in Chapter 7. Since all waves through the core are longitudinal like *P*, the one letter *K* is the only symbol we need. The main core refractions are therefore written *PKS*, *SKP*, and *SKS*. There are also some rather more distant but not unimportant relatives that have been reflected inside the core itself. The main ones are *PKKP* and *SKKS*, and there are also some like *PKPPKP* that have been able to pass right through the core in order to be reflected back from the surface of the Earth on the opposite side of the globe (Figure 16).

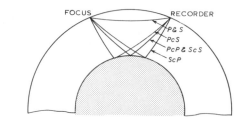

Fig. 14: Reflections from the core. The upper part of the diagram shows the paths of waves reflected from the boundary between the mantle and the core, and the graph below shows their times of travel.

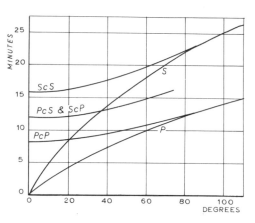

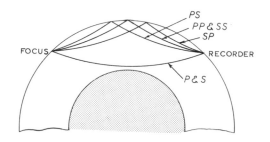

Fig. 15: Single and multiple reflections at the Earth's surface. The upper diagram shows the paths of waves reflected once only, with and without change of type. Below are the paths of singly and doubly reflected P-waves.

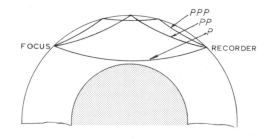

Fig. 16: Core phases. The phase **PKP** *arises from simple refraction by the cores.* **PKKP** *is internally relected within it, while* **PKPPKP** *emerges to undergo internal reflection at the surface on the far side of the Earth.*

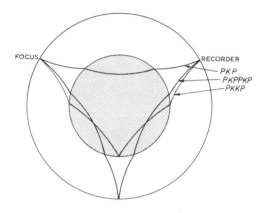

Because it has had so far to travel, *PKPPKP* arrives a long time after most of the other phases, and it is not difficult to mistake it for the *P* of a new shock. If you trace out these paths on the different diagrams, you will not find it hard to work out how the different phases are named, and to imagine the paths of some of the more unusual ones like *PKPPKPPKP* and *PKSP*.

It should be mentioned that seismologists in a hurry sometimes write *P'* as a shorthand for *PKP*, so that *PKPPKP* becomes *P'P'* and so on, but we shall not use this notation again in this book.

We have already looked at a simple travel-time curve showing the direct waves and the core reflections. Figure 17 is a much more complete diagram, including most of the commonly recorded phases. In a large earthquake many more are possible, and at some distances they can appear quite prominent.

There is still one important class of wave to be considered. These are the surface waves, which are often the most prominent part of a record. They are often called *L*, or 'long' waves, since they oscillate more slowly than either the *P* or the *S* type, and they travel round the outside of the Earth instead of passing through the interior. Closer study shows that they are a mixture of two different kinds of wave — Love waves and Rayleigh waves, named after their respective discoverers. Both of these men showed mathematically that waves of this kind could exist before they were identified on seismograms. Love waves are a transverse movement, rather like *S*, but moving only in a horizontal plane. They are guided around the outside of the

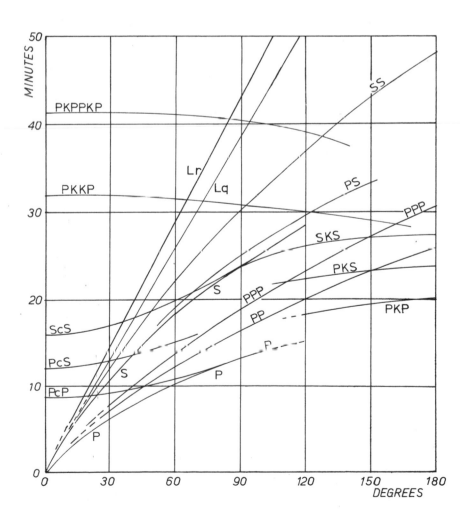

Fig. 17: A travel-time curve. Seismologists use charts like this to help them identify the waves that appear on their records. These curves are for a shallow earthquake, and only the more common arrivals are shown.

Earth by continuous reflection between the upper and lower boundaries of the surface layers. They have no vertical component at all (Figure 18).

Rayleigh waves, on the other hand, have quite a prominent vertical component, and are a kind of 'up and over backwards roll', which starts with a push in the direction of travel, then up, back, down, and push again (Figures 19 and 20). Both of these waves travel rather more slowly than *S*, and the Rayleigh wave is slower than the Love wave. When we need to distinguish them, we call the Love waves L_Q, from the German *Querwellen*, cross-waves, and the Rayleigh waves L_R.

Something has already been said about deep-focus earthquakes. More than half the world's earthquakes occure within the crust, that is to say, within 30 or 40 kilometres of the surface. In 1922 Professor F. J. Turner, who was then in charge of the *International Seismological Summary*, reported that some of the readings being sent to him would make sense only if it were assumed that the origins of these shocks were several hundred kilometres deeper than the normal ones.

For a number of reasons, seismologists were reluctant to believe this. It conflicted with what they thought they knew about the condition of the material below the crust, and Turner had also reported instances of 'high focus', so high indeed that on any reasonable assumption about the normal depth of earthquakes they would have been up in the air. Part of the difficulty was that there are no deep earthquakes in the parts of the world then covered closely with recording stations. It was not until 1928 that Professor Wadati showed that the waves from certain Japanese earthquakes arrived almost simultaneously at all the near stations, and put the reality of deep shocks beyond question. The deepest shocks so far recorded occur near the Tonga-Kermadec Trench to the north-east of New Zealand, and in the region south of Sulawesi in Indonesia. Their foci are almost 700 km below the surface.

This is a convenient place to mention that the focus is sometimes called the *hypocentre*. The term was used by early seismologists to distinguish the true origin below the ground from the centre of shaking on the surface. Since it means 'beneath the centre' it does not fit easily into modern thinking and is hard to reconcile with *epicentre* which is quite correctly 'upon the centre'. At the present time hypocentre is enjoying a vogue among American seismologists. The reason for it is obscure.

Records of deep-focus shocks look very different from those of shallow ones. To begin with there are few surface-waves, and the seismograms are complicated by the appearance of a new set of reflected phases. It will be recalled that a *P*- or an *S*-wave can be reflected near the mid-point of its path to produce the phases *PP* and *SS*. When the shock originates below the surface, there is also a reflection very close to the epicentre. Because its path from the focus to the surface is so short, we denote this first leg of the journey by a small letter, so that the phases are called *pP* (read as 'little pP'), *sP*, *pS*, *sS*, and so on. A glance at Figure 21 will show that the time of travel for *pP* or *sS* will not be very different from that of *P* or *S*. Each phase in the record can therefore appear double or triple, and the inexperienced observer can mistake the record for that of two earthquakes which have become superimposed because they happened within a few seconds of one another. These phases give us one convenient method of working out the focal depth. Core

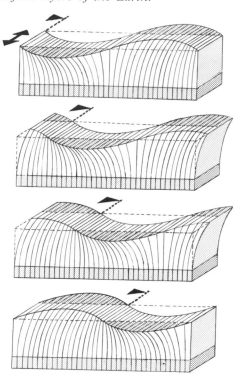

Fig. 18: A Love wave. Love waves are one kind of surface wave. The particles have a transverse motion, rather like S, but they can move only in a horizontal plane and the waves are confined to the surface layers of the Earth.

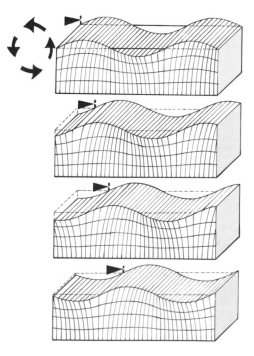

Fig. 19: A Rayleigh wave. Rayleigh waves can travel only on the surface of the Earth. The particles move in ellipses, rolling over and over backwards as the wave moves on.

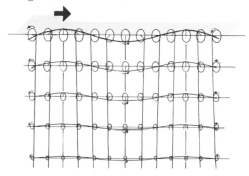

Fig. 20: Particle motion in a Rayleigh wave. Below the Earth's surface the displacement of the particles becomes less and less until the movement dies out altogether.

reflections such as *ScS* are also helpful, and in New Zealand the phase *sScS* has been used. New Zealand seismologists are very grateful for the good network of stations at the antipodes, in Europe. The phase *PKP* is often very well recorded in Sweden and gives a valuable check on the depth of New Zealand shocks.

With so many waves to be expected in an earthquake record, how does the seismologist sort them out? Fortunately it is often possible to pick the *P* and *S* waves just by looking at the record. This tells how far away the shock is, and reference to tables of travel-times helps to fit in the rest of the picture. The method of working most seismologists use is to draw out the tables of travel-times in the form of a graph, with the time scale the same as that of their records; that is to say, if the seismograph drum turns through 30 millimetres a minute, then 30 mm are made to represent a minute on the graph. He takes a narrow strip of paper as long as the record of the earthquakes he wishes to interpret, and makes a pencil mark on it opposite the beginning of every prominent phase. He can then lay the tape on top of the curves, keeping the first mark on *P* (or perhaps *PP* or *PKP* if it is a very distant earthquake) and moving it about until the other phases give the best possible fit.

When the phases have been identified, their times of arrival must be measured. If the arrivals are sharp and clear, this is done to a tenth of a second; but if the movement is very small, or there is a heavy background of microseisms, it is not always posible to be quite sure of the point on the record at which a movement begins, particularly for the waves of longer period.

In all record interpretation experience plays a big part, and in difficult cases it is often wiser to wait for information from other stations before attempting a final measurement of the records. Most observatories work in two stages. The first step is to select the well-recorded shocks and to read the time of the first arrival, which is usually *P*, or *PKP* if the shock is very distant. Some stations also read *S*, and *pP* if the shock is deep. The readings are sent as quickly as possible to a regional or an international centre that will undertake the determination of a preliminary epicentre. The most important of these international centres is the National Earthquake Information Service of the United States Geological Survey, and has offices near Denver in Colorado.

The NEIS now carries on a service started by the U.S. Coast and Geodetic Survey early in World War II. Large observatories in many countries send in their readings daily by urgent cable, and the NEIS works out approximate origin times, epicentres, and focal depths, the accuracy of which is astonishingly high. About twice a week lists of the epicentres and the data on which they are based are prepared and sent back to the contributing observatories by airmail. Once a month, they are arranged in chronological order and printed, thus becoming available to anyone interested in earthquakes at a very modest charge.

In most seismic countries, the headquarters of the national recording network arranges to provide very rapid information about large local shocks to the civil defence authorities, and many of them are also the centres of regional groupings providing less speedy but often more accurate determinations for shocks within their region.

European data are handled by the Bureau Central International de Séismologie in Strasbourg, and UNESCO has sponsored the organization of Regional Centres in Lima and Manila. In New Zealand and Japan, where the major networks are under government

Fig. 21: Depth phases. In deep-focus earthquakes additional phases like pP *arise from internal reflections at the surface of the Earth close to the epicentre.*

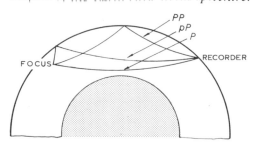

control, the stations in Wellington and Tokyo carry out most of the functions of a regional centre, and in the vast territory of the U.S.S.R. there are centres that look after Central Asia and the Far East as well as the central station in Moscow.

International cooperation is not limited to producing preliminary epicentres. The International Seismological Centre, with its headquarters at Newbury in Berkshire, England, attempts a final summary of all the world's earthquakes. It is financed by contributions from more than twenty countries, and collects not only the preliminary epicentre information from the other services, but station readings from the many stations that do not contribute to the rapid services. The *Monthly Bulletin* of the I.S.C., which appears about two years after the earthquakes, lists all of the readings, and a new set of epicentres worked out in a standard manner. In keeping with its international character, the Centre has much of the computing and typesetting done in England, and then sends the *Bulletin* to Bangkok for printing. From time to time, the Centre also produces regional catalogues, maps, and a bibliography.

Although it was not set up until 1964, the Centre had had a distinguished predecessor, the *International Seismological Summary*, which had been doing similar work since 1923, but had run into financial trouble after the war, and needed reorganizing to take advantage of electronic computing methods. Even that was not the beginning, for the origins of the *I.S.S.* can be traced to the information of an International Seismological Association at a meeting in Strasbourg in 1903, and earlier still John Milne, who had returned from Japan in 1895 to settle in the Isle of Wight, began at once to collect the station registers from a world-wide network of stations sponsored by the British Association for the Advancement of Science, and to publish summaries of their readings.

The *International Seismological Summary* and the *Bulletins* of the I.S.C. contain a mountain of data, but many stations still find it useful to publish monthly or annual bulletins of their own containing more detail than it would be practicable to include in the *Summary*. A typical listing in such a bulletin looks something like this:

		h	*m*	*s*	*μ*	*sec*	
1953 Aug. 15	iP!	17	32	06	50	3	△=83° *h*=N
	PP		34	17	10	7	*M*=7·4
	PcP		35	51			
	eS		40	33	75	5	
	(SS)		42	04	20	8	
	L$_Q$		46·3				
	L$_R$		47·1				
	Max		53		250	18	

In it, there are some symbols that have not yet been explained.

When a phase has a sharp beginning, we prefix its symbol with an *i*, which stands for impulsive; and if it is very sharp indeed, we may even follow it with an exclamation mark. On the other hand, a movement may be so small, or the background of microseisms so heavy, that it is not easy to judge just what particular instant is the true beginning of the particular phase. Such a reading is labelled *e*, for emergent. Sometimes a sharp *P*-phase appears to be preceded by a slight 'curtsey', or small movement of the trace beforehand. In such a case the phase is written *ei*.

All phases will not agree precisely with a set of theoretical travel-time curves, and even a good seismologist is frequently uncertain of the true identity of some of the phases on his records. If he is not sure of the interpretation, he puts the name of the phase in brackets. On the other hand, a question mark means that the movement may not have anything to do with the earthquake at all, and could just as well be a prominent microseism, somebody working the cellar, or an insect in the works. The column headed μ (the Greek letter *mu*) is a measurement of how much the ground moved when that particular phase arrived. μ stands for microns, or thousandths of a millimetre, so it is obvious that the movements are not as a rule very big. The column headed 'sec' is the period, or time of swing of the ground movement. The final column gives the estimated distance ($\triangle$) in degrees, the depth of focus (h) in kilometres, or 'N' for normal depth; and the instrumental magnitude (M) of the shock which is explained in Chapter 11. Individual stations vary their procedures slightly, but the main pattern is always very similar, and there is no difficulty in following bulletins in Greek, Russian, Turkish, or Japanese!

To conclude the chapter, which is already a long one, let us review the characteristics of some typical records at different distances (Figures 22 - 27). Up to about 5°, the main phases are P and S, the periods are short, and there are no obvious surface waves. From 20° to 40° P, S, and L can be clearly picked out, and the reflected phases PP and SS, are usually present. The main S-phase remains prominent in records up to 90° or 100°, but round about 80° there is a certain complication of the record resulting from the almost simultaneous arrival of SKS, S, and ScS, so that wrong identification is only too easy. Beyond this distance PS and PSP begin to show quite clearly. Records in the shadow zone (103° to 142°) present quite a changed appearance. Unless the earthquake is large, there will be gaps between the phases in which little but microseisms can be distinguished. The first phase is generally PP, followed by PPP, or PKS; and PS and PSP are prominent $SKKS$ is stronger than SKS. At very great distances 'textbook' records are seldom obtained, but PKP is well established as the first movement. The records are also complicated by phases which have gone the long way round, and traversed more than half the Earth.

Fig. 22: Seismogram of a near earthquake. These are the three components of the record of an aftershock of the Inangahua earthquake in May 1968 made on short-period Benioff instruments at Wellington. The distance of the epicentre was 2°·2, and the magnitude of the shock 4·3.

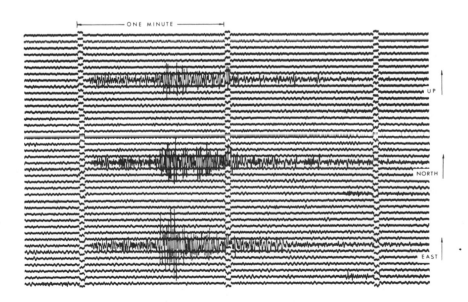

Distant earthquake records. Records of three shallow earthquakes at increasing distances. All three were made on Press-Ewing instruments, the first two at Wellington, and the third at Scott Base. Only the vertical component is shown for the two more distant shocks. Note that the time-scales differ, to allow reproduction as large as possible.

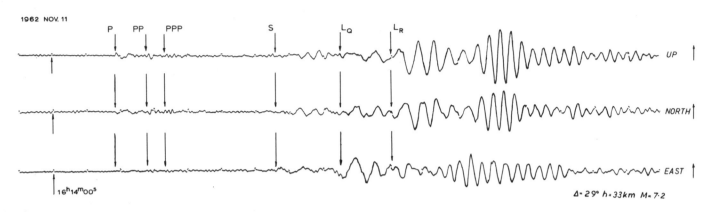

Fig. 23. Santa Cruz Islands, 1962 Nov. 11.

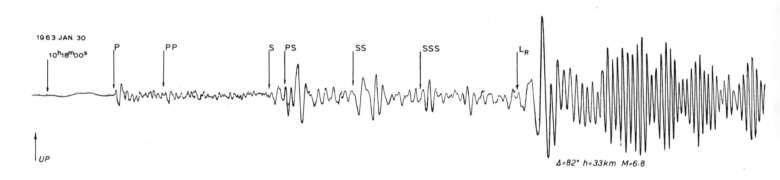

Fig. 24. South Sandwich Islands, 1963 Jan. 30.

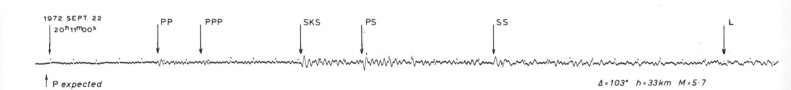

Fig. 25. Taiwan, 1972 Sept. 22. Scott Base lies just within the shadow zone, and P is not recorded.

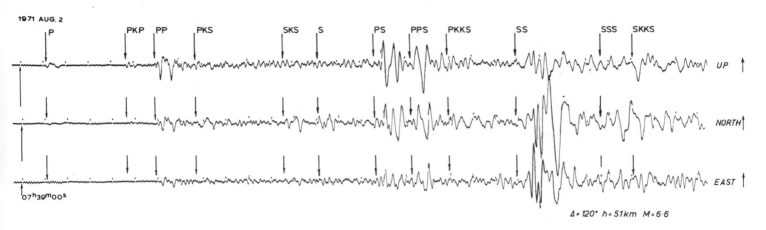

1971 AUG. 2

P PKP PP PKS SKS S PS PPS PKKS SS SSS SKKS

UP

NORTH

EAST

07h39m00s

Δ = 120° h = 51km M = 6·6

Fig. 26. *A complex record showing the many phases that can be identified in the seismograms of earthquakes at great distances. The record was made at Scott Base, of a shock in Hokkaido, 1971 Aug. 2.*

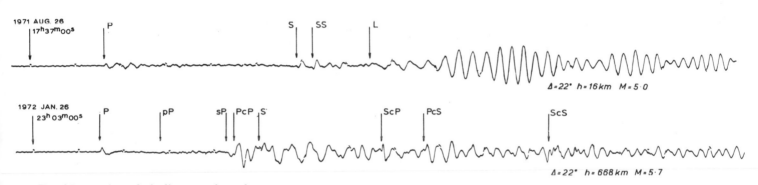

1971 AUG. 26
17h37m00s

P S SS L

Δ = 22° h = 16km M = 5·0

1972 JAN. 26
23h03m00s

P pP sP PcP S ScP PcS ScS

Δ = 22° h = 668km M = 5·7

Fig. 27. *Deep and shallow earthquakes. Both these vertical component records were made on Press-Ewing instruments at Wellington. The upper one is a shallow shock in the Loyalty Islands, and the lower one a deep shock near Fiji. The shallow shock has produced more surface waves, but the record of the deep one shows additional phases.*

5 Preliminary probing

PROSPERO: Deeper than did ever plummet sound,
  I'll drown my book.
              Shakespeare, *The Tempest*

There is a story told about Sir J. J. Thomson, the discoverer of the electron, which should be more widely known. He was being asked, as many scientists are, what use could be made of his discoveries. 'Let us suppose,' he said, 'that at the time of the Franco-Prussian war, the nations had become alarmed at the great number of wounds in which pieces of bullet were still lodged, and could not be located; and that when the peace treaties were signed, the nations had agreed to offer a large premium to be paid to the man who could devise the most efficient method of finding these foreign bodies. What would have happened? Probing would have become a fine art, and the human body a pincushion — but we should not have discovered X-rays.'

The history of science offers many examples of discoveries that have found important applications in quite unrelated fields, and of the problems that have been solved by men who were looking for something quite different. If the early seismologists had worked in countries where earthquakes were a serious social problem, and had been dependent upon 'practical' politicians for their money, the effort that went into the study of the structure of the Earth could easily have been diverted to premature searches for a method of earthquake prediction, or to designing the details of earthquake-resistant buildings soon to be outdated by changing fashion and developments in structural engineering. If that had happened, we might still be without the most directly useful technique that seismology has developed — that of seismic prospecting. But this is to begin the story in the middle.

In 1910, there was published the study of an earthquake in Kulpa Valley, Croatia, in October of the previous year. The author, a geologist named Andrija Mohorovičić, noticed the records made at stations close to the epicentre did not show simple *P*- and *S*-phases, but had in addition a secondary movement following each of them. This, he suggested, could be explained if the outermost portion of the Earth were supposed to consist of a crust some 60 km in thickness, resting on top of the mantle. As we shall see, there have been great arguments about this figure, and seismologists are still discussing the nature of the outer portion of the Earth; but Mohorovičić had shown them a method of using local earthquakes to explore it. How does the method work?

Suppose that we have a series of seismographs spread out along a line from the origin of an earthquake, assumed to be at the surface of the Earth (Figure 28) and that the Earth has a crust about 30 km thick. (This is a better estimate for most big land areas than Mohorovičić's 60 km.) Let us further suppose that in the crust a *P*-wave travels at a speed of 6 km/sec, and in the mantle immediately beneath it at 8 km/sec. At a station within about 100 km of the epicentre, the first wave to arrive will be the slow one travelling directly along the path between the focus and the station. Simple

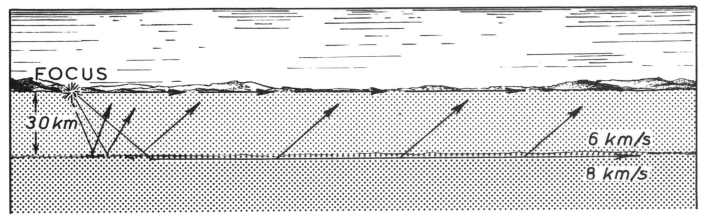

Fig. 28: The origin of crustal pulses in the records of near earthquakes.

arithmetic tells us that if the station is 50 km away the wave will take a little over 8 seconds for the trip; for 100 km between 16 and 17 sec; and for 300 km, 50 sec. We call this phase *Pg*, and if we draw a graph for it like the ones we drew for waves in the deeper parts of the Earth, we find that it is a simple straight line (Figure 29).

In addition to *Pg* there will be a second wave recorded. This has travelled by a less direct path, first going down to the base of the crust at 6 km/sec, and then travelling in the mantle at the faster 8 km/sec. Finally it must come up again at the slower speed to reach the recorder. This wave is called *Pn*, and is really the same wave that we called *P* when talking about distant earthquakes.

Because of its indirect route, the travel-time of *Pn* is a little harder to work out. It goes down a slanting path to the base of the crust, at an angle that depends upon the ratio of the speeds above and below the boundary, and comes up to the recorder again at exactly the same angle. At stations close to the origin *Pn* is later to arrive than *Pg*, as it has farther to go, but at greater distances its higher speed in the mantle enables it to overtake and become the first wave to arrive. At very short distances, where there is not room for a wave to go up and down at the correct angle, *Pn* is not recorded at all. Instead there is a reflection from the base of the crust, the reflected wave going up and down more steeply until right at the origin it goes straight down and straight up, taking 10 seconds for the double trip.

Fig. 29: The travel-time of crustal pulses. These times assume a model crust 30 km thick in which the velocity of P-waves is 6 km/sec, overlying a mantle in which the velocity is 8 km/sec.

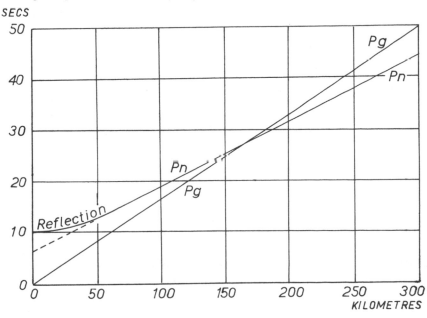

The travel-times of *Pn* and *Pg* in our imaginary crust can be summed up in a little table:

	Pg	Pn
50 km	8·3 sec	12·8 sec
100	16·6	19·1
150	25·0	25·3
200	33·3	31·6
250	41·6	37·8
300	50·0	44·1

These values are not exactly the same as those in the real Earth, but they are approximately right and make our sums a little easier. With this model, a proper *Pn* could not be recorded at distances much less 70 km, and it would overtake *Pg* between 155 and 160 km.

Mohorovičić had to look at this problem the other way round, as he did not know either the speeds of the waves or the thickness of the crust to begin with. Let us look at it from his point of view. First he would have to work out where the earthquake was, and find the distances to his various recording stations. Then he could plot the arrival times on a graph like Figure 29. The slopes of the two lines would then give him the speeds of the two waves, and the distance at which the lines intersected would enable him to work out the thickness of the crust.

The base of the crust is now known as the *Mohorovičić Discontinuity*, or to those with less flexible tongues as the Moho. Seismologists everywhere were anxious to obtain better measurements of crustal thickness, but it proved unexpectedly difficult. There were not enough recording stations, the timing was not good enough, and the phases were not sharp enough to be measured accurately. A further complication made its appearance. In most parts of the world more than two pulses were recorded, suggesting that there were more than two layers (Figure 30). Not only was this so, but the variations in wave-speed that were reported made it obvious that different seismologists were not all measuring the same thing. In spite of this, most of them wanted to claim world significance for their results, and for a brief time of madness new layers were being added to the Earth's crust at a rate of about one a month!

An obvious solution to the problem was to use artificial explosions instead of earthquakes. They could be accurately timed and located,

Fig. 30: Crustal pulses in the record of a near earthquake. The upper record shows the multiple phases due to the layering of the crust that are found in records of shallow earthquakes. The lower seismogram is one of a deep shock, and shows only simple P and S arrivals.

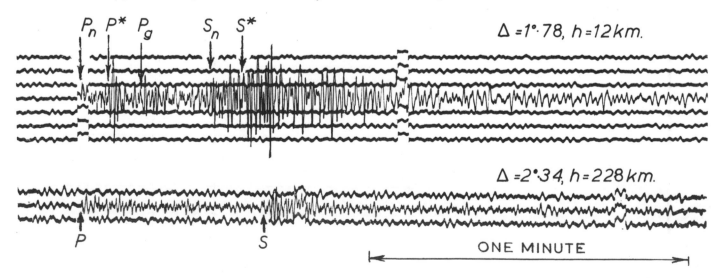

P_n P^* P_g S_n S^* $\Delta = 1°·78, h = 12 km.$

$\Delta = 2°·34, h = 228 km.$

P   S   ONE MINUTE

and they could be recorded on a special network of stations set up beforehand in the best places. At this point practical men began to take notice. Other hidden layers beneath the Earth's surface might be discovered by searching for them with seismic waves. The big oil companies were particularly interested in a method that could check the geologists' guesses about the way the strata they mapped at the surface of the Earth behaved at greater depths, without the costly trouble of drilling through hundreds of metres of rock to see whether some fold in the strata had trapped oil. The answer could now be obtained with a small explosive charge and a couple of dozen portable seismographs. Soon the big oil companies were providing money for geophysical research and the development of more convenient instruments.

The seismometers used by the modern oil prospector are known as *geophones*, and are smaller and more rugged than the ones used in observatories. Two factors make this possible. First of all, they can have short periods, as they are to be used close to the source of the vibrations, and secondly, they need have only a moderate output as they are almost always used with electronic amplifiers.

Plate 10: Artificial earthquakes. When a seismic shot is fired, a little of the energy is usually wasted in blowing ground-water from the drill-hole. In desert conditions, where conventional drilling is not possible, many shallow charges may be placed in a regular pattern and exploded together, with even more spectacular results. For very shallow surveys, and in places where the use of explosives would be undesirable it is sometimes possible to get enough energy by dropping a heavy weight.

Plate 11: A drilling rig. In order to make the most efficient use of the explosive charge it is usual to drill through the surface material into more solid rock.

Seismic prospecting has often to be carried out in undeveloped countries, in conditions varying from tropical deserts or jungles to the Arctic, and the equipment must be both rugged and self-contained. It is usual to mount it in a convoy of trucks, which may include servicing workshops and living quarters for the operators.

Under normal conditions the explosion is generated by a small plug of gelignite lowered down a hole about ten metres deep (Plate 10). This hole is necessary to get below the soil and weathered rock at the surface, so that the force of the explosion can be communicated to the ground as efficiently as possible. The convoy therefore includes drilling equipment and water-tanks to supply 'lubrication' to the point of the drill (Plate 11). When it is not possible to drill a suitable hole, elaborate patterns of small charges may be used instead of a single shot (Plate 10). At the other extreme, a sufficiently large shock may be obtained by dropping a large weight (Plate 10) or even tapping the ground with a hammer!

In a simple recording truck, of the kind that is still widely in use for scientific purposes, there is provision for recording the outputs from up to twenty-four geophones, which can be connected at intervals of about 30 metres to a cable run out from a drum at the rear. The amplifiers and filters can be so arranged as to turn each geophone into a pick-up of almost any characteristic likely to be useful. Twenty-four light-beams from the twenty-four galvanometers record side by side of a strip of photographic paper about ten centimetres wide. The truck carries facilities for developing the records, and radio equipment both enables the operator to keep in touch with the shot-firer, and automatically records the instant of the shot on the photographic paper along with the galvanometer traces. A built-in electronic clock puts precise timing-marks on the paper at intervals of 0·01 sec.

Plate 12: A modern seismic recording truck.

Equipment in the most modern trucks has become very elaborate (Plates 12 and 13), and in a large convoy things like the radio and photographic equipment acquire whole trucks of their own. Records are now very often made on magnetic tape, or in more complicated patterns than the old wavy line on a strip of paper. There is often a computer and an associated cathode-ray tube display. The magnetic tape record can be played back through a series of different filters, so that the best combination can be chosen, and the waves being looked for are not lost among confusing background movements.

Although oil companies have been responsible for much of the expenditure which has been needed for developing modern prospecting equipment, there are many other uses to which it can be put. In New Zealand, seismic surveys have been used to examine the dam-sites for our hydro-electric power stations, in connection with the search for geothermal power at Wairakei, and in the exploration of coal and other mineral resources. In this way, seismology is giving the answers to many problems which can scarcely have occurred to the early pioneers of earthquake study.

Plate 13: Seismic prospecting. Inside the recording cabin. The outputs from as many as 48 geophones can be recorded either on paper or on magnetic tape. The equipment includes a computer and a cathode-ray tube display for use in the field.

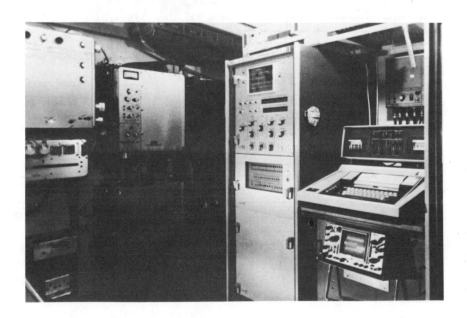

The technique I have described is' known to the prospector as *refraction shooting*. In recent years it has been supplanted to a large extent by the reflection method, which is in many ways more straightforward, since it uses a direct record of the echoes from the boundaries between the rock strata beneath the surface. The geophones used to record reflections can be placed nearer to the shot-point than those used in refraction measurements, and this saves a great deal of time in laying cable for the geophone spread. Early seismic prospectors were forced to use the refraction method, because their geophones and amplifiers were able to record only the time of arrival of the first impulse with any clarity. By using modern geophones in conjunction with amplifiers and filters of known frequency characteristics, and automatic volume control to limit the effect of the first movement, the arrival of subsequent reflections can be clearly identified on the record (Figure 31).

Geophysical methods of prospecting for oil have perhaps been too successful, leading to the premature depletion of a limited resource. During the 1950s, when the possibility of shortages first became apparent, methods were developed for undertaking seismic surveys at sea (Plates 14 and 15). These have resulted in the exploitation of a number of previously unknown submarine oil and gas fields, first in the shallow waters of the Gulf of Mexico, later in the North Sea, off the coasts of North Africa and New Zealand, and in many other parts of the world.

We shall not end the chapter on a note of big business. Hydrographers have used seismic methods to obtain needed information about the sediments on the sea-bottom, and geologists use them for a multitude of purposes that have little to do with the

Fig. 31: Reflection prospecting. This is a portion of a record made on Farewell Spit by a seismic unit of the Geophysics Division of the New Zealand Department of Scientific and Industrial Research. The shot was fired at the centre of a spread of 24 geophones. After the arrival of the direct wave (on the left) the traces are confused for a short time, but the ground is relatively steady again by the time the waves reflected from the solid bedrock under the less consolidated material of the Spit arrive. The instant of firing the shot is marked by a deflection of the third and fourth traces from the top, and the numbered timing-lines are a tenth of a second apart. The section of record reproduced here occupied less than a second.

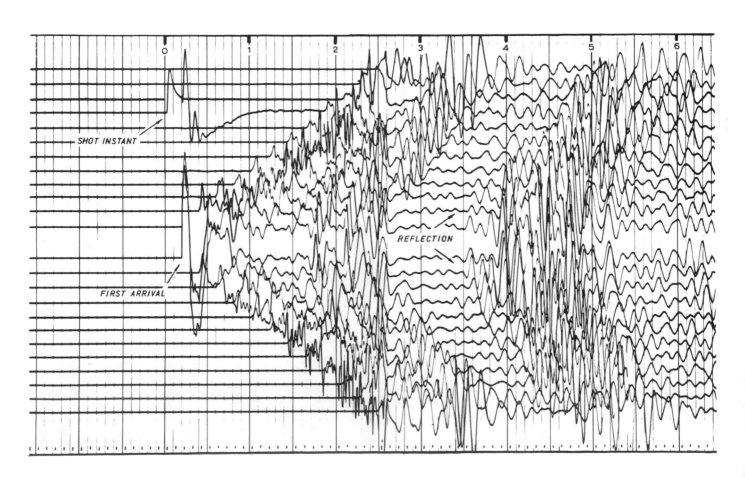

SHOT INSTANT

FIRST ARRIVAL

REFLECTION

Plate 14: Seismic work at sea. The research vessel Explora, *intended for seismic, magnetic, and gravity measurements at sea.*

economic exploitation of minerals. Less expected was their value to the archaeologist.

Ground that has been dug over in the past does not transmit seismic waves so readily as ground that has not been touched, and buried masonry behaves differently from its surroundings. Readers who may fear the seismologists will establish another powder-magazine in the Parthenon can rest assured that for work on this small scale no explosives are needed. The necessary shock is produced by dropping a weight. By using a combination of geophysical methods, it has now been made reasonably certain that there are no undiscovered chambers concealed within the Great Pyramid, but the most celebrated occasion on which seismic exploration was used in archaeology was in 1951 when Father Daniel Linehan, a Jesuit seismologist, disposed his geophones about the church of Saint Peter in Rome. He was able to avoid a great deal of fruitless digging that might have endangered the structure, and lead the archaeologists to an ancient tomb that could contain the bones of Saint Peter himself.

Plate 15: Prospecting in shallow water. This is a sea-going version of the seismic truck, intended for use close to the coast. Cable for the geophones is carried on the large drum aft of the recording cabin.

6 Down to rock bottom

The Earth doth like a snake renew
Her winter weeds outworn
                    Shelley, *Hellas*

What we have learned of seismology so far does nothing to explain why there should be earthquakes at all. If we set aside the small tremors that result from landslides, collapsing caverns, erupting volcanoes, and a few other minor sources of vibration, we find that nearly all earthquakes are the result of the geological forces that build mountains and shape the other major features of the Earth's surface. The study of these forces and their effects is called *tectonics*, from the Greek *tekton*, a builder, and the kind of shocks with which we shall in the main be dealing are called tectonic earthquakes. To understand their nature and their consequences we must learn both the source of the forces responsible, and about the material they act upon.

Judging from all the things we can find on its surface, the Earth is made of rock. Huge masses of rock stretch upwards to form mountain ranges; there is rock beneath the ooze of the ocean floor; the beds of our rivers are strewn with rocky boulders; and the sands of our beaches are ground-up rock. The lava that flows from volcanoes cools to form rock, and the material that is drilled from tunnels, mines, and wells is once again rock.

There are many different kinds of rock, and everyone is familiar with the names of some of them — granite, basalt, limestone, and so on. Geologists have grouped them into three main classes — *sedimentary*, *igneous*, and *metamorphic*. At the surface of the Earth, sedimentary rocks are by far the most plentiful, covering about three quarters of the total land area. The average depth to which they extend has been estimated at about a kilometre or two. They are not original features of the Earth's surface, but the product of an important process that is still going on.

It would be wrong to think of a geologist as a man who is concerned only with long-dead fossils and things that happened millions of years ago. He is probably more aware of the constant change and renewal of his surroundings than other people. Every rock that is exposed at the surface of the Earth, or *outcrops* as we say, is subjected to weathering, which gradually breaks it up into small fragments. In high mountain regions, alternate freezing and thawing makes the process a comparatively rapid one; but the chemical action of water on the material of the rock, the blasting of wind-driven sand, and grinding by glacier ice all play a part in the process of disintegration.

Once the rock mass has been reduced to small enough fragments, it is carried away and sorted by wind and water. Sometimes, the material can be moved bodily by the current, and in times of flood the amount of material shifted can be very great; sometimes the process is the gentle one of solution, but in the end the result is the same — the rocks of the mountain ranges are moved gradually to the coast. Material carried along rivers and watercourses enlarges the channel by scouring the bed and eroding the banks. Every year the Mississippi River moves more than four hundred million tons of material.

Plate 16: Sedimentary rocks. Regular annual floods have built up layer upon layer of material that has become compressed and hardened to form this sandstone at Roche Percée, near Bourail in New Caledonia.

During transportation further breaking up occurs, and the angular chips that make up the mountain shingle-slides become rounded gravel in the beds of the rivers of the plains. At the coast, the waves take a hand, adding material from the coastal cliffs to that brought down by the rivers, and depositing the broken and pulverized material on the sea bottom, where it is able to consolidate under the pressure of the superimposed material to form new rocks.

The nature of the new rock that is formed will depend upon the type of material that is being deposited. For example, very fine particles cannot come to rest in water that is running swiftly, or is churned up by breaking waves. The details of the process of deposition have been very carefully studied, but for our purposes it is sufficient to notice its importance. As time goes on, and more and more material accumulates, the distribution of currents alters, the depth of the sea changes and the supply of weathered material may now come from a different part of the mountain range and be different in texture or chemical compositon from that originally deposited. The rocks formed on the sea floor consequently lie in a series of superimposed layers (Plates 16 and 17).

Plate 17: The geological column. These cliffs near Cape Kidnappers, south of Hawke Bay, show alternating beds of sandstone and pumiceous material. Some slight tilting has occurred, but the oldest rocks still remain at the bottom, and the most recent at the top.

Material brought down by the rivers is not the only possible source of the sediment needed for rock formation. Limestone, for example, is a most important exception, although it is still a sedimentary rock. In this case, the material deposited originates in the sea itself, particularly where it is warm and shallow, and consists mainly of the shells and skeletons of dead sea creatures, which sink to the sea floor. When there is no admixture of other material we get a pure chalk or limestone; but under certain conditions they may serve merely as a kind of natural cement to bind material brought down by the rivers, or transported along the coast by ocean currents.

The superimposed layers of rock that result from the process of sedimentation are called *strata*. They have roughly parallel surfaces, and vary in thickness according to the rate at which the material accumulated and the time for which the deposition continued. In a series of undisturbed strata, the oldest rocks will lie at the bottom, and the youngest at the top. Sedimentary rocks often surround the shells or skeletons of animals and plants, which become buried in the sediments when they are being accumulated. These remains are known as *fossils* (Plate 18); and if they are well enough preserved to let us identify them, they give an important clue to the age of the rock. The types of creature living together have changed throughout geological history, so that if we find a similar set of fossils in two different rocks we can be fairly sure that they were laid down at about the same time. For example, a South Australian sandstone might contain the same fossils as those in a dissimilar rock from New Guinea, showing us how to piece together the sequences of strata in the two places. The complete sequence from the very oldest to the most recent is known as the *geological column*. The problem of dating a given geological event thus becomes the same thing as finding its correct place in the column (Figure 32).

It is not easy to determine how long the different geological periods lasted, but good estimates can now be made by using measurements

Plate 18: Fossils. The remains of dead plants and animals become incorporated in the rocks, and help the geologist to assign them a date. These scallop-like Monotis *shells lived in the Triassic period, some 200 million years ago. They measure about 30 to 40mm across.*

of the amount of radioactive material in the rocks. A schoolboy who knows the names of England's kings and queens in their right order knows that something which happened in the reign of Charles II took place before something in the reign of George IV, even if he doesn't know the dates of each reign. If he had a rough idea of the average length of a reign, he could make a good guess at the number of years involved. In the same way, a geologist knows that a Cambrian rock is older than a Jurassic one, and that he has got his events in the right order, even if he is uncertain of the speed of the complete process.

It is seldom that more than a limited section of the geological column is to be found in one place, so that the deciphering of the whole story of the Earth is a laborious process. Profesor Cotton has likened it to an attempt to assemble a complete book from a great pile of damaged copies which have been torn into groups of a few pages. A list of the geologist's periods with recent estimates of their lengths is given in the Appendix.

In many parts of the world, the volcanoes have long ceased to be active. We could not surprise the ordinary dweller in Indonesia, Japan, or Hawaii by telling him that the rocks on the nearby hillside had once been molten lava, and the soil of his fields hot ash, but it might surprise the people in parts of Scotland, the United States, or France of which our statement would be equally true. The second important type of rock is to be found in these places, as well as in places where volcanoes are still active. Such rocks are called *igneous*, a name which indicates their fiery origin. Sometimes they actually

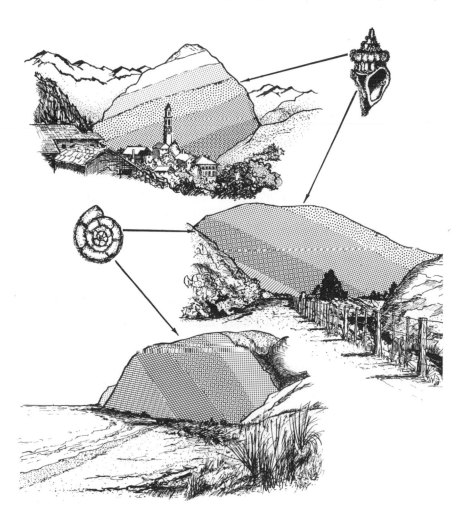

Fig. 32: The geological column. The complete geological column must be pieced together by comparing the fossil sequences in the strata of many separate localities. Remember that the fossils determine the age of the rocks and not their composition. A limestone may have been formed in one place at the same time as a sandstone was forming somewhere else.

came to the surface of the Earth in their hot condition, and flowed as lava from some volcanic vent; in other cases they have forced their way upwards through the underground strata, only to solidify and remain buried until erosion exposed them at the surface. In either case, they were once hot enough to flow with a greater or less degree of freedom, until they cooled or crystallized into their present form. Since they must once have been deep in the Earth, they are of great interest to the geophysicist, as they help to confirm his deductions about the nature of the Earth's interior.

The third main class, the *metamorphic* rocks, occupies an intermediate position between the other two classes. In its original form, a metamorphic rock may have belonged to either, but deep burial and subjection to heat and pressure, the behaviour during cooling and crystallization, or the heat from a nearby igneous intrusion have so changed its characteristics that it is necessary to describe it as a new kind of rock. The divisions between the three classes are not quite clear cut, but they are nevertheless very useful distinctions.

Changes of the Earth's surface are not a one-way process. The rocks of our land areas, igneous, metamorphic, and sedimentary, would seem from the account I have given to be alike destined to erosion, transportation by rivers, and deposition on some distant sea floor. This is only half the story. Since three-quarters of the land area is composed of sedimentary rocks, it is obvious that at some stage some of the sea-bed must once again become dry land. This is mainly the result of the process known as *orogenesis*, or mountain-building. The details of this process are still very speculative, and we shall have to return to them again.

It seems probable that the building of a mountain range begins with the filling of a shallow basin with a great mass of sediment (Figure 33). As the sediment accumulates, the supporting floor of the basin is further deformed and depressed. This structure is called a *geosyncline*. Because the floor of the geosyncline is forced to a greater depth than its original one, it is weakened by the higher temperature. Under the influence of compressional forces in the Earth's crust, the prism of sediment is folded and buckled, and dry land appears in the form of a new mountain range. By this time, the old continent which was the source of the sediment will have been largely eroded away, and the new mountain range will greatly alter the drainage pattern. Erosion will proceed as before, possibly contributing to the formation of a new geosyncline and a further period of mountain building. In this way a cyclic process comes into action, affording some justification for the claim of an early geologist that there is 'no trace of a beginning, and no prospect of an end'.

One result of mountain building is the widespread disruption of the geological column to which I have referred. Although we can find fairly extended sequences of strata, they have to be looked for carefully, and the rocks are often found bent and folded into strange shapes, cracked and shattered by the magnitude of the forces at work upon them (Plate 19). The process is a slow one, but the results are far-reaching.

Throughout geological history, periods of active mountain-building have alternated with periods of comparative calm during which major sedimentation proceeds. These orogenies have been sufficiently widespread for the major divisions of the geological column to be traced over large stretches of the globe. It is therefore possible to use the same broad time-scale everywhere, making only

Fig. 33: Mountain-building. A: Sediment from the land is deposited in a shallow sea. B: A geosyncline is formed. C: Compression of the crust raises a chain of fold mountains.

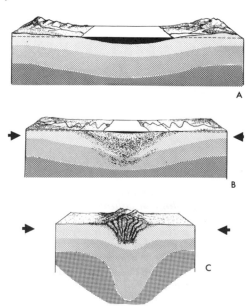

Plate 19: The geological column disrupted. This contorted and fractured limestone at White Rock, in the eastern Wairarapa, shows how rock can behave under sufficient heat and pressure. It would be difficult to work out in detail all that has happened to this formation.

minor changes to allow for local peculiarities, though it is possible that stratigraphers will protest at this summary treatment of their problems.

The story of mountain-building as we have just outlined it is unsatisfactory in a number of ways. Great compressional forces are needed to fold the geosynclinal sediments, but we have not explained where they come from. The geologist can tell us what has happened, but he cannot tell us why. The reason is probably that the cause lies too deep in the Earth to have left clues in the surface rocks. In the next chapter we shall see how physics can probe a little deeper.

7 Inside the Earth

Our souls, whose faculties can comprehend
The wondrous Architecture of the world.
      Christopher Marlowe, *Tamburlaine*

The Earth is a ball 12 700 kilometres in diameter, revolving about the Sun at a distance of nearly 150 million kilometres. By drilling we have been able to pierce less than ten of the six and a half thousand kilometres that lie between us and its centre and even these drill-holes provide a most inadequate sample of the outer parts. The rest of our knowledge has been laboriously pieced together from indirect evidence, the greater part of which has come from seismology, but astronomy and the other fields of geophysics have also played an important part.

As the Earth spins on its axis and journeys about the Sun; the Sun, the Moon and the other planets lie sometimes on one side of its equatorial bulge, and sometimes on the other. As a result, their gravitational pull gives the Earth a wobble. This wobble is called *nutation,* and it can be measured by taking accurate sightings on distant stars. The amount of wobble to be expected depends upon the way the internal mass of the Earth is distributed. If all the heavy parts were concentrated near the outside like the rim of a fly-wheel, for example, it would be much harder to disturb than if it had a uniform structure all the way through. By the end of last century astronomers were fairly sure that there was a heavy lump in the centre, and we have already seen how Oldham was able to use seismic waves to prove it in 1906, and Gutenberg to make an accurate measurement of its size a few years later.

Until a few years ago most scientists believed that the Earth began as a very hot body, and that most of its subsequent behaviour could be explained on the assumption that it had been cooling down ever since. Recently these ideas have undergone many changes. Some astronomers still think that the material of the Earth was once ejected from the Sun or torn from it by the gravitational pull of some passing star, but most now believe that it was formed from cooler matter, gathered from space by the Sun's attraction, or as part of the process that formed the Sun itself.

There is little doubt that the interior of the Earth is hot. Measurements in mines and deep drill holes show that for every kilometre we go down the temperature rises about 25° C, so that at no great depth we should expect to reach a point at which all rocks of the kind we meet at the surface would melt and become something like the lava that flows out of volcanoes. Some people, like the characters in Georg Büchner's play, have found this alarming:

FIRST CITIZEN: You're not frightened, surely?

SECOND CITIZEN: Well you see, sir, the Earth has a very thin crust — very thin, sir — very thin. I always fancy you might drop right through if you stepped into a hole like that. One has to tread very carefully indeed, sir, very carefully indeed. You might break through . . .

A little reflection should convince us that the rapid rise in temperature we observe at the surface cannot continue, for if it did, the material at the Earth's centre would be hotter than the Sun itself. Most of the Earth's heat seems to be due to its present radioactivity, rather than a relic of its past history. There is more than enough radioactive material in the crust alone to account for the whole of the measured outward heat-flow through the surface. It seems quite clear that if the Earth was not originally molten, it must soon have become so when sufficient material had concentrated about its original nucleus. The big problem for the geophysicist is whether it is at present heating or cooling.

The three main divisions of the Earth — the crust, the mantle, and the core — must have formed quite early. Gravitational attraction would concentrate the heavier elements in the central core, and help the lighter constituents of the mantle to separate out and form the crust. In 1799 Henry Cavendish carried out his famous measurement of the mass of the Earth, and found that the planet as a whole had a mean density that is almost twice as great as the average of the surface rocks. It is natural to ask what other materials are present in the deeper interior.

One line of argument has been based upon the chemical analysis of meteorites, which are generally supposed either to be the remnants of a disrupted planet, or to be surplus material left over when the formation of the major planets was complete. It is hard to know how far the meteorites reaching the Earth's surface are a representative sample, but there are two main groups, the *stones,* which have a predominantly silicate composition, and the *irons* which are metallic. The two types can not unreasonably be considered to parallel the existence of the core and the mantle of the Earth.

We shall now see how far these deductions are borne out by the behaviour of seismic waves, beginning with the crust, which behaves in a more familiar way than the deeper parts of the Earth, and work our way downwards to the centre.

In the previous chapter we saw how refracted waves can be used to measure the layers that make up the crust. In the upper part of it where geological processes have free reign, the situation, if not exactly chaotic, is at least complex. The speed of a *P*-wave can be as low as two kilometres per second, or it may reach six or more according to the nature of the rocks, but in most regions the base of the crust is marked by a sharp rise in velocity. The level at which this takes place is the Mohorovičić discontinuity, and just beneath it the velocity is nearly always a little above 8 km/sec.

The thickness of the crust is very variable. Beneath the continents, it is usually about thirty to thirty-five kilometres, but whenever there are great mountains standing far above the average level of the surface, there is nearly always a corresponding 'root' underneath. Measurements in Tibet have disclosed thicknesses of more than seventy kilometres.

Just as high mountains mean thick crusts, deep oceans mean thin ones, and there are differences in the structure of continental and oceanic crusts. A selection of cross-sections is shown in Figure 34. In the continents the basement material beneath the cover of surface sediments is usually hard crystalline rock, chemically acidic, and of a kind that the seismologist usually calls granitic, though geologists will hasten to insist that they are not always granite. Beneath the granitic layer is a second one of more basic rocks, usually described as basaltic but sometimes called 'intermediate'. There is often a sharp change in velocity between the two layers, at a boundary known as the Conrad discontinuity, but in some places there is a more gradual transition distributed throughout the crust.

In the thinner oceanic crusts the granitic layer is missing, and it used to be said that under the deepest oceans all we could expect to find above the Mohorovičić discontinuity was a few hundred metres of ooze and five or six kilometres of sea water, but more recent measurements show that there is nearly always several kilometres of basaltic material, with the base of the crust about ten kilometres below sea level.

The waves from near earthquakes and explosions are not the only source of information about the nature and thickness of the crust. Another powerful technique uses the records of surface-waves. The method depends not upon their time of arrival, but upon details of their structure that will be easier to understand if we begin by clearing up the meanings of some of the terms that seismologists use when talking about waves.

Figure 35 shows an ordinary enough wave of the kind that mathematicians call a *sine wave*. One of the most important things about sine waves is that you can build up waves of any other shape at all (including ones with sharp corners) by adding together a sufficient

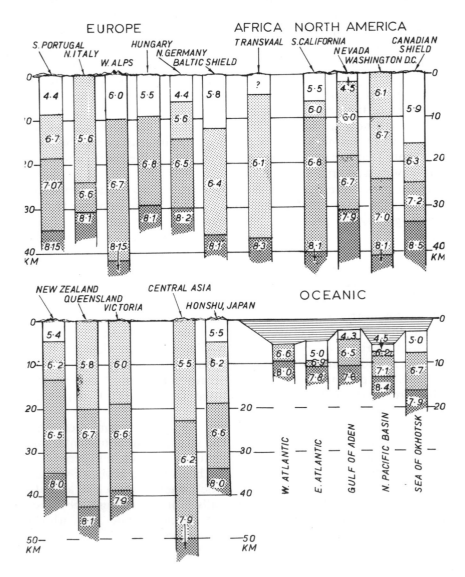

Fig. 34: Typical cross-sections of the crust. The depth of the Mohorovičić Discontinuity is much greater in continental than in oceanic regions. It is usually marked by a sharp rise in the velocity of P- waves to about 8·1 km/sec. The contintental crust is often divided into an upper granitic and a lower basaltic layer, and may be overlain by widely varying thicknesses of sediment.

number of sine waves of different sizes. In this simple kind of wave, if B, F, and J are successive crests, and D, H, and L successive troughs, the distance from B to F, F to J, D to H, or H to L is the same. This distance between corresponding points is called the *wave-length,* and is often represented just by the Greek letter λ (lambda).

The difference in height between the crests and the troughs, PQ, is sometimes called the *amplitude,* but that name is more usually given to PA, the maximum swing in one direction. When I use the word 'amplitude' I shall mean PA.

If the wave is moving, a certain number of crests will pass a fixed point every second. This number is called the *frequency* of the wave. The frequency, velocity, and wavelength are connected in a very simple way:

Velocity = frequency times wavelength $v = n\lambda$,
Frequency = velocity divided by wavelength $n = v/\lambda$

Since the frequencies in which a seismologist is most interested are generally less than one a second, he more often refers to the *period.* This is the time interval between the arrival of two successive crests, and is the reciprocal of the frequency. That means, a frequency of half a cycle per second is a period of two seconds, one third of a cycle a period of three seconds, and so on. A frequency of one cycle per second is often called one Hertz.

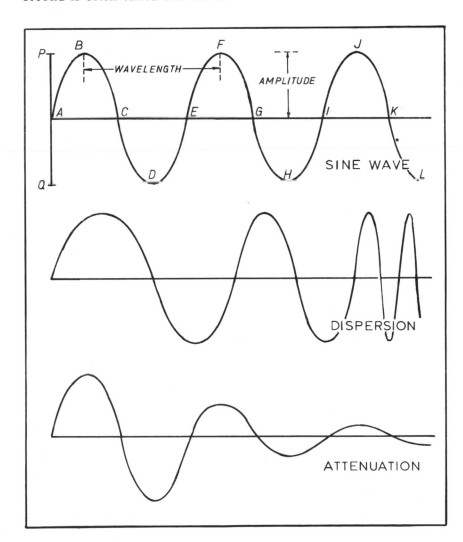

Fig. 35: Wave motion. The distance between the successive crests or troughs of a wave is called the wavelength, *and the maximum excursion from the zero position in either direction the* amplitude. *The sine wave shown at the top has a constant wavelength and a constant amplitude. If the wavelength changes with time, as in the middle example, the wave is said to be* dispersed, *and if the amplitude decreases as in the lower example it is said to be* attenuated.

If we look at the tail end, or *coda* of a seismogram, where the L-waves are recorded, we will see that the waves of longest period apparently arrive first and that shorter and shorter ones come progressively later. This process is known as *dispersion,* and it results from the fact that although an earthquake produces surface-waves of many different periods all mixed up, they travel at different speeds, depending on their period, and gradually sort themselves out as they travel. If we know when and where an earthquake took place, we can work out the speed of travel for waves of each particular period, and plot the result in the form of a graph called a dispersion curve. The shape of the curve we get will depend upon the thickness and composition of the outermost layers of the Earth along the whole path between the epicentre and the recording station.

Surface-wave measurements are evaluated by a rather tedious trial-and-error process. First you must guess the likely thickness and speed of travel in each layer of the crust, and then use your model to calculate a dispersion curve. Finally, you compare the result with the curve you obtained from your earthquake record. If they don't fit, you change some of your figures, and try again. Fortunately, the electronic computer has relieved us of a great deal of this drudgery, and it is usually possible to find a model that fits the observations quite closely, even when there are complicated changes in crustal thickness along the path. Figure 36 shows how Love waves and Rayleigh waves behave when they travel over paths that are mainly continent or mainly ocean.

There are, of course, other ways of getting information about the crust. The geologist has obtained useful data by analysing the kind of lava that comes out of volcanoes in different parts of the world. Precise measurements of the pull of gravity tell us whether the rocks beneath us are heavier or lighter than normal. Measurements of electric currents in the ground, and of the Earth's magnetic field can also provide information about the deeper parts of the crust. All of these studies help to complete the picture we get from seismic refraction measurements and surface waves.

Below the crust, we are no longer concerned with rocks of a familiar kind. At a depth of 30 km, the temperature is about 1200° C. and we might expect them to melt, but they do not become liquid. The great weight of material on top prevents it. Nevertheless, they gradually lose their individual identities, and become fused into one great mixture. Some small localized variations in composition remain, but the diversity that is typical of the crustal rocks has gone.

Perhaps the best way to think of the physical condition of the rocks at this depth is to liken them to solid pitch. Even if it is so solid that it can be shattered by a hammer blow, it will still flow and spread if you leave a lump on the bench overnight. If we treat it gently, it behaves as a liquid; but if we apply sudden forces to it, it behaves like a brittle solid. As far as waves are concerned, the upper part of the mantle is elastic, but for the slower processes of geological deformation, it is plastic, and within it slow movements are taking place.

Among the most important of these movements are those due to convection, and we shall consider their effects in a later chapter. Convection is the transfer of heat from one place to another by bodily movement of the hot substance. A body of rock that is heated by contact with hot material in the deep interior of the Earth will expand, becoming less dense than its surroundings, and consequently tending to rise. On nearing the surface, it is able to lose its heat and, contract, thus becoming denser and sinking again. This process sets

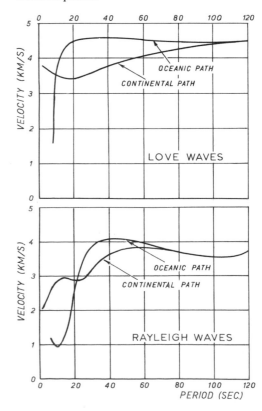

Fig. 36: Dispersion of Love and Rayleigh waves. When the speed of the components of a complex wave depends upon their period, the resultant wave is dispersed. The way in which a surface wave is dispersed depends upon the structure of the crust along the path it travels. The graphs show the differences in behaviour of waves that have travelled over typical continental and oceanic paths.

up great circulating convection currents, ascending and descending as they convey heat from the interior of the Earth.

Because the descending currents are denser than the rising ones, there are regional differences in the composition of the mantle, but here we shall consider only how its properties change with depth. Very broadly speaking, seismic waves travel faster and faster the more deeply they penetrate into the mantle. Just below the Mohorovičić discontinuity the velocity of *P*-waves is about 8·1 km/sec, and this increases to 13·6 km/sec at the boundary of the core. The corresponding figures for *S*-waves are 4·4 and 7·3 km/sec. There is no obvious change at a depth of 700 km, the greatest depth at which earthquakes occur, but deep earthquakes are confined to certain limited parts of the Earth, and we can expect any associated changes in the physical properties of the mantle to be similarly localized.

The speed of a seismic wave depends upon the density and the rigidity of the material through which it is travelling. An increase in density will slow it down, and higher rigidity will make it go faster. At greater depths the material should be more and more compressed by the increasing weight on top, but the fact that the speed of the waves increases shows that the increase in density must be less rapid than the corresponding increase in rigidity. However, there are some exceptions to the general rule which were first noticed in connection with the behaviour of sound-waves from explosions in the deep ocean.

In the oceans, it gets colder quite quickly down to a depth of about fifteen hundred metres, where the temperature is close to freezing point. At greater depths the decrease takes place much more slowly. Since the speed of sound in water depends on both the temperature and the pressure, the result of the two acting together is to make it travel more slowly at this depth than either above or below it. If we fire a small explosive charge at this depth, not all the waves will be able to reach the surface. Unless they leave the source at a great angle to the horizontal they will be bent backwards and forwards and trapped within a narrow channel. Most of them are transmitted to very great distances in this way before they are ultimately absorbed. The explosion of small bombs containing only a few kilograms of explosive can be recorded quite easily at distances of several thousand kilometres. This sound channel in the ocean is called the SOFAR layer, and it has been suggested that ships, rafts, and aeroplanes in distress could use it to signal their whereabouts to specially equipped listening stations by firing a small charge.

In the uppermost part of the mantle, between the base of the crust and a depth of about a hundred kilometres, something similar goes on. This region is known as the *asthenosphere* (from the Greek *a*, without, and *sthenos,* strength). The rocks in it have been weakened by the increase in temperature to a greater extent than they have been consolidated by the weight of material on top. The result is that the speed of seismic waves in this region drops below that at the base of the crust. At still greater depths the effect of the increasing pressure is to make it rise again, and so form a low-velocity channel like the one in the ocean. This channel interferes with the travel-times of *P*- and *S*-waves recorded at distances between about 15° and 20°. Professor Caloi of Rome University first realized that the fall in velocity in the asthenosphere was responsible, and that waves were being channelled through it like sound waves around a whispering gallery.

The rocky material that lies above the asthenosphere is called the *lithosphere*, from the Greek *lithos*, a stone. Older writers used the term lithosphere to mean the crust. We now apply it to a much thicker region — how thick is hard to say, for there is no sharp boundary like the Mohorovičić discontinuity to define it.

The asthenosphere channel is not the only low-velocity channel in the Earth. Professor Gutenberg has suggested that in many parts of the world there could be one within the crust. Under the influence of heat and pressure, quartz changes its physical state, and this change should occur at a depth of about ten kilometres, producing the drop in velocity needed to create the channel (Figure 37). In continental regions waves have been detected that appear to have been directed through the channel. Its presence affects our estimates of the thickness of continental crusts by a few kilometres, but oceanic ones are less than ten kilometres thick and do not contain a channel.

This interpretation would dispose of two long-standing difficulties. When we measure the speed of the waves produced by an explosion at the surface of the Earth, we get a slightly higher value than we obtain when we measure earthquake waves. Since they are known to be the same kind of waves, and to travel through the same rock, this is ridiculous. If there were any difference, we would expect the earthquake waves to take the deeper path and to have the higher velocity. By assuming that the earthquake foci lie in the low-velocity channel, Professor Gutenberg was able to explain the observed results quite satisfactorily. At the same time, it was possible to avoid the odd result that *P*- and *S*-waves from some earthquakes did not appear to leave the focus at the same insant.

In 1957 and 1958 the world's geophysicists organized a special programme of cooperative research projects known as the International Geophysical Year. This resulted in a great many additional crustal studies, and in the establishment of new seismograph stations in Antarctica and other parts of the globe that had previously been inadequately covered. The success of the operation was so apparent that in 1960 Professor V. V. Beloussov of the Institute of Physics of the Earth in Moscow suggested that there should be a further programme directed towards the study of the upper mantle. Most geophysicists agreed with him that the answers to many puzzling questions were likely to be bound in the region immediately beneath the crust.

One of the most spectacular schemes intended to contribute to the Upper Mantle Project was an American proposal to drill a hole right through the crust and to obtain a sample of the mantle for direct

*Fig. 37: The crustal low-velocity channel. If the velocity of waves at any particular depth in the Earth is less than at depths above and below it, waves that leave the focus of an earthquake at that depth in certain directions are trapped within a 'low-velocity channel'. In this sketch the velocity has been assumed to increase from 6 km/sec. at the surface to 7 km/sec. at a depth of 10 km. It then falls again to 6 km/sec. at 15 km., and increases once more to about 7·5 km/sec. just above the Mohorovičić Discontinuity. Waves directed steeply upwards from the focus, as at A, can reach the surface directly as a normal *Pg phase. Those directed steeply downwards, as at D, are reflected from the discontinuity. If a little less steeply inclined they are refracted by it, as shown at C, travelling beneath the discontinuity and returning to the surface as* Pn. *Over the range of inclinations intermediate between these groups, the waves are trapped within the channel, as at B.*

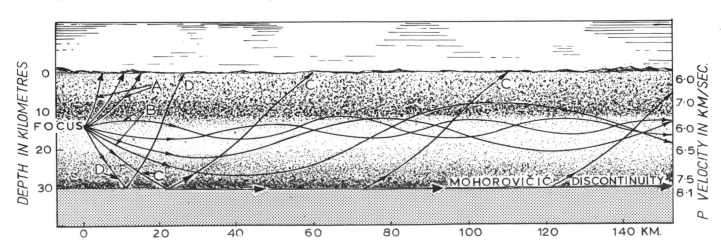

study and analysis in the laboratory. Under most land areas the Mohorovičić discontinuity lies beneath at least twenty or thirty kilometres of rock, so it was decided to drill the Mohole (as it had been irreverently christened) through the comparatively thinner oceanic crust, working from a floating barge. Enormous technical difficulties were expected, but it turned out that the political ones were even greater. In 1966 the U.S. Congress decreed that Project Mohole should be abandoned, we are still without a sample of the mantle.

Fortunately the less ambitious parts of the Upper Mantle Project went ahead more smoothly, including some deep drilling in several parts of the U.S.S.R., more crustal thickness measurements and some fresh work on seismic travel-times. We shall return later to consider the processes going on in the upper mantle, many of which have only been understood within the last decade.

When the Mohorovičić discontinuity is ultimately pierced, what can we expect to find beneath it? Chemically, the mantle is composed for the most part of silicates of magnesium, with lesser amounts of iron and aluminium oxides and traces of sodium and calcium. If we had to name an actual rock the most likely one seems to be a dense ultrabasic one called dunite, which is mainly olivine, but this is at best an informed guess.

The change from mantle to core is abrupt, occurring within a few kilometres at most. Two changes are involved – a change of material, and a change of state.

At the core boundary, the *S*-waves meet an impenetrable barrier, but *P*-waves can continue, although their speed is once again reduced to 8·1 km/sec (Figure 38). On the surface of the Earth, inability to transmit *S*-waves is regarded as a most important sign that a material is a liquid. Although the core is liquid by this test, it is misleading to think of it as behaving like water. A reliable analogy is difficult to find, and we must be content to think of the material of the core as quite unlike anything we have ever met at the surface of the Earth. The core is much denser than the mantle. The density of the whole Earth is about 5½, whilst the average of the surface rocks is only about 2½ times as heavy as a corresponding bulk of water. In the mantle, the density averages less than 5, so that there is a good deal of weight to be made up in the core, which has a density of 10 to 12 for most of its bulk, and may rise as high as 16 or 17 at the centre. Some geophysicists think that this great density is due to a concentration of heavy metals, like iron and nickel, whilst others think it can be accounted for merely by supposing that the atoms of the materials forming the rest of the Earth have been changed under the pressure so that they can be more tightly packed together in the core. This is a question which is not likely to receive a final answer for a long time.

The existence of a sharp boundary between the mantle and the core gives us a further clue to the Earth's internal temperature. At this depth, it must be hot enough to melt the metal of the core, but not so hot that it can melt the silicate material of the mantle in contact with it. This sets quite narrow limits, and the probable temperature works out at about 3600° C. Since the core is metallic it is a good conductor of heat, and there cannot be much further rise of temperature within it.

I have already hinted that the core is not a simple structure with the same properties all the way through. In 1936, Miss Inge Lehmann, the Danish seismologist, examined records of a number of large earthquakes, including the New Zealand shocks at Murchison and

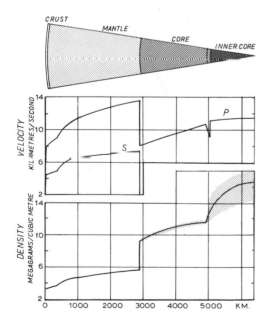

Fig. 38: Density and seismic wave velocity inside the Earth. The velocities of P- and S- at different depths within the Earth are known within fairly close limits. The densities deduced from them are less certain, particularly in the outer and inner core, as indicated by the shading in the lower graph.

Hawke's Bay in 1928 and 1931. It was clear from these records that a *P*-type wave was arriving at stations which should have been within the shadow zone. This can be explained if there is an inner core, about 1250 km in radius, and of rather greater density than the outer portion. When naming a phase which has travelled through the inner part of the core, we use the letter *I* if it is a *P*-type wave, and *J* if it is an *S*-type wave. The phase *PKIKP* has now been definitely observed, but the existence of *PKJKP* is still very doubtful. If it exists, there are reasons to believe that it will not be very strong, so that we can expect it only in big earthquakes. It is probable for other reasons that the inner core is solid, but a record of *PKJKP* would provide a welcome proof. Figure 38 shows the way in which the density and the velocity of seismic waves change with depth below the Earth's surface. We are now in a position to draw a complete picture of the interior of the Earth, and this has been done in Figure 39.

Fig. 39: The Earth's interior.

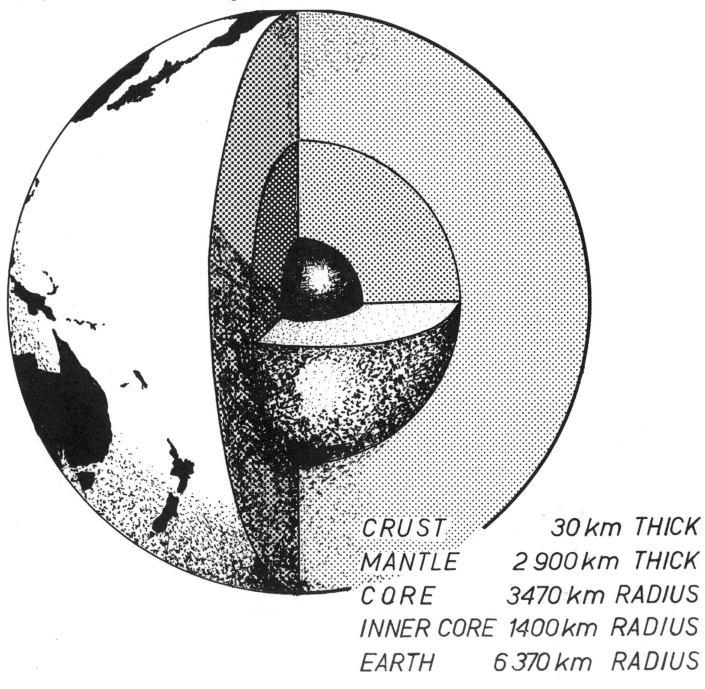

CRUST   30 km THICK
MANTLE   2 900 km THICK
CORE   3470 km RADIUS
INNER CORE 1400 km RADIUS
EARTH   6 370 km RADIUS

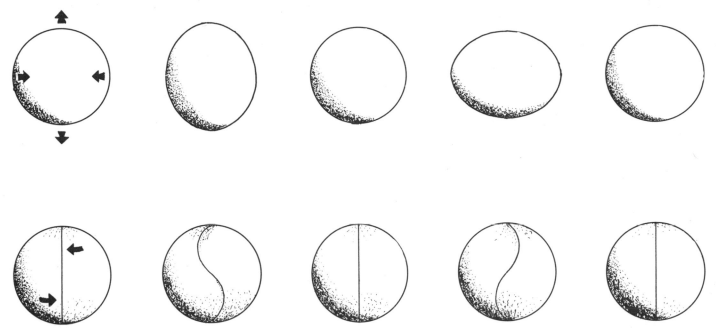

Fig. 40: Free oscillations of the Earth. Very large earthquakes can set the whole Earth vibrating. There can be radial movements that distort its shape, as in the upper set of diagrams, or transverse movements that leave it the same shape but distort the surface, as in the lower set.

Although we àre reasonably sure that the inner core is solid, its density is very uncertain. It is unlikely to be less than 15, and on some reasonable assumptions it could be as high as 18 or 20. The study of surface-waves of very long period offers a possible way of finding out.

The longer the period of a surface-wave, the deeper are the parts of the Earth involved in transmitting it, so the introduction of ultra-long-period seismographs means that the usefulness of surface-waves is no longer limited to the study of the crust. First the properties of the mantle, and more recently those of the Earth as a whole have been investigated with their help.

Very large earthquakes like those in Chile in 1960 and Alaska in 1964 have set the whole bulk of the Earth in vibration like a great jelly. Two basic kinds of wobble are possible, known as the *torsional* and *spheroidal* modes (Figure 40). In torsional oscillation the surface of the Earth is displaced sideways, the simplest case being when the two opposite hemispheres move in opposite directions. During spheroidal vibration the particles move in and out radially, so that the Earth alternately bulges at an equator and stretches at the poles, in the manner of a rugby football. This kind of vibration is like that of the outside of a great bell, or it can sometimes be seen in a suspended water-drop.

These oscillations are of course very slow, the deep fundamental note having a period of nearly an hour, and there is a complicated series of overtones. The exact period of this note, the relationship of the overtones to it, and the way the whole series of vibrations dies away are all related to the distribution of density and elasticity throughout the whole bulk of the Earth. Once vibrations of this kind have been started, they take a very long time to die out, and suitably designed pendulums can still detect them several days after the earthquake.

8 Continents and oceans

Some force whole regions, in despite
O' geography, to change their site:
      Samuel Butler, *Hudibras*

The fact that there are continents and oceans needs an explanation. If the Earth began as a molten mass surrounded by vapours, it might very well have ended up as a smooth ball covered to an even depth by sea. Studies of the crust have shown that the continents and oceans are different in structure, thickness, and chemical compositon. It is simpler to see why these differences, once they have arisen, should persist.

Compared with the radius of the Earth the thickness of the crust is small. The difference in average level between the continents and the ocean floors is smaller still, a mere five kilometres. To be sure, it is nearly twenty kilometres from the bottom of the deepest ocean trench to the summit of Everest, but these large departures from the average are unusual, and the processes of geology are active to reduce them. The basic difference in level between continent and ocean, however, is in a different category.

If we were to float a number of pieces of wood of different shapes and sizes in a trough of water (Figure 41) we would find, provided that they were all made of the same kind of wood, that a big block sticking a long way out of the water also went well down underneath, while a thin plank that was almost awash didn't go far under the water at all. The comparatively light material that makes up the continents rests upon the denser material of the mantle in a way that is not very different from floating. If each bit of the continent could find its own level independently, we could expect the bottom of the crust to lie very much deeper under the mountain ranges than it does beneath the plains, and the base of the thin oceanic crust to be nearer the surface than the base of a continent. This kind of balance is known as *isostasy*, from the Greek *iso*, equal, and *stasis*, standing.

There are several indications that isostasy is operating in the Earth. Waves from near earthquakes that have to pass under mountain ranges are delayed by their roots, for example, but the usual method of investigation is to make measurements of gravity.

Imagine that we have hung up a plumb-bob somewhere in the middle of a great continental plain (Figure 42). Below us the light rocks of the crust and the material of the mantle underneath them lie in even layers stretching away in all directions. Under these conditions the pull of gravity will make the bob hang straight down, pointing to the centre of the Earth. Suppose now that without altering anything else we pile a mountain range on top of the crust, to one side of the bob. There is now more mass on that side than the other, and the gravitational attraction of this mass will try to pull the bob a little in its direction.

When we make measurements near real mountains, we find that their pull has very little effect. The reason is that underneath, the mountain has a root sticking down into the mantle. This root is composed of the same kind of rock as the crust, and drives out

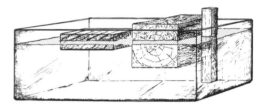

Fig. 41: The principle of isostasy. The distance to which a floating block extends beneath the surface can be judged from the amount that appears above it.

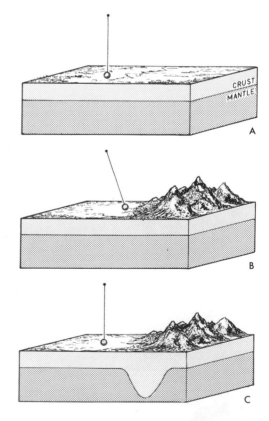

Fig. 42: Deflection of the plumb-line. When there are no local irregularities, a plumb-line hangs vertically, pointing in the direction of the centre of the Earth, as in A. The gravitational attraction of a large mass like the range of mountains in B should pull it to one side, but if the mass of the mountain is compensated by a root of light crustal material driving out part of the heavier mantle, the total mass on all sides of the bob remains the same, and it continues to hang vertically, as in C.

enough of the heavy material to leave the same total mass on all sides of our pendulum.

Regions in which the balance is perfect are said to be isostatically *compensated*, and large parts of the Earth seem to be very close to the condition of balance. In others the balance is upset, and we say that there is a *gravity anomaly*. Measuring the displacement of a suspended plumb-bob is difficult, but portable instruments called gravimeters (Plate 20) have been devised to simplify the mapping of the Earth's gravitational field. Basically they are no more than a delicate spring with a weight hanging from the end. When the pull of gravity on the weight increases, the spring gets longer, and when the pull is removed it contracts again. In practice, the changes in pull are very small, so the springs have to be very delicate, and protected against changes in temperature and mechanical damage. Even then, there are problems in interpreting the readings, for complicated allowances have to be made for the configuration of the country, for the height above sea-level, and for departures from normal density in the near-by rocks due to localized geological peculiarities.

The gravity anomalies in uncompensated regions may be either positive or negative. Regions where the pull is greater than normal will have a tendency to sink, and those where it is less will tend to rise. There are many reasons why anomalies should exist.When mountain ranges are eroded away, and their rocks transported to the sea by rivers and dropped on the bottom, the trim of the continental rafts is

Plate 20: Gravity measurements. Differences in the pull of gravity at different places on the Earth's surface can be measured with portable gravity-meters like this one being used in the Antarctic. The part of the meter that responds to the varying pull is enclosed in a vacuum, and is rather like a vertical seismometer. For transportation it is placed in a sprung and padded compartment in the aluminium cylinder seen standing behind it.

upset, but the material beneath the crust yields only slowly, and it takes time for them to reach their new stable positions. Under these conditions, the mountain ranges have a continual tendency to rise, and the crust beneath the shallow seas where the material is deposited becomes warped downwards. These differential processes cause strains in the region between.

Isostatic forces alone are insufficient to account for all the folding, fracturing, and uplift that is evident in the rocks around us. The crust is also stressed by the slow but powerful movements of the mantle beneath, generated ultimately by the Earth's internal heat.

Each of the continents contains a nucleus of very old crystalline rocks. Most of its former relief has been weathered away, but it has been untouched by the processes of deformation and tilting that are so much in evidence at the active continental margins. To all appearances these stable nuclei, which are known as *shields*, have been unmoved, if not since the beginning of time then at least since the pre-Cambrian, which for most human purposes approximates to the same thing. Appearances deceive. The continents are floating rafts, and rafts can move without disturbances to the cargo.

As long ago as 1620 Francis Bacon was struck by the similar shapes of the coastlines on opposite shores of the Atlantic, but it was not until 1910 that Alfred Wegener, a German meteorologist, seriously suggested that they had once been united, along with Australia and Antarctica, to form a single super-continent that he called *Pangaea* (Greek for 'all the land', Figure 43). Pangaea was supposed to have remained in one piece until about the beginning of the Mesozoic, when it rifted into pieces that gradually moved apart to become the present continents. This hypothesis is known as *Continental Drift*.

Geologists quickly found that the similarities between formerly united pieces of Pangaea went far beyond a similarity in general shape. Whole sequences of rocks in widely separated continents were found to match in extraordinary detail. Botanists and zoologists, who had previously insisted that there must once have been now

Fig. 43: Continental drift. The present continents are probably fragments of a single primitive continent called Pangaea, which broke up in the Mesozoic era about 150 million years ago. The pieces have since drifted apart and their shapes have been modified. In the reconstruction above Africa and the Americas are easily recognized. Australia and India nestle against eastern Antarctica. The Indian fragment later collided with Eurasia and became part of it.

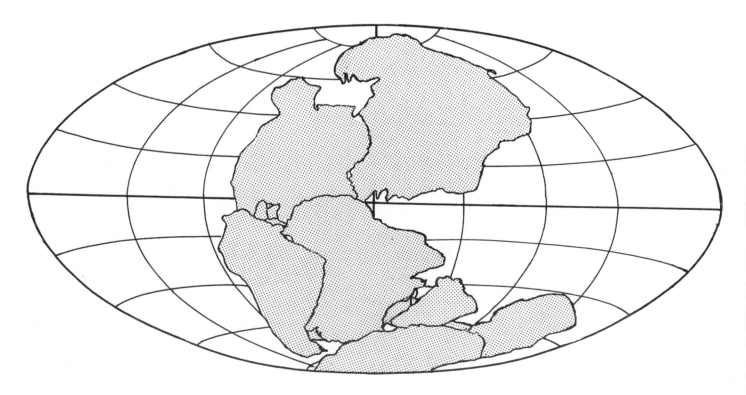

sunken land-bridges across the oceans to account for similarities in plants and animals, gave the hypothesis a warm welcome.

Geophysicists were less enthusiastic. They were prepared to grant that for the purposes of isostasy the continents acted like great rafts of granite floating on the denser material beneath; but although that material was plastic, they knew that it was also extremely viscous, and they knew of no forces great enough to move the rafts apart. Wegener had written of *Polflucht*, a flight from the poles. This idea they were inclined to dismiss as German mysticism. Yet geophysicists were gathering data that could only be explained by supposing that something of the kind had in fact occurred. The clues lay in the magnetism of the Earth.

The Earth is a magnet, but not because of the permanent magnetism of the iron and nickel in the core. At that depth the temperature is far too high for permanent magnetism to be possible. The fact that a suspended lodestone or compass needle would point towards the pole has been known since very ancient times. At the end of the sixteenth century it was realized that it did so only approximately, and that the direction in which it actually pointed slowly changed. This happens because the Earth's magnetic field varies in a rather complicated way.

To begin with, it has two parts, one originating within the Earth itself, and the other resulting from an interaction between the ionosphere (the electrically charged layer of the upper atmosphere that reflects radio waves) and streams of electric particles emitted by the Sun. An eruption of sunspots or solar flares can upset the balance of this interaction, causing magnetic storms during which radio communications are disrupted and auroral displays may be seen; but these storms are short-lived and less relevant to seismological problems than the slower changes that affect the internal field.

The core of the Earth is fluid, and it is a good conductor of electricity. The fluid is in motion, and there are electric currents circulating within it. Taken together these movements constitute a kind of self-exciting dynamo, which generates the internal magnetic field. This dynamo has a most important property. It is unstable. While the Earth's rotation ensures that the magnetic poles remain somewhere close to the geographical ones, a very small disturbance in the internal currents could make the entire external magnetic field reverse its direction, so that the end of a compass-needle that had previously pointed north would now point south.

This kind of upset has not occurred in historic times, but we do not have to go far back into the geological past to find that the rocks contain a record of many such reversals. The study of this magnetic record is called *palaeomagnetism*, and provides the most persuasive evidence for the reality of continental drift and the existence of convection currents within the mantle.

A rock can become useful for palaeomagnetic study in a number of ways. When substances are heated beyond about six hundred degrees Celsius they lose their magnetism, but if they are allowed to cool again in the presence of a magnetic field they become re-magnetized in the direction of the field. The natural magnetism of igneous and metamorphic rocks is therefore a record of the direction of the Earth's magnetic field at the time they cooled. Sedimentary rocks can also preserve a record. While magnetic particles are floating, they behave like tiny compass-needles, so that under calm conditions they are deposited on the bottom all pointing the one way, aligned in the direction of the field. In a very thick stratum it may be possible to follow the changes in direction from the time the oldest material was deposited at the bottom until the most recent was formed at the top. Even artificial materials like the clay bricks in the ancient hearths and ovens uncovered by archaeologists have proved useful to the palaeomagnetician.

The practical difficulties of palaeomagnetic work are very great, for there are many ways in which the original magnetism of the rock could have been disturbed, but by taking many samples a reasonably consistent story can be pieced together. After proper allowance has been made for reversal of the field, the orientation of a continent at the times its rocks were formed can be worked out, and its wanderings traced. The details of the story differ a little from the one originally told by Wegener, but it is now generally accepted that large bodily movement of the continents has taken place.

Magnetic measurements at sea are a less tedious business than the collection of carefully-oriented rock specimens and the delicate laboratory measurements called for on land. All that is needed is to tow a continuously recording magnetometer behind a ship, and because the geological history of the ocean floors has usually been less disturbed than that of the continents, the elaborate mapping needed before proper allowance can be made for the tilting and folding of the rocks since they acquired their magnetism is also unnecessary. This is fortunate, for the difficulties facing a marine geologist are daunting.

The sea covers seventy percent of the Earth's surface. Most of our geological knowledge has been gathered from the other thirty percent, and no matter what allowances we make, geology alone is bound to give us a distorted picture. Oceanographers realized that corrective measures were needed, and in the 1950s, particularly at the time of the International Geophysical Year, a great many important oceanographic cruises were made. The Americans were active in both the Atlantic and the Pacific, the Russians tackled the Pacific and the icy problems of the Arctic, and the French, the Japanese, and the Danes also mounted major expeditions. Their enormous contributions to biology and their work on ocean currents, sea-temperatures, and salinities do not concern the seismologist. What does is the detailed mapping of the topography of the ocean floor, the sampling of the sediments on the bottom, and the measurement of their thickness by seismic methods.

It was already known that the Atlantic was divided into eastern and western halves by a great range of submarine mountains that poked above the surface in Iceland, and in a chain of smaller islands like the Azores, St Helena, and Tristan da Cunha. It was also known that similar ridges crossed the floors of the other oceans. What was new was the realization that these mid-oceanic ridges are connected to form a single great system that branches and snakes its way over most of the globe.

There were other puzzling discoveries. One was that none of the sea-floor sediments was very thick, and that all of them were very young. The oldest bottom-samples then found were Cretaceous, about 135 million years old. To explain this two American oceanographers, R. S. Dietz and H. S. Hess, revived an earlier suggestion that the sea floor was in motion. In 1963 F. J. Vine and D. H. Matthews of Cambridge University realized that the magnetized rocks on the sea bottom contained proof of it.

It had been observed in the North Atlantic, the Antarctic, and the Indian Oceans that bands of magnetic anomalies lay parallel to the

Fig. 44: Magnetic striping of the sea floor. This diagram shows the symmetrical pattern of oppositely magnetized rocks on the sea floor on opposite sides of the Reykjanes Ridge, south of Iceland.

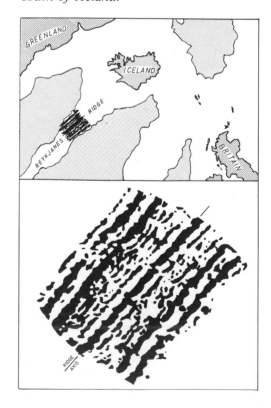

crest of the oceanic ridges, and that the patterns on opposite sides of the ridge were almost mirror images of one another. This was not easy to explain. What Vine and Matthews suggested was that the basalt lavas that make up most of the sea floor originated in the volcanoes that are found along the ridges, and were then carried outwards by convection currents in the material underneath. When the lavas cooled, they became magnetized by the Earth's field, and the reason why the striped pattern was the same on both sides was that every time the Earth's magnetic field changed polarity, the new lavas were magnetized the opposite way round (Figure 44).

In this new way of looking at things the ocean floors have become huge conveyor-belts carrying material outwards from the submarine ridges, and the pattern of magnetic striping provides a measure of the rate at which they are moving. In most places it is only a couple of centimetres a year, but in the course of geological time it can move continents, and provide the horizontal forces needed to build mountains, and to fold and fracture the crust.

What happens to the material reaching the ocean margins? There are two possible answers. It can pile up and form mountains, or it can be drawn into the mantle by the now descending convection current. In either case, we can expect to find a region of vigorous geological activity, and we shall return later to consider what happens in more detail. One thing that happens is the occurrence of earthquakes, and we must first see how seismic activity fits into the overall pattern of crustal movement.

9 How earthquakes happen

The emperor Justinian prohibited, under penalty of death, certain kinds
of sexual offences, together with blasphemy and the practice of
swearing by the hair of one's head, on the grounds that such
practices notoriously provoked thunderbolts and earthquakes. This seems
to me a sound reason. One cannot tolerate conduct which causes
earthquakes any more than one can tolerate conduct which
leads to riot and disorder.

A. H. Campbell, *Justice and Toleration*

We are now ready to leave the broad association of earthquakes with
the development of the Earth's geological and geophysical features
and consider how the slowly accumulating tectonic forces are
transformed into a sudden burst of seismic waves.

The crust of the Earth is fractured in many places. When the rocks
on either side of a fracture have been displaced so that the strata no
longer match, the geologist calls the crack a *fault* (Plate 21). The
forces that produced it may have been forces of compression, or
tensions, or shearing. Each will result in a different kind of
displacement, and this is the basis of the usual method of classifying
faults. Figure 45 shows the basic kinds of movement possible, their
names, and the names given to the different parts of a fault. Plates 22
to 28 show the actual appearance of faults of different kinds in a
variety of settings.

Normal faults are usually considered to be the result of tension,
and *reverse* faults the result of thrusting. Because the movement is
along the direction of the *strike*, the name given to the bearing of the
fault trace, *transcurrent* faults are also known as *strike-slip* faults.
When the opposite side of the fault moves towards the observer's
right the movement is said to be *dextral*, or *right lateral* and *sinistral*
or *left lateral* when it moves to his left. Transcurrent movement may
of course be accompanied by a greater or lesser amount of normal or
reverse movement, but it is usual for one or the other to predominate.
The word normal should not be taken to imply that this kind of fault
is more usual than the other kinds.

The total displacement of a fault has usually taken place in several
steps. In any particular region, the forces responsible tend to go on
acting for long periods of time; but this is not always the case. They
may be transferred elsewhere, be interrupted and renewed, or may
even reverse their direction.

Geologists have noted that the appearance of fresh fault-breaks on
the Earth's surface, or renewed movement on existing faults has
sometimes accompanied a large shallow earthquake. The first clear
instance to be reported was in 1819 when an earthquake near the
present border of India and Pakistan resulted in some 1500 deaths,
and a fault-scarp some three metres high rose across the coastal salt
flats of the Rann of Kutch. This became known as the Allah Bund, or
God's Dyke, from its similarity to the levées thrown up by the local
ruler for irrigation purposes.

After the San Francisco earthquake of 1906, H. F. Reid examined
the impressive transcurrent movement that had affected three or four
hundred kilometres of the great fracture known as the San Andreas

Plate 21: Geological faulting. Where the Nukumaru Fault reaches the coast it appears as a break passing through cliffs about 6 metres high. Because of surface erosion, the right side is higher than the left, but an attempt to match the corresponding rock layers will show that it is the left side of the fault that has moved upwards.

Fault, and the deformation of the country for some distance on either side of the fault trace. As a result of his observations he put forward the hypothesis known as the *elastic rebound* theory.

Plate 22: Vertical faulting. This famous picture was taken in 1891, and shows the faulting at Midori in the Neo Valley that accompanied the Mino-Owari earthquake. The almost vertical scarp is six metres high, but inspection of the road on the right will show that there has also been a sinistral movement of about four metres.

Fig. 45: Geological faulting. The upper pictures show the three main types of faulting. In most real faults tension or compression is combined with shear, and any one of the three may predominate. The strike of a fault is what seamen would call its bearing — the angle its trace makes with a north-south line, measured from north towards the east.

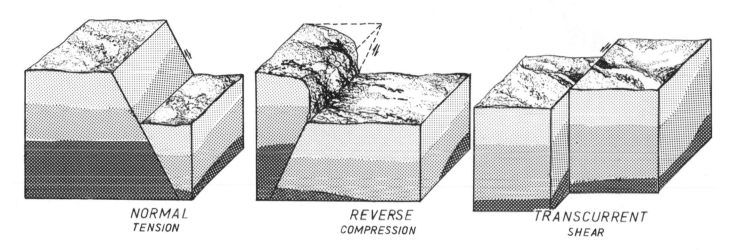

NORMAL
TENSION

REVERSE
COMPRESSION

TRANSCURRENT
SHEAR

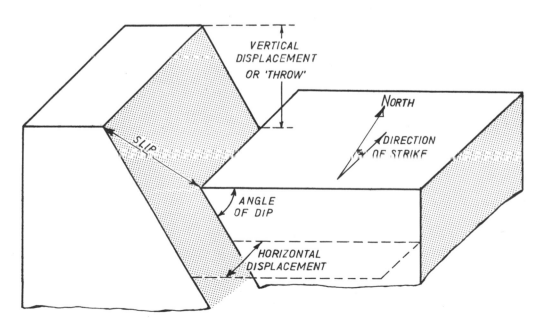

VERTICAL DISPLACEMENT OR 'THROW'

NORTH

DIRECTION OF STRIKE

SLIP

ANGLE OF DIP

HORIZONTAL DISPLACEMENT

Plate 23: Vertical faulting. This fault scarp at Quiches, in the Peruvian Andes, is three metres high and appeared in the Ancash earthquake in 1946.

Plate 24: Transcurrent faulting. Faulting during the Imperial Valley earthquake in 1940 displaced the rows of trees in this Californian orange-grove.

Plate 25: Transcurrent faulting. A sinistral movement of about four and a half metres that occurred in the Dasht-e-Bayaz earthquake in Iran in 1968. When there is little vertical movement, as in this case, the surface trace is often quickly destroyed by erosion and human activity.

Plate 26: Mole tracks. The appearance of a fault trace often depends as much upon the nature of the surface as upon the movement of the underlying rocks. In soft ground a common effect is the appearance of what the Japanese call 'mole tracks'. This example comes from Sampazari, in western Anatolia, and made its appearance in the Mudurunu Valley earthquake in 1967.

Plate 27: Faulting and topography. Faulting can often be distinguished from superficial slumping by its relative independence of the topography. The downhill side of this fault in the Nimbluk Valley, near Boskabad in Iran, moved upwards about thirty centimetres in the Dasht-e-Bayaz earthquake in 1968.

Plate 28: The stronger wins. When this fault break in the Turkish earthquake at Gediz in 1970 encountered a grove of trees, it found it easier to divert through the soft ground than to break the roots of the trees.

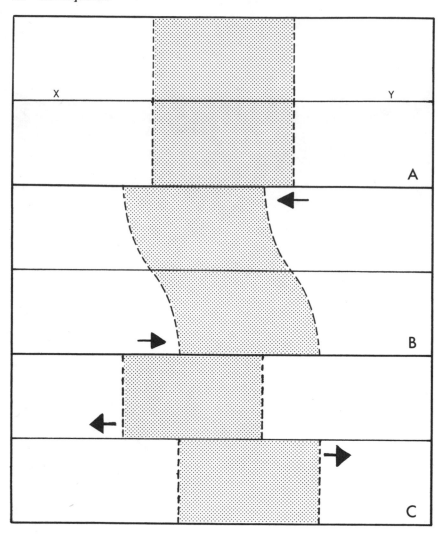

Fig. 46: Elastic rebound. The top figure shows a tract of country whose weakest rocks lie along the line XY. Regional forces slowly distort it until it assumes the shape shown in B, at the same time storing elastic energy in the rocks. When the accumulated strain. becomes too great for the strength of the rocks they break along the line XY, releasing their stored energy in the form of earthquake waves and creating a geological fault, as shown at C.

Suppose that Figure 46A represents a tract of country perhaps 50 or 100 kilometres across, and the weakest rocks in it lie along the line XY (which could for example be an old fault). Imagine that the broken lines are very long straight fences built at right angles to the line of weakness, and that the country is being slowly deformed by regional forces in the crust. In time the fences will assume the shapes shown in Figure 46B. All the time this has been going on — and the process may go on for a century or more — elastic energy is being stored in the rocks, just as it is when we wind a spring. Eventually the strain may become so great that the weaker rocks can no longer resist it, and they suddenly break along the line of weakness. This releases the stored energy, as if the coiled spring were suddenly let go. On either side of the break the rocks rebound to their unstrained positions. The movement is greater near the break and becomes less and less as we go away to either side. It is the waves set up by this sudden rebound movement that we call an earthquake.

The block diagram (Figure 47) shows the same process in a slightly different way. The movement can be horizontal as shown here, or vertical, or a combination of the two, according to the manner in which the rocks had been strained. If Reid is correct earthquakes are not a sudden abnormal happening, but a return to normal after a prolonged period of strain.

The elastic rebound theory has not been without its critics. In 1927 two Japanese observers reported that the fault trace of the Tango earthquake did not appear until *after* the destruction of their houses. Similar observations had been made in 1891, and this has led some Japanese seismologists to maintain that faulting is the result of earthquakes and not the cause. It should be remembered, however, that a mechanical failure of this kind must develop from some definite point of greatest weakness. This point is the focus of the earthquake, and it is generally buried at some considerable depth. The rate at which the fracture can spread from the focus is less than the speed of seismic waves, and the maximum shaking will in all probability precede the appearance of the dislocation at the surface. If the main energy release did not take place in a limited area, and in a comparatively brief instant of time, a seismogram would present a very complicated appearance, instead of the comparatively orderly sequence of pulses we can observe.

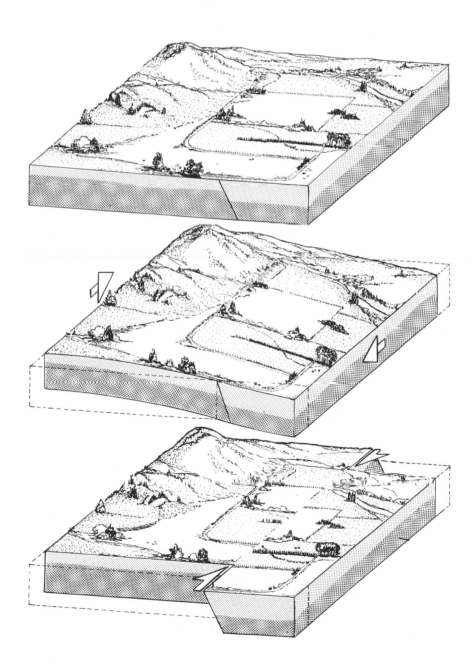

Fig. 47: Elastic rebound. This block diagram of a landscape traversed by a fault shows its gradual distortion by regional stresses until the strain is released by an elastic rebound along the fault.

The rebound theory certainly gives a satisfactory account of the deformations that can be observed at the surface of the Earth, but examination of surface faulting can tell us little about conditions at the focus, several kilometres underground even in the shallowest shocks. It could be that most of the energy comes from something other than elastic strain, and that surface faulting is only a form of earthquake damage. In the early 1960s this was the view of most New Zealand seismologists, and some of their Japanese colleagues agreed. For several decades the seismologists of Europe and America had been busy with problems to which the actual mechanism of the earthquake was irrelevant, or in which it was at most a minor consideration, and serious physical objections to the theory seemed to have been overlooked.

We have seen that earthquakes occur, at least in some parts of the Earth, down to depths of about 700 km. Because of difficulties in measurement, we cannot be so sure whether there is a shallow limit, but the shallowest shocks of any great size have focal depths of a few kilometres at least. As we penetrate deeper and deeper into the Earth, the pressure and the temperature both increase. The increase in pressure means that the frictional forces acting to prevent a fault from moving also become greater and greater. At the same time, the increasing temperature makes it easier for the rocks to deform and flow. Unless the rocks are fairly rigid, it is not possible for them to accumulate enough elastic strain energy to overcome the friction, and faulting by simple brittle fracture would probably become impossible at any depth greater than that of the very shallowest earthquakes. Dr. E. Orowan has estimated that at a depth of 600–700 km, the friction would be at least a thousand times the strength of the rock. For reasons of this kind, many seismologists who found elastic rebound a satisfactory explanation of shallow earthquakes had reservations about deep ones. If there were really two quite different sorts of earthquake, why did they produce such similar records, and why did they tend to happen in the same parts of the world?

Doubts were to be strengthened by a discovery in California where the rebound theory had originated, and where belief in it was very strong. In 1948 a wine-grower near Hollister had built himself a new reinforced-concrete winery. A few years later, the walls on opposite sides of the building had cracked. As time went on, the cracks became wider, and the concrete slabs that made up the floor were displaced. The building had been so sited that part of it lay on one side of the San Andreas fault, and the rest on the other. Although there had been no earthquake strong enough to damage the building, and certainly no earthquake strong enough to cause a visible fault-break, the opposite sides of the fault were slowly creeping along at an average rate of about one or two centimetres a year. No building could be expected to stand up to that sort of treatment. Seismographs and instruments for measuring the amount and the rate of the creep have been installed, and although it is found that local earthquakes speed up the movement temporarily, the steady movement appears to be unrelated to earthquake activity.

This is not the first time creep has been observed. As far back as 1932, it had been found that oil-wells drilled through the Buena Vista fault in Kern County, farther to the north, were being sheared off by continuous movement of this kind. The number of faults transfixed by oil-wells or straddled by wineries is not great, and it is still uncertain how general fault creep will turn out to be. Several New Zealand faults are now being watched to see if creep is taking place, but so far none has been detected. If strain can be continuously relieved in this way, it is clear that there will be no stored energy to produce the waves radiated from a large earthquake.

A final objection was based on the very small number of earthquakes that were known to have produced fresh fault movements. In 1954 Professor C. F. Richter considered that there were only thirty-six 'clear and well authenticated cases', and among these there are some that could be questioned. Since then closer observation has added significantly to the list, but even when due allowance is made for shocks under the sea and in other inaccessible places the total number of examples is surprisingly small in comparison with the yearly total of recorded earthquakes.

In spite of these apparently strong objections, few seismologists would now question the broad correctness of the elastic rebound theory. Three lines of research have silenced the objectors. The first was the result of a shift in attention from the Earth's surface to a renewed concentration on events at the actual focus. The theory of the method used to study them was first worked out by H. Nakano in about 1922, and it had been extensively applied by Kawasumi and other Japanese seismologists over the next two decades, but instrumental limitations and the small number of good recording stations had limited their success, and it had found little application outside Japan.

Let us imagine the origin of an earthquake to be surrounded by a sphere, just big enough to enclose whatever is going on, with the focus of the shock at the centre of the sphere. If we join the focus to each recording station by a line along the path the *P*-wave takes, each line will pass through the sphere at some different point. Now, if the first movement that reaches the station is a compression, the corresponding point on the focal sphere must have moved outwards, and if it is a rarefaction, the point must have moved inwards. If we can collect records from enough stations right round the Earth, it should be possible to build up a picture of what happened at the focus.

In practice, these studies are very difficult. Not every earthquake begins with a clear movement, and many stations turn out to have only emergent phases, almost lost in the background of microseisms. It is also difficult to get a set of observations well spaced around the focal sphere, not only because seismograph stations are unevenly scattered around the globe, but because the layered structure of the

Fig. 48: First-motion studies. The first movement recorded at a particular seismograph station may be either towards it (a compression, C) or away from it (a dilatation, D). The stations that record compressions and dilatations are usually distributed in alternate quadrants about the epicentre. This can be used to work out the direction of the fault-plane and the direction of movement, but the results are ambiguous. A dextral movement of the fault shown in A produces the same pattern of compressions and dilatations as a sinistral movement on one at right angles to it, as shown in B.

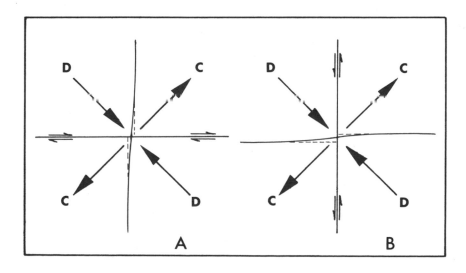

Earth bends the rays in such a way that for shallow shocks all the waves from the top half of the focal sphere reach the surface within a hundred kilometres or so of the epicentre. In theory we would need half our stations within this distance to get proper coverage. Fortunately the position is a little better for deep-focus earthquakes.

There is a still more serious problem. The results are ambiguous. Figure 48A shows a fault with its plane perpendicular to the paper. The direction of regional strain is such that rocks on the upper side of the fault will move to the right. When this strain is suddenly released by elastic rebound, all the seismographs in the quadrants marked C should record compressions, and those in the alternate quadrants marked D should record dilatations. Figure 48B shows a second fault, at right angles to the first, but with a sinistral instead of a dextral movement. The pattern of compressions and dilatations is the same in both cases.

If the earthquake mechanism were not some kind of shearing movement, some very different patterns of first motion could be expected. Explosions, for example, should produce nothing but compressions, and collapses should produce only dilatations, provided that there was no change of shape. If there were a change of shape at the same time as the change of volume a quadrantal pattern, or even something more complicated, could be superimposed upon the simple pattern of compressions or rarefactions.

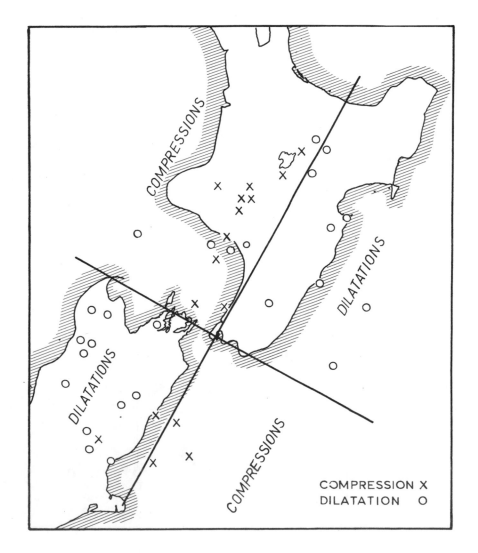

COMPRESSION X
DILATATION   O

Fig. 49: First motions at Wellington. If all the faults in a region have much the same orientation, as is often the case, the earthquakes that produce compressional first motions at a particular station and those that produce dilatations are distributed in alternate quadrants.

In spite of the difficulties first-motion studies became a very popular field of research during the 1960s, particularly careful work being done by the teams of workers under Dr. J. H. Hodgson in Canada, Professor Keilis-Borok in the Soviet Union, and Professor Honda in Japan. Although the confidence that could be placed upon the observations of a single earthquake was small, regional patterns were found and these lent support to the developing ideas of sea-floor spreading and plate tectonics.

When there are dense networks of recording stations, it becomes possible to apply first-motion techniques to local earthquakes. In many parts of the world large concentrations of portable instruments have been used to record very small shocks in limited regions for short periods. The large numbers of clear first motions recorded during these projects are of great value in understanding the patterns of regional strain, and how they vary with depth.

When the faults of a region share the same general orientation, a single station is sufficient to show the sense of movement. In central New Zealand, for example, most active faults run in a roughly north-east or south-west direction. Figure 49 shows the direction of the initial movements observed in Wellington for a number of shallow earthquakes. Granting the assumptions involved, the map suggests that there is a dextral displacement, that is, that the north-western side of the faults moves north-eastwards with respect to the south-eastern side. This is in accord with the geologists' observations of the faults at the surface.

The second line of research was mathematical. Professor Leon Knopoff in California and Dr. M. J. Randall in New Zealand worked out in detail the kinds of wave that would be radiated by different possible source mechanisms. Their results showed not only whether the first wave would be a compression or a rarefaction, but what amplitude it would have, and what proportion of P-type and S-type waves were to be expected. Dr. Ari Ben-Menahem worked back from records of surface-waves to conditions at the focus, and other American seismologists concerned themselves with details of fault-rupture and the waves it generated. All of these studies showed the importance of some form of shear, as the elastic rebound theory indicated. What had been little more than a qualitative hypothesis was becoming a proper mathematical theory.

The final and most recent line of study has removed the objection that at quite shallow depths friction would effectively prevent a fault from moving. Laboratory work on the behaviour of rocks at high pressures showed that the presence of liquid in the pores of the rock could result in the lubrication of a crack that would otherwise have been locked. This idea was supported by the observation that an increase in the number of earthquakes had followed the impounding of water in a number of large dams. In these cases, however, increases in pressure on the lake bottom were also involved, and it is not possible to be sure of how great a part the water is playing. More startling evidence of the importance of water was obtained near Denver, Colorado, in 1962. The United States Army, wishing to get rid of a surplus of toxic gases, dissolved them in water and pumped them down a well over three and a half kilometres deep. By the end of 1965 more than 700 earthquakes had been recorded in an area which had experienced none since 1882, and the frequency with which they occurred was linked with the amount of pumping. We shall return to this question of fault lubrication in a later chapter.

10 Where earthquakes happen

...the smoke and stir of this dim spot
Which men call Earth.
                    John Milton, *Comus*

One Thursday in February 1750, an earthquake was felt in London. Most New Zealanders have felt earthquakes, and so have most Japanese, but most Englishmen have not and there was much alarm. The alarm increased when a second shock followed four weeks later. Now, as John Wesley once observed, 'there is no divine visitation which is likely to have so general an influence upon sinners as an earthquake', and it is no surprise to learn that the churches were full the following Sunday, and that the recent 'divine warnings' provided most of the preachers with their text. Their number included the Rev. Dr William Stukeley, M.D., F.R.S.

Stukeley believed that earthquakes were due to electricity, and later expounded his views to the Royal Society in three papers that have earned him a corner in the history of seismology; but whatever natural agency was involved, Stukeley had no doubt that the hand of God was ultimately responsible. 'The chastening rod' he told the congregation of St George's Church, Bloomsbury, 'is directed to towns and cities, where there are inhabitants, the objects of its monition; not to bare cliffs and uninhabited beaches'. It was a reasonable guess, but it could not have been supported by observation.

During the nineteenth century a number of attempts were made to compile systematic catalogues of earthquakes, so that by the time the seismograph was invented the broad pattern of the world's seismic belts was known, and Montessus de Ballore had made the important observation that they approximated closely to the belts of young fold mountains.

Plates 29 and 30: Weak buildings. In many parts of the world the high casualty rates in moderate earthquakes are a direct result of the traditional building practices. The inherent weaknesses of piled stones or sun-dried brick can be only slightly improved by wooden framing, and even this may be beyond the resources of the people. These examples are from Turkey, but similar ones could be found in South and Central America, and in other parts of the Middle East. Intensities as low as MM VIII could destroy structures of this kind. Below, Plate 29 (rubble); opposite, Plate 30 (adobe).

There are still many uses for lists of damaging earthquakes, but they have serious limitations as a basis for the study of seismicity. Where there are no people there are no observations, and a large part of the Earth's surface is unwatched. At the other extreme, the large numbers of casualties that are often reported from some parts of South America, North Africa, and the Middle East indicate the folly of housing dense populations in buildings of piled rubble and mud brick, rather than the number and severity of the earthquakes in those places (Plates 29, 30). For an undistorted picture instrumental records are essential.

Figures 50 and 51, which are taken from Gutenberg and Richter's classic *The Seismicity of the Earth,* show the epicentres of all the large earthquakes in roughly half a century. Although the maps were drawn in 1954, and the accuracy of some of the early epicentres is low, they are still the best maps available for showing the relative vigor of the activity in the main seismic regions. Unfortunately there are some quite active regions in which all the shocks were too small to be included. The most serious omission is the activity that follows the mid-oceanic ridges. The ordinary shallow shocks and the deep-focus ones have been shown on separate maps so that they can be distinguished more clearly.

The mid-oceanic ridges are seen very clearly in Figure 52, but in these maps no attention is paid to magnitude. As a result the western United States, where there are many recording stations and very small shocks can be detected, appears far too active.

The active belts in which most earthquakes occur lie at the edges of stable regions which are not entirely without earthquakes, but in which the shocks are infrequent and usually small. The most vigorous of these active belts follows the greater part of the Pacific margin, and is characterised by both deep and shallow activity, which are not exactly superimposed. A second and only slightly less active belt joins it in the southern Philippines, and passes through Indonesia, Burma, and the Himalayas to the Meditteranean. It closely parallels the great mountain ranges and is often called the Alpide Belt.

When these belts are examined in detail, it will be found that they are not strictly continuous. The maximum depth of the activity, the relative positions of the deep and shallow shocks, and the patterns of association between the earthquakes and other geological and geophysical features vary strikingly from place to place. On small scale maps the individual segments merge to give an illusion of continuity which is nevertheless the result of a real tectonic pattern we shall discuss further.

Compared with the activity of the Circum-Pacific and Alpide belts, the seismicity of the mid-oceanic ridges is minor, the earthquakes being neither so numerous nor so large.

There are two kinds of region that are characteristically stable – the great ocean basins, and the continental shields – but they may contain active fractures such as the African Rift Valley – which has volcanoes as well as earthquakes – and the line of activity crossing South Australia from Spencer's Gulf to Lake Eyre. Perhaps the only part of the Earth that can validly claim to be earthquake-free is Antarctica. This is something of a seismological puzzle, as Antarctica has both young mountain ranges and active volcanoes, which seem to be associated with earthquakes in most other places. A proper understanding of this would probably teach us something important about the mechanism of earthquakes.

Professor F. F. Evison has pointed out that it is useful to classify

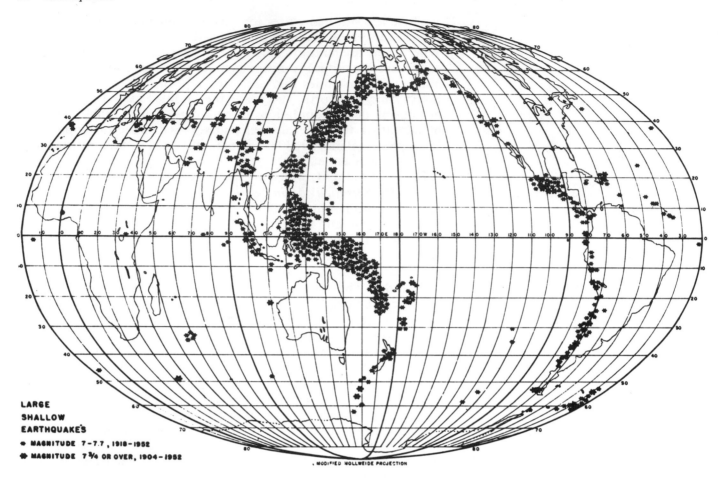

LARGE
SHALLOW
EARTHQUAKES
✦ MAGNITUDE 7-7.7 , 1918-1952
✸ MAGNITUDE 7¾ OR OVER, 1904-1952

. MODIFIED MOLLWEIDE PROJECTION

Fig. 50: Seismicity of the Earth. Epicentres of large shallow earthquakes, 1904 — 1952. (From Gutenberg and Richter.)

seismic regions as symmetrical or asymmetrical, according to their relationship with other geophysical features like volcanoes, gravity anomalies, and submarine trenches. The symmetrical systems, which include the mid-oceanic ridges and the rifts, are not so active and all the earthquakes are shallow. In the asymmetrical systems, the deeper shocks are increasingly displaced to one side of the shallow activity.

The ideas of continental drift and spreading of the sea floor provide a possible explanation of the world pattern and of the differing arrangements of geophysical features. The hypothesis that has been developed is known as *plate tectonics*.

According to this idea, the outer layers of the Earth behave like rigid plates that fit the main body of the Earth like loose caps, which are free to move about. Their thickness is a matter of some controversy. They must be substantially thicker than the crust, or they would not be able to withstand horizontal pressures without breaking. On the other hand they cannot extend below the weak layer in the asthenosphere, which probably provides the surface on which they slide. About 100 kilometres is therefore a likely figure. There are seven main plates, shown in Figure 53, and a few minor platelets needed to complete the pattern. The plate boundaries lie along the mid-oceanic ridges and active continental margins, following the belts of seismic activity.

Assuming that the plates are not immovably jammed together, there are three things that could be happening at a boundary between two plates – they could be moving apart, they could be driven together, or they could be slipping sideways with respect to one other.

At the mid-oceanic ridges they are being forced apart, and the force responsible is thermal convection in the Earth's mantle. Rising currents are injecting lavas that are continually being added to the edges of the plates (Figure 54) creating new sea-floor and forcing it outwards, leaving a record of the process in the pattern of magnetic stripes already described in Chapter Eight.

Convection depends essentially upon circulation. Rising currents of hot material must be balanced by descending currents of the material that has cooled. These descending currents are to be found near the active continental margins, and in the neighbourhood of the deep submarine trenches. This is confirmed by measurements of heat-flow taken with probes forced into the sea bed, and in drill-holes on land. There is little difference in the figures on land and at sea, but near the ridges the values rise to several times the average.

Where two rather similar plates collide, the result may be a chain of fold mountains. Contact of this kind between the Indian and Eurasian plates is the basic explanation of the Himalayas. Where the plates are dissimilar and there is a descending convection current, the situation becomes more complicated. The ocean floor is pulled downwards producing a submarine trench, but the continental material consisting of lighter rocks is unable to sink, and rides over the top. The result is a *subduction zone* in which the material of the ocean floor is once more carried downwards until the rising temperature melts it and absorbs it again into the mantle.

The presence of the descending material reveals itself in several ways. Being cooler and denser than the surrounding mantle it creates a gravity anomaly, it alters the appearance of the seismograms of earthquake waves that have had to pass through it (Figure 55), and it

Fig. 51: Seismicity of the Earth. Epicentres of large deep and intermediate earthquakes, 1904 — 1952. (From Gutenberg and Richter.)

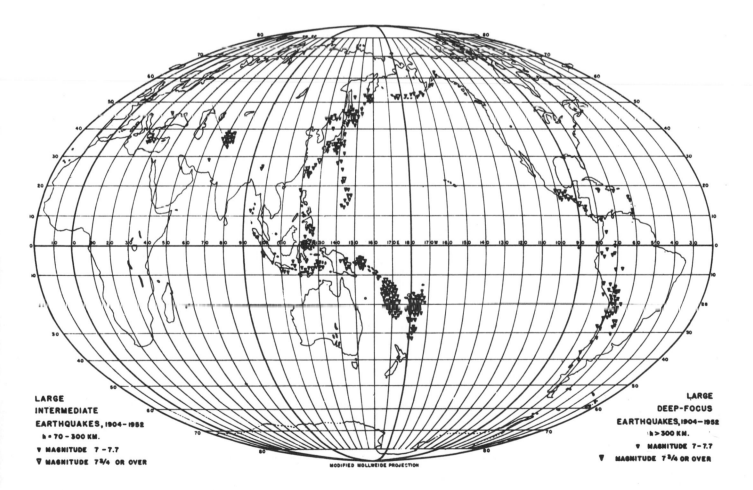

LARGE
INTERMEDIATE
EARTHQUAKES, 1904–1952
h = 70 - 300 KM.
▽ MAGNITUDE 7 - 7.7
▼ MAGNITUDE 7¾ OR OVER

MODIFIED MOLLWEIDE PROJECTION

LARGE
DEEP-FOCUS
EARTHQUAKES, 1904–1952
h > 300 KM.
▽ MAGNITUDE 7 - 7.7
▼ MAGNITUDE 7¾ OR OVER

traps the energy of the deep-focus earthquakes that occur within it, giving them very characteristic isoseismal patterns.

Deep-focus earthquakes are found only where there is descending material of this kind. Some writers call the volume within which the foci of deep shocks occur the 'down-going lithospheric slab', and others call it the *Benioff zone,* though Dr Hugo Benioff's view of these regions was not very like the one held now.

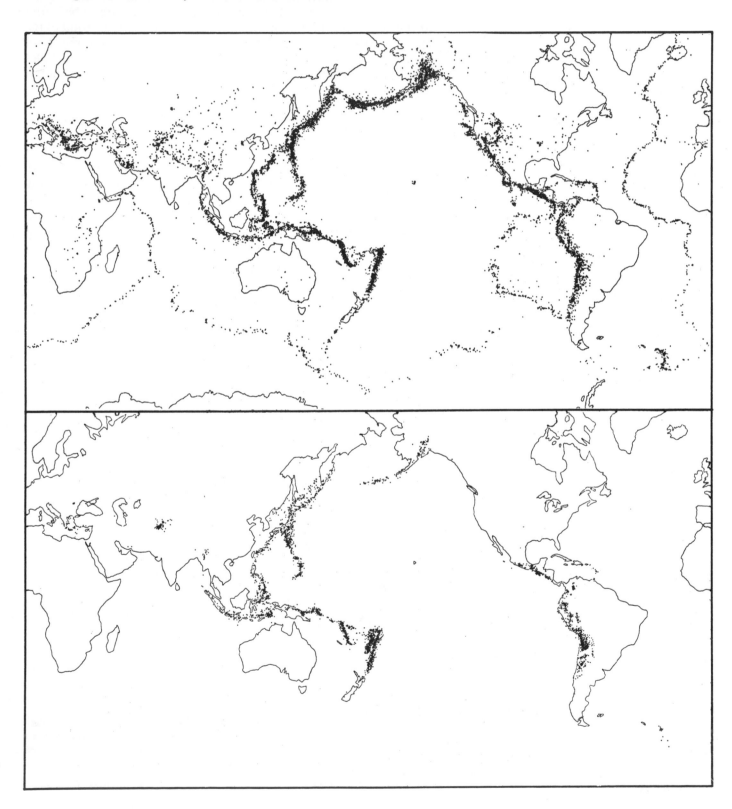

In both symmetrical and asymmetrical regions the different geophysical features – earthquakes, volcanoes, gravity anomalies and so on – occur in a definite pattern. That of the mid-oceanic ridges is the simpler of the two. Shallow earthquakes occur close to the axis of the ridge, along which there is usually a central rift or chasm. There are active volcanoes, emitting fluid basaltic lavas that cool to produce the pattern of magnetic striping on the ocean floor. The age of the volcanoes increases with their distance from the axis of the ridge.

The essentially asymmetrical features of a subduction zone are most clearly seen at active continental margins and in the formations known to the structural geologist as *island arcs* (Figure 56). These great arcuate systems occur along many segments of the Pacific margin, the most spectacular example being the Aleutians. On the outer, convex side of the arc there is a deep oceanic trench, with a narrow but active belt of shallow earthquakes just inside it. Here the values of gravity are lower than normal, and there may be a few small islands where the ocean bottom again rises in a ridge, as in the Mentawai Islands off the south coast of Sumatra. Within this ridge, the gravity again becomes normal, but continues to increase. The earthquakes become rather deeper, with foci at perhaps 50 or 100 kilometres. Then come the main islands of the arc, usually formed in the Cretaceous or Tertiary period, and often having active volcanoes. These are sometimes violently eruptive, and emit stiff andesitic lavas. Further inland, there is an older or secondary arc with extinct or nearly extinct volcanoes, and earthquakes at depths of about 200 kilometres. Continuing still further there may be a shallow sea before the continent proper is reached. The seismicity does not always continue, but if it does, its depth goes on increasing up to the maximum of about 700 kilometres.

Not all the features enumerated are present in every asymmetrical system; indeed, it would be difficult to find an example in which they had all been adequately observed, but when they do occur they

Fig. 52: Seismic geography. The upper map shows the epicentres of shallow earthquakes, and the lower one those of earthquakes with focal depths of 100 km or more from 1962 to 1967. They show the positions of the mid-oceanic ridges and the deep earthquake zones very clearly, but since the magnitude of the shocks shown is not the same everywhere, they give a distorted picture of the relative seismicity of the different zones. (After Barazangi and Dorman.)

Fig. 53: Plate tectonics. The Earth's lithosphere is divided into a number of rigid plates at the boundaries of which most of the world's earthquakes occur. The names of the main plates are shown, and minor platelets are identified by numbers: 1 Philippines Plate, 2 Cocos Plate, 3 Caribbean Plate, 4 Nasca Plate, 5 Arabian Plate.

Shading indicates the main zones of deep earthquakes, and the arrows indicate the directions in which the plates are believed to be moving.

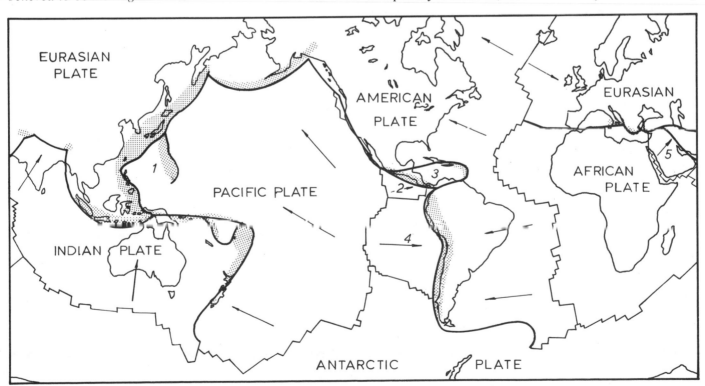

EURASIAN PLATE

AMERICAN PLATE

EURASIAN

AFRICAN PLATE

PACIFIC PLATE

INDIAN PLATE

ANTARCTIC PLATE

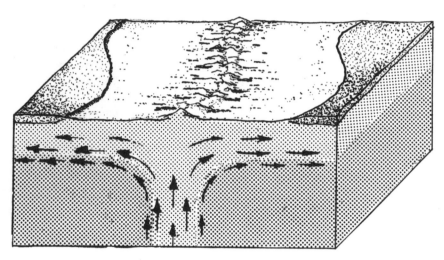

Fig. 54: A spreading ridge. Rising convection currents produce vulcanism along the mid-oceanic ridges, adding material to the edges of the lithospheric plates that make up the sea floor, and driving them apart.

occupy the relative positions that have been described. The minor differences betweeen island arcs and active margins are adequately explained as the result of differences in the more superficial parts of the structure.

If we consider the number of earthquakes that occur at different depths we find that about two thirds of them are shallow, and that

Fig. 55: Attenuation in a subduction zone. Two seismograms of a small deep earthquake on January 6, 1977 (Magnitude 4·5 and depth 189 km). The wave paths to Tuai, where the upper record was made, lie within the lithospheric slab and high frequency vibrations are recorded; but the paths to Karapiro (lower record) lie mainly in the asthenosphere, and the more rapid movements are missing.

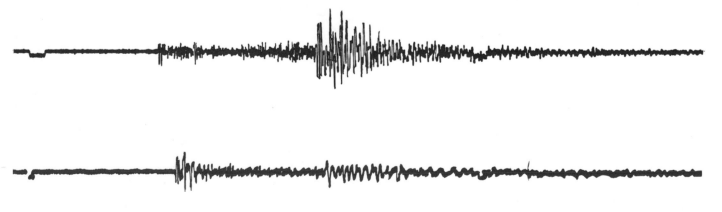

Fig. 56: Subduction beneath an island arc. Shallow earthquakes occur over the whole breadth of the arc, but deeper shocks are confined to the descending lithospheric slab.

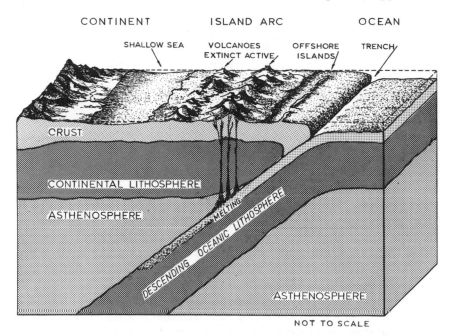

less than five percent have depths greater than 450 kilometres. At this depth there is a minimum, but an average based on world figures is unlikely to mean very much, as the detailed pattern varies greatly from place to place, and there are often complete gaps in the range. In New Zealand there are no shocks at all between 380 and 550 km, and similar gaps exist in Kamchatka and in South America.

Most really deep shocks occur around the Pacific or close to it, the deepest known shocks being at about 720 kilometres beneath the Flores Sea. The striking exception to this rule is a shock near the Straits of Gibraltar in 1954, which had a depth of 640 km. Otherwise it is rare to find depths of more than 100 km outside the Pacific. The main exceptions are in the eastern Mediterranean, particularly in the Vrancea district of Romania; and in the Hindu Kush where a vigorous grouping of shocks at about 220 km marks the western end of the Himalayas.

11 Sizes and numbers

It is shaped, sir, like itself, and it is as broad as it hath breadth; it is just so high as it is, and moves with its own organs . . .

Shakespeare, *Antony and Cleopatra*

So far we have talked rather loosely of large and small earthquakes. It is of course possible to compare one with another by giving the number of people killed, or the value of the buildings destroyed, but these things are not really measures of the earthquake itself. They depend upon outside factors like the density of the population and the level of social development in the shaken region.

Maximum felt intensities depend a little more directly upon the earthquake, but even they can be upset by secondary factors. A small variation in depth produces a big change in the size of the felt area and the way the intensities are distributed, and if the epicentre lies off the coast or in rugged and inaccessible country it may be impossible to get a direct estimate of the maximum intensity. A really satisfactory measure has to sum up the total effect of the earthquake and must be easily worked out from the records of existing seismograph stations.

The way to get such a measure was found by Professor Charles Richter of the California Institute of Technology, who devised the scale of earthquake magnitudes. The *magnitude* is a measure of the total energy in the seismic waves. The number used indicates the maximum amplitude of the trace that would be recorded on a standard kind of seismograph put at a standard distance from the earthquake. The instrument chosen was a Wood-Anderson torsion seismometer with a period of 0·8 seconds, critical damping, and a magnification of 2 800, but the magnitude can be found from other instruments at other distances by fairly simple calculations.

On this scale, any earthquake with a magnitude of eight or more is a very big one indeed. The largest shocks of which we have instrumental records were the Colombia-Equador earthquake on Jan. 31, 1906, and the Sanriku earthquake in Japan in 1933, both of which reached magnitude 8·9. Judging from its felt effects the largest shock ever was the Lisbon earthquake in 1755, which might have reached 9, but there is now no way of telling for certain. The San Francisco earthquake in 1906 and the one in Alaska in 1964 reached 8·3 and 8·4 respectively, but the only New Zealand earthquake to approach magnitude 8 was the South-west Wairarapa shock in 1855. The biggest since there have been seismographs was the Hawke's Bay earthquake in 1931, with a magnitude of 7·9.

Any earthquake much above magnitude 7 can be a major disaster if it happens near a populated area, particularly if it is in a part of the world where the buildings are poor. A magnitude 5 shock can damage chimneys and plaster, and break goods stacked up in window displays. Most of the small felt shocks in New Zealand have a magnitude of at least $3\frac{1}{2}$, but in California where the shocks are shallower, earthquakes of magnitude $2\frac{1}{2}$ are often reported. It is unusual for shocks smaller than magnitude 2 to be felt anywhere.

The size of the smallest shock possible is not easy to determine, but a value not far below magnitude 0 seems likely. Magnitude 0 is just a number on a scale; it doesn't mean that there is no energy in a shock that size, any more than a thermometer reading of $0°C$ implies that there is no heat left in the bulb. For very tiny earthquakes we use minus magnitudes, just as we use temperatures below zero when it gets sufficiently cold. No matter how big or how small an earthquake is, it can be assigned a magnitude. Journalists who write of the Richter scale 'of 12 degrees' are probably confusing magnitude with intensity, and those who write of the 'open-ended Richter scale' are stating the obvious. They never seem to find it necessary to point out that our scales of mass, length, time, temperature, and electric power are also 'open-ended'.

It is important to stress the difference between the total energies given on the magnitude scale, and the felt intensities of the modified Mercalli, MSK, and Rossi-Forel scales. A shock has different intensities in different places – as many intensities as there are observers – but it has only one magnitude, even if the estimates of it made by different observatories disagree. Newspaper, radio, and television reporters the world over seem desparately anxious to keep the public confused about this, their usual method being to substitute the word 'force' for magnitude and intensity alike, apparently considering the proper terms too technical for their readers. A more subtle gambit is to insert the words 'on the Richter scale' after any unqualified number in the original report. It is a great pity that so many reporters think that their duty is done when they have obtained a number from the nearest observatory. The earlier generation of newsmen who printed homely descriptions of the happenings in their neighborhood have left stories of permanent scientific value.

Having berated journalists for confusing the public about the magnitude scale, the seismologist must also admit to a degree of guilt. The original magnitude scale, as we have seen, depended upon the records of a Wood-Anderson seismograph. In California and New Zealand, where there were networks of these instruments, it came into general use almost at once, but in other parts of the world different instruments were in use, and the Wood-Anderson ceases to be useful for shocks at distances beyond about 1 000 kilometres. It was natural that attempts should be made to apply the scale to the teleseisms recorded on long-period instruments.

The first result was a magnitude scale that depended upon surface-waves. It was intended to give the same numbers as the original scale, but closer study showed that there were small differences. To distinguish the two scales, seismologists now call the original local magnitudes M_L and the surface-wave magnitudes M_S. The differences are not serious for large shocks, but below magnitude 5 the values obtained from distant records may be as much as half a magnitude too low.

There are two difficulties facing a magnitude scale based on surface-waves. The first is that deep-focus shocks do not generate them, and the second is that their amplitudes are seriously reduced when the path to the recording station follows a route with complicated changes in crustal structure. In order to get round these troubles Professor Gutenberg suggested using a quantity he called the 'unified magnitude', which depended upon the amplitude of body-waves like *P, S,* and *PP*. This turned out to involve even bigger differences from the original scale. There is reasonable agreement for shocks of magnitude 6·6, but above this the unified magnitude (usually written m or m_B) falls increasingly below the Richter magnitude, so that a shock with a unified magnitude of 8·0 would have a Richter magnitude of about 8·7. Below magnitude 5, m is slightly greater than M_L.

Unfortunately not all seismograph stations make it clear which magnitude they are reporting, and although the differences are not very important in the middle range, they can be serious in the case of large shocks that attract a great deal of public interest. The U.S. National Earthquake Information Center often quotes m, and this becomes transposed in the course of transmission by teletype. The term 'Richter magnitude' should be reserved for the original M, which will be used for all magnitudes quoted in this book, the distinction between M_S and M_L being made in the few cases where it is important.

Although the magnitude of an earthquake is related to its total energy, the relationship is not quite straightforward, for the scale is a 'logarithmic' one. Instead of its steps being equal they increase in a regular way, so that the amount of additional energy in any particular step is about 27 times that in the previous one. Thus, a magnitude six shock releases 27 times as much energy as a magnitude five, and 27 times 27, or 729 times as much as a magnitude four.

There are many more small earthquakes than big ones. Over the range of magnitudes from about 2 to 8 the number of shocks increases about eightfold for each decrease of one magnitude step. Over the whole Earth there are about twenty shocks each year that exceed magnitude 7, nearly a thousand over magnitude 5, and over 100 000 that are strong enough to be felt. Of course this trend cannot go on indefinitely. If it did we should have to put up with a continuous tremble from a succession of minute shocks, but the total number of shocks picked up by our seismographs cannot be far short of a couple of million a year.

We can be thankful that the eightfold relationship breaks down at the top end too, so that there is a limit to the size of earthquakes. The strength of the rocks sets a limit to the amount of elastic energy that can be stored. To reassure the timid that this is not mere theorizing, we can point out that if the relationship still held for very big shocks we would have a magnitude ten earthquake about every ninety years. Such a devastating event would shake the whole Earth, and we can be quite sure that nothing so catastrophic has happened in all recorded history.

If we know the magnitude and the focal depth of an earthquake we can deduce a great deal about its effects in a given place, but the uncertainties that remain can be of serious practical consequence to engineers. The same amount of energy can be released in different ways. It may have been stored in a small but highly-strained region, or it may have come from a much larger region strained to a smaller extent. This will affect the spectrum of the radiated waves, that is to say, what proportion of the energy will go into waves of any particular frequency. A highly-strained source region produces a large drop in stress and radiates a much greater proportion of waves of short period than would come from a larger source region and a smaller drop in stress. Which kind of shock we can expect will depend upon the strength of the rocks involved, and the degree to which they have been previously fractured.

Long-period records can be used to work out a quantity that supplies much of the missing information. It is called the *moment* (from the Latin *momentum,* importance), and is related to the drop in stress and the amount of movement of the fault. A comparison of the magnitude and the moment of a shock reveals whether a high or a low stress-drop was involved. The volume of the source, the displacement of the fault, the magnitude, the moment and the drop in stress are all connected, so that if we can find any three of them, we can calculate the other two. The moment is not so easy to work out as the magnitude, but Dr S. J. Gibowicz has found a method that can be used for routine work, and the moments as well as the magnitudes of many shocks are now available.

Earthquakes do not happen at regular intervals, but they are not completely random events. If an earthquake has just occurred, the probability that there will be another in the same area is increased. To put things less formally, most big earthquakes are followed by aftershocks.

The simple elastic rebound theory does not make it at all clear why these aftershocks should occur. If the main shock releases the energy stored in the strained country, why doesn't the fault go on moving until all the strain is gone? The accumulation of enough energy to unlock the fault again after it has once stopped moving should take considerable time; yet the early aftershocks are sometimes almost as big as the main shock itself. It had often been suggested that the main shock might re-distribute the remaining stresses in the area, so as to make energy available which could not be released by the first shock itself, and that the fault, once it had been unlocked, would probably move more easily if it hadn't had time to cement up again. A few years ago, Dr Hugo Benioff, who designed the seismograph already described, made a study of the magnitude of these small shocks and their relation in time to the main shock, and has been able to put forward a much more convincing explanation. In order to understand it, we must first make a study of what happens to materials when we compress them.

Suppose we have a sample of rock in our laboratory, which can be squashed in a special hydraulic press, and some means of measuring just how much we squash it. If we apply the pressure, and leave it for a long time, measuring the change in bulk from time to time, we will get results which can be plotted on a graph like Figure 57. When the pressure is first applied, at A, the rock will immediately contract to a smaller bulk, B. If we continue to exert the same pressure, it will continue to contract for a long time afterwards, but at an ever decreasing rate. When the point C is reached, we release the pressure again. The rock recovers at once, but it does not come right back to its original size. It comes back quickly to D, so that CD represents the same amount of change as AB, and then takes its time about the rest of the recovery. This recovery process is known as 'elastic afterworking' or 'creep-strain recovery', and Benioff considers that it is responsible for aftershocks.

Elastic rebound can release only the stored energy corresponding to CD; this causes the main earthquake. But stress across the fault is immediately set up again as the elastic afterworking takes place. This energy is released in small aftershocks, for the fault can move more easily and extend further now that it has been freed by the movement causing the main shock. By adding up the energy stored in a sequence of aftershocks, and plotting it on a graph, Dr Benioff has been able to show that the creep strain recovers in exactly the way that would be expected from laboratory studies of the effect of pressure upon rocks. One very curious thing happens. In most cases, the strain is a mixture

Fig. 57: Elastic creep. When pressure is applied to a sample of rock, part of the compression occurs at once, but very slow contraction continues to take place for a long time afterwards. When the pressure is released the first part of the contraction is immediately recovered, but the rest is only very slowly released during a period of 'elastic afterworking'.

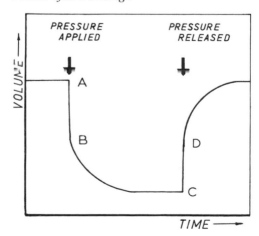

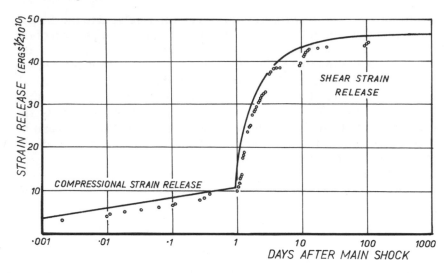

Fig. 58: An aftershock sequence. This graph shows the strain released in the series of aftershocks that followed the Cheviot earthquake on January 10th, 1951.

of compression and shear. When both types are present, no shear energy is released until all the compression has gone. Because of this, the graph is broken into two portions of different shape; and the shapes are those laboratory experiment has led us to expect. Figure 58 shows the graph for the sequence of aftershocks which followed the Cheviot earthquake of 10th January, 1951.

After a shallow earthquake in an average tectonic setting the biggest aftershock is very often a little more than a magnitude smaller than the main shock, a statement sometimes called 'Båth's Law' after the Swedish seismologist who first noticed it. The number of shocks occurring becomes less as time goes by until the aftershocks merge with the normal activity of the region, but in any group of shocks the proportion of large to small ones stays much the same. This means that the biggest aftershock may come long after the main earthquake, and it is quite possible for large shocks to happen near the end of a sequence.

The shallower an earthquake is, the more likely it is to have aftershocks. At depths greater than 100 km extended sequences are rare, but it is quite common for deep shocks to occur in pairs or groups of three of nearly equal magnitude, at intervals that range from three or four minutes or less up to several days or perhaps weeks.

Groups of shallow earthquakes can sometimes take on the character of an earthquake swarm. Swarm earthquakes are usually small but very numerous, and of much the same magnitude, so that it is not possible to pick a principal member of the group. Small swarms are fairly common in both New Zealand and Japan, but they are also known in Europe, in Tasmania, and in other places where the normal level of seismic activity is low.

12 Earth waves and sea waves

They take the rustic murmur of their bourg
For the great wave that echoes round the world.
Tennyson, *Idylls of the King*

There is a limit to the useful magnification of a seismograph. The Earth is never completely still. If our instrument is sensitive enough, we will record small continuous movements even when there is no earthquake. They are called *microseisms*. If the magnification is great enough to show the microseisms, there is no advantage in increasing it any further, as the only effect will be to confuse the record. Microseisms are very regular in period, generally in the range from four to six seconds, although there are others of shorter period which can be quite troublesome to some seismographs. Their amplitude is not constant, but changes from day to day. Occasionally violent 'microseism storms' occur (Figure 59) when they become so large as to make the records unreadable.

Some microseisms, especially the short period ones, are probably due to human activity. If the recording station is near a town, the short period vibrations will largely disappear at night when heavy machinery in the factories is stopped, and the amount of traffic falls. We can get away from these disturbances to some extent by putting the recorders in suitable places, but there are still natural microseisms to be dealt with. It has long been known that they are less troublesome inland than near a coast, but the exact way in which the earth waves and the water waves are connected has only recently come to be understood.

When there are long straight coasts or lines of cliffs, it has been suggested, the constant breaking of the surf could generate waves in the ground, and be recorded as microseisms. There is no doubt that some microseisms do originate in this way, but when an attempt was made to track down the source of others, it was found to lie far out to sea.

During the Second World War special networks of seismographs, known as tripartite stations, were set up on the islands of the Caribbean Sea in the hope that the microseisms they recorded would turn out to have a close connection with major weather disturbances. It was found that they had their origin at the centre of intense meteorological systems such as tropical cyclones, and that the specially designed seismographs could be used to follow the movement of the storms. After further study it was found that ocean waves set up by the storm exert a kind of pumping action on the sea bottom, and communicate their energy to the Earth. Once started, these trains of waves will travel many thousands of kilometres, but suitable equipment will usually enable the various separate sources to be distinguished.

Although the method showed promise, seismographs for recording microseisms have not become a regular part of the weather forecaster's equipment. Some further research into North Atlantic storms was carried out in Denmark, and the Royal Observatory in Hong Kong has found the microseisms recorded on its standard instruments of some value in following typhoons, but radar and satellite techniques seem destined to drive the seismologist from the field of storm warning.

In addition to these storm microseisms, which have periods in the range from four to six seconds, and the artificial machinery and traffic vibrations of a second period or less, there are other short-period movements which result from quite local meteorological conditions. Chief among these are rain microseisms and frost microseisms, whose names are sufficiently self-explanatory.

Microseisms are for the most part a mixture of the different types of surface wave, and although their main origin appears to be linked with storms over the ocean and a few great lakes, there is only a small decrease in their amplitude as we travel inland. They can still be recorded in such places as the centre of the North American continent, and at the Soviet stations in Central Asia. It is quite possible that the presence of the low-velocity channel in the crust may play some part in the fact that they can be efficiently transmitted over such vast distances.

Now that meteorologists have spurned the microseism, the seismologist is likely to resume his traditional view that microseisms are nothing but a nuisance. They certainly make it very difficult to find good recording sites on small islands. New Zealand seismologists with a responsibility for much of the South-West

Fig. 59: A microseism storm. A section of a record made at Christchurch on a Galitzin seismograph. Each line covers a period of about 7 minutes, and successive traces are half an hour apart. The increase in microseism level was associated with the passage of a meteorological front.

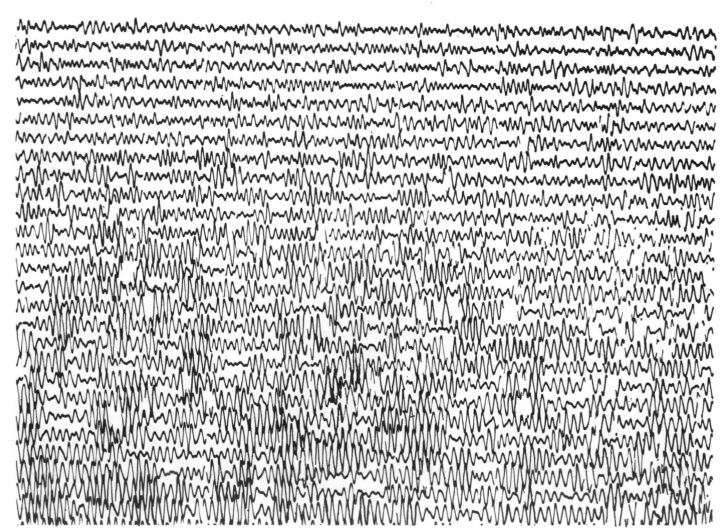

Plate 31: Tsunami damage. The great Alaskan earthquake in 1964 created a wave 12 metres high, devastating buildings, docks, and railway yards along the shores of Prince William Sound.

Pacific and a country that contains no place more than sixty or seventy kilometres from the sea look with some envy at the quiet stations at Charters Towers in Queensland and Chieng Mai in northern Thailand, whose instruments run at several hundred times the sensitivity of their own. At Scott Base, beset by Antarctic storms for part of the year, the magnification can be raised when the ocean freezes over for the long polar night.

The best known link between earthquake waves and the waves of the sea is the *tsunami* or seismic sea-wave that can follow a large earthquake under the sea. Tsunamis are popularly known as 'tidal waves', but they have nothing to do with tides, and as there *is* such a thing as a tidal wave it is better not to run the risk of increasing the confusion. The Japanese word tsunami, which is now in fairly wide use, really means 'harbour wave'. Since the effects of seismic sea-waves are frequently most severe in narrow estuaries and bays the term is both appropriate and convenient.

The way in which a tsunami is started is not completely understood. It is clear that water must be displaced when there is faulting, slumping, or uplift of the sea-bed, but Professor Gutenberg has established a number of cases in which the epicentre of the shock was clearly on land, and it seems that the passage of surface-waves across a shallow continental shelf or perhaps along a submarine canyon can sometimes start a sea-wave.

Earthquakes can also set up wave movements in ponds and lakes. The water in a lake or an enclosed arm of the sea has a natural tendency to 'slop' at some particular frequency that depends on its size and depth. If this frequency coincides with that of the earthquake waves the water will resonate, and the waves will be magnified as if by a seismograph. These oscillations are called *seiches*, and they may be set up by the wind and other causes besides earthquakes. The passage of a tsunami or a large storm wave past the entrance to an enclosed harbour has sometimes set the water inside it into seiche oscillation.

The very largest earthquakes seem to be particularly effective in generating seiches, possibly because the very long-period waves still have an appreciable amplitude at distances far beyond that to which the shock can be felt. After the great Lisbon earthquake in 1755 seiches were reported from France, Italy, Holland, Switzerland, England, and even from Norway and Sweden, some 2 800 kilometres from the epicentre. After the Assam earthquake in 1950 there were oscillations recorded on the depth gauges of several English reservoirs, and also observations in Scandinavia. It is also on record that a seiche caused by an earthquake in the Aleutians put a sudden and undignified end to a formal gathering beside a swimming pool in Texas.

Tsunamis can be extremely destructive, and some of the stories told about them are so alarming that it is not easy to separate fact from fiction, but their destructive power is not apparent until they reach a coast. In deep water the waves are extremely wide from crest to crest, so that they cannot be detected by shipping even when they are several metres high. Their speed depends upon the depth of the water, and when shallow water is reached the wave is abruptly slowed down, so that the front piles up and breaks with tremendous force, particularly if it is confined within an estuary or a narrow bay. Even a wave only one or two metres high can damage small vessels moored in shallow water by bumping them on the bottom, and can be powerful enough to destroy boatsheds and coastal roads and embankments (Plates 31, 32, 33).

Once a tsunami has been started it can travel for many thousands of kilometres with little diminution in size. Tsunamis from South

Plate 32: Tsunami damage. All that remained of Hawaiian beach houses and coconut palms after they had been struck by a tsunami 7 metres high in 1975.

Plate 33: A tsunami wave. The tsunami that followed the Niigata earthquake carried these boats against the bridge at Iwafune, and is still flowing up the river.

American earthquakes have proved troublesome in New Zealand, Japan, and Hawaii, which has also been affected by tsunamis from Japan and from the Aleutians.

Very large tsunamis are fortunately rare, but around the Pacific Ocean they are frequent enough to pose a serious problem, and a regular warning system has been organized. This has its headquarters in Hawaii and depends upon the cooperation of major seismograph and tide-gauge stations in many countries. Stations that record an earthquake that could possibly have generated a tsunami radio sufficient data for Hawaii to determine the epicentre, and if it proves to be a submarine earthquake to ask the nearest tide-gauge stations to watch for abnormal movements of sea level. Although the speed of a tsunami can reach more than 600 kilometres an hour in the open ocean, there is still time for many places to get an estimate of the arrival time and probable size of the wave, so that shipping and people in coastal areas can be warned and if necessary evacuated.

The tsunamis that affect Hawaii most often come from the Aleutians, and warning is given by the tide-gauges on the Alaskan and Canadian coasts, but in the Aleutians themselves and in Japan the earthquakes responsible are often too close to allow much time. However, the Japanese have arranged for urgent telegraph messages to be passed from any place that is affected to the places the wave has not yet reached. The Soviet authorities operate a similar system in Sakhalin and Kamchatka.

The greatest seismic sea-wave on record is perhaps not strictly a tsunami. It occurred at Lituya Bay in Alaska in 1958. Here a magnitude eight earthquake set off a great landslide that fell into the bay and shot one wave over an opposite spur, removing the forest to a height of over 500 metres, and sent another down the bay to break at a height of 290 metres on the far shore. Two fishing vessels were sunk with the loss of two lives, and some ten square kilometres of forest were destroyed. There have been some other large waves started by landslides, but no earthquake has been involved. It appears that the record for a normal tsunami is still held by the wave that struck Cape Lopatka, at the southern tip of Kamchatka, in 1737, breaking at a height of 70 metres.

Not all countries with earthquakes off their coasts have a tsunami problem. Something in the contour of the sea-bottom or the mechanism of the shocks prevents the generation of a wave. This is true of New Zealand. The magnitude eight South-West Wairarapa earthquake in 1855 raised a long stretch of coast and disrupted tidal patterns in Cook Strait, but does not seem to have caused a large wave. The only clear instance of a locally generated tsunami was in 1947 when the wave that followed a moderately large shock off East Cape washed away the bridges over small streams along the coast to the south, and damaged a small seaside hotel.

Waves of distant origin are more often observed. Early in 1976 a shock near Raoul Island in the Kermadecs generated a wave that gave the many pleasure-craft in the bays of the Northland peninsula some anxious moments. Fortunately the earthquakes of the Kermadec region, like those nearer to New Zealand, do not often cause tsunamis, even though large shocks are fairly frequent. The most troublesome waves have come from Chile. In 1868 waves from a Chilean earthquake reached New Zealand with sufficient force to attract general attention in the ports on both coasts, and there was a drowning in the Chatham Islands.

Similar surges followed another Chilean shock in 1960, and disrupted shipping movements in the port of Lyttelton for some hours. Upsetting as this was, it was much less serious than the effects of the same tsunami in more distant parts of the Pacific, such as Japan, where it attained destructive force. The difference can be explained by the presence of the Campbell Plateau, a large area of comparatively shallow water to the south-east of the South Island. When the wave reaches the outer edge of this, it is forced to slow down and a large part of its energy is dissipated before it reaches the New Zealand coast.

Sometimes the sea gives warning of the approach of a tsunami by withdrawing before the wave arrives. When this happens, it is wise to make for high ground at once, but curiosity frequently gets the better of people and leads them to explore the area of sea-bed that has been uncovered. This withdrawal does not always take place, and is certainly not a reliable enough effect to be used as the basis of a warning system.

One or more secondary waves may follow, at intervals of an hour or more, and the disturbance can upset normal tidal patterns for some days.

Japanese observers have sometimes recorded flashes of light at sea before the arrival of a tsunami. There is no reason to doubt the reports, and it has been suggested that they might be caused by disturbance of the small marine organisms that make the wake of a ship so luminous in tropical waters. Whatever the truth of this, it still affords no basis for any kind of practical warning.

The frequency with which tsunamis occur is hard to determine. The only lists that have been published are obviously very incomplete, and can often offer only a guess at the position of the epicentre responsible. Sizes are seldom given, and do not mean very much unless they are measured on an open coast or in deep water. Even small islands may sometimes cause a large 'shadow' and protect the places on the far side quite effectively. It would seem that the Pacific has one or two a year, but that the majority of them are quite small.

13 Earthquakes and volcanoes

BANQUO: The earth hath bubbles, as the water has,
      And these are of them.
                Shakespeare, *Macbeth*

Many people associate earthquakes and volcanoes. In New Zealand we have plenty of both; but the earthquakes do not happen just because there are volcanoes in the Tongariro National Park and hot springs at Whakarewarewa. Volcanoes and earthquakes are different outcomes of the same underlying geological processes, and there is therefore a broad similarity between the world pattern of earthquake belts and the pattern of active volcanoes.

When we discussed the interior of the Earth we saw that it was hot, but that there was no world-wide layer of molten lava just below the surface, waiting to pour from any convenient hole. The enormous pressure of the overlying rocks effectively prevents melting. Nevertheless, there are localized exceptions. The circulating convection currents in the mantle can create 'hot-spots' beneath the oceanic ridges, or the surface material being carried downwards at an ocean trench or a continental margin may become molten during the process of re-absorption. The molten material formed in this way is called *magma*, and is able to force its passage through cracks and along lines of weakness in the solid material.

Usually it does this by a comparatively unspectacular process known as *intrusion*. The magma, having forced itself a certain distance through the crack, or along the interface between strata, solidifies to form a *dyke* or a *sill* of igneous rock. If the conditions are suitable, and the magma behaves in a less controlled manner, a volcano may result.

Eight or nine hundred of the world's volcanoes can be considered active, but there are often long periods of quiescence, and the school geography book's distinction between active, dormant, and extinct volcanoes is often hard to make. At any one time, only a few of them are in eruption, no more than twenty or thirty in a typical year.

A volcano starts as a vent through which escaping gases and ash can reach the surface. Scoria, pumice, ash, and so on piles up around the vent, and usually builds up the typical cone-shaped mountain. The rate of growth of the cone is often extremely rapid. At Parícutin in Mexico the local farmers knew of a hole in a paddock that kept reappearing whenever they filled it in, so they gave up and left it to form a small pit. One afternoon in February 1943, the pit cracked across and began to send up a small column of greyish ash. Twenty-four hours later, lava and scoria were coming out and piling into a cone fifty metres high. By June it had reached the village three kilometres away, by September it had destroyed it, and the lava covered some twenty-five square kilometres. After two years, the cone was five hundred metres high, but the eruption had begun to slacken, and nine years after it started, it stopped. This is one of the few cases in which a volcano has been studied right from birth.

It is usual to distinguish between the molten magma still within the Earth and the lavas that issue at the surface, losing dissolved gas and steam before they cool and solidify. The streams of molten lava and the explosions of burning gas are often spectacular, particularly at night, but the temperature of the molten material is seldom more than about 1 200° C. This is only just sufficient to keep it molten, an indication that we are dealing with a comparatively superficial process.

Lavas differ greatly in chemical composition, the two extremes being represented by the very liquid basaltic lavas that erupt along the mid-oceanic ridges to form the sea floor, and by the acid andesitic lavas that come from the volcanoes of the island arcs and continental margins. Most people regard the graceful cones of Fujiyama, Egmont, or Mayon as the typical shape of a volcano (Plate 34), but this is true only of those emitting fairly stiff andesitic lavas. Basaltic volcanoes, like Mauna Loa in Hawaii, or Kilimanjaro in northern Tanzania are gently dome-shaped, like an inverted saucer. In some cases, basaltic lavas may be so liquid that they do little more than fill the hollows in the ground, but repeated eruptions of this kind from many neighbouring fissures can build up great plateaus, like the Deccan Plateau in India, consisting in all of some seven hundred thousand cubic kilometres of erupted material.

Plate 34: An andesitic cone. Merapi volcano in central Java, during the eruption in 1961. Lava is spilling from the left-hand side of the crater.

Plate 35: A vulcanian eruption. Mt Ngauruhoe, in the central North Island, during the eruption in 1975. This explosion on February 19 was accompanied by a small earthquake of magnitude 3·4. The large blocks that are being hurled within the cauliflower cloud are about twenty metres across.

Plate 36: A nuée ardente. During the eruption of Merapi in 1961 a nuée cut this broad path through the jungle on its lower slopes for a distance of several kilometres, and left it covered in thick white ash.

Plate 37: A nuée ardente. One of several villages at the foot of Merapi destroyed by the nuée in 1961. This one stood at the side of the path and did not experience its full force.

The potential destructiveness of a volcano depends to a great degree upon the kind of lava it habitually emits, and it is possible to classify volcanoes by their usual manner of eruption, but most of them change their habits in the course of time. The quietest type is the Hawaiian eruption, which is seldom violent. Instead, the volcano prefers to pour out quantities of very liquid basalt, building up a mound of scoria close to its vent.

In the next type, like Stromboli, the lava is still basaltic in composition, but much less liquid, and is often thrown up in gas fountains and small explosions. The Vulcanian type, named after the original Vulcano, also in the Lipari Islands off the coast of Italy, has an even stiffer type of lava, composed of more acid rock which tends to harden inside the crater. Volcanoes of this type often send up great clouds of fine ash in a 'cauliflower' cloud, and the wind disperses the material over very wide areas (Plate 35). In New Zealand there are thick deposits of ash from ancient eruptions of this type all over the Tongariro-Taupo region in the centre of the North Island. The last type of volcano, the Peléean, is named after Mont Pelée in Martinique, the scene of a disastrous eruption which destroyed the town of St. Pierre in 1902. These volcanoes send out what are called *nuées ardentes* — dense clouds of gases and incandescent material which tumble over the edge of the crater and roll swiftly down the slope (Plates 36, 37). The lava in these volcanoes is so stiff that it can form an apparently solid plug in the mouth of the vent. Sometimes the pressure underneath forces the plug high into the air to form a 'spine'. The material is soft, and soon erodes away when exposed to wind and weather. The spine of Mont Pelée was originally a most impressive affair several hundred metres in height.

Between eruptions many craters fill with the water that drains from the surrounding slopes, and a crater lake is formed. The crater wall is often little more than a pile of ash in which a breach can easily be formed, either by further volcanic action, or because the wall can no longer support the growing weight of water behind it. When this happens a turbulent mass of ash, bolders, mud, and snow may be carried down the mountain side at great speed. This is called a *lahar*, or volcanic mudflow (Plate 38). New Zealand's worst railway disaster occurred when a lahar from the Ruapehu crater lake carried away a bridge over the Whangaehu River in the Tongariro National Park. All through the park there are rocky mounds composed of material deposited by past lahars. A crater lake is not essential to the creation of lahars. In Indonesia there have been instances where heavy rainfall has been sufficient to start serious mudflows.

The explosions that accompany a violent eruption can send waves through the Earth that can be recorded on seismographs and may even be felt as earthquakes. Most of these explosions take place either in the crater or in the vent of the volcano, but sometimes there are underground explosions or movements of magma that can truly be called volcanic earthquakes. Compared with the tectonic earthquakes to which most of this book is devoted volcanic shocks are usually very minor affairs. This is because most of the energy of the explosion goes into the air as a sound wave rather than into the ground, and because the comparatively weak rocks fracture before very large pressures or strains can build up.

When the air-wave from a great eruption strikes a building, the shaking can be mistaken for an earthquake. Waves of this kind can travel very great distances. Sounds from the great eruption of Krakatoa in 1883 were heard from Sri Lanka and northern Thailand to Alice Springs in central Australia. Big noises are not always heard at shorter distances, as the sound is carried more effectively in the high atmosphere, and there is a zone of silence around the volcano itself. Explosions of Ngauruhoe and Ruapehu that were not heard in the National Park area have been reported from Taranaki and from Wellington suburbs over two hundred kilometres away.

In most countries where there are dangerous volcanoes close to centres of population, the authorities have organized some kind of a watch for impending eruptions. Unfortunately volcanoes are so individual in their habits that it is often difficult to know what to watch for. It is usual to install a seismograph, but many eruptions are well advanced before the first earthquakes are recorded. Other indications, like increasing ground tilts, or changes in the temperature of hot springs and crater lakes are often better pointers to a coming eruption.

Volcanic earthquakes and crater explosions are most frequent when the volcano is visibly active. When the activity is on the increase nearby seismographs show a kind of movement known as *volcanic*

Plate 38: A lahar. Ash from beside the crater lake of Mt Ruapehu swept down the mountainside, cutting a path through the snowfield.

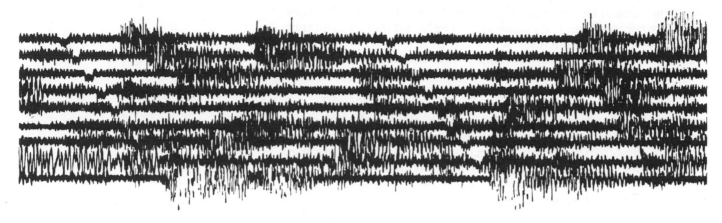

Fig. 60: Volcanic tremor. Explosions and shallow earthquakes against a background of volcanic tremor, recorded on Raoul Island during the 1964 eruption.

tremor. This takes the form of very rapid vibrations, generally less than half a second in period. When tremor first appears, it lasts only for an hour or two at a time, but as the activity of the mountain increases, it becomes more violent, and increases in amplitude. When the eruption is at its height, it is much less regular in appearance, not so much because the period changes, but because the vibration keeps changing phase; that is to say, it breaks off in the middle of a movement, and begins all over again. Hawaiian volcanologists have suggested that the tremor may be caused by molten lava rushing past the edges of projecting underground strata, making them vibrate like the reeds of a mouth-organ. Shimozuru has found that the tremor is a mixture of body-waves and surface-waves, and that the more deep-seated its origin is, the longer its period becomes. He suggests that as the magma releases its gas to become lava, rhythmical oscillations of the lava can be set up in the underground conduits and in the vent of the volcano, and these generate the tremor.

The seismogram shown in Figure 60 was obtained by the New Zealand expedition to Raoul Island in the Kermadec group during an eruption at the end of 1964. Explosions in the crater and shallow earthquakes centred beneath Denham Bay appear against a background of volcanic tremor many times the amplitude of the normal microseisms, and of much shorter period.

Regions in which there are active or recently extinct volcanoes, like parts of Japan and the North Island of New Zealand, often experience earthquake swarms. These are outbreaks of numerous small to moderate earthquakes, no one of which can be clearly identified as the main member of the group. From May to December 1922 the small township of Taupo experienced an outbreak that has been quoted in several textbooks as a typical swarm. There were many hundred shocks, the largest of which caused minor damage, surface faulting was observed a few kilometres to the west, and a stretch of the lake shore subsided about two metres.

In 1922 this area was sparsely populated, and there were no seismographs capable of recording local shocks. It now seems probable that a moderate earthquake was responsible for the faulting, and that what followed was a normal but unusually vigorous sequence of aftershocks. At the end of 1964, however, the same district experienced a more typical swarm. There is now a permanent seismograph station at the Wairakei geothermal electric power station, a few kilometres to the north, and it was possible to move portable recorders to the district. In normal periods the Wairakei seismograph records about five close shocks a month. At the peak of the swarm it recorded over nine hundred in one day. The foci turned out to lie under the western part of the Lake, not far from the bays where the fault traces appeared in 1922, but there was no sign of renewed fault movement.

Public opinion tended to blame the occurrence upon the exploitation of geothermal steam, but no changes in the quantity or the quality of the steam were noticed by the power-station staff, and none of the field investigators who regularly measure spring and bore-hole temperatures reported anything abnormal. Few true swarms have been reported from non-volcanic regions, but their link with volcanic activity is at best indirect, and it cannot be claimed that the mechanism that produces them is properly understood.

We saw when discussing island arcs that the earthquakes directly beneath active volcanoes were often at a depth of about 150 kilometres. The French volcanologist Claude Blot has suggested that deeper earthquakes over a wider area may also be involved in the eruptive process, pointing to a number of sequences that begin with a deep earthquake, continue with shocks that get shallower and closer to a volcano, and end with a volcanic eruption. Although his statistics are superior to those commonly employed in political argument, they have not been good enough to convince most geophysicists and his hypothesis at present remains an interesting suggestion.

Dr Trevor Hatherton of the New Zealand Geophysics Division and his Californian colleague Dr W. R. Dickinson have discovered an interesting relationship between the depths of the earthquakes under andesitic volcanoes and the amount of potash present in their lavas, which increases as the earthquakes become deeper. This kind of analysis should give us additional information about the physical as well as the chemical properties of the material at the depths at which melting occurs.

The subject of volcanism is wide enough for a book in its own right, and only an outline can find a place in a book about earthquakes, so we shall say nothing of hot springs, boiling mud-pools, or geysers. Readers who want to know more will find them discussed in books on geology, some of which are listed in the Appendix.

14 Earthquake prediction

CASSANDRA . . . Destroyed again, and this time utterly!
CHORUS: She seems about to predict her own misfortunes . . .
Of your prophetic fame we have heard before,
But in this matter, prophets are not required.
Aeschylus, *The Agamemnon*

Astronomers can predict eclipses and other spectacular conjunctions of the heavenly bodies with an accuracy that is in no small degree responsible for the respect with which their more dubious speculations are treated. The meteorologist's predictions, if less reliable, are accurate enough to exact a measure of confidence. The seismologist, who issues no warnings, is frequently chided for neglect, and if he protests that prediction is none of his business, he is left in no doubt that most people think that it should be.

At first sight, it would seem that an earthquake prediction would need the astronomer's kind of accuracy before it was of any use at all. A prediction that there will be a disastrous earthquake in California on 5th November, or that Manila will have a big earthquake within the next few years, even if correct, affords little basis for practical action. It is not possible to evacuate all California, or even to bring business to a standstill.

After New Zealand's disastrous Hawke's Bay earthquake in 1931, when more than 250 of the inhabitants of Napier and Hastings were killed, a local seer claimed that he had 'correctly' predicted it. In fact, he had placed the centre south of Hawke's Bay, in the Wairarapa, but a distance of a hundred and fifty kilometres is little hindrance to a determined prophet. Had the authorities believed his warning, it is not improbable that the inhabitants of Masterton, the chief township of the Wairarapa, would have been evacuated to Napier or Hastings to become additional casualties. As it was, they escaped with a severe shaking.

Prediction of individual earthquakes will need to specify the time, place, and size of the shock with high accuracy, or at the very least provide a good indication of the degree of uncertainty involved, or they will do more harm than good.

It is not only the soothsayer whose predictions can pose problems for the civil authorities. Quite recently an English academic (not a seismologist) considered that he had found a method of predicting earthquakes, and decided to tell the press. He added that he was expecting a large one in New Zealand. The British press passed the news on by cable. Fortunately their New Zealand colleagues decided to get expert comment before printing the story, and only very timid souls were upset. New Zealand's official displeasure was conveyed to the prophet, who is understood to have muttered darkly about interference with academic freedom.

Even it if were precise, the prediction of an individual earthquake could bring only problems to a community whose buildings had not been designed to withstand it. Something might be done to minimize casualties, but knowledge of the impending losses would result in social and economic confusion. This would be even worse if false predictions could be issued maliciously. Fortunately one useful kind

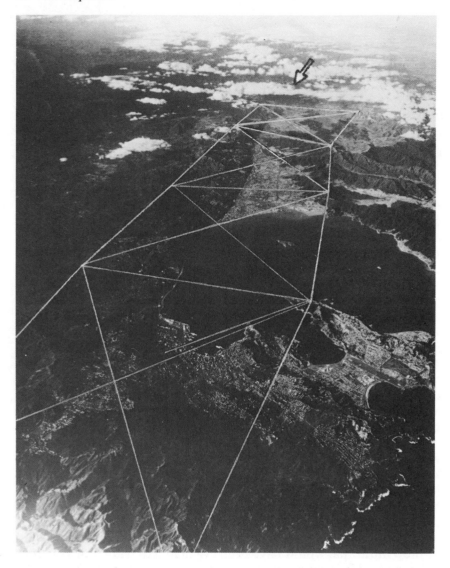

Plate 39: Regional strain. Repeated surveys of this network of triangles across the Wellington Fault are being undertaken in order to keep track of the accumulation of regional strain which could lead to an earthquake. Similar work is being undertaken near many active faults. The fault follows the western (left hand) side of the harbour and the Hutt Valley beyond it to the north.

of prediction is possible. The statement that 'During the next 100 years, this bridge will have to withstand ten shocks of intensity seven or more' is quite useful to the design engineer. Seismologists have concentrated upon making reliable statements of this kind, to be embodied in building codes and zoning provisions, but this does not mean that they have given up hope of making more precise forecasts.

Early seismologists spent much time looking for regular periodicities in the times at which earthquakes occurred, but without success. As the elastic rebound theory gained acceptance it became clear that the build-up of the forces responsible for the shock was a slow process, and that what should be looked for was some form of 'trigger' that determined the exact instant at which the stored energy would be released. If no trigger were involved, exact prediction would be very difficult indeed. We should need to know the exact dimensions of the fault, the strength of the rocks that surrounded it, the roughness of the surface, how much force was pressing the faces together, and many other uncertain quantities before we could have any hope of estimating the amount of strain needed to start it slipping.

It is a simpler matter to detect the accumulation of strain. Accurate surveys repeated at intervals should reveal whether a tract of country is being deformed or not. These have become much simpler and cheaper since radar instruments for the precise measurement of distance supplanted the older methods of triangulation with a theodolite. Surveys for this purpose are now being made regularly in California, Japan, and New Zealand (Plates 39, 40). As the Japanese seismologist Suyehiro pointed out to a meeting of American engineers many years ago, it is no use worrying about the trigger being pulled until you know whether the gun is loaded, particularly as the earthquake-gun will go off without the trigger being pulled when the charge in it has grown large enough.

Changes in pressure have always been considered among the more likely triggers. Tidal loading and a variety of meterological factors come under this heading. Some investigators have looked at planetary attractions, but these are so much smaller than other variable forces at work that they are unlikely to have the deciding effect. Nevertheless, if an earthquake is just on the point of happening, a very small effect indeed could determine its precise instant.

Signs of triggering are possibly present during aftershock sequences and swarms, when the conditions for another earthquake can be considered more than usually favourable. For example, R. C. Hayes found that the aftershocks of a Cook Strait earthquake in early 1950 tended to be more frequent when the tide was falling and the barometer lower than normal. Similar observations have been made in Japan. In the Himalayas and in the Mississippi Basin it has been reported that the frequency of small tremors is linked to flood conditions, a high rate of change in the intensity of the flood being likely to trigger off minor swarms.

Dr T. H. Heaton of the California Institute of Technology points out that what probably matters is the relative rates of change of the triggering and the tectonic stresses. The gravitational pulls of the Moon and Sun affect not only the water in the oceans but the solid body of the Earth, raising a tide that can change its radius by as much as forty centimetres. This creates elastic strains that change much more rapidly than the slowly accumulating tectonic strain released in

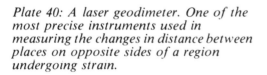

Plate 40: A laser geodimeter. One of the most precise instruments used in measuring the changes in distance between places on opposite sides of a region undergoing strain.

an earthquake. Whether the tidal change is big enough to act as a trigger should depend upon the orientation of the fault. He examined 107 shocks in which this was known and found that large shocks within the crust appeared to be triggered if the fault displacement was vertical or oblique, but not if it was transcurrent. This was what his mathematical analysis had suggested. Deep shocks did not appear to be triggered. He does not think that shocks smaller than magnitude 4 should be triggered, as the rate of change of the other forces involved would, on our present theories, be greater than that of the trigger. So far he has not been able to check whether this suggestion is true.

Most countries have some popular tradition of 'earthquake weather'. In his *French Revolution* Carlyle remarks that 'Hope ushers in a revolution as earthquakes are preceded by bright weather', but most Englishmen, Shakespeare among their number, have pictured earthquakes as the fitting climax to a storm:

LENNOX: The night has been unruly: where we lay

　　　　Our chimneys were blown down . . .

　　　　. . . some say the earth was fev'rous, and did shake.

MACBETH: 'Twas a rough night.

LENNOX: My young remembrance cannot parallel a fellow to it.

The Japanese consider that earthquake weather is hot and humid. Omori examined the weather conditions during eighteen major Japanese shocks spread over 530 years, and found that twelve of them happened on fine days, two on cloudy days, and four on rainy days. This tells us more about the Japanese climate than it does about the earthquakes.

The rescue operations that followed New Zealand's Hawke's Bay earthquake in 1931 were aided by an abnormally long period of fine weather, but the Murchison earthquake two years previously occurred in an equally abnormal period of storm and rain. Local folk-lore has it that earthquake weather is hot and still.

Instances are known when the sharp change in barometric pressure that accompanies the passage of a meteorological front has coincided with a local earthquake, and Richter observes that in California, minor shocks tend to increase at the beginning of the rainy season, when large air masses are shifting and the load on the Earth's surface is consequently changing. If pressure changes play any great part in triggering earthquakes we might expect shocks under the sea to depend greatly upon the tides, as the daily changes in pressure on the sea bottom as they ebb and flow are ten times greater than the changes in air pressure. Nothing of the kind has been observed.

It is widely believed that a sharp increase in the number of small earthquakes heralds the approach of a large one, but this is the exception rather than the rule. Except in the case of the shocks that precede a volcanic eruption there are seldom more than one or two foreshocks, and there is no way in which a foreshock can be distinguished from the normal minor activity until after the main event.

Japanese seismologists have observed that some large earthquakes have been preceded by abnormal tilting of the ground, and special tiltmeters were installed to study the matter more closely. Although further instances were recorded, they had no success in finding any kind of regular pattern. Tiltmeters are not easy to keep in good adjustment, and there have been few attempts to duplicate or follow up the Japanese work.

The most promising work so far began in Soviet Central Asia. For many years Soviet seismologists have made a particularly close study of the earthquakes in the Garm district of Tadzhikstan. In 1962 Kondratenko and Nersesov announced that they had found a regular pattern of changes in the speed of seismic waves that had crossed a part of the region about to have an earthquake.

Under normal circumstances the speeds of *P*- and *S*-waves through most kinds of rock have almost exactly the same ratio to one another; the *P*-wave is about 1·77 times as fast as the *S*. If, however, the rocks are under very great strain the ratio falls, until when they are just at the point of breaking it is a little above 1·5.

The Russians kept a watch on the waves from the small earthquakes that are always occurring in the district and found that when they had passed through an area about to have a larger earthquake their velocities were abnormal. Low velocity-ratios developed and persisted for quite long periods, and just before an earthquake they suddenly returned to normal. The size of the earthquake depended upon the time for which the abnormal conditions had persisted (Figure 61).

The first problem in using this effect for prediction is that the region in which abnormal velocities are found is quite small – only a few tens of kilometres even in the case of a large shock. Several methods of detection have been tried. The one used by the Russians was originally devised by the Japanese seismologist Wadati, and depends on having about a dozen or more stations at close range. If the *S*-*P* interval at each station is plotted against the time of arrival of *P*, the points lie on a straight line whose slope represents the ratio of the velocities. An alternative method, which has been tried in New

Fig. 61: Premonitory changes in velocity. The small circles represent individual measurements of the ratio between the velocities of P- and S- waves that had crossed parts of the Garm district of Soviet Central Asia in the months preceding two moderate earthquakes. In each case the ratio fell slowly some months before the shock and returned rapidly to normal just before the earthquake took place.

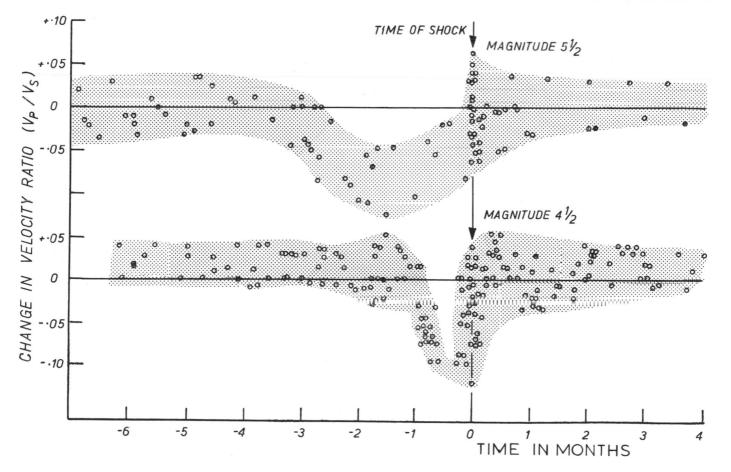

Zealand and in the U.S.A., depends upon recording the arrival of *P*-waves from distant shocks at a station actually within the region of abnormal velocity. If the region is strained, the waves arrive later than the travel-time tables suggest they should.

So far, most predictions have been made long after the event. Seismologists have looked through their records to find an earthquake close to a seismograph station, and then found that the anomaly was there beforehand. In New Zealand it was present before the Gisborne earthquake in 1966, and in California the speed of *P*-waves fell three and a half years before the San Fernando shock in 1971. Both Russian and American seismologists have been making cautious predictions in private with some success, though the shocks predicted have been small. The best publicised prediction so far was of a magnitude 7·3 earthquake in the Liaoning province of China in early 1975 (Plate 41). Reports indicate that the Chinese authorities felt sufficient confidence in the prediction to ask people to leave their homes, offering the inducement of outdoor movies! Most people complied, and although many houses were destroyed there were few casualties.

It was some time before the pioneer work of the Soviet seismologists attracted attention elsewhere. When it did, the first problem was to find out whether similar velocity changes occurred in

Plate 41: Earthquake prediction. Chinese seismologists successfully predicted the Liaoning earthquake in 1975, but although casualties could be minimized, there was no way of preventing the economic loss represented by the damage to this factory and the office building opposite.

other parts of the world, or whether they were due to some local geological peculiarity of the Garm district. Once it became clear that they were not a purely local effect, it was natural to ask why they happened. It was easy enough to understand why the velocity-ratio fell, but what caused the return to normal that seemed to be most significant in deciding the instant of the shock?

The answer that is most generally accepted was given in 1972 by Amos Nur of Stanford University. He suggested that the explanation was *dilatancy*. Dilatancy is a curious phenomenon with a curious history. It was discovered as long ago as 1886 by Osborne Reynolds, an English physicist who was looking for the properties of ether, the mysterious all-pervading medium that was then thought to be responsible for transmitting light and radio waves. He found instead that he had come upon a general property of almost every granular substance, like sand or piles of grain.

In 1972, few seismologists had heard of dilatancy, although it was familiar to engineers working in the field of soil mechanics, and in 1965 Dr F. C. Frank had published a review paper in an American journal drawing attention to its possible involvement in the mechanism of earthquakes. What is dilatancy? Suppose the grains in a heap of rock particles are packed as closely as possible, and we try to compress it further. We can compress it in the direction of our push, but it will move out in other directions to compensate. As it was already packed as tightly as possible, the only way in which it can change its shape is by dilating and occupying a bigger total volume. The odd thing is that in the process it becomes stronger, probably as a result of the increased pressure between the grains at the points of contact, and it is consequently in a condition to store still more elastic strain before it eventually collapses.

A complication arises when the pores of the dilatant material are filled with fluid. This is the case with the rocks inside the Earth. At shallow depths, ground-water is present, and farther below there will be magmatic material that can move through the pores of the more solid rock. When external pressure causes the rocks to dilate, they do so by increasing the volume of pore space, more probably by the formation of minute cracks than by rearrangement of the grains. Since the spaces that contain it are now bigger, the pressure of the pore fluid must fall, but beyond the dilatant region it will remain normal, and there will be a flow of liquid into the region until the pressure is once again equalized. As this happens the dilatant rock loses its increased strength. When the pressure of the pore fluid falls, the velocity of *P*-waves through the region also falls, returning to normal when the pressure deficiency has been made good by the influx of fluid from beyond the strained region.

We can now describe the elastic rebound process in more convincing detail. As regional strain builds up towards breaking point tiny cracks begin to form in the rocks, and they become dilatant. In the dilatant condition they become stronger and can store further strain, but while this is going on fluid from beyond the dilatant region is flowing in and weakening them once again. They are already strained beyond their normal capacity, and the rate at which they fall in strength determines the instant of failure (Figure 62).

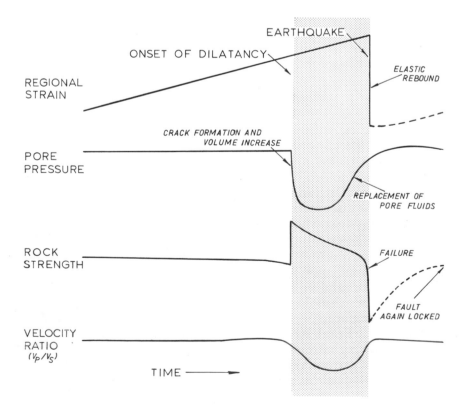

Fig. 62: *Dilatancy and earthquake mechanism. When regional strain increases sufficiently the rocks become dilatant. The pressure of the fluid in the pores falls, increasing their strength and making it possible to store more strain. As the fluid is replaced the strength of the rocks falls again, triggering an elastic rebound and producing an earthquake.*

If this dilatancy theory of earthquake mechanism is correct, keeping a watch on *P*-waves or changed velocity ratios may not be the only way to detect dangerous conditions. It may now be possible to find some pattern in the apparently erratic uplifts and tilts that Japanese seismologists have reported, and geophysical measurements of the movement of ground-water may be simpler to make than purely seismological measurements.

One method that the Russians have found promising is to measure the electrical resistance between buried electrodes several kilometres apart. As the ability of rocks to carry an electric current depends to a large extent upon the amount of pore fluid they contain, the resistance can be expected to rise when they become dilatant. By changing the spacing between the electrodes and the strength of the current it is possible to test rocks at different depths. A less obvious method that was tried in the Garm region depends upon the fact that many crustal rocks are to a greater or lesser extent radioactive. When cracks open in the rock, the area in contact with the ground-water increases, and the result is to increase the amount of radon it absorbs. This can be watched by sampling the water in deep wells, and testing it with a geiger counter in a laboratory. Before long, a number of reliable methods of detecting dilatant regions should be available.

If these methods live up to present hopes, the warnings will come in two stages. The first alert can be given when a region has been dilatant for long enough to produce a significant earthquake. The longer it is delayed, the bigger the expected shock will be, but how big a shock a given delay implies depends upon the strength of the rocks and the rate at which strain accumulates. It will therefore have to be found for each particular region, but it seems likely that there will be at least a year's warning of a shock of magnitude 7. The danger period and final alert would begin when the anomalies started their return to normal. The speed at which they do this will depend upon the porosity of the rocks and the availability of fluid. It will certainly be different in different regions, and in some places may well vary seasonally. The final warning could come only days before the shock, but indications are that the alert will be soon enough to be useful.

Professor F. F. Evison has noted a pattern of events that has preceded several earthquakes in New Zealand and California. First, there is a closely-grouped set of earthquakes of about the same magnitude that he calls the 'premonitory swarm'. This is followed by a period called the 'premonitory gap', during which there are no earthquakes in the region nearby. Eventually there is a 'main earthquake' whose size depends upon the size of the 'swarm' earthquakes and the duration of the gap. The 'swarm' is believed to attend the opening of the cracks that signal the onset of dilatancy, and the gap to last thoughout the dilatant period. The possibility of basing predictions upon this pattern is obvious, but there are difficulties in distinguishing 'premonitory swarms' from other similar groupings of earthquakes, and there have not so far been any indisputable successes. Russian and Japanese seismologists have also reported a decrease in the number of small earthquakes in the period preceding a major shock.

The discovery of changes preceding a shock by some days gives some support to the popular belief that birds and animals can sense that an earthquake is imminent. There is no difficulty in explaining periods of warning of half a minute or so. Many creatures are more sensitive to sound and vibration than humans are, and at least some instances of apparent prescience are due to the animal's response to the weak P-wave of a shock in which humans could feel only the S.

It is much harder to verify and explain the persistent reports of animals being disturbed for a day or more before the shock, and most long-period predictions by animals remain open to question. It now seems possible that the reports of abnormal behaviour of sheep and cattle some 15 minutes before the Inangahua earthquake in 1968 and other similar reports are accounts of animal response to some preliminary ground deformations that were not perceptible to humans. There were no instrumentally recorded foreshocks.

Similar stories are told of the sensitivity of fish, which can be seriously affected by the passage of strong P-waves through the water. Numbers of dead fish apparently killed by submarine concussion have been observed after many large earthquakes from the South-West Wairarapa shock in 1855 to the Alaskan earthquake in 1964.

Professor Tsuneji Rikitake, Director of the Earthquake Research Institute of the University of Tokyo, has drawn attention to a curious consistency in the length of warning that we can expect different kinds of precursory signs to give. It depends upon the magnitude of the coming shock, and applies to changes in wave-velocity, earth currents, radon content of ground-water, changes in the rate of fault creep, and a number of other possible indicators. For a shock of magnitude 3 we can expect only about one day's warning, but for one of magnitude 4 the time is about 10 days. For a magnitude 8 shock we would have 25 or 30 years in which to prepare. The fact that a number of different indicators all give similar results raises hopes that a practical method of prediction is at last in sight.

The problem of what to do with a prediction remains. Few seismologists would feel that their duty had been done when they had telegraphed their warning to the Prime Minister, and many of them are trying to interest sociologists in finding out what the public response to a prediction is likely to be. The ordinary citizen is unlikely to welcome the news that his house is likely to fall down in an hour or two, but that the City Council is turning on free movies in the town square.

There can be little doubt that the social and economic consequences of issuing a prediction will be serious, but exactly what is likely to happen depends a great deal upon the nature of the prediction. At present, it looks as if the seismologist will first issue a long-term warning, perhaps some years in advance, and then gradually make the time and place of the shock and its probable magnitude more and more definite as the time of the shock gets nearer. Once such a prediction is published, insurance and property values are likely to be seriously upset, there may be a movement of population, new constructional projects are likely to be postponed, and there may be unemployment among people engaged in painting and repairing buildings. On the other hand, camping gear, fire extinguishers, and emergency rations could be in demand, with shortages and high prices following.

An important distinction should be made between a prediction the source of which may or may not be worthy of belief, and a warning, which should be an official instruction or advice to take some definite action. Even those governments and local bodies that have been active in the field of civil defence, and have excellent plans for dealing with unexpected disaster, have so far thought little about the consequences of prediction.

Even more serious from the legal and administrative point of view would be the adoption of a suggestion by some American geophysicists that the earthquakes of California could be controlled. What they suggest should be done is to drill holes along the San Andreas fault, several kilometres deep, and about half a kilometre apart. They would then pump fluid from a pair of holes, and force it into a third hole between them. This should trigger off an earthquake, but its magnitude would be limited by the fact that the fault was locked at the two outer holes. By moving systematically along the fault they could remove the regional strains before they became dangerous, and California need experience only minor shocks. The cost of the project would be no more than a few thousand million dollars.

Whatever the prospects for prediction or control, it is certain that earthquake casualties and economic loss can be greatly reduced if we turn our ingenuity and our labours to framing sound building codes, and devising better methods of construction.

15 Safe as houses

They dreamt not of a perishable home
Who thus could build.
  William Wordsworth, *Ecclesiastical Sonnets*

In the confusion that follows an earthquake there are more urgent tasks than the compilation of statistics, and it is no easy matter to estimate the total of the damage and loss of life they have caused. Even official figures can be misleading. Some countries habitually minimize disasters, while others exaggerate the casualty figures in the hope of increasing the flow of aid. When the horrifying results of the Tang Shan earthquake in 1976 have finally been assessed, however, the figure of a million deaths in the last half century is unlikely to prove an under-estimate.

By and large, earthquake disasters can be prevented. It is not earthquakes that kill people, but the things we build. Purely natural phenomena, like landslides and tsunamis, certainly play a part, and lack of foresight and the limitations in our engineering skills take their toll, but whenever there are big casualty figures it is usual to find the combination of a poor country, dense population, and primitive building methods. It is not necessary to have a large earthquake.

Plate 42: Inadequate cross-bracing. Proper diagonal bracing of the lower floor might have prevented this damage to a top-heavy warehouse at Port Ahuriri in the Napier earthquake of 1931.

Plate 43: Chimneys. In most private houses, the chimney is the biggest earthquake hazard. This picture shows the very common fracture at roof level, which occurs at an intensity of about MM VII or VIII. Modern chimneys usually contain reinforcing rods which prevent the top from falling, but do not prevent the crack and the resultant fire danger.

In 1960 a shock with a magnitude of only 5·8 caused ten to fifteen thousand deaths at Agadir, in Morocco. At Quizvan in Iran in 1962, where the magnitude was 7·1, the death toll was over twelve thousand; while the Chimbote earthquake in Peru, with a magnitude of 7·7 and the complicating factors of landslide and flood, killed sixty thousand. Delving further into the past we find that Chinese historians recorded the deaths of 830 000 people in the Shansi earthquake in 1556. This is the greatest total ever claimed, but it cannot be dismissed as fiction. In 1920 another shock in the same region killed 100 000, a figure that was equalled in Tokyo in 1923 and doubled at Nan Shan in 1927.

In this context the loss of 700 people in the San Francisco earthquake of 1906 hardly ranks as a disaster. The 256 deaths in New Zealand's only serious calamity, the Hawke's Bay earthquake of 1931, do not reach half the annual total of deaths on the road, but they are avoidable deaths, and it is right to be concerned. The engineering seismologist must see that not only our homes, offices, shops, and factories, but our roads, dams, bridges and public utilities can withstand any earthquake they are reasonably likely to experience.

If we look at the details of a felt intensity scale, like the modified Mercalli scale given in the Appendix, we see that serious damage to well-built structures should occur only in quite large earthquakes, even if no particular measures have been taken to make them resistant; but even in developed countries we cannot assume that all buildings are well-built, or that there has been no deterioration with age.

In New Zealand, where most people live in what Englishmen would call wooden bungalows, and Americans term single storey frame houses, the average man is probably safer than in countries where it is usual to live in a brick apartment block. The typical house is firmly bolted to a reinforced concrete foundation with broad footings. The framing is adequately cross-braced, and the covering of overlapping weatherboards nailed to every upright gives it further help in resisting deformation, though not always enough to prevent cracking of the plaster on the interior partitions. The older houses have a tin roof of galvanized corrugated-iron sheet fixed to wooden rafters with lead-headed nails. This fashion gave place to tiles, and later to flat roofs covered with fabric, tarred, and sanded. Still more recently, steep gables have again become the vogue, and there has been a return to galvanized iron and aluminium, which can now be produced in sufficient length to span the building in a single piece. A variety of sheet plastic materials, and squares of metal with ceramic coatings that imitate tiles or shingles are also in use. In some instances, a veneer of bricks replaces the weatherboarding, but stucco is now uncommon.

From the point of view of safety in an earthquake, the tiled roof was a step back from the tin one. Tiled roofs are heavy – many times the weight of the structure which has to support them – and some varieties absorb more than their own weight of water. This results in a top-heavy building, and the situation can only be partly relieved by additional cross-bracing of the framework. The warehouse at Port Ahuriri seen in Plate 42 is an interesting example of the behaviour of a top-heavy building with inadequate cross bracing. This was taken after the Hawkes Bay earthquake in 1931. Tiles are easily dislodged in a shake, and even if they do not cascade to the ground and strike the passers-by or the occupants of the building as they rush outside, they will probably be so badly cracked that they are no longer watertight.

It is sound advice not to run outside in an earthquake, whatever the building you may be in at the time.

The maximum violence in a destructive shock is generally reached within ten seconds of the first tremor, and all that can be done is to follow the advice of Dr. Bailey Willis: 'Stand still and count to forty. At the end of that time, it makes no difference what you do.'

The best thing to do, Dr Willis's advice notwithstanding, is to get under some part of the structure which is reinforced, such as a doorway, or under a strong desk or table that will support the weight of anything that collapses on top. Falling material is responsible for

Plate 44: Bricks and tiles. The cracks in the walls of this house at Inangahua show that bricks are not always stronger than the mortar that holds them together. Falling tiles have caused many deaths. The combination of an inadequately braced chimney and a tiled roof is to be avoided.

Plate 45: Differences in natural period. The difference in period between the tower of the Hastings Post Office and the rest of the building resulted in its collapse. Although a passer-by was killed, the occupants escaped uninjured.

most earthquake casualties, and as a rule more rubble falls into the streets than inside the buildings. In the Hastings Post Office the tower collapsed, killing a passer-by, but there were no casualties amongst the people inside.

Fortunately, there is seldom serious structural damage to the wooden house. The frame has considerable resilience, and can put up with a great deal of distortion before anything snaps. This flexibility does, however, contribute to the most common type of damage – a cracked pan in the water-closet. Since the cistern is fastened to the wall and the pan to the floor, a comparatively mild shake in the right direction will break it. Isolated instances are reported in shocks of strength between MM IV and MM V, but this is exceptional. Perhaps there is a case for flexible plumbing.

Damage to the water-closet is inconvenient, but hardly dangerous. This is not the case with the next most common form of damage – cracked and fallen chimneys. These begin to fall about MM V. Builders assure me that there is no reason why a properly erected chimney should ever fall, but they undoubtedly do. Some 20 000 chimneys in Wellington and the Hutt Valley were in need of attention after the Masterton earthquakes of 1942. The most common types of failure are a separation of the bricks, often along a diagonal or in a kind of X-pattern, or a snapping off at roof level (Plate 43). Individual bricks, or even the whole top section of the chimney can crash through a roof. Sentimental attachment to the open fire is responsible for the largest single earthquake hazard in the country.

The failure of brick buildings is often attributed to the use of poor mortar, but a careful examination of Plate 44 will show that in a number of cases the strength of the bricks themselves has been exceeded. It is most important that the corners of brick buildings, and those portions which may try to vibrate independently of the rest of the structure, should be well tied together. The failure of towers, like the one on the Hastings Post Office (Plate 45) is probably quite as much due to a difference in natural period from the rest of the building as to any inherent structural weaknesses.

It may be thought that the danger is limited to that of being hit by a falling brick. This is unfortunately not the case. Failure due to separation of the bricks is the greater hazard, but its operation is indirect. This occurrence of secondary damage is a commonplace to the insurance man. A small earthquake may, for example, break a pipe, and the escaping water may damage large quantities of stored goods. In any large earthquake, community services such as water, gas, and electricity are put out of action. Under these circumstances many a housewife is tempted to prepare a meal, or at least to boil tea on the open fireplace. If the chimney has a crack concealed behind the

Plate 46: Inertia. This water-tank has a well-braced metal stand that could probably have withstood the shaking, but the tank was not fixed to it, and the scratches on its underside record the story of its wanderings.

Plate 47: Chimneys. Not everything that breaks falls down at once. Happenings like this increase the risks in aftershocks. The twisting of this tall factory stack probably indicates an intensity of MM VIII — but note that the tiled roof seems to be intact.

Plate 48: Inverted pendulum. A tall support for a large mass needs to be strong. Brickwork is too brittle for a job like this.

woodwork, the risk of fire is very great. Once a fire starts, the normal fire-fighting services are not available to put it out. This is not just a far-fetched possibility. Records of the great San Francisco shock, and several more recent Japanese ones, show that the damage by fires lit after the earthquake was many times more costly than that caused by the shock itself.

There are two main factors in earthquake damage: resonance with the incoming waves, and inertia. The hazard from inertia seems to be less obvious to members of the public and the ordinary small builder. When the ground beneath an object moves, it will have a much greater tendency to resist the movement if it is heavy, like the water-tank shown in Plate 46. Hot-water cylinders that are constrained only by their supply and outlet pipes have been responsible for a great deal of expensive secondary damage that could have been prevented with a simple ring of nails around the base. Heavy wardrobes and bookcases are all too seldom screwed to the wall behind, and stoves, refrigerators and pianos are almost never secured in any way. All of these can move about (or more correctly, tend to 'stay put') in quite moderate earthquakes.

Securing the contents of our buildings may be in large measure a matter of common sense, but it is no use bothering if the buildings themselves are going to fall down. How can we design buildings that are adequate to resist the earthquakes they are likely to experience?

Even in the epicentral regions of magnitude eight and a half earthquakes, some buildings have been left standing. A crude approach would be to copy them, and to forbid other types of construction, but most communities would consider this too harsh a restriction upon their development. We must find out why buildings collapse, and apply the principles to new planning and design. From the beginning it was clear that this approach would involve both the study of earthquakes and the study of structures. It was rather longer before it was realized that the properties of soils and foundations, which form the connection between the earthquake and the building, are equally important.

Even if the earthquake engineers can solve these problems, some element of risk is likely to remain. When the question is posed in the abstract, most people will say that this is not acceptable; yet in other fields – in transport, in public health, and in damage from tempest, fire, and flood – they undoubtedly face far greater risks than they do from earthquake. It is possible to analyze these events and arrive at some kind of a measure of public acceptability. Most engineers and framers of anti-seismic laws would say that their aim was to bring the risks well within this limit at the least possible cost. A world without risks of any kind is an unattainable ideal.

During an earthquake, a building behaves like a crude kind of seismograph, responding to the incoming waves in accordance with its natural period and damping. The design of a seismograph is purposely kept simple, so that its behaviour can easily be calculated, but most buildings are rather complicated structures. The different parts may have different resonances, and different degrees of internal damping and friction, and these may vary with the amplitude of the imposed vibration. Analyzing the different components of the response is not an easy matter, and finding the characteristics of the incoming waves in a strong earthquake is no less troublesome a problem.

The records of observatory seismographs are of only limited help. They are too sensitive to produce clear records of near earthquakes unless they are very small, and they have the additional disadvantage that the speed of the recording paper is usually insufficient to open out the shape of the waves, so that the higher frequencies and the details of the wave-form cannot be adequately studied. Special strong-motion instruments have therefore to be used. They do not operate continuously, but have a trigger that starts the recording paper moving whenever there is a fairly strong earthquake. It can therefore move at high speed without using awkwardly large and expensive quantitites of paper. The first second or so of the record is lost while the paper gets up speed, but this is not usually the destructive part of the earthquake.

The small number of good strong-motion records available for study is still a matter for concern. We do not know where and when a large shock will happen, and it is difficult to lay a trap for one. In California and Japan the owners of large buildings are now compelled to install strong-motion seismographs, and in New Zealand, the Department of Scientific and Industrial Research has

Plate 49: Framed masonry panels. The reinforced-concrete frame of this exhibition building at Skoplje saved it from collapse, but the brick infilled wall shows the typical X-pattern cracks resulting from shear.

Plate 50: Unreinforced brick. The first storey of this brick apartment building in Skoplje failed and collapsed, leaving the upper floors comparatively intact.

Plate 51: Complete collapse was common in the Andean townships affected by the Chimbote earthquake in Peru in 1970. Streets filled with rubble add to the difficulty of rescue operations.

Plate 52: Look both ways. This light tropical structure walled with mats has a relatively heavy roof. The end walls are probably stiff enough to resist a thrust at right angles to the page, but some kind of bracing was obviously needed on the mat-covered sides.

spread a network of instruments across the country, and the Ministry of Works has built strain-gauges and other measuring devices into a number of its larger engineering structures. In spite of efforts like this in many parts of the world, no one has yet obtained a good record within the zone of maximum intensity for a magnitude eight shock.

The reinforced concrete or steel-framed building, which is typical of most of the larger constructions today, possesses both strength and flexibility; and although there may be superficial damage to partitions and curtain walls, they can be expected to remain substantially sound after even a large earthquake. In fairness to architects and builders, attention should be drawn to the fact that the great majority of well-designed modern buildings will survive all but the largest shocks, but much more attention needs to be paid to the problems of secondary damage and fire.

There is more to making a building earthquake resistant than constructing it of suitable materials and seeing that there are no loose bits to fall off, though small buildings and private houses can usually be made safe by applying simple rules-of-thumb embodied in local by-laws. The design of skyscrapers, factories, bridges, refineries, dams and the like calls for a more elaborate procedure.

Plate 53: Traditional and modern. Two lessons from New Guinea. The foundations of the native building are without bracing, while the wall of the concrete block store had no reinforcing.

Plate 54: Lateral movement of the decking broke these bridge piers at Lianoning.

Plate 55: Poor bracing. The light unbraced foundations of this San Fernando building were inadequate to resist the sideways forces of the mass above.

Plate 56: Frame distortion. Poor bracing and a heavy roof caused the distortion of this San Fernando home.

One of the earliest approaches was to lay down some definite horizontal acceleration that the building must be designed to withstand. This had the advantage that the engineer could use the design techniques he was accustomed to use when considering wind loadings, and could often combine the wind and the seismic factors and handle them together. The value of the acceleration adopted was usually about a tenth of the acceleration due to gravity. Experience has shown that normal buildings designed in this way perform quite well in most earthquakes, in spite of the fact that strong motion seismographs show the actual accelerations developed in even moderately damaging shocks to be much greater.

Plate 57: Wooden houses. Wooden frame houses are good earthquake risks, provided they are built on an adequate foundation. Ground subsidence at Anchorage during the Alaskan earthquake in 1964 tilted this building without causing serious structural damage.

Plate 58: Fires follow earthquakes. After the 1931 earthquake, fire soon gained hold on the business centre of Napier. Very many large earthquakes have been followed by fire.

Plate 59: Rival neighbours. The differing periods of these two buildings at Niigata made them respond to the earthquake with different kinds of motion, so the stronger battered the weaker.

Plate 60: A building vibrator. The vibrator of the University of Auckland's School of Engineering attached to the parapet of a building. The two outer wheels revolve in the opposite direction from the centre one. A range of different weights can be bolted to them eccentrically.

The reason for the discrepancy seems to be that the maximum accelerations developed are associated with periods that are shorter than those of most buildings, and are not characteristic of the whole duration of strong shaking. With the help of the information now being gathered the engineer can begin his calculations with a 'design spectrum' that specifies the strength of the building at certain definite frequencies.

Where the earthquake risk is believed to vary in different parts of a country, the code may contain zoning provisions varying the resistance required. In New Zealand the acceleration specified varies from 0·08 to 0·16 times that due to gravity.

In Japan, a more elaborate method is used. The country is divided into three regions, in which values of 0·2, 0·15, and 0·1g respectively are taken as standard. These regional values are then multiplied by a factor varying from 0·5 to 1·5 which depends upon the building and upon the type of subsoil on which it is to stand. This type of code is gradually being replaced by a more elaborate consideration of the dynamic characteristics of the building, particularly in the case of tall or otherwise unusual structures.

Analysis of a design must establish not only that the building is strong enough to resist foreseeable earthquake forces, but that the movements during the shock are not excessive and alarming to the occupants. In the case of tall tower-like buildings the displacements can be very large before there is any chance of structural damage, but the truth of this statement will not necessarily be obvious to someone caught twenty storeys above the ground during an earthquake. Apart from this, the contents of the building may be thrown about, blocking stairs and exits.

The general availability of electronic computers has greatly changed the approach to practical design, and makes it possible to consider structures which would have been out of the question a few years ago, not because the principle on which their design depends was unknown, but because the necessary calculations would have been too laborious to be economic.

What if, in spite of all precautions, there is a shock large enough to cause severe structural damage? The designer has still a measure of control over the part of the structure that will fail first, and it is usually possible to arrange things so that the occupants of the building will be safe, even if the damage is so bad that it will have to pulled down and replaced.

If the movement of a building during an earthquake is to be limited, it must be well damped. Damping devices function by absorbing energy, and a common arrangement is to arrange that certain sections of wall will bear the brunt of the damage. New Zealand engineers have been experimenting with disposable components that can be built into bridges and similar structures. These can be metal links or sections that are intended to be strained and deformed far beyond their elastic limits, or piston devices that use the unwanted energy to force lead through a small aperture. After a severe shock these components can be readily removed and replaced.

It is important to see that the natural period of a building is not too close to the predominant period of earthquake waves. This period can be calculated from the stiffness of the materials and the way in which the weight is distributed, but these can be difficult to estimate, and the addition or removal of internal partitions or the storage of heavy goods can change it markedly. Fortunately it is possible to measure the period of a completed building by recording its vibration in high winds, or by shaking it artificially with a vibrator.

Fig. 63: A building vibrator. Equal weights revolve in opposite directions. When they are in the vertical position as at 1 and 3 the centrifugal forces cancel out, but in the horizontal positions they act together to produce a horizontal force on the axle X Y, alternately directed to the right as at 2 and to the left as at 4. The gearing to produce the rotation of the weights, the variable speed motor and its controls, and the frame for clamping the vibrator to the building are not shown.

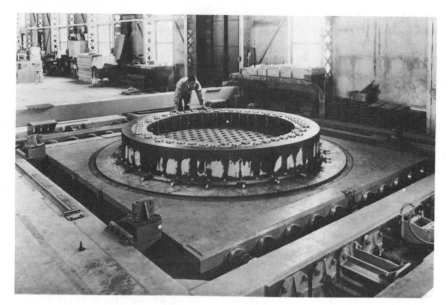

Plate 61: The large shaking-table at the Building Research Laboratory of the Japanese Ministry of Construction can support a load of 17 tons and shake it with a vertical acceleration equal to that of gravity and a horizontal one twice as great. The period of vibration can be adjusted over the range from about 0.2 to 0.9 seconds. Here it is shown with the bottom section of an atomic reactor in position for testing.

A building vibrator consists of a set of rotating weights driven by a variable-speed motor and geared to rotate in opposite directions (Figure 63, Plate 60). Each of the weights exerts a centrifugal force upon the axle XY. In positions 1 and 3 the forces pull in opposite directions and cancel out, but in position 2 they combine to pull the axle and the framework that carries it to the right. Half a revolution later, in position 4, the weights are again together, but the pull is now to the left. The machine therefore generates an alternating force F with a frequency that depends upon the speed of the motor. So that the machine will not have a tendency to twist, the weight A is split into two halves, and B revolves in between them. This is much less trying for the gearing and the bearings. There are various ways of connecting the vibrator to the building. The actual size of the weights used depends on how safe it is to shake the building, and how sensitive a recorder is available to measure the vibrations. In America, certain old buildings due for demolition have been turned into vibration laboratories and literally shaken to pieces!

Not all vibration studies have to made on full-size buildings. Sometimes it is sufficient to use a model, or to test only part of the structure. The Japanese Ministry of Construction has a very large shaking-table (Plate 61) which was used to test the components of a nuclear power-station.

Another approach is to use an electrical analogue. An analogue is an electrical circuit in which the values of the components are arranged to give them a response to electrical vibrations that can be compared with the mechanical properties of the building. An ingenious photo-electric device converts the record of an earthquake into a varying electric current that can be passed through the analogue, which is then studied by the techniques of electrical engineering. The results can finally be reinterpreted in mechanical terms that will apply to the real building.

We have already mentioned the importance of the ground on which a building stands. An American study has shown that the intensity on good and bad foundations at the same distance from the epicentre can in exceptional cases amount to as much as four degrees of the modified Mercalli scale. These variations can be studied by examining damaged cities, but only strong-motion records on a variety of foundations will really give the engineer the information he needs. It is certainly a sound practice to build on a rock foundation, and to avoid building different parts of the structure on different kinds of subsoil, such as partly on rock and partly on filling. One of the most unsatisfactory foundations appears to be alluvium – the material brought down by rivers, to build up the floors of their valleys. Japanese results indicate that a foundation of alluvium has the effect of absorbing small earthquakes, but it amplifies the vibrations of the larger ones. Unfortunately, old river terraces make apparently desirable building sites, and many ports have grown up at the mouths of rivers.

The foundation characteristics of a building-site can be directly investigated by boring drill-holes, and in the case of large buildings, this is almost invariably done. It is desirable that the building regulations for a large city should be based on wider knowledge than can be gleaned from a limited number of arbitrarily spaced holes. In Japan, a method of investigating the subsoil by observing 'micro-tremor' has been used. It is found that the character of the continuous background of microseisms and artificial vibrations at a given site depends upon the nature and depth of the unconsolidated material

Plate 62: Liquefaction of subsoil. The weight of this building at Niigata drove it so far into the loose sandy foundation that the ground storey was almost buried, and the canopy over the entrance door became a vantage point.

Plate 63: Sand craters. When shaking compacts loose subsoil, the ground-water is forced out, bringing quantities of fine sand and mud to the surface through craters like these. The upper picture was taken in Charleston, South Carolina, in 1886, and the lower one in Niigata in 1964.

near the surface. A sample record can be made in a matter of minutes, and it has proved possible to identify three or four main types of subsoil in this way. Large cities like Tokyo, Yokohama and Osaka have been completely mapped.

No building can be much safer that the ground it stands on. When some kinds of clay are shaken they will flow like a liquid, with unfortunate effects upon any buildings on top (Plate 62), and one of the results of the settlement of unconsolidated gravel is to drive out the ground-water, along with quantities of fine sand and mud (Plate 63). Few people expect an earthquake to leave them standing up to the knees in swirling muddy water that seems to have appeared from nowhere (Plate 64). Railways and roads cannot always avoid areas of bad ground of this kind, and bridges and embankments are often the vulnerable points in any network of communications (Plates 65 to 69).

Perhaps the hardest problem that remains in the field of engineering seismology is posed by the existence of old buildings that are valued for their beauty or their associations. Even when expense is a secondary consideration, strengthening measures may destroy the character that makes the building worth preserving. New Zealand

Plate 64: Ground water. Expulsion of ground water by the 1964 earthquake brought traffic in Niigata to a standstill and drove citizens to the roof-tops.

Plate 65: Broken communications. Both road and rail links with Inangahua were severed by the earthquake in 1968. A section of road crossing filled ground has slumped, and the railway tracks have been buckled by the movement of the ballast.

does not face the problem of whether a York Minster or a Leaning Tower poses an unacceptable seismic hazard to its citizens, but the very absence of ancient buildings in a young country makes us most reluctant to destroy any building of character. Should an ornate Victorian building facing a main thoroughfare be allowed to remain? If the ornamentation is well secured to a sound structure, there is probably no reason why it should not. The problem is often to find out whether this is so without doing damage. The old plans and specifications may no longer exist, and if they do, they are still no guarantee that the workmanship was sound.

With the passage of time even our newest buildings will weaken and the history and sentiment that surrounds the older ones will increase. With the growth of public regard we can also expect a greater willingness to spend money on preservation. Further research should lead to better techniques of strengthening. In the meantime we should not lightly make the decision to destroy all 'potential risks', and before we grant the humanitarian proposition that no building is worth a human life, we should ponder upon the number of fatal accidents that now attend the construction of our dams, railroads, bridges, and major buildings, without giving rise to public outcry.

Plate 66: Bridge piers. Movement of the piers of the newly-completed Showa Bridge at Niigata caused the decks to collapse. An old stone bridge with wide piers was unharmed.

Plate 67: Bridge approach. Even if the decking of the Showa Bridge had not fallen (see Plate 66) getting on to it would have been a problem. The approach has subsided and cracked because of inadequate compaction and failure of the side walls. Note also the sand craters in the foreground.

Plate 68: The weakest link. Design of this New Guinea bridge apparently stopped at the abutments. Subsidence of the approach has left a wall across the road.

Plate 69: Temporary diversion. Several bridge-spans have collapsed, putting this elaborate traffic fly-over near San Fernando out of action. The earthquake responsible, with a magnitude of 6·8, must be considered only moderately severe.

Plate 70: Poor foundations. The fate of these identical apartment buildings at Niigata depended wholly upon their foundations. All were strong enough to resist the shaking, but some have tilted, one is completely overturned, and others are quite unharmed. Note the sand craters in the foreground.

Plate 71: Soil creep. This soil cracking and building damage was caused by movement down a comparatively gentle slope during the Liaoning earthquake.

16 Zoning and insurance

TAMBURLAINE: I will confute those blind geographers
That make a triple region in the world
Excluding regions that I mean to trace
And with this pen reduce them to a map.
Marlowe, *Tamburlaine*

Earthquakes are more common in some parts of the world than others, and it is possible to make generalizations about which regions are active and which regions stable. In stable regions, precautions against earthquake are unnecessary; in regions with a history of repeated destructive earthquakes it is equally obvious that something should be done. The enforcement of suitable building codes and insurance against economic loss are two possible counter-measures.

Where there have been earthquakes in the past, there will almost certainly be earthquakes again. Unfortunately, human memory is short, and the earthquakes of even a generation ago are often forgotten. The history of countries like Korea and Japan, which have kept earthquake records for centuries, reveals a further problem. Periods of activity alternate with periods in which there are few or no earthquakes. In countries like New Zealand that have only recently been inhabited, and in those whose inhabitants have only recently become civilized, it is difficult to learn much from history; but once it is known that there are earthquakes, any prudent administration must consider whether its building-laws should contain provisions for anti-seismic design, whether these provisions should be enforced over the whole country or only in part of it, and whether the provisions should vary in stringency from place to place. The division of a country into regions having different anti-seismic building codes is known as seismic zoning.

Seismic zoning is not the same thing as studying seismicity. It may, for example, be quite reasonable to insist upon a higher degree of earthquake resistance for a building that could collapse into a busy city street than for one that is surrounded by open country, even though earthquakes are equally likely in the two places. The degree of shaking experienced is markedly dependent upon the subsoil, and a building erected upon thick gravels needs to be stronger than one on hard bed-rock nearby. Less stringent regulations may be needed for a storage warehouse than for a theatre or cinema that could be crammed with hundreds of people, or for a dam that would flood a populated valley if it were to burst. All of these factors may legitimately influence zoning, but they have nothing to do with seismicity, and the seismologist is rightly indignant when considerations of this kind are represented to be his scientific findings about earthquake risk.

In countries with a long recorded history and a dense population, such as Japan, it is useful to draw maps showing the highest recorded intensity in each town or city. If the region, again like Japan, is a very seismic one, most places that are going to have earthquakes will already have had one, and the map will give a fair estimate of the likely intensity. Maps of this kind indicate the minimum precautions.

The longer the history on which they are based, the better they are likely to be; but it is unwise to trust them in matters of detail. The disastrous earthquake at Niigata in 1964 occurred in a region with a record of lower seismicity than other parts of Japan. It is therefore necessary to supplement the lessons of history with other investigations. Two lines of approach are used – geological mapping, and the instrumental study of the smaller earthquakes.

We have seen that there are many more small earthquakes than big ones, the number of shocks of any particular magnitude being about eight times the number of the magnitude above. By recording the number of small shocks in a limited period we can therefore get a rough idea of how often to expect a large one. Of course the exact relationship between the big shocks and the small ones varies from region to region, but it is wise to assume that where small shocks are frequent, larger ones are possible. How much further it is possible to go is a matter of controversy. In the Soviet Union special expeditions have been sent to several of the Central Asian republics to assess the seismicity. Dr M. V. Gzovsky and his colleagues consider that from their studies in the Tyan Shan, where they recorded earthquakes down to magnitude 2 or less for one or two years, they have been able to produce a reliable evaluation. While active regions can certainly be found in this way, it would be rash to conclude that because no shocks were recorded in so brief a time the region was inactive.

With the very sensitive portable seismographs developed over the last few years it is possible to record and locate even smaller earthquakes than was done in the Tyan Shan. A small network of stations can be installed in a district and left for a few days or a week until a reasonable number of shocks has been observed, and then moved on until a whole region has been covered. These so-called *micro-earthquake studies* have now been carried out in both North and South America and in New Zealand, and have thrown light on a number of tectonic problems. They can, for example, establish what parts of a fault zone are at present active and where the fault is locked, but there are obvious dangers in using these short-term studies to predict long-term trends.

Many kinds of geological observation are of value for seismic zoning purposes. If one part of a geological unit is seismically active, it is reasonable to assume that the rest of it shares the same risk. We have seen that a close relationship exists between large earthquakes and geological faulting, and precautions are obviously necessary in any region where conspicuously active faults have been mapped. Few earthquakes have been recorded along the central portion of New Zealand's Alpine Fault, and on parts of the San Andreas Fault in California, but no seismologist would suggest that we should relax precautions in those areas because they have been inactive in recent times.

Soviet scientists have been very active in the field of what they call *seismic regionalization*. This is rather more than simple zoning. It involves a most careful synthesis of all the lines of seismological and geological argument. Data are frequently collected by special large expeditions like the one already mentioned, and historical documents are searched for accounts of past earthquakes. Soviet geologists place much less emphasis upon faulting than most Americans or New Zealanders would do, concentrating instead upon the identification of zones with contrasting geological history, particularly where vertical movements are involved, and regarding the regions of transition from one zone to another with suspicion. In the parts of the world with which they are concerned, these are more often marked by 'flexures' than by great faults of the type that is familiar around the Pacific.

Faulting is not the only geological evidence of past earthquakes. Many shocks are accompanied by uplift, subsidence, or tilting of large tracts of land. This can be inferred from changes in shore-lines and beach terraces, by the position of wave-cut platforms in relation to the present water-level, and from geomorphological features, such as small streams in which the rate of down-cutting has suddenly increased. Extensive areas of landslide may be explicable only on the assumption that there has been a large earthquake, and so on.

Important as this evidence is, it is essential to stress that it is admissable only for the purpose of *extending* the zones arrived at by direct consideration of the positions of the known earthquakes and of the distance to which the effects of a large earthquake can extend. The absence of a fault, or of any other geological feature, does not establish that there have been no earthquakes; and the fact that only small shocks have been experienced in the past does not establish that this is the upper limit of their possible size.

No part of New Zealand is far from a known earthquake origin, and until recently a uniform code of anti-seismic building laws was recommended for the whole country. In spite of strong representations from seismologists, a new code has been introduced, which slightly increases the requirements in some areas, but reduces them in others that include two of our largest cities, one of which has since suffered minor damage from a shallow magnitude 5 shock almost directly beneath it.

National zoning schemes, at least in a free enterprise economy, usually concern themselves only with the question of public safety. It should be possible for the citizen to emerge alive (and preferably uninjured) from a damaged building. The man with a large capital investment in property may look at the matter rather differently. Even if his building is still structurally sound, it could cost him a great deal to repair and repaint cracked plaster and the like. He will probably look for insurance cover. It is in this context, rather than in that of zoning, that studies of earthquake frequency are important. The infrequent earthquake is as destructive as the frequent one, and failure to plan for it cannot be excused by telling injured men whose city lies in ruins, 'I didn't say that this wouldn't happen – only that it wouldn't happen often'. A degree of earthquake resistance sufficient to protect life is the minimum acceptable standard for any building in a seismic area. Whether it is cheaper to pay higher insurance or to strengthen the plaster may reasonably be left to the owner.

Geological fault-lines are not narrow zones of exceptional earthquake risk. A structure that actually crossed a fault would naturally be in danger if the two sides of the fault were to move but few buildings are in this position. Ground movement close to faults that have moved appear to be simple displacements rather than wave-motions, which become predominant only at some distance away. A building on solid rock near a fault is more likely to be safe than one on a poor foundation a kilometre or more from it. If there is a zone of crushed or broken rock at the fault, it would be unwise to build on it, but this is because of its fractured nature and not because of its nearness to the fault. So firmly does the public believe in the potency of faults that seismologists are more asked for a 'map of the faults' than for the information about earthquake risks that the inquirer really needs. The whole of a country like New Zealand is intensively faulted, but in many cases the age of the fault is very difficult to determine. The geologist knows that a fault must be younger than the youngest rock it cuts, and is consequently able to classify a number of them as 'Recent'. But Recent, to the geologist, may mean any time in the last twenty-five thousand years, and the fault may have no intention of moving again. The only certain proof that a fault is active is the knowledge that someone has seen it move. Earthquakes have sometimes resulted in a hurried re-classification of faults. The White Creek Fault, which moved in the Murchison earthquake in 1929 was previously though to be 'dead'. If an inquirer really does want to know about faults, he should be referred to a geologist. Geologists asked for information about earthquake risks should see that the questioner talks to a seismologist.

There is widespread belief that certain people live 'on the earthquake line', where shocks are more strongly felt than they are in neighbouring places. The announcement is often made with a kind of pride, and as far as I can gather, the 'line' is pictured as a kind of wriggly snake stretching its erratic and sinister length across the countryside. Many towns have localities which are reputed to lie on it. In Wellington, at least, the places I have heard so described are in the older parts of the city, where the buildings are undoubtedly more shaky. Certainly, not all parts of a city will feel an earthquake with equal intensity, but the reasons are related to the differences in foundation, and the 'earthquake line' is a pure fiction.

There may be room for argument about the appropriate degree of strengthening needed to make a building earthquake resistant, but if the existing level is adequate, there is as little excuse for raising it in some centres as there is for lowering it in others. Insistence that earthquakes are necessarily less frequent and less severe in areas that are without known active faulting can only be described as irresponsible. The unhappy coincidence of this view with lay misconceptions about faults diverts attention from the implications of the earthquakes that lie beyond the boundaries of the area of Recent transcurrent faulting, and from the fact that we are almost totally ignorant of the submarine geology off the shores of our long and narrow country.

In many parts of the world, zoning ensures that protection is given to people who would otherwise be without it. In New Zealand it must result either in the people within the supposed zones of lower risk being denied it, or in those in the high-risk zones being put to unnecessary expense.

Increasing attention is being given to the small-scale variations that result from the differing foundation conditions to be found within a single zone of earthquake risk. Measurements made in large earthquakes have established that the intensities reached on poorly consolidated ground may be several degrees higher than those on solid rock nearby. The assessment of these variations within the primary zoning scheme is known as *microzoning*.

Microzoning is usually based on the results of several different kinds of survey, because of the practical difficulties that face most techniques in a busy built-up area. Gravity surveys can be used to follow changes in the depth of the bedrock beneath alluvium and artificial fill. Direct geological surveys are possible to some extent, and samples of soil and rock from the exploratory drill-holes on building sites can be examined in the laboratory. In addition, portable seismographs can be used to record the frequency and amplitude of the microtremor. This is usually of artificial origin, but the response of the soil to artificial vibrations is an indication of its probable behaviour in natural earthquakes. The tremor shows sharp changes in character when the recording point is moved from one type of foundation to another. When all the available information has been pooled, a map can be drawn to show the troublesome areas. Microzoning studies have now been made in a number of Japanese and New Zealand cities, and in parts of California. The results of the different methods used are in good agreement.

Seismic zoning problems are linked to the problem of earthquake insurance, but the zones established for insurance and for building purposes should not necessarily be identical. Structural problems arise almost entirely from the larger earthquakes, but the total of the insurance claims that arise from damage to goods and to non-structural fittings in small shocks may be very great. The frequency of occurrence of the smaller shocks, and the relative numbers of shocks of different magnitude therefore become important. A further difficulty is that people in regions of low seismicity are unlikely to seek earthquake insurance, so that unless it is linked to some other risk such as fire the risks cannot be properly spread and premiums become high, perhaps unrealistically so.

The insurance scheme operated by the New Zealand Earthquake and War Damage Commission was started by the government after the Masterton earthquakes of 1942, and provides compensation to owners for damage resulting from earthquake, enemy attack, and certain other natural calamities. It is funded by a small compulsory surcharge added to the premiums for fire insurance, including the insurance of motor cars. When a property is mortgaged, half the surcharge can be recovered from the mortgagee.

By New Zealand standards, the sums involved are large. In a quiet year, the amount paid out for damage in minor shocks totals only a few thousand dollars, but a shock of magnitude 5 is sufficient to send the payments up by tenfold. Since the fund was established, the largest shock has been the magnitude 7 Inangahua earthquake in 1968. Although most of the townships affected were not large, and were some distance from the epicentre, payments rose to over two million New Zealand dollars.

The weaknesses of the scheme have been the difficulty of arranging re-insurance outside the country, the fact that public opinion and state intervention has forced relief payments to people carrying no insurance, or in some cases when the seismic origin of the damage was open to question. There is continued pressure from rural interests to have the fund cover damage from flooding, landslide, and similar misfortunes that have often been aggravated by their own commercial activities.

Insurance is not a method by which payment for damage can be avoided; it merely spreads the payments in time and place. The Earthquake and War Damage Commission therefore devotes some of its resources to encouraging improved standards of building, and generously aids the New Zealand National Society for Earthquake Engineering with grants for publication and research. It is interesting that payments from the fund have gone to all parts of the country from the extreme north to Stewart Island. This lends support to the seismologists' view that New Zealand should be treated as a single zone of substantially uniform earthquake risk.

17 Earthquakes and the bomb

. . . they contend not about matter of fact, nor can determine their
controversies by any certaine witnesses, nor judges. But as long as they goe
towards peace, that is Truth, it is no matter which way.

John Donne, *Biathanatos*

The use of explosions for seismic prospecting has been so successful
that the observatory seismologist has sometimes been a little envious
of his colleague in the field. The use of natural earthquake records for
investigating the internal structure of the Earth is limited by
uncertanties in the time and place and the depth of the shock.
Controlled explosions need have none of these disadvantages, but a
great deal of explosive is needed to generate elastic waves as well as an
earthquake can. Until the last war, most big explosions were
accidental, and although the place was known, the time was not, and
no special recording arrangements could be made. As soon as the war
was over, seismologists in many countries succeeded in persuading
the military authorities to make surplus ammunition available for
crustal-structure studies, or at least to explode it in such a way that
the records would be of scientific value. For example, the
seismologists of Europe cooperated in recording the great explosion
at Haslach, in Germany, and on the island of Heligoland. In New
Zealand, tons of naval depth-charges were exploded together in
Wellington harbour, and recorded at mobile stations up to 150
kilometres away. All this was very gratifying, but the fortunes of war
threw up a seismological tool of even greater potency – the atomic
bomb. The pity is that soldiers and politicians consider (on grounds
that are at least questionable) that they are better able than
seismologists to decide how it should be used.

From the very beginning, seismograph records of atomic bomb
explosions were made, but the first few were of limited value. At the
first test in New Mexico, no proper record was made of the shot-
instant, because of the 'somewhat confused and emotional
circumstances'. Similar considerations no doubt obtained at
Hiroshima and Nagasaki. The Bikini test was a different matter.
Satisfactory records were obtained as far away as in California, and
Gutenberg and Richter were able to estimate its magnitude.

About the time of the International Geophysical Year, Professor
K. E. Bullen was leading an international agitation to have a number
of bombs specially exploded for crustal structure and upper mantle
studies. Those proposals proved politically unacceptable, but since
then a number of nuclear tests have been studied in some detail,
including the British test at Maralinga, in Australia, and most of the
American ones. The Maralinga test was of particular value, as the
region is without natural earthquakes, and it looked as if the crust of
a major continent was likely to remain unexplored for a long time.
Meanwhile, Professor Bullen was collecting routine recordings of
nuclear explosions made at ordinary seismological observatories,
and was able to use them both for the revision of the standard travel-
time tables, and to convince the military authorities that there were
certain facts they could not hope to keep secret. Since then, shot-

instants and other information necessary for seismological studies have been more readily made available.

Important as this work was, it was soon to become secondary to the problem of nuclear test detection. Agreement to ban nuclear explosions in the atmosphere had been reached, and it seemed likely that underground tests would be banned as well, if only it were possible to detect infringements. Explosions in the atmosphere are easy to detect – and so too, in fact, are underground ones. The difficulty is that the underground ones are almost, if not completely, indistinguishable from earthquakes (Figure 64). If agreement on a test-ban is to be reached, the problem will have to be solved. If it is, the only people to regret it will be the seismologists! Meanwhile, government money for earthquake research has become available to an unprecedented extent, and it is extraordinary how many fundamental seismological problems are now said to be closely bound up with the detection of underground nuclear explosions.

Although the detection of underground nuclear explosions was technically possible, the existing seismograph stations in many parts of the world were too thinly spaced, and had only obsolete equipment.

A committee of American seismologists pointed out that many more good stations would be needed if clandestine tests were to be adequately policed, and that if the characteristics distinguishing bombs from explosions lay in the finer details of the records, it would be desirable for all the recording stations to have identical equipment. If this ideal was to be reached, the instruments would have to come from the same factory, and stations in many different countries would have to be persuaded to install them. As most of the stations would not want to replace their existing equipment, the only possible method of persuasion would be to give them instruments for nothing. This the United States government generously decided to

Fig. 64: Which is the bomb? The upper seismogram is of a nuclear explosion 180 km from the recording station at Tinemaha. The lower one is that of a natural earthquake 181 km away, in almost the same direction. The distance between the test site and the epicentre was 43 km. (After Press and Archambeau.)

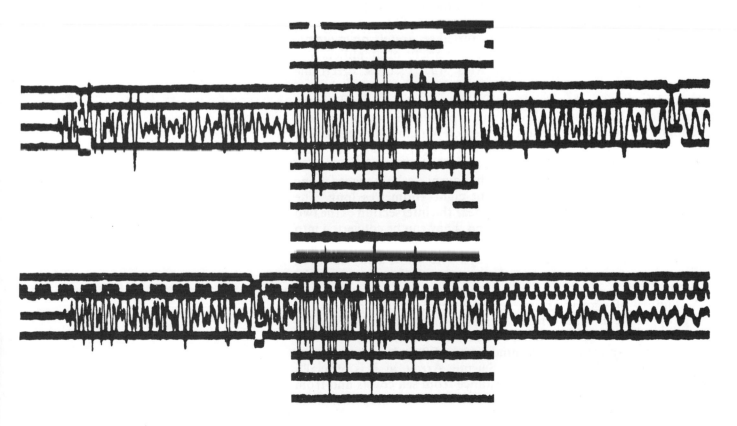

do, and there is now a World Network of about 120 Standard Seismograph Stations. Each has two sets of three-component instruments, Benioffs for the short periods, and Press-Ewing seismometers for the long. The equipment also includes an accurate electronic clock and a radio receiver for uniform timing, instruments for calibration, and for copying photographic records. Stations retain their own records if they wish, but the United States Geological Survey maintains a central archive from which copies of any record from any station can be obtained for a few cents. The only large parts of the Earth now without standard stations are Canada (except for one in the far north), China, and the Soviet Union, but part of a standard set is being operated in Moscow. New Zealand controls four standard stations.

We have seen in a previous chapter that the upper limit to the useful magnification of a seismograph is set by the background of microseisms. These are a little less troublesome below the surface, and several recently-developed seismometers are small enough to be lowered to the bottom of drill-holes a hundred metres deep.

There is another way in which we can counteract the effect of microseisms, by combining the outputs from seismometers a short distance apart. The records of a distant earthquake made at two places a kilometre or so apart are very much alike, except for a small difference in arrival time, depending upon the direction from which the earthquake waves are coming. The background of artificial disturbances at the two stations, however, is likely to be different, and in most cases, the microseisms will not be coming from the same direction as the earthquake. If we displace one of the records slightly to allow for the time-difference, we can superimpose the earthquake records, but not the unwanted background. By spacing out many seismometers in a regular pattern, known as an 'array', and combining the outputs electrically after introducing suitable time-delays, it is possible to construct an instrument that will detect very small earthquakes (or bombs) at great distances. The output of each seismometer in the array is usually recorded separately on magnetic tape, and can be played back through a variety of amplifiers and filters before or after combination with other records. Electronic computers automatically determine the appropriate time-delays to be introduced, and what combination will give the seismologist the information he wants about any particular event. Array seismographs are a powerful aid to research of many different kinds.

In 1962, the United Kingdom Atomic Energy Authority set up an array of twenty seismometers at Eskdalemuir, in Scotland. They are mounted on concrete foundations in shallow pits evenly spaced along two lines at right angles, each about eight kilometres long. The signals are fed to a central laboratory near the intersection of the two lines, and recorded upon magnetic tape. They can be converted into conventional paper records, or subjected to electrical filtering and intercomparison in many different ways. The whole array has been calibrated by exploding naval depth-charges in the North Sea and the Irish Sea.

A number of similar arrays, using different layout patterns, is being operated in the United States. A still more impressive installation at Billings, Montana, best described as an array of arrays, is spread over an area about a hundred and fifty kilometres square.

The site of the Large Aperture Seismic Array, as it is officially called, was chosen because of its distance from sea coasts and from human activity, and for its geological uniformity. Altogether there are 525 seismometers grouped into twenty-one clusters known as 'sub-arrays'. Each sub-array consists of twenty-five instruments, disposed along six radii of a circle 7 kilometres across (Figure 65, Plate 72). In order to reduce background noise still further, the seismometers are placed at the bottom of drill-holes 120 millimetres in diameter, lined with metal pipe and set in concrete. Most of the holes are 65 metres deep, but the centre one in each array is slightly larger and goes down 170 metres (Figure 66).

The signals from the separate seismometers in each sub-array are fed to an underground vault where they are amplified and electrically transformed into a suitable form for transmission by micro-wave radio link to the data-centre at Billings, some 200km away. At Billings two electronic computers compare and record the signals from the seismometers and make periodical checks and calibrations of the seismometers and their associated electrical equipment (Plate 73).

Fig. 65: A seismic array. At the top left is a plan of the great seismic array in Montana. Each of the dots represents a cluster of seismographs laid out in the pattern shown on a larger scale at the right. The cross-section at the bottom shows the central seismometer at a depth of 170 metres, and the four shallower instruments along the same radius of the pattern at a depth of 65 metres.

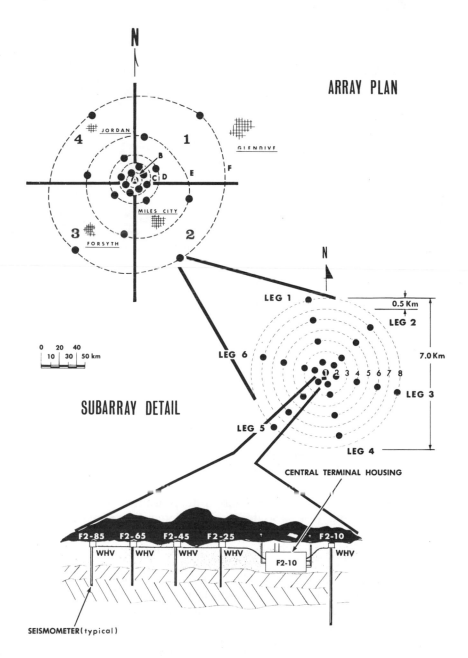

Plate 72: An array seismograph. An aerial view of one of the twenty-one sub-arrays that make up the Large Aperture Seismic Array in south-eastern Montana, U.S.A.

The cost of this gigantic instrument was over seven and a quarter million dollars, one million of which was spent on the computers and other equipment in the data-centre, over one and a quarter million on the drill-holes, half a million on seismometers and amplifiers, and the rest on buildings, radio links, land-lines, and fencing. The data-centre has a staff of seventeen, only one of whom is a seismologist. Another fifteen men are needed for routine maintenance of the array.

When we have recorded a suspicious event, whether by using an array, or at a conventional station, how are we to know whether it is a bomb or not? Figure 65 shows how similar earthquake and explosion records can be when the earthquake and the bomb are at almost the same distance from the recording station. The more obvious characteristics of the records seem to result from the ground structure, rather than from the mechanism responsible. It is possible that accurate depth measurements could help us. If the origin of the shock was more than a few kilometres deep, it must certainly have been an earthquake. But good depth measurements are not easy, and in order to make them we need records from places very close to the origin. In the event of a clandestine test, we are not likely to have them.

It was at first thought that observations of the direction of the initial movements on the seismograms would give a very simple method of distinguishing between bombs and earthquakes. We saw that an earthquake due to elastic rebound should give rise to a pattern of compressions and dilatations in alternate quadrants. In an explosion, it was argued, the pattern should be much simpler. All the ground particles near the source move outwards and nothing but compressions should result. It was also suggested that because the mechanism was all compressional there should be few S-waves or none at all.

Fig. 66: A bore-hole seismometer. This is the arrangement used for each of the separate seismographs that make up the Montana array. The casing of each borehole ends in a 'well-head vault' consisting of a section cut from an ordinary 200-litre oil-drum, covered with a metal 'coolie hat' to keep out the rain. The vault contains an amplifier and the end of the land-line that feeds the signal to the centre of the sub-array. The stand at the bottom of the hole is a help in getting the seismometer into a vertical position.

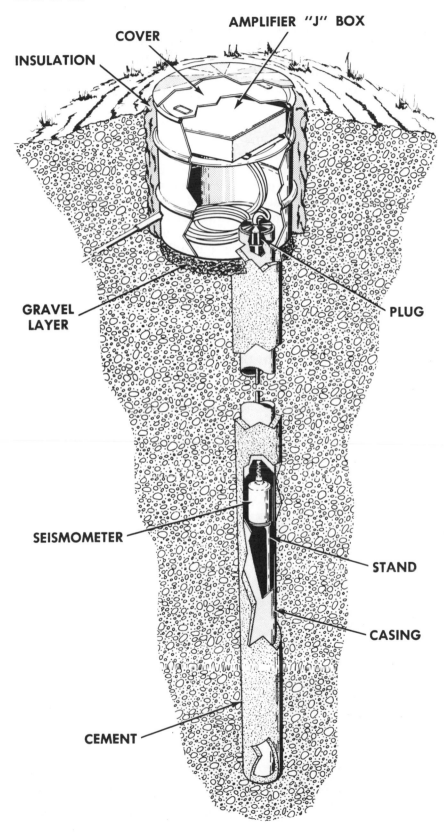

COVER

AMPLIFIER "J" BOX

INSULATION

GRAVEL LAYER

PLUG

SEISMOMETER

STAND

CASING

CEMENT

This is certainly not so. Even when conditions near the source are very uniform some shearing is inevitable, and shear strains already present in the surrounding rock can be released. Most records of atomic explosions therefore show significant S-phases, though small prospecting explosions sometimes do not. At present the most readily detectable difference between bombs and earthquakes seems to lie in the proportion of body waves to surface waves; that is, there is a difference in the magnitudes determined from the different phases. Taking all the methods now available together, it seems that the number of doubtful cases can be made small enough to make a ban on underground testing politically practicable, and at the time of writing new discussions on the subject have been announced.

Many members of the public are concerned that underground testing may increase the number of natural earthquakes taking place. Indeed, some of them accuse seismologists of concealing the 'fact' that such an increase followed the French tests in the atmosphere at Mururoa Atoll. For their part, seismologists have not attributed any significance to the fact that the period of the tests was one of less than normal seismic activity in the south-west Pacific.

The possibility that a large explosion could trigger an earthquake is not entirely without substance, but only in an area in which an earthquake would in any case occur. If the regional strain were already very close to causing elastic failure, the arrival of large elastic waves from an explosion might be enough to carry the rocks beyond their breaking strain and initiate rebound, but an event of this kind would only be possible when a natural shock was imminent. The bomb could determine *when* it occurred, but not *whether* it did.

We can be reasonably sure that if triggering of this kind is possible it does not extend to any great distance from the source. A 5 kiloton bomb radiates roughly the same energy as a magnitude 5 earthquake. If a bomb of this size could trigger earthquakes, we should expect the waves from the several hundred natural shocks of magnitude 5 that take place every year to set off further shocks, and the really large earthquakes to have spectacular repercussions in distant places. In brief, they don't. There are many highly creditable reasons for opposing atomic testing, but this is not one of them.

Plate 73: Data centre. Inside the data centre at Billings, Montana, where the signals from the 525 seismographs that compose the Large Aperture Seismic Array are electronically correlated and recorded.

18 Out of this world

OTHELLO: It is the very error of the Moon;
She comes more near the Earth than she was wont.
Shakespeare, *Othello*

Fig. 67: Lunar seismograph stations and moonquakes. This sketch map shows the positions of the seismographs that are or have been operating on the moon and the epicentres of some of the moonquakes they have detected. By terrestrial standards 'normal' moonquakes are very deep indeed.

Geophysicists studying the basic structure and tectonics of our planet have been known to complain that there is only one Earth. It is very difficult to know whether the things you have discovered are terrestrial accidents, or true of planets in general and therefore of prime importance. Since November 1969 when an American Apollo space mission successfully placed a seismograph on the Moon the situation has become a little better. There are now five stations operating (Figure 67, Plate 74).

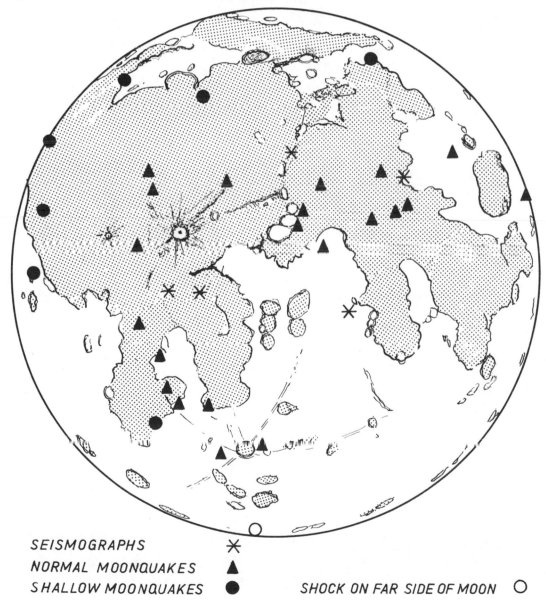

SEISMOGRAPHS ✳

NORMAL MOONQUAKES ▲

SHALLOW MOONQUAKES ●   SHOCK ON FAR SIDE OF MOON ○

Plate 74: Lunar seismology. The Apollo II spacecraft carried four seismographs to the Moon, three long-period instruments and a short-period vertical-component one, which is seen in close-up in the smaller picture. The astronaut is standing just behind the seismometer assembly, on either side of which (facing east and west) are the solar panels that provide the power supply.

Before the first instrument was landed, seismological opinion about the existence of moonquakes (or *selenoseisms* if you insist upon a word in the classical tradition) was divided, but it was readily agreed that a seismograph on the Moon would yield a great deal of needed information. The impact of meteorites could probably be recorded, it would certainly be possible to record the impact of landing spacecraft, and if all else failed explosive charges could be detonated. In one way or another, knowledge of the Moon's interior would be forthcoming.

The first problem was to develop a seismometer that could withstand the shock of an unmanned landing. Seismologists took to dropping seismographs out of helicopters and even to firing them like circus artists from small cannon. Unfortunately the first attempts to land an instrument failed, and even when there was an astronaut on the spot the recordings looked so strange that he was accused of stumbling over something, but in the end things sorted themselves out.

There are interesting differences between earthquakes and moonquakes, and the internal structure and the wave-transmitting properties of the Moon have turned out to be rather different from those we expected. Compared with the Earth, the Moon is seismically quiet. Nearly all the shocks are very small. Over a year the total energy they release is barely sufficient to make a shock much bigger than magnitude 2, but they are fairly numerous and the recording stations are sensitive enough to pick up between 600 and 2 000 shocks a year, depending on the site. This does not include the very small 'thermal moonquakes' that accompany the abrupt temperature change at lunar sunrise and sunset. These tiny shocks seem to be the result of small-scale cracking and slumping of the surface.

Three larger kinds of disturbance are picked up. First there are the impacts of falling meteorites, though it has turned out that there are not nearly so many big ones as terrestrial meteor observations had suggested. Next there are the normal moonquakes, which turn out to originate at depths between 600 and 900 kilometres, and could not be regarded as 'normal' on Earth. These seem to come from a limited number of foci, perhaps fewer than fifty. The seismograms of different shocks from the same focus are almost identical with one another, and each focus seems to become active at some definite time of the month. Tidal forces apparently account for this. There are peaks of activity 14 days apart, and secondary peaks at intervals of 206 days, which would coincide with the Sun's contribution to the tidal forces.

The last type of moonquake is very shallow, and may result like terrestrial earthquakes from the release of crustal stress. So far only about a dozen of these have been observed, and there is no obvious pattern in their positions or times of occurrence (Figure 67).

Lunar seismograms are very different in appearance from those of earthquakes (Figure 68). The movements are much higher in frequency, and reverberations continue for a very long time. It is hard to pick out definite phases, and there are no clear surface-waves. The very dry condition of the rocks on the lunar surface is thought to be responsible, but we still have much to learn about wave propagation on the Moon.

The interior of the Moon, like that of the Earth, has three main divisions, but their properties are rather different. By using the records of artificial shocks, meteorite impacts, and the larger moonquakes, it has been possible to build up a travel-time curve for

P-waves for distances up to about 1 000km. The phases *PP* and *PPP* have also been identified (Figure 69).

Compared with the Earth's, the Moon's layers are comparatively irregular, and contain large inhomogeneities. The crust is about 60 kilometres thick, and within it the average *P*-velocity is about 6·7 km/sec. Higher velocities can be found not only in the basalts that form the floors of the great lunar seas (the *maria* as they are called), but also at the base of the crust where they may in some places amount to a kind of high-velocity layer. Below the crust the velocity rises to 8 km/sec., and remains fairly uniform to the base of the mantle, which extends to a depth of about 700 kilometres.

The core is not at all closely analogous to that of the Earth. Astronomical measurements have shown that the Moon's mean density is only 3·3, so that no great quantity of metal could exist. The lunar core does not seem to transmit *S*-waves, or at least does not transmit them well, but it appears to be solid, and the explanation seems to lie in its lack of strength. It might therefore be appropriate to describe it as a lunar asthenosphere, and the mantle above it as the lithosphere. Conditions at the boundary are complicated, and it may be far from smooth.

These lunar studies provide a first glimpse of the contributions that seismology can make to planetary astronomy. By the time this book

Fig. 68: Moonquakes. Seismograms of normal and shallow moonquakes and of a meteorite impact. The two upper traces in each case are from long-period horizontal component seismographs, and the lower ones from long- and short-period verticals. Note the gradual build-up and slow decay of the vibrations. (After Nakamura et al.)

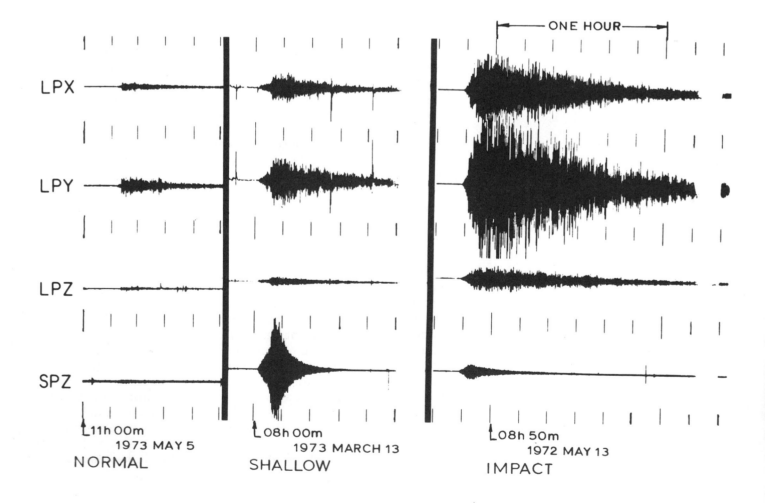

ONE HOUR

LPX

LPY

LPZ

SPZ

└11h 00m
1973 MAY 5
NORMAL

└08h 00m
1973 MARCH 13
SHALLOW

└08h 50m
1972 MAY 13
IMPACT

is in print it seems likely that the two Viking missions will have landed seismographs on Mars. Getting their information back to Earth will be more difficult technically than getting it back from the Moon, but it is believed that the problems have been solved. Each of the stations will have a life-time of only 90 days, and the two of them will be running together for only half of that time. What we already know about Mars suggests that the structure and tectonics will be more Earth-like than those of the Moon, and it should not be long before marsquakes (*areoseisms*?) join the earthquakes and the moonquakes as subjects for seismological concern.

In November 1976 a seismometer placed on the Plains of Utopia by the Viking space-craft recorded what appears to be a shock of about magnitude 6.

Fig. 69: Internal structure of the Moon. A cross-section showing the size of the lunar crust, mantle, and core, and the foci of normal and shallow moonquakes.

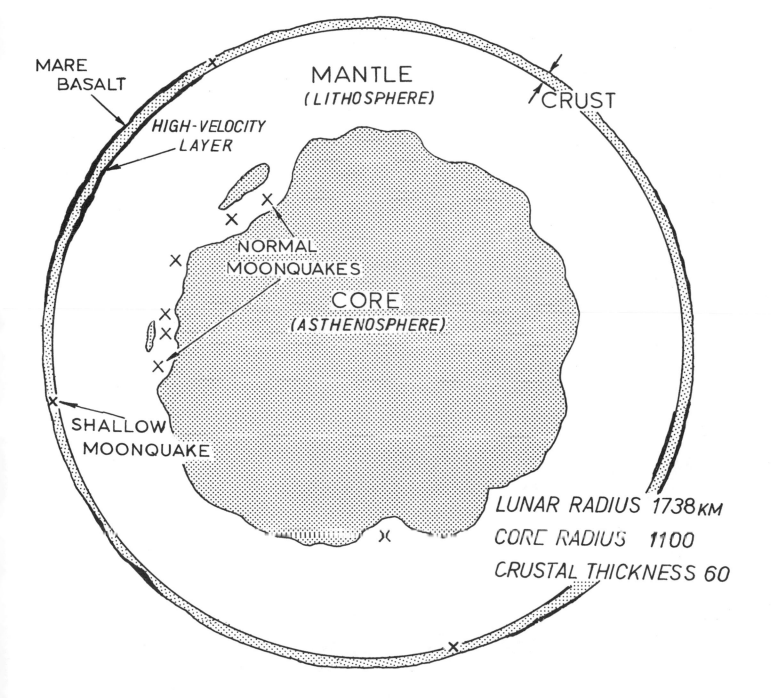

19 More seismic geography

JACQUES: . . . strange places cramm'd
       With observation . . .
       Shakespeare, *As You Like It*

We have already described the distribution of the world's seismic belts and stable areas, and seen how both the broad pattern and the local character of the activity are explained by the plate-tectonic hypothesis. In most parts of the world I have visited, seismic and otherwise, the active regions best known to the general public seem to be California and Japan, perhaps because the more vigorously active countries are less developed, or because the work of their seismologists is less well publicised. Both these places, like New Zealand, lie on the margin of the Pacific Plate, but in the three cases the nature of the contact with the neighbouring plate is different, and the character of the seismicity differs accordingly. Let us examine it in more detail.

Plate 75: San Andreas Fault. An aerial view of a section of the San Andreas Fault, showing how the spurs of the hills have been truncated by successive horizontal movements of the fault.

Of the three, California is the simplest. Here the great San Andreas Fault (Plate 75) marks the contact between the Pacific and the American Plates. Periodical transcurrent movement along this fault (or one of the subsidiary faults related to it) gives rise to shallow earthquakes, but there is no subduction or overthrusting of either plate to produce deep-focus activity. The smaller shocks in particular are often very shallow, and as a consequence are felt only over a small area, even when people at the epicentre feel quite high intensities. Californians feel fewer shocks than New Zealanders, but the ones they do feel are more alarming! The pattern of epicentres (Figure 70) and the pattern of faults (Figure 71) are closely similar, explaining the early readiness of American seismologists to accept the elastic-rebound theory. By comparison, Japan and New Zealand offer complicated problems, but they are far more typical of the Pacific margin as a whole. The basic simplicity of the Californian pattern is not at all usual.

New Zealand's Alpine Fault, which follows the western slopes of the Southern Alps (Plate 76, Figure 76) offers many geological parallels to the San Andreas Fault of California, but its existence could not easily be deduced from maps of New Zealand earthquakes (Figures 72, 73 and 74). Although the level of activity varies, and some parts of the country may experience a temporary quiescence, shallow shocks are experienced in all parts of the two main islands. It

Fig. 70: Earthquakes in California. This map shows the epicentres of the earthquakes that occurred over a period of about three months. The broken line shows the area within which the shocks could be reliably detected and located.

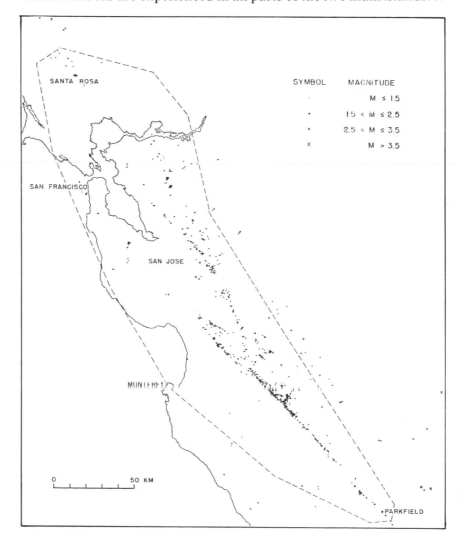

is nevertheless possible to distinguish two important groupings. The shocks of the Main Seismic Region (Figure 76) cover most of the North Island except the Northland Peninsula, and the northern parts of the South Island. Those of the Fiordland (or Southern) Region are concentrated in the south-western part of the South Island. Between the two lies the Central Seismic Region which is by no means inactive, but is less seismic than the other two regions.

There are no deep-focus shocks in the Central Region, but they occur in both the Main and Fiordland Regions. Those of the Main Region lie within a zone that crosses it from the Bay of Plenty to Nelson and Marlborough (Figures 74 and 75). With the exception of a small group of shocks that lie about 600 km below northern Taranaki, the deepest earthquakes are at the northern end of the zone. Going southwards, the maximum depth becomes less in a regular way, until the deep and shallow systems merge. This system of foci, which has sometimes been called the New Zealand Sub-Crustal Rift, is of the kind that many writers call a Benioff Zone, and is now considered by many seismologists to mark the position of the descending edge of the Pacific Plate.

The deep activity in Fiordland is much more tightly grouped than that in the north. The epicentres all lie close to Lake Te Anau, and the focal depths are about 100 or 120 km. These are the southernmost deep shocks to be found on the western side of the Circum-Pacific Belt.

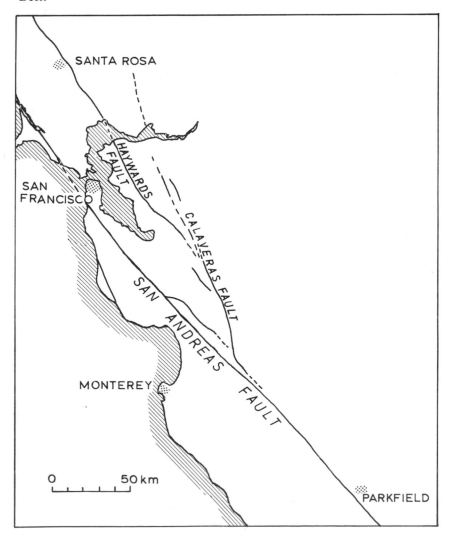

Fig. 71: Faults in California. Major faults in the area shown in Figure 70. Earthquake activity in California closely follows the pattern of geological faults apparent at the surface.

*Plate 76: The Alpine Fault, following
the western side of the snow-covered
Southern Alps in the South Island of
New Zealand. This photograph, taken
from an orbiting satellite, shows over
150km. of its length from the Grey River
to the Franz Josef Glacier. The large
lake at the northern end is Lake
Brunner, and that at the south Lake
Mapourika, with the Okarito and
Saltwater Lagoons on the coast to the
north of it.*

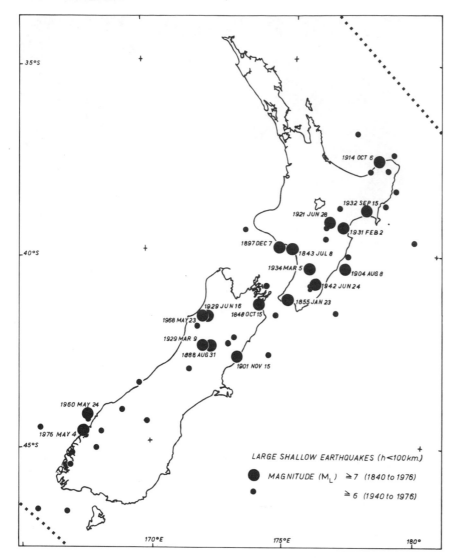

LARGE SHALLOW EARTHQUAKES (h<100km.)

MAGNITUDE (M$_L$)   ≧ 7 (1840 to 1976)

≧ 6 (1940 to 1976)

Fig. 72: Large shallow earthquakes in New Zealand. The south western part of the South Island is very sparsely inhabited. The present distribution of magnitude 6 earthquakes suggests that the historical record of shocks in that part of the country is very incomplete. Magnitudes of shocks before 1929 have been estimated by comparing their felt effects with those of instrumentally recorded shocks.

Considering the configuration of the earthquake activity and the position of the other geophysical features of the region (Figure 76), it appears that under the North Island the edge of the Pacific Plate is being thrust or pulled beneath the edge of the Indian Plate, while in the Fiordland Region, it is the Pacific Plate that is on top. The transition between the two arrangements, in which the Alpine Fault must play an important part, is naturally complex.

The arrangement of geophysical features in the Main Seismic Region is broadly that of an island arc. There are both active and recently extinct volcanoes, and the North Island is crossed by a major negative gravity anomaly. Off its east coast lies the submarine Hikurangi Trench. All of these features and the belt of deep earthquakes are roughly parallel and in the relative positions to be expected, though there are important variations in the finer detail. There is a narrow gap and an offset between the New Zealand deep-focus activity and the great system that continues the Circum-Pacific Belt north-eastwards to the Kermadec Islands and Tonga.

It is clear that the Fiordland system is oriented towards the Tasman Basin rather than towards the Pacific, but its geophysical features are less well marked. There are no active volcanoes, and older volcanism is represented only by the Otago Peninsula (close to

Fig. 73: Shallow earthquakes in New Zealand. This map shows the activity in 1971 and 1972. The broad pattern persists from year to year, but the details change. The absence of a shock reaching magnitude 6 is unusual, and activity in the Central Region is somewhat above average. The absence of shocks in the Northland Peninsula and the south-east of the South Island, however, is normal, though neither of these regions is permanently without shocks.

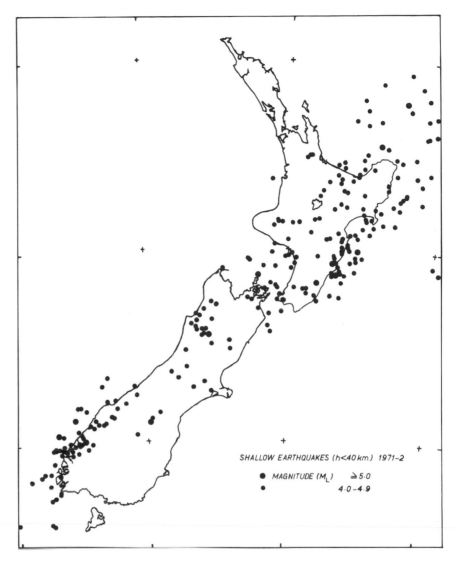

SHALLOW EARTHQUAKES (h<40 km.) 1971–2

● MAGNITUDE (M_L) ≧5.0

• 4.0 – 4.9

Dunedin) and the tiny Solander Island, in the western approaches to Foveaux Strait. Although there is deep water very close to the west coast there is no well-defined trench, and the arrangement of the gravity anomalies, positive and negative, is not quite that conventionally expected. Fiordland is a rugged area, covered with dense forest and for the most part without permanent inhabitants. Close seismograph stations have been established only within recent years, and other geophysical data are just becoming available.

The Northland Peninsula was until recently believed to be quite without earthquakes, but in November 1963 a small shock was felt near Kaitaia in the far north of the peninsula. On Christmas Eve a further shock, of about magnitude 5¼ did some minor damage. Since then there have been several smaller shocks in the same area, and in other places between there and Auckland. The publicity brought to light accounts of earthquakes felt in the Bay of Islands in 1914, and it is now clear that no part of New Zealand is without its earthquakes. Occurrences like this are a warning against too fine a division in seismic zoning schemes.

So far as we know, New Zealand is spared from the very largest earthquakes. Only two, the semi-legendary *Hao-whenua* in about 1460 and the south-west Wairarapa earthquake in 1855, seem likely to have had magnitudes as high as 8. Both the historical record and

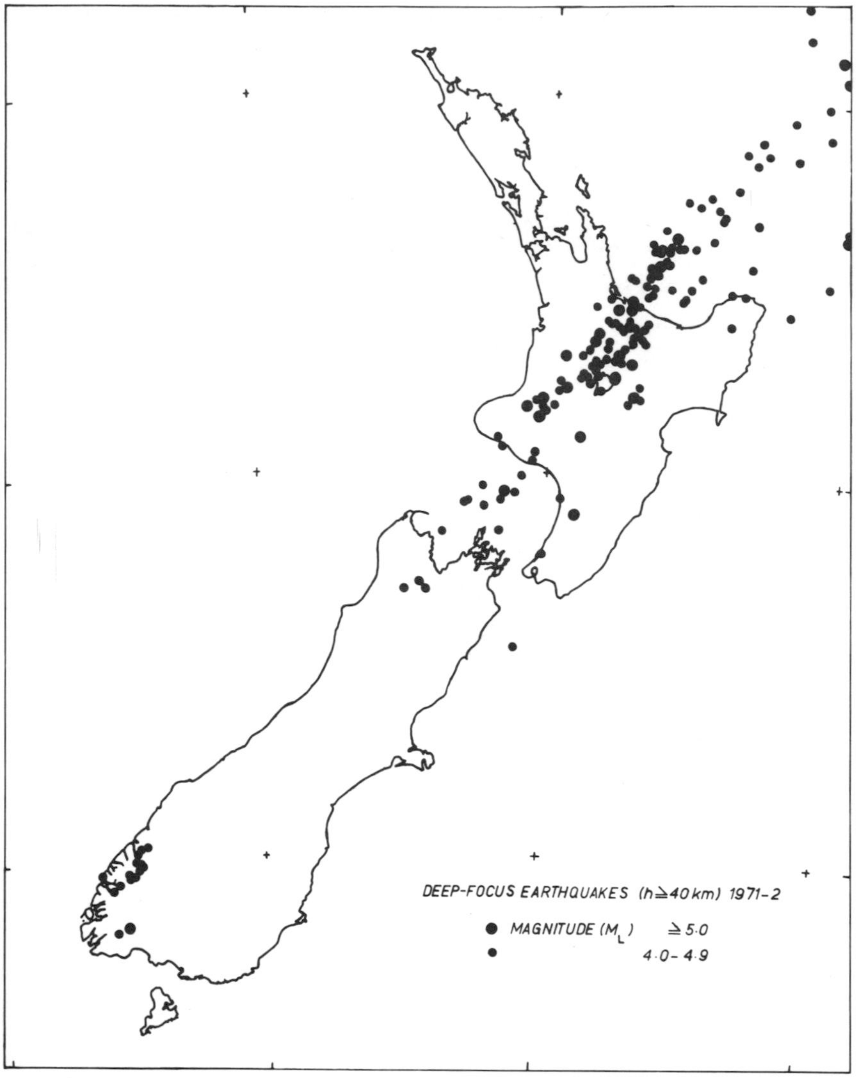

Fig. 74: Deep earthquakes in New Zealand. Epicentres of sub-crustal earthquakes in 1971 and 1972. The two separate systems of deep activity are clearly shown.

the pattern of the smaller activity suggest that on the average shocks as big as these do not happen more than about once a century, but magnitude 7 earthquakes can be expected about once a decade. Fortunately, few of them have happened close to large towns. There is a list of these shocks and an epicentre map in the Appendix, and some of the larger or more interesting ones are described in the next chapter.

Japanese earthquakes arise from the relative movement of the Pacific and Eurasian Plates; but we find that as in New Zealand the meeting of the plates has produced a rather complicated structure. The line of seismicity that extends southwards from Kamchatka through the Kuril Islands and Hokkaido divides in central Honshu, and the inner branch that follows the main axis of Japan through Shikoku and Kyushu is a secondary one. The main activity turns abruptly to the south-east and follows a chain of small volcanic islets that includes the Bonin and Volcano groups. This change in direction is shared by the gravity anomalies, the volcanoes, and the submarine trench off eastern Japan (Figure 77). Geologically it is marked by a great volcanic depression known as the Fossa Magna, which crosses central Honshu and contains a number of important cones, including Mount Fuji. The deep-focus earthquakes of the outer system extend beneath Honshu and the Japan Sea to the Asian mainland, but in the

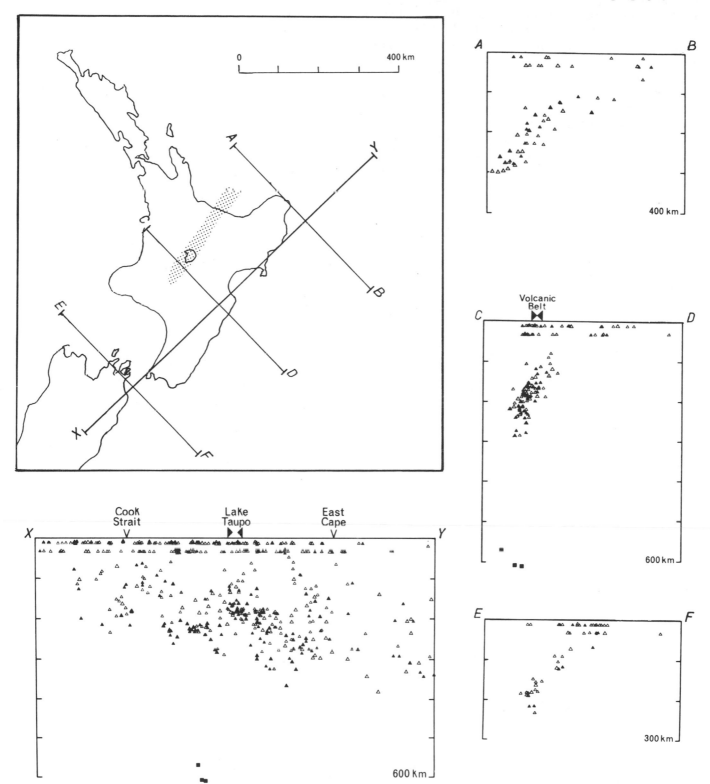

Fig. 75: Deep earthquakes in New Zealand. These cross-sections of the Main Seismic Region show that the foci lie within a restricted volume that may indicate the extent of a down-going lithospheric slab. Note the compact group of isolated shocks at a depth of about 600 km. The shading on the map indicates the active volcanic region. (Cross-sections after Hamilton and Gale.)

inner system there are breaks in both the line of volcanoes and the deep seismicity that last almost to Kyushu. In terms of plate tectonics, the inner and outer systems embrace a Philippines 'platelet' (Figure 53) or in older language, northern Japan has an arcuate and southern Japan a block-type structure.

Japan's long civilization has produced a very detailed historical record of its past earthquakes, though China can boast an even longer one. The earliest reliable record of a Japanese earthquake dates from A.D. 416 and, for central Japan at least, the record of large events becomes very complete after the great Nankaido shock in 684. Imamura, who has catalogued 66 destructive shocks between 1596 and 1935, considers that over that period shocks in even remote parts of the country were adequately covered.

There is doubt whether the Colombia-Equador earthquake on January 31, 1906 or the Sanriku shock off the east coast of Honshu on March 3, 1933, both of which Richter has assigned magnitudes of 8·9, was the largest since instrumental records have been available; but there is no doubt that from the human point of view the Chinese Tang Shan earthquake on July 27, 1976 was the greatest natural disaster in modern times. Only the sketchiest accounts of the catastrophe are yet available, but about half a millon people lost their lives. This is the highest death toll in any earthquake in the last four

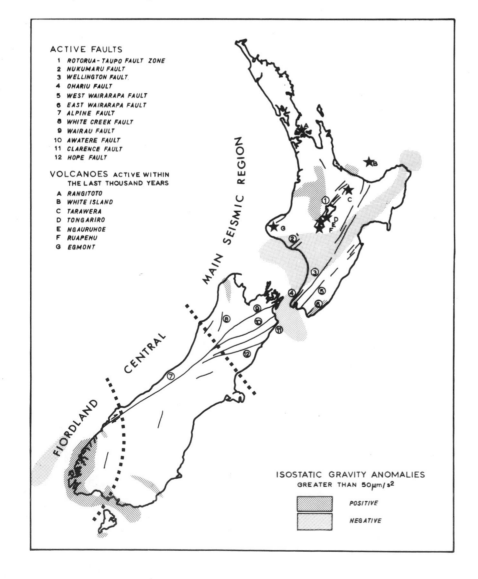

Fig. 76: Seismotectonic features of New Zealand. The relationship of the three seismic regions to the active volcanoes, major faults, and gravity anomalies. The close relationship between the earthquakes and the surface faulting found in California (Figures 70 and 71) is not present in New Zealand.

Plate 77: Regional uplift. White bands of dead barnacles and other marine growths record the uplifting of the island of Awa Shima and nearby parts of the coast of Honshu in the Niigata earthquake of 1964.

centuries, and the second highest in all recorded history. The only comparable event of which we have an adequate account is the Kwanto earthquake on September 1, 1923, which almost completely destroyed Tokyo and Yokohama, two of the most densely populated cities in the world. Official figures record the deaths of nearly a hundred thousand people.

The Kwanto earthquake, which is usually called after the province most severely affected, was in fact centred about 80 km south-west of Tokyo near the island of Oshima in Sugami Bay, and many of the smaller towns about the bay were badly damaged by the tsunami that followed. In some of the smaller inlets it reached heights of up to twelve metres and there were many drownings; but the tsunami had its advantages: it extinguished many fires that would otherwise have been uncontrollable.

Plate 78: Faulting and uplift. Displacement of the Hanning Bay Fault in the 1964 Alaskan earthquake. The white coating on the rocks at the left consists of the bleached remains of dead sea creatures lifted above water-level. The whole area has been raised, but the land on the left of the fault has come up some three metres more than that on the right.

Plate 79: Transcurrent faulting. Many photographs of distorted fence-lines have been published since this one was taken by Alexander McKay at Glynn Wye in north Canterbury in 1888, first establishing the importance of transcurrent movements. The displacement was about three metres.

Fig. 77: Japanese deep earthquakes. This map shows the relative positions of the deep earthquakes, the Japan Trench, the Fossa Magna, and the active volcanoes. Shallow earthquakes have not been shown.

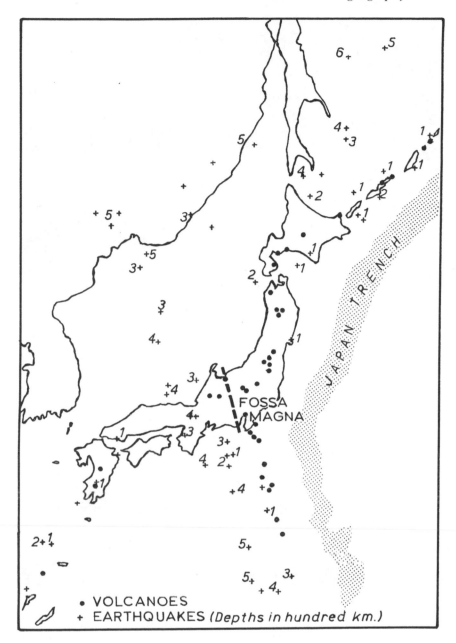

FOSSA MAGNA

JAPAN TRENCH

• VOLCANOES
+ EARTHQUAKES *(Depths in hundred km.)*

Plate 80: Kwanto earthquake, 1923. This picture, taken from a military aeroplane, shows the many separate outbreaks of fire which gave rise to conflicting streams of refugees.

Plate 81: The ruins of Tokyo after the Kwanto earthquake and subsequent fire.

Plate 82: Refugees in a Tokyo park after the Kwanto earthquake.

In Tokyo and Yokohama, the enormous death-toll was due to fire, and not to collapsing buildings. Japanese homes have traditionally been made of wood, with internal partitions of light sliding paper-covered frames. They are heated with portable charcoal braziers, which can easily tip and ignite the woven matting that covers the floors. In the hour that followed the earthquake, over a hundred fires had been located by the fire department, but with the telephone and alarm systems out of action and the streets becoming increasingly jammed with refugees there was little they could do. The streams of fugitives, many of them carrying inflammable belongings on handcarts, converged upon the bridges of the Sumida-gawa River, not realizing that the danger from which they were fleeing was equally serious on both sides. The bridges themselves caught fire, and no escape from the heat was to be found even in the river, down which flaming debris was drifting. Fire has been a complication in many earthquake disasters, to the extent that many Americans think of the destruction of San Francisco in 1906 as a great fire rather than an earthquake, but it did not match the horror and tragedy of the events in Tokyo in 1923.

The details of the ground movement in the Kwanto earthquake still puzzle seismologists, though we should not be surprised to find that a shock of magnitude 8·3 is a complex event, and some of the movements observed should undoubtedly be attributed to the larger aftershocks. Imamura believes that there was at least one very large one under the land to the north of the main epicentre.

Japanese seismologists carried out a very precise survey of the area affected (Figure 78). Assuming that trig stations some 80 kilometres to the north were still in their original positions, they found that the whole of the Boso Peninsula and the land about Sugami Bay had moved to the south east. On the peninsula the displacements were as great as four and a half metres, but they became progressively less inland, being less than a metre on the far side of Tokyo and eventually becoming undetectable. The island of Oshima, on the other hand, seemed to have moved nearly a metre to the north. As well as the horizontal movements, they also found an uplift of about two metres around the bay.

What happened beneath the waters of the bay has still to be sorted out. Some of the changes in depth reported by the Japanese naval party that prepared the new charts can possibly be explained by slumping, but the deepest part of the bay seemed to have become about 200 metres deeper, and there were other subsidences twice as big.

In the open ocean it is often reasonable to attribute apparent changes in depth to uncertainty in the position of the survey ships, but when 83 000 soundings in a land-locked bay are involved this seems less likely. The alternative is to assume movements larger than in any other known earthquake, and most seismologists assume some defect in the survey made before the earthquake.

In 1923 the school of seismological research established by Milne had lost something of its initial impetus, but as a result of the Tokyo disaster the Imperial Earthquake Research Institute was set up at Tokyo University, and a new period of vigorous Japanese research began. Californian research was a little slower to begin, but the report of the commission that investigated the San Francisco earthquake of 1906 and the elastic rebound theory put forward by Reid as a result are major seismological landmarks.

The San Francisco shock on April 18, which like the Kwanto earthquake had a magnitude of 8·3, occurred in a surprising year. In 1906 at least seven other earthquakes are believed to have reached magnitude 8. The Colombia-Equador shock on January 31 with a magnitude of 8·9 contends with the Sanriku earthquake in 1933 for the title of largest instrumentally recorded shock, and a Chilean shock on August 17 reached 8·6. It is not size alone that makes an earthquake remembered.

The great earthquake in 1906 is not the beginning of California's earthquake history. Shocks had been felt by explorers in the eighteenth century, and they were familiar to the fathers of the Spanish missions, several of which were seriously damaged. In 1812 forty people were killed when the church at San Juan Capistrano collapsed, and the year became known as the 'year of earthquakes'. There were large shocks near San Francisco in 1836 and 1838, and one near Fort Tejon in central California in 1852. The Owens Valley earthquake in 1872 was the first to become the subject of a geological report.

Relative movement along the Californian faults is carrying the western coast of the state northwards at an average rate of a few

Fig. 78: *Ground displacement in the Kwanto earthquake. The arrows show the direction of the permanent ground movement revealed by comparison of precise surveys made before and after. the shock. Their lengths are proportional to the amount of the displacement. The locations of a number of places mentioned in the text have also been shown.*

Fig. 79: *Transform faulting. The transverse fractures that break up the mid-oceanic ridges are believed to be transform faults. Most earthquakes occur on the segment of the fault between the sections of the ridge. Here the sense of the movement is opposite to that which would be inferred from the displacement of the ridge, because of the spreading from its crest.*

centimetres a year, a process that must eventually bring about a *rapprochement* between the citizens of Los Angeles and those of San Francisco, who live on opposite sides of the San Andreas Fault.

In size and extent the San Andreas is very similar to the Alpine Fault in New Zealand, but instead of ending in opposing overthrusts, the San Andreas Fault is related to a series of submarine fracture-zones that had been puzzling geophysicists ever since they became known in the 1950s. These too are transcurrent faults, but of a kind that was called *transform faults* by Professor J. Tuzo Wilson, the Canadian who succeeded in explaining them in 1965. Transform faults occur where a mid-oceanic ridge has been fractured, and the sections displaced laterally. The result is a fracture with different rates of spreading at adjacent points on the opposite sides (Figure 79). The seismicity of mid-oceanic ridges is often associated with these transverse fractures.

Considered as a disaster the San Francisco earthquake in 1906 falls well short of the horror that occurred in Tokyo in 1923, but the destruction of a great city by earthquake and fire is never a small matter. It is estimated that some 700 people died and 28 000 lost their

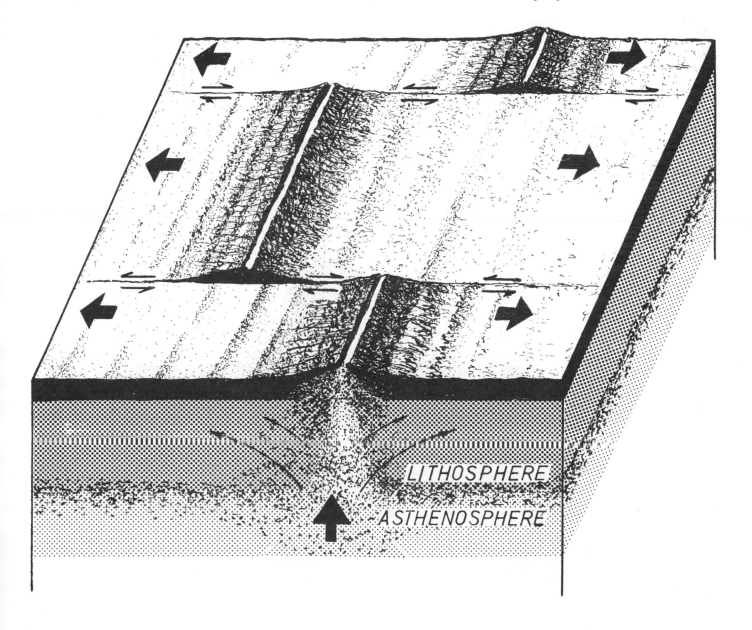

LITHOSPHERE

ASTHENOSPHERE

Plate 83: San Francisco earthquake. Fire added greatly to the devastation in 1906. Broken water-mains and rubble-strewn streets, hampered attempts at fire-fighting.

homes. The greatest damage was in the business area of the city, built mainly upon land reclaimed from the bay. The subsequent fire was confined to an area of just under ten square kilometres only by the decision to dynamite rows of buildings that were still standing. Many of the water-mains had been disrupted, and in the absence of isolating valves the pressure soon fell in the sections that had remained intact. The total value of the property lost has been put at about four million dollars.

The shock had a magnitude of 8·3. The value is particularly well known for so early a shock, as the Investigation Commission had the foresight to collect and publish seismograms from all over the world. In very large earthquakes it is probably misleading to talk about the epicentre, for the source must have an appreciable size, but it is usual to assign a point on the San Andreas Fault about 50 kilometres north-west of the city. The fresh fault breakage that resulted is the longest on record for a single shock, even if we accept the minimum estimate of 300 kilometres. In places the fault passes beneath the sea, and there are other observational difficulties. Richter suggests that the true value is nearer 430 kilometres. The amount of the displacement varies greatly, reaching a maximum of nearly five metres north of the Golden Gate, leaving aside an offset of seven metres in soft ground near Tomales Bay, which is probably a surface effect and not a true indication of the fault movement. The displacement is almost all horizontal. No change in level of more than a metre was reported anywhere, and in most places there was little or none.

The area of damage follows the fault for well over five hundred kilometres, but it is only about eighty kilometres wide. This unusually pronounced elongation is probably due in part to the extent of the faulting, but differences in geological foundation account for some of it.

20 Some famous earthquakes

> . . . The strong-based promontory
> Have I made shake, and by the spurs pluck'd up
> The pine and cedar:
>
> Shakespeare, *The Tempest*

Earthquakes have always been the subject of rumour and exaggeration. That ancient gossip writer, Pliny, tells of twelve cities in Asia overthrown by earthquake; and Seneca records the birth of two new islands, Thereon and Therea. In 740 'The Citie of *Constantinople* was so wonderfully shaken with an Earthquake an whole yeare together, that the Emperour thereof, and all his people, were constreyned to dwell abroade in the fields vnder tents and pauilions, for feare that their houses & buildings would fall on their heads.'

The theoreticians of classical antiquity have not left seismology much of permanent value. Aristotle, who often has something interesting to say even when he is wrong, ascribes earthquakes to winds imprisoned in underground caverns, and so lays the basis for popular beliefs about earthquake weather.

Instrumental seismology begins in China, where Chang Heng devised a seismoscope in A.D. 132. It was a nice blend of artistry and practicality. Round the outside of a tall jar containing an inverted pendulum was a ring of carved dragons' heads, each holding a ball in its jaws. When the pendulum moved, one or more balls was dislodged and fell into the open mouth of a frog stationed below in a suitable place to swallow it.

It is not only the great disasters that are recorded in history. 'Tis since the earthquake now eleven year,' says Juliet's nurse, and Shakespeare himself no doubt felt the earthquake of 1580. This shock forms the subject of a pamphlet by Thomas Twyne, which contains more good sense and accurate observation than the modern reader would expect from the title – 'A fhorte and pithie difcourfe concerning the engendring, tokens, and effects of all Earthquakes in Generall; Particularly applyed and conferred with that moft ftrange and terrible worke of the Lord in shaking the Earth, not only within the Citie of London, but alfo in moft partes of all Englande: VVhich hapned vpon VVenfday in Eafter weeke laft paft, which was the fixt day of April, almoft at fixe a clocke in the euening, in the yeare of our Lord GOD. 1580.'

Twyne's views upon the cause of earthquakes, like those that Shakespeare has put into the mouth of Hotspur, are basically Aristotelian, though he does not understate the part played by God's wrath. He is nevertheless a keen observer and an accurate reporter, and his account became a pattern for many that followed it, both in the Old World and the New.

We do not know the magnitude of the earthquake in the Shansi province of China in 1556, which is reliably supposed to have killed over 830 000 people. Although it is the worst seismic disaster on record, it is not likely to have been the largest known earthquake. That title is usually accorded the Lisbon earthquake of 1755, which possibly reached magnitude 9.

The epicentre of the Lisbon shock is believed to have been at sea, perhaps a hundred kilometres off the coast of Portugal. Because of the unusually widespread occurrences of seiches it has been difficult to establish the limits of the felt area. It was certainly more than 1 500 kilometres in radius, extending from the Azores to Italy, and from England to North Africa. Seiches were reported from as far away as Norway and Sweden, over 3 500 kilometres from the epicentre. We can safely dismiss statements that it was felt in the New World as reports of unrelated shocks.

The damage to Lisbon was very great. In 1755 the city had about 230 000 inhabitants, nearly 30 000 of whom were killed, according to conservative estimates. Great numbers of people were in the churches, for it was All Saints' Day, and the time of the first Mass. The shock was followed by a tsunami about seven metres in height, and by fire.

The disaster shocked all Europe, and the moralists and the wiseacres were not slow to make capital of it. Voltaire, in a preface to his *Poem on the Disaster of Lisbon* rebukes people who contended that 'The heirs of the dead would now come into their fortunes, masons would grow rich in rebuilding the city, beasts would grow fat on corpses buried in the ruins; such is the natural effect of natural causes'; but he secured the earthquake a more permanent place in literature by the reference in *Candide*.

'The earthquake is nothing new,' said Pangloss. 'The town of Lima in America experienced the same shocks last year. The same causes produce the same effects. There is certainly a vein of sulphur running under the earth from Lima to Lisbon.' Many of the learned men of the age would probably have agreed. The rest of the report is less factual, but reminds us again that in former times, natural disasters of this kind were more the occasion for examination of the national conscience than for investigation and taking practical measures against a recurrence. 'The University of Coimbra had pronounced that the sight of a few people ceremonially burned alive before a slow fire was an infallible prescription for preventing earthquakes; so that when the earthquake had subsided after destroying three-quarters of Lisbon, the authorities of that country could find no better way of avoiding total ruin than by giving the citizens a magnificent *auto-da-fé*.' This was no doubt as efficacious as the products of Joseph Addison's 'impudent mountebank, who sold pills which (as he told the country people) were very good against an earthquake'. It may be noted that the University of Coimbra is now equipped with seismographs.

It is not possible to give an account of every major earthquake from those times to the present, but a list of the more important ones is given in the Appendix. Europe has fortunately been free from further disasters on the scale of the Lisbon earthquake, whether in consequence of the *auto-da-fé* or not I venture no opinion. Other parts of the world have not fared so well. The New World was by no means earthquake free, and in the New England colonies, the settlers speculated on whether the 'electrical substance' drawn from the air by Mr Franklin's new lightning-rods might not be responsible.

It cannot be too often stressed that areas of minor seismicity are not free from the risk of larger shocks. Lisbon is not in a region of high activity, and the Mississippi Valley where the New Madrid earthquakes occurred in 1811 is even less active. The epicentral region was not densely settled at the time, but several of the shocks were of destructive intensity. Richter suggests that the largest of them, on December 16, was the largest known earthquake in what was then the territory of the U.S.A. It was felt in Boston, 1700 kilometres away, and in other places from Canada to New Orleans. Both its size and its location present a challenge to tectonic theory.

Another part of the United States not usually considered liable to earthquake is South Carolina, but Charleston was badly damaged in 1886. This shock was one of the first to be the subject of an extended geological report, and there are some excellent photographs (Plate 63).

Modern seismological observation, however, should begin with the visit of Robert Mallet to the area affected by the Italian earthquakes in 1857. In 1862 he published *The Great Neapolitan Earthquake of 1857; the first Principles of Observational Seismology*. These two volumes are finely illustrated with coloured lithographs, and are a seismological classic. Damaged towns and villages are described in detail. The direction of overthrow of buildings and monuments, the nature of the forces needed to produce the damage, and the patterns of isoseismals are all carefuly discussed, and an attempt is made to frame general principles. Mallet was not content just to describe damage. He was also an experimenter. He investigated the speed at which earthquake waves could travel by using charges of gunpowder to generate a shock, observing their

Plate 84: Raised beach terraces at Turakirae Head, east of the entrance to Wellington Harbour, preserve a long history of vertical movement of the coast, probably associated with ancient earthquakes. Sudden uplifts have left a succession of terraces, the edges of which are marked by lighter bands. The beach between the water-line and the first of these was first exposed in the West Wairarapa earthquake of 1855, and the next one above it in about 1460. The probable dates of the higher terraces are roughly 1100 B.C. and 2900 B.C. The slightly tilted steps on the more distant headland are the remnants of a still older beach, cut by the sea during the Pleistocene, at least 100 000 years ago.

arrival by watching the surface of a shallow bowl of mercury. He was also responsible for coining many of our technical words, among them seismology, isoseismal, and seismic focus. The earthquake was not a big one, unless we measure its importance by the contribution to knowledge which resulted from it.

Members of Captain Cook's expedition to New Zealand felt an earthquake in the Marlborough Sounds, but the country's earthquake history begins in about 1460. Maori traditions give details of a large shock near Wellington about that time, accompanied by impressive coastal uplift. The present Miramar Peninsula ceased to be an island, and there was a further addition to the series of raised beach-terraces at Turakirae (Plate 84). Here a whole set of terraces records successive uplifts going back for at least 6 500 years.

Organized European settlement of New Zealand dates from 1840, when the newly-arrived colonists felt their first shock. Thinking that the natives were trying to pull down their houses, they sprang from their beds and seized swords and pistols to do battle with the adversary. Three years later a more severe shock struck Wanganui. Houses and a church were damaged and a Maori was buried in a landslide; but the seriousness of the earthquake problem was not realized until 1848 when the Marlborough earthquake on October 16 destroyed or damaged most of the buildings in Wellington (Plate 85). Three lives were lost when an aftershock brought down an already damaged wall.

This earthquake has often been credited with the formation of the prominent 'Earthquake Rent' that can be followed along the side of the Awatere Valley for a hundred kilometres. Of course no single earthquake was responsible for the Awatere Fault, and on this occasion it did not move at all. Historical research has recently come upon clear descriptions of fault movement in the Wairau Valley, parallel and to the north west of the Awatere, which was not explored until some years later.

So large a shock within ten years of the founding of the city should have warned the colonists that special building measures would be needed in their new home, but the warning went largely unheeded. They discussed whether the shock had been caused by gas becoming ignited in a cavern under Cook Strait, propped up their damaged buildings, and went on building new ones in the same style as the old. In 1855 the lesson was repeated.

The 1855 earthquake is the only New Zealand shock in historic times believed to have reached magnitude 8. It originated on the South-West Wairarapa Fault on the far side of the Rimutaka Mountains, about 25 kilometres east of the city. There was vertical movement of up to three metres, and possibly surface breakage over about 50 kilometres, as well as uplifting of the coast and the shores of Wellington Harbour. Except for the Indian shock in the Rann of Kutch in 1819, this was the first occasion on which faulting had been observed to accompany an earthquake, and it became well-known to geologists from an account published by Lyell in his *Principles of Geology*.

Wellington had grown rapidly since 1848 and many of the new buildings were destroyed. It was realized that timber structures had fared relatively well, and the city authorities became divided upon whether fire or earthquake was likely to prove the greater hazard in the future. Eventually they settled upon brick for the central city, though most Wellingtonians still choose to live in a wooden house.

There have since been several serious fires, but there was to be no more serious earthquake damage in the city until the Masterton earthquakes of 1942.

Christchurch, like Wellington, has experienced large earthquakes, though there has never been an important epicentre quite so close. One of the more amusing aspects of Christchurch's troubles has been the difficulty of providing the cathedral with a fitting spire. The upper portion has been destroyed several times, in spite of a number of ingenious expedients, such as mounting the cross on top to swing like a pendulum, and having it consecrated by a bishop hauled to the top in a bosun's chair. Nevertheless, the present arrangement, in which the upper part is of wood, has maintained a suitable architectural composure for many years. The greatest of the Canterbury shocks occurred in 1901 near Cheviot, or Mackenzie as the township was then called. The government geologist of the time, Alexander McKay, published a very readable account of this shock. It begins with a summary of the views then commonly held concerning the cause of earthquakes, reviews the earlier earthquake history of the

Fitzherberts Store.

Ordnance Store.

Colonial Hospital.

Hickson & Co.

Plate 85: Marlborough earthquake, 1848. These sketches of damaged buildings in Wellington are the earliest pictorial record of the effects of earthquakes in New Zealand.

district, describes the damage he observed, reports the opinions of the local farmers, and concludes with an anecdote about a horse which died of fright.

The main shock was on 16th November, and on the 20th, McKay left Wellington for Christchurch, where he examined the cathedral spire, noticed that there had been a slight shift, and that 'some repairs had been effected'. The journey to Cheviot involved both rail and coach, as the train did not then run beyond Amberley; but he arrived at 4 p.m., just in time for an aftershock, which he did not feel. He remarks with some asperity upon the 'eagerness of the Press after the smallest item that deals with what is called "stricken Cheviot"', for he seems to have been deeply impressed by a common aspect of moderate earthquake damage. It is not obvious except at close range. From about a kilometre away 'the township looked the very ideal of a country town, in nothing peculiar save that it was smokeless because there were no chimneys'. When he entered the town, however, he found that the streets were littered with glass from broken windows, and most of the inhabitants, having pitched tents in the paddocks and harnessed the buggy for a quick retreat, had gathered at the post office to discuss the last aftershock.

The damage he found was of the kind usual with wooden buildings. They had moved from their foundations, the chimneys had fallen – in many cases through the roof – and contents were badly disarranged. Superficial cracks and slumps appeared along the roads. On the following day, 'a strong nor'-wester continued to blow, which made it impossible to do any photography, and rendered work of any kind very unpleasant'.

He records one of the earliest instances which has come to my notice of the direction of approach of an earthquake wave being determined by two people in telephone communication, one feeling the shock before the other. In this case it gave clear evidence that the shock originated to the north of Parnassus, a conclusion McKay had reached on other grounds. This was at variance with local opinion in Cheviot, which held that the shock had come from the east, or from the sea. These were honest opinions, but there were also some tall stories current. Mount Cookson, a limestone formation, was reported to be in eruption; and the bed of the Waiau River had been seen to open, first engulfing the water, and then as it closed again, forcing it to discharge in spouting columns which played to a height of ten metres! This story could have some foundation in the formation of sand craters.

The two earthquakes that have remained uppermost in the minds of the New Zealand public are the Murchison (or Buller) earthquake of 1929, and the Hawke's Bay earthquake in 1931. The Murchison earthquake, in which 17 people died, was the first New Zealand shock in which there had been a large loss of life.

Murchison, from which the shock has taken its name, is a small settlement of only 300 people built on narrow river flats where the steeply-gorged Buller River is joined by two tributaries. The valley is nowhere more than a kilometre wide, and the hills rise abruptly at its sides for twelve or fifteen hundred metres. It is one of the wettest parts of New Zealand, the shock occurred in mid-winter, and the weather had been exceptionally bad. The conditions were favourable for landslides, and many spectacular slips occurred, cutting roads and damming rivers. Many casualties were the result of the landslides, and others occurred in the flooding that followed the bursting of the temporary dams.

The hardships faced by the survivors are the material from which legends are made. The townships of Westport and Nelson, from which Murchison generally obtained its supplies, had themselves been damaged, and the roads were cut. The Public Works Department did what it could to shelter the homeless in sodden marquees put up in the school grounds, but it was five days before the road to Nelson could be opened again. No sooner had the town been evacuated and left in the care of a few watchmen than the real refugees began arriving from the remoter valleys.

Hoping to find shelter in Murchison, more than thirty women and children, sick and elderly, had made their way over thirty kilometres of landslides, and through bush so thick that tracks had to be cut.

Karamea had been completely forgotten. The tiny settlement had not been seriously damaged, but the road to Westport which was its only link with the outside world was cut in so many places by slips and washouts that it no longer existed, and food was running desperately short. A settler along the road walked the fifty kilometres to Westport in search of help, but it was not to arrive until a pioneer aviator was able to land his Tiger Moth on the beach fully two weeks later.

The earthquake, which had a magnitude of 7·8, was felt in all parts of New Zealand. Two members of the Geological Survey, M. L. Ongley and H. E. Fyfe, who made an exhaustive field study of the epicentral region found that the whole region had been uplifted, but that the eastern side had moved more than the western, causing a rift along the White Creek Fault, a feature that had previously been regarded as inactive. Where the fault crossed the main road, it left a vertical barrier five metres high.

Plate 86: Landslide. One of the many large landslides triggered by the Inangahua earthquake. This one temporarily dammed the Buller River, creating a further hazard for places down stream.

This shock seems to have been an unusually noisy one. The sounds may have been intensified by concentration in the narrow valleys, but they also travelled more than 100 kilometres through the high atmosphere and descended again in Taranaki. Weather conditions at other places at the same distance were not suitable for hearing them, but close to the epicentre noises like rolling thunder and bursts of artillery fire accompanied the aftershocks for many weeks.

New Zealand was badly shocked by the Murchison earthquake, but the Hawke's Bay earthquake that followed two years later was an even more serious disaster (See Plates 3 and 45). This time the towns of Napier, Hastings, Gisborne, and Wairoa – in all about 30 000 people – lay within the area of destruction. Of these people 256 were killed. The business areas of Napier and Hastings were almost totally destroyed, and fires completed the work of the earthquake.

The shock, on the morning of February 3rd, 1931 (local time) was centred within about 25 kilometres of Napier, and had a magnitude of 7·9. There was only minor faulting, but a tract of land some 90 kilometres long and 15 kilometres wide was raised by amounts up to 3 metres. Near Napier itself the rise was about two metres, draining large areas of the Ahuriri Lagoon and providing New Zealand with another fourteen square kilometres of territory, on which the city has since built its aerodrome.

About two weeks after the main shock a remarkable event occurred at Sponge Bay, near Gisborne. Men working on the beach saw a boulder bank rise from the sea, without previous warning, and without any tremors they could feel. The top of the bank is more than two metres above sea level, and its area is nearly a hectare.

Since 1931 New Zealand has not had an earthquake as big as those in Murchison and Hawke's Bay. On June 24th, 1942 a shock of magnitude 7 with an epicentre near Masterton badly damaged older buildings in an area that extended to the city of Wellington. There were no deaths, and only minor injuries, but the necessary repairs were a severe burden on the manpower of a country that was then at war. This shock resulted in the introduction of the Earthquake and War Damage Insurance scheme.

On May 24th, 1968 there was a magnitude 7 earthquake at Inangahua, about 35 kilometres from Murchison, which again brought down major landslides, one of which caused two deaths (Plate 86; see also Plate 65). An isoseismal map for this shock was given in Chapter One. The improved seismograph network, and the fact that parties of geologists and portable stations to record the aftershocks could be rushed into the area within a few hours of the event have made this the best studied New Zealand earthquake. The area is not densely populated, but there was serious damage to houses, bridges, railway lines, and underground pipes. In the month that followed the main shock there were fifteen aftershocks of magnitude 5 or more.

21 Some recent earthquakes

. . .Is this the scene
Where the old Earthquake-daemon taught her young
Ruin? Were these her toys?

P. B. Shelley, *Mont Blanc*

The year 1960 is among the most tragic in recent earthquake history, not only because of the catastrophic effects of the magnitude 8·5 Chilean earthquake in May, and the disastrous tsunami that followed it, but because of the disproportionately severe consequences of several earthquakes of moderate size that occurred in countries whose traditional building methods are faulty. On 21st February, a magnitude 5·5 earthquake killed forty-seven people in the Algerian village of Melousa, and on 24th April, 450 inhabitants of Lar and nearby villages in Iran were buried beneath the ruins of buildings destroyed by a shock whose magnitude was only $5^3/_4$, among them two hundred children parading in a festival procession through the narrow streets. A shock of the same magnitude that struck Agadir on the night of 29th February levelled the old city to the ground, and destroyed about half the buildings in the modern business centre. Over a third of its population was killed. Another third was injured. So many dead lay beneath the fallen masonry that orderly identification and reinterment was out of the question. The area was bulldozed flat and abandoned.

It can be argued that the Agadir earthquake was something of a freak. The last time a major earthquake occurred in this part of Morocco was in 1731, and the event appears to have been forgotten. More recent minor shocks were dismissed as of no importance. It had certainly never been suggested that Agadir lay in a major seismic zone, and even now many seismologists would feel that something larger than a magnitude $5^3/_4$ earthquake is needed before a place can be admitted to that category. After all, a shock of that size happens somewhere on Earth every three or four days. The other unusual circumstances are the shallow focal depth, estimated from the limited extent of the damaged area to be only 3 or 4 kilometres, and the fact that the epicentre lay within a kilometre or two of the town. When the radius of the area of damaging intensities is so small, it seems particularly unfortunate that this area should contain a city, and that the buildings of that city should be so poorly constructed.

What sort of place was Agadir, and how far was the disaster avoidable? The origins of the city are lost in antiquity. In the sixteenth century the Sherif Moulay Mohammed wrested it from the Portuguese and built the Kasbah; but after the earthquake of 1731 it suffered a decline until the early years of the present century when the natural advantages of its safe anchorage and the attractiveness of its fine sandy beaches were again recognized. Its importance as a port and a tourist centre increased, and in the expanding industrial area sixty canneries prepared sea-foods and agricultural produce for export.

It need not surprise us that the buildings of the Moroccan quarter fared badly. The old stone masonry was held together with a mortar of mud and sand, and roofed with anything from timber and corrugated iron to reinforced concrete slabs. The fate of so many attractive modern-looking hotels, apartment blocks and public buildings is more disturbing; but in most cases the appearance of quality was confined to the smooth outer plaster skin. Behind lay unreinforced stone masonry and inadequate mortar. The few reinforced-concrete buildings fared better. Although most of them lacked adequate cross-bracing, they did not collapse completely like the unbonded masonry.

Unlike Morocco, Chile is a country with a long history of large earthquakes. The epicentre of the magnitude $8\frac{1}{2}$ earthquake on 22nd May was in the south of the Arauco peninsula. It was almost immediately followed by great numbers of aftershocks, some of them large, spread over almost the whole length of the country; and it is not always clear which shock was responsible for any particular damage. The cities of Concepción and Valdivia were badly shaken, but many of their newer buildings conformed with effective codes imposed after a large earthquake in 1939, and performed well. Older masonry structures dating from before the introduction of the code were less fortunate.

Most of the phenomena associated with large earthquakes were observed in Chile — ground uplift in some regions, subsidence and consequent inundation in others, seiches in the lakes, landslides that dammed rivers, and mysterious lights in the air. Water-saturated clay soils flowed from beneath buildings, leading to their collapse, and blocking waterways, streams, and harbours. Two days after the shock the volcano Puyehue, 650 kilometres south of Concepción, erupted for the first time since 1905. Almost the only earthquake phenomenon that was not observed was surface faulting, though this has not stopped geologists from publishing maps showing a 'probable causative fault' in the sea.

The tsunami that followed was the most serious for many years. Not only were many of the coastal towns of Chile itself inundated,

Fig. 80: Alaskan uplift and subsidence. The zones of uplift and subsidence in the great earthquake of March 27th, 1964, as mapped by Dr George Plafker of the U.S. Geological Survey. Surface faulting was observed only at the southern end of Montague Island. The area in which aftershocks occurred is almost identical with the zone of uplift.

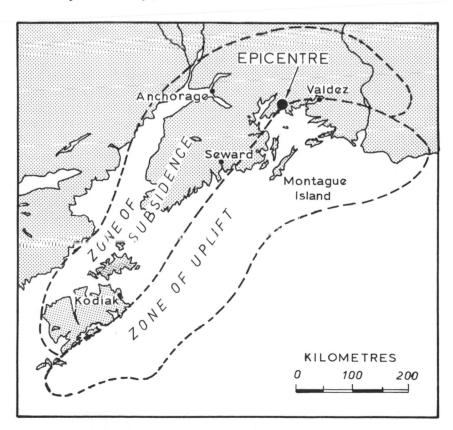

but the wave crossed the Pacific and caused damage around its entire perimeter. In Hawaii there were sixty-one deaths, in spite of the fact that the authorities had advised evacuation of the danger areas. Japan also suffered many casualties and extensive damage to coastal property and port installations. In New Zealand there was only minor damage.

Poor buildings of the type that made the Lar, the Agadir, and the Melousa earthquakes so disastrous were also to be found at Buyin-Zara. This region of Iran experienced a larger shock, of about magnitude 7, and the casualties were proportionately higher. Some twelve thousand villagers and much of their livestock were killed. Dr N. N. Ambraseys, who visited the area under UNESCO auspices, reports that those seismologists who had studied the area considered it to be 'the least seismic in the country', and that even the oldest villagers had never felt a shock strong enough to alarm them. The survival of old buildings and bridges in the area showed that nothing approaching the severity of the present shock could have occured since 1630. Most of the buildings were made of adobe-brick, and few survived the shaking. No major cities lie close to the epicentre, but the intensity in Teheran was great enough to crack plaster and to cause panic. People leapt from first-storey windows, lost control of vehicles, and fled from homes and places of entertainment.

This earthquake was accompanied by conspicuous faulting extending for over a hundred kilometres, probably occurring in at least two stages. Seiches, changes in the flow of springs and wells, and small mud-fountains were also reported. There is an apparently well-authenticated report of 'earthquake lights'. Thirty-nine people reported an orange-red glow over Rudak, a region in which there is no electricity supply. The glow was followed by a sound like a low-flying aeroplane. The Chilian apparition already mentioned was described as bluish-green.

The magnitude 6 earthquake at Skoplje, in Yugoslavia, on 26th July, 1963, provides yet another instance of the disastrous consequences of a moderate earthquake in a city that had chosen to ignore obvious precautions. Moderate earthquakes are not uncommon in other parts of Macedonia, and historical records show that Skoplje itself was destroyed twice before, in A.D. 518, and again in 1555. Many of the damaged buildings were new; but although the regulations specified anti-seismic precautions, it appears that they had frequently been waived as a natural result of impatience to repair the ravages of war, and to house the people of a rapidly-growing city with as little delay as possible. The gamble did not come off (Plates 49 and 50). Some of the building failures in the new areas were as spectacular and disastrous as those in the Old City, where many picturesque one-storey adobe houses and shops with tile roofs dating back several centuries managed to survive. On the other hand, there were only minor breaks in the water and sewerage systems. Poor foundations were an important factor in the disaster. The city lies on the late Tertiary sands and gravels of the Vardar basin, varying in thickness from three metres to eighty or more.

A surprising feature of the Skoplje earthquake was that no fire followed it. It seems that the greater use of electricity for domestic heating and cooking is at last reducing what was once the greatest of earthquake hazards. On the other hand, it must be remembered that the shock took place at a quarter past five on a summer morning.

On 27th March, 1964, an earthquake of magnitude $8\frac{1}{2}$ occurred at the northern end of Prince William Sound, Alaska. Although some faulting was observed on Montague Island, the enormous extent of the areas of uplift and subsidence is by far the most striking geological consequence of the shock. The area of aftershocks, which extends from near Valdez to the southernmost tip of Kodiak Island is almost exactly the size and shape of the South Island of New Zealand (Figure 80). Several of these aftershocks had magnitudes of 6 or more, and were therefore considerable earthquakes in their own right.

The wide publicity given to the effects of this earthquake upon the city of Anchorage has diverted attention from the fact that the epicentre was 130 kilometres away, and that other cities, such as Valdez and Seward, though just as close, were much less severely damaged. Much of Anchorage was built upon a thick tongue of old glacial moraine. Layers of sand and gravel underlain by ninety metres or so of unstable clay and poised above a steep submarine slope were held together by permafrost. It is not surprising that such a material proved unable to withstand shaking.

The chief engineering lessons from this shock are not to be found in the prestressed concrete flats that collapsed because of inadequate anchoring of the tensioning cables, or in the buildings that lost precast decorative panels inadequately tied to their facades, but in the many structures, ranging from small wooden houses to large city buildings, that remained in one piece after their foundations had

Plate 87: Superficial slumping. Much of the damage at Niigata, like that at this railway-station, was due to consolidation or slumping of poorly-compacted ground.

failed completely, leaving them bridging gaping chasms, or tilted at improbable angles (Plate 57). Ordinary well-constructed buildings have a surprising resistance to shaking, but no building can be safer than the site on which it stands. Much of the effort now directed to discussing differences in the frequency of earthquake occurrence would be better directed to the adequate study of differences in foundation characteristics. This lesson was to be repeated three months later in Japan.

Niigata is a city of about 340 000 inhabitants, situated on a low-lying sandy area at the mouth of the Shinano River, on the west coast on northern Honshu, the largest island of Japan. Just after 1 p.m. on 16th June, 1964, an earthquake of magnitude $7\frac{3}{4}$ occurred at sea about 70 kilometres north of the city. Casualties were few – twelve dead in Niigata itself, and as many more in nearby townships and the surrounding countryside. Most of the larger buildings were modern structures of reinforced concrete. They survived the shaking, but were badly damaged by the behaviour of the poor foundations.

About a third of the city subsided, by as much as two metres in places, as a result of compaction of the sand being shaken. Simultaneously, ground water was expelled through 'sand volcanoes', around the edges of heavy buildings, and through large fissures, so that pedestrians found themselves up to their knees in swirling muddy water. Flooding of this kind was worsened by a combination of high tide, and a small tsunami (Plate 33). These halted the normal flow of the river, which burst its banks and turned the streets within half a kilometre into temporary channels, in some of which the current was strong and deep enough to float motor vehicles. Bridge spans collapsed when the piers moved as a result of foundation failure (Plate 66), the runways of the aerodrome were cracked and under water, and the seventy tanks of the oil refinery caught fire. The fire spread to neighbouring houses, and destroyed 300 of them. Its cause is unknown. No outbreaks occurred elsewhere in the city. Electricity, water-supply, sewerage, and other city services were disrupted.

Apart from the flooding, which in some areas had not subsided after three days, the most spectacular effect was the tilting of many large and otherwise undamaged buildings. One of a group of eight similar four-storey reinforced-concrete apartment buildings overturned almost completely (Plates 70 and 88), and all of them sank some distance into the ground (Plate 62). The overturning took place slowly, and a newspaper report has it that a woman hanging out washing on the roof of the tilted building was able to ride down gently and to step off at ground level.

There has been no greater disaster in the Southern Hemisphere than the Peruvian earthquake of May 31st, 1970. The magnitude of the shock was 7·7, and the epicentre was about 25 kilometres off the coast to the west of Chimbote, a coastal port with a population of about 120 000. There are modern reinforced concrete buildings in Chimbote, and steel-framed factories, but the prevailing form of construction is adobe, which is used for most of the houses, some of which are two storied.

In the towns and villages over a radius of about a hundred kilometres, the adobe collapsed. Many of the better buildings were on poor foundations, and there was widespread liquefaction of the soil. It comes as no surprise that nearly 500 people died in Chimbote, but the total estimated loss of 70 000 lives, 50 000 injured, and 800 000 left homeless is staggering. The reason was the debris avalanche of Huascaran.

Plate 88: Improvisation. Realizing that their toppled apartment block is still in one piece, these Niigata citizens decided to return home and live on the walls.

Plate 89: Restoration. After the Liaoning earthquake, Chinese farmers begin the task of clearing the ejected mud and rubble from their roads and fields.

Plate 90: The Huascarán avalanche. The Plaza de Armas in Yungay before and after the catastrophic lahar triggered by the Chimbote earthquake in 1970. Only the palm trees remain to mark the former position of the town.

Nevado de Huascarán is an Andean peak 6 768 metres high lying just over a hundred kilometres due east of Chimbote. From its sheer western face an enormous mass of rock capped with ice and snow broke away and swept down the Llanganuco Valley towards the town of Yungay and the village of Ranrahirca. There had been avalanches before, even without the stimulus of an earthquake. In 1962 one of them had almost wiped out Ranrahirca, but Yungay was considered safe, for between it and the path of the avalanche there ran a spur some 250 metres high. In 1970 it was not enough; a lobe of the debris swept over the ridge.

Yungay had been a picturesque place with a handsome square and a cathedral. All that remained of it was a small part of the cathedral wall and four palms that had stood in the square. Of the 18 000 inhabitants, 15 000 were missing. In less than five minutes the debris had fallen three kilometres and swept forwards twelve. In Yungay, Ranrahirca, and other villages in its path, twenty-five or thirty thousand people lost their lives (Plate 90).

The Yungay avalanche was a giant lahar. Its highly fluid character is clear from the mud splashed on to the valley walls, from its great speed, and its ability to cross the dividing ridge. At the start it was probably ten or fifteen metres thick, but it quickly thinned as it travelled, and only three metres of debris were left in the Yungay town square. In it were huge boulders, some weighing as much as a hundred tons.

It is well to close with this reminder that we have not yet solved the whole earthquake problem. We have the examples of Yungay, Niigata, and Anchorage to show that even if buildings designed in accordance with a modern building code will not shake to pieces, the siting of our cities, towns and individual buildings is still in need of study.

Plate 91: Lahar debris. A close-up view of some of the material that composed the Huascarán avalanche.

Plate 92: What now? After the Niigata earthquake, homeless citizens confront the blaze of the fuel storage depot.

Specialized structures like dams and bridges and ever taller buildings continue to challenge the seismic engineer, and a host of secondary problems remain unsolved. Most of our water, electricity, and drainage systems are vulnerable at one point or another, and so are our roads, railways, docks, and aerodromes.

In many parts of the world, seismic zoning is leading to improved building codes. In others, as is unfortunately true of my own country, ill-informed pressure groups are able to use it as an excuse for relaxing existing precautions. The earthquakes at Niigata, Agadir, and Buyin-Zara all occurred in regions supposed (on inadequate grounds) to be safer than regions a few hundred kilometres away. The precautions taken by a wise community will not only provide a degree of resistance adequate for the prevailing level of activity, but must also provide for the infrequent large earthquake that is possible in regions of minor seismicity, or which falls outside the known limits of an active area.

Appendix

If a man will begin with certainties, he shall end in doubts;
but if he will be content to begin with doubts, he shall end
in certainties.

Francis Bacon, *The Advancement of Learning*

Facts and figures

In bringing this survey of present-day seismology to a close I am
conscious of how much has been left out. There is nothing about
laboratory experiments on the behaviour of materials under high
temperature and pressure, the ramifications of modern tectonic
theory have barely been sketched in, and whole regions of the Earth
seem to have been dismissed with little more than a mention.

But I hope it is possible to see what seismology is about, and how
many branches of physical and geological knowledge can be brought
to bear upon it. Few of us who claim to be seismologists can discuss
more than a handful of specialist problems with any authority.

This final section of the book brings together some tables of figures
and lists of historical events which the reader may care to have for
reference, and lists a few of the books that may help the student who
wishes to go further.

The size of the Earth

More than two hundred years ago French scientists began a battle to
establish an international standard of length based upon the size of
the Earth. The *metre* was intended to be one ten millionth part of the
distance from the equator to the pole, which they established by
carrying out a heroic series of geodetic measurements between about
1790 and 1820. They incidentally laid the foundation of modern
gravity observation.

International agreement to adopt the metre and its associated
standard of mass the kilogram has now been reached, and most
countries have either made the change to the units of the Système
International or are in the course of doing so. S.I. units have
therefore been used throughout this book, but the accompanying
official recommendations concerning preferred multiples (which
would deprive us of so useful a unit as the centimetre) have been
passed over whenever popular usage seemed likely to part company
from official edict. My most wilful offence has been to use 'ton' to
mean metric ton throughout. When tons avoirdupois no longer
appear in the problems of school arithmetics, and short tons and long
tons have vanished from commerce, the form *tonne* should become
as rare in English as *gramme* is now.

Geophysicists, who saw no reason to express densities in four figures when they needed only two or three, have decided to adopt the
allowed unit *megagrams per cubic metre* ($Mg\ m^{-3}$), which yields
exactly the same numbers as their old *grams per cubic centimetre*.
Thus, honour is preserved on both sides, and the old advantage that
densities and specific gravities taking water as 1 are expressed by the
same numbers is still retained.

Polar diameter of the Earth	12 714 km
Equatorial diameter	12 757
Mean radius	6 371
Radius of the core	3 473
Radius of the inner core	1 250
Depth to the core	2 898
Depth to the inner core	5 121
Mass of the Earth	$5 \cdot 98 \times 10^{24}$ kg
Volume of the Earth	$1 \cdot 083 \times 10^{21}$ m^3
Mean density of the Earth	$5 \cdot 517$ Mg m^{-3}

The geological column

Years ago	Era	Period	Duration (years)
	Quaternary	Recent	25 000
		Pleistocene	2 million
2 million			
	Tertiary or Cainozoic	Pliocene	10 million
		Miocene	13 million
		Oligocene	15 million
		Eocene	20 million
		Palaeocene	10 million
70 million			
	Secondary or Mesozoic	Cretaceous	65 million
		Jurassic	45 million
		Triassic	45 million
225 million			
	Primary or Palaeozoic	Permian	45 million
		Carboniferous	80 million
		Devonian	50 million
		Silurian	40 million
		Ordovician	60 million
		Cambrian	100 million
600 million			
	Pre-Cambrian or Eozoic	Pre-Cambrian	
Age of Earth's crust: 4 500 million years.			

Felt intensity scales

The version of the modified Mercalli scale given below is an abridged one intended only to give an indication of the main features of scales of this kind. There are strong arguments for using intensity scales adapted to local needs, and any reader who is called upon to make a practical assessment of damage is advised to look at the versions given by Richter (*Elementary Seismology,* pp 136 - 139) and Eiby (*New Zealand Journal of Geology and Geophysics 7*: 108 - 133, 1963). The most accessible English version of the MSK scale is probably that given by Båth (*Introduction to Seismology,* pp 125 - 128).

I. Not felt except by a very few under especially favourable circumstances.

II. Felt only by a few persons at rest, especially on the upper floors of buildings. Delicately suspended objects may swing.

III. Felt quite noticeably indoors, especially on the upper floors of buildings, but many people do not recognize it as an earthquake. Standing motor-cars may rock slightly. Vibration like the passing of a truck. Duration estimated.

IV. During the day, felt indoors by many, outdoors by few. At night, some awakened. Dishes, windows, doors disturbed; walls make cracking sound. Sensation like heavy truck striking the building. Standing motor-cars rocks noticeably.

V. Felt by nearly everyone; many awakened. Some dishes, windows, etc., broken; a few instances of cracked plaster; unstable objects overturned. Disturbance of poles, trees, and other tall objects sometimes noticed. Pendulum clocks may stop.

VI. Felt by all; many frightened and run outdoors. Some heavy furniture moved; a few instances of fallen plaster or damaged chimneys. Damage slight.

VII. Everybody runs outdoors. Damage negligible in buildings of good design and construction; slight to moderate in well-built ordinary structures; considerable in poorly built or badly designed structures; some chimneys broken. Noticed by persons driving motor-cars.

VIII. Damage slight in specially designed structures; considerable in ordinary substantial buildings with partial collapse; great in poorly built structures. Panel walls thrown out of frame structures. Fall of chimneys, factory stacks, columns, monuments, walls. Heavy furniture overturned. Sand and mud ejected in small amounts. Changes in well water. Disturbs persons driving motor-cars.

IX. Damage considerable in specially designed structures; well-designed frame structures thrown out of plumb; great in substantial buildings, with partial collapse. Buildings shifted off foundations. Ground cracked conspicuously. Underground pipes broken.

X. Some well-built wooden structures destroyed; most masonry and frame structures destroyed with foundations; ground badly cracked. Rails bent. Landslides considerable from river banks and slopes. Shifted sand and mud. Water splashed (slopped) over banks.

XI. Few if any (masonry) structures remain standing. Bridges destroyed. Broad fissures in ground. Underground pipe-lines completely out of service. Earth slumps and landslips in soft ground. Rails bent greatly.

XII. Damage total. Waves seen on ground surfaces. Lines of sight and level distorted. Objects thrown upwards into the air.

Magnitudes and energies

The magnitude of an earthquake is a measure of the total energy radiated in the form of elastic waves, but this is not strictly speaking the full total of the energy released, for the elastic rebound process is a far from efficient generator of waves. Part of the stored elastic strain is converted into heat. Evidence of this may appear in metamorphism of rocks close to the surface of the fault break, or as a rise in the temperature of the ground water in nearby wells and springs. How much of the total energy becomes heat is very difficult to estimate.

In scientific terms, energy is power to do work, whether it takes the form of heat, or electricity, or elastic waves, or anything else. Energy is measured in joules. Formally a joule (J) is the work done when a force of one newton (N) is displaced through a distance of one metre in the direction of the force; and a newton is the force which, applied to a mass of one kilogram, will give it an acceleration of one metre per second per second (1 m s^{-2}).

The relationship between the energy of the elastic waves in joules and the numbers of the magnitude scale is not beyond argument, but most seismologists now use an equation derived by Markus Båth:

Log $E = 5\cdot24 + 1\cdot44M_S$ (joules).

Magnitudes on the M_L and m_B scales must first be converted using the equations:

$m = 1\cdot7 + 0\cdot8 \ M_L - 0\cdot01 \ M_L{}^?$, and
$m = 0\cdot56 \ M_S + 2\cdot9$.

The domestic unit of electric power, the kilowatt (kW) is equal to 1 000 joules per second. Båth has pointed out that the annual power consumption of Uppsala, his home city, which has about 100 000 inhabitants who use some 290 million units a year, could be supplied by appropriately harnessing an earthquake of magnitude 6·8. One of magnitude $8^3/_4$ would keep them going for over six hundred years, but they would get through a magnitude $1^1/_2$ in well under a second!

Attempts have sometimes been made to compare earthquakes with nuclear bombs, but it cannot be done very exactly and the appropriate conversion factors are still being discussed over international conference tables. The kind of rock in which the bomb is exploded has a lot to do with the efficiency of the wave generation. According to American sources you need to explode 10 kilotons in alluvium to get the effect of 1 kiloton in hard rock. Soviet experts have claimed that they get the equivalent of a shock of magnitude 4·6 to 4·8 from a 1 kiloton bomb, while the Americans say that 2 kilotons are needed to reach magnitude 4·0. The data in the following table are therefore presented with some diffidence.

M_S	Joules	
0	$1\cdot7 \times 10^5$	Values for very small shocks are unreliable
1	$4\cdot8 \times 10^6$	
2	$1\cdot3 \times 10^8$	
$2^1/_2$		Smallest felt earthquakes
3	$3\cdot6 \times 10^9$	
4	$1\cdot0 \times 10^{11}$	
5	$2\cdot7 \times 10^{12}$	Smallest damaging shocks Dunedin earthquake, 1974
$5^1/_2$		Bikini bomb
5·9		Agadir earthquake, 1960
6	$4\cdot4 \times 10^{13}$	Skoplje earthquake, 1963
$6^1/_2$		'Nominal' (20 kiloton) atom bomb
6·8		San Fernando earthquake, 1971
7	$2\cdot1 \times 10^{15}$	Inangahua earthquake, 1968
7·8		Buller earthquake, 1929
7·9		Hawke's Bay earthquake, 1931

8	$5 \cdot 7 \times 10^{16}$	A 5 megaton bomb?
		Aleutians underground test, 1971
8·3		San Francisco earthquake, 1906
8·4		Chile, 1960; Alaska, 1964
8·9		Largest recorded shocks:
		Colombia, 1906; Sanriku, 1933
9	$1 \cdot 6 \times 10^{18}$	A 300 megaton bomb?

Earthquake statistics

The following table is based on data for the 47 years from 1918 to 1964, compiled by S. J. Duda:

Magnitude	Number of shocks per decade	Energy release per decade
8·5 – 8·9	3	156×10^{16} joules
8·0 – 8·4	11	113
7·5 – 7·9	31	80
7·0 – 7·4	149	58
6·5 – 6·9	560	41
6·0 – 6·4	2 100	30

Smaller shocks are very numerous and the data are less reliable. Gutenberg and Richter place the number of earthquakes per year above magnitude 5·0 at a little under a thousand, and that above 3·0 at about fifty thousand.

Because tectonic regions differ so greatly in size, it is difficult to compare the seismicity of one country with that of another, but the following table compiled by Markus Båth may be helpful. Nearly all the seismic energy is released in the larger shocks, so he has considered only the shocks of magnitude 7·9 or more, for the years 1904 – 1964.

Region	Percentage of total seismic energy release	Energy per degree along the belt
Alaska	4·3	$6 \cdot 1 \times 10^{16}$ joules
Western North America	1·0	0·8
Mexico – Central America	4·2	2·3
South America	16·4	6·4
S. W. Pacific – Philippines	26·5	7·0
Ryukyu – Japan	15·8	13·5
Kuril Islands – Kamchatka	5·8	7·0
Aleutian Islands	3·0	2·9
Central Asia – Turkey	16·9	5·6
Indian Ocean	4·5	–
Atlantic Ocean	1·6	–

The total energy released within the stated limits of time and magnitude was $2 \cdot 4 \times 10^{19}$ joules. About 77 percent of it was released in circum-Pacific areas.

Historical earthquakes 1500 — 1902

The following list covers the period in which reliable information is available down to the general availability of instrumental records. It has been drawn mainly from John Milne's *Catalogue of Destructive Earthquakes.* All European earthquakes of Milne's Class III (which destroy towns and devastate districts) are included. Outside Europe, I have listed a selection of Class III shocks likely to be mentioned by general writers. To these are added some less intense shocks of special seismological interest, or connected with other historical events.

Dates may differ by one day from those in other accounts, as it is not always certain whether writers are using local time or Greenwich time for their records. They have all been given in the present calendar, as the change from 'Old Style' took place at different times in different countries.

The names printed in capitals are often used for convenience as 'proper names' of the earthquakes to which they refer, but it is usual to state the year as well in order to avoid ambiguity.

1505	July 6	Persia, Afghanistan
1509	Feb. 25	Calabria, Sicily
1509	Sept. 14	Turkey
1510	Jan. 10	Bavaria
1511	Mar. 26	Adriatic
1514	Apr. 16	Zante, Greece
1531	Jan. 26	Spain, Portugal
1549		Persia
1556	Jan. 24	Austria, Bavaria
1556	Jan. 26	SHANSI, China
1590	Sept. 15	Central Europe
1596		Nizhni Novgorod
1609	July 15	Kansu, China
1612	Nov. 8	Southern Europe
1618	Aug. 25	Switzerland
1622	Oct. 25	Kansu, China
1638	Mar. 27	Italy, Greece
1658	Aug. 20	Philippines
1663	Feb. 5	St. Maurice, Canada
1670	Jan. 17	Central Europe
1679	June 4	Caucasia
1687	Oct. 20	Lima, Peru
1688	Apr. 11	Italy
1688	June 5	Italy
1688	July 10	Asia Minor
1692	June 7	Jamaica
1693	Jan. 9	Italy, Sicily
1693	June 11	Malta
1703	Jan. 14	Italy
1703	Dec. 31	ODOWARA, Japan
1706	Apr. 10	Iceland
1710	May-June	Algiers
1718	Dec. 10	Cyprus
1719	May 25	Turkey
1721	Apr. 26	Persia
1727	Nov. 18	Persia
1728	Nov. 28	Philippines
1730	July 8	Chile
1730	Dec. 30	Hokkaido, Japan

1737	Oct. 11	Calcutta
1741	Apr. 24	Italy
1751	May 24	Chile
1755	Nov. 1	LISBON, Portugal
1757	July 9	Azores
1759	Oct. 30	Asia Minor
1763	July 29	Hungary
1766	Oct. 21	Venezuela
1767	July 11	Zante, Greece
1773	June 3	Guatemala
1783	Feb. 5	Calabria, Italy
1786	Feb. 5	Greece
1786	Mar. 9	Southern Italy
1789	Sept. 30	Perugia, Italy
1790	Apr. 6	Transylvania
1791	Nov. 2	Greece
1796	Feb. 26	Asia Minor
1797	Feb. 4	Ecuador, Peru
1799	July 28	Italy
1802	Oct. 26	Eastern Europe
1805	July 26	Italy
1810	Feb. 16	Candia, Greece
1811	Dec. 16	NEW MADRID, U.S.A.
1812	Mar. 26	Venezuela, Colombia
1819	June 16	KUTCH, India
1822	Nov. 20	VALPARAISO, Chile
1823	Mar. 5	Southern Italy, Sicily
1823	May 7	Central America
1825	Jan. 19	Greece
1827	Sept.	Lahore, India
1828	Mar. 7	Siberia
1829	May 5	Turkey
1832	Mar. 8	Calabria, Italy
1833	Aug. 26	North India, Tibet
1835	Feb. 20	CONCEPCIÓN, Chile
1840	July 2	Armenia
1846	Aug. 14	Central Italy
1847	July 31	Nicaragua
1847	Oct. 8	Chile
1847	Nov. 16	Java, Sumatra
1848	Oct. 15	MARLBOROUGH, New Zealand
1853	Apr. 21	Sheraz, Persia
1853	Aug. 18	Greece
1855	Jan. 23	WELLINGTON, New Zealand
1856	Oct. 12	Mediterranean
1857	Jan. 8	Southern California
1857	Dec. 16	The NEAPOLITAN, Italy
1858	Sept. 20	Greece, Turkey
1859	Mar. 22	Ecuador
1860	Dec. 3	Central America
1861	Feb. 16	S. W. Sumatra
1864	Jan. 12	Chile
1867	Jan. 2	Algiers
1868	Aug. 13	CHILE-BOLIVIA
1868	Aug. 16	Ecuador
1870	Oct. 5	Mangone, Italy
1872	Mar. 20	OWENS VALLEY, California, U.S.A.

1875	Mar. 28	New Caledonia
1875	May 18	Colombia, Venezuela
1877	May 9	IQUIQUE, Chile
1879	Oct. 18	S. Hungary, Roumania
1880	Feb. 22	YOKOHAMA, Japan
1880	July 18	Philippines
1882	Sept. 7	Central America
1883	May 3	Tabriz, Persia
1883	July 28	Cassamicciola, Italy
1883	Aug. 27	KRAKATOA (Eruption)
1883	Oct. 15	Greece
1885	Mar. 27	Greece
1885	Aug. 2	Russian Turkestan
1886	Aug. 27	Greece
1886	Aug. 31	CHARLESTON, S. Carolina, U.S.A.
1889	July 28	Kumamoto, Japan
1891	Oct. 28	MINO-OWARI, Japan
1893	Jan. 31	Greece
1893	Apr. 17	Greece
1894	July 10	Turkey
1895	Jan. 7	Khorasan, Persia
1895	May 13	Greece, Turkey
1896	June 15	SANRIKU, Japan
1896	Aug. 26	Iceland
1897	June 12	ASSAM, India
1897	Sept. 21	Philippines
1898	July 2	Hungary
1899	Jan. 22	S. W. Greece
1899	Sept. 10	YAKUTAT BAY, Alaska
1899	Sept. 30	CERAM, E. Indies
1900	Mar. 22	Japan
1900	Oct. 9	Alaska
1902	Apr. 19	Central America
1902	Aug. 21	Philippines
1902	Dec. 16	Turkestan

Important earthquakes since 1903

This list begins in 1903 because that is the first year for which reasonably accurate and complete instrumental magnitudes are available. It contains all shocks with magnitudes of 8·0 or more, and a selection of smaller shocks that have been the subject of important researches, or have attracted unusual public attention.

From 1903 to 1954 the magnitudes quoted are those given in Gutenberg and Richter's *Seismicity of the Earth*, with appropriate amendments taken from Richter's *Elementary Seismology*. From 1955 to 1965 they are from Rothé's *La Séismicité du Globe* and should be completely consistent with the earlier figures. For later shocks, no authoritative listing of magnitudes exists. Reference has been made to Båth's *Introduction to Seismology*, to values of M_S quoted in the *Regional Catalogue* of the International Seismological Centre, and to monographs on the individual earthquakes. Where appropriate the statistical corrections derived by Rothé have been applied.

Date	Epicentral region	Magnitude	Focal Depth
1903 Jan. 4	Tonga	8±	400 km
Jan. 14	Mexico	8·3	
Feb. 27	Java	8·1	
June 2	Aleutians	8·3±	100 km?
Aug. 11	Thessaly, Greece	8·3	100 km
1904 June 7	Sea of Japan	7·9	350 km
June 25	Kamchatka	8·3	
June 25	Kamchatka	8·1	
Aug. 27	KOLYMA, Siberia	8·3	
Dec. 20	Costa Rica	8·3	
1905 Jan. 22	Celebes	8·4	90 km
Apr. 4	KANGRA, India	8·6	
July 9	S. W. of Lake Baikal	8·4	
July 23	S. W. of Lake Baikal	8·7	
Sep. 8	CALABRIA, Italy	7·9	
1906 Jan. 21	HONSHU, Japan	8·4	340 km
Jan. 31	Colombia-Equador	8·9	
Mar. 16	KAGI (Chia-i), Taiwan	7·1	
Apr. 18	SAN FRANCISCO, California	8·3	
Aug. 17	Aleutians	8·3	
Aug. 17	Chile	8·6	
Sep. 14	New Guinea	8·4	
Dec. 22	SIKIANG, China	8·3	
1907 Jan 14	KINGSTON, Jamaica	–	
Apr. 15	Mexico	8·3	
May 25	Sea of Okhotsk	7·9	600 km
Oct. 21	KARATAG, Tadzhikstan	8·1	
1908 Mar. 26	Mexico	8·1	80 km ±
Dec. 28	MESSINA, Sicily	7½	
1909 Feb. 22	Fiji	7·9	550 km
Mar. 13	Honshu, Japan	8·3	80 km
July 7	Hindu Kush	8·1	230 km ±
1910 Apr. 12	Ryukyu Is.	8·3	200 km
June 16	Loyalty Is.	8·6	100 km
1911 Jan. 3	TYAN SHAN, Turkestan	8·7	
Feb. 18	FERGHANA, Pamir	7¾	
June 15	Ryukyu Is.	8·7	160 km
1912 Aug. 9	Sea of Marmara	7·8	
1913 Mar. 14	Molucca Is.	8·3	
1914 Nov. 24	Mariana Is.	8·7	110 km
1915 Jan. 13	AVEZZANO, Italy	7½	
May 1	Kamchatka	8·1	
Oct. 3	NEVADA, U.S.A.	7¾	
1916 Jan. 13	New Guinea	8·1	
1917 Jan. 30	Kamchatka	8·1	
May 1	Tonga	8·6 ±	
June 26	SAMOA	8·7	
1918 Aug. 15	Caroline Is.	8·3	
Sep. 7	Kuril Is.	8·3	
Nov. 18	Banda Sea	8·1	190 km
1919 Jan. 1	Tonga	8·3	180 km
Apr. 30	Tonga	8·4	

1920 June 5	Taiwan	8·3	
Sep. 20	Fiji	8·3	
Dec. 16	KANSU, China	8·6	
1921 Nov. 15	Hindu Kush	8·1	215 km
Dec. 18	Peru	7·9	650 km
1922 Nov. 11	ATACAMA, Chile	8·4	
1923 Feb. 3	Kamchatka	8·4	
Sep. 1	KWANTO, Japan	8·3	
1924 Apr. 14	Philippines	8·3	
June 26	S. W. of Macquarie Is.	8·3	
1925 Mar. 1	QUEBEC, Canada	7·0	60 km
Mar. 16	Yunnan, China	7·1	
June 28	MONTANA, U.S.A.	$6^3/_4$	
1926 June 26	RHODES, Dodecanese Is.	8·3	100 km
1927 Mar. 7	TANGO, Japan	7·9	
May 22	KANSU, China	8·3	
1928 Mar. 9	Indian Ocean	8·1	
Dec. 1	Chile	8·3	
1929 Mar. 7	Aleutians	8·6	
May 1	SHIRWAN, Iran	7·1	
June 16	BULLER (Murchison), N.Z.	7·6	
June 27	South Sandwich Is.	8·3	
1930 Nov. 20	IZU, Japan	7·1	
1931 Feb. 2	HAWKES BAY, N.Z.	7·9	
Oct. 3	Solomon Is.	8·1	
1932 May 14	Celebes	8·3	
May 26	Tonga-Kermadec Trench	7·9	600 km
June 3	Mexico	8·1	
1933 Mar. 2	SANRIKU, Japan	8·9	
1934 Jan. 15	BIHAR, India	8·4	
June 29	Celebes	6·9	720 km
July 18	Santa Cruz Is.	8·1	
1935 Apr. 20	Taiwan	7·1	
May 30	QUETTA, Baluchistan	$7^1/_2$	
Dec. 28	Sumatra	8·1	
1937 Apr. 16	Tonga	8·1	400 km
1938 Feb. 1	Java	8·6	
Nov. 10	BEHRING SEA	8·7	
1939 Jan. 25	Chile	8·3	
Apr. 30	Solomon Is.	8·1	
Dec. 21	Celebes	8·6	150 km
Dec. 26	ANATOLIA	7·9	
1940 May 24	Peru	8·4	
1941 June 26	Burma	8·7	
June 27	Central Australia	$6^3/_4$	
Nov. 25	West of Portugal	8·4	
1942 May 14	Equador	8·3	
Aug. 6	Guatemala	8·3	
Aug. 24	Brazil	8·6	
Nov. 10	South of Africa	8·3	
1943 Apr. 6	Andes	8·3	
May 25	Philippines	8·1	
June 30	Celebes Sea	6·8	700 km
July 23	Java	8·1	90 km
Sep. 6	Macquarie Is.	7·8	
Sep. 10	TOTTORI, Japan	7·4	

1944 Dec. 7	Honshu, Japan	8·3	
1945 Jan. 12	MIKAWA, Japan	7·1	
Nov. 27	Indian Ocean	8·3	
1946 Aug. 4	West Indies	8·1	
Nov. 10	ANCASH, Peru	7·3	
Dec. 20	Shikoku, Japan	8·4	
1948 Jan. 24	Philippines	8·3	
June 28	FUKUI, Japan	7·3	
Oct. 5	ASHKHABAD, Turkestan	7·3	
1949 July 10	TADZHIKSTAN	8·0	
Aug. 22	S. Alaska	8·1	
1950 Feb. 28	Hokkaido, Japan	7·9	340 km
Aug. 15	ASSAM	8·7	
Nov. 2	Banda Sea	8·1	
Dec. 2	New Hebrides	8·1	
Dec. 9	Andes, Argentina	8·3	100 km
1952 Mar. 4	Hokkaido, Japan	8·6	
July 21	KERN COUNTY, California	7·7	
Nov. 4	Kamchatka	8·4	
1953 Mar. 18	N. W. ANATOLIA	7·2	
Nov. 25	Honshu, Japan	8·0	
1954 July 6	FALLON, Nevada, U.S.A.	6·6	
Sep. 9	ORLEANSVILLE, Algeria	6³⁄₄	
Dec. 16	Nevada, U.S.A.	7·1	
1955 Feb. 18	QUETTA, Pakistan	6³⁄₄	
April 1	LANAO, Philippines	7·6	55 km
1956 June 9	KABUL, Afghanistan	7·7	
July 9	SANTORIN, Greece	7·7	
1957 Mar. 9	Andreanof Is.	8·0	
Apr. 14	S. of Samoa	8·0	
Jul. 28	GUERRERO, Mexico	7·8	
Dec. 4	Outer Mongolia	8·3	
Dec. 13	Iran	7·2	
1958 July 10	S. E. Alaska	7·9	
Nov. 6	Kuril Is.	8·7	75 km
1959 Jan 2	Brittany	5·2	
May 4	Kamchatka	8¹⁄₄	60 km
Aug. 18	HEBGEN LAKE, Montana, U.S.A.	7·1	
1960 Feb. 21	MELOUSA, Algeria	5¹⁄₂	
Feb. 29	AGADIR, Morocco	5·8	
Apr. 24	LAR, Iran	5³⁄₄	
May 22	Arauco, CHILE	8·4	
1961 June 1	Ethiopia	6³⁄₄	
June 11	LAR, Iran	6³⁄₄	
Aug. 31	Peru-Brazil border	7³⁄₄	629 km
1962 Sep. 1	BUYIN-ZARA, Iran	7¹⁄₂	
1963 Feb. 21	BARCE, Libya	–	
July 26	SKOPLJE, Yugoslavia	6·0	
Oct. 13	Kuril Is.	8¹⁄₄	60 km
1964 Mar. 27	ANCHORAGE, Alaska	8·4	
June 16	NIIGATA, Honshu, Japan	7¹⁄₂	

1965	Mar 28	Chile	7½
1966	Aug 19	VARTO, Turkey	6·9
1967	Jul 30	CARACAS, Venezuela	7·1
1968	Jan15	Sicily	6·1
	May 16	TOKACHI, Japan	7·9
	Aug 1	CASIGURAN, Philippines	7·7
	Aug 31	DASHT-E-BAYAZ, Iran	7·2
	Oct 14	MECKERING, W. Australia	7·2
1969	Feb 28	Off coast of Portugal	7·9
	Jul 25	E. China	6·1
1970	Mar 28	GEDIZ, Turkey	7·4
	Apr 7	Luzon, Philippines	7·7
	May 31	CHIMBOTE, Peru	7·7
1971	Jan 10	West Irian	8·0
	Feb 9	SAN FERNANDO, California	6·8
	May 12	BURDUR, Turkey	6·8
	May 22	BINGÖL, Turkey	6·7
	Jul 9	ILLAPEL, Chile	7·7
	Jul 14	Solomon Islands	8·1
1972	Jan 25	Taiwan	7½
	Jul 30	S. E. Alaska	7·6
	Dec 23	MANAGUA, Nicaragua	6·2
1973	Jan 30	MICHOACAN, Mexico	7½
	Jun 17	Hokkaido	7·7
1974	Oct 3	Peru	7·6
	Dec 28	PATTAN, W. Pakistan	6·2
1975	Feb 4	LIAONING, China	7·4
	Feb 11	GUATEMALA	7½
	May 26	N. Atlantic	7·9
	Jul 20	Solomon I.	7·9
	Sep 6	LICE, Turkey	6·7
	Oct 11	S. of Tonga	7·8
1976	Jan 14	Kermadec Is.	8·0
	May 6	FRIULI, N. Italy	6½
	Aug. 16	Mindanao	7·9
	Jul 27	TANG SHAN, China	8·0

New Zealand earthquakes

This list is included not only because of its obvious interest to New Zealanders, but because there are few other regions of moderate seismicity for which data are available to compile such a list. The epicentres of the larger shocks have been shown in Figure 72. The list includes all earthquakes believed to have reached magnitude 7 and a selection of other shocks that have attracted public interest or occurred in unusual places. Data for historical shocks are based upon information collected for the author's *Descriptive Catalogue of New Zealand Earthquakes* of which only the sections covering the years 1460 to 1854 have so far been published. Magnitudes of early shocks have been assigned on the basis of their felt effects. Instrumental data are taken from the annual *New Zealand Seismological Reports* and from special studies of individual shocks. In the period from 1860 to 1940 minor revision of some epicentres and magnitudes has still to be carried out. New Zealand dates have been used.

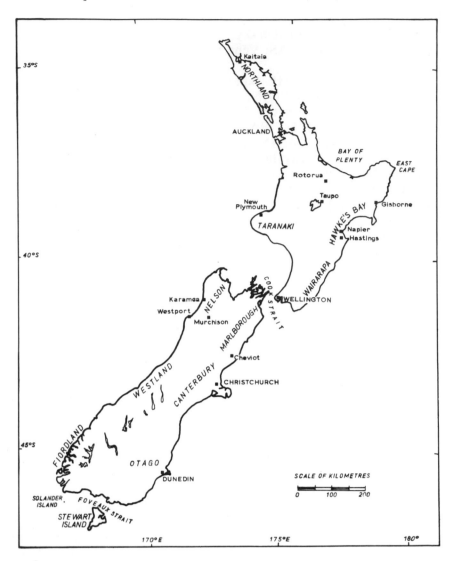

Fig. 81: New Zealand showing the principal place-names mentioned in the text. Geological faults and active volcanoes are identified in Figure 76.

Latitudes and longitudes of major epicentres are given, but readers unfamiliar with New Zealand geography may find Figure 81 helpful. All place-names used in the main text have been included.

1460±: Wellington. Possibly magnitude 8. Known in Maori tradition as *Hao-whenua*, the land swallower.

1773 May 11: Queen Charlotte Sound. Captain Furneaux of the *Adventure* records that his shore-party 'felt some two shocks of an earthquake but received no kind of damage'. The first New Zealand shock reported by a European observer.

1826: Fiordland. Uncertain traditions based upon the reports of sealers and whalers strongly suggest that a very large earthquake occurred about this time.

1843 Jul. 8: Wanganui. Magnitude not less than 7½. Building damage and large landslides, resulting in two deaths.

1848 Oct. 16: N. E. Marlborough. Magnitude 7·1. Intensities reached MM X in the lower Wairau Valley, and there was serious damage to buildings in Wellington. Sometimes mis-called the Awatere Earthquake in spite of contemporary reports describing faulting in the Wairau. It is also mis-dated by up to three days because of confusion with aftershocks. Three deaths in the large aftershock on October 19.

1853 Jan. 1: New Plymouth. Magnitude about $6\frac{1}{2}$. The strongest known shock in this part of New Zealand. Fallen chimneys and other minor damage to buildings and goods.

1855 Jan. 23: S.W. Wairarapa. Probably magnitude 8·1. Extensive faulting and coastal uplift. Destructive in Wellington, severely damaging in Wanganui. Five deaths.

1863 Feb. 23: Hawke's Bay. Building damage and ground fissures at Napier. Felt over most of the country. Information still very incomplete.

1876 Feb. 26: Oamaru. Some damage to buildings. Unusually large for this part of New Zealand.

1886 Jun. 9: Tarawera eruption. New Zealand's greatest volcanic disaster. Earthquakes were felt, but there is little evidence that they were severe.

1888 Sep. 1: North Canterbury. Magnitude about 7. Faulting at Glynn Wye provided one of the earliest observations of transcurrent movement.

1891 Jun. 23: Mouth of the Waikato River. Magnitude probably well over 6. An unusual location. Damaging in Raglan and Kawhia. Chimneys overthrown in Auckland.

1895 Aug. 18: Taupo. Magnitude over 6. Damage to buildings. Landslides and fissures. Possible surface faulting.

1897 Dec. 7: Wanganui. Magnitude 7. Damaging in Wanganui. Felt from Auckland to Timaru.

1901 Nov. 17: Cheviot. Magnitude 7. Damage and landslides in North Canterbury. One death.

1904 Aug. 9: Off Cape Turnagain. Magnitude $7\frac{1}{2}$. Damage at Castlepoint.

1914 Oct. 7: East Cape Peninsula. Magnitude 7 to $7\frac{1}{2}$. Damaging intensities in the eastern Bay of Plenty. One death.

1914 Nov. 22: East Cape Peninsula. Magnitude $6\frac{1}{2}$ to 7. Felt over the whole North Island and south to Oamaru, but little damage reported. Possibly deep.

1917 Aug. 6: North Wairarapa, 40°·8S, 176°·0E. Magnitude above 6. Felt from Auckland to Cheviot.

1921 Jun. 19: Hawke's Bay, 30°·3S, 176°·4E. Magnitude 7. Focal depth about 80 km. Felt from Auckland to Dunedin. Minor damage over much of Hawke's Bay.

1922 Jun. 19: Taupo District. Many aftershocks. Often described as an earthquake swarm. Surface faulting and subsidence to the north west of Lake Taupo.

1922 Mar. 9: Arthur's Pass, 42°·5S, 172°·0E. Magnitude 6·9. Epicentre in thinly settled mountainous country. Felt over the whole country except the Northland Peninsula.

1929 Jun. 16: Buller, 41°·8S, 172°·2E. Magnitude 7·8. Destructive in the Murchison district, with numerous landslides and faulting. 17 deaths.

1931 Feb. 3: Hawke's Bay, 39°20'S, 176°40'E. Magnitude 7·9. Destructive. Intensity reached MM XI at Napier. Regional uplift. Minor faulting. 256 deaths.

1931 May 5: Poverty Bay. Magnitude above 6. Damage in the Gisborne area.

1932 Sep. 16: Wairoa, 38°·9S, 177°·55E. Magnitude 6·8. Damage in Gisborne and Wairoa.

1934 Mar. 5: Pahiatua, 40°·5S, 175°·6E. Magnitude 7·6. Damage in southern Hawke's Bay and northern Wairarapa. One death.

1942 Jun. 24: Southern Wairarapa, 40°·9S, 175°·9E. Magnitude 7·0. Damaging in the Wairarapa and Wellington.

1942 Aug. 1: Southern Wairarapa, 40°·95S, 175°·8E. Magnitude 7·1. Because of its greater focal depth (55 km) intensities were substantially lower than on Jun. 24.

1950 Feb. 5: South of the South Island 48°·5S, 164° E. Magnitude 7. Felt in parts of Otago and Southland.

1950 Aug. 5: South of the South Island 50° S, 164° E. Magnitude 7·3. Felt about Foveaux Strait.

1953 Sep. 29: Bay of Plenty, 37°·3S, 176°·8E. Magnitude 7·1 Focal depth 300 km. Very widely felt, with only minor damage.

1955 Jun. 12: Seaward Kaikouras, 42°·8S, 173°·3E. Magnitude 5·1. Minor damage in Cheviot district.

1958 Dec. 10: Bay of Plenty, 37°·2S, 176°·9E. Magnitude 6·9. Focal depth 330 km. Isolated damage to chimneys as far from the epicentre as Blenheim.

1960 May 24: Fiordland, 44°·2S, 167°·7E. Magnitude 7·0. Epicentral region sparsely inhabited. Minor damage to goods and plaster near Lake Wanaka. Not felt in the North Island.

1962 May 10: Wesport, 41°·65S, 171°·32E. Magnitude 5·9. Damage to chimneys, brick, and plasterwork, valued at $250 000. No casualties.

1963 Dec. 23: Northland, 35°·1S, 173°·5E. Magnitude 5·2. Damaged chimneys, house foundations, water-tanks and stacked goods in the area east of Kaitaia. Earthquakes in the Northland peninsula are rare. Before this event the region was considered aseismic.

1966 Mar. 5: Gisborne, 38°·52S, 177°·85E. Magnitude 6·2. Damage to older buildings on poor ground. Many cracked chimneys. Some gas and water mains broken.

1966 Apr. 23: Cook Strait, 41°·64S, 174°·52E. Magnitude 6·1. Damage to chimneys and household goods in Seddon.

1968 May 24: Inangahua, 41°·72S, 171°·94E. Magnitude 7·0. Large landslides. Serious damage to wooden houses, bridges, railway lines, and underground pipes. Fault breakage. Three deaths.

1972 Jan. 8: Te Aroha, 37°·58S, 175°·69E. Magnitude 5·1. Minor damage to chimneys, furniture, and goods.

1974 Apr. 9: Dunedin, 45°·97S, 170°·52E. Magnitude 5·0. Damage to chimneys and goods valued at $250 000. The largest known shock in eastern Otago.

A short book-list

Although seismology finds a place in several recent books intended to present the earth-sciences to the man in the street, few of them have earthquakes as a main concern, and many of those that do cannot be recommended without serious reservations. It is better for the reader who would like to know more to go straight to the experts. First on any list must come C. F. Richter's *Elementary Seismology* (W. H. Freeman and Co., San Francisco, 1958) which deals further with many of the topics discussed in this book, and contains a detailed and critical bibliography. It should make clear that although plate tectonics and what has been hailed as 'the new global seismology' provide a framework within which seismicity and tectonic processes can be viewed advantageously, they have destroyed less of the previously accepted picture than their more enthusiastic advocates sometimes imply.

Markus Båth's *Introduction to Seismology* (Birkhauser Verlag, Basel and Stuttgart, 1973) has a more physical and less geological approach and demonstrates that a very balanced picture of the rest of the world is to be obtained from its author's base in Uppsala. Elementary mathematics are used to very good effect without interrupting the flow of a very readable book. At a more elementary level J. H. Hodgson's *Earthquakes and Earth Structure* (Prentice-Hall Inc., New York, 1964) covers its author's special interests very well, but falls short of covering the ground implied by its title. Readers who find that the lack of formal studies in physics is an obstacle to understanding may find O. M. Phillips's *The Heart of the Earth* (Freeman Cooper, San Francisco, 1968) a help. Bruce Bolt's *Earthquakes: a Primer* (W. H. Freeman and Co., San Francisco, 1978) has some excellent descriptions of recent earthquakes and treats problems of current research interest.

Of geology texts that adopt an up-to-date standpoint *Understanding the Earth* edited by Gass, Smith, and Wilson for the Open University Press (Artemis Press, Sussex, 1971) and Press and Seivers's *Earth* (W. H. Freeman and Co., San Francisco, 1974) are recommended. The same publishers have collected a series of articles that appeared in the *Scientific American* between 1952 and 1973 under the title *Continents Adrift*. A standard text that has opened the door for several generations of students is Arthur Holmes's *Principles of Physical Geology* (Nelson, London, 3rd ed. 1978).

Engineers who would like more seismological background than is given in most books on structural design will find *Earthquake Engineering*, edited by Robert L. Wiegel (Prentice-Hall, Englewood Cliffs, New Jersey, 1970) of interest. Bolt, Horn, Macdonald, and Scott's *Geological Hazards* (Springer Verlag, Berlin, Heidelberg, New York, 1975) contains detailed case-histories of some recent disasters.

Many well-illustrated technical reports on particular earthquakes have appeared in the last few years, ranging from the many volumes dealing with the Alaskan earthquake in 1964 and the San Fernando earthquake in 1971, and the exhaustive Japanese reports on the Niigata and Tokachi-Oki shocks to the briefer summaries produced by UNESCO reconnaissance teams. Among good non-technical accounts of large earthquakes are Noel F. Busch's *Two Minutes to Noon* (Arthur Barker, London 1963) dealing with the Kwanto earthquake in 1923, and Monica Sutherland's *The San Francisco Disaster* (Barrie and Rockliff, London, 1959). With this should be perused William Bronson's extraordinary collection of photographs *The Earth Shook, The Sky Burned* (Doubleday and Co., New York, 1959). T. D. Kendrick's *The Lisbon Earthquake* (Methuen, London, 1956) is a scholarly work in the best sense, setting the disaster against the thought and social background of the times.

Two books that should appeal equally to the reader who likes to see for himself in the field and to the reader who expects books to save him the effort are *Earthquake Country* by Robert Iacopi (Lane Book Co., Menlo Park, 1964), which takes him on a conducted tour of the San Andreas Fault, and *Rugged Landscape* by Graeme Stevens (A. H. and A. W. Reed, Wellington, Sydney, London, 1974). This deals in fascinating detail with the structural history of central New Zealand and seems likely to become a geological classic. Both books are beautifully illustrated.

The standard work on world seismicity is still Gutenberg and Richter's *Seismicity of the Earth and Associated Phenomena*. A facsimile of the 1954 edition has been issued by the Hafner Publishing Co. (New York and London, 1965), and the data have been continued to 1965 by J. P. Rothé (*La séismicité du globe*, UNESCO, Paris, 1969. Parallel French and English texts). These contain detailed epicentre maps for the whole Earth, with the shocks classified by magnitude and focal depth.

Readers who would like to take a wider look at geophysics might begin with *Global Geophysics* by Tucker, Cook, Iyer, and Stacey (English Universities Press, London, 1970), and then proceed if their mathematics will allow it to F.D. Stacey's *Physics of the Earth* (John Wiley and Sons, New York, London, 1969). A seismological text on the same level is K. E. Bullen's *Introduction to Theoretical Seismology* (Cambridge University Press, 3rd ed. 1963). Those unable to follow Bullen's mathematics might still find interest in his excellent bibliography.

Three valuable books have appeared while this one was being written. *Geological Hazards* by Bolt, Horn, Macdonald and Scott (Springer Verlag, Berlin, 1975) has valuable chapters on earthquakes, tsunamis, and volcanoes together with interesting material on topics less closely related to earthquakes. B. A. Bolt's *Nuclear Explosions and Earthquakes: The Parted Veil* (Freeman, San Francisco, 1976) takes a commendably international view of both the technical and the political problems involved. *Earthquake Prediction and Public Policy*, the report of a commission of the U.S. National Research Council (U.S. National Academy of Science, Washington, 1975) for the most part avoids sociological and administrative jargon and sets out the issues clearly. Differences in public reaction and social values would prevent most countries from applying many of the conclusions, but the methods of enquiry will repay study.

Finally, a corner must be found to mention a few of the more important technical journals. Only two — the *Bulletin of the Seismological Society of America* and the *Journal of the Earthquake Research Institute,* Tokyo — are mainly seismology. Among those dealing more widely with geophysics are the *Geophysical Journal,* the *Journal of Geophysical Research, Izvestiya Akademii Nauk SSSR (Seriya Geofizicheskiya),* which is available in an English translation, and *Tectonophysics.* For engineers there are *Earthquake Engineering and Structural Dynamics,* the *Bulletin of the New Zealand National Society for Earthquake Engineering* (which in spite of its title has an international circle of contributors and readers), and the *Proceedings* of the triennial World Conferences on Earthquake Engineering.

Index

Place-names that are used as the names of an *Earthquake* or a *Fault* are listed only under those headings unless other information is given. Seismic phases are grouped under *Phase*, but *P-wave*, *S-wave* and *L-wave* have separate entries.

Music from Within

Music from Within
A Biography of the Composer
S C Eckhardt-Gramatté

by Ferdinand Eckhardt
edited by Gerald Bowler

The University of Manitoba Press

Unless otherwise indicated, all illustrations are
courtesy of the author.

Cover illustration and frontispiece after
a lithograph by Walter Gramatté, 1923.

This book has been published with the assistance of
the Canada Council.

Cataloguing in Publication Data

Eckhardt, Ferdinand
  Music from within

Includes index.
ISBN 0-88755-136-X

1. Eckhardt-Gramatté, S.C., 1899-1974.
2. Composers—Canada—Biography.
I. Bowler, Gerald, 1948-   II. Title

ML410.E32E19   1985   780'.92'4   C85-090187-1

I have no favourite composer and I make a distinction only between good music and unprofessional or layman's music. I never care to lean on a style, past or present, and particularly not on the so-called contemporary or experimental "avant-garde" style. Experimenting means that one is looking for something not yet found. Styles are secondary but quality comes first and will remain. I recognize everything which is done with skill and honesty. I deplore dilettantism, dishonesty and mere unconditioned desire for novelty.

S. C. Eckhardt-Gramatté, 1969

Contents

Foreword

When we first conceived the idea of publishing an abridged version of Ferdinand Eckhardt's monumental biography of his wife, I promised to contribute a foreword, something which would give at least an outline of the different sources and versions of his work. As the actual process of editing drew to a close this last week – closely coinciding with the tenth anniversary of Sonia's death on 2 December 1974 – I turned my attention to fulfilling my promise. I called my good friend Ferdinand and told him that I would like to get together with him to refresh my memory about the facts. A couple of nights later I met him at a performance given by the Manitoba Trio; with a look of pride and considerable self-satisfaction, he produced from his pocket three sheets of paper and gave them to me with the comment, "Here is what you need."

Even at a glance it was obvious that what he had given me was indeed what I *needed*, but not what I had *sought*. Rather than a bare-bones outline of bibliographical data, Ferdinand had produced poetry: an ode, a paean, a eulogy. I can do no better by way of introduction to this volume than to reprint those three sheets almost exactly as Ferdinand gave them to me. I have exercised only the lightest editorial hand. These are *his* words:

Suggestions for the Foreword by Dr. Herman Keahey to the "Sonia-Book":

This book on the life of the composer S. C. Eckhardt-Gramatté reads like a novel. It is dramatic, in parts scandalous, it is full of humour, shows an almost religious belief in her vocation, and is particularly filled with passion and deep love.

Incomprehensible, like the place of her birth, her age, her lineage, she shows many faces – like the approximately one hundred portraits which her first husband, the painter Walter Gramatté, made of her, almost all of them with a different expression, none that was merely flattering, some even with a hidden criticism.

Great musicians, like Edwin Fischer, Stokowski, Casals and Sir Ernest MacMillan, believed in her work. But, in spite of the enthusiasm of some critics, there were others who rejected her music almost violently. Let me give two examples not cited in this book: in a letter to Gramatté in 1928, she describes her *rencontre* with the Swiss conductor Ansermet, who admitted "that she writes remarkable things, incomprehensible, rich and sincere, but she does not follow the laws that are imposed upon music. A law made by oneself is no law; it is a passport which one issues to himself. Such a passport has no value; only a passport from the police counts." Against this stands what Casals wrote about her in 1935: "S. C. Eckhardt-Gramatté is a born musician. She is a musician by God's favour. All her compositions and her violin- and her piano-playing are manifestations of this favour, and provide us with the feeling of abundance, of rich gifts of the kind that can only be endowed by nature."

11

This biography was conceived over a number of years, starting shortly after her death in 1974. Written over a decade, it may contain certain inconsistencies in facts and ideas which have only developed gradually, in part through the finding of new sources and biographical materials. But the book, after all, is based on forty-five years of close relationship with the composer and her individual personality. It is certainly not unbiased, but it is for the most part built up of her entirely plausible statements found in letters, diaries and other writings – even little notes, which seem to exist by the hundreds.

She wrote many of her dreams down almost immediately following them, and she frequently wrote letters to the deceased – to Gramatté, her mother and her brother. These sources are chosen from a large archive of documents, critiques and programs, correspondence with a world of musicians, artists and friends, and even trivial correspondence with manufacturers and domestic personnel.

All of her writings were in one of three languages: French, German or English, according to where she lived or how she felt. Some of her letters (and all of her mother's) are in French, but some of hers are also in English, like the description of her early youth in England. The largest part of the documentation, however, is in German, and it was in that language that I wrote the original version of this book. I later translated it into English and had it edited by Gerry Bowler to make it more acceptable to English-speaking readers.

Hers was a creative life which very often tended to go to extremes, one in which she sometimes felt that she did not exist personally but was a legendary character. Particularly in respect to her early work, she stated that she wrote what she felt, not how one was supposed to compose. But after the years with Trapp, and after the Viennese experience, she confessed in a weak moment: "Now I am a composer," and she meant it in the sense of the Latin root: to consciously form, to put together.

She was exposed to many criticisms for various reasons, for her unworldliness, for human weaknesses, for some naivité in the compositions of her youth, but mostly because of the conventional prejudices of her fellow human beings and the changing trends of her day. Up to the time she was fifty, people – even professionals – were concerned with the question: Can women compose? Always prepared to give a quick answer, she would say: "My notes have no pants and no skirts!"

T. Herman Keahey
15 December 1984
Winnipeg

Editor's Preface

The book which you now hold, *Music from Within*, first began life in quite a different form. The earliest biography of S.C. Eckhardt-Gramatté, begun shortly after the composer's death in 1974, was a two-volume work in German by her husband, Dr. Ferdinand Eckhardt. Based on the author's recollections and on his wife's memoirs, dreams, letters, notebooks and documents, this 550-page typescript was later translated into English by the author. This translation had the virtues of comprehensiveness, but its length and style did not commend it easily to a Canadian reader. It has been my chief task as editor to make Dr. Eckhardt's story accessible to an English-speaking audience. In preparing *Music from Within* for publication, I have tried to lay as light a hand as possible on the narrative and let the voice of its author and his personal view of his subject shine through.

Those readers, or future biographers, who wish to get closer to the sources will find that the privately published unabridged versions, both German and English, are on deposit in libraries in this country and in Europe, as are the twenty-four volumes of the *Selected Works of S.C. Eckhardt-Gramatté*. The photographs, memoirs and other primary documents are, for the most part, in the possession of the author.

Early Childhood

The origins of Sophie-Carmen Eckhardt-Gramatté are shrouded in legend. In one account, she was born in Moscow; in another she was born in Paris; a third story places her birth on a train travelling west through Europe. The identity of her real father is a mystery. There is no official documentation for her early years. From these uncertain beginnings she fashioned a life full of incident and tragedy, yet rich in emotion and creative genius. It is my purpose here to tell you the story of the life of the composer S. C. Eckhardt-Gramatté (or Sonia, as she was called by her friends), to show how she developed as a woman in the centre of turbulent times and as an artist always following the promptings of the music she felt from within.

Anyone who seeks to understand the personality of this woman, known first as Sophie-Carmen Fridman, must understand that of her mother, Catharina. The child took so much of her musicality and temperament from her mother that any biography of Sophie-Carmen must begin with one of Catharina. Born in 1862 into the aristocratic family of a Russian military officer and his Parisian wife, Catharina de Kochevskaia was educated at St. Petersburg's fashionable *Institut pour jeune filles nobles*. Here she excelled in the French language and at the piano. Her talent on the piano drew not only the flattering attentions of Tsar Alexander II but also the notice of the renowned pianist and composer Anton Rubinstein. Rubinstein gave her a few lessons and seems to have engendered in her the desire to become a professional pianist, an unthinkable ambition in a young Russian noblewoman of her time. In this, Catharina showed the rebellious streak that she shared with her siblings – her brother Nicolas was a poet and freethinker who was exiled to Siberia for his political opinions, her sister Sophie was enmeshed in a spiritist cult and her sister Marie (we are told) bore an illegitimate child.

Scarcely eighteen and against the will of her family, Catharina went to Moscow where she worked as a governess so she could study at the conservatory. Her teacher was Nicolas Rubinstein, who took Catharina as his pupil on the recommendation of his brother Anton. Shortly after, in March 1881, Nicolas died of consumption, but Catharina continued her studies at the conservatory where she became the student of, and later assistant to, Paul Pabst. Before his death, however, Rubinstein had introduced Catharina to the family of Count Leo Tolstoy, who eventually hired her to teach the children French and piano. Her relationship with the family was a close and happy one which lasted for twenty years.

Despite her early successes, Catharina's life was not to be a happy one. Many of her troubles stemmed from her marriage to the blind businessman Nicolas Karlovich de Fridman. At first their relationship went smoothly: his interests prospered and they had two children, Nicolas (whose pet-name was Colja) and Sophie (also called Szonja). However, after a time his business foundered, debts mounted and he sought consolation in the arms of other women. When Catharina discovered that he was conducting a liaison with his secretary she turned to her sister Sophie, who was a devotee of spiritism. Sophie arranged a seance for Catharina to ask the spirits' advice about her marital problems, and Catharina, who confessed to dabbling at various times not only with spiritism but also Islam, Judaism, Calvinism, Methodism and Confucianism, did so. Upon learning of this, de Fridman went into a rage; their unstable relationship became an intolerable one and the couple separated in April 1895.

De Fridman threatened to take the children away and, indeed, shortly after, placed his daughter in a convent. Catharina then became obsessed with the fear that he would someday take away Nicolas, going so far as to pierce a laundry basket with air-holes so that the boy could hide there in case of a sudden swoop by agents of her husband. Her fears proved correct. One day in the winter of 1897, her lodgings were invaded by members of the secret police and she and Nicolas were taken to police headquarters where, after a hideous confrontation with her husband, her son was wrested from her.

Catharina left no stone unturned in her struggle to regain her children. She prepared a petition for the tsar and threw herself in front of his horse, hands outstretched, to gain his attention. In the following excerpt from the petition, we can see evidence of the passionate and emancipated spirit that Catharina possessed (and which she was to pass on to Sonia):

It is the fruitful woman who is considered inferior inside as well as outside the home, who is a slave. It is the mother of the family who must surrender all power, who must renounce her own fortune, and who may be deprived even of her own children. And yet it is she who is guardian and joy of the hearth, the order of the household' it is she who cares for and comforts her husband and family, who raises the hope of the nation. She is the heart and soul of the family, the seed of posterity. From the day she fulfills the highest function of nature she surrenders her own freedom, the very thing which can exalt or lay a woman low. Unmarried a woman is master of herself; married she becomes subordinate to a man, is no longer master of her earnings, and cannot even defend herself in court without authorization from her husband. She surrenders all personal and legal rights, not to mention her social life. She can even be deprived of the thing closest to her heart – her own child.

The tsar responded to her determined efforts (Catharina had sent copies of the petition to the tsar's wife and mother) by decreeing that the daughter Sophie should spend all of her vacation time with her mother and that the son Nicolas should so spend half of his. Outwardly Catharina accepted this but inwardly she was determined on full custody of her children and also on revenge.

Catharina eventually succeeded in having Nicolas legally returned to her care but she was also bent on humiliating her husband. What form this humiliation and revenge took and its relationship to Sonia's birth are open to question.

I shall tell you first the story as Catharina herself told it and as Sonia was led all her life to believe.

Among Catharina's music students was a young man who called himself Xavier Friedman, who had been having an affair with her sister Marie. Marie's husband, Henry Sandeau, was teaching French in Siberia and when Marie became pregnant by Xavier and delivered a baby girl, she gave the child to her sister. Catharina said that she would later adopt the child.

Meanwhile the twenty-three-year-old Xavier had decided to switch his attentions from Marie to Catharina; he tried to persuade Catharina that she was the perfect "spiritual" woman for whom he was seeking. Though he was given to posturing (he claimed that he was of noble German stock, had virtually the identical surname as hers and was being persecuted because of his Jewish antecedents) and was thirteen years her junior, Catharina found him attractive enough to be the instrument of her further revenge. She agreed to become his mistress and soon, to her joy, became pregnant by him. Her plan was then to smuggle her children out of Russia and set up home abroad, most likely in England where her sister Sophie had obtained a position as mathematics teacher in a Gloucestershire school. After whisking young Nicolas off to England, Catharina returned to Russia using the name Marie Claire Leontine Maurice. It was there, in Moscow, on 6 January 1899 that she gave birth to Sophie-Carmen, who was usually addressed by the diminuitive, Sonia. (I must add that at times Catharina claimed Sonia was born in Paris or on the train to Paris but that Sonia always believed she was born in Moscow.)

Such was the story that Catharina told Sonia and the one she published in a book, *How and Why Sophie-Carmen Was Born*. Sonia, throughout her life, believed most of its details and was always convinced that the absent Xavier was her father – she thought, for example, that Xavier was a mathematician and that it was from him that she had derived her sense of music as "mathematics of the spheres." It is, however, a story that is open to some question and the attempt to unravel the mystery of Sonia's paternity is as interesting as the tale Catharina told. You may read of my attempt to do so in the epilogue at the end of this volume. However, in the absence of hard evidence to the contrary, we must settle for Catharina's account.

The child's birth was not registered, nor was the baby baptised. Catharina wished to leave no documentary trace of her daughter lest de Fridman find her and take her away as he had her other children. When she had enough money to travel, Catherina took her baby daughter to England where she was reunited with her son Nicolas and sister Sophie. Together they joined a colony called Whiteway in the Cotswold hills, which was founded on Tolstoyan principles of free love and communal property. Here, idealistic intellectuals abandoned bourgeois conventions such as marriage, money and private ownership in an attempt to live off the fruits of the earth. On wash days, for example, artists, professors and Hegelian philosophers would stride into the forest to chop wood for the fire, haul water and then pitch in to help the women with the laundry. After a short stay at Whiteway, the sisters realized that they would need money even in a communal economy, so Catharina took a series of jobs as music teacher and "lady's companion" at various places in England. Sonia went with her and naturally grew up hearing music all the day long. That the constant exposure to music was an influence on Sonia can be seen in the story the mother told in later years about scolding her daughter for running off without telling her where she was going. Sonia, then less than three years old, is said to have apologized and explained, "I often forget to tell you where I am going because music is always in my ears....Listen! Can't you hear it?" When told that no one else could hear the music, Sonia replied, "But it is quite distinct. If I had an instrument I would play it. Couldn't you at least get me a piano?"

Catharina's stay in England did not last long. Concerned with money problems and obsessed with obtaining custody of her oldest daughter, she returned to St. Petersburg and got a position as a governess. Her sister Sophie took young Nicolas to Switzerland where Catharina felt he would receive a better education than he would in Whiteway. They decided to leave little Sonia behind in the care of the commune. Sonia's memories of those days were not happy ones. It was, to begin with, a terrible shock for the child to lose her family. The people with whom she was placed did little to ease the pain. They used her as a drudge and locked her in the basement or attic for episodes of misbehaviour, which may have happened frequently since Sonia was, even in those days, possessed of a fierce independent temper. During one period of confinement she had been placed high atop a stack of trunks in the belief that she could not climb down from so dangerous a perch. In an attempt to escape she fell off and injured her spine. To make matters worse, money sent to her did not seem to reach her. Hygiene was lacking too – Sonia was found to be suffering from both lice and scabies when her mother returned. (In fairness to the people at Whiteway, however, it must be said that Sonia occasionally spoke well of some of them, especially Miss Nellie Shaw, with whom she and her mother maintained contact after leaving England.)

Meanwhile in Russia, on learning the whereabouts of her daughter in Moscow, Catharina had abandoned her position as governess in St. Petersburg and went to Moscow. Her sister Sophie had also returned to Moscow, probably for medical reasons (she suffered from an internal tumour) and there she convinced de Fridman that he should allow his daughter to live with her. Unbeknownst to de Fridman, Catharina began living with her sister and her daughter in a little basement suite while she earned enough money as a music teacher for her passage out of Russia. By Christmas of 1903 she had sufficient funds and so, leaving sister and daughter in Moscow, she travelled to Lausanne for a visit with Nicolas, to Paris to arrange a new home and then to England to rejoin Sonia.

It had been well over two years since the two had parted and Catharina was so anxious to be reunited that on reaching a nearby town she could not wait for the coach to Whiteway and walked almost nine miles to the colony. In the words of Catharina's memoirs:

In spite of the warm welcome that was bestowed upon me, my thoughts were elsewhere and I excused myself. I was hardly out of the door when I caught sight of her, yes it must be her, the beautiful little girl running down the hill, followed by the other children. What joy! She must have sensed that she would now be loved like the others, and that she would no longer be alone. When I ran toward her and took her in my arms, I knew that she recognized me. Very excitedly she began to talk to me in English but I couldn't understand a word....She couldn't understand me any better when I spoke to her in French; but we both laughed. We understood each other in spite of the language barrier – we knew that we loved each other.

Sonia's memory of their reunion was just as touching as she recalled being ecstatic on learning that she had a mother like all her playmates did. She remembered the gratitude that she felt when she discovered that a button had been sewn back on her dress and she realized that her own mother had done it for her. After a short stay in Whiteway during the early months of 1904, Catharina and Sonia left England for a new life in Paris.

Paris

Sonia arrived in Paris at five years of age, very much the product of her stay at Whiteway – she was a vegetarian and spoke only English. Her mother was still using the alias Maurice, and Sonia was dubbed Carmen Maurice. After staying in a series of cheap, bedbug-infested hotels, she and Catharina settled into a sixth-floor walk-up at 50 Faubourg du Temple. The apartment lacked a real kitchen, and Catharina had to prepare her own meals for the first time in her life. Though their lodgings were spartan, the rooms had beautiful big windows and a view of the Eiffel Tower. At night the flashing light from the top of the tower would wink into their apartment and the young Sonia would reach out her little arms to catch this "comet" before it disappeared.

Catharina gave music lessons to earn her way in the world. While her mother gave instruction to not-very-gifted students, Sonia would sit quietly underneath a table covered with a large cloth, playing with home-made toys and gradually absorbing the elements of music. To encourage her daughter's musicality, Catharina decided to buy Sonia a piano from a shop on the Boulevard de Sébastopol. Catharina selected a piano, but it was out of tune. Sonia, grimacing, refused to accept it and pointed out another piano which she felt was up to her standards. Later Catharina bought Sonia a quarter-sized violin and within a few months Sonia was playing Beethoven's "Romance" and some of Mendelssohn's *Lieder ohne Worte* by ear. She also began to improvise on the piano and, at the age of six, dictated pieces to her mother, which became part of her collection, *Pieces From My Childhood*. It was not long before the countless theory lessons that Sonia had listened in on quietly took hold and she realized that she knew, without having been taught, how to write notation. However, she kept the knowledge of this discovery from her mother lest she be made to study even more. Catharina had decided not to send Sonia to school but to educate her at home by teaching her French grammar, arithmetic, and the fables of La Fontaine, which had to be learnt by heart. Evidently Sonia, who as a child suffered from acute laziness, felt this course of studies was arduous enough without having to learn music theory as well.

It was not until she was seven years old that her mother decided to begin Sonia's formal musical education by reading her the life stories of great composers. This piqued her interest and she began to listen to music much more consciously. Sonia continued to hide her knowledge of musical theory from her mother and began to compose in secret, hiding in the bathroom to write down the little pieces that she heard within her. Finally, the dreadful day arrived when Catharina proposed to begin teaching her the notes. Sonia could dissemble no more and confessed that she already knew them and had begun to compose. Her mother was astonished and embraced her, saying, "If you continue to work like this, you will be a great composer some day."

Despite her ability to learn quickly, Sonia must have been a difficult pupil. Her character bordered on the untameable and when she decided to make a stand there was little anyone could do to move her from her chosen position,

Sonia with her mother in Whiteway,
England. Sonia lived with foster parents
in a Tolstoyan colony there when her
mother had to return to Moscow to earn
a living.

Sonia with her first quarter-sized violin, Paris, 1904. When Sonia was only five years old, her mother took her to Paris where she bought her a piano and a violin. When she was not quite nine, Sonia entered the Conservatoire de Paris and began giving concerts when she was only eleven. But from the age of six, she preferred composing to practising.

no matter how unreasonable it was. Once, when she detected a printer's error in a sight-reading exercise, she refused to play the piece as written. Her mother tried to coax her but Sonia remained obstinate and sat silent. Finally in her frustration Catharina threw her in a dark closet hoping that the punishment would prompt Sonia to obey. After a few screams and kicks on the door, however, Sonia settled down and amused herself by playing marbles with some cherry stones she found on the floor. In fact she began to enjoy herself and refused not only to give the required musical answer but even declined to come out at all, saying that she would rather spend time in the closet than learn. On other occasions Sonia would react to discipline by screaming as if her throat had been cut, bringing neighbours to pound on the door, enquire as to the trouble and give advice as to how to bring the hysterical child to her senses. A petty dispute with her mother over a choice of underwear sent Sonia into a fit during which she locked herself into one of the communal toilets. Some neighbours counselled a gentle approach to the problem while some less patient ones called for Sonia to be sent to a reformatory. Eventually the caretaker had to break down the door and hold the thrashing, screaming child until the police arrived to calm the inhabitants and return Sonia to her mother.

Another exasperating characteristic was her ability to think of trick after trick to avoid the tedium of lessons. These ploys included deliberately untuning her violin, and moving the clock that was used to time her practising forward by fifteen minutes. Catharina's patience must have been infinite as she sought ways to make her daughter finish her lessons. She foiled the untuning gambit for a time by gluing the violin pegs into place – of course when the strings stretched the violin was unplayable and was eventually broken in an attempt to remedy the situation. When Catharina at last discovered that Sonia learned best when she was praised mildly and left to practise on her own, lessons went much more smoothly.

Catharina's financial situation was always precarious and she could not afford the fees charged by professional music teachers, so when she learned of free lessons given by municipal evening schools she resolved that the seven-year-old Sonia would attend. The lessons for beginning students started at ten p.m., so Sonia was put to bed after tea and awakened when it was time to leave. For the first lesson, she and her mother walked through a driving downpour to the instruction hall and arrived to find, in a poorly lit room, forty-three other students scratching away on their violins, tuning up or practising as they awaited the arrival of their one teacher. When Master Sabathé finally arrived and began the class, pandemonium broke out, with forty-four violins playing and one harassed professor shouting correction and encouragement. Sonia's excellent sight-reading and playing were enough, however, to distinguish her, even in this musical bedlam, and Sabathé suggested getting her into the class for advanced students.

The advanced class began at an even later hour, eleven or eleven thirty p.m., but these classes had only twenty students and they played one at a time. As the eight-year-old Sonia awaited her turn, she would play with her doll, from which she was inseparable. She had joined the class near the end of the semester but had no trepidations about the required examination piece, which she quickly learned. When examination day arrived, Sonia was the only student to play it from memory and performed with precision and good phrasing. However when she received no prize for her efforts, her sense of outrage and injustice rendered her mute – she could not speak for five days, even to her mother. This was not to be the last time that she was to feel robbed of musical honours; her reaction would not always be a deferential one.

Catharina's next step was to try and enroll Sonia in the famous Conservatoire de Musique, but she faced two difficult barriers. The first was Sonia's age (she was too young by at least a year) and the second was her illegitimate birth – it seemed that the conservatoire was not prepared to accept bastards. These problems might have deterred a mother less resolute than Catharina but she was adamant that her daughter should receive a first-class musical education. It is uncertain how she achieved her ambition, but she either provided false papers or simply "sweet-talked" the conservatoire's secretary, and Sonia was registered at the school as Sophie-Carmen Friedman. (The slight change in surname was probably due to Catharina's desire to pun on the German word *Fried*, or *peace*, consistent with her philosophy at the time.) This name change created a problem in that they had been living openly as the Maurice family. A change of neighbourhoods was thus in order. Catharina told the people of 50 Faubourg du Temple that they were leaving the country, sold their few pieces of furniture and moved to a different Paris address, 12 rue Richer.

The period before the First World War was a great time to be in Paris and interested in the arts. Catharina would take Sonia to concerts, and among the great performers she saw were Sarah Bernhardt and Pablo Sarasate. Sonia found the great actress a disappointment: Bernhardt was by then long past her prime and Sonia's French was still not good enough for her to appreciate a lengthy program. Sarasate was much more inspiring as he played the "Zigeunerweisen" on one of his two Stradivarius violins. It was a performance which Sonia never forgot and she later said that Sarasate was one of those artists, like Picasso, who always stayed young and kept their ability to communicate with their audience. (Two of Sonia's treasures in the years to come were the tailpiece of one of Sarasate's violins and one of his business cards, which were given to her after a private performance.)

With her new documents, Sonia was able to enter the conservatoire on 3 September 1908, winning admittance in an almost unprecedented way, as a student of both violin and piano, and astonishing her examiners with her prodigious skills on both instruments. Such skills soon attracted patrons, and Sonia began to receive stipends from members of the Rothschild family, Madame Armand Glotz and others. These stipends allowed her to continue her musical studies.

We lack abundant documentation for her years at the conservatoire. However, we do know the names of several of her teachers. Mme. Chené taught her piano, Professors Brun and Remy taught her violin, while Vincent d'Indy instructed her in chamber music. At various times she won the praise of Gabriel Fauré, the director, and Camille Saint-Saens, who served as an examiner. We can also say with certainty that Sonia proved to be the same sort of student at the conservatoire that she had been for her mother – brilliant but occasionally lazy and obstinate. When she had decided that her piano teacher was incompetent (Sonia labelled her unmusical, a bad teacher and possessed of the sterility of a music box) she refused to do the assigned work and instead spent her time composing and preparing the examination piece. Her senior violin instructor quarrelled with Sonia over the correct fingering technique and drove her from the lesson, shouting, "Who is teaching here, you or I?" It was the same Professor Remy who recorded in 1910 that Sonia was a "very gifted student who would make great progress if she did not spend so much of her time composing." A year later his opinion of her was that she had truly extraordinary abilities and could "soon develop into a remarkable virtuoso if she would be more obedient. Oh, if the director could only convince her to work, learn and study slowly!"

It seems that her compositional talents were ignored at the conservatoire and that her teachers wished to see in her only a piano or violin virtuoso. It is almost incomprehensible that those at the school should have overlooked such a large part of her talent, especially with examiners such as Claude Debussy and Maurice Ravel. Fauré was certainly aware of Sonia's love of composition – "Étude de Concert," published in 1910, was dedicated to him. On the other hand, it is easy to see why they concentrated on her instrumental skills – they were of the highest calibre. At the conservatoire she won first prizes in both piano and violin and she gave concerts in Paris, Geneva and Berlin as an eleven- and twelve-year-old that drew enthusiastic reviews. One Berlin critic said: "She used the bow with such verve and elegance and was such a master of her instrument, so confident, that the Kreutzer Sonata was truly enjoyable. It could not have been played better by a mature artist." When the German impresario Hermann Wolff, who engaged her for the 1911 Berlin concert, was told that Sonia would play the Kreutzer Sonata by heart, he exclaimed, "This is impossible! Only Pugno, Joachim and Ysaye ever played that work from memory." Sonia's reply was, "Pugno, Joachim, Ysaye and *me*." It is important to note that at these concerts Sonia played some of her own compositions and, in fact, in 1911 gave a concert in Paris which consisted totally of her own improvisations. (The program mentions that the purpose of the recital was to raise money for a new violin.)

Given such rapid musical progress and Sonia's sensitive pride, it is not surprising that she would react adversely to the slightest criticisms of her talent offered by the conservatoire. Few at the school, however, could have expected the vehemence of her reaction to the results of her final violin competition in 1913. Competing against men of eighteen and twenty, Sonia seems to have done creditably – her teachers and patrons were certainly well pleased with her efforts. However she did not win first prize. This sent Sonia into a rage and she decided to quit the conservatoire and to leave France entirely. Before

doing so, she wrote the director an incredibly undiplomatic letter which reveals so much of her passionate personality that it is worth quoting at some length:

December 13, 1913

M. Fauré:

Ever since I began studying at your "incomparable school" I have received, and still receive, anonymous letters which predict that at the Conservatoire I will never achieve anything....Since I see that these anonymous letters, which must come from very well-informed people, are continuing to harass me, I do not want to waste any more of my time in this "incomparable school" (as only the French call it)....I will leave Paris and the French with pleasure and disillusionment.

What did I gain by having worked so well? They showed me the door!

I asked the reason for this injustice but received no word of response! Yes, this is one more way in which this "incomparable school" encourages students as well as develops their talents.

These little papers of enormous size which you call "First Prize" are not good for anything but earning a living. You refused it to me; you have disinherited a gifted and worthy student! Therefore I am leaving with pleasure and laughter. It is a pity that I spent so much time at your institution.

In 1911 when I played so well, and did so well in sight-reading, on a mediocre violin in a hall like the Odeon, you awarded me the last of the honorable mentions....First prize, first mention, went to my fellow-student Quiroga-Losada who also played very well, but sight-read very badly....It was at that time (though I was not independent and still a young child), it was then that I should have left! I felt it with all my soul, the soul of a premature child! I felt the forces of wickedness against me, the jealousy so widely spread here, the injustice of which I was so frightened!

It was partly the fault of my beloved mother who let herself be influenced (against her nature and principles) by our friends and patrons who encouraged me to continue at this nasty "incomparable school". Now my mother is letting me be free....I am finishing once and for all, I have had enough.

The Director of the Conservatoire de Musique in Paris is a charming man, and a remarkable director....I wrote to this director and asked him why I was being shown the door. I asked for an interview – but nothing! I could not get an answer nor an interview, under the pretence that the letter was addressed to his home! What a crime! And yet, Monsieur G.F. is neither God nor the Czar.

I also see that the opinion of a professor like M. Remy has no value. After the competition he embraced me several times in the foyer, in the presence of Moreau and others, repeating to me in English, "Perfect! Perfect!"

If you had had any insight, you would have been more understanding,...since you had heard me at quite a few competitions and at several examinations when I was still very small, you knew that with my temperament I would not have played the Lalo Scherzo in such a lukewarm way - although that was how my professor at the Conservatoire wanted me to play (and who repeatedly said "perfect, perfect" while embracing me).

It was amusing to hear M. Remy whisper into my ear before I went on to the podium: "Give it all, your whole soul, your everything and let go!" Ha! He had to wait for this moment to tell me that! All year long he had cut my wings and, at the very end of the year, at the very last moment, he says, "Fly, fly, unrestrained, with all your soul!"

What is even more amusing in this Paris Conservatoire of Music is that the main emphasis seems to be on character! It seems that this Conservatoire is more a correctional institution than a school of music! "Yes" the mothers of these students would tell me, "Let's hope that you will become famous through your character, your kindness and also (?!) your talent." Ah, "character", "kindness", "talent" - what a mixture! A Russian salad! "Kindness"! - I do not work to become a philanthropist!

To judge others, to pretend to bestow awards, when all these judges are inclined to make errors, to be partial! These competitions are complete nonsense! Judge yourself first - then you will see what your conscience tells you. The moment you judge others, in this moment, shut your eyes tightly, examine your conscience, go to the very bottom of your soul and - confess all! I know that because you want to feel important, you won't acknowledge anything. You will even say, "Even better that this Sophie-Carmen Friedman has left; we are rid of her."

And then the stories which will be told about me - this will be so easy for you all to do, even those fellow-students who seemed to be so nice, and who invented the story that I was supposed to have said that I was superior to Beethoven. Ha! Are they finished with these refined inventions? And the Conservatoire is not much better. To show that I was progressing with the steps of a turtle they could have at least given me, as they have done before, one more "mention", this time the second last!!! Luckily for me, this was not done.

When I simply say that I have talent and only need to develop it, then witness the exasperated faces of those imbeciles who tell me: "That is immodest, Mademoiselle. You cannot say you have talent." I reply, "Surely when a person makes music his profession, it would be nonsense to do it without having talent, inborn or acquired...."

Do you like to pretend? Do you like that? This is a simple statement of facts, it is not presumptuous.

S. C. Friedman

One can only wonder at the reaction of Fauré and the staff of the conservatoire upon receiving this letter. They had certainly not, despite Sonia's repeated avowals, "shown her the door"; they had only rated her lower than others in a violin examination. Sonia may have been right in her accusations of biased

judging (two of her teachers agreed with her claims) but her letter was obviously written in a state of high emotion and its arrogant tone can have done her no good. My overall conclusion of this quarrel between Sonia and the conservatoire is that such "elite" institutions might be useful for average students but that brighter students will most likely only run into trouble because they are not willing to walk in the usual path of mediocrity. It was Sonia's opinion that her years at the conservatoire were wasted and that she progressed in spite of, and not because of, her lessons there. In this judgement she may well have been right.

Catharina decided that they would go to Germany. Before leaving, Catharina took the precaution of securing for Sonia a set of official papers that could pass without question in their new homeland. How Catharina went about doing this is a mystery, though Sonia remembered her mother saying that she had once paid a man ten francs to pose as her husband. The result was the following document:

Prefecture des Departments Seine:

On December 19, 1913, 3 h p.m., Nicolas Xavier Friedman, born January 14, 1869, in Graudenz (Germany), day labourer, and Catharina de Kochevskoi, born December 7, 1862, in Staradoub (Russia), professor of music and languages, living in Paris (Quai des Celestines, 54), have declared that the child with the first names Sophie-Carmen, born January 6, 1899, rue de la Hachette No.... (5th District), which has not yet been registered, is the daughter of the above named.

In the presence of Louis Boucherez, public servant, rue de Feuillantine 9 and Charles Grymonez, mechanic, living rue Paul Bert 18, after information and in presence of Arthur Taire, deputy of the mayor of the 5th District of Paris, since the declarer is illiterate.

Signed, notarized and stamped, Paris, February 16, 1914.

It must have strained the credulity of the officials who drew up this document to put much faith in the truth of a union between the highly refined professor of languages and music and an illiterate day labourer. Perhaps they just had a Gallic faith in the irresistible power of love.* In any event, Catharina's declaration was accepted, Sonia received her papers, and off they went to Germany, "the true home of music."

---

* In 1919, just before Sonia was about to be married, she pressed Catharina to tell her more about this episode. Catharina obliged and wrote to a man who may have posed as her husband. When Catharina wrote to "Monsieur Hassan," she received a reply from his relatives who said that he had died in the war and that they did not care to be mixed up in the sort of dirty business in which he once engaged.

Berlin

The decision to move to Germany is in many ways a mysterious one. It was taken in the face of the growing probability of a European war, a threat about which Sonia and her mother seem to have been almost completely ignorant. Neither Sonia nor Catharina spoke German; nor does it appear that they had any friends or close contacts to whom they could turn for advice or employment. Furthermore they were now accompanied by Catharina's oldest daughter, Sonia's half sister, Sophie, who had suffered from a serious mental illness requiring care in an asylum. To make matters worse, Sophie's spirits seem to have been quite low – yet another uprooting may well have sent her into a severe depression. And yet, without resources and seemingly with no motive other than to spite the conservatoire and its faculty, these three women moved to Berlin in the early months of 1914, taking rooms across from the Philharmonie on Bernburgerstrasse.

We know little of their first months in Berlin. Sonia gradually learned German on her errands to shopkeepers, and she would often seek the peace of the Tiergarten as a place to work on her compositions undisturbed among the trees. Catharina seems to have had no job and the little family relied on remittances from Russia for its income. The insecurity of their position was brought home forcefully with the outbreak of the First World War in August of 1914. The start of hostilities between the German and the Russian empires meant that there would be no more transfers of money across these borders. At a stroke, the three women were rendered paupers. Their landlord let them stay until the beginning of October, but when their lease expired they found themselves out on the street, searching for a place to sleep in the park.

On their first autumn night in the open, a cold rain began to fall. Sophie, who had grown used to certain comforts, was seized by mental agitation and began demanding to go home. Sonia criticized her for her lack of spirit and her mother tried to calm her but Sophie's disturbances continued. The trio attempted to keep warm on a wet park bench; a policeman passed by and, seeing their plight, gave them an address where help might be found. After an unsuccessful trip to this address the women returned to their bench. Sonia and Catharina went into a light slumber but they were awoken by the sound of Sophie's voice. They looked around to find Sophie talking intimately with a stranger. When Sophie realized that they were awake she took the stranger's arm and led him up a dark lane. Indignantly Sonia ran after them and forced Sophie to return; Sonia's determination made her older sister obey like a child. However when they fell asleep again Sophie disappeared once more and returned only after a long time and with no explanation for her absence.

The next day they spent shuttling from place to place, trying to get relief from organizations such as the Red Cross. In the evening, as they walked down the Schoenhauser Allee, Sonia stopped her mother in front of a large beer garden in which loud music was being played. She went in and asked to see the manager, explaining that she would like to exchange her musical

French, and her style is splendid, but I did not like her touch on the violin.... (Suzanne) brought her to Schnabel. He likes her performance but he does not like her character. She is not very modest and can talk enough for three; she is also a bit conceited. Schnabel thinks that she might be treated as an idol here at home, but her family should realize that there are other idols besides her. Her voice is not supposed to be good.

What a revealing look at Sonia! These diaries also mention Catharina, describing her as an old woman, though she was only fifty-three at the time. Again from Suzanne:

July 29, 1915

This morning by surprise I went to see Sonia's mother. Ah, what a dreary apartment house. Just a hole at the top of a winding staircase!...a dreadful hole paved with bricks, with a terrible smoky stove in the corner,...an upright piano in the middle...and on a pitiful iron bed, under blankets nibbled by worms, this poor old almost naked woman was weeping into her wrinkled hands; while Sonia, with eyes raised, in a white dress like an angel, improvised amazingly. It would need the pen of Maupassant to describe this moving scene. Since I don't have it, nobody will ever know what went on in my soul today....I was there, sitting on a miserable bed crying....In front of me, a portrait of Tolstoy was pinned to the wall.

The introduction to Suzanne was a very profitable one for Sonia. Suzanne arranged bursaries for her (primarily from the Mendelssohn family), found her a new place to live, rent free, and gave Sonia one of her father-in-law's violins, a Guarneri copy of the French maker J. B. Vuillaume. More important, she introduced her protegé into Berlin's better musical circles.

One of the more interesting engagements which grew out of Sonia's newly found recognition was a 1916 acting role in Strindberg's *Traumspiel*. She played Edith, a small part which called mainly on her pianistic talents. The character was to be physically ugly, and every night Sonia had to submit to being painted in wrinkles and dressed in unattractive costumes. The following year she acted in Wilhelm Stueckler's *The Street to Steinach*, for which she was paid the tidy sum of twenty marks nightly. Through her theatre connections she began a relationship with the actress Maria Orska, and soon grew very fond of her. On Maria's birthday Sonia brought a silver bowl inscribed with the name "Maria" and filled with lilies of the valley. Because it was early, Maria was still dressing, but she invited Sonia into her bedroom where Sonia saw an array of expensive underwear the like of which she had never seen. The two met frequently, went for walks and took drives in Maria's automobile.

Orska also introduced her to the wealthy socialite, Edith Andrea, a sister of the industrialist and politician Walther Rathenau. This acquaintanceship might, but for Sonia's tactlessness, have done much for her career. At a gala at Andrea's

house, in a French-style gallery with white and gold mirrored walls, Sonia played Chopin's Polonaise with such feeling that the elderly writer Emil Strauss came and knelt before her. When she saw the admiration and enthusiasm on the guests' faces she felt she was in paradise and wished that she and her mother could be lifted out of all their worries. Her hopes were raised when Mrs. Andrea spoke of Sonia moving in with her family, becoming a "fourth child" and teaching her children music. However, after several days went by and Sonia had heard no more about this idea, a package arrived in the mail with a letter praising Sonia highly and enclosing a valuable brooch which Mrs. Andrea hoped she would always wear and remember her by. While the brooch was a pretty enough token, it did not put any food on the table. Sonia expressed her disappointment to some friends, who advised her to write a letter in this vein to her benefactor. The tone of the letter must have shocked the woman. A cheque came by return mail but there was no personal note, and Sonia had lost a friend and patron. (Years later Sonia wrote an apologetic letter to Mrs. Andrea but received only a rather frigid reply.)

During the war, Sonia continued to compose, writing during these years the symphonic pantomime, *Zyganka*, a piano arrangement of Paganini's "Campanella" and piano accompaniments to some of Paganini's caprices. Sonia's desire to compose was, at this time, straining her relationship with her patrons, who wanted her to concentrate on performing. She was beginning to present their pressures on her. Before the monthly scholarship cheque was handed over, Sonia was given a lecture on the generosity of her patrons, how little she appreciated their help, how slow she was in developing a repertoire, how much time she was wasting in composing and how much any other musician in her position would have done with such aid. Moreover these scholarships carried conditions restricting her choice of a teacher and instrument and limiting her to one musical field. Sonia, however, had decided not to tie herself to just one teacher until she had developed a style of her own. Besides, she had not found any personality to her liking. For some time she worked on the violin with Bronislav Hubermann, who taught her much about bow-hand technique, but before long they parted ways. One day in 1918 when Sonia went to Suzanne to pick up her cheque, she was told that she would have to make this cheque last as long as possible, since her patrons, disappointed by Sonia's failure to develop a concert repertoire, had decided to discontinue their support.

Thus Sonia fell from the good graces of the upper classes. Though it was a harsh blow, she still had friends in artistic and musical circles, such as Philipp Scharwenka, Eugene d'Albert and Helene Warschauer, who kept up their encouragement and sometimes gave financial support. It was in these circles that Sonia met the man who was to become her first husband, Walter Gramatté.

Sonia was introduced to Gramatté at a literary evening for young poets which he hosted in his studio in 1919. Her first impressions of him were of his gentleness and amiability, but in the crush of visitors he seemed to pay little attention to her. A year later Sonia was playing in a private home when she noticed some of Gramatté's graphics on the wall. Especially touching was one entitled *Tired*. Thinking that the artist must truly have suffered to have been able to depict weariness in such a way, she mentioned that she would like to meet Gramatté some day. Her host, boasting that Gramatté was one of his best friends, said he would call him and invite him to come over immediately. And, sure enough, despite the lateness of the hour and his having just arrived back from Hamburg, Gramatté consented to a short visit. At their introduction Sonia shook Gramatté's hand so strongly and so unfemininely that he was more frightened than attracted. However, when he heard her play, all superficial observations were forgotten and he saw only the musician in her.

Eight days later the same host gave a little dance party at which Sonia was invited to play and to which, she was told, Gramatté was also coming. At the party, however, things rapidly got out of control. All the guests wore masks and costumes and capered in rooms lit only by dim Chinese lanterns. Sonia was encircled, for a time, by a gang of over twenty semi-nude men and women who tried to touch her hair. Her job, it turned out, was to accompany a half-dressed woman singing vulgar cabaret songs. The party grew wilder and more erotic. Sonia tried to escape but the outside door was locked and she could not find the key. Suddenly the doorbell rang. "Oh," said the hostess, "a new guest." "Or the police," called out a voice from one of the dark corners. The excitement grew as the doorbell rang again and again. Finally the key was found, the door opened and there stood Gramatté. Sonia's heart nearly stopped beating in relief. He later told her that one glance was enough for him to see what was happening. He greeted Sonia and then took the host aside, telling him that he found it outrageous that she had been lured into such a situation. Then he asked her if he could walk her home, and Sonia agreed.

Outside they walked for a long time, the moon high in the sky as they spoke about themselves and their works. Suddenly Gramatté stopped in front of a house, which was his, and suggested they talk a little more inside. Without hesitation Sonia agreed and boldly walked through the rooms of his lodgings, shocking him with her free and easy ways. He made Turkish coffee which they drank from old porcelain cups while sitting on a low couch and they talked until past daybreak. She told him her life story; he told her his. They were not in love – their personalities were too different for that – but it was clear that they shared something special. As he walked her home in the morning he told her that he would soon be travelling to Hamburg but that he would call her on his return.

Weeks went by with no word from Gramatté. Sonia confessed to her mother that she now thought that he was like all the rest who had promised much but who soon forgot. Then one day the phone rang – Gramatté was back. Sonia invited him to her apartment, spending her last pennies on chocolates and fruit. Impressed by the way they had sat so informally on his couch the last time they had met, she tried to make her surroundings less bourgeois by removing the large table from the middle of the room and scattering cushions on the floor. He arrived, as was his custom, hours late, saying that he had been etching some plates which could not have been abandoned without damage. He then told Sonia that he had spent his time in Hamburg arranging a concert for her and contacting wealthy people who might be persuaded to set up a stipend for Sonia which would allow her to compose without financial worry.

The concert in Hamburg was not the financial success that the two had hoped it would be. To be sure, a fund for Sonia was set up, but after two months the payments arrived only irregularly. The real importance of the trip was the closeness that was developing between Walter and Sonia. Later the two journeyed to a country cottage in Gremsmühlen, which was owned by friends of Walter's; there they spent the summer working on their art and relaxing in the sun. As their relationship grew, Walter began to think of marriage. When he proposed, Sonia's answer was brusque. She recorded this reaction in her memoirs:

My reply was short and abrupt: "Never!" But I already loved him so much that I wanted to be his life companion forever, though I did not want to get married as I had been brought up not to be feminine, nor did I even feel feminine. I can still see Walter begging me to marry him, which he did with such unique grace that I felt a feminine response within me for the first time in my life. Though quite honestly I did not want to hear anything about getting married, I became his wife before God in that dear little house.

The two had the same pet name for each other: Hulele or Hull, chosen only for its soothing sound. But the course of their love did not run smoothly at first. This was mostly due to Sonia's strong, not to say explosive, personality. Many times she offended Walter with her wild temper but he never stopped loving her and slowly tried to melt all the wildness away. The following entry from her journal gives a vivid example of this sort of behaviour:

One evening a large number of friends were gathered and I was asked to play. This was always a terrible trial for me. (When I was still a prodigy I loved to play for others!) After they succeeded in persuading me, I went to the concert grand. But what a box! Usually in revenge for such situations I would take out, on the poor instrument, my rage on the lady of the house who expected me to play on such a lame piano. With some very high and hard wrist-strokes I played a few notes but the keyboard got stuck–speechless–and the whole piano looked as if it had a few teeth missing. Some of the strings… jumped out of the piano casing. I finally smashed the piano lid down with a loud bang in the middle of my playing…and I ran out.

Everyone was silent. The lady of the house was horrified, but kept her dignity. Ashamedly she stuttered, "Yes, yes, the concert piano is worn out and I should at least have had it tuned." The worst was still to come. I ran outside and stumbled in the dark garden until I reached our little house. Shortly afterwards, Walter came. He told me how wonderfully I had played, that everyone has been utterly enthusiastic, that the lady of the house had

Sonia moved to Berlin shortly before
the outbreak of the First World War.
Together with her half-sister and her
mother, she lived in one small room on
the Bahnhofstrasse.

Sonia's mother, Catharina Fridman-de
Kochevskaia, was an intellectual and a
distinguished pianist. She was a pupil
of Nicolas Rubinstein and taught piano
and French to the children of Leo Tolstoy
for twenty years.

excused herself many times and that also he had suffered with me while I was playing. He kissed my eyes.

One of their most frequent sources of disagreement was Sonia's jealousy over his male friends. He was a man with many friends and Sonia saw each of them as a threat or as a competitor for Walter's time and affection, an attitude which sadly continued even after their marriage.

There were other barriers to their relationship – their families. Walter's parents had objected to the speedy end of his first marriage to Hetta Lindhorst and had little good to say about Sonia. They were solidly bourgeois and could not appreciate either Sonia's musical career or the gypsy-like life of her family. For her part, Catharina was too emotionally dependent on Sonia to easily accept her relationship with a man. By this time, her other daughter, Sophie, had been institutionalized for her mental problems once again, and her son, Nicolas, lived his own life in Paris, leaving only Sonia on whom Catharina could lavish her love.

But how did Walter eventually convince Sonia to be his wife? He did it by promising to honour her independence. He told her that the marriage need only be a formality and that she would be as free after the wedding as she had been before. Marriage, he said, would only be a form of protection for Sonia, a way to avoid life's daily worries and expenses. She would have nothing to do but compose, and if she found marriage not to her liking, then she could divorce him at any time. It was the last promise that proved convincing, and Sonia agreed to marry Walter on 31 December 1920.

At two o'clock in the morning on the night before their wedding, Sonia was awakened by tapping on her bedroom window. Walter stood there, totally distraught. He said that he could not sleep and had been walking for hours in the Tiergarten. He had been having second thoughts about their marriage and asked Sonia to think it over carefully one more time. Sonia, who had hesitated for some time before agreeing to marry Walter, had by now become very definite on the matter. She told him firmly that there was going to be a wedding, that her brother Nicolas had travelled all the way from Paris for it and that Walter should stop worrying and go home. But for all that, Sonia did not get back to sleep and nervously lay awake all the rest of the night.

The usual last-minute delays that attend every wedding day occurred. When the time came to take the taxi to the registry office, Sonia's mother could not be found. Since the hour was late, they thought they would have to leave without her, but then someone remembered that she had been seen going to the hairdresser's. Catharina, who had never in her life set her hair in curls, made this gesture to hide her grief at losing Sonia. Saying only that she had wished to make herself pretty for her darling daughter, she joined her waiting family. The wedding party was small: Walther Merck was the witness and Catharina, Nicolas, Robert Friedlander, Irmela Dulong and Leopold Huber-mann, brother of Bronislav, were the guests. The ceremony was brief and without frills, but afterwards the guests went to the couple's home where they drank champagne and broke a glass against the wall for good luck. Such crockery-smashing, merry-making and Sonia's playing unfortunately angered their downstairs neighbour. He stormed upstairs and threatened to break in with an axe if they did not stop the noise. Walter, pale and trembling with excitement, took his pistol and told the neighbour that he would fire through the door if he did not leave immediately. It was an interesting end to a wedding day and, unfortunately, a portent of future relations with other neighbours sensitive to noise.

Sonia and Walter

Wedded life was not without its problems. Early in the marriage, Sonia suddenly grew very ill, stricken with uncontrollable shivering and convulsions. The doctor diagnosed a kidney infection and for days she hung between life and death with Walter watching over her as a faithful nurse. Sonia's recovery took several weeks, and during this time Walter painted two portraits of her: *Tired Girl with Cyclamen* and *The Convalescent*. Because they were short of money in these days, they had to sell these two fresh from the easel, a wrenching experience because his whole heart had gone into the pictures during those terrible weeks.

The greatest problem the couple faced in 1921 was the incompatibility of their two arts under the same roof. Though they had two large and comfortable studios in their apartment, it soon became clear that Sonia's noisy vocation could not coexist with Walter's quiet one. In addition there was the violence of the neighbour's reaction to be considered every time Sonia practised. By chance they recounted their plight to Minna Tube, the opera singer and estranged wife of Max Beckmann, who told them that she owned an empty house in the suburb of Hemsdorf which they could make use of. Delighted by this news, Sonia and Walter decided to sublet their apartment and make the move to the vacant house, a move which was accomplished in April 1921. At first, life in Hemsdorf was idyllic and extremely productive. Sonia had a large music room and Walter a huge studio with a very high ceiling. They were so involved in their respective work and saw so little of each other during the day that they communicated by telephone, arranging to dine together. Often one of them would say, "I still have half an hour's work to do before the next break," or "I can't right now, I'm in the middle of an important job." They would spend their evenings together and then, late at night, during Walter's favourite working hours, he would work under artificial light. During the months in that house he completed eight oil paintings and a large number of water colours and graphics. Sonia began new compositions and also reworked and finished her pantomime, *Zyganka*, for which Walter did the stage design, presenting her with two portfolios of wonderful drawings and sketches. They decided to change the pantomime's title to *Der Träumende Knabe (The Dreaming Boy)*.

Their idyll was shattered, however, when winter came and they discovered that they could not heat the house. The winter was a severe one, coal was unavailable due to rationing, and the roof leaked. They tried to regain their old apartment but the artist to whom they had sublet it refused to give it up even when offered good money. The housing shortage in Berlin made it impossible to find other accommodation and so, after sleeping on sofas in friends' apartments or in a tiny rented room, first Sonia and then Walter moved to Paris. In February 1922 they moved back to Berlin and tried unsuccessfully to regain their apartment through the courts. For most of that year the couple lived with Sonia's mother in a little studio which ironically was next door to the one they were struggling so hard to get back. The flat had one large room, lit only by candles, and was filled with suitcases and trunks. It seemed to Sonia that it had always been so, that she had grown up with these pieces of luggage. Ever since Catharina had left the security of Russia, she always appeared ready to move yet again. She never seemed to want to buy furniture and lived, filled by a restless spirit, as if she were constantly on tour. To preserve a sense of decency and not have to sleep in the same room as the two women, Walter curtained off a little utility room filled with yet more luggage and slept on a folding camp bed. It was here that the first signs of his mortal illness appeared in chronic coughing and back pains. He began taking medication, but his symptoms grew worse.

It is to Walter's great credit that during this painful time in this tiny room he was still in control of his creative powers. Here he produced a number of self-portraits, many graphics, the lithographs, *A un sal collegue* and *Three People in One Studio*, as well as his oil portrait of Catharina, which he called *La Quasi Diogène*. However, his ill health and frustrated resentment at not being able to find a suitable home often prevented him from working or even leading a normal life. On the night of 31 December 1922, their second wedding anniversary, Walter was in bed with a fever. Suddenly he began to cry and beat, with clenched fists, on the wall, the wall that separated him from his old apartment. In their rage and grief, he and Sonia then conceived a mad plan of revenge, a plan to set fire to the roof of the studio next door and drive their tenant out. Sick as he was, Walter wanted to get out of bed and crawl on to the neighbour's roof. Eventually, Sonia saw the danger to Walter in scrambling over a steeply pitched roof on a winter's night in the grip of a fever, and she persuaded him to remain inside with her.

A great deal of Walter's misery stemmed from not having a proper place to work, but much was also the result of enforced prolonged contact with Sonia and her mother. In a letter written the day after the feverish revenge episode, Walter told his friend Hermann Kasack about the strain of living with two people for whom it was a tremendous effort just to smile. He revealed in February 1923 in another letter: "I am very often absolutely desperate from being together with Sonia and her mother so much." He took to going out by himself, drinking coffee and reading the newspapers somewhere, and not returning home until two or three o'clock in the morning. Finally the situation grew unbearable and the couple decided to separate temporarily: Sonia was to go to Paris and Walter would remain in Berlin, staying with friends and pursuing the lawsuit against their tenant. But before this happened, Walter returned home with the news that he had found an apartment. It was just one room and was insanely expensive, but it was large and, at last, offered some privacy.

Their apartment was in the aptly named Haus der Kuenstlerinnen, or House of Women Artists, a block divided into a number of studios. Walter used curtains and furniture to create a living room, a kitchen, a music room and, by the window, an area for him to paint in. The apartment was crammed full of his works. In Sonia's bedroom was the lithograph, *Self-Portrait Under Trees* and *Fight*, while above Walter's bed hung the huge *Dying Forest*. Above the sofa

On 31 December 1920, Sonia married the Berlin expressionist painter Walter Gramatté, who gave her the opportunity, for the first time in her life, to compose without worrying about daily expenses.

Oil by Walter Gramatté, *The Convalescent*, January 1921. Shortly after the
wedding, Sonia fell ill with a kidney
infection. Soon after her recovery,
because of her "noisy vocation," she
and Walter had to give up their studio.

was the mystical *Still-Life with Clock and Tulip Pot* and everywhere were crates of finished pictures, frames, palettes, etching equipment, easels and presses. In these cramped conditions, Walter worked on his art and Sonia practised her violin. In the evenings after closing hour she would go to the Steinway store to practise her piano and compose. Walter would stay at home and paint in the silence until two or three o'clock in the morning when he would go and pick Sonia up. Between 1922 and 1924, Sonia wrote or published eight pieces, including the accompaniment for the Paganini caprices, the "Danse de Nègre," the first and second violin suite, the first piano sonata and the first three violin solo caprices. In 1923 the overture to *The Dreaming Boy* was performed in Hamburg where she also played her first violin suite and one of her piano sonatas to approving reviews. One stated: "It is overpoweringly beautiful to see this young artist, full of victorious vigour, expressing her own musical fantasy." Another said: "She is a versatile, genuinely strong and exceptionally gifted musician," while yet another called her "an ingenious personality, and a musical talent with an active and fertile imagination in these our over-intellectual times."

Despite these creative successes Walter and Sonia had reached the end of their patience with living conditions in Germany. Walter's letter to Martha Rauert, the wife of his most important collector, explained:

We are very seriously considering emigrating to Spain. We can't go on like this anymore. I am not leaving my homeland out of cowardice but because the Fatherland cannot provide a home for two people, a home where they can devote themselves to their work. You can best see how hard it is on, and how sad it is for, poor diligent Sonia who finally believed that she had found a homeland. She has had a little bit of Russia, five years of England, nine years of France and now Germany – with the possibility of moving yet again. Believe me, it is hard, very hard....When I think of my friends it is even harder, although I have Sonia's love at my side which gives me courage and her enveloping confidence which gives me strength....Perhaps we shall be happier there.

On 7 February 1924, the two boarded the tiny steamship Neapel in Hamburg and set sail for Spain. The trip was full of adventure. Before the ship had left port it collided with another vessel, resulting in a delay for a harbour-police investigation. They next encountered icebergs and then ran aground on a sandbar. Once afloat again, the ship became lost and, by the time it had returned to its proper course, it was in the midst of a storm of hurricane force that lasted three days. Sonia was not a good sailor and burdened poor Walter by continually moaning that fortune tellers had warned her not to go to sea before her thirty-first year, and if they should drown now it was Walter who had forced her into the trip. Finally, when the Neapel reached Valencia at five o'clock in the morning it crashed into a smaller Spanish boat, smashing it completely and sending passengers running to the deck in their underwear. The only good thing about the trip was the inspiration it provided for Sonia's *Biscaya* Suite, her second piano sonata.

For anyone coming out of postwar Germany with its shortages and inflation, living in Barcelona in 1924 must have been a wonderful experience. There was no shortage of accommodation. Sonia and Walter soon found a house of suitable size with a beautiful garden. The climate seemed to be good for Walter's health and they soon made a number of friends in the local German community. The country and its people fascinated them. They took trips by car and boat to Majorca, Madrid, Cadiz, Toledo, Seville and elsewhere, enjoying the bull-fights, the music and the cabarets.

For Sonia these years in Spain were rewarding musically. Inspired by Spain she wrote the *Majorca* Suite (her third violin suite), the solo violin concerto, the first piano concerto and the "Spanish Dance" of the third piano sonata. She made valuable contacts in Spain as well. She met Igor Stravinski and Richard Strauss in Barcelona where they were attending festivals of their music. Stravinski seems to have paid her little notice but Strauss listened to Sonia play some of her works and invited her and Walter to his home in Garmisch. In Barcelona she was also closely acquainted with Pablo Casals, whom she had met through Suzanne Joachim-Chaigneau. For him she also played her new works and received in return the warmest of recommenda-tions. Life for Walter seems not to have gone as well in Spain as he had hoped. Though he was sometimes able to work, the problem of having both a noisy and a quiet artist under the same roof persisted. Perhaps he felt, more than Sonia did, that he was isolated from his surroundings. In Spain he found neither contact with artists working in a similar vein nor buyers for his works.

During the years they lived in Spain, they returned to Germany for occasional visits. In 1925 Sonia gave a series of concerts with Edwin Fischer, playing both her own compositions and those of Bach and Mozart. At the Bechsteinsaal in Berlin she gave a solo performance which premiered her violin concerto and which drew extravagant praise from the critics. Kurt Singer of *Vorwaerts* said: "She proved herself as pianist, violinist and composer and in each of these fields she has something to say....She is a musical Amazon who is loaded with explosive moods." The *Allgemeine Musikzeitung* exclaimed; "What a breed, what a temper, what a fascination! And how freely she expresses herself on the instruments out of which she coaxes the most unique effects." The *Berliner Morgenpost* stated flatly: "She is the first female who has something to say as a composer."

Walter returned to Berlin in the summer of 1926, determined to find a suitable apartment for the two of them. In October Walter wrote to Sonia: "For the first time in years I can see an end. I can hardly comprehend the whole thing. My faded hopes are built up again...." By November they were esconced in what proved to be the last apartment they shared. Despite finding a place to live, they were not happy in 1927. Part of their problem was financial – they were very low on funds and could afford neither Christmas nor birthday presents. When Walter attempted to borrow a mere fifty marks from his father he received a harsh lecture which listed every expense his parents had incurred for him and which blamed their penury on Walter's and Sonia's pursuit of careers in

Oil by Walter Gramatté, *At the Harmonium*, 1922. For several years after the war, Sonia and Walter could not find a decent home and place to work, and they lived, partly separated, with friends. Sonia was obliged to practise in the Steinway store after closing hours. At home all she had was a harmonium.

the arts. Sonia's efforts to win an advance on her fees for touring were similarly rebuffed.

Another element in their unhappiness was Sonia's emotional depression brought on by a lack of recognition. She felt herself misunderstood and unappreciated by the musical establishment in Berlin and reacted bitterly to what she perceived as snubs by more famous musicians. She yearned vainly for a close friend to advise her musically. Moreover she was cursed yet again by neighbours unappreciative of her need for constant and noisy practise. This time it was Herr Grossmann, who lived beneath them, who threatened to take them to court if Sonia did not cease to make noise. After much quarrelling, the two parties reached a compromise, the details of which Walter outlined in a letter to the Grossmanns' representative:

My wife is not going to work for five hours as Mrs. Grossmann would allow but for six. However this amount will probably never be used, except shortly before concerts. It could be exceeded during periods of composition...for nobody can take the responsibility of forcibly interrupting inspiration; at least no one who had the faintest idea of an artist's creativity or had even a spark of respect for cultural work in this field would dare to do this. My wife's working time will, if possible, be divided between the morning and the afternoon, but in general there will be complete silence at ten o'clock. Off and on when we have artists or musicians as guests, this time limit might be exceeded as well; this practice is common in all houses in Berlin. I hope Mrs. Grossmann will not consider violin playing to be a disturbing noise – we of course consider that beyond commitment. This is my last effort to settle this conflict.

Unfortunately this compromise did not put an end to the squabbling. Later, after what Sonia claimed was only an hour of violin practise at nine in the evening, the Grossmanns charged upstairs, screaming and ringing the doorbell for twenty minutes. Sonia was saved by another neighbour but Grossmann continued to rave about "that Russian gang...those Polacks" and to vow that he would strangle the beast.

Though Sonia felt herself neglected by the music world she was, in fact, in some demand. On 21 March 1927, the world premiere of the second movement of her first piano concerto, with Sonia at the piano, took place in Lübeck under Edwin Fischer. It had been intended that the entire concerto be played but rehearsals were plagued by the problem that was to haunt Sonia all her composing life – there were too many mistakes in the parts. Consequently Fischer decided to play only a portion. It was, incidentally, to be the only time that Walter was to hear one of Sonia's larger orchestral works. In June, Sonia went on a nine-concert tour of Spain and North Africa, a trip which inspired the composition of two more violin caprices. One was occasioned by the island of Majorca and the other, the "Danse Marocaine," by a concert in the Moroccan garrison town of Melilla, which Sonia described in her diary:

At eight o'clock in the morning, I took a trip around Melilla. It was magnificent! The gypsies, the camels, the market, the snake dance, the blind flautist, the home of the tribal chief, the other concert in the Sultan's palace, the baths, the dance of "Fatima," the Moors with whom we had tea, there was such a beautiful little girl who was only fifteen years old.

(It seems that Sonia had made a big hit with the young officers of the garrison who swarmed around her. They drove her around the city and also picked up the young "Fatima" who gave an impromptu dance in front of their cafe.) In November, Sonia gave a concert in Hamburg, which she was to repeat in Lübeck two months later, consisting entirely of her own compositions and including the second piano sonata, the Polish Dance, the Violin Solo Concerto, sections of the third violin suite and the fourth and fifth violin caprices.

These apparent successes do not seem to have lifted Walter and Sonia from the deep depression in which money troubles and career disappointments had placed them. Their letters from this time reveal a strong belief in their own merits and an ingrained pessimism about the chances of ever being recognized. An example is Sonia's reaction to the success of a one-man show of Walter's works at Berlin's Ferdinand Moeller Gallery in October 1927. In the following journal entry her attitude changes swiftly from one of outright ebullience to despair:

It is shortly before six!
Wall is still at Moeller's. In ten minutes Wall's big exhibition
will close.
The press was a success!
Attendance was excellent!
Two prints sold!
Tomorrow is the first and we hardly have any money.
It is always the same.
Money, money–we need only money–not a superfluous amount, but enough to live. Now Wall, my Wall, my unique dear artist-comrade, with whom I wish to share our fates forever–whether it be external success or disappointment, be sure of yourself. You express yourself so uniquely in your art, and at the moment you are the only one who is working so honestly. You would never express yourself dishonestly in a stroke here or there which you didn't feel within, in the hope that no one would notice. You were always too modest in your great art. Why must it be that these deeply-felt strokes, sounds or word-pictures are regarded as holy only after the great birth into the other world, that is, after death. Why can't we have the satisfaction of seeing the fruit in our worldly lives, the enjoyment of seeing the fruit of our tree?
My dear Hull, don't despair!

It must not be thought that Sonia alone was of this depressed state of mind. Walter, as we can see in the following excerpts from letters to her in 1927, shared her feelings of alienation and desperation.

Etching by Walter Gramatté, *Bird Woman*, 1922. Like her music, Sonia's personality and her physiognomical expressions were inexhaustible.

Photograph of Sonia and Walter, probably taken in the mid-1920s during a short stay in Germany at Sudeck's summer resort in Ahrenshoop on the Baltic Sea.

Etching by Walter Gramatté, *Tired Woman*, 1923. In spite of housing problems, Walter was relentlessly active in his art, creating, among other works, about a hundred portraits of his wife in oil, water colour, drawings and graphics.

My Hull, don't worry about things which are deplorable. You yourself have abandoned all thoughts of fame. You think of it sometimes because you regard fame as useful, but you have never been so small as are almost all the other musicians, to strive for fame out of vanity. Oh, how wonderful they all think they are, how important they feel, they would rather eat dirt than give up their fame which they think is so important for their meager spiritual life. You have nothing in common with any of them. Nothing. The two of us are going to live and soon we will live better....We shall work and we will have all the happiness which man can enjoy on earth. We are of royal blood through our own perception.

Now I think we have both recognized what this dear human race is all about, and that we do not belong to them. Why give them the highest and receive nothing in return?

The year 1928 was a year of mixed fortunes for the couple. It was dominated from the beginning by Walter's increasingly poor health. He had been growing constantly weaker and this weakness kept him from working regularly. With fewer and fewer pictures to sell, their income dwindled dangerously low and they went deeper into debt. There were weeks at a time when they did not dare answer the doorbell for fear they would find a creditor presenting them with another unpayable bill. Then one Sunday in spring Walter suffered a coughing fit which would not stop and which exhausted him utterly. Sonia stood helplessly by as Walter shakily stood up, looked into a mirror for a long while and then looked at his handkerchief, which showed blood stains. He then went over to Sonia and took her into his arms and said, "My Hull, I believe you shall have me for only one more year."

On the very day in which they realized that Walter was dying, a telegram arrived from Paris: "Famous orchestra conductor Stokowski wants to hear you. Bring your violin. Expenses will be paid. Come immediately. Sincerely, Marraine." They were doubtful, but a second wire arrived: "Come right away, Marraine." Very well, Sonia would come right away, but how? There was only enough money for next month's rent and nothing else. Walter decided that a gamble was in order: use the rent money for the fare to Paris and trust in the promise of reimbursement for expenses. It took three days for Sonia to pack and arrange for a passport and then she and Walter stood at the train station, each of them excited by Sonia's prospects but uneasy at leaving the other. Out of this emotional farewell grew two works of art. From Walter's description of standing on the platform watching her train pull away Sonia composed the seventh violin caprice, "The Red Light of a Departing Train." Inspired by his mood of farewell, Walter executed the etching, *Myself, Resting My Head In My Hands.*

Arriving in Paris on 6 May, having had no sleep, Sonia went to the home of her "god-mother," Suzanne Joachim-Chaigneau, where the interview with Stokowski was to take place. Exhausted and having had no time to practise, she thought of how important her audition was to herself and her dying husband.

She grew nervous and her hands started to tremble. When Stokowski arrived, she offered him the music to follow, but he replied charmingly that music was to be heard and not seen. He expressed no preference when asked whether he would like to hear Sonia's own compositions or music from the classical repertoire, so with a little prayer she launched first into three of her violin caprices. Stokowski at first seemed surprised, but he asked to hear more. Sonia then played her Violin Solo Concerto, a movement from her piano concerto and finally the "Procession Funèbre."

Stokowski's reaction was very encouraging. "How can you play violin and piano so well and at the same time be such a good composer?" he asked. When Suzanne explained Sonia's situation to him, he offered at once to help. He immediately cabled his manager in New York to arrange concerts for her under his direction with an honorarium of $600 per evening. To clear up her immediate financial problems, he advanced her $500 from his own pocket, saying, "Just so you will be able to work quietly without any worries. I am doing this for your great talent. You may return this money to me from your concert income but if that should prove too difficult, there is no need to do so." The opening concert was set for 1 May 1929. His parting words to Sonia were: "We will meet again at the morning rehearsal on May 1st in the Philharmonia in Philadelphia. Until that time work as hard as you can."

On receiving this news, Sonia cabled Walter in Berlin: "Are saved. American contract perfect. Payment in advance." But before receiving the cable, Walter indulged in some glum fantasizing about what he thought would happen and which he included in a letter to Sonia written on the evening of her audition.

Little angel! By now you will have played but no wire has arrived. Mr. Stokowski will not have had much time. He certainly will not have risked more than an hour in his search for talent. With the most polite phrases he will just disappear into Switzerland where he will indulge in good, wholesome Swiss milk to gain strength [to search] for more geniuses. Don't be sad, and above all, don't be disappointed. Success never comes when it should.

The unfathomable depths of Walter's depression can be gauged by this letter written *after* he had received his wife's good news:

The telegram came this morning at 7 a.m. I did not open it right away. I couldn't. But after I had read it, and even later, tears rolled from my eyes; tears of joy for your achievement and of sorrow that you had achieved it, because this will be just the beginning of the real hard times. Why don't I have enough to care for you, feed and dress you properly? Then I would keep you far away from the kind of life that is now awaiting you. You will be far away from your quiet little home for a very long time and well-dressed ignorant people will be around you day and night to exhaust you. Oh, if you could only earn

Sonia developed a special technique for
violin as well as for piano. Her bowing
technique could probably be traced
back to her study with Hubermann.

In spite of housing problems during the early 1920s, Sonia enjoyed her first enduring composition period and gave concerts on both violin and piano. She was hailed by critics as "a musical phenomenon...perhaps the only one of her kind which has ever been born."

enough in a short time so that we could build our little house, but I can't see this happening so quickly. Perhaps by that time you will be ill. I will be separated from you for long periods of time, and even now, I fear this.

After her audition, Sonia returned to Berlin, but only for a short time. She felt that in order to prepare for her American tour, which was almost a year in the future, she needed undisturbed peace for her composing and practising. Leaving Walter in Berlin, she settled into a little summer house in Barbizon, outside Paris. During the day Sonia worked under artifical light because the windows were covered with blankets. She saw the sun only when she took a short break for lunch at a neighbouring *pension*. Sleeping little, she was able to work ten or twelve hours a day, mostly on transcribing her pieces for orchestral accompaniment. Her only relaxation was reading the letters Walter sent her almost daily. These letters are loving but full of despair and unhappiness at her absence. In later years Sonia was to reproach herself bitterly for overlooking his needs and the cry for understanding in his letters. At the time, however, she was preoccupied with her work and preparing for a breakthrough in her career. Even when Walter was unable to care for himself and had to move into his parents' home, Sonia remained working in Barbizon.

In addition to writing music in the months she spent in France, Sonia wrote her first set of memoirs, which have been preserved and from which I have drawn much of my narrative. Not only do they tell us of the events of her daily existence but they also let us look into her mental and spiritual life. She was approaching thirty, always a time of reflection, and on the brink of possible musical stardom. It must have seemed a good time to sum up her life and to set down her dreams for the future. In the introduction to these memoirs Sonia revealed much of herself when she said:

If one day I succeed and my wishes be granted, I will still have a suffering heart and ears sensitive to the music of the poor unfortunate souls who are crying. My desire would be to help them as well as myself, but because I am so powerless and such a little thing in this great universe, it is really an impossible task for me to be happy. Although I sense a maternal feeling within me, and I ardently wish to have a child to whom I could give a little bit of the happiness which I have never known myself, I believe I shall never have one. I already love it too much to let it suffer here on earth with us. Either it would suffer for himself when unhappy, or it would suffer for others when it sees them unhappy. I would like to finish my life by being useful to my loved ones, my mother, my Wall, my sister; and if possible, by extending my help to those around me, and not to see the same beginning again in a new being made of my blood and skin, as much as perhaps I would like it....I will try my best to concentrate, searching my soul, purifying myself to develop the great calm which must reign within, so that consistent work will help to develop the language given to me here – music. Perhaps then God will hear me.

Meanwhile, back in Germany, Walter Gramatté was nearing the end of his life. So low were his physical resources that he was forced to stop his painting altogether, a thing which caused him almost as much pain as Sonia's absence. He resented (as who would not?) his own helplessness but feared for Sonia after his death, telling her in one letter, "Perhaps I have seen many things worse than they actually were, but then perhaps not even bad enough. For man is the most dreadful creature living on this earth, and to think of you alone among them – what a thought for me." In another note to her we can see both his pessimism and spirituality as he discusses the same topic: "Fate has so much harm in store for you, so especially much, that after suffering through all these trials you should not become confused. Stick close to me and to the good that you, I am sure, shall inherit at the end of this earthly life. You will be lifted into a higher sphere which has nothing to do with people, for you are a chosen being."

Sonia finally returned to Berlin in early November and found Walter very near death. With money received from her new American patrons, the Adler family of Chicago, she took Walter to Hamburg where he was placed in the Eppendorf Hospital. Later he was moved to a private clinic owned by his friend and doctor, Professor Paul Sudeck, but despite all this care his condition grew unmistakably worse. Throughout Christmas, New Year's Eve (their wedding anniversary), Sonia's birthday in early January and until his death, Walter was surrounded by friends and the countless flowers which they brought. His letters mention Christmas and birthday festivities and the orchids, lilies, carnations, potted plants and a palm tree about his bed. His body, however, grew continually weaker and in the early hours of 9 February 1929 Walter Gramatté died.

Sonia was devastated by grief. Only the presence of her brother, Nick, who had rushed from Paris to be by her during her husband's last hours, prevented her from taking her own life. Nick performed a further service by arranging for the transport of the body and accompanying it back to Berlin on one of the coldest nights of the century. The funeral service took place at the Wilhelms-hagen cemetery where Walter's father had bought a double plot. The eulogy was given by Hermann Kasack.

Though cared for by friends such as the Heckels and Schmidt-Rottluffs, Sonia was in no condition to carry on with the American tour. (Indeed it was months before she could bring herself even to touch a violin or piano.) Stokowski was informed and he made arrangements for a series of concerts in Philadelphia and Chicago for the autumn of 1929 instead of for the spring.

In the meantime, Sonia concentrated on ensuring that Walter Gramatté would not soon be forgotten. To this end, she endeavoured to keep their apartment in the Neue Wintersfeldtstrasse as unchanged as possible, with paints and brushes prepared as if waiting for Walter's return. In addition, Sonia spent more of the advance money on photographing his works, framing the pictures and matting the water colours and prints. Many of these pictures were of Sonia herself, for it was her face that had filled Gramatté's art. In over one hundred

When they had finally settled in a lovely
apartment at 29 Neue Winterfeldt-
Strasse, Walter had been ill for a long
time. He died in February 1929. During
Walter's last months, Leopold Stokowski
engaged Sonia for a series of concerts
in America which she undertook in the
fall of 1929. When she returned, she
decided to give up playing and devote
herself completely to composing.

portraits, in oils, water colours, drawings and graphics, he had sought to capture the elusive physiognomy of his wife.

Just as Sonia had touched Walter's artistry, so did he play a great role in shaping her life and work. It was their marriage that allowed her to concentrate on the creativity of composition without the burden of trying to exploit her instrumental virtuosity for material gain. Moreover, Walter deeply affected the type of music that Sonia chose to compose. Influenced by her husband's introversion, her works became increasingly loaded with contemplative and emotional expression. This can be heard in the first three piano sonatas, the violin solos, the slow movements of the violin suites, the concerto and the violin caprices. Certain of her works were directly inspired by Gramatté's art, such as the Improvisation for Flute and Piano, drawn from the water colour, *For Hulele*; and the piano caprice, "Aufschrei" ("Scream") was inspired by his drypoint of the same name.

Walter influenced Sonia's personality in other ways too. As much as their finances would allow, they had travelled together. Germany and its seacoast, France, Switzerland and, above all, Spain touched Sonia's spirit and music. Walter educated her eye not only to the beauty of nature, the landscape and the sea, but also to that which lay in everyday things: home, furniture, carpets, porcelain and glass. Gramatté made a reflective and contemplative person out of the gypsy; she was changed into a person who loved home above everything. Finally he brought her friends, artists with whom she was to share attachments until the end of her life – the painter couples Schmidt-Rottluff, Heckel and Kaus; the writer couples Kasack and Koeppen; and perhaps above all the Sudeck family.

Sadly, there was a dark side to Walter's influence upon Sonia. As surely as he had supported her in life, his death was to haunt and torment her for years to come. I have mentioned already how close Sonia was to suicide in February 1929. For a long time afterward, the thought of death was with her constantly and wherever she went she carried twenty Veronal pills, which had been described to her as an effective way of ending her life. I believe that she needed this security during the many crises she endured. Though outwardly decisive and self-assured, inwardly she was insecure, deeply wounded and, I dare say, almost lunatic and somnambulistic.

The depth of her suffering over Walter's loss may be seen, for example, in the shrine she made of their apartment – an altar to a dead artist. She also made the ninth day of each month a remembrance day of his death; for as long as she was in Berlin she dedicated that day to Walter. She also undertook monthly pilgrimages to his grave.

Her torment is also clearly evident in her letters. In one written to herself she stated: "Psychological illness gnaws on me and makes me unable to master upcoming tasks and thus this eternal longing for an inner solution, for divine peace....I must have around me certain flowers of death and mourning, a certain cult of glorification and solemnity." She also wrote to her dead husband. In a letter from Christmas 1932 she wrote:

69

I shall build an altar for you, Hull: There is a gentle rain outside and your spirit is all around me....I feel so exhausted and empty. My strength is gone and tears will not fall, although I live, day by day, in deep mourning. I constantly have this terrible vision before my eyes....Outside it is raining softly on your, "our", grave. Hull, on this very evening, in front of your altar, I would like to gain the strength I need to find the way to you. May the invisible world, the unreachable world in which you live, soon become visible to me. If I should find you, give me your hand the way you did when you were here on earth, and we will not desire anything more than rest. May my existence burn and sink down like the candles on this altar, so I may glow again in the other world.

Just as revealing of her troubled mental state as her letters are her dreams in which she was in contact with the dead. On All Souls' Day, 1932, for example, Sonia recorded this dream: On a dark, windy night Walter appears bearing two flowers for her; he then disappears. Sonia finds herself in bed with the door to Walter's studio open to reveal flowers, a coffin, and her mother – dead. As the fourth anniversary of Walter's death approached, she again dreamt that he had returned, this time to tell her that he was being allowed to paint once more. She tells him that she has kept all in readiness for him but wonders how she will explain the new works he is to produce. She is told that she must keep his return a secret and pass his paintings off as posthumous. Sonia then offers to be dead in his place but a strong wind blows shut the door between them and when it is reopened Walter is gone. The sense of hopelessness and despair that marks these dreams is particularly evident in an episode from 1934. In this vision Sonia witnesses brutal forces dragging a soul toward a deep pit in order to extort his agreement to a pact. Sonia, armed with a club, wants to help, but is powerless to intervene. In order to save a loved one, he agrees to the pact but cannot write. Instead he paints a portrait of himself with a rope around his neck, under a red moon. Sonia approaches. This saddens the soul but enrages the brutes who attack him and his painting. Sonia realizes she cannot save the soul but has been saved by him.

With her life in such turmoil, it is not surprising that Sonia did not succeed in her American tour in the way that she had hoped. She journeyed to the United States in October 1929 and her first concerts were scheduled for 1 and 2 November in Philadelphia under Stokowski. Sonia had planned to play part, if not all, of her piano concerto as well as the Violin Solo Concerto to which she had wished to add an orchestral accompaniment. In addition, she was to play several shorter pieces including the three violin caprices, "Isla de Oro," "Danse Marocaine" and "Elegie," for which she had also written orchestral parts. However, the rehearsal in Philadelphia revealed that the horn parts of the piano concerto were written in a different key from that which the Americans were accustomed to playing in and she had to change the parts at the very last minute. (It is possible that there were other shortcomings in the instrumentation, for Sonia, at that time, did not have much experience in orchestration.) The exhausting task of rewriting left her no time to practise on her instruments and the program was shortened to include just two of the violin caprices with orchestra and the middle movement of the piano concerto which was dubbed "Konzerstueck" for the evening. For an encore Sonia performed part of the Violin Solo Concerto.

After her stay in Philadelphia, Sonia travelled to Chicago, where she stayed with the Adler family while rehearsing for her concerts under Stock. Sonia felt no better about the result of these than she had about those under Stokowski; she concluded that she had not been sufficiently prepared for her American tour. She then spent several weeks in New York meeting and hearing musicians such as Heifetz, Iturbi, Elman, Bauer, Mengelberg and Menuhin before returning to Europe aboard the Ile de France. Also aboard the ship was Jose Iturbi, for whom she had had a secret passion dating back to her days in Paris when she had watched him practise. Iturbi seems to have treated her with condescencion and arrogance, but Sonia, who usually had no time for this sort of behaviour, was too insecure to object.

Though not as successful an event as she might have hoped, the American tour was not without some significance in Sonia's life. Her financial gain from the trip was very real. It allowed her to improve her home and better display Walter's art works. Sonia spent money on framing and matting some of the works and made herself into a curator of their collection. On rare occasions when she had to part with one of Walter's pictures she would take it aside, talk to it and kiss it goodbye, believing that having lived with it so long it was like a valued friend. Another effect of the American visit was a change in her style of dress. From the time of her relationship with the actress Maria Orska, Sonia's apparel had a certain masculine look. Shortly before her trip, the Adlers had come to Berlin and criticized Sonia's choice of clothing. Therefore, on the advice of her sponsors, she changed to a more feminine mode and bought a wardrobe of casual outfits, cocktail gowns and evening dresses. She continued to wear the new outfits for a time after her return as kind of a disguise, a way of masking her grief and emotional collapse. Gradually, however, she returned to the sort of style she had worn earlier.

For over two years after her trip, in the midst of a depressed economy, her monthly remittance from the Adlers was practically her only income. Stokowski's encouragement and support continued, for a time at least, unabated. He had plans to make her a house composer and hoped that she would produce a new work for him every year. (Though Sonia continued work on a piece called *Gedenkstein*, a memorial in music for Walter, the years after Gramatté's death were not good ones for planning any large work.) Another result of the American tour, based on discussions with musicians there, was a determination to completely change both her violin and piano techniques. This she did with great decisiveness and by August 1930 she wrote in her notebook: "I have overcome the mechanical change. I can continue."

I cannot end this discussion of the effects of Sonia's American tour without mentioning that she had attracted a suitor for her hand in marriage while in the United States. It was Marcus Grossmann, who was, I believe, vice-president of one of the big steel companies in America. He sought Sonia's favour and proposed marriage to her, promising that she would have none of the obligations usually connected with the position, except managing the social arrangements of his household. Since Sonia was in a very bad financial situation at the time, she naturally considered his proposition. Grossmann continued to press his suit during several visits to Europe, but Sonia was indecisive. In the end she decided to marry me.

Sonia and I

How did I meet Sonia? Shortly after I had gone to Berlin in 1929, I was asked by the Viennese art magazine *Die graphischen Künste* to write an article called "Berlin Graphic Arts After the War." I agreed and began to interview many of the artists about whom I had already heard. When I asked two of them, Schmidt-Rottluff and Heckel, if they knew any young and interesting artists, they both recommended that I see the widow of Walter Gramatté, who had died the year before. On the afternoon of 8 April 1930, I rang the doorbell at Sonia's apartment. Many times later she would describe jokingly how, before entering, I forcefully blew my nose and announced: "You know why I came." She had wanted me to get a general impression of the apartment and Gramatté's art but at that moment I didn't care too much about such things – I wanted to see the graphics. Somewhat disappointed, she took me to the graphic cabinet and I started to go rather quickly through the matted prints. Again she was disappointed in my behaviour. However, I soon returned, slowly and carefully, to each of the prints I had examined. "Ah," she thought, "perhaps he is not so superficial after all!"

I was sufficiently interested in Gramatté's work to think that much could be written about his artistry. I do not wish to conceal that I was also fascinated by this little woman with her assertive manner, determined voice and rather accentuated movements. She was dressed in a dark jacket and, as was the fashion for afternoon tea at the time, in a black hat with a little dark veil that covered part of her forehead. She offered me one or two glasses of sweet vermouth and little sandwiches and dainties, a gesture which rather baffled me. I remarked that this was the first time that I had been offered anything on such visits. She replied that it would not hurt to interrupt such concentrated work for a moment to take some refreshment. It was apparently the usual form of hospitality in the home of the Gramattés.

No further visit followed for about a month and it was early May before I went to see her again. From that point, however, I began to work on Gramatté and my visits became much more regular. A small example of how close we were growing can be seen in an episode from June 1930 when a zeppelin called The Deutschland came to Berlin. Sonia had intended to go to Tempelhof airport to see this great dirigible and had cleaned her gloves in preparation. Unwisely she had used gasoline as a cleaner and left the container open near the burning gas stove. There was an explosion and Sonia was badly burnt on her hands and face. In her pain it was me whom she called on for help and who summoned the doctor.

After she had spent the summer visiting the Sudeck and Merck families in Ahrenshoop and Hamburg, she returned to Berlin where we began to see much of each other. I visited her apartment and we went to concerts and the homes of her friends. It was jarring for some of these people to see another man at the side of Walter's widow and it took time for them to accept me. Through friends of mine Sonia was introduced to people in the Prussian

Ministry of Culture who might have proved valuable. For some reason, however, Sonia did not impress them.

It was Sonia's relationship with me which led to the final break between Sonia and her American patrons. The Adlers had sent her monthly cheques throughout 1931 but they saw her only as an instrumental virtuoso and were beginning to doubt her genius for composing. The Great Depression seems to have affected even such a wealthy clan as the Adlers, for in 1932 they sent a letter stating that their ability to be of financial assistance was coming to an end. Accompanying the letter they sent a concert program which included a short biography of Schubert in which, underlined in green ink, was a statement that the composer had suffered through periods of misery and hunger. It was meant, I suppose to be consoling but it was really rather tactless. The Adlers were still interested in helping Sonia emigrate to America, but she wished to remain close to me. And since the Adlers showed no interest in assisting in my immigration, Sonia stayed in Germany and contact with the Adlers was broken off.

By the late autumn of 1931, I had moved into Sonia's apartment. My financial situation was rather desperate; the banking crisis in the United States had deprived me of the money I was getting from writing articles in American art magazines. I could not afford my studio on the Kaiserdamm and indeed had to leave with unpaid debts. Sonia allowed me to move into a studio in her seven-room apartment as an honorarium for doing a book on Gramatté's graphic art, for which I had just finished the manuscript. I had been deeply impressed by the humanity in Walter's letters and had started to copy and collect them in 1930. As a result, I was able to include in my book about him all the parts which referred to his art. To my knowledge this had not been done before.

It was around this time that Sonia began to compose again after the hiatus brought about by Gramatté's death. One of her earliest efforts resulted from most peculiar circumstances. In the summer of 1931 Sonia and I went on holiday to Limone, on Lake Garda in the Italian Alps. One evening, after watching a magnificent moonrise over the lake, Sonia was stricken by an attack of sleepwalking with hallucinations. On the following day she had a high fever and convulsions. There was no doctor nearby and communications were very primitive so our innkeeper did her best and summoned the village midwife. Labouring under some incredible misapprehension, the woman arrived – bearing, under her arm, a gigantic enema syringe! Sonia submitted to this bizarre treatment but its only effect was a rather decisive movement of the bowels. There was no improvement in her illness until time gradually cured it. That night, however, she dictated to me the vision which she had had while under the influence of her fever, a vision in which she heard the theme to what became the "Grave Funèbre." She copied this down the next day and eventually wrote parts for a chamber orchestra. Thus did she and the midwife collaborate to deliver one of Sonia's first compositions since Walter's death.

A major event in Sonia's musical career occurred in January 1932 with the first complete performance of her first piano concerto, parts of which had been played in the late twenties under Edwin Fischer and Stokowski. Now it was played in its entirety by the Berlin Symphony under Ernst Kunwald, with Sonia at the piano. The orchestra was under-rehearsed, which infuriated Sonia, who had underwritten part of the cost of the production with money given her by the Adlers, and at the last practice she stormed out in protest. Despite this, she won the admiration of the conductor, Kunwald, who called her a female Rubinstein, and the program, when performed, won popular acclaim. Sadly, the critics were less enthusiastic, partly because of a prejudice against female composers. After the performance, when Sonia's admirers were crowding so closely around her that I could not get through, I thought that I spied Mrs. Grossmann, our neighbour from downstairs whose husband had threatened Sonia's life if she did not quit playing music. When I told Sonia this, her reaction was, "Impossible!" There was every reason for this response. Not only had Grossmann and his wife reacted violently to Sonia's practising but there had also been an incident when Grossmann died. One night earlier that year, our faithful caretaker, Mrs. Papenfuss, had come up to our apartment in a state of agitation. "Mrs. Gramatté, Mrs. Gramatté," she exclaimed (accentuating the first 'a' like every Berliner did), "please stop playing. Mr. Grossmann is dying!" "What!" said Sonia. "He is dying? Well then, he shall go to Heaven, or rather Hell – that would be more appropriate for him – with music." And she continued playing, and playing quite vigorously too, the Chopin Etudes. Yet, here was Mrs. Grossmann attending Sonia's concert. And even more surprising, the morning after the concert, there was the delivery of a huge congratulatory arrangement of flowers with a card from Mrs. Grossmann. "Now," I said, "there is no getting around it. You must go and thank her." "Never!" said Sonia quite categorically. "Never!"

Finally Sonia agreed to go, but she stipulated, "I am not going to shake her hand, and I am certainly not going to take my gloves off." That afternoon we rang the bell at Mrs. Grossmann's apartment and she greeted us, a tiny elderly lady. Sonia advanced with her hands behind her back and I followed immediately to prevent any possible retreat. Sonia started the conversation somewhat abruptly. "Mrs. Grossmann," she said, "you sent flowers to me. That was very kind of you. Thank you very much."

Mrs. Grossmann took a deep breath and said slowly, "You know, Mrs. Gramatté, if ever anyone knew that concert it was I, because you had practised it for many months. But I never imagined how beautiful it could sound in a concert."

At this, Sonia softened a bit. Then she said, "Mrs. Grossmann, I know you also play the piano occasionally. If you don't mind I would like to show you a few things, especially how to play that Mozart sonata more effectively." I have told this story many times, as "Sonia's Greatest Success" and to raise a monument to the integrity of Mrs. Grossmann.

Though Sonia could sometimes appear gruff or unfeeling, she was capable of the most touching sorts of spontaneous kindness. One cold February evening in the early 1930s, Sonia, with her violin in hand, stopped in front of a shoe store to do some window shopping. While wondering which pair she could buy to replace her battered old ones, she overheard the conversation of two prostitutes standing nearby. The younger, still in her teens, complained that she had had nothing to eat all day. When the two had parted, Sonia approached the young prostitute and asked the way to the subway. It was just around the corner but Sonia pretended not to know that and the girl offered to take her there. On the way, Sonia noticed a milk bar and exclaimed, "Oh, milk! I am so thirsty for some. Would you join me, may I invite you?" And so Sonia and the prostitute chatted away for a quarter of an hour, mostly about how bad business had been that day.

At the time of the premiere of the piano concerto, plans were also under way for a memorial exhibition of Walter Gramatté's work. Sonia had always longed for such an exhibition, but it took three years before all was in readiness and through the influence of friends Walther Merck and Professor Paul Sudeck the exhibition opened in Hamburg on 17 February 1932. At the opening, Merck gave the introductory speech and Sonia played the second movement of the Violin Solo Concerto while hidden from view, so that the music seemed to come from above. The exhibition in Hamburg lasted a month and then it moved on to Kiel, Bremen and Bielefeld. At this time the collection was divided: part went east to Danzig, Koenigsberg and Chemnitz; the rest went to Münster (where Sonia gave a concert before the opening) and to Goettingen, Giessen and Stuttgart. Toward the end of the tour the National Socialists (Nazis) came into power and the shows in Stuttgart and Chemnitz were closed prematurely. The exhibitors feared political demonstrations against their galleries because Gramatté had been branded a "degenerate" artist. We therefore recalled the exhibitions and displayed the art on the walls of our apartment.

Another project that occupied us during these years was our attempt to make recordings of Sonia playing her own music as a way of documenting her unique treatment of the piano and violin. We hoped to defray the costs of this project by selling the recordings (they were short-playing 78s, less than five minutes per side) by subscription to friends and other interested people. Unfortunately there was little interest beyond our circle of friends and the only lasting results of this plan were three, still-existing but badly-scratched recordings of Sonia playing some of her violin caprices. In 1936 we tried again to record Sonia, this time with Dr. Ludwig Koch, the famous recording engineer who later became so popular in England for his recordings of birdcalls. He recorded the Violin Solo Concerto first, then the Bach Chaconne and finally the third piano sonata. At this time the techniques of record-making were very primitive, yet they were complicated. Unlike today when the best parts of several performances can be spliced together, no corrections to something already recorded were possible. Also the format was the 78-rpm disc, which allowed for only four to four-and-a-half minutes of music per side. Because of these limitations the Violin Solo Concerto was spread over eight sides, and for each side there had to be four to six masters made from which to choose the best. The recording procedure was a terribly strenuous process because even the smallest mistake necessitated another waxing. I remember, for example, that the recording sessions were scheduled at night when there were likely to be fewer extraneous noises. Even so, one of the best waxes was ruined by the sound of an airplane passing overhead and another was spoiled by the barking of the watchdog in the courtyard. (In spite of all this, the technical quality of these 1936 recordings was excellent. One set which I kept untouched was used as the basis of a 1980 "Masters of the Bow" edition produced by Jim Creighton of Toronto.) When the records were issued it was found that Sonia's recordings of the Bach Chaconne found their best market not in Germany but in Japan!

Just as the Nazis had interfered with the exhibitions of Walter's art, so did they and their ideology restrict Sonia in her career. First, National Socialist theory saw a woman's place as in the home, a breeder of strong sons for the "master race." Nazis were not in favour of women as composers of modern music and consequently concerts of her work were arranged increasingly rarely. Second, and much more damaging, was the belief that Sonia was Jewish – a belief which arose because of her maiden name, Friedman. It was only in 1938, after a long period in which Sonia found it difficult to get work, that I discovered this. One evening after a pleasant interview with the music-ologist Professor Hans-Joachim Moser, who had expressed a desire to write an article on Sonia, Moser turned to Sonia and asked bluntly, "Now tell me Mrs. Gramatté, what are you really? Are you Jewish or not?" Very surprised, we asked him where he could have got this idea and he replied, "You are in the *Juden ABC.*" He then told us of the handbook of "non-Aryan" musicians which all Nazi offices and music organizations possessed and in which Sonia (presumably because of the name Friedman) had been listed since 1932! Though I got her name removed from the third edition of this handbook, the damage had already been done. (I must say that Sonia was less upset about her inclusion than the fact that her birth date was listed in 1892, seven years earlier than she was actually born.) I learned later that the Nazis kept a close eye on Sonia for a long time, questioned fellow tenants about her friends and visitors and even thought that she might have been a Russian spy. Ironically, because the Nazi newspaper *Völkischer Beobachter* had once reprinted, in a mutilated form, an article of mine on German museums, people for a time assumed I had influence in National Socialist circles and cultivated me for favours I might do them. These approaches were in vain for I had no such influence and could do nothing for our Jewish friends such as Jasha Culberg. Jasha had wanted to form an orchestra with Sonia as first violinist but could get nowhere. He found his musical career, like Sonia's, blighted by the Nazi regime.

Despite these setbacks, Sonia's creativity was never completely interrupted. Starting in 1932, she wrote four piano caprices, the first based on Walter's *Aufschrei (Scream)*; the second was based on *Gute Ruh (Rest Well)* and was our way of saying good-night; the third was based on *Meeresmuschelperlchen (On an Aquarium)*; and the last was based on *Wohin? (Where To?)*. In February

1934 she began writing the *February Suite*, her only major violin-piano work. It ended up being called the *Wedding Suite*, for we were married on the twenty-fourth of that month.

Late in 1933 I had been offered a job with a drug company by an old friend of the Gramattés from Barcelona, Dr. Reinhold Krebs, who knew the financial predicament that we were in. He also knew that, after a controversy I had engaged in with German museums, there was little future for me in the art world until the political climate changed. As I had had previous experience in the field of advertising through my connections with art, painting and graphics, and because I was familiar with publishing houses, he asked me to accept this position of advertising manager with the Bayer Company. After discussing the proposition with Sonia, I decided that it was the only possible solution. It meant that I would have to give up my profession of freelance writer and art critic, because my contract specified that I was to write only for the company. (However I realized later that Krebs, as a much more experienced man, had demanded this to prevent me from being endangered politically through my writings.) It also meant that we would have to move to Cologne and divest ourselves of the apartment which had been so convenient and in which we had been so happy. Neue Wintersfeldtstrasse 29 was close to the subway, the little park where we would sit on a bench on hot summer evenings, a Munich Hofbräuhaus where we would have a beer with a radish and a pretzel, the Scala cabaret, and Schlichter's, a gourmet restaurant where we would sometimes go if we had a bit of extra money. Around the corner was the garage where we stored Lilli, a six-cylinder Wanderer-Limousine that made travelling much easier for us. Luckily, before I could find us a new apartment in Cologne, the company was reorganized and part of the central advertising department of which I was to be head was transferred to Berlin. We were very happy to be able to stay. Not only was our apartment so convivial but also Berlin was an artistic and musical capital. Sonia would have suffered in leaving it.

Because of my job at Bayer, we were freed from our most pressing financial obligations. My wages were nothing exceptional but it did mean that for the first time I could offer Sonia some security. Thus it was possible to seriously consider something we had long talked about – our getting married. Sonia had some reservations. She did not wish to give up the name Gramatté and feared that in marrying me she would in some way be violating her loyalty to Walter. In the end she put these fears aside and we decided to marry.

When we announced our news we received congratulations and presents from all our friends and families. From Sonia's brother Nick, who owned Les Moulières, a country estate with large gardens and greenhouses near Toulon, France, came a package of artichokes and mimosas. The story of our trip to the customs office to claim the gift shows Sonia in a typically mischievous light. When it was revealed to the customs officers what was in our package, we were told instantly that importing plants and flowers into Germany was strictly prohibited because of the potato-beetle menace. "What can we do?" we asked, only to be told there was no remedy. They had been ordered to be strict on this point. At this, Sonia immediately grew agitated, but I tried to deal with the officials. I explained how much it would mean to my wife to have this present which had been grown on her brother's own land. At the same time, I was taking a ten-mark note out of my wallet and idly playing with it. It was all to no avail.

Sonia cried, smiled and finally grew loudly outraged, only to be told that she was insulting the law. I smoothed the ruffled official feathers and pleaded for at least a few stems of the mimosa. Impossible, unless I presented verification from the Plant Biological Station that the flowers were not contaminated with the potato beetles. After forty minutes of frustrated argument, I gave up and dramatically slammed the door. Outside in the cold air I paused to calm down and exchange glances with Sonia. Coyly, she opened her coat to show that she had hidden two stolen stems of the mimosa. We broke into laughter, not caring whether or not we had brought the potato beetle into Germany.

Our wedding took place at the Schoeneberger city hall on a Saturday morning, with only two of our friends, Siddi Heckel and Dr. Eduard Petertil, as witnesses. After the ceremony, when we came out of the city hall, we were surprised by a brass band made up of four unemployed musicians who played for newlyweds to earn a little money during those hard times. Afterward, we had a small wedding luncheon with our two friends and celebrated with a bottle of Rhine wine and a ragout of mussels. Later that afternoon we went to the Grunewald where we amused ourselves by watching the hundreds of love-hungry toads which we found in pairs everywhere – a very timely event! Our rings bore the inscription "MLgD" which means "*Mein Leben gehört Dir*" (My Life Belongs to You"). I think both of us kept that promise.

Our marriage changed our daily lives very little. Sonia slowly recovered her inner strength and, as we can see from the letters, she continued to write to the dead Walter. Though they are touched with a certain longing and melancholy, the letters are free of the desperate tone that marked earlier missives. This is evident in a letter written about the time I took a journey by airplane to England:

My Hulele in Heaven,

Should your eyes ever touch this little planet Earth and notice little Hull whom you once loved and who will love you eternally, please listen to my prayers. Move the clouds and wind protectively, guide the attention of the pilot, carry the plane in your hands and bring my boy back to me. You yourself know what I can do alone in this world. I have only one wish and that is that the three of us shall one day be united in a more hospitable world and that we shall always be happy like three little angels.

My job with Bayer had its up and downs, but an exciting time came in 1936 with the Berlin Olympics. My office opened a movie production centre; its main task was to cover the Olympic games. Though the exclusive rights for

35-mm. film were given to Leni Riefenstahl, we were able to join with the Agfa firm and make a 16-mm. movie. We had a large crew working for us, including sixteen cameramen, and together we covered the Olympics from start to finish. Though Sonia and I had never been interested in sports before, we watched from the first day to the last, seeing the entrance of the athletes and the lighting of the Olympic flame, hearing the Olympic hymn especially composed and conducted by Richard Strauss, and watching many of the contests themselves. It was not just the athletics which moved us but the experience of such a grand and peaceful competition among so many young people from around the world.

The year 1936 was an important year in the career of Sonia as well as for me, for it was then that she began to study with Max Trapp. Trapp was a composer of some note, whom Stokowski had recommended Sonia contact years earlier. Through a chance encounter with Hitler in 1933, Trapp had been vaulted into the forefront of the German musical scene as one of the few competent non-Jewish musicians and was accorded respect and power which, of course, at the time, did no harm to him or his students, including Sonia. (After the war, however, Trapp's Nazi connections put him in a bad light and he and his music suffered oblivion.) Working with Trapp in master classes at the Prussian Academy of the Arts, Sonia studied composition and instrumentation, her first project being the Passacaglia and Fugue. At first Sonia refused to believe that she could write a fugue, but with Trapp's encouragement she found that she could. The Passacaglia and Fugue was first performed at the Berlin Sing-Akademie in 1938, conducted by Trapp because the musicians, partly out of arrogance, but perhaps with some justification, refused to take Sonia's direction.

Though Sonia's composition techniques grew more deft under Trapp's tutelage, she had some misgivings about the whole creative process, as we can see in this letter from the late 1930s:

The newly revised "coda" has been much praised. It is said to have been made very cleverly but I have my own thoughts on that. In the end I would rather trust the laws of nature than the man-made ones. The work which constantly has to solve new problems creates a new form. It is the task which produces the form, not man. The human mind has to obey the task and not vice-versa. I shall never again write as genuinely and as nicely as I did before, because now I am too aware. That shows, in spite of everything I am able to compose naturally without having studied, that I can adjust myself to do everything which is demanded by modern taste. But composing with that certain inspiration I possessed up until the "Gedenkstein" is lost. A child remains a child until it has reached the age of puberty. Maturity has its beauty as well, but there are limits. I never wrote immaturely or childishly but I was a child at heart and my compositions were free of affectation. My compositions were pure and uncomplicated and they expressed my inner feelings. I was a poet in music but now I am a knowlegeable composer. I compose in the true sense of the word, offering unbiased abstract values to the public. Now I simply put one note after another, while, before, oh before, my heart would weep. I could hear the weeping and play it. Then smiling would overcome my tears. Today we are nothing but robots. People become excited when millions of soldiers, like marionettes, all make the same movement with one sharp jerk – because they don't know how to write poetry any more.

But despite these thoughts, Trapp's instruction and connections proved valuable to Sonia. Stokowski's advice had been sound, for through Trapp's teaching she gained a mastery of counterpoint, the fugue and instrumentation which was to stand her in good stead during her whole career. He introduced her to the famous Silesian Quartet and Sonia was asked to compose for them. Others who appreciated Sonia's genius during these years were Louise Fischer-Thielemann and Viennese pianist Angela Janowski, both of whom often played Sonia's compositions. However, there were many in the music circles of Berlin in the 1930s who did not find it worthwhile to have to pay the royalties that were due modern composers and so avoided playing contemporary music altogether. Many expressed an interest in Sonia's music but, in the end, did nothing for her. Among such were Wilhelm Furtwangler, who repeatedly promised her that he would perform her music but never did, Nathan Milstein, the violinist, and the great Jascha Heifetz, who examined her Violin Solo Concerto and claimed he would add some of her smaller pieces to his repertoire.

In my opinion, there were two reasons that Sonia was unsuccessful in her approaches to famous artists. The first was that Sonia was naïve in believing that these well-known performers would play a work by an unknown composer. She did not realize that the arrogance of these people would prevent them from accepting the work of someone who had not yet "made it." In fact she was told this explicitly by Hubermann who, when asked if he would include some of Sonia's work in one of his programs, said to her, "Yes, but first you must be recognized." Her reply, "But Hubermann, you are great enough a musician and an authority to grant recognition," was apt but fell on deaf ears. The second reason Sonia was unsuccessful in attracting well-known performers was that her music was extremely difficult technically and required real effort and considerable time to master. Her scores are complicated and not at all easy to perform, which must have discouraged many from adding her works to their repertoires. Perhaps she would have had better luck in approaching young and unknown artists.

Though we often travelled and went to the theatre and concerts, our social activity in the 1930s revolved mainly around our large circle of friends. Every visit in their or our homes was a very special event in our lives, characterized by a festive atmosphere, little presents and a celebration of quiet dignity. Though occasionally we were part of a larger party, usually our get-togethers consisted just of two couples. I remember our visits to the Heckels, the Kauses and the Schmidt-Rottluffs – all were quiet evenings with a simple but well-chosen supper and, afterward, the showing of their works. Heckel especially loved conversing, and our visits always extended into the late hours of the night. Once we had trouble parting at all and I think we left his studio at three in the morning. We then walked up and down the street between the Emserstrasse and the Neue-Wintersfeldtstrasse for over two hours, engaging in lively discussion and parting at five-thirty a.m. It was Heckel who gave us, one Christmas, a water colour of the famous clowns and acrobats, the Rivels, whom we had once seen with him and his wife, Siddi, at our local cabaret. Schmidt-Rottluff gave us for our wedding a picture of a pot of cyclamen, the same flowers that Walter and Sonia had given him in 1925. Nazi Germany in the 1930s was a difficult time for artists, and I was glad to be of some help to these two friends of ours. I persuaded Dr. Krebs to engage Schmidt-Rottluff to draw some glass window designs for the Bayerhaus in Berlin and to buy some water colours from Heckel. Unfortunately these, together with the entire building where I had my office, were destroyed in the war-time bombing of Berlin.

There were many other friends whom I cannot forget: the Kasacks and the Koeppens, for example, with their ties to the literary world, and the lawyers Paul Rauert and Fritz Schwarz, who had handled the negotiations with the angry Grossmann. Friends who collected Gramatté's art included Dr. Felix Emmel and his wife, who possessed two of Walter's early oil paintings on a gold background, and Rosa Schapire, a Hamburg art historian who had been one of the first to be interested in his art. She emigrated to England in the 1930s and Sonia never forgave her for leaving Walter's work behind and yet taking her collection of Schmidt-Rottluff pictures. The Sudeck family in Hamburg and the Krebs family in Cologne were always offering us their hospitality and we owed a debt of gratitude and love to both.

During those years, we had two friends whom I must mention especially. The first was Walther Merck, who had been one of Gramatté's closest companions. He came to Berlin only twice a year, but always made a point of visiting us. He had a reputation as the most unpunctual of persons but, once he had arrived, his visits would always last until after midnight as we opened bottle after bottle and engaged in spirited conversation. His last visit in 1938 was unforgettable. On New Year's Eve we went to Lutter and Wegener, the famous restaurant portrayed in Offenbach's *The Tales of Hoffmann*, to drink a bottle of wine. Sonia stayed at home to finish an assignment that she had set for herself. Merck and I, both a little tipsy, returned home as we had promised at around ten-thirty p.m., intending to celebrate the rest of the old year and the start of the new with Sonia. While we were between the first and second floors, the elevator stopped and would not budge. At first we laughed and joked about how funny it would be if we had to stay in the elevator over New Year's. We could look through the slit in the door and into other people's apartments and see them eating, drinking and celebrating with their guests. We pressed the alarm bell but got no response. Finally we found the situation unbearable and we started screaming for help. At last a woman heard us and called down to ask what had happened to us. After hearing of our predicament she ran to find a janitor or an electrician, but New Year's Eve was the wrong night to locate one, either at home or at work. When she returned without success I told her to phone the fire brigade and, though shocked at this prospect, she did so. Around eleven-thirty p.m., the firemen arrived with their usual loud alarm and were led into the house. They were rather helpless in the face of our problem and could only guess at solutions. In the end they broke down an iron door to get into the machine room and found a handle with which they could lower the elevator safely to the next floor. When we were free it was about five minutes to midnight. I gave a tip to the brave firemen and locked the house door behind them. In the meantime I had sent Merck to tell Sonia what had been going on. The woman who had helped us previously had asked whether she should inform Sonia, but I had told her not to, lest my wife be too upset. When I walked upstairs and neared the third floor, I heard much yelling and screaming from Sonia. I arrived just in time to prevent Sonia from physically attacking Merck whom she was blaming for our tardiness and for causing her so much worry. While Sonia continued to insult Merck, I slipped into the kitchen and grabbed a bottle of champagne, opened it and filled the glasses just in time for twelve o'clock. With a loud "Happy New Year!" we resolved the situation and we laughed merrily as we told Sonia what had happened. Even later, the story was good for a laugh. We often told friends about our experience and how I might have spent one year to the next in an elevator.

Of the last friend I will mention here, Count Alexander Brockdorf, I have a much sadder story. He was a very special friend with whom it was a great pleasure to converse as he was an intellectual, well read and informed about the arts. In 1932 he had published a book entitled *Ur-We-We: Uranische Weltwende (Uranian World Turning Point)* in which he had included ten of Gramatté's pictures. He was General Secretary of the All-German Association, a national organization which favoured a united and greater Germany, but he was opposed to the Nazis. In fact, in 1932, he had been attacked and beaten by a gang of Nazi storm troopers. When his father died, he asked Sonia to perform at his funeral and she played the second movement of her Violin Solo Concerto. One early morning in the spring of 1939 the Gestapo came to his house to arrest him. Brockdorf asked for permission to go to the washroom and there he shot himself. At his funeral Sonia played her "Grave Funèbre," which did nothing to win the hearts of those in power. They noted everything that happened at the burial.

In my narrative, I have not mentioned Catharina, Sonia's mother, for some time. That does not mean that she did not play an important, if unhappy, role in Sonia's life. When I first met her mother in late 1930 or early 1931, she was already a helpless and bizarre old woman, with whom I found it impossible to carry on a conversation. I believe that, when Sonia married Walter, Catharina's spirit was broken. She never recovered from this blow, preferring to play the role of a prematurely old woman. Since her birth, Sonia had been the focal point of Catharina's life. She tried to give her third child what she had missed in her own youth – freedom and music. About the same time as Sonia left her mother's life to marry, Catharina's beloved sister Sophie died in Russia of cancer. With the blow of these losses, Catharina seemed to withdraw into herself and become resigned to await death. In the early 1920s she still corresponded with a number of people and wrote books on theosophy, paid for, I imagine, by her regular remittances from her son Nick in France. However, as time went by, she became more eccentric. She became quite a sight in the neighbourhood; she was well known to everyone for her strange appearance and poor dress as she shuffled along slowly with her walking cane, long white hair and blue glasses. She could not have been easy to deal with on a daily basis – sometimes she behaved as if she were blind and, since she had a poor command of German, tried to speak only French.

After we were married, Sonia and I took over financial responsibility for her from Nick. We paid her rent and expenses but she lived by herself in a studio on Emserstrasse that looked like a rubbish heap. She called herself a "quasi Diogène" and certainly lived almost as unpretentiously as the philosopher of old did. Sonia did not visit Catharina regularly but did so as often as possible. She saw to it that the apartment was kept orderly and tidy, and, from time to time, cooked for her or brought her food that could be warmed up. When Catharina came to our place, which was very seldom, she was almost submissive and would speak highly about me. She would speak a few words of German and then switch immediately to French, often abruptly interrupting the conversation to talk to Sonia (whom she called Sophie-Carmen, the name she insisted others use in her presence) or to herself. Frequently she was simply incoherent. Once in awhile she would sit down at the piano and play pieces of Chopin or others she remembered from her youth, inexpressively in fragments between periods of walking around. Usually she would stay only for a short time and would soon shuffle off, pleading the urgency of other commitments. She was always infinitely grateful for any favours one would do her. Sometimes we took her out in the car for Sunday excursions, which she seemed to enjoy very much. She would contemplatively watch the landscape but say very little. Sonia would treat her like a little child or a small animal, commanding her to do things, and Catharina would respond unwillingly. When the two were left alone they would immediately fall into debates and disagreements over which the mother would jump up and disappear. Catharina's independent existence came to an end one day in 1938 when we arrived at her apartment to find her unconscious, apparently from an accidental overdose of sleeping pills. We then had no choice but to place her in a Catholic nursing home in the Waldstrasse, where she was able to get regular care and where Sonia could visit her easily by car. Many letters exist from this time which testify to the weakened mental state of Catharina and the worry that Sonia invested in making sure that her mother was getting the attention that she needed from the staff. All this changed, however, when we were forced to move to Vienna.

Late in 1938 Dr. Krebs informed me that my advertising department in its present form was no longer needed because of the growing likelihood of war.

He offered me a transfer to the company's scientific division and, following my retraining, a position in either Leipzig or Vienna. I chose Vienna but first had to take a five-month course in pharmacy and medicine in Leverkusen.

The company's reorganization, my enforced absence and the necessity of finally leaving Berlin made Sonia very unhappy. She suspected intuitively that there was more to the shakeup than met the eye and felt that we were being treated unjustly. (We discovered much later that she had been correct. Intrigue among certain colleagues had been the actual cause of the disbanding of my department.) In her letters to me during my retraining she expressed herself with the utmost bitterness. She railed against those unknown forces which she thought to be doing us harm. I include these remarks partly to show the depth of her feeling and partly to demonstrate the vigour of her linguistic expression. From a letter of 11 February 1939: "Haemorrhoids, with blood in the excrement, and cancer shall grow at the assholes of those who attempt to disturb our peace! As my work is going well, I feel strength in me and I can tell you that our enemies had better be careful. We caught the ping-pong balls, but we have thrown those shitballs back against their numb brains. Be assured it will go well!" She was no less vehement when she wrote again on February 18: "The devil will get those who have done this to us. Their rear ends shall be fried, mustard put on and a carrot shoved up their assholes. When they run around naked they will look ridiculous with a tail in front and a tail behind. I could invent many things to sweeten the lives of these intriguing people."

While I was away in Leverkusen, Sonia found life alone to be tedious and depressing. She complained that inspiration was elusive, and that the silence in our apartment was so deep that one "could hear a flea pee." The high point of her week was her study with Trapp. Her letters are full of talk about their work together and her progress at composition. At times she disagreed with him and almost lost faith in his teaching abilities when she thought that he had advised her incorrectly about the symphony that she was working on. Though she blamed him for costing her two or three weeks' labour on this and for almost bringing her to the point of total collapse, she expressed her gratitude for his guidance. Trapp himself thought that Sonia had come to him at just the right stage, he felt that his musical understanding had matured only after the age of forty. One of the pieces which they worked on together was the first of her string quartets, which was premiered in Breslau in November 1939 by the Sileslan String Quartet. Sonia was in raptures about their playing and also appreciated the fact that they admired her composition, even though they confessed that they found it extremely difficult. At this remark, Trapp smiled proudly and said, "You know, Mrs. Gramatté, you should write on your Quartet: 'For Musicians Only!'"

Sadly, war was almost incvitable. Brockdorf's death depressed and frightened Sonia as did the incessant talk of the imminence of war. She dreaded hearing each new speech by Hitler, was disgusted with politics, and vowed to have nothing to do with it, saying that it brought only death. Knowing that a storm of war was gathering in Europe, she prayed that it not break until she and I had passed from this earth. As the situation grew worse, government restrictions grew tighter and more irksome. This little note written on May 1939 shows how this touched our lives: "The *Luftschutz* [air-raid wardens] got me again. Tomorrow, on the tenth, is a new course on 'Self-Defence'. I am writing the following on a card: 'Please exempt me from this course, because of my profession. I have to go to the Music Festival in Dusseldorf, and when I come back, we will be moving to Vienna. Heil Hitler! E.'"

Before we left for Vienna we said good-bye to our beloved apartment in a special way – we asked Heckel to make us a sample book of the different colours from each room. The colours which Gramatté had surrounded himself with were very striking as they reflected aspects of his personality and provided effective backgrounds to his pictures. Heckel took small samples from the painted wallpaper and added the colours which he could not peel off, thus creating a memorial book which Sonia and I kept for years before we donated it to the Brücke Museum in Berlin.

Though our hearts were heavy at leaving the apartment that had meant so much to us, we little knew at the time that our departure would prove to be a blessing. During an air raid on Berlin a few short years later, our building was hit by a bomb and reduced to a smoking pile of rubble and ash. But knowing nothing of this, or any other of the joys or heartaches to come, we left the Neue-Wintersfeldtstrasse for Vienna. It was 1 June 1939.

Vienna

In Vienna we found an apartment on the Mariahilferstrasse, the same street on which I had been born. Our new flat was large, with the charm of a huge Schönbrunner chandelier in the music room and a balcony with a wonderful view. Sonia and I decided to redecorate it in the colour scheme of our place in Berlin. We had a red room for practising music, a blue room for Sonia and an ochre room for my studio and bedroom. From the previous tenant we bought some nineteenth-century gold and white furniture which, with the red rug, gave the room a rather grand appearance, wonderfully suited both for practising and for receiving guests. Of course we had also brought our Bechstein piano, the Spanish oak furniture and all our other impedimenta. As the movers struggled with all this, sweating in the summer heat, one heaved a sigh and said, "My this is thirsty work!" Sonia, completely misinterpreting the worker's remarks, replied, "The water here in Vienna is so good. I will bring you a jug right away."

There were some disadvantages to our new home. For one thing it was terribly noisy. The Mariahilferstrasse was a busy street and we had to put up with not only the usual noise of automobiles but also the starting and braking of streetcars at a stop across the road from us. Unfortunately for me, it also proved difficult to heat in the winter. Each morning before breakfast I had to clean, fill and make a fire in one of the two stoves in the red room. During the day, depending on outside temperatures, we might have to add briquettes but, unless it was very cold, the one large stove was a sufficient heater.

Though the Viennese music season had just ended as we arrived, we did not mind. Once settled in, we took a vacation at Gmunden, just outside Orth Castle, where, from our garden, we could jump directly into the lake for a swim. Back in Vienna we were happy enough. I had found a car to replace our Lilli, and things were going well with my new job. However on 1 September 1939, war was declared and what followed was six years of deprivation and misery. Blackout orders for the city were put in effect and we had to throw black shades over the windows. There were restrictions on many things, including the use of cars. Soon, because of a gasoline shortage, I had to leave it in the garage where, robbed of its tires, it remained for the remainder of the war. Worst of all, food became scarce.

In the beginning, Sonia suffered some difficulties because of her obvious Berlin accent – Germans were not popular in Vienna at that time and were called *Biefkes*. Once at a grocery store, Sonia asked politely if she could have some potatoes, but she used the un-Viennese expression *Kartoffeln* instead of *Erdäpfel*. The shop clerk said rudely that there were none available – they could be obtained only with a ration card. As Sonia stood there, another shopper complimented her on her thick fur coat and Sonia told her that it was Russian bearskin. "Oh," said the other, "How did you come by Russian bear? Are you Russian?" "Yes," said Sonia, "I was born in Russia." "So," said the shop clerk, "you aren't from Berlin then." Turning to her husband, she said,

"Paul, go bring the lady two kilos of potatoes."

Government restrictions also applied to artistic life. Our friends back in Germany, like Heckel and Schmidt-Rottluff whose art was not approved of in official circles, were being given a difficult time. First they were denied exhibitions and then they were denied permission to paint at all. Government inspectors intruded on them to ensure that they were really not practising their art. Works by men like these, including some by Gramatté, were taken from museums and a travelling show was put together to show the German people the nature of this "degenerate" art. This exhibition came, in turn, to Vienna. I tell now the story that I have often told about myself, that of the museum director who once stole a picture from an exhibition.

It was clear to us that these pictures were soon destined to be destroyed by the Nazis, and Sonia and I were determined to rescue Walter's work from such a fate. We chose a rainy day and a late hour when there would be few people about. I sauntered up to the picture we had decided on, and, quick as a flash, it disappeared under my baggy raincoat. In the same exhibition we saw an oil painting by Heckel and debated taking that to safety as well. However we discovered it was too large and when we considered that, if caught, we would have less excuse stealing a Heckel than we would stealing a Gramatté, we left it hanging there. It was a decision we often regretted.

A great blow came on 25 September, when the nuns told us by telegram that Sonia's mother had died. That evening, after the first shock and severe weeping, Sonia and I took the train from Vienna to Berlin. I gave the conductor a good tip so that we might have the compartment to ourselves. Sonia sobbed and whimpered all night.

The next morning, after we drove to the nursing home in the taxi, we found Catharina lying in her bed and Siddi Heckel with her. Her dead face had a beautiful expression and for the first time I noticed that her features resembled Beethoven's. Around her were some flowers, and a single candle was burning beside her bed. With a borrowed camera, in the weak light of the candle, I took several photographs. The burial took place the following day at Wilhelmshagen, where we had a double plot not far from that of Walter Gramatté. There was no priest at the funeral and only a handful of mourners was present. I was the only man among the following: Siddi Heckel, Hildegard Gramatté, Walter's mother, the maid, and another woman from Wilhelmshagen, a friend of mother Gramatté's. Suddenly Sonia approached the grave, seemingly calm and unmoved, and began, in French, to speak the moving words which she wrote down two days later on my request.

Surely no one but myself understood them. While I could not speak, the tears streaming down my face, she spoke beautifully and without a tear to the very end. She had not told me a word of this before. She must, however, have considered the words carefully. This speech was an example of the unique willpower and concentration that she had always shown in her concerts.

Oh, my poor little angel, dear mother! The last moment, supreme and sacred, at which we all arrive some day, has come. We, your five children and some of our nearest friends, are re-united here in the most intimate embrace. We have come to give you a last testimony of our veneration and our love. Taking the sacred soil into our hands, each of us: Here, the salute of your son Nicolas, your small Colja, that of your poor oldest daughter, Sonja, neither of whom could be present, and here – myself – Sophie-Carmen, your little Benjamin, who brings you her humble salute, burning with love, the angel of the sky, Walter, the angel of the earth, Ferdinand, and the representatives of our dear friends.

You have not only been an exceptionally good and excellent mother, to the children, hard-working and courageous, showering us with devotion and limitless love, but you were a great artist in your time with the finest soul. It is from you that I have inherited my talent, and it is to you that I owe becoming a composer. You will see, Maman, that I will take care of this precious gift with which you have entrusted me, to make it bloom one day as you had always desired and dreamed. I will always regret that you will not be able to see it bloom yourself.

It is for me to thank you especially from the bottom of my heart for everything you have done for me – above all, for the insight to have me raised as a real musician from the start. I admire, today like never before, the way you raised and nourished me until the day when I could do so for myself, without the aid of a father, without any fortune, having lost everything in our poor Russia of old. How brave you were to struggle so valiantly through life, without being deterred by any circumstance or by all the sadness.

With your departure we three, the last living members of our small family which is waning to an end, remain. Today I take this opportunity to wish, my adored mother, that you will find the peace and rest which you more than deserve and to which you have not passed without great sorrows and constant material difficulties, in the infinite and unknown world to which you have been sent.

Now I wish you final happiness and that heaven will grant you that. I address one last ardent prayer to God, I express it with great fervor, propelled by the great expanse of my soul, that we will see you again some day there in that world. Oh, to see each other again and never to be separated. Let heaven hear me!

Later, when you are able, protect us with your spirit from the war, us, the poor beings of the earth, and especially our Ferdinand. My dear mother whom I adore, my dear sweet angel, au-revoir, au-revoir to a better world.

Here, these red roses and white lilies, will cover your grave which will shortly close for all eternity, this poor little icy-cold grave which I am covering with hot tears and on which rests all the warmth of my love for you.

Let there be peace between us all.
In the name of the Father,
In the name of the Son,

In the name of the Holy Ghost,
Ainsi soit-il.

Amen.

Her tombstone read:

**CATHERINE DE FRIDMAN-KOCHEVSKAIA
TROIS ENFANTS TE PLEURENT
SOPHIE NICOLAS SOPHIE-CARMEN**

On the evening of the burial we met with Professor Trapp and his wife in an inn by the train station of Friedrichstrasse in a ghostly, dark Berlin, and that same night we went back to Vienna.

Three weeks later the news came that Sonia's sister had also died, in the medical establishment in Wittstock on the Dosse. We had taken her there in 1934, shortly after our wedding, because life would have become unbearable for all of us had she stayed with us, and Sonia feared that our marriage might be jeopardized.

From then on, the death of her mother cast deep shadows on Sonia's life, particularly in the months following. She could never forgive herself for having left her mother to die alone, despite the fact that it was her mother who refused to leave Berlin and move with us to Vienna.

In 1939 and 1940, Sonia wrote frequently in a notebook that was entirely dedicated to her mother:

May 9, 1940.

This poor dear angel that I loved so much, that I adored more than myself; if I had not married I would have never left her. I would have had her beside me and would have cared for her to the last minute. It was impossible. Nothing is more cruel than separation without the possibility of seeing one another again, and I do not forgive destiny for having submitted us to such a great misfortune under which I will suffer until my last breath. I give myself entirely to her memory.

Though she continued to mourn her mother's passing and to berate herself for not being with her mother at the end, she did find some comfort in Vienna in my family. We spent a great deal of time with my parents, with whom Sonia had in common love of music and love of me, and my sister Mia, whose husband was away at the front. Sonia enjoyed as well the company of Mia's children and those of my cousin Ernst Witting. She gave Harald Witting piano lessons for a long time, gave Mia's son Harry violin instruction and taught my niece Ricki the cello. My nephew Wolfgang also took piano lessons from Sonia, and Robert, the youngest, plays Beethoven and Schubert piano sonatas to this

day. Sonia also got along well with the elderly widow Tante Grete, who lived in the same apartment building. Her daughter-in-law, Martha Bauer, was a great friend to Sonia too, and counselled her in matters of style.

Gradually we made our way into the musical life of Vienna. We started by attending as many concerts as possible and by making friends in the business. Through my father's old music teacher, Henriette Ribarz, we met Emmy Zopf, who had played Sonia's "Danse de Nègre" in the 1930s. She introduced Sonia to the music teacher's circle as well. The more official musical people in the *Musikverein* were more difficult to approach, since it was dominated by the organist, Franz Schuetz, who had taken a dislike to Sonia. The composer in the concert house, a Professor Reidinger, was not a fan of Sonia either. He could not totally ignore her but, where he could, he held her back. The Philharmonic showed no interest, nor did the Vienna Concert House Quartet. Oswald Kabasta of the official Austrian radio station, RAVAG, had no time for Sonia and thus prompted this bitter note from April 1942:

Until now, I was so naive as to believe that one could go directly to a musician and the music, good music, would speak for itself. But now I set aside that foolish misunderstanding once and for all. You can only reach musicians the long way, either through force or through connections, through extortion or through giving personal advantage. But not just through the music. Kabasta treated me abominably.

Sonia had more luck with the conductor Dr. Hans Weisbach. He performed several of Sonia's works over the next few years, starting with the Passacaglia and Fugue, which was broadcast on the radio. He then gave an evening performance of the Capriccio Concertante. The first string quartet was first played by the Silesian and then the Vienna Hübner Quartet. The Mozart Quartet then decided to play the piece too and, in fact, had already had several rehearsals when they were drafted into military service. Sonia's first and second violin duos were performed in Salzburg by the Steiners, husband and wife, who were very enthusiastic about Sonia.

An old colleague of mine from university, the musicologist Dr. Andreas Liesz, also proved to be a devotee of Sonia's music but only after a rather strange introduction to it. After a chance meeting with him, I invited him over for tea but told him nothing about Sonia. We talked lightly about many things including music and then I idly remarked, "By the way I have become a patron of the musical arts. I am very interested in this one composer." I then played him the record of the first string quartet and he exclaimed, "Who is this composer? I must know this composer!" I then put on the records of the Violin Solo Concerto and by now he was totally flustered, saying, "Don't pull my leg anymore! Who is it?" "The composer is in this very room," I said. At this he sprang up, astonished. "But Eckhardt, you never told me that you composed!" "Not I," I said, pointing to Sonia, "but she." After a few seconds of silence he understood and we all began to laugh. From that moment we were firm friends

Our home in Vienna was the centre of
many musical activities. Success followed
success for Sonia, and in 1950 she
received an Austrian State Prize for
composition.

Sonia and I were married in 1934, and in 1939 we moved to my native Vienna, where Sonia made a significant impression on the musical scene.

and he took quite an interest in Sonia's music, introducing her to people in the university's Faculty of Music.

Sonia went to Breslau in October 1939 to supervise the rehearsals of the Silesian Quartet and then Sonia and I went to their performances in Berlin and Dusseldorf. At the Dusseldorf performance something extraordinary happened. At the time in the program when it was customary for the composer to come to the stage, Sonia did so, but the applause suddenly stopped. Her first thought was, "Now come the eggs and rotten apples." But it was nothing like that. To conceal the fact that the composer was a woman, the program contained only the name S.C. Eckhardt-Gramatté, and in Dusseldorf, where Sonia was unknown, the audience expected a man. When she suddenly

It was in Vienna that Sonia finished her first symphony, which was premiered in Breslau in 1942 under Philipp Wüst. The conductor had to postpone the premiere because of the difficulty and length of the work. Knowing of Sonia's temper, Wüst also requested discreetly that she not come to the first rehearsals lest there be too many time-consuming disagreements. However, after the first rehearsal, Sonia received a telegraph requesting her immediate presence in Breslau as there was a host of problems that needed sorting out. Sonia rushed there to confront Wüst, who told her that he wanted to drop the third movement, the trio and the reprise of the scherzo, as well as other critical parts of the symphony. Wüst, a true Bavarian, was quite excitable, and of course Sonia fought like a tiger for the integrity of her work. The tension at the rehearsals grew very heavy, especially when the two disagreed about how a particular section should be played. Wüst would yell at Sonia from the podium and Sonia would yell back from he seat in the last row. During the fourth rehearsal Sonia and Wüst yelled out their mutual disagreement until she finally shouted, "Oh, play it how you like. It's all the same shit to me!" After a deathly silence, the orchestra burst out laughing and the tension was instantly dispelled.

Wüst, however, continued to make unhelpful remarks. For example: "Mrs. Gramatté, how do you want this? The way you have it written? It sounds horrible. Very well, gentlemen, play it like that then."

Our friend Schätzer, the concert master, tried to mediate in a diplomatic way. When Wüst said, "Mr. Schätzer, don't you think it would be better to leave that out?" he replied, "Quite right, Herr Generalmusikdirector, you are right. It is much better like that." Pause. Longer pause. "Maybe we could also do it the way it is written here." And that is the way it was done. He also told Sonia not to worry, that by the second-last rehearsal Wüst would have been so completely won over that she could wrap him around her finger.

He was right. Wüst and the orchestra grew friendlier and friendlier despite the rigorous demands of the piece. In fact the orchestra supported Sonia greatly and they, thanks in part to the members of the Silesian Quartet who occupied the first desks, were very well prepared for the performance. Trapp, who also had an engagement in Breslau, appeared for the final rehearsal and intervened to ensure that the last of the disagreements was settled to Sonia's satisfaction with the reprise of the scherzo reinstated. So, in the end, aside from a few insignificant changes, the symphony was played in its entirety with the tempi the way Sonia had wanted them.

On the Sunday before the premiere, musicologist Dr. Tröger spoke about the modern symphony and Sonia's work in particular to over two hundred people at the local university's science of music seminar. Sonia explained the themes and main elements of her symphony and then listened as a capable music critic intelligently dissected her work. It was a novel, and not unpleasant, experience for her. Tröger also wrote an introductory newspaper article which appeared in the Breslau paper the same day.

The symphony was played on consecutive nights to sell-out audiences of two thousand people. Wüst and the orchestra had worked hard and perceptively on the piece and gave a wonderful performance. Our friends Krebs and Trapp were in attendance for both nights and were able to witness for themselves the huge success of Sonia's work. The press loved it and so did the audiences – Sonia was given nine curtain calls. Even Wüst was completely captivated. He told Trapp, "That woman says more in three bars than another in a whole symphony." He promised to take the piece on tour to other cities and arranged a performance in Dresden, but the exigencies of war prevented it. There were other benefits from the Breslau success, however. Recordings were made of the first performance, recordings which were useful for playing for conductors or others interested in finding out more about Sonia's music. Most important, however, was the confidence that she gained. She now knew, after hearing a first-rate performance of one of her creations, that she was in control of her compositional techniques for major works and that her work was of considerable merit.

By the summer of 1942 there was a growing possibility that my exemption from the military would not last long and that I might soon be inducted into the armed forces of the Third Reich. I saw one possibility of avoiding this dubious honour and that was to move to the Bayer office in Leipzig, which had one draft-exempt position open. Accordingly Sonia and I moved to Leipzig where we stayed in the apartment of Lise Sudeck, whose husband was at the front. While there, we took side trips into the Erzebirge mountains and to Dresden, where Konrad Hansen was giving master classes. In Dresden Sonia and I went to the opera *Tosca* conducted by Böhm. Sonia was no great fan of opera. She could tolerate Wagner for his musicality and great instrumental techniques but Puccini proved to be another matter. When it came to the famous martyr scene, where Tosca must listen to Cavaradossi's cries of pain, it was too much for Sonia. She was anything but a sadist and could take no more. She stood up, grabbed my hand and said, "Let's go!" Everyone in our row had to stand up to let us pass. The audience was, of course, furious and scolded us as we scrambled out: "Stay at home then, if you are not musically inclined!"

Our sojourn in Leipzig ended abruptly with my call to military service on 22 July 1942. I was to receive my basic training in the barracks in the old little city of Hainburg on the Danube, just ten miles from Vienna. Sonia was not prepared to be separated from me and so she too moved to Hainburg to be as near as possible. The town's available housing was all taken by other soldiers' wives, so Sonia moved into a rather primitive house owned by a kindly woman named Frau Fasching. At first Sonia slept in the attic with the bats, and later, when it got colder, in the basement laundry room with the mice. There was, of course, no piano for her to work on. There were sausages hanging from the low, dusty ceiling, stacks of onions and lard and piles of coal and wood. The basement window revealed only the shoes of the passers-by and when I was due for a visit, Sonia would try to guess which feet were mine and rush to the door. It was by no means comfortable, but there she stayed and watched daily as I was mistreated on the parade ground; we forty-year-old recruits were treated like disobedient schoolboys. Though it was not easy for me, for Sonia it was much worse, as these excerpts from her letters show.

From a postcard to Franz Schätzer:

Every day Ferri's fate hangs by a thread. I have not written a single note since Ferri's call to duty. My Piano Concerto is getting nowhere. I cannot decribe to you what we are going through. His superior is a brute, who takes a sadistic joy in ordering around one of the "intelligentsia," a "doctor." Almost daily he has to clean out the latrine, peel potatoes, heave heavy loads of potatoes on his back and, at night, has only a plank bed without sheets or pillows but lice to make up for that!! Pig sty! Not to mention his valuable time! It is a waste of energy, time and achievement. I have become poor, my nerves are worn through....By the way, I am living like a soldier. Instead of lice I have mice in my basement. At first I was terrified each time the mouse traps sprang shut at night.

One evening while I was on sentry duty, Sonia approached me wishing to chat, and I was forced to send her away. She wrote me a letter of rebuke which reveals so much of her deep love and her essentially poetic passion that I reproduce it here in full:

Night on duty, October 6/7, 42, Hainburg:

My dear heart!

Too bad that you chased me away tonight. Was it because you were afraid of being seen? I would have known how to camouflage myself in the dark. I have learnt it, too. In the meantime, with your fear, you are destroying a tender web, that romantic meeting of two souls on a starry night. I got up without any effort, after four hours of sleep, with a sad sort of happiness thinking that maybe I would see that dear slave whom I love so much. Maybe he will say something to me, or I to him, that will lighten our souls for these two hours and carry us on, invisibly with lightly-coloured feathers into another, unreal, world-away from the reality of our situation. A creative person sees and feels things with a different heart, different eyes, and is not afraid if he is armed with love. And then I had to return home. From you I received only fear. Because I was searching for something else, I will not be able to transform your words into music. I was looking for my Boy, not the frightened soldier who sent me "home". Isn't my soul in danger there? Isn't that the nourishment it is seeking from the other soul that is bound to it? Isn't that a bit of a risk, the dark forest noises, the mysterious whispering of the trees, the barely-moonlit paths, the view from the other end of the path? Isn't it worth it, to see you? Is it more important that I sleep behind a bolted door....

I am cold. You did not send me any sweet words; not because you did not feel them, but because you were choked by the ghastly atmosphere of that stinking two-by-three metre barracks watch-room.

You have your soldier's life and don't even feel attracted to me, otherwise you would not be in that shack. Go ahead. Do your duties so that they can't get to you on the outside. But don't go past me as if you did not know me. A secret-sign, a quick tender word is more important than a Kafka-sleep. It is now 2:30. In half an hour you can lie down. At least I was with you for a short while.

Throughout my spell of military duty Sonia maintained an air of outraged indignation and an incomprehension of the realities of my situation. For example, she believed that my being ordered to carry heavy objects around was bad for my health and ordered me not to lift fifty-kg. sacks of potatoes ever again. She hated the plight I was in and had only scorn for my fellow soldiers, once describing them as "minor bipeds." Her greatest fear was that I would be sent to the Russian Front. I was able to get the occasional leave to join her and those moments together, away from the discomforts of a conscript's life, were precious to both of us. After one such furlough, in which we were together for her birthday in 1943, Sonia expressed how much these shared moments meant when she wrote:

We are still living in the memory of those five days of freedom in our little home. We were so close together during those hours. We live in a dream, too, but the only difference is that reality is so oppressive that we wish that real life were the bad dream. In spite of that we are so rich! We know the strength of love the way few people do and this alone helps us overcome everything including all the meanness and adversity.

I don't want to start the new year without first thanking you from the bottom of my heart for everything, everything that I have enjoyed because of you. The most beautiful years of my sad life have been spent at your side.

By early 1943 Sonia found herself able to begin composing again. In January she started work on her second string quartet, which she called "The Hainburg" because of our experiences in that garrison town. Written in a flood of inspiration, the first movement of the piece is very stormy and might

be thought of as an accusation against the injustices that Sonia sensed in the world. However, her composition coach, Max Trapp, was not pleased with the work when Sonia first showed it to him and told her that the music did not suit the instruments for which it had been written. Sonia once again began to doubt his critical judgement. Moreover, his refusal to introduce her to Böhm, after a concert which she had travelled to Berlin to hear, hurt her personally. However, she was still reluctant to part company with Trapp. To her credit she kept composing under the very trying circumstances of life in Frau Fasching's basement, and eventually her views on "The Hainburg" Quartet won Trapp over. The piece was premiered in the fall of 1943 by the Breslau String Quartet. The performance was a success but, sadly, it was the last time we ever saw the members of the group, three of whom were killed in useless sacrifice during the last months of the war.

There soon developed a growing number of musicians who had heard about Sonia and who wished to study with her. Some, like Angela Janowski, who played Sonia's works at public concerts, were never charged for their lessons. Others paid what they could. Sonia's best student was a tall, thin, blonde girl from the Baltic region, Vally Taette, who was very musical and who had, in Sonia's opinion, the best piano hands that she had ever seen. One of Taette's old teachers from the Horak Conservatory believed so much in her talent that she paid for her lessons. Taette came often until one day she failed to appear. We never heard from her again. Was she dragged off? It was not an uncommon occurrence in Vienna at that time. Sonia grieved for her very much.

By late 1943 I had been transferred from Hainburg to a less dangerous posting, in Vienna. I was then able to join Sonia at the series of house concerts which we gave in our home to gatherings of sixty to eighty people. Strangers as well as good friends attended; Nazis and Jews rubbed shoulders. All were linked by a love of music. It was here that many works, including some by Anton Heiller and Kurt Lehrperger, and Sonia's string duos, received their premieres. It was also here that many musical contacts were made.

It was through personal contact that Sonia continued to attempt to get her compositions performed. Sonia talked to most of the leading people in the German and Austrian musical scene, trying to interest them in her work. Some, such as the Prague String Quartet, and the conductors Weisbach, Furtwängler and Abendroth, expressed a desire to perform something of Sonia's but nothing developed from these contacts. Others were even more disappointing. In June 1943, after a long correspondence with the radio executive Kabasta, Sonia travelled to Munich to play recordings of her symphony for him. He listened to them at the radio station with his wife. Just as the record ended, Kabasta stood up, took his hat and cane and said goodbye. When Sonia asked him to give her his reaction, he only answered. "That's not for me." The whole scene was painful for his wife, but finally she ran after her husband like a little puppy. There was not even a word of acknowledgement that Sonia had come so far to see him.

There were other setbacks. The Mozart Quartet was to have played the C-Sharp Minor Quartet in a series of concerts and were rehearsing it. Sonia received compliments on her piece from those who had heard it in rehearsal. Unfortunately two members of the group were called for military service and all performances were cancelled. The same piece was to have been played in Graz by the Silesian Quartet but they too had to cancel their concert. Other arrangements fell through because of travel difficulties, personal differences or the deaths of some of the musicians who were willing to play Sonia's work.

All these difficulties were frustrating, but they were insignificant in comparison to the threats posed by the war, which was drawing ever closer to Vienna. By 1943 the city was subject to regular bomber attacks, and I was assigned to air-raid duties, ironically at cultural sites such as the National Library and the Künsthistorisches Museum. During the next year the air attacks occurred almost daily and Sonia and I spent many hours sitting in the coal cellar of our apartment house on the Mariahilferstrasse, listening to the bombs fall on Vienna. On 7 February 1945, the city suffered its worst attack. The Opera, the Burgtheater, and the Küntshistorisches Museum were hit and the houses on either side of us were badly damaged. When we finally emerged into the light, Sonia sobbed so uncontrollably that people were moved to ask, "Why are you crying? Did something happen to you?" They did not understand that she was crying from the terrible tension.

In the final weeks of the war, the bombing grew so intense that we moved many of our treasured possessions, such as Gramatté's paintings, the Bechstein piano and Sonia's manuscripts, out to my parents' house in the suburb of Pressbaum. It was in that house that I hid in March and April 1945 to avoid being conscripted into the *Volkssturm*, an effort by the Nazi authorities to form an army of old men and children. (I had already been unexpectedly discharged from the regular army in November 1944.) For forty-eight hours the war raged all around us and we were ordered by the military to stay in the basement. There was an artillery duel over our house and tanks fought in the street as retreating German troops battled Russians before our eyes. A few dozen S.S. men dug themselves into the nearby woods and resisted tenaciously as the Russians poured over the mountain by the hundreds. My whole family, including my sister's children, stood on the balcony and watched, fearlessly and with cold hearts, as battles took place only eight hundred meters away.

It was clear that we were about to be occupied by the Red Army. Sonia and I packed our favourite things away: we rolled up a few of Gramatté's most beautiful paintings and took two metal boxes containing negatives of Sonia's works. We covered the boxes with blankets and tied them onto an axle with two wheels. We were now ready to leave as refugees. But in the end we decided to stay and face our fate. This decision proved to be a good one. Those who did leave lost everything – all the abandoned houses were plundered by both the native citizens and the Russians. After a few days they looked like the worm-eaten skeletons of animals left on the street.

The following night the Russians came into our house. With the first ones we were quite unsuspecting, and when they demanded and gestured unmistakeably towards my watch and gold chain, I handed them over without protest. In earlier years I had often wondered what I would do if I were attacked by robbers in the woods at night, and this robbery happened approximately the way I had envisioned it. Sonia was rather less compliant. After taking a few other things, they asked for Sonia's two gold wedding rings which had been a gift from Gramatté, and which she always wore on her hand. She resisted, not wanting to give them up. When the Russians were about to take them off by force she began to cry out. "Fine," said one, "then we will just take off the finger," and took out his bayonet. You can imagine how Sonia felt. She let out such a blood-curdling scream that the second Russian, gesturing widely, said "*Nitschevo* – leave her be, we'll do without the rings." My father, who was hard of hearing, had retreated into the bedroom on the top floor when he saw the way the situation was developing. We noticed his absence only after some time, for what was happening around us was so upsetting that we could not really concern ourselves with anything else. When I went up to the bedroom some time later to look for him, I found him sitting on the edge of the bed, sobbing loudly. He had thought that we had all been killed, and in his weakness had not had the courage to look for us.

Most of the plunderers just wanted gold or money, or, what was even more in demand – wine and schnapps. When they had drunk their fill they were even more dangerous. As a precautionary measure, we had dumped the last bottle of liquor into the cesspool. Others were mainly on the hunt for women, and no female between the age of twelve and eighty was safe from them. Some time later, I spoke with a gynecologist from a hospital in Vienna and he told me that the number of women that had received serious tearing injuries in these weeks was incredible. Our lives were threatened by soldiers with bayonets and rifles about seven times. Once I was ordered to find some girls for the soldiers, and could only say that I did not know where any were. Another time, I tried to prevent them from taking my father's boots and his camera, but finally gave up, because my life was more important to me than all the boots and cameras in the world.

However, many of the Russians were good-natured. We had heard it said that the Russians were very fond of children, and I found that to be the case. My sister constantly had her three children around her and was in the sixth month of her fourth pregnancy. When the Russians set up a depot for provisions in a neighbouring house a few days later, they sent us no less than ten kilos of the best meat – "for the children."

Sonia, who had never before been in a position to support herself through her work, became the most important person in the household in those days – the only supplier of food for the whole family. Because she could speak Russian, even if it was just in broken sentences, she could converse with the soldiers, and soon she had found a method of mastering the invaders. She would greet the Russians in a very friendly manner, and then would immediately begin to question them about where they were from, what they did in civilian, and all about their families. She told them that she had been born in

Moscow. She gave them no break, but kept them holding their breaths continually. Since the Russians found very few people in Austria with whom they could talk, they fell into the trap. However, it was a horrible strain for Sonia to be constantly talking with these soldiers from nine in the morning to three in the morning, for about two weeks.

After two weeks Sonia had a short-lived nervous breakdown and I thought that everything was lost, but by then the time of greatest danger had ended. While almost everyone else had gone hungry, we could not complain, for Sonia had always had something organized, so to speak. Sometimes we would go to the bakery and handle bread for the solders (under very strict surveillance, of course) and here and there a loaf would slip out of our hands and fall onto the not-too-clean street, for our consumption. Understandably, we were quite nervous about this job. On other occasions Sonia would go to the field kitchens and would be given a pot of soup in which potatoes and pieces of meat were not scarce.

Sonia always carried a bunch of strings with her in those days so she could carry home things that she had begged or seized. One noon she came upon a clearing, not far from the well-known institute for bringing up young girls, Sacré Coeur, where a small group of Russians had just settled down and set up a field kitchen. Just then a requisitioned cow was brought and slaughtered on the spot and was left lying on its back with its legs in the air. Sonia saw this unique opportunity and immediately went up to one of the older soldiers, who seemed to be the cook and the one in charge. For these sorts of circumstances she told her standard story, which was that she had a family of ten to feed at home. This of course was true, if you counted the children and the adults. "Yes, my little one," said the cook, "you will get some." Sonia watched expectantly as the soldiers pulled the skin off the cow. Then each of the soldiers cut off a good piece of meat. After a few minutes there was little left of the cow but her intestines and skin, which lay on the ground, along with the hocks. When Sonia saw this, she was very disappointed and went crying to the cook and said, "And what am I supposed to get? You promised that I would get a good piece, too." "Right," said the cook, "you can have the hocks." And with an axe and a huge knife he chopped off the hocks. Once she had recovered from her first shock, Sonia, who was not lazy, pulled out her string, shouldered two hocks and pulled the other two behind her, simply dragging them home. We had been anxiously awaiting Sonia, and finally saw her coming, slowly, sweating and gasping, her clothes covered in blood. I have never seen her as exhausted as she was that day. It was quite a chore skinning the hocks but from all our effort the family had wonderful soup made from the marrow.

Much later I heard that the conduct of the Russian soldiers was nothing extraordinary for those days. If I am correctly informed, it was an established custom of war that conquering soldiers could plunder for twelve days. Moreover, the soldiers always said that many objects, such as cameras, watches, and high boots, had military importance.

When we returned to Vienna a few weeks later, sitting in an open truck on a load of firewood, we could see that the city was a pile of rubble. On the Mariahilferstrasse there were dead horses and burnt-out tanks in front of almost every house. The human corpses had already been taken away. Luckily, not too much had happened to our home. The outside windows were all shattered, of course, but we had taken the inner ones out before and placed them safely in the back of the apartment. Some stray grenade shrapnel had ricocheted into the room and had damaged various pieces of furniture.

There was no water, no gas and no light in Vienna, but we got used to that. It was fantastic to see the way the street righted itself again. People met, friends came together, the first newspapers appeared again. The Russians handed out their first provisions, dried green peas, to many who had literally starved for two or three weeks. We found, however, these peas were spoiled and worms had gotten into them. But the people of Vienna found a remedy. If they left the peas in water overnight the worms would come out and float to the top, and then the peas could be cooked and eaten. Since the Russian commandant was called Koniev, the Viennese called it Koniev beef. You can imagine what a dubious pleasure it was to be in the same room as people who had nothing but peas in their stomachs!

In our quest for food, it was vitally important to have the right contacts. We knew some farmers in the Sarleinsbach area from whom we could obtain food by barter. They lived under rather primitive conditions, without electricity, and coveted an ancient hand-powered Singer sewing machine that had belonged to Sonia's mother. It was so disreputable-looking that even the Russians had not bothered to steal it, but to us it meant fresh, nourishing food. We traded the machine to the farmers for two kilos of butter, two large chunks of bacon, many eggs, ten kilos of flour, ten kilos of potatoes and other goodies, all of which we placed in two large suitcases for the return trip. We were to travel home by night in the back of an open truck with thirty others. There was a certain element of danger in all this, since our food was considered contraband by the Austrian police and we would have to pass through their roadblocks before reaching Vienna. I explained our situation to the driver, who hid the suitcases behind his seat where he thought they would be out of sight and safe from confiscation. Unfortunately, the police searched rather more carefully than we had hoped and discovered our two cases. I was questioned about their contents but professed ignorance of what was inside, even when they pointed out the flour seeping from one bag. I was told to open them up but I denied that I had the key. I tried to bargain for the return of our property but my fellow-passengers were growing impatient and, in the end, they seized the cases and I could only win a receipt for them. Sonia, who loved good food and hated injustice, was grinding her teeth in fury. "I told you something would go wrong!" she exclaimed. "And all because of that stupid driver. But I'm telling you, we will get those things back, even if I have to go to the prime minister. I won't let them have the suitcases!" As we jostled along in the back of the truck in the middle of the night Sonia would not sleep and spoke of nothing else but whom she could contact to win return of our food.

When we arrived in Vienna in the morning, I began trying to see who could help us. The Austrian authorities, the police, the interior ministry, were useless. We petitioned the Russians themselves, again with no luck. We tried two other of the four Allied occupation forces: the British and the Americans. The British were too proper and said they could never interfere in the affairs of the Russian zone while the Americans, though very sympathetic, also professed an inability to help. Finally a friend of mine claimed a friendship with a high-ranking French officer and volunteered to introduce Sonia to him. The next day they journeyed to the barracks where Sonia was presented as Madame Gramatté, a distressed Frenchwoman whose property had been seized. The officer was only too glad to help and dictated a letter to the effect that Professor Eckhardt had been carrying the suitcases in question under his authority and requested their prompt return. I hitch-hiked back into the Russian zone and presented the letter to the police in St. Poelten. With this talisman in hand they led me into a large storeroom packed to the ceiling with suitcases, parcels, sausages, hams and other food. I pointed out my two cases and was allowed to carry them back to Vienna. At home I ran up the stairs and, placing the suitcases in front of the door, rang the bell. Without opening up, Sonia demanded, "With or without?" "With, of course," I said. "Great!" she exclaimed and let me inside where together we danced for joy and celebrated. Three cheers for the French! Only they knew what it was like to have suffered as we were suffering then.

The people of Vienna collected themselves quite quickly and tried to overcome the physical difficulties. They would get water from any remote well and wait into the middle of the night for the electricity to come on. (Because of shortages, electricity was supplied during the day to only the most important food stores and other industries.) People would go to sleep with the light switch on. When the electricity was turned on at two or three in the morning and the light would suddenly be lit, they would jump out of their beds, quickly cook the meal for the next day on their electric cookers, fill hot-water bottles with hot water, and go back to sleep. In this way they could even have warm water to wash with. When it got cooler in the fall, they would put a number of hot-water bottles into a warming box insulated with crumpled newspaper so they could heat themselves the next day. By doing this, we could welcome visitors, even on cold days, by wrapping everyone up in blankets and giving each of them a few hot water bottles, one above and one below. Thus, social life went on.

Political and artistic life resumed as well, with new people in positions of power. Sonia and I benefited by these changes. The International Society for Contemporary Music, which had been dissolved in 1938, was reconstituted and Sonia was among the charter members. I was an associate member. The society took the lead in arranging for concerts and Sonia found that her pieces, especially her string duos and piano caprices, were being played with great frequency. I involved myself with opening relations with the West through the founding of the Austria-America Society. Because of my American contacts and my skill as a writer I was asked by my old friend Alfred Stix to work for him in the museum system. Stix, who as a monarchist, had been removed from his pre-war position by the Nazis, was now general director of all art history museums. He wanted me to develop a division of art education. This was a new field for Austrian museums, who saw their role as primarily one of research, but I gladly accepted the challenge. The work involved countless tours, lectures, radio shows and newspaper writing, but to me it was a great pleasure.

While I was doing this, Sonia was growing more involved with the musical life in Vienna. She was increasingly well connected with organizations such as the Universal Edition and the Cultural League, whose members were interested in her music. In 1946 she wrote, for the Philharmonic Winds, the Wind Quartet. It was often played and was recorded as well. That same year she wrote the two string trios for the Steinbauers, an all-woman group. In 1947, the "Ruck-Ruck" Sonata was written for the outstanding clarinettist Friedrich Wildgans, who had survived a number of Nazi concentration camps. The next year, Sonia's biggest production was the second piano concerto, which she herself played at the Musikverein, the orchestra conducted by Eugen Jochum. There were too few rehearsals to achieve a real understanding among soloist, orchestra and conductor by the night of the performance, so, when Sonia felt that Jochum was slowing the orchestra, she took it on herself to speed things up, hoping the players would follow. They did, and the piece was a success with the audience. The acerbic reaction of the critic Max Graf gives a vivid impression of Sonia and her music:

The Piano Concerto, played by the composer herself, thundered into the great Musikverein hall like a waterfall…. The piano roared and droned; the passages flooded over the keys; the masses of chords seemed almost to crush the Bösendorfer grand piano completely. Energy was not lacking in the little woman at the piano who played her composition herself. She could have chased a whole battalion of male pianists into flight, and this music critic, who belongs to the weaker sex, is amazed by this energy, power and amazon-like furor….The piano concerto of the lady with the steel hands is artistically designed….[combining] the friction of the parts, the pressed-together chords, the hardness of the tone, the compressed harmonies, the combination of hard, flashy and poisonous sounds, the raging brass, the whispering piccolo and the free harmonies. The audience of today accepted this music with appreciative applause and covered the little woman, who had constructed this cast-iron concerto, with approbation. In this music, besides the tremendous strength of sound, there is also contained a great spiritual power.

Sonia was clearly a success in the Musikverein. In both 1947 and 1948 she was awarded a prize for her compositions. She was given a trifling amount of money, but it was an honour nonetheless. Her reputation was growing. The reception given her triple concerto and her "Ruck-Ruck" Sonata (based on

In Vienna, Sonia developed the pedago-
gical talents which she had inherited
from her mother. Here she shows the
basics on the violin to her nephew, Pierre
de Fridman, in 1949.

the Swabian folk-song "Mädle ruck, ruck, ruck an meine grüne Seite") showed that she could write for wind instruments. As a result, she was commissioned in the spring of 1950 by Dr. Hans Sittner to write a bassoon concerto for the American bassoonist, Gloria Soloway. This Sonia did in time for the Ausseer Music Festival at which the concerto, which quickly became one of Sonia's most-played pieces of that period, was premiered. During the rehearsals, which were held in our home, we grew to like Gloria. On one occasion her pencil fell from the rather unstable music stand and, holding her bassoon, she found it difficult to bend over to pick it up. Sonia, who was playing the piano part, obliged her by retrieving the pencil. The pencil dropped repeatedly and eventually Gloria grew to expect that Sonia would pick it up for her. At the next rehearsal the same thing happened but instead of fetching the dropped pencil, Sonia merely said, "Never mind, I have another," and gave one to Gloria. Again and again pencils dropped but each time Sonia had a replacement, and each time Gloria's amazement grew – she did not know that Sonia had brought along a store of pencils just for the pleasure of seeing the look on Gloria's face.

Not only did Dr. Sittner arrange for this commission, but he also tried to get Sonia a teaching position at the Music Academy. He set up a demonstration before the teaching body and Sonia displayed her technique. Several of her students came along to perform as well. Unfortunately, this demonstration was poorly attended, so Sittner arranged another, at which it was compulsory for teachers to attend. They did so, but were obviously not taken with Sonia and in a secret ballot voted not to accept her as a colleague. She was apparently "so very different" and they felt she would not fit in at the academy.

In the autumn of 1950, Austria revived the practice of awarding state prizes in music, a custom that had lapsed in 1938. The prize of appreciation that year was awarded to the uncrowned king of Austrian composers, Joseph Marx, and prizes for the advancement of music went to Armin Kaufmann, Felix Petyrek and Hans Jelinek. Awarded an honourable mention was the composer S. C. Eckhardt-Gramatté, an astonishingly gratifying reward for a woman who had only appeared on the Austrian music scene eleven years before. The prize meant a great deal to Sonia. It was to be only the first of many tokens of recognition she was to receive in the years to come.

Of just as much importance to her as prizes was the fact that her music was increasingly finding enthusiastic players and an appreciative audience. One of her greatest fans and promoters was Franz Litschauer, who, with his all-female orchestra, began playing Sonia's compositions in the 1940s, starting with the Concertino for Strings and later doing the Triple Concerto and the Bassoon Concerto. His wife, Frieda Litschauer-Krause, was a cellist who also appreciated Sonia's work. She premiered the Duo for Two Cellos with Senta Benesch and, as part of the Steinbauer Quartet, also performed Sonia's chamber music. Numerous other groups ranging from professional to amateur gave her work an extremely wide hearing in those years and provided a stimulating milieu in which to work.

The musical world of Vienna during those years was not without its political side, as can be seen by the rivalry which existed between the radical International Society for Contemporary Music (IGNM) and the conservative Austrian Society for Contemporary Music. Sonia had earlier drifted away from the former and had been a founder of the latter, but she was not an unconditional adherent of any school. She had taken in a few lectures of Webern's but was scarcely a disciple of his or of Schönberg's – she believed in music and not dogma or the latest trends. Some respected her for this; others did not. When, for example, Sonia was asked to write a violin concerto for the IGNM's 1952 international festival, there was some controversy and doubt about the funding. Eventually, however, it was agreed that there would be an honorarium for Sonia, that Herbert Häfner would conduct and that Walter Schneiderhan would play the solo. It was an exciting time for Sonia but I could share in it only vicariously as I was sent on a tour of America during the Salzburg Festival. In New York I haunted the Austrian consulate daily, trying to find an account of the performance in the Austrian newspapers. Finally, I found such an article and read in disbelief the headline, "Herbert Häfner's Last Concert." During the concert Häfner had dropped dead on the podium! My first thought was that it had happened during Sonia's piece and I also could not help thinking that perhaps a disagreement with her had triggered the fatal stroke. I immediately cabled Vienna to learn the truth of the matter. Within a few days I received the news that Sonia had played no part in it at all. The death had occurred in the piece before hers and in the resulting grief and confusion, her concerto was not played that night. The concerto was eventually premiered in February 1954 with Schneiderhan again the soloist. The performance was recorded, but the tape was destroyed and an excellent rendition of the second violin concerto was lost forever.

During the late 1940s, Sonia turned increasingly to writing for the piano, encouraged by her successes with the piano caprices and the second piano concerto. However, she was also interested in composing orchestral works and it is not surprising that she started a piece that combined orchestra and piano. About this time, Sonia had come to regard her first piano concerto as outdated. She then decided to take its third movement, which she still thought had some potential, and rework it, this time for two pianos. The result was her "Markantes Stück" which was performed at the Vienna Festival in 1952 by the Vienna Symphony under the German conductor Schüchter. Though Sonia herself played one of the pianos, she was not pleased with the performance – perhaps in reaction to Schüchter, who was unpleasant and did not seem to like the piece. Despite this reaction and the difficulty of the work, it is one of Sonia's most interesting.

Two other compositions from Vienna in the early 1950s deserve mention. The first is another one commissioned and published by the IGNM, her fifth piano sonata, in which she used the twelve-tone system, not blindly, but as it suited her. This was inspired by a ride on a gondola car where Sonia became fascinated by the sounds of cowbells, voices in the Alps and the dizzying effect of the grand expanse of space. A somewhat later piece was the sixth piano sonata, another piece with an interesting history. In 1928 she had written the third movement of the fourth piano sonata which she hoped Paul Wittgenstein, the one-armed pianist who had been disabled in the First World War, would play. Sonia also played this left-handed movement quite often as a novelty. After the end of the Second World War, the pianist Robert Wallenborn, who was with the occupying American army, suggested that she write him a movement for the right hand, so that he could play the two pieces together. This was the sort of challenge Sonia liked and within a few days she had finished the second movement. The obvious next step was to write a third movement for both hands. This turned out to be more difficult, since it was not easy to find a way to make the two themes match. But eventually inspiration struck and the third movement was written, combining with the first two to produce her sixth piano sonata. Like much of Sonia's work, it is not easy to play, but it proved to be popular at concerts.

It must not be thought, however, that the two of us lived only for music or art. We enjoyed our holidays to the fullest, especially after enduring the war years, when vacations were an unthinkable luxury. We loved the mountains of Austria and spent parts of several summers hiking through them, soaking up the beautiful landscape and visiting old buildings of artistic merit. We sometimes returned to Germany to visit old haunts such as the ruins of our apartment house, dear friends like the Sudecks and the Krebs, and exhibitions of Gramatté's art. In 1951 Sonia and I made our first trip into the heart of Italy. We visited Rome where we were struck, not only by the architecture, but also by the countless gardens and fountains that made the city seem like a single great park. So charming did we find Rome that we seriously thought about spending our old age there. From the Eternal City we journeyed to Florence and fell in love with the architectural harmony we found in the proportions of its squares, palaces and museums.

But wherever we went Sonia was always inspired by her surroundings and could not cease composing. On one of our trips to upper Austria we stayed during a hot summer night at a small village inn. This was in the days before insecticide, when the only way we could get to sleep without being devoured by mosquitoes was to kill all the bugs in our room before going to sleep. We succeeded in eliminating most of the insects that night but there was one we just could not get. After a lengthy hunt we gave up and decided simply to pull the covers over our heads for protection while we slept. During the middle of the night I awoke to find Sonia moving about with the flashlight on. When she perceived that I was awake, she said, "I've got it!" "So, you've got it," I said, still half asleep, "well, thank God." "Yes," she said, "I've finally got the theme for the second movement." In spite of my interest in Sonia's music I could not really respond at the time to the happy announcement. Instead, I turned over and went to sleep thinking about how peculiar things got sometimes when married to a composer.

A little-known facet of Sonia's career as a composer was her attempt to write

At the second summer festival for music students in Bad Aussee, Sonia's Bassoon Concerto was premiered by American bassoonist Gloria Soloway. This photograph, taken during the festival, shows Sonia with conductor Hans Swarowski and his wife (fourth and third from right) and eighteen-year-old Alfred Brendel (left).

Among Sonia's countless friends was a Dutch couple, Mr. and Mrs. Smith, who both played in the Frankfurt Radio Orchestra. One day she met them in Salzburg, accompanied them to the train station and into the coach. Sonia suddenly realized that the train had started to move and happily stayed with them until they arrived in Munich, where she boarded a train back to Salzburg.

an opera. This attempt occurred in Vienna in 1952 when she was approached by our friend Hans Sittner, who had been impressed by a libretto entitled *The Innkeeper of Ghent*. Written by Elmira Koref, the work was based on Charles de Coster's *The Honeymoon*, a tale about the tragic love of an innkeeper's daughter set against the backdrop of Carnival. Sonia was not in the least bit interested in trying her hand at opera and was even less enthusiastic after she had read the libretto. I, however, found the work had a certain charm – it was naïve and primitive but possessed a true kind of "folk art" all the same. I read parts of it aloud to Sonia and finally she grew interested enough to begin writing music for it. Within a short time she had parts of the overture and two scenes. In the first scene the disbelieving mother chases the doctor from the room of her dead daughter, while in the second, the mother and maid sing a lament with the thick-headed houseboy who was secretly in love with the girl. Sittner brought over four singers, two male and two female, and with Sonia at the piano, they rehearsed the scenes. All present were excited about the project, Sittner going so far as to call Sonia "a second Alban Berg" and telling her she should henceforth write nothing but opera. However when the enthusiastic Sittner took Sonia's compositions to the librettist, Frau Koref was horrified. She objected not to the music but to the gender of the composer. "What!," she said. "Two women? Impossible! That would be a joke – the whole world would laugh at it! No, I could never let that happen to my libretto!" Instead, she sent her work out to a number of male composers, including Richard Strauss, none of whom were interested. For a short time Sonia was furious; she had spent her time and skill on a futile venture, but soon she was engrossed in another, more gripping, project – our move to Canada.

Canada

In 1952 I had the opportunity of working in the United States as a guest of the State Department with the task of studying the educational aspects of the American museum system. I had originally meant to stay only three months but the chance to participate in an international symposium on museum education led me to prolong my stay, with grants from the National Gallery and Metropolitan Museum of Art, to eight months. Though I hated to be away from Sonia for such a length of time, the trip was to prove a highly important one in our lives since it helped lead to our move to Canada.

While I was in Washington, D.C., I was offered the position of director of the Winnipeg Art Gallery. My name had been proposed by Dr. Richard Hiscoks, who had known me from his work in Vienna with the British Council, and who was teaching at the University of Manitoba. On hearing of the offer, my first reaction was to go to the *Encyclopedia Britannica* and look up its article on Winnipeg. What I read was not encouraging. But I was persuaded to take a short trip to Winnipeg to better assess the situation. What I saw there left me even more uncertain about accepting the position. My greatest worry was taking Sonia out of the Viennese musical environment, where she was beginning to achieve success and put down roots, and transplanting her to a prairie city in North America. On the other hand, there was my own career to think about. Though I loved my work at the Art History Museum, the newly appointed director, Dr. Ernst Buschbeck, was creating an unhappy work situation for me. An unpleasant and arrogant fellow, he had returned to Austria convinced that I was a Nazi and even carried around my fifteen-year-old article from the *Völkischer Beobachter* in his briefcase to remind him of his dislike of me. In the end, it was Sonia's strong support for the idea of a change that convinced me, and we decided to move to Canada in September 1953.

After this first painful decision, others had to be made. We could transport some of our belongings, but other possessions, equally precious or meaningful, would have to be left behind. Naturally, the piano, all the music and manuscripts, Gramatté's paintings, other art work and my own books and papers had to be taken along. With great reluctance we left behind Gramatté's red and blue carpets, the Biedermeier furniture which had been part of Sonia's life since her teens and which she had scrimped to buy, the gorgeous Schönbrunn crystal chandelier and countless other pieces of silver, furniture and glass.

Before Sonia and I left Vienna, we were the guests at a reception jointly tendered by the Music Academy and the *Verein der Museumsfreunde*. Over two hundred people attended and heard some of Sonia's music played. Farewell speeches were given by our friend Dr. Sittner and by Dr. Allmayer-Beck, and I spoke a few words in reply. The next Saturday morning, Sonia and I left Vienna by train, stopping to visit friends in Stuttgart, Frankfurt, Paris and London before boarding the great Cunard liner Mauretania at Southampton. Unlike Sonia and Walter's infamous voyage to Spain, the crossing to New York was mercifully calm.

Our first destination in Canada was Montreal. As our train crossed the America-Canadian border, I left my seat for a moment and returned to find Sonia being quizzed by a customs officer. He asked her about the violin which she was clutching and which she had held throughout the entire trip. Knowing that it was a valuable instrument and fearful of being forced to pay duty on its importation, Sonia foolishly said, "It's nothing very special; it's just a new one." This is exactly what the officer was waiting to hear, that she was trying to bring in a new violin, and it took all my powers of persuasion to convince him that it was an old instrument after all and to let us enter Canada without having to pay duty.

In Ottawa I called on the Austrian *chargé d'affaires,* Dr. Peinsipp, with whom I had lunch at the Château Laurier. There, something interesting happened which was to have important consequences a few years later. As Peinsipp and I entered the restaurant, I noticed Lawren Harris sitting with another gentleman. I had met Harris in Winnipeg the previous autumn when John MacAuley had given a party for the two of us, and I was delighted that we recognized each other now. I went over to his table, where he rose and exclaimed, "So you've arrived! Welcome to Canada." After shaking his hand, I went off to rejoin my companion.

After we had sat down at our table Peinsipp hardly spoke, and I thought to myself, "Lord, what an unfriendly person." But after a moment he asked: "Who was that gentleman you were talking with?" I replied, "Lawren Harris, the famous painter from the Group of Seven." "Ah," he said and fell silent again. After a while he asked, "Do you know that he is sitting with a very important person?" Having just arrived and knowing no one, I showed no special interest. Only later did I discover that the other gentleman was Harris's cousin, Vincent Massey, the governor-general of Canada. Through Peinsipp's mind must have run some such thought as, "Here is this Eckhardt, coming to Canada as a stranger and the first one to greet him is a gentleman dining with the governor-general. He is our man." I believe that it was at this moment that his plan took shape to name me the Austrian consul in Winnipeg.

From Montreal we travelled to Toronto. Here we met old friends, listened to the Toronto Symphony and met its conductor, Sir Ernest MacMillan, and attended an exhibition of the Group of Seven, where we were introduced to A.Y. Jackson and Vincent Massey.

It was also in Toronto that we encountered an unmusical waitress. One hot evening we had slipped into a bar for a cold glass of beer. Sonia was eager to acquaint our friend Wolfgang Grunsky, whom she had not seen in years, with the score of her second string quartet. She was softly humming its theme when the waitress appeared at our side. "Excuse me," she said, "are you singers?" "No," we replied. "Then would you mind not singing in here?" she said. Apparently the management considered us a group of drunks whom they feared would any moment wish to burst into song.

Our train left for Winnipeg by night. Though we had booked space in the sleeping car, Sonia could not sleep and, instead, stayed awake, staring out of the window. As we passed Sudbury, its rocky landscape bathed in the lunar light, Sonia in the lower berth took fright and called up to me, "Dear Boy, where are you taking me? It looks like the moon." Her unease and uncertainty about the sort of country we were venturing into could not have been relieved by another incident which took place as the train entered the outskirts of Winnipeg. She had spotted an old wooden shack plastered with an advertisement for the Bank of Montreal and had asked, "Will that be our bank?" Absently, I replied, "Yes, probably." This answer alarmed Sonia, who was thus led to believe that in Canada banking transactions took place in decrepit shacks.

We were met at the station by Joseph Harris, president of the Winnipeg Art Gallery, and we were soon swept into the social life of Winnipeg's artistic community, with invitations from Harris, Professor Richard Hiscocks, Leonard Heaton and Mrs. Edith Motley. A story about one such social engagement will reveal how we were gradually introduced to the city and its customs.

One of our first invitations was to attend an enormous party at the Harris's, where we were introduced to everyone from the lieutenant-governor on down. Sonia was asked to pour tea and, as a European unaccustomed to this rite, she asked me what to do. In my ignorance I replied that I supposed that they were short of staff and she was being asked to help out, but that on no account should she refuse. So she sat down at one end of the table and when the guests came she soon got into the routine of asking them: "With or without sugar?" "Milk or lemon?" "One lump or two?" After a while, the woman at the other end of the table, pouring coffee, asked her, "Mrs. Eckhardt, are you musical?"

"Yes," replied Sonia, "I suppose so."

"And do you play an instrument?"

"No. People play me."

"What do you mean by that?....Oh, you're a composer! Mrs. Sharp, we have a celebrity in our midst; Mrs. Eckhardt is a composer."

And so all the women, who had certainly already known what Sonia did in life, began talking with her.

Despite these and other social welcomes, our early life in Winnipeg was harder for Sonia than it was for me. I had my work at the gallery, but Sonia was virtually unknown and neglected as a musician. When I was negotiating the terms of my employment the previous year I had explored the possibility of a position for Sonia, but the people with whom I was dealing were mostly from the art world and did not wish to complicate matters by including Sonia's problems. They were anxious to convince me that, once my position was consolidated, hers would immediately follow. This, I came to realize, was a mistake and it was to be some time before Sonia's unique talents were recognized in Winnipeg. (Even the local professional body representing music teachers was wary of admitting Sonia to its ranks.) I have often wondered why this should have been so and have come to two conclusions. The first is simply that her international nature seemed very exotic and strange to many and their reaction was naturally one of reserve. The second explanation is that most of the people she first encountered played only a minimal role in the city's musical life and she may have made them envious or insecure about their own positions. It was not that she encountered outright opposition, but among the leading lights of the Winnipeg Symphony Orchestra (WSO), the CBC and other musical circles there was a much greater interest in satisfying the public's taste for familiar masterpieces than in helping to give birth to new works.

It was only when we had rented a house on Oakwood Avenue in Riverview and the Bechstein grand piano had arrived that Sonia was able to begin to show off her musical talents for our guests. Among the earliest to hear Sonia's works in Winnipeg was Yehudi Menuhin, who was in the city to give a concert. He agreed to listen to several of Sonia's recordings but, since we had no record player at the time, we all had to troop down to the Bay and hear them there. He spent an hour listening and congratulated Sonia on her instrumental mastery in her Violin Solo Concerto but showed no interest in playing any of her works himself. He confessed that, aside from a Bartok piece dedicated to him, he included no contemporary works in his program and had no students to whom he could recommend Sonia's compositions.

Glenn Gould was among those who came to our Oakwood Avenue home and heard Sonia play and talk. In those early days he was little known and welcomed a bit of friendly advice from Sonia. After he had spent an hour running through his String Quartet, op. 1, no. 1, Sonia ironically told him that the piece would require four professional page turners, or else come to grief with the Musicians' Union, since he had quite forgotten to write the necessary pauses to allow the players to turn their pages. To our amusement, he took this advice a bit too literally. When we later heard the work on the radio, Gould had inserted so many rests that in some places only a couple of instruments were playing at a time. I cannot say however that he ever again sought out our company and in later years he turned down any connection with the Eckhardt-Gramatté Competition on the grounds that he opposed competitions in principle.

A less reclusive guest was Malcolm Troup. Sonia initially did not take to this brilliant Canadian pianist living in England and, indeed, spent all of our first luncheon together arguing with him. She said privately to me, "He is like all the rest. He talks too much." And yet when we went that evening to his concert, Troup had hardly played ten bars before Sonia turned to me and said, "He really is a great pianist." That was the beginning of a friendship that has lasted to this day. When we asked him to be one of the judges for the first Eckhardt-Gramatté Competition, he did not hesitate a moment before accepting.

But despite this stream of musicians through our first Winnipeg home, it was still a struggle to bring Sonia's work before the public. In fact, the year 1954 passed without Sonia being heard publicly. This did not mean, however, that she was not working; naturally her composing life continued. One day in late 1953, after arriving home from the gallery, I was surprised to hear the opening of a song for which Sonia herself had written the words. It was the first of the "Four Christmas Songs," written, I believe, out of a feeling of loneliness and homesickness. I improved the German text and she finished the work over the next few days. Three more songs followed: the second about Christmas lights, the third about the joy of family life in the holiday season; and the fourth about the bright winter sunlight reflecting off the snow. Though Sonia at first wrote the songs for *a capella* choir, she later added an instrumental accompaniment.

Though Winnipeg was neglecting Sonia's talents at this time, other musical circles were not. New York was the site in February 1954 of a rendition of her Bassoon Concerto by the Little Orchestra, under Thomas Sherman, with Bernard Garfield as soloist. About the same time the Vienna Symphony was playing the piece that had been postponed because of its conductor's tragic demise, the Concerto for Violin and Orchestra. Both were fine performances and well received but it was not until early 1955 that Sonia made her first public appearance in Winnipeg.

Her Manitoba debut came in March of 1954, when she played her own fifth and sixth piano sonatas on CBC Radio's Distinguished Artists series. But even this did not seem to be enough to attract interest. Indeed, it was nearly a year before another local concert of her work was given. This was at the University Chamber Music Group's performance of her "Nick" Trio, in February 1956 with Richard Guymonpré, Ed James and Peggie Sampson playing. Other concerts soon followed. In the next month Sonia played the fifth piano sonata at the same Wednesday Morning Musicale in which brother and sister Ann and Victor Pomer played the Violin Duo no. 2. A week later, Walter Kaufmann and the Winnipeg Symphony gave a performance of the first movement of the Symphony in C and in May came the "Ruck-Ruck" Sonata for the Canadian Citizenship Council.

In the end it didn't matter that these were only minor performances. What was really important in those first years in Winnipeg on Oakwood Avenue was the circle of friends we developed. This was particularly true of the relationship that grew between us and the musical couple, Ann and Ed Pomer-James. Along with Peggie Sampson, Ann undoubtedly did the most to introduce Sonia into the Winnipeg music community. (It was, for example, through the influence of those two women that the Manitoba Registered Music Teachers' Association finally relented and admitted Sonia as a member.) The Pomer-James's three-storey house on Harvard and Wilton was a veritable musical factory. Both Ed and Ann played in the WSO and both of them taught privately at the house. Music poured out of all rooms as they taught simultaneously and as waiting students practised in other rooms. The house gave the impression of a multi-chambered conservatory, and for a long time I toyed with the idea of writing an operatic libretto about just such a place, filled with a wonderful cacaphony.

It was into this infinitely elastic house that Sonia and I came to live during the summer of 1955. Our lease had run out on our Oakwood Avenue home and Ann and Ed offered to put us up temporarily in two attic rooms. So we had our furniture and piano stored and moved in there in June 1955; Sonia and Ann arranged, happily, that Sonia's violin instruction would be considered our rent. Then, just after settling in, we left on our first trip to Europe since coming to Canada.

When I had agreed to take the job as director of the Winnipeg Art Gallery, one of my conditions had been that I be granted a paid leave every two years to travel to Europe for three months of research, study or improving the museum's contacts in the art world. So, in the summer of 1955, we went travelling. After stops in Washington, New York and Paris we journeyed to Germany, where I gave a series of lectures on New York's Museum of Modern Art, and where Sonia and I had many happy reunions with old friends. We also spent time in Vienna, where we still had our flat on the Mariahilferstrasse, and in Zürich, where we visited the Heckels. From there we went to Spain, full of memories for Sonia from the years that she and Walter had spent there in the 1920s. I had never seen the country before and Sonia was bursting to show me the places and sights that she had first seen thirty years before.

We first visited Barcelona and saw the houses that she and Walter had occupied. We also saw some of the people and scenery that became part of Gramatté's art. We had planned to travel from Barcelona to Madrid by train in a first-class carriage but when we went to a travel agent we found that only third-class seats were available. Having heard many horror stories about the Spanish railway system, we were prepared for the worst and I gave the conductor a sizeable tip to get us into first-class as soon as possible. However, when we boarded the train we were pleasantly surprised to see how clean the carriage was. We shared our compartment with two soldiers, two other men, and a widow who was travelling to fetch her son from his school. The widow was sitting beside us and Sonia, who wished to practise her Spanish, engaged her in conversation. The woman proceeded to tell us her life story, which, mercifully, was rather interesting. Then, after two hours of recitation, the woman opened up her lunch and offered to share it with us. In return for the repast of roast chicken, we offered cakes and chocolate. We were then treated to a spectacle we never could have seen in first-class – in the next compartment two young girls were singing beautiful Spanish folksongs in falsetto. We were enjoying ourselves so much that when the conductor finally came to fetch us into better seats our companions cried, "You really can't leave us now!" Sonia and I agreed and, thanking the conductor, we stayed for the rest of the trip.

In Madrid we visited that most conservative of museums, the Prado, with its great collection of Spanish art by Velazquez, Goya and El Greco, which somehow failed to move us. We journeyed to Toledo, Cordova, Seville and, for Sonia and me, the highlight of the entire trip, Grenada. What can one say about the fairy-tale palace of Alhambra or about the choirs of nightingales singing in the trees surrounding it? Everyone should experience this delight as Sonia and I did.

On our return to Canada we resolved to do as the Canadians did and to buy a house. This was easier said than done and, with the searching and waiting for occupancy, it was 3 September 1956 before we moved into 54 Harrow Street. It was a long-standing dream which had finally come true. For the first time in our lives we had a house we could call our own. Even though it was not yet paid for, we felt that it was ours and from the first moment Sonia loved

When, in 1955, Sonia visited Pablo
Casals during his exile in Prades,
France, he gave her a photograph with
the following dedication: "To the quite
young Sonia, whom I have known,
whom I have admired and whom I will
always admire."

it. Now she could play her piano to her heart's content, even at three in the morning if she wished.

On the outside, the bungalow was white with pink trim and had a typically Canadian reddish-grey roof. But the inside was quite un-Canadian and yet not typically European either – let's call it "international" or, even better, "just very personal." Soon we had the house's interior painted in our favourite colours. The largest room, according to local usage a combination living- and dining-room, we had done in red and blue and Sonia's bedroom in mauve with a gold ceiling. The kitchen, with its golden-brown cupboards, we painted ivory with a lemon ceiling. However, the most striking thing about the interior was our collection of paintings, which stood out against the dark walls with an almost mystical glow. The house was a little Walter Gramatté museum, but there were other pictures as well: the Schieles, the water colours by Schmidt-Rottluff, Heckel and Laske and Klimt's *Woman in a Feathered Hat*. With the old Spanish furniture, they formed a harmonious whole, although not everyone appreciated this. When some of it was shown a few years later at the Guggenheim Museum in New York, people would come up and exclaim, "We didn't know that you had so many things!" "Remarkable." I would reply. "You must have seen them in our house. They have been there all along." (But many have no eyes for this kind of art, though the example we set may have done something to change some attitudes.)

To us our little house was splendid, for it met all our needs. Sonia spent nearly all her time here and was delighted that she could now work as she pleased. Her piano stood by the window and during her breaks she could look outside. She took the keenest interest in her surroundings: the crocuses in spring, the birds and the squirrels, the youngsters on their way to Kelvin High School across the street. In summer she took her rest periods in the garden, tying up plants, pulling out weeds and picking flowers for the house which was always full of blossoms. The smaller the flower, the greater her delight; she loved the faces of pansies, the scent of the lilies of the valley and carnations, the festive colours and shapes of the dahlias, gladioli, zinnias, nasturtiums, clematis and the few roses we had. (We were always having to plant new roses to replace those lost to the killing Manitoba winter until we finally gave up in discouragement.) Sonia dried many flowers and in this she had an especially skillful hand, taking away the water at just the right time. We had roses which kept their dark red colour, nearly a macabre black, for as long as twenty years. In winter I took great care to always have fresh flowers about. Sixty to eighty pots of bulbs, including hyacinths, crocuses, narcissi, daffodils and tulips, were started in the cold cellar and brought up into the warmth to bloom. When the last asters ceased blooming and the late chrysanthemums finally died after braving the snow and the branches which we had gathered with their red, brown and yellow leaves had faded, the first Christmas cactus was ready to bloom indoors. Shortly after the last potted daffodils had lost their blooms in spring, Sonia and I were out gathering prairie crocuses. Then, in the garden, the first tulips came out, followed by lilies of the valley, bleeding hearts, cornflowers and peonies, until the full richness of summer flowers returned once more.

Such was our house. Here we lived, made music, worked and welcomed our many guests. Among these was the man who became one of our greatest friends, Lorne Watson, director of the School of Music at Brandon University. Lorne was greatly impressed by Sonia's piano technique, began to study with her on the weekends he spent in Winnipeg, and conceived the idea of writing a book on Sonia's unique piano technique. It was also Lorne who caused the rearrangement of our livingroom. Originally our piano had been on the west, the shorter side of the room, but Sonia feared that when Lorne leaned against it, as was his habit, the piano would one day crash through the wall. Consequently we moved it to the east side where there was more elbow-room. However, from this time on Sonia was uneasy because people coming in and out of the house could see her from behind as she sat at the piano. In this she resembled Beethoven, who hated anyone surreptitiously listening to him play.

As we grow older, death claims, with increasing frequency, those we know and love. So it was that, as Sonia entered her seventh decade, death took two men in Sonia's family, causing her grief in different ways. In the summer of 1959, our travels had taken us back to Europe, where again we visited places and people from Sonia's past. In England we visited Whiteway, where Sonia had spent her earliest childhood. Later, we went to the French Riviera where we visited her brother Nick's first wife, Renée. How sadly ironic then that not long after our return to Canada we should receive a cable from Nick's second wife informing us of his death.

Sonia and Nick had spent only a few years together, at Whiteway. While she was quite young he was taken to Switzerland to study and he saw Sonia only briefly during a visit at Easter 1914. In 1920 he went to Berlin for the wedding of Sonia and Walter, and over the next nine years was visited several times by the Gramattés, or Sonia alone, at his home in Paris. When Walter lay dying, Nick hurried to Hamburg and dissuaded Sonia from her impulse of suicide. During the 1930s, Sonia saw nothing of him until the two of us visited him on the Riviera, where old family differences erupted and Sonia left in a huff after only two days. Between then and his next visit in 1947 he left his wife, Renée, to take up with their teen-age housekeeper, who was able to give him his long-wished-for son and whom he eventually married. After he had visited us in Vienna he sent along his wife, Olga, and their child, Pierre. Shortly after, the family emigrated to Caracas, Venezuela, and, when we too emigrated, a lively correspondence sprang up between Sonia and Nick. The main theme of their letters was always the same – Sonia tried to persuade Nick to come to Canada while he wanted us to move to Caracas or, at least, visit him there.

In the summer of 1959 Sonia wrote to him from Whiteway. It angered Nick to think that she should visit their old home without him. This was, however, not all that Sonia did to upset him. During our stay with Renée, who was leading a very sad life, Sonia learned some things about her brother which caused her, on our return, to write him a letter of angry reproach. This letter came as a great blow to him. According to his new wife, Nick grew so angry that he "turned

green." Olga, in fact, believed that their angry correspondence contributed to the stroke Nick suffered in November, the one from which he died. Sonia was stricken with grief and guilt as this letter shows. Written (originally in French) on the first anniversary of her brother's death, it shows the passionate side of Sonia as she reviews Nick's life and pursues their disagreement beyond the grave:

14 November 1960

You left still bearing resentment towards me – you were unjust to me up to your very last breath. You accused me of being foolish, wicked, egotistic, for not having been helpful to anyone, for being tactless, stingy and ungrateful. You sent back the very last letter in which I tried to explain myself and our misunderstandings and to tell you that I loved you in spite of these misunderstandings which got worse from one letter to the next. You replied that I was not to write and then you wrote one of those letters that I found impossible to believe could have come from you. I've kept it to remind myself of how badly you treated me.

To die unreconciled and harbouring such feelings of hatred is unforgiveable. I have suffered so much at your death and I promised at your grave that I would not abandon Pierre and his mother if they stuck to me. I shall do all I can to help them, even though you blamed me for having done nothing in my whole life to help anyone. I have kept this reproach to myself for a whole year. This is the anniversary of the last day of your life, a life as wasted as my own. We've been unlucky and life has given you only a son, whose studies you've not even been given the time to oversee. He is on his own. You left too soon.

But tragedy began in our family on the day of your birth and your life ended before you could carry out your duty to your son. As for me, what is left? Should I die in some catastrophe, would we both have a chance to wipe out our debts? I am so weary. I pray that Ferdinand will be strong enough to keep going and maintain his health which is already in jeopardy as he so often gives way to fatigue. Now I shall have no family left, except Pierre – if he can care for me a little – to remind me of you. I pray that you, in whatever heaven you are, will forgive me and that your spirit will find that peace which you so needed here below.

This day I have devoted entirely to you. In my prayers I express the burning desire to see you again, one more time. I hope that we will see a little of each other in the other world; blood calls out to blood. I am desolate that you left me nothing, not even a kind word. At least God may reunite us after death – we who had the same mother.

I remember those rare occasions in our life when we saw each other. When I was a tiny child in England we were together, you and I, at Whiteway. We so longed to return to that place we were together when I was still a baby, and try to understand why we were taken away from that dear simple

Visiting Marc and Vava Chagall in
St. Paul de Vence in 1959. An oil of Vava
is the second-last painting of Walter
Gramatté.

place. You, my beloved brother, were already old enough to have seen terrible things in Russia. The secret police tore you from your mother's arms after those three days of captivity, the third without food. Under threat of starvation she had to give you over to your father. And what did he do? He tossed you into the cadet corps, only to revenge himself on your mother. You, a soldier! What a vile fellow, that Russian, to have disrupted your whole life. He was the reason too that you never found an occupation. You became a colonel and that's all you ever did. The rest was just a haphazard life with only Renée to help you. And yet after those thirty years together you left for someone younger. Well, that was none of my business. Now that you've a son, he is the important thing and I will try to counsel him as best I can, if he cares just a little for us. If he doesn't then the last member of our family will have gone for me, and I can only live for Ferry and wait for our collection to be preserved for the future. Life has been harsh and sad for me. Our mother had no life at all; you hated her and showed no feelings for her. And your little sister is gone. She had no life either. You though, had your moments of ease, especially in your early years with Renée when she managed you so well.

For me it was only the constant struggle for survival, disjointed career. Only Ferry has a real profession and a job that he does well – though he too suffers from injustices that eat away at his morale, and his health seems to be declining like mine. There is nothing now but to pray that Providence will grant us time enough to carry things through to a successful conclusion – or at least that we will not be forced, like you, to quit in the middle of the road.

May God keep your soul and may Heaven watch over us here on earth, over Pierre, his mother and both of us, especially Ferdinand.

Within a year news of another death reached Sonia, but this time her shock was of a different sort. The death was that of Dr. Fritz Hinkelmann, the husband of Walter Gramatté's sister Hildegard. What shocked Sonia was that Fritz had been buried in the grave with Walter, in the spot reserved for her own body! I was in New York when this information arrived and learned of it all in a letter from Sonia:

I received such dreadful news from Hildegard. Fritz has been buried in our grave plot. That is too much! She begs you to pacify me – yes, she knows me well enough. "The two men will understand each other so well; they got along so nicely while they lived," etc. Never in their lives!

I didn't want to do anything hasty and therefore I am waiting until you tell me what to do. I am absolutely speechless! At first I wanted to cable them that they must not interfere with my property without my consent! But I didn't. I am so upset. Fritz will have to be moved; I won't let him stay there. No! This was the man who came to me after Walter's death, quoting the law, saying I had no claim on Walter's estate because I had had no children by him. To have that man beside us is intolerable! Hildegard arranged all this and then tells me I can still be buried above Walter. I will never agree to that and yet she asks me how she should put the birth- and death-dates on the stone. That tops it all! I will ask Karl [Schmidt-Rottluff] to tell her that he designed the monument for Walter and me alone. She writes that the cemetery authorities have new rules. All right, they should deal with me and not dispose of my plot behind my back!

We soon sorted things out and Fritz was moved to the grave of Walter's father. When we visited East Berlin the next year to see the grave site and call on Walter's family, we said nothing about the matter at all.

Not all the news in 1960 was bad, however. Early in that year I was named the honorary consul for Austria in Manitoba and Saskatchewan, a posting I owed to Kurt Waldheim (later secretary-general of the United Nations). From this point on we had a great many more business and diplomatic obligations in addition to gallery and musical interests. Many of these obligations were discharged at parties in our newly renovated basement, where we entertained visiting ambassadors, choirs, figure skaters, artists, teachers and Sonia's students, sometimes crowding in as many as 107 guests. At the end of each party there was always apple strudel, Viennese sausage and the potato salad for which we became famous. In the first years we found it difficult to offer wine to people used to whisky but soon our friends became glad to sample a good Austrian vintage. (Some of our parties were held in the garden, but in this we found both the mosquitoes and the ban on drinking out of doors to be nuisances.) For smaller dinner parties, Sonia and I collaborated on making the meals. She cooked her incomparable soups and French vegetables while I prepared the meats, especially my renowned wiener schnitzel, and desserts. The latter included all the Austrian specialties such as cherry-, apricot-, and plum dumplings, palatschinken, diplomat cake and others. If guests protested that they could eat no more, I told them the joke about Mrs. Pollak's three guests and the leftover schnitzel. If they *really* couldn't eat any more, I advised them to run three times around the house and then see if they could manage some more apricot dumplings.

The year 1960 was also the year of the Canada Council's international convention of composers held in Stratford, Ontario. It was a measure of Sonia's growing recognition in Canadian musical circles that she was invited to a gathering that included Taktakischwilly, Sutermeister, Varese and Hoeller and others. I accompanied Sonia and when we registered I was asked, "Did you bring your wife?" "No," I replied, "She brought me."

We met several other Canadian composers, among them Oskar Morawetz, and we spent a great deal of time with Sir Ernest MacMillan and his wife, Louise. We also encountered the Sao Paulo critic, Frankenstein, who remembered Sonia's Chicago debut in 1929. The music varied from experimental works by Varese and Badings to a popular concert by Roy Harris and his American Youth Orchestra and it all helped contribute to a highly successful conference. Sonia came away pleased, since she won a commission for a wind quintet.

There were soon to be other successes. In early 1961 Sonia was informed that she had shared, with Germany's Ilse Michaelis-Fromm, the joint first and second prize in the second GEDOK (Society of German and American Women Artists) international composer's competition for orchestral works. Later that year Sonia and I travelled to Europe and the Middle East, seeing everything from my family's ancestral home in Pleidelsheim to the Holy Sepulchre in Jerusalem and travelling, in a way unthinkable today, through Lebanon by taxi. The musical highlight of the trip, however, was our stop in Mannheim for the GEDOK festival week where Sonia reacquainted herself with her European contacts and where we heard the performances of the prize-winning compositions including her own Triple Concerto. An anecdote from this trip reveals Sonia's quick tongue and her tendency to blame me when something went wrong. In Greece after a night's stay at a little hotel, we had a late breakfast and emerged to find the interior of our car quite hot. Sonia's priceless remark was: "You've left the car standing out in the sun again all night long!"

But no matter how sharp her remarks, Sonia loved me dearly and could always find time to write a letter as touching as the following:

April 28, 1962

My dearest,

Today is the beginning of your seventh decade…a serious reminder that we must husband our time. Only a year ago at this time we were in such peril. Then came that wonderful trip to the East, taken together.

Having lived through so much good and evil, may heaven grant us the necessary strength to round out our lives, although we are somewhat exhausted after so much hard work.

And now I lay my life at your feet. Take my poor tortured soul into yours. It is so easy to persevere when we are together. This way we're sure to have a smile on our lips and some hope of fulfillment. May your mother live a long time, but most of all – stay with me, just we two. Find the strength you need to begin a new year which will bring you many better things;…may heaven help us and may I be able to help you.

In the summer of 1962 I was forced to leave Sonia in Winnipeg while I under-took a tour of museums in the United States. Sonia wrote to me constantly and one topic she always discussed in her letters was the creation of her third string quartet. These letters are unmatched in showing the pains and joys of Sonia's creative processes. Anyone who seeks to understand her as a composer can scarcely do better than read the following passages from the letter of 8/9 May:

I began the Third String Quartet out of pure curiosity, without at all being in the mood for it. The first movement went well technically, but I was still not involved – it was rather a duty. The second movement was the same. After I'd been at it for a couple of days I foolishly tried to go on. It went slowly. When your letter came today, I felt so happy to know you to be the way you are, that I first replied in music, wonderful music. It has been such a long time since I've written something full of feeling and so well; it is not the stuff the younger generation throws together just for the sake of being avant-garde.*

The second movement was completed the same day. A heavy load dropped from me. The movement is so beautiful; I had written it for myself in advance, "Farewell to this World." And the whole is sustained in perfect consistency. Everything is to be soft-pedalled until the end of the last phrase. Then (long pause) as you've always suggested, if you remember an open movement without conclusion, a Quo vadis. After endless duration an outcry. And in the end, exhiliration is what emerges from this unreal movement. And the last measures of the final phrases will be plain, earthly, without pedal, an mf ending without an ending, "Never the last!"†

12 May 1962:

Today I did the instrumentation for the lovely second movement and the parts for the V-1 and V-2. I played them through myself on the violin, with bowing, fingering, etc., so that no one can say they are too hard or unplayable. I'll ask Dr. Kosic to play the viola parts for me in June and Peggie or Lynn, the cello. After breakfast I hope to get on with the third movement. Frühstück! Spätstück at a quarter past eleven. Got into bed around three. But the work goes ahead; slowly but surely.

16 May 1962:

I'm always at work; I feel so tired, but am not conscious of it. Suddenly, in a moment, it hits me and I drag myself around. Why and for what reason? It's just feeling sorry for myself, as if I were already in the beyond, and I see

---

* This attitude toward her work can also be found in a letter written in 1966: "All through these last years, I have never felt compelled to music....I feel somehow frightened to start a new work. In other words, I do not really want to write any work for the small group of musically competent people left in the world, when the flashy, splashy, daring New Music is in such demand at the present time, regardless of its quality. Just daringly new, that's all. It becomes just a business for those close to the producers....These cheap, ephemeral works, are either experimental or just daring: to be new, a quick sell for the day, forgotton tomorrow already. Bluff works only on first hearing; at second hearing it reveals the sterility and non-musical quality."

† "Never the last!" was a phrase that had great significance in our lives. It meant "May this never be the last occasion we enjoy a time like this!" and was used between us when we were sharing a golden moment or when toasting each other.

myself as I am. I cry, but in this silent room. I am so tired; I collapse for a few minutes, then realize, how absurd, that I have to finish, I must, and ten minutes later I will sit down at the piano again like a clod of earth and go on working.

20 May 1962:

I still fuss over the third movement, having come near to the half-way mark. It may be that it will be a very subtle, good one – but I am fond only of the second movement, the unique one which I wrote for the two of us.

21 May 1962:

The third movement has come quickly to me. It's a very witty one, not boring and it appeared to me after the first calculation. I'm getting interested and I'm beginning to like it. I would like to finish it tonight.

24 May 1962:

Quite unexpectedly, the third movement. It is a dance of the skeletons, terribly odd in its theme, grotesque. In between there is always this inspiring bow with the repeated rhythm and a dry silly sf, sf tune, a mindless but frolicsome melody which I think will be quite an original touch. I'm having great fun with it. It's only that I'm so slow – is this a *chant de cygne*? Second movement, a farewell; the third, the Danse Macabre. In any case it's the last piece of chamber music I shall write.

28 May 1962:

Third String Quartet, First Movement
Intellectual music, counterpoint, on earth with both feet on the ground. Well done – I feel perfectly distanced from it. Composed on my own, just to compose, something at all! Used only musical technique. Again, well done.

Second Movement
Farewell! All in mute – surreal above the earth, but not yet on the moon – two souls floating in the sky, a beautiful, quiet atmosphere made with a pattern of four notes only. The theme is divided into five quarters (4 notes in 5/4) and brings an interesting slide of harmonic changes, starting low, winding up to the firmament. As well the violin harmonics say farewell on the fourth (interval) which was taken from the progressive scale mark at the beginning of the second movement. After this it vanishes – the mute comes off! On earth again, we hear the people left behind – and they too have a short farewell (same two fourths) to say it ends with a question, "Quo vadis?" No answer, no end!

Third Movement
Vivo et molto ritmico. Bones! Skeletons, bones, ghosts walk to march music –
a grotesque theme with drums which alternates between the instruments,
passing it from one to the other. The theme consists of twelve tone and
filing patterns (note patterns and music intervals are the same thing). The
note patterns come to an excess, two times, and exhaust themselves. Then
there is a dissonant chord after the wild dance, as a wearied rest. The patterns
still whirl up and up, round and round, break, and that sad tune comes back –
while others in pizzicati, or even in tremolo, bowings go through the whole
short movement. All three movements are short; three, four minutes, no more.
All four instruments, the quartet element, play cooperatively while getting
weak and divided into two groups of two instruments.

Fourth Movement
A fine harmony which will be very short and is a "short prayer."

Fifth Movement
This will be – should be – a run in race with life, a sort of quick-breathing thing.
I thought this would interest you. The whole conception of the work is not a
private statement but is approachable by anyone.

29 May 1962:

The third movement is as good as finished but I still must polish it and the
ending is not yet written, though not much more can be done with it.

Often I'm so tired that I find myself asleep, standing up. My eyes burn and
ache (too many little notes), my eyelids droop. If I lie down at night: I haven't
slept for three nights in a row. It has been like this since you went away.

30 May 1962:

If you come home in time, you'll see the lilacs, the tulips, the little pink tree
outside the kitchen window and the blue hyacinths near the sleeping sculpture.

Last night at 3:30 I finished the third movement, but it all has to be looked
over carefully. The fourth movement is already begun but shivers run up and
down my back when I think that in two or three weeks it will all have to
be copied

I'm so tired – deadly tired. I went to bed after the third movement around
four in the morning, and again I couldn't sleep. By eight I was sitting down
with the fourth movement. I feel asleep when Deidre was playing. I woke
up at her first mistake – that was what woke me.

12 June 1962:

I heard your voice and immediately I had inner strength enough for work. I think I might have found the first two beats. It's sometimes so difficult to decide the right direction.

Today I've been so weary that instead of working I'll draw the curtains and try to get some sleep.

Just imagine, I was asked to lunch for one o'clock at the Berry's. I was working, working and one o'clock went by unnoticed. At 1:30 Ed arrived in the Cadillac to fetch me. I was on the telephone to Marta Hidy and couldn't go to the door....I didn't know who was knocking; maybe it was for the consulate, maybe it was the Watchtower. Luckily I said, "Marta, please hold the line," and I saw Ed standing there waiting to pick me up. He had to wait five minutes longer before I was ready to go. I apologized for having completely forgotten while I was composing. It was so awful but I made up and they came back to our house for coffee. It was good coffee. I played the quartet for them, the second and third slow movements, so all is now well.

13 June 1962:

Today I've had a fabulous inspiration and I've begun the fifth movement making use of all the open strings while a stupid, primitive melodic theme in sixteenths is running along uninterruptedly. It will be very short because I'm fed up with this unmusical town and because the ears of Midas can't take in too much music, only a few drops of straight alcohol. They are weak like eunuchs - brains, ears, tails - nothing works after a few minutes of real listening.

I am closing this letter while still in the midst of my fifth movement - a real case of diarrhoea. It will sound almost popular: I am making fun of the people listening to me. It will be daring to fool around in that fifth movement - just daring. People deserve to be mocked - *cochons*!

Your girl with the long, sharp teeth. Better not approach me, folks! I am in the right mood to kick you out of my world.

Your Frightened Girl

I am barking because I am so scared - just like a little dog.

In 1963 Sonia and I took another trip to Europe and this time spent the first part of our tour in Scandinavia. Though we visited museums in Sweden and Denmark and the newly recovered archaeological treasure, the ship Vasa, just lifted from Stockholm harbour, the highlight of our stay was the Stravinsky festival. Swedish radio was presenting several works of the master, conducted by Stravinsky himself with his assistant, Kraft, directing the rehearsals. We attended nearly all the run throughs. We had occasion to speak with Stravinsky numerous times and were dismayed to find how unpleasant a fellow he was,

even with his wife and Kraft. At the concert we heard that the audience showed little enthusiasm for his newer works but received the *Firebird Suite* wildly. We wondered how a composer must feel when his new creations attracted so little interest while a fifty-year-old piece caused such a sensation. We wondered if he had even noticed.

Our trip continued southward, taking us to Germany and to Detmold, where we visited the music school so popular among the Mennonite community of Winnipeg. We found it a most agreeable milieu and enjoyed our stay with David and Viola Falk, but we soon continued our travels. In Geneva, Switzerland, Sonia went to Vidoudez, the violin maker, and bought a bow made by François Nicolas Voirin (1833–85), a pupil of Vuillaume, the maker of her Joachim violin. She paid 850 francs (about $250) for the bow and was overjoyed because, at only fifty-four grams, it was so light and gave such wonderful *sautillé*. At Vidoudez's she also fell in love with a David Dechler violin, dating from Rome in 1723. Unfortunately, at $3,000, it was too expensive for us and we had to leave it behind.

Though we enjoyed this trip immensely, it is fair to say that our return to Europe in 1965 was much more eventful. In East Berlin we entered into negotiations with the National Gallery which, a short time before, had taken over the collection of Gramatté pictures deposited with Hildegard Hinkelmann and restored them. We also had to deal with the East German Ministry of Culture for the return of these works to Sonia's ownership and permission to take them back to Canada. In return we promised to give the National Gallery the *Portrait of Rosa Schapire*, which they had selected for this purpose. On this trip we saw Leopold Reidemeister who had taken an early interest in Gramatté's work and who was now eager to set up a Gramatté exhibition at the Brücke Museum, which was then just being organized.

Later in our trip we made a most important contact – Erich Kretschmar, the bassoonist of the Leipzig Radio Orchestra. He had written to Sonia in Canada suggesting that he play the Bassoon Concerto as the orchestra had already played the Triple Concerto in a broadcast. Now, in 1965, he wanted to include the Wind Quintet in one of his programs, and so he twice entertained us hospitably despite food shortages in East Germany. The result of our contact was a very creditable performance of the quintet.

As we travelled from Leipzig to Bremen we paused briefly at Wilhelmshagen where a sad duty awaited us in the graveyard. Because of over-crowding in the cemetery, the authorities had obliged us to give up Sonia's mother's burial plot. So, over twenty-five years after her death, the body of Catharina was exhumed in our presence. The coffin lid was partially preserved and there was positive evidence of the remains. We placed all the big bones – the small ones were hopelessly dispersed – in a small wooden box, which we placed in Walter's grave. The skull was astonishingly well preserved, with long locks of white hair still there. Sonia could not help taking it in her hand and laying it in the box on a bed of leaves and flowers. No one could have performed this labour of love with more reverence and dignity than she. She wrote this note to her dead mother shortly after:

the patterns still [3] whirl up and up round
and round ___ break, and 'always
that __sad tune__, arco ___ (while other)
in pizzicatti ___ or tremolo (bowings)
goes through the whole short
movement ___

___ [all three Movements are short
3, 4 Minutes no more __]
___ Playing /co-operatively all 4 Instruments
Quartett Element ___ ___
then ending ___
while getting week ___ and divided in
2 and 2 Instruments ___ ___

For the first time in her life, in our home at 54 Harrow Street in Winnipeg, Sonia was fully free to compose or to play whenever it was convenient for her, day or night. She was a passionate worker and sat at the piano composing in the early hours of the morning and late at night. (Photograph by Ivan Kotulski.)

A page of a letter from Sonia to me in 1962, concerning her third string quartet.

The final bars of Sonia's third string quartet, 1964.

After seeing with my own eyes how time has consumed everything that remained of the poor body that enclosed your spirit here below, where you suffered so much, I felt all the closer to you, my poor little *maman*. It is as if I must soon follow when our task here is done.

By the early 1960s, Sonia had carved a niche for herself in the musical community of Winnipeg, combining her composing with a career as a teacher of a distinctive and highly successful piano technique. In a letter drawn from the same correspondence in which she exposed so much of her struggles as a composer, she shows a teacher's pride and concern as she talks about her brightest student, Deidre Irons, in the midst of a Winnipeg competition:

8/9 May

Dear Boy,

You've flown off and left me here all by myself. I am not going to describe my feelings because you know me so well. We know each other so well except for those little things we would rather spare the other. To bear problems alone is always more difficult than when with someone else.

Deidre played extra well. She made some tiny mistakes in the first passages which only she and I could detect....G. played only a Brahms sonata but with a terrible fiddler whom I can't even call a violinist. None of them could cope with the piano bench, the most amateurish thing you can imagine. They played everything p, pp, or when there was an f, only mf. No power at all, not even this boy whom you once saw, who came first in the senior TV competition. When he played the Khachaturian, it was like Mickey Mouse. Then out came Deidre in a bright red party dress with long sleeves....I thought when the others couldn't play with any strength it might be because of a poor piano. But that girl came on stage and crashed over the piano beautifully and seemingly with no effort at all.

Of course the new technique can produce ruinous results on any piano if one lets it, because, as you know, we make use of the whole body – it doesn't take much to make the touch heavy. Deidre said to me, "When I heard those chickens, I thought there was something wrong – perhaps they were wrong on technique or the piano was bad. When I got there I had to do something about it. Well, I added body weight and it was no strain at all."

I had several phone calls of congratulations. Ann rang to say she was speechless about how Deidre had developed. The hall was full; everyone was talking about it. But it will be much harder on the seventeenth of May and the fourteenth of June when young H. plays Khachaturian. If he plays properly and if Deidre makes little mistakes in the Campanella, he may just win first prize – people love gentle playing.

141

In 1953, we moved to Canada. Sonia
was soon successful in obtaining paid
commissions for compositions and
began teaching. The most successful
student was Deidre Irons, now a well-
established pianist and teacher in
New Zealand.

Sonia took her vocation as music teacher very seriously. She excluded no one on financial grounds, and if a pupil could not pay she tried to get them scholarships from the Canada Council or from private patrons such as Mrs. Collum, Ms. Richardson or Mrs. Rileigh. The lessons were usually lengthy, never less than two hours and often up to three. They were seldom dry and were most always punctuated with laughter and sprightly conversation.

The pupil closest to Sonia's heart was Deidre Irons, who came in September 1957, and stayed over seven years. She was a girl of considerable talent, having achieved a measure of success in Winnipeg, Regina, Calgary and Toronto, as well as on CBC. Working with Sonia, she mastered the Schumann Piano Concerto, going on to Beethovon, Brahms and Prokoviev and eventually playing Stravinski's Piano Concerto with the WSO under Victor Feldbrill. Under my own tutelage she studied German and took lessons in art history and literature.

The break came in October 1964 when Sonia wanted to enter her in a competition in Vienna for which she had already secured expense money from the Canada Council. Deidre instead announced that she had other plans. Several people had whispered in her ear that she ought to find another teacher. Though Sonia thought it too soon for this, Deidre went first to Weiser in Minneapolis and later to Serkin at the Curtis Institute in Philadelphia. Sonia could not and did not try to hold her and when she realized it was all over she wished to hear no more of Deidre and broke off all contact. I remember hearing Deidre play in a pops concert with Mitch Miller; we sat in the balcony with Sonia overcome by sadness and was crying at what she heard. For Sonia, Deidre's departure was the worst blow since her mother's death.

There were other talented students. Sonia's best violin pupil was Gwen Thomson but, as a good friend of Deidre's, she left about the same time. Hanny Unruh (later Labuhn), Wanda Konrad (later Becker), her sister Martha Jantzen and Matthea Schludermann were all serious students of the violin. Piano students included Matthea's daughter, Ulrike, Rose Cowan, Lilian Karpinka (later Kuschmarek), Douglas and Debbie Kuhl, Donna Semelka and Emmanuel Ax. Ax was interesting but stayed only a couple of months. Sonia took a great deal of trouble with him, even making an exception in allowing his father to attend his lessons and to rap him on the head if he did anything wrong. Ax later studied in New York and Israel and won the Rubinstein Prize and an international reputation. Sonia often said that she could have made something of him had it not been for his father's interference.

Sonia also taught cello and composition and received many musicians who came for coaching before examinations and concerts. Perhaps the most rewarding experiences for her were the opportunities she had for sharing her experience and knowledge with musicians who were less her students than her colleagues, musicians such as Lorne Watson and Peggie Sampson.

Lorne, director of School of Music at the University of Brandon, was fascinated by Sonia's piano technique, and from 1960 on he came to Winnipeg every second week to work with her. He had used the technique as the subject

143

Sonia was a deeply emotional person
with an artistic temperament, but she
was always full of humour and could
have a good laugh.

of his doctoral dissertation at Indiana University, and for years he made further notes with the intention of writing a book about it. He played Sonia's works constantly, premiering, with Peggy Sampson, the Duo Concertante for Cello and Piano and also giving performances of the second, fifth and sixth piano sonatas and the "Ruck-Ruck" Sonata, with clarinetist Jim Manishen. Lorne made good use of Sonia's teaching abilities, bringing her to Brandon for recitals, round-table discussions and demonstrations before audiences of university students and teachers.

Peggie Sampson was a professor of cello and strings at the University of Manitoba. She had worked for a time with Casals. She came to Sonia to improve her technique, concentrating mainly on her bowing. Though Peggie was a mature artist, she did not mind discussing her work fully and indeed lost no opportunity to praise Sonia and acknowledge how much she owed her in the development of her own art. She became Sonia's friend, patron, pupil and interpreter *par excellence*. To Sonia who, like her mother Catharina, was an excellent teacher, these discussions with an expert artist were a real encouragement.

Sonia and I had spent many years protecting and promoting the art of Walter Gramatté. At last in 1966 his work achieved a large measure of recognition in Canada. This was achieved mainly at the Gramatté Exhibition at the National Gallery in Ottawa, whose director was Jean Boggs. The museum's chief curator, Dr. Robert Hubbard, helped me organize the exhibition and together we brought out a comprehensive catalogue with colour illustrations and excerpts in French and English from Walter's letters. This was the first of a series of exhibitions that took the collection to Winnipeg, Saskatoon and throughout Germany. We caught up with the travelling show in Berlin at the Brücke Museum in 1968. The setting, in this intimate gallery surrounded by the pines of the Grunewald which Walter loved and included in his paintings, was ideal. Many of Walter's friends, including Leopold Reidemeister, who had established the gallery and his wife Ursel, attended this first proper exhibition of his works in Germany since 1927. The actor Dr. Tappart read selections from Walter's letters and members of Radio Free Berlin's Orchestra performed Sonia's second wind trio.

Five months before this moving ceremony, an accident in Winnipeg had sad results for Sonia. Shortly before Christmas 1967, Sonia slipped and fell on the ice in front of our house and broke her left arm. She hit her head on the pavement and lay unconscious in the bitter cold until the sound of passing cars revived her and she was able to crawl into the house. (She later wrote: "Only my keen ears saved my life. The loud car horns made me think that a student had played a wrong note.") She called me at the gallery and I urged her to do nothing until I could rush home. However in her distress she called a friend who was a doctor and he arranged for her to get into a hospital. Examination showed, as I had feared, that the arm was broken at the wrist. The doctor set it but departed that very evening, leaving Sonia in the care of a substitute.

Sonia's anxiety can well be imagined. Her hands were everything to her and anything that threatened her work could only cause her immense worry. In addition, the arm gave her a great deal of pain; in spite of medication she could get no sleep at night. The bandage seemed too tight. The pain increased daily and her fingers swelled up, turning blue. She feared she would lose her hand. After Christmas, the substitute doctor removed the bandages, but did not put the arm back in the cast. However, by the time the original doctor returned sometime after New Year's, the wrist bone had slipped and was protruding. In addition to the broken wrist, Sonia also suffered a torn tendon between the thumb and the first finger, which had gone undetected. Despite the doctor's assurances that it would turn out all right and despite prolonged therapy, the arm was permanently impaired. Sonia could not even get her fingers around her violin – a disability which she never got over. The torn tendon also reduced her hand span, and instead of reaching two notes above the octave on the piano, she could reach only one.

This accident cast a shadow over all her life. Again and again she compared herself with Beethoven, who had lost his hearing; she lamented that fate had robbed her of the use of her hands. Though Sonia eventually recovered movement in her arm, she never again played the violin. Everything she had planned to do was left undone. The following excerpts from her journal in early 1968 show the extent of anxiety and frustrated rage:

19 January 1968

At four o'clock today it will be four weeks since I had the accident with my left hand, which has caused me so much damage. I saw my hand before it was X-rayed – so awful.

I so hope it will not remain crippled. No octaves, can't hold the violin. I can't even reach beyond the first position with the fourth finger. My God, why must this happen to me when I have so much to do? Life is so senseless. Here we live as if blind.

26 February 1968

Have begun to work, but very little. My hands, my poor hands hurt so much and are useless for my special technique. I must have been cursed from birth. The greatest pain comes when one has found a great love and loses it – to be endowed with a great talent, and then to have it die prematurely, when the hand can no longer express what heaven puts in the heart. What a fate! What a senseless existence! Life brings such fleeting pleasures which must be paid for so dearly.

29 February 1968

Ran through the Bach Prelude in G for the first time, but tears streamed down my cheeks because I could hardly do it – and for the last four notes my

Boy had to hold the neck of the violin, so it would not slip with the movements of my hand.

Even three years later she wrote:

The loss of my hands, what is gained by that? Nothing but torture for the artist who needs them as a means of expression. And now that these tools are taken away from him, what is left? To the end of his days it breaks his heart every time he hears another violinist or pianist! His hand twitches at every phase he himself has played and knows so well. He knows every note and his very being bleeds. A senseless existence based on total waste.

We tried to forget all this pain and inconvenience during 1968 with trips to Europe and to the West Coast of Canada. Here, after watching me wade in the frigid ocean, Sonia sketched out an andante movement which was to become the beginning of the second movement of the fourth violin solo suite called "Pacific." Such trips were among the high points of our life together. We loved the freedom that our car gave us (we owned a series of five Volkswagen Beetles). We roamed the countryside of Canada: the prairies, lakes, forests and, at harvest time, the broad fields that are mirrored in Sonia's *Manitoba* Symphony. In the summers we often went to the Rockies, resting and enjoying the grand scale of nature, watching the mountains, valleys and animals, and studying the mountain flora. We stayed in inexpensive cabins and motels where we could read and write on rainy days. Sonia often took her work along and even practised on her two-octave silent keyboard in order to keep her fingers limber. In hotel rooms she copied, corrected and made orchestrations. (One odd habit of hers which I must mention was that whenever she stayed more than twenty-four hours in one place, she had to rearrange the room to her liking. She would shift the furniture around and take great care to put her work table in a good light. More than once I can recall the chambermaid coming in and thinking she was in the wrong room.)

Once we were back at home, life could be wonderfully cosy and concentrated. The many practical appliances of a modern Canadian house made life easy and cooking an enjoyable break from work. Sonia spent her leisure time reading and listening. She subscribed to musical journals which she carefully studied and annotated. She listened to radio musical programs but increasingly watched television, enjoying the opportunity of studying the techniques of great musicians. She loved to observe the closeups of their fingering, their bowing and their touch on the piano. In this way she increased her knowledge of instrumentation and of instruments which she had never studied so closely before, such as woodwinds and brasses. This experience was invaluable to her in her composition of "Fanfare," to give one example.

For the first time in her life Sonia became interested in current events, in the affairs of politicians and the issues of the day. She began to read magazines and newspapers and cut out articles of interest – on natural disasters,

This 1967 photograph clearly shows
Sonia's unique piano technique.
(Photograph by Ivan Kotulski.)

Notes on the Eckhardt-Gramatté piano
technique.

9) _Barres_ are only a helpful for composers to communicate writting 6ique and make the rtards understandible. They do not always mean rythme, nor show always a _down-beat_, etc—

10) Try never to repeat a phrase _twice_ the same way; there should be a dynamic difference between the ~~two~~ times— if they are not meant to be (echo.) black and white: f. p. only— to give a colour to it—

11) Mostly _trillers start slowly_ if the mouvement is a slow one

12) In classical music = If two notes are played and the 2^{d} same one has a triller

animal stories and the inevitable misery, cruelty and arrogance of the human condition. She had a whole string of television favourites with a pronounced weakness for romantic drama. She knew the family problems of all the characters and waxed enthusiastic over their dramatic talent. To accommodate this fascination, we placed the television in the corner of her room so that she could watch from bed.

Sonia loved to fill our home with her collectibles. In an early-Victorian corner cupboard she kept valuables such as a yellowed mask of Beethoven, Japanese netsukes, old crucifixes and a small baroque relic of St. Joseph. Not all her treasures were necessarily worth much money; she loved her collection of dried flowers, shells and animal figurines. She loved a little wooden bear which was always a symbol of her years in Berlin; she also loved an image of a Christchild in a nut-shell, which was part of our Christmas wherever we went. There were tiny horses from Sweden, little pigeons from Mexico, tin figurines, glass animals and Christmas angels. She called all this her "museum" and would never fail to bring it to the attention of guests from the gallery world, saying, "Here I am the director and president and have neither a board nor committees."

Sonia could give away as well as collect. In fact, one of her great pleasures was choosing and bestowing little gifts for visitors to our house. Sometimes the gifts were unusual flowers, orchids if she could afford them, anemones, or cyclamen of the striking colours that Gramatté loved to paint. Sometimes they were practical gifts such as shawls, handkerchiefs or little bottles of perfume – these she would stock in order to have them ready to give away on special occasions. Sonia especially loved to give things to children and kept on hand a variety of gifts, like rubber balls or balloons or kaleidoscopes. Every Hallowe'en she had nuts, apples, candies and oranges ready. When the children came singing to our door she gave each of them something, but not before turning and twisting the treat in her hands with fiendish delight and watching the impatience mount in the unfortunate children. She always kept some chocolate or candies for the paper boy and for neighbourhood children. When we lived on Oakwood Avenue it was not unusual to hear kids outside our house shout, "Candy, lady! Candy, lady!"

It was not until the 1960s that Sonia finally began to play a prominent part in musical life of Winnipeg and to achieve the recognition which she deserved. In Berlin she had won critical acclaim but had not been admitted into the inner circles, and in Vienna her growing acceptance had been thwarted by our move. Now, after Sonia had been in Canada for a decade, her works began to be played widely and she received commission after commission.

At this time the third string quartet, the Concerto for Orchestra and the Wind Quintet were finding receptive audiences as were the Nonet and the second wind trio, two chamber works written for University of Manitoba students. The Piano Trio, commissioned by Marta Hidy, received an outstanding performance from Hidy, Edmund Bishé and Chester Duncan. This was also the time in which one of Sonia's best-known works, the Symphony Concerto for Piano and Orchestra was first seeing the light of day.

Sonia and German Ambassador
Dr. Oppler at the opening of the Walter
Gramatté Exhibition at the National
Gallery in Ottawa, 1966.

At first Sonia had named the piece the Third Piano Concerto. Then she thought of it as the Duo Concerto for Piano and Orchestra but finally settled on its present name as a way of stressing that it was not only a piano concerto and that the orchestra part was fully symphonic. She began it in late 1966 and we have a note of hers from 11 December stating: "Today I began the Second Movement, Concerto for Piano and Orchestra. May Heaven help me get on with it! I have to work so hard in a world of Midas ears."

It was not an easy birthing process. In January she wrote that she had begun the third movement a fourth time and that it was getting longer and longer, like a rubber band. When she finally finished the concerto she became hysterical from the excitement and I had to calm her down. The CBC agreed that it should be considered one of their commissions, that it should be recorded and that Anton Kuerti should be the soloist. While she was in Toronto for one of the rehearsals, an incident so typical of Sonia took place. We arrived late to the rehearsal and, because the orchestra had started with the second movement, Sonia did not immediately recognize her work. She remarked to me as we sat down, "Oh, that's a modern work too." A few bars later she said, "And not badly written." Ten seconds later she caught on and there was great merriment. The broadcast went well but it was not until 1970 that RCA made the recording available in Canada.

Sonia had long contemplated writing a second symphony and finally, in 1969, after she had complained to officials of the WSO that they had never approached her with a commission, she learned that the WSO would underwrite such a piece. The result was the *Manitoba* Symphony, in honour of her adopted home. After an epic wrangle with the copyist, Sonia delivered the work in a televised ceremony to Maitland Steinkopf, the provincial secretary. The symphony received its premiere on 7 November 1970 with the WSO under Piero Gamba.

Flowers had begun arriving at the house early that day and Sonia's excitement mounted. She had had a gold jacket made to go over her black dress, wanting for once "to look like Liberace." The symphony was placed in the middle of the program, a strategy that allowed the musicians to start with Dvorak's seventh symphony and get well into their stride. During Sonia's work, the players shone and Gamba's conducting was superb, eliciting a warm response from the audience. In the following weeks the WSO played the symphony at the National Arts Centre in Ottawa and at Massey Hall in Toronto; the Ottawa performance garnered a better response from audience and critics than the Toronto one did. The only unpleasantness about the whole affair was the bill from the copyist, who charged $3,000 in excess of the amount set aside for the job.

While galas, applause and new dresses are the glamorous part of a composer's life, most of Sonia's time was spent in the hard effort bringing a musical idea to life. If in her early years she had been notoriously lazy, this was not the case in her maturity – she often said that she would rather be known as a hard worker instead of a genius. Though no one could force her to work when she was not feeling inspired by her "music from within" and might often go weeks without working, when she set herself a musical chore, it was impossible to keep her from her task. When she was in the midst of a piece she would sit at the piano day in and day out, at times for weeks on end, working through her ideas, orchestrating or stubbornly proofreading and correcting scores. It was not unusual for her to work long into the night, for she loved the silence of the wee, small hours and the chance for pure concentration that they gave her – it was only then that she said she could hear the music of the spheres. Because she was a perfectionist, she would go over one piece of music again and again until she felt satisfied. She would play the theme, vary it, repeat the original so as not to forget it, write it down, erase it, repeat it, write it down once more, only to erase it again.

When at work she could be either quiet or full of life. Mostly she liked to be alone and uninterrupted by such things as the telephone or the mailman or by the need to rest and to eat. However, there were other occasions when she could let her hair down. In full swing, she could become quite animated, talk happily to herself for hours and, when ten fingers were not enough to express what she wanted on the piano, she would hum and sing. She could get quite loud when excitement about her work gripped her. She would laugh and rejoice when she saw everything working out, or perhaps she might jump up and run around the room. I have even known her to throw herself on the floor in an excess of enthusiasm, roll over like a dog, scream and laugh convulsively and then dash back to the piano. In these good moments she liked to share her feelings about the piece and would tell me about it or perhaps call a friend and play the developing work over the phone.

In some ways, writing a piece of music is the easiest part of a composer's life. Perhaps the most difficult part of it all for many is the job of convincing artists, conductors and publishing houses to bring the music to the listening public. In this cause, Sonia was indefatigable in promoting her work and contemporary music in general. Whenever we were in New York, for example, she repeatedly called on music publishers to interest them and to sound them out. One such visit to Schirmer's produced the response that, though there was little demand for large contemporary pieces such as symphonies or chamber music, there was a demand for opera. Consequently Sonia turned her thoughts back to opera and, at the suggestion of our New York friend, Herman Herrey, she began an association with the playwright Eugene Ionescu. He and Sonia agreed that she would begin work on the music for a libretto based on his play, *Johnny and the Omission*. However, when she approached Schirmer's with the project, they showed no interest and the opera was sadly abandoned. Sonia also contacted prominent conductors – Susskind, Avison, Ozawa and Mehta – but these contacts too were fruitless. Many of the great artists who passed through Winnipeg or whom Sonia encountered on our travels were subjected to her relentless campaign of interesting them in contemporary music and in getting them to play her works. Her methods can be seen in her relationship with the violinist Ruggiero Ricci. When Ricci visited Winnipeg in 1966 he had already received a letter from Sonia inviting him to meet and

153

Sonia at the rehearsal of her second
symphony, the *Manitoba* Symphony,
under Piero Gamba, with the Winnipeg
Symphony Orchestra at Massey Hall in
Toronto, 1970.

discuss her compositions for the violin. He came for a two-hour visit and listened to parts of her Violin Solo Concerto. His reply reveals why it was so hard to interest the more renowned musicians in new pieces. "This is a big work," he said. "It can only take the place of another concerto of this size and quality but no one will want an unknown work to be put on a program replacing a Mendelssohn, Bartok, Beethoven or Tchaikovsky. Everyone wants to hear what they know, particularly if it is written in the old style. Besides, I have no time to learn a new work when I am giving a hundred concerts a year." Undaunted, Sonio tackled Ricci again eight years later at the Shawnigan Lake Summer School, where he was giving master classes. He listened politely to the tapes we had brought of the violin caprices nos. 4, 5, 6, 7, 9 and 10 and studied some of the scores, but his response was, "I am not here to foster composers, only to play the violin."

It is greatly to Sonia's credit that such rebuffs never deterred her from her objectives and that she never stopped promoting the cause of her music. To know where she drew the strength necessary to carry on in the face of discouragement, one must understand at least a part of her deeply felt philosophy of life. To Sonia, one's existence on this earth was not a happy one, but rather one filled with struggle and tragedy, especially for the sensitive and artistic, who comprised a tortured but privileged elite. In her journal she wrote:

I wrote everything in my music but I did not write it for this world. This, at least, is compensation, to write for the gods and not for mortals – those people who pass arrogantly by, ignoring it, satisfied only with themselves.

There are few gods among us and those few mostly know each other. To get to know one another, a great sensitivity of feeling and thought is necessary. A person needs time to develop that, time alone which is so rare. To be alone allows one to go deep into oneself. The struggle for existence, for mere existence, uses up so much strength and what is left is weakened by exhaustion....We gods need private time to dive down into ourselves, to meditate, to find ourselves, to be alone, far away from all the "animaux inferieurs", to meditate and enjoy the sun before it goes down into eternity.

Why is everything so difficult for the good gods here on earth, and so easy for these inferior people who eat, enjoy their money but remain as animals?

Therefore, being a composer, or at least an uncompromisingly honest one, meant that one was in for more than one's share of setbacks but that, as part of an invisible elect there were responsibilities to one's art and to other artists.

There was also the strength derived from her belief in an afterlife. Time and again I have quoted from her prayers and exhortations to her dead loved ones to care for those still alive and the expressions of hope that we would all meet again on the other side of the grave. Because of Catharina's modern open-mindedness about religion, Sonia had not been brought up in any particular denomination. She had no time for the trappings and ceremonies of conventional faiths but she was, at heart, as deeply religious a woman as I have met. Even if she was never sure about the exact nature of the Deity (one of her prayers began, "If God *is*...") when hard times assailed her or when discouragement followed discouragement, it was the thought of a life beyond this one that sustained her. At Easter 1974, she wrote: "Born to live a short time is the Present. Death, the Past; rebirth, the Future and the Eternity: All in All." The theosophy that her mother imbibed from Tolstoy clearly remained with Sonia and gave her hope for the future.

Recognition

The year 1970 brought Sonia a treasured form of recognition. In May, Brandon University conferred honorary doctorate degrees upon her, on Dr. P. H. T. Thorlakson, the head of the Winnipeg Clinic, and on Tommy Douglas, the first leader of the New Democratic Party. Sonia, robed in a red and blue gown, a blue cap with gold tassel and a red and blue hood (the colours of the School of Music), watched as two hundred students knelt to receive their degrees, fearing that she would have to imitate them. Thankfully, she found she was required only to stand when her citation was read by Professor Lawrence Jones. That evening we attended a great smorgasbord and dance and then, with Lorne Watson, Peggie Sampson and our friends the Noonans, we conducted a post mortem of the day's events. She deeply treasured her doctorate and loved people to use her title.

A hand reached out of the past in July 1970. Robert Adler, son of Max Adler, Sonia's patron forty years earlier, phoned from Kenora, Ontario, where he was on a fishing expedition. Though he was a young man when Sonia visited the United States in 1929, he had nursed a secret admiration for her all these years and now wanted to see us. The next day we drove to Kenora and spent a few pleasant hours with him.

Robert recounted how, some time before, a music society in Chicago had given a talk on some of his father's musical protegés. He had kept in touch with many of them but he had lost contact with Sonia. (It was eventually Harold Joachim, curator of the graphics collection at the Art Institute of Chicago, who informed him that Sonia was married to the director of the Winnipeg Art Gallery.) Robert told us that he still had a host of friends from the music world, including Isaac Stern, and promised that he would gladly bring Sonia's work to their attention. Accordingly, after his return to the United States, we sent him recordings; we also sent material to those contacts he suggested. Unfortunately all we ever received from Stern and the others were polite, negative replies.

One work written in 1970 waited a long time for its first performance. This was the Concertino for Gamba and Harpsichord commissioned by Peggie Sampson. Unfortunately, after placing the commission, Peggie took a postion at York University, leaving Sonia to puzzle through the special instrumental requirements of the piece on her own. Peggie asked one of her Winnipeg students to help, but Sonia could arrange only one discussion with the girl, at which they discussed gamba tuning.

When the work was finished in November 1971, Sonia sent it off to Peggie Sampson for approval, since it was her habit to discuss a commission with the client before putting it into final form. Sonia had earlier discussed the harpsichord aspect of the piece with Lawrence Ritchey of the University of Manitoba, but Ritchey had doubts about the instrumentation. Sampson turned down the work, a rejection which greatly upset Sonia, who thought highly of the concertino. Though Sonia reworked it for cello and piano, at Peggie's suggestion,

The house in Winnipeg became a
perfect artistic environment, combining
old Spanish and early Canadian
furniture and the art of Walter Gramatté.
(Photograph by Ivan Kotulski.)

the piece was never played by her. So intense was Sonia's commitment to her music that this disagreement caused her to take offence at Peggie, and it took more than two years before I was able to effect, despite Sonia's reservations, a reconciliation between the two. To Peggie's credit, she never lost faith in her friendship with Sonia and continued to refer to her in warm and enthusiastic terms. (Eventually the concertino received its premiere. In 1984 Delores Keahey and Dorothy Bishop performed it as written for piano and cello.)

Aware of the weak position of Manitoba composers in relation to that of their colleagues in Toronto, Montreal and Vancouver, Sonia spent a great deal of time in 1970 working on a project to unite the province's composers in a single organization. With the help of some colleagues, she drew up a proposed program and distributd it to elicit the response of the musical community. The following passage outlines the purposes of what she called the Manitoba Composers' Group:

1 To promote the creation and performance of contemporary music, and especially the music of Manitoba composers;

2 To foster the understanding of contemporary music – regardless of its style;

3 To aspire to the highest possible level of performance in these works as only carefully rehearsed and authentic performances are fair to the contemporary composer;

4 To emphasize the role of the composer in musical life and in our society. Without the composer of the past we would not be able to enjoy music which is today one of the most essential elements in civilization. Without the contemporary composer, music could not regenerate itself in a meaningful way;

5 To create a centre for the music (manuscripts, records and tapes) of Manitoba composers, so that everybody who wants to study or use them for performance can get them....

6 To stimulate or organize performances or even festivals of Canadian (Manitoba) music;

7 To assist talented young musicians in the performance of contemporary Canadian works;

8 To influence performers (particularly those connected with the CBC, Canadian symphony orchestras, choirs, music schools and schools at large) to put a greater emphasis on contemporary Canadian and Manitoban work;

9 To influence all organizations which support musical aims in a financial way (the Canada Council, the different levels of government, the various educational organizations) to make their support conditional on the principle that the creators of music are not neglected in the process.

The Manitoba composers whom Sonia saw at the core of this undertaking were Victor Davies, Chester Duncan, Walter Hekster, Leslie Mann, Arthur Polson, Robert Turner and, naturally, herself, though she also hoped to involve patrons such as the CBC, the WSO and the universities. However, despite the group's laudable objectives, the scheme aroused no great enthusiasm in the musical community and it failed through lack of support. Sonia's plans were not forgotten though. In the early 1980s her dream of a composers' group was realized with the formation of the Manitoba Composers' Association. In its constitution, the association consciously echoes Sonia's original plans, and the group acknowledges the inspiration of her example, stating boldly what she said before: Without new composition, music could not regenerate itself.

In 1971 my work and Sonia's coincided. The Canada Council and the Winnipeg Art Gallery had commissioned her to write "Fanfare," a work for eight brass instruments, to be played at the opening of the new gallery building. I had prepared an impressive opening exhibit drawing on some of the finest works from museums in Canada, the United States and Europe and the official ceremonies were to be conducted by Princess Margaret and the Earl of Snowden. However, disaster struck in the form of a walkout by the construction union, who threw up picket lines and brought work on the new building to a halt. I had to cancel the exhibit and I advised against continuing the opening ceremonies as they had been planned.

Despite my misgivings, the plans went ahead unchanged and on 25 September the building was inaugurated. The weather had turned nasty overnight and a cold wind was blowing as Princess Margaret, in a light blue dress, was seated on the east side of the building with the other guests of honour. The musicians who were to sound the fanfare every fifteen minutes were members of the Musicians' Union and thus reluctant to cross a picket line, even though the line seemed to have been abandoned for that day. Consequently they positioned themselves on the top floor of the Bay parkade across the street. The wind was blowing in a contrary direction and carried the sound of their playing *away* from the gallery so that when the speeches ended and the princess remained standing at the entrance, the music could scarcely be heard. She also went inside too soon. So "Fanfare" was really enjoyed only by those standing next to the trumpeters.

"Fanfare" was performed again two weeks later at a pops concert. The performance was not all that effective because the players remained in their places in the orchestra. My suggestion of having it played in front of the stage was rejected because the musicians would have been considered soloists and thus have had to been paid double.

The year 1972 was a year of highs and lows. The high point was our trip to Europe for a summer of travel and recreation in Italy, Switzerland, Germany and Austria. The low point was definitely reached on our return to Winnipeg when a tumor on my neck flared up, requiring ten operations and highly painful skin grafts. Though the ordeal was hideous for me, it was worse for Sonia, whose nature was sensitive. During my stays in the hospital, Sonia was fierce in her defence of me, and the doctors soon learned that she meant business. She watched over me constantly and sometimes hid herself behind curtains to maintain her vigil when she knew her presence was not officially approved.

165

Sonia's beloved Bechstein piano, which she obtained with the help of friends early in 1928. At home on Harrow Street, she could work at the piano and also watch the birds and trees and the passing students from Kelvin High School across the street.
(Photograph by Ernest Mayer.)

It is also interesting to see how this crisis prompted Sonia to again write imaginary letters to the spirit of long-dead Walter and to invoke the ghost of Catharina as well:

Hull, if your soul does exist and is not destroyed with the body, let it be with our boy! Pray with me that we'll pull through, so that we may go on working together and being together. Heaven hear our prayer! Oh, my dear boy, why must all this be?

Thank heavens, today he has got through so far. Thank you, mother, and you, Walter, as well, if you've helped us along! If only the garden flowers would bloom when you are home again. I am now a little more at peace.

Your dear little girl

After my recovery, a bit of rest and recuperation was in order. We achieved this with a trip to Hawaii in February 1973. Sonia and I visited four islands, admired the scenery, watched the sea and the sea life, peered into volcanoes and generally let the warm air of the South Pacific work its soothing magic on two battered souls seeking release from the rigours of a prairie winter.

Later, that summer, we returned to Europe for another working holiday. Though our tour was plagued by a car with recurrent clutch problems, we achieved much. In Sierksdorf, Germany, for example, we visited the Schmidt-Rottluffs for the last time that Sonia would ever see them. In Frankfurt we attended the opening of an exhibit, which I had sent over, of the works of Canadian artist Ivan Eyre. In Nuremburg we visited Dr. Veit, of the Germanic National Museum, to whom we had recently sent copies of Gramatté's letters for the archive of artists' letters. In Austria, our itinerary included a visit with Kurt Waldheim and performances of Mozart arias by Janet Baker singing with the London Symphony Orchestra and of the world premiere of Orff's "De temporum comedia" under von Karajan. The latter performance received a deservedly lukewarm response.

The year 1974, my wife's last, was one of triumph for her. Early in the year, on 26 and 27 February, we saw her Triple Concerto receive two performances in Ottawa from the National Arts Centre Orchestra under Mario Bernardi. To increase our joy in the event, our arrival in the capital coincided with our fortieth wedding anniversary.

At our invitation, Sonia's nephew, Pierre, and his family came up from Boston, where he was studying at the Massachusetts Institute of Technology, for the occasion. When their flight arrived, there was no one we could recognize as Pierre until a bearded individual came up to us and exclaimed, "Aunt Sonia!" She had to overcome the shock of finding her nephew looking like a hippie but recovered to give him a hearty welcome. He and his wife and son stayed with us at the Château Laurier and gave Sonia much joy. The next day, an excellent interview with Sonia was printed in the *Ottawa Citizen*. In it, Pierre and his family were also mentioned. The headline to the article read "Beethoven and I." It was revealed that Beethoven and Sonia had several things in common:

"The three doctors": Ferdinand Eckhardt, Sonia and Lorne Watson. In 1970, she received an honorary doctoral degree from the University of Brandon.

Celebration of the twentieth anniversary of my appointment as director of the Winnipeg Art Gallery, 1973. It was always with great joy that Sonia participated in my successes. (Photograph by Ernest Mayer.)

An "official" snapshot of Sonia by
Toronto photographer Walter Curtin,
RCA, June 1974. She appears somewhat suspicious here, since she did not
feel at ease about being photographed
that day. (Photograph by Walter Curtin,
RCA.)

both were musical and both had a nephew for whom they cared very much. An interview that did not go so well was one with the local CBC station in which Sonia, egged on by the interviewer, was a little too unguarded in some of her opinions about colleagues, critics and other musicians, many of whom she was actually on good terms with. It took all my influence to keep them from playing that tape. It would have hurt the feelings of many and done Sonia no good.

The rehearsals for the concerto seemed to go well. The whole atmosphere at the National Arts Centre was ideal, and both performances went splendidly. We and the family sat, of course, in the *loge d'honneur*; Pierre junior beat time with his hands and feet as a sign of his musicality. Bernardi and the orchestra later travelled west with the Triple Concerto, giving performances in Windsor, Winnipeg, Edmonton, Calgary, Regina and Saskatoon. In all there were ten performances, a record for consecutive performances by one group of any of Sonia's compositions.

In May and June the CBC Festival in Winnipeg devoted a whole evening to her work. Lorne Watson played two movements of the second and all of the sixth piano sonata. He and Jim Manishen played the "Ruck-Ruck" Sonata and the Purcell String Quartet did the third string quartet. Later in the festival, Sonia's "Hainburger" Quartet was played with Leonard Isaacs, Director of the University of Manitoba School of Music, giving a long and perceptive introduction.

All over North America that year people were playing Sonia's music. The Purcell Quartet played the third string quartet on its tour of western Canada. Lorne Watson played the sixth sonata at the University of Indiana, and Karin Redekopp performed the fifth sonata at four concerts in the United States. Sonia's student, Wanda Toews, embarked on a series of concerts in Canada and the United States, always playing Sonia's first sonata. At the Manitoba Music Festival, eighteen-year-old Douglas Finch won the highest prize, the Aitkens Trophy, with his rendition of Sonia's fifth sonata, a piece he later played to take second prize at the National Music Festival in Toronto. Arthur Polson and Eugene Kowalski, in the last concert Sonia ever attended, played her second violin duo at the Winnipeg Art Gallery in a recital broadcast by the CBC. Finally, there was the radio documentary on Sonia and her work that was presented over the entire CBC network in November 1974.

The documentary was the brainchild of Lorne Watson and John Roberts of the CBC. Preliminary discussions took place in 1972 and Sonia was the first to be interviewed, in June of that year. Later interviews were recorded with a number of people acquainted with Sonia and her music, including Keith MacMillan, son of Sir Ernest, Kenneth Winters, Anton Kuerti, Peggie Sampson, Victor Feldbrill and Marta Hidy. In 1973, recordings and videotapes were made of Sonia at the University of Brandon where she opened Canada Music Week and gave lecture demonstrations of eight of her compositions to the students. (This, incidentally, was where the possibility of an Eckhardt-Gramatté Competition was first explored.)

Among Walter and Sonia's closest friends were Brücke painter Karl Schmidt-Rottluff and his wife, Emmy. Schmidt-Rottluff designed the grave monument for the cemetary plot in Wilhelmshagen, East Berlin, where Sonia and Walter are buried.

A visit with Erich Heckel, another
painter from the Brücke movement,
and his wife Siddi, at Lake Mammern,
on Lake Konstanz, in 1969. The Heckels
were among Sonia's most intimate
friends.

Sonia surrounded herself with flowers
whenever she could afford them.

Finally, after several delays, the two-hour documentary was broadcast in two parts on 13 and 14 November 1974. Listening to it was Sonia's last great pleasure in life. The program was lively, without a trace of the boredom that usually infects such material. The interviews with Sonia were vital and witty, the contributions of the others were invaluable, and the musical interludes made it all come alive. The fact that not all the comments were flattering (in fact some were downright critical) only made the documentary more interesting. Its importance as a sign of Sonia's acceptance as a major musical figure in Canada was clear, and the documentary seemed to signal that the chance for even more achievement and recognition was great. How little we knew what lay in store.

Sonia's Death

I have described our various trips in detail because they were so important to Sonia and to me. That we were able to travel on our small budget so extensively, visiting all parts of Canada and the United States, the Middle East and every European country west of the Iron Curtain, is a tribute to Sonia's genius for organization and her bent for economy. She would always carry a hotplate cooker in her luggage to make tea or coffee or to boil an egg. Not surprisingly our bags were very heavy, since Sonia also insisted we take along pots and pans as well as plates, cutlery and napkins. Under every set of circumstances she tried to maintain her sense of decorum and style. She loved these travels and looked forward to another European trip in November 1974 and to our excursion the following February to Tahiti and Fiji. To my great sorrow our trip to Germany was our last together.

It was a trip prompted, in part, by my retirement after over two decades as the director of the Winnipeg Art Gallery. My staff gave me a wonderful farewell party on 30 August 1974 and I looked ahead to putting my library in order and organizing Sonia's music and press clippings. Above all, however, I sought the freedom to travel widely and to see as much of the world and as many of our friends as we could.

On the weekend of 17 November we travelled to Brandon, where Sonia gave a master class to some of the senior music students and where we heard a performance of the "Ruck-Ruck" Sonata. We partied, unwittingly for the last time, with Lorne Watson, Edna Knox and other Brandon friends and then journeyed back to Winnipeg to catch our plane. By 23 November we were in Frankfurt.

For the next few days we visited friends, including Hanna Bekker, and had dinner with Hildegard Weber, the music critic of the *Frankfurter Allgemeine Zeitung*. When we had recovered from the effects of the flight we went to Cassel to speak with Dr. Voeterle of the Bärenreiter Publishing House. Later that day we saw Tolstoy's play, *Powers of Darkness*, and visited art galleries. As we travelled about, Sonia, who loved flowers, spotted a beautiful bunch of orchids in the Cassel station. We realized of course that it would be foolish to carry them about and so forgot any idea of buying them. After a warm meeting with Dr. Georg Schaefer in Schweinfurt, who showed us part of his art collection and treated us to champagne and roast duck, we journeyed to Stuttgart for a stay with our old friend Maria Kasack.

On the morning of 29 November we negotiated about the possibility of future broadcasts with Dr. Gerhard Wienke of South German Radio. After lunch I proposed that we take a taxi back to Maria's but Sonia cried, "Must you spend even more money?" and so I agreed that we should catch a bus. As the bus neared Maria's neighbourhood I realized I did not know exactly where to get off and I stood up to question the driver. I motioned Sonia to remain in her seat but in her impatience she decided to follow me. I suddenly heard the passengers behind me shriek and turned to see that Sonia had tripped and fallen. With the help of others I managed to get Sonia off the bus and into Maria's house where I laid her on the couch.

When the doctor finally arrived he thought matters serious enough to have Sonia taken away by ambulance and admitted to the hospital. The X-rays showed that the injury was a fracture of the thighbone; an operation was scheduled for the following Monday. The chief surgeon, Dr. Gerhard Richter, did all he could to reassure me and said, "There is no great cause for alarm. We do these operations twice a week." To be quite sure in my own mind, I telephoned my surgeon-friend, Helmut Remé, in Lübeck, who talked with Dr. Richter about Sonia's condition and the intended treatment. He agreed that the operation was the only course open and I went and sat with Sonia until that night.

The next few days were naturally full of anxiety. I spent as much time as I could at Sonia's side and when not there paced the hallways, talked to doctors, slept fitfully or took coffee with Maria. Maria told me then that Walter Gramatté's first wife, Hetta, had died a year before.

On the afternoon before the operation, Sonia was very animated, entertaining the nurses and orderlies with her stories. Later she and I talked and she reviewed her whole life: she brought up memory after memory. There was the Paris of her childhood with the view across the rooftops to the Eiffel Tower and the piano room where she had practised hour after hour. She spoke of her life with Walter and how he had sketched her at their first meeting. Finally she assessed her place in the music world: "Hindemith, Stravinsky and Khachaturian – and I come next with Penderecki and Lutoslawski." Just after six o'clock she was given an injection to kill the pain and to help her sleep, and I left.

The next morning I was at the hospital much too early, so I walked the grounds and stared up at her window. At last I slipped into her room where she was awaiting the anaesthetist. There was time only for a brief farewell, a kiss and outstretched hands before she was wheeled away. She had looked at me so trustingly and felt so confident.

She had spent her last waking moments on this earth writing me a letter. Her words reveal her thoughts on mortality, our marriage and her place in contemporary music:

December 3, [sic] 1974

Dear Boy:

If I have shown you the bad side of my character so often, I believed I was – no, I am – the only one who reveres and loves you so much that I'd lay down my life for you if need be. You're one of the rarest beings, for whom one would have to look a long time before finding. I was the luckiest woman in the world to have found you and haven't done enough for you. It was possible to protect you sometimes only by showing my teeth the way a bulldog does…in order to gain respect for both of us and give us a chance to get ahead.

Here below we can count on nothing.

We are still protected from above and our thanks ascend to Heaven where we have our own angels - those who were once here by our sides and who have been called away before us.

We two are also angels on earth. We can hope only not to be separated prematurely from each other because we want to be together to finish a few things and until we find our other angels in Heaven.

I have the feeling that, senseless though it seems, this will soon be over. So take heart; "just wait and pray this". We'll get back into our old routine and everything will be O.K. "We'll forget this like a nightmare" and go on with our plans. The handle of the blue soup cup was stuck together by Mrs. May - this fracture will be knit up and I'll be able to run about again.

This whole business has made me even more suspicious than before, that's all. Who knows what good may come of it all?

The entire operation will only last an hour, and then after another two hours I'll be awake again and back with you.

If it should go wrong, however, you'll be the poorer because you'll have lost someone who holds you in awe and loves you so much, more than myself. You are such a saint that I've feared for you - for angels don't belong on earth.

But we'll be back together until we finish what we still have to do.

Amen.

Your Girl in an extremely difficult situation.
The pen does not write any more.

Karl Olga Hospital, Stuttgart
Monday, December 2.1974
12 midnight

I have thought on thee
          -Schubert*

Later, when the effect of the sedative was clearly causing her to make spelling mistakes, she wrote:

Shestavovith [sic]
Katatschurian [sic]
      Ludoslawsky [Poldianer]
      Panderewsky [sic]
J. Nepomuk David
      More advanced than Hindemith
This approximately the order in which I place myself - however, my second movements have always had more weight.

*These are the last words of the first song in Schubert's *Winterreise,* which
 we had enjoyed together so many times.

The operation was to have lasted an hour, ending about ten o'clock. At eleven o'clock the doctor came to tell me she was dead. Taciturnly, he told me that the operation had gone well but as the wound was being sewn up Sonia's heart collapsed. He opened the chest cavity and administered cardiac massage for twenty minutes but to no avail. Stunned and desperate, I listened, but I didn't know what to do.

Sometime later – I don't remember how long I waited – she was brought back into the room, quite unchanged. She looked as if she were sleepling peacefully. With the matron's help we bound up her jaw and put a pillow between it and her chest to close her mouth. When the nurse left I kissed Sonia, fell down beside the bed to ask pardon if I had ever hurt her and commended her soul to God and His angels. My prayers for her recovery having failed, I now wished only not to lose my head.

It took a while before I knew what to do. I found a telephone and called my colleague Dr. Guenther Thiem of the Staatsgalerie, asking if he could provide me with a photographer and a sculptor to make a death mask. While I waited, I went to a florist's and bought orchids the colour of those Sonia had longed for a few short days earlier. Late in the afternoon I selected a plain oak coffin and arranged for its transport to Berlin. Back at the hospital we took Sonia's body to a cool room and I placed the orchids on her breast.

The sculptor, Guenther Weinreuter, arrived at eight. His preparations and the covering of the face with graphite powder were frightening to watch. When the job was over I washed her face and hair and, for lack of anything better, we dressed her in the light-blue pyjamas she had brought to the hospital. Years later, while going through her mother's papers, I found the following note copied in Sonia's hand:

When they bury me,
Let them put between my poor hands
(if cruel nature allows)
These few photos of my children
Now dead and gone.

Maman

In the confusion at the Stuttgart hospital I could not find any of the pictures of her mother, Walter or myself that I could have given Sonia. All I could find was a small leather case of photographs from which she was never separated. I could not bear to part with it, however, so I folded her poor hands and put her publicity brochure and the orchids on her breast. May my dear girl forgive me for not doing better than this. I still reproach myself for it. The next morning I went to the studios of South German Radio and gave Dr. Wienke two recordings of Sonia's music. In the following days he played them and broadcast Sonia's obituary.

The funeral was scheduled for Friday, 6 December, in East Berlin. I accompanied the van with the coffin as it drove silently through the snowy night. As we neared Berlin the landscape of the north German plain grew increasingly familiar and I thought about how often Sonia and I had travelled the same roads in our pre-war Lilli. When we reached the city, the body was taken to East Berlin burial authorities while I went to the home of my friends the Reidemeisters to await the funeral.

Knowing Sonia to have been a person both deeply religious and yet wanting little to do with the Church, I asked the pastor for a very simple service. There were only five mourners: myself, the Reidemeisters, and Ursel and Christoph Hinkelmann. The music was all Sonia's own (as she herself had requested) played on my little Sony cassette recorder. The slow movement of the Duo Concertante for Cello and Piano, as played by Peggie Sampson and Lorne Watson, one of the most beautiful and transcendant things Sonia ever wrote, rang out clearly in the church. The pastor then read those immortal lines from Ecclesiastes: "To every thing there is a season, and a time to every purpose under heaven; A time to be born and a time to die...." He followed this with Albrecht Goes's poem:

Does our worldly heart not feel
if so much power of love dies?
Does a life mean so little;
can it be replaced so quickly?
We do not know,
and call it irreplaceable
what was taken out of our heart
by almighty death.

Paths, repeatedly walked on,
how do you end suddenly in thickets?
Voice, so familiar to us, lonely, are you afraid?

They, whom he took away,
this secret changer,
are they silent in dark sleep?
Do they listen to a distant song?
Perhaps they are
just comfortably leaning on the fence,
still neighbours and friends
to all that goes on here.

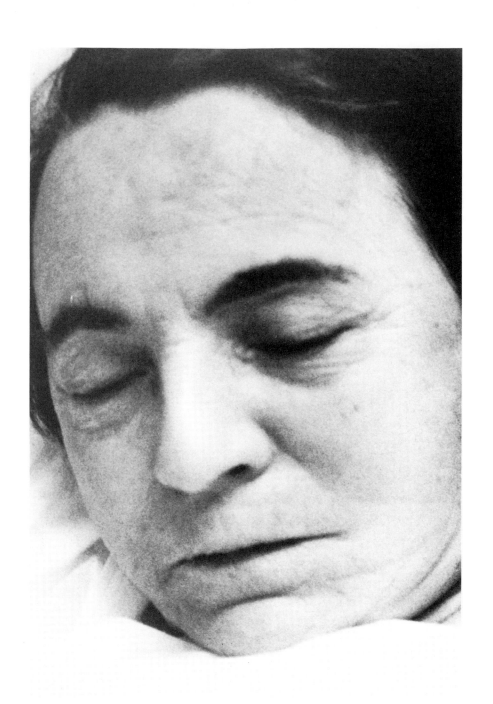

Sonia died on 2 December 1974 during
surgery following an accident on a bus
in Stuttgart, Germany, in which she
broke her hip.

Oh, would that, if we called them
they would come, these blessed relieved
ones.
Oh, let it be, that forever
they will lovingly be on our path.

At the end of the service I played a passage from the second movement of the first string quartet as it had been performed in 1939 by the Silesian Quartet. The coffin was taken into the churchyard on a little wheeled cart. Then came that terrible moment, standing at the graveside, when I saw my beloved's coffin going down into the ground. The parson said a few words and recited the Lord's Prayer. I threw the big wreath of poinsettias into the grave; I can still hear the sound of how it fell with a heavy thump onto the coffin. Then I strewed a handful of dust. And so Sonia lay in her grave with Walter and her mother.

The Legacy of S.C. Eckhardt-Gramatté

Sonia left much behind her. There was, for instance, a significant body of unfinished work and work that had yet to receive its first performance. Found in her estate after her death was her last composition, the Concert Piece for Cello and Orchestra. Tsutsumi had been inspired enough by tapes of the violin caprices which Sonia had played for him at Banff to ask for a work for the cello. She obliged him by beginning the piece in the late summer and early autumn of 1974. They had originally agreed on the seventh caprice but Sonia found it unsuitable for cello solo and so rewrote it for cello and orchestra. Tsutsumi visited Winnipeg in September and suggested a few small changes which were made. The work was completed before we left for Sonia's last trip, but she never lived to hear it played. A trumpet concerto, meant for the Winnipeg trumpeter Ramon Parcells, had been started in 1972 and was resumed two years later. Unfortunately, Sonia did not proceed past the first movement and it remains unfinished in her estate. Another late composition, the seventh piano sonata, remains in embryonic form. I am not certain whether or not Sonia wrote it on a commission from Anton Kuerti, but it does date from the time he was playing her Symphony Concerto and, in her enthusiastic way, she did wish to dedicate something to him out of gratitude. I know that she showed him the beginnings of the piece and she got the impression that he did not like it. Though this may have just been one of her whims, she was hurt and set the work aside.

One of the most interesting of the works Sonia left behind her was the collection, *Pieces From My Childhood*, which dates from the Paris of her sixth to twelfth years. The earliest were improvised on the piano and later dictated to her mother. Many of these were her interpretations of the alphabet, trying to give each letter its own character, though in some cases the letters were a composer's initials. Sonia seems to have composed, or at least begun, two separate alphabets, one for lower and one for upper-case letters, so that some letters were treated twice. In the 1930s she began copying part of the alphabet and I hoped that she would record this work, but she was always too tired or not in the mood for such a project. During her life only the letters A and B were put on tape. Recently, however, the entire collection was put into publishable form by Lorne Watson for Waterloo Publishing and recordings were made with students from the University of Brandon and Manitoba Music Teachers Association playing the pieces. There is also a collection of short character pieces, most with no separate titles and which may be identical to "Something Short." For a time she gave these early pieces opus numbers and seems even to have subdivided them into numbered sections to make them seem more grand. Many of these were destroyed, but some were preserved and reworked and played for me or for intimates over the years. I have already mentioned the completed Concertino for Gamba and Harpsichord, written for Peggie Sampson but not acceptable to her. It was not until nine years after Sonia's death that this piece was premiered.

individualistic way. She was influenced a little by us I guess, if only because we listened to her, but she took over and influenced us, undoubtedly for the better. The natural tendency of a Winnipeg artist, subject to the pressures of his trade, is to compromise, to become all soft with sympathy and fear – and to weaken; but Sonia Eckhardt was honourably without compromise, a vital and vivid figure who was an inspiration to all those who just catch a glimpse of what it means to be faithful to the highest standards of art. For the rest of us, the public of Winnipeg, to whom she gave work after work – well, she believed (with Oscar Wilde) that "art should never try to make itself popular. The public should try to make itself artistic." And some-how she brought it off. Rather than being quelled by provincialism or the philistine prairie squint, she became our most creative citizen….The death of a heroine of music is not a matter for rejoicing exactly, but there is some-thing positive in it when she leaves us at the height of her powers, unimpaired, carrying her gifts and her strength to the grave. And so the next chapter is hers too, if we get the message.

Epilogue: The Search for Sonia's Father

I am not utterly convinced by the story of Sonia's parentage and birth which was related by her mother, Catharina, and which I have set out in the first chapter. The story has its inconsistencies and often raises more questions than answers. Prompted by these anomalies, by discussions with Sonia and by things found among her papers after her death, I embarked on a quest for the truth behind the fables, for the real story of Sonia's father. The search took me from Winnipeg to Moscow, to Paris, to Berlin and the Lake Country of England. Whether I found the truth in the end is a question I leave to the reader to answer.

Sometime between 1906 and 1916 Catharina wrote a book entitled *How and Why Sophie-Carmen Was Born*. It was a conscious attempt at creating a dramatic and romantic mythology around her daughter, the musical prodigy. Catharina's myth-making bent can be seen in her choice of pseudonyms: Catherine Kalwähr or Calvary. The book was printed in St. Petersburg but appeared in a French and a German edition. In this work, Catharina described her tenant, pupil and lover, Xavier, at great length. He was at that time a student, poor but handsome. He rented a room and occasionally played piano duets with her. In the course of this close contact he developed an unmistakable attraction for her, which Catharina says she rebuffed. Though Xavier had originally introduced himself under a pseudonym, being of Jewish descent and afraid of pogroms, he soon revealed that his name was really Nicolas Xavier Friedman. He was of noble stock, but was modest about it; he was born in Graudenz, Germany.

Catharina's older sister Marie was married to a Frenchman, Henri Sandeau, who was teaching in Siberia. When Marie, attractive and pleasant, came to Moscow for an extended visit, she caught Xavier's eye and the two were soon involved in an affair. In time Marie announced that she was pregnant and gave birth to a baby girl, whom she sent to her sister in Moscow. When Catharina received the child, she was so enchanted with it that she decided to declare it her own. She also declared that her estranged husband – from whom she had been separated for some time – was the child's father. She took the matter to court and, with the help of one of the best lawyers in Moscow and the testimony of her cook (who claimed that de Fridman's coachman stayed with her in the kitchen while his master visited Catharina), she convinced the courts to declare de Fridman's paternity official. The child of which she took custody was named Sophie-Blanche.

As far as Catharina was concerned her revenge was incomplete, and when Xavier renewed his suit she found herself falling in love with "this tall handsome child." She agreed to a liaison with the express purpose of conceiving a daughter that she could bring up as a musician. Her purpose was achieved in the birth of Sophie-Carmen. Because of Xavier's Jewish name he felt himself in danger, and when warned by friends in the government of renewed persecution, he told Catharina he would accompany her and the baby to England under the name of Darbitschof. Once in Britain, he secured himself a teaching position at a college in Ambleside, Scotland.

Let us examine some of the improbabilities in this account. Perhaps the most obvious is the almost identical surnames they had. Catharina herself seemed more than a little defensive about this "coincidence." She took pains to describe how many Friedmans she knew, starting with her tailor and wine merchant, her lawyer, a painter and the pianist Ignaz Friedman. The mere fact of having a Jewish-sounding name was scarcely enough to endanger him particularly since Catharina avows that Xavier had papers attesting to his Protestant religious connections. Apparently de Fridman was never subject to any kind of persecution because of his name. Far more likely is Xavier's fear of official action springing out of radical political activites. We know that Catharina's brother was harassed for such activities and exiled to Siberia. The attribution of Jewish blood to Xavier then may have served two purposes: it would have given a plausible cover to his fears and flight, motivated in fact by underground politics, and it would have given Sonia an edge in the music world. Catharina, who was clever and calculating, was not beyond ascribing a partly-Jewish past to her musically talented daughter, knowing the number of Jewish friends and patrons that she had or would encounter.

So far, I have been writing as if the existence of Xavier was undoubted. To be sure, Sonia did not doubt it. She believed that he had once visited her and her mother in Paris, that he was a dark-eyed mathematician, intelligent, violent and energetic. In addition, among Catharina's papers that Sonia preserved, were three photographs, supposedly of him, one of them a double portrait with Catharina. However, when examined, these photographs only increase the suspicions about Xavier. This is because none of the photographs is an original print – in fact the double portrait is a crude fake. It consists of a photograph of two drawings which are glued on the back of a Moscow photographer's base. The inscription on the back reads: "1899 – that's us together – Kabschi-schitzka (a pet-name of Catharina) – we love each other – to my wife, friend – Sascha." Since Sascha is a diminuitive of Alexander and since I am told by Russians that the Russian inscription is clumsy and ungrammatical, the mystery only deepens. The other photographs are also based on a drawing, the original of which I saw in Europe and which, I assume, Sonia must have destroyed when she came to Canada. This strengthens my doubts about the authenticity of the portrait, since Sonia would scarcely have destroyed the only existing drawing of someone she believed to be her father. After examining photographs of Sonia taken around 1915 and comparing them to the image of Xavier, I have finally come to the conclusion that the portrait was in fact one commissioned by Catharina and that it was based on a picture, not of Xavier, but of Sonia! (We will see later, in the case of Sophie-Blanche of whom no real photographs exist, that Catharina was given to the practice of substantiating imaginative characters by displaying pictures of them based on drawings.)

Did Xavier leave any other traces? In my search for Sonia's father, I visited Ambleside in March 1979 to see if eight decades had obliterated all record of a Russian-German professor of languages at the local college. First came my discovery that Catharina had "misplaced" Ambleside. It is, in fact, in northern England, not Scotland. When I journeyed there and inquired about the college, I was referred to a local teacher-training institute for girls which had been founded in the 1890s. I was shown a large folio with the names of all students, but there was no record of the teachers. No one could tell me if there had ever been a teacher of Russian around the turn of the century who had also taught German.

Though I found out little at the college, I was not finished in Ambleside. I interviewed ten elderly locals, some over 90, to see if they had any recollection that might lead to a trace of Xavier, but all to no avail. There was an excellent local-history archive at the library which I visited and, because of Sonia's belief that he had died around the end of the First World War, I also combed the local cemetery in search of a gravestone with Xavier's name on it. In neighbouring Kendal, I did research in the archives of County Hall, to which some records from Ambleside had been transferred. The director of the local museum, Miss Burkett, was a woman whom I had met by accident in Leningrad three years before. Miss Burkett gave me the opportunity to publish an article about my quest and a picture of Xavier in the museum's magazine, *Quarto*, in the hope that someone reading it might be able to provide me with helpful information. I was also interviewed extensively by the local newspaper, *The Westmoreland Gazette*, but neither article yielded any fruitful response. I had no better luck in London, where at the central records repository in St. Catherine's House I examined dozens of folios up to 1920 for a death notice of a Dobre-, Dabre-, Davre-, Dobrechev, Darbitschof or any similar name. Because I could find no trace of Xavier, I concluded either that he had lived in Ambleside under another name or that he had left England and died elsewhere. Perhaps his tempestuous and radical nature took him back to revolutionary Russia. One might be tempted to think that he had never existed at all, but Catharina's descriptions of him seem so real that I believe he must have existed. What I doubt is that he was Sonia's father.

If we have doubts about Xavier, we may have sufficient reason to look elsewhere for a father for Sonia. We may find one behind the story of the child Sophie-Blanche. To back up Catharina's assertions about this child are: Sonia's belief that she once knew Sophie-Blanche, but that she had died young; and a list in Catharina's handwriting in which she compares the development of her three children at various ages with that of Sophie-Blanche. However, one of the most interesting parts of the story that Catharina tells about this love child, which she supposedly took on as her daughter, is the fact that within a very short time, the girl is utterly lost. As in Xavier's case, there *are* pictures which purport to be of the child. In one picture, she is in the arms of Catharina's oldest daughter, Sonja, and in another she poses with a walking stick. But again, as with Xavier, they are photographs of drawings, the originals, or reproductions of which, I have in my possession. Moreover, on the back of one there is an inscription in Catharina's handwriting reading:

"S. Carmen, one year and 7½ months old, in boy's dress, so that she could pass the border." In her book on Sonia's birth, Catharina claimed that Sophie-Blanche and Sophie-Carmen resembled each other "like one drop of water another one." This, of course could explain a portrait of one being labelled with the name of the other. However on a page of the remant of another (apparently earlier) edition of her book is an extremely interesting passage. Handwritten by Catharina, in lilac ink, obviously meant for Sonia, was this inscription: "You know very well, that the story of Sophie-Blanche, which I told you was only to make you younger. I have told you this and asked you to keep the secret, like my mother, who had such confidence in me that... anything she told me would never, never be told to another." If we take this astonishing sentence at face value (always dangerous when dealing with a statement of Catharina's) it means that the entire story of Sophie-Blanche, and thus the Marie-Xavier liaison, is a figment of the mother's imagination.

The reason that Catharina would wish to make Sonia out to be younger seems obvious. It is the same reason Beethoven and Mozart, as children, were presented as younger than their true ages, making their youthful musical talents seem even more prodigious. For her concerts in Paris, Geneva and Berlin, it was certainly to Sonia's advantage that her mother claimed that her child was perhaps two or three years younger than she actually was. However, Sonia's youth was indeed a barrier to her entering the Paris Conservatoire. Here Catharina claims that she had to make Sonia pass as an older child.

If we accept these speculations as fact for a moment, might we not reasonably conclude that the child Sophie-Blanche was really Sophie-Carmen, and that Sonia might then have been born, not in 1899, but in 1897 or even 1896? If this is so, another motive for Catharina's lying about Sonia's age emerges, that is, the possibility that Sonia might really have been the daughter of the hated de Fridman, from whom Catharina was separated in 1895. A passionate woman who despised her spouse might well seek the double satisfaction of ensuring that her daughter was considered legitimate by ascribing the paternity to her husband and still spreading the story of an adulterous affair with a handsome younger man. (I must say here that Nick always maintained that Sonia and he shared the same father as well as the same mother.)

There is circumstantial evidence that would tend to argue for Sonia being older than Catharina portrayed her, for example, a photograph of Sonja, Nick and baby Sophie-Carmen together in Russia. Now, if we believe Catharina's statement that Nick was in England studying in 1899, we must ascribe an earlier date to the picture and thus make Sonia older. Also arguing for an older age is Sonia's memory of attending school in England. She might have been dragged along with older children, her foster parents happy to have her temporarily out of their hair, but we must not discount the obvious – that she actually was of school age. However, there is also circumstantial evidence, and I think it is strong, to support a birthdate of 1899. The stories of her earliest days in Paris, how she tried to gather the light beams of the Eiffel Tower, how she played with cherry pits in the dark closet, and how she screamed in protest over the choice of underwear, seem to be more appropriate to a child of five than one of eight. There is the letter from Vincent d'Indy, her professor at the conservatoire, dated April 1913, in which he calls her *"mon cher infant,"* a form of address perhaps unsuitable for a sixteen-year-old. Finally there is the admission date to the conservatoire of 3 September 1908. It is difficult for me to believe that Catharina would have waited until Sonia was twelve when she could have enrolled her at nine.

Where has this search for Sonia's father taken us? I fear we are no nearer to being certain of his identity now than when we began. There are arguments for and against de Fridman, for and against Xavier. In her book, Catharina spoke affectionately of other men, such as her husband's secretary, and Boiko, her son Nick's private tutor. Her teaching work took her into the households of a number of other aristocratic Russian families. Let me then add another name here and indulge in some interesting speculation. Catharina was for many years employed in the home of Count Leo Tolstoy, and it was a long-held belief of some of Sonia's friends (though not of Sonia herself) that Tolstoy was her father. We know that Catharina was an ardent admirer of Tolstoy, and we are told by the diary of Suzanne Joachim-Chaigneau that in Berlin Catharina kept a portrait of him on the wall above her bed. The person who, according to Sonia, provided the lawyer in the de Fridman paternity case was none other than Tolstoy. We also know that Catharina lived with the Tolstoys at times, not only at their country estate of Jasnaja Poljana, but also in their Moscow residence. In this context I find it suggestive that (as it was pointed out to me when I visited the Tolstoy home) at the end of a long hallway, right across the corridor from the writer's private studio, was the governess's room.

I started my quest for Sonia's father with doubts and now at the end of this book, I have replaced them with different doubts. I can say definitively that the sole person who could have answered this question truthfully was Catharina, and in many respects she seems to have been a woman oblivious to truth. This is not to say that she was a liar or even mentally disturbed. She was a complex, sensitive, well-educated woman, who was deeply affected by the tragedies in her life and, when faced with difficult situations, resorted to imaginative solutions. (To a certain extent Sonia shared this tendency and was prone to embroider details, which in time she sometimes came to believe.) Catharina set out more than eighty years ago to create a mythology around her daughter, a mythology useful to herself and to her child – and in this she succeeded. What else can be said about Sonia than what I said in my first chapter, that the origins of the composer S. C. Eckhardt-Gramatté are shrouded in legend?

Selected Works

ORCHESTRA

Skelettenspiel. 1923. Ms
L'Île. 1923 (Saskatoon 1978). Ms
Prozession Funèbre. 1928. Ms
Weihebild. 1924–35 (Cologne 1935). Ms
Tanzbild. 1924–35. Ms
Gedenkstein. 1932–37. Fragment. Ms
Passacaglia and Fugue. 1937 (Berlin 1937). Ms
Symphony No. 1 in C. 1939–40 (Breslau 1942). CMCentre
Capriccio Concertante. 1941 (Vienna 1942). CMCentre
Concertino for Strings. 1947. String orchestra (Vienna 1948). CMCentre
Molto Sostenuto. 1938–52 (Winnipeg 1977). Ms
Concerto for Orchestra. 1954 (Winnipeg 1954). CMCentre
Symphony No. 2 "Manitoba." 1970 (Winnipeg 1970). CMCentre
Ziganka, 1920. Ballet suite, fragment. Ms
Der Träumende Knabe, 1923. Overture (Hamburg 1923). Ms

VOICE

Four Christmas Songs. 1953–54 (Winnipeg 1977). CMCentre

SOLOIST(S) WITH ORCHESTRA

Piano Concerto No. 1. 1926 (Berlin 1932). CMCentre
Grave Funèbre. 1931 Viola, chamber orchestra (Winnipeg 1977). Ms
Piano Concerto No. 2. 1942–46 (Vienna 1948). CMCentre
Triple Concerto. 1949. Trumpet, clarinet, bassoon, orchestra (Vienna 1950; UE 1952). Ms
Bassoon Concerto. 1950 (Bad Aussee 1950). CMCentre
Markantes Stück. 1925–52. Two pianos, orchestra (Vienna 1952). CMCentre
Concerto for Violin and Orchestra. 1950–51 (Vienna 1954). CMCentre (Walter Schneiderhan)
Piano Concerto No. 3 "Symphony-Concerto." 1967 (Toronto 1968). CMCentre (Kuerti)
Symphony Concerto for Trumpet and Orchestra. 1972–74. One movement. Ms
Konzertstück for Cello and Chamber Orchestra. 1928–74 (Ottawa 1981). Ms (Tsutsumi)

Also arrangements of several Paganini *Caprices* in various combinations. 1928

CHAMBER

Ein Wenig Musik. 1910. Piano trio (Winnipeg 1979). Vieu and Vieu 1912

Paganini Caprices for Violin, 1, 16, 17, 24. 1918 or earlier. With piano accompaniment. Simrock 1922

Lagrima. 1926. Cello, piano (Brandon 1975). Ms

February Suite. 1934. Violin, piano (Leverkusen 1935). CMCentre

String Quartet No. 1. 1938 (Breslau 1939). CMCentre

Quartettsatz. 1942 (Winnipeg 1985).

String Quartet No. 2 "Hainburger." 1943 (Breslau 1943). CMCentre

String Trio No. 1 "Triotino." 1947 (Vienna 1947). CMCentre

String Trio No. 2 "Nicolas Trio" 1947 (Vienna 1949). CMCentre

Duo for Two Violins No. 1. 1944 (Vienna 1944). Ms

Duo for Two Violins No. 2. 1944 (Vienna 1946) Oesterreichischer Bundesverlag 1949

Duo for Viola and Cello. 1944 (Vienna 1944). CMCentre

Duo for Two Cellos. 1944 (Vienna 1947). CMCentre

Wind Quartet. 1946. Flute, clarinet, bassetthorn, bass clarinet (Vienna 1946). CMCentre

"Ruck-Ruck" Sonata. 1947. Clarinet, piano (Vienna 1947). CMCentre

Duo Concertante for Flute and Violin. 1956 (Winnipeg 1957). CMCentre

Duo Concertante for Cello and Piano. 1959 (Saskatoon 1959). CMCentre

Woodwind Quintet. 1963 (Toronto 1963). CMCentre

String Quartet No. 3. 1962 – 64 (Winnipeg 1964). Ber 1978(?)

Nonet. 1966. String quartet, wind quintet (Regina 1967). CMCentre

Piano Trio No. 2. 1967 (Winnipeg 1968). CMCentre

Concertino for Cello and Piano. 1970 (Winnipeg 1984). Ms

Fanfare. 1971. Eight brass (Winnipeg 1971). Ms

WORKS FOR SOLO VIOLIN

Suites for Solo Violin No. 1 and 2. 1922. Simrock 1924

Suite for Solo Violin No. 3 "Mallorca." 1924. Eschig 1925

Concerto for Solo Violin. 1925 (Berlin 1925). Ms

Ten Caprices for Solo Violin. 1924 – 34. Ms

Suite for Solo Violin No. 4 "Pacific." 1968 (Toronto 1970). Ms (Hidy)

WORKS FOR PIANO

Pieces from my Childhood. 1905 – 12. Fourteen alphabet letters. Waterloo 1980

Pieces from my Childhood. 1907 – 14. Fourteen character pieces. Waterloo 1980

Etude de concert. 1910. Mercier 1910

Campanella. 1918 or earlier. Arranged after Paganini-Busoni. Ms

Danse de negre. 1922. Simrock 1924

Sonata No. 1. 1923 (Hamburg 1923). Simrock 1924

Sonata No. 2 "Biscaya." 1923–24. (Barcelona 1925). CMCentre
Kosak. 1924. Ms
Sonata No. 3. 1924–25 (Berlin 1925). CMCentre
Cirque de Village. 1925. Ms
Trepak. 1926. Ms
Sonata No. 4 "Hulele." 1927–31 (Berlin 1932). CMCentre
Six Piano Caprices. 1931–48. Ms
Introduction and Variations on Theme of my Childhood. 1936 (Berlin 1936). Ms
Sonata No. 5 "Klavierstück." 1950 (Vienna 1950). ISCM 1952
Sonata No. 6 "Drei Klavierstücke." 1928–52 (Vienna 1952). CMCentre
Tune for a Child. 1972. Ms
Ten Paedagogical Pieces. 1973. Ms

RECORDINGS

Concerto for Solo Violin (violin, Eckhardt-Gramatté) and Bach *Chaconne* (violin, Eckhardt-Gramatté) ODEON Berlin 1936. Both newly edited on "Masters of the Bow" 31, Discopaedia, Toronto, 1980.
Duo Concertante for Cello and Piano and *Piano Sonata No. 6* (cello, Peggie Sampson; piano, Deidre Irons) RCA Victor CC/CCS–108, 1967.
Symphony Concerto for Piano and Orchestra (Alexander Brott, Anton Kuerti) RCA Victor LSC-3175, 1967-   .
Triple Concerto (National Orchestra, Mario Bernardi) CBC SM 272, 1977.
EGre Plays EGre (four records, a documentary of the composer as violinist and pianist, twenty-four works), Discopaedia, Toronto 1981.
10 Caprices for Violin Solo (Francis Chaplin) "Masters of the Bow" Discopaedia, Toronto 1985.
Anthology of Canadian Music 21 (five records, narrator Lorne Watson) Radio Canada International, Montreal, 1985.
Concertino for Cello and Piano Dorothy Bishop, Delores Kaehey, in preparation). *"Fanfare" in Composers Brass Group,* Music Gallery Edition, Toronto 1981 –

Also, S.C. Eckhardt-Gramatté, *Selected Works*, 23 volumes (one more in preparation), published by the estate of S.C. Eckhardt-Gramatté.

Note: This list (apart from the section on recordings) was first published in the *Encyclopedia of Music in Canada* (University of Toronto Press, 1981), p. 294. It has been updated and corrected by the author.

Index

The text of this book
was photoset by
B/W Type Service Ltd.
in Helvetica
and has been printed
by D. W. Friesen & Sons Ltd.
in Altona, Manitoba
Canada

Designed by Norman Schmidt

400 10/23

For Denise, - Spark Joy! -

the
J☘Y
of
CANNABIS

75 Ways to Amplify Your Life Through the Science and Magic of Cannabis

MELANIE ABRAMS • LARRY SMITH

sourcebooks

Published by Sourcebooks
P.O. Box 4410, Naperville, Illinois 60567-4410
(630) 961-3900
sourcebooks.com

Library of Congress Cataloging-in-Publication Data

Names: Abrams, Melanie, author. | Smith, Larry, 1968- author.
Title: The joy of cannabis : 75 ways to amplify your life through the
   science and magic of cannabis / Melanie Abrams, Larry Smith.
Description: Naperville, Illinois : Sourcebooks, 2022. | Includes
   bibliographical references and index.
Identifiers: LCCN 2021052666 (print) | LCCN 2021052667 (ebook) |
Subjects: LCSH: Marijuana--Psychological aspects | Marijuana--Physiological
   effect. | Marijuana--Therapeutic use | Cannabis--Psychological aspects |
   Cannabis--Physiological effect. | Cannabis--Therapeutic use
Classification: LCC BF209.C3 A27 2022 (print) | LCC BF209.C3 (ebook) |
   DDC 394.1/4--dc23/eng/20211104
LC record available at https://lccn.loc.gov/2021052666
LC ebook record available at https://lccn.loc.gov/2021052667

Printed and bound in Thailand.
IG 10 9 8 7 6 5 4 3 2 1

CONTENTS

INTRODUCTION

FLOWER POWER

What if there was a safe and (increasingly) legal substance that could make you happier, more productive, and more creative? What if we told you this substance was not actually a substance but a flower, one with all-natural powers that makes music even more beautiful, food even more delicious, and sex even sexier? This magical flower—one that is both two thousand years old and also in the midst of a renaissance—is (drum roll, please) *cannabis*. And in this book, we're going to tell you where it's from, where it's going, and how you can use it to amplify almost any part of your life.

We are, we bet, like many of you, two of the more than 200 million people in the world who use cannabis. And we are fortunate enough to live in one of the many states where cannabis is fully legal (for adult medicinal and recreational use). With each passing year, more and more states are joining the ranks of those that have legalized cannabis for medical and/or recreational use. More cannabis means more pleasure, more connection, and more joy to the world.

Melanie has enjoyed the magical flower since the day it was legalized (or *maybe* a few days before) and is a Type A personality who could not be more grateful for an industry that has fine-tuned strains, strengths, and delivery systems, all designed to perfect her happy high. Larry was a casual college smoker who initially took a detour after one too many strong pot brownies. Now he navigates a dispensary with appreciation and expertise and has fallen back in love with cannabis and its many pleasures (and after years of insomnia, he's never slept better).

Like many of you, we are fast-moving, high-achieving modern weed users. Sure, we love a beer or a glass of wine at the end of the day, but we prefer THC. Not only does cannabis deliver a magical mood, but flower in all its forms is better for our bodies and our minds. With weed, there are no hangovers, no damage to the vital organs, no drunk dialing the ex. It's a substance that heals, not hurts—just ask the millions of people who use cannabis to treat everything from cancer to epilepsy to migraines. It's part of the mainstream now, and it's here to stay. It's here to be consumed safely, thoughtfully, and—it goes without saying—legally. Check your state's laws...now check again. The legal cannabis train is moving fast and could be stopping in your state before you know it.

In the third decade of the third millennium, the stigma of being a "slacker stoner" is gone. This book is for the new breed of cannabis appreciators: smart and functional adults who enjoy an entertaining inebriant and are rapidly realizing its

> **Cannabis not only delivers a magical mood, but flower in all its forms is better for our minds and our bodies.**

wide array of benefits. It's for your friend who prefers spending twenty dollars for a week's worth of nightly tokes rather than fifty dollars on a single night at a bar. It's for the mom or dad who was glad to partake when their pals passed the pipe and is now ready to have their own stash. It's for the millennial as comfortable announcing their affection for a good strain as a good pour of Old Forester. It's for the millions of people who already know—or are quickly finding out—all the things cannabis can do for their creativity and productivity, their heads and hearts.

In the pages that follow, we identify six key pillars of life and discuss how cannabis can amplify each. By expanding the mind, moving the body, unlocking creativity, boosting productivity, fortifying meaningful connections, and sparking joy, you'll soon see how life can be higher and happier through the science and magic of cannabis. For some, these ideas will further awaken their love for an elixir they're already familiar with. For others, this in-depth look into all things cannabis will pique their curiosity and inspire them to be part of the golden age of this ancient flower.

These ideas aren't just about making the mundane miraculous, although

0

The number of reported cannabis deaths in history. You would have to consume 1,000 pounds of cannabis in an hour for it to kill you, which you can't, and so it won't.

you'll find some of that (trust us when we say lacing up your running shoes will never be the same). Rather, they are about letting cannabis enhance your life. We're pretty sure you know that cannabis gives you access to new ways of seeing, thinking, and doing, but just lighting up doesn't always get you there. And that is the reason we wrote this book. Think of us as your guides to the activities that pair best with cannabis's ability to make you a better you and life's rich pageant a little richer.

How do we know so much? We took one for the team and did the research. We completed the field studies, sourced the science, and curated a set of seventy-five life-enhancing experiences, augmenting them with just the right strain and delivery system. The activities make the most of our sensory touchstones: food, music, sex, nature, and more. But there are also the experiences we found under the radar—the surprising, the strange, the profound, the silly, the awe-inspiring, the soothing, the significant.

Each of our six sections begins with an introduction that takes a deep dive, relaying the science and stats with, we hope, comforting clarity. We've also enlisted a number of bold thinkers to share their expertise on how getting high can rekindle and enhance everything from gardening to yoga to rediscovering your inner child (sometimes with an actual child).

This book is designed to be picked up and opened to any section, enjoyed high or not, left on your bedside table or passed around with a pre-roll on a beach blanket. If you're newer to cannabis, start with our "Toolkit" (page 6) and get a quick lay of the land, from the many delivery systems you can choose from to what to know before your first trip to a cannabis dispensary.

As cannabis becomes ever more optimized, safe, and legal, millions of new users are discovering its benefits. To you, we say: Welcome. We are delighted to be your cannabis concierges. For readers who've been enjoying herb for years, we know what you're thinking: How can the joy of cannabis be contained in just one book? We feel you on that, friends. And still, like so many of life's pleasures, all things in moderation.

Cannabis has changed our lives. We hope it changes yours.

—Melanie Abrams and Larry Smith,
Oakland, California

TOOLKIT

"Cannabis isn't harmful, but prohibition is. Cannabis can provide food, fuel, fiber, medicine, and a spiritual connection. There are so many benefits from this one plant: for health and wellness, for extended patience, for waking up creativity, for enhancing the sounds of music, the taste of food, or the touch of your lover. Cannabis turns an argument into a dialogue, a walk in the park into a spiritual experience."

STEVE DEANGELO,

CALLED THE "FATHER OF THE LEGAL CANNABIS INDUSTRY"
AND FOUNDER OF HARBORSIDE HEALTH CENTER, ONE OF THE
WORLD'S LARGEST MEDICAL-CANNABIS DISPENSARIES

WHAT IT IS

A FLOWER BY ANY OTHER NAME

Weed, Pot, Marijuana, Reefer, Mary Jane, Kush, Ganja, Grass, Bud, Herb, Dank, Dope, Skunk, Flower, the Green, the Goods, the Devil's Lettuce, Laughing Grass, Chronic, Shrek's Pubes

You can smoke it, you can vape it, you can eat it, but what exactly *is* it? That fragrant green flower we all know and love is known by many names, but the botanists (and all the cool kids) know it by *cannabis,* its genus classification. If you paid attention in science, you'll remember that below the genus classification is the species, and cannabis has (surprise!) three of those. You're probably familiar with *sativas* and *indicas,* but have you heard of *Cannabis ruderalis*? Probably not, and that's because it has a super low THC concentration. In other words, it won't get you high. So we're thinking you're more interested in those other species (also called strains). But first we need to break some unsettling news to

CANNABIS: A Brief History of High Times

2737 BC: Oldest reported reference to the cannabis plant. *Shen-nung Pen Ts'ao Ching*, a Chinese pharmacy book, notes cannabis has over 100 medical uses, including treating gout, malaria, and rheumatism.

500 BC: Phytochemical analysis indicates that cannabis plants were burned in wooden braziers during mortuary ceremonies at the Jirzankal Cemetery in the eastern Pamirs region of Central Asia.

7

you: there's a good chance everything you know about the differences between sativas and indicas is a lie. Take a minute. We understand.

Indicas vs. Sativas vs. Hybrids

Most of us have been told that you choose an indica for a relaxing full-body high, a sativa for an energizing cerebral high, and a hybrid for something in the middle. It's not that this may *never* have been true, but as John McPartland noted in his study published in *Botany and Biotechnology,* "distinguishing between 'sativa' and 'indica' has become nearly impossible because of extensive cross-breeding in the past forty years," so what you think is a couch-lock-inducing indica may actually be a couch-lock-inducing sativa.

Whether we're talking about an indica or a sativa, we're still only beginning to understand how cannabis affects the body. Blame the U.S. federal government, which classifies cannabis as a Schedule I drug, a product with "no currently accepted medical use and a high potential for abuse." No medical use equals strict restrictions on clinical trials; few clinical trials equals not a whole lot of info on how cannabis works in our bodies. As such, the importance of cannabis's entire

• **480 BC:** Classical Greek historian Herodotus reports that the Scythian people inhale hemp-seed smoke vapor for enjoyment and use in rituals. Much to the Scythians' disappointment, Cheetos will not be invented for another 2,400 years.

• **1200s:** Cannabis is introduced to the Arab world and consumed as an edible before the era of smoking begins.

chemical makeup is just starting to make itself known. So while sativas grow tall and thin and indicas grow short and stout, it's most likely a strain's chemical profile—the cannabinoids and terpenes—that determines how it affects you, not its physical features.

Still, the force is strong in anecdotal evidence, and our ongoing personal research still finds us preferring cannabis labeled a sativa to an indica. Our advice: try to hold both contradictory truths at the same time as you look for your favorite cannabis product. Cognitive dissonance, used judiciously, is good for something.

1300s: Soudoun Sheikouni, the emir of Joneima in Arabia, prohibits cannabis use in what is likely the earliest recorded banning of the plant.

1583: King Henry VIII issues a proclamation for farmers to grow cannabis.

Cannabinoids

Cannabinoids are the chemical compounds found in cannabis that are responsible for helping with pain, nausea, anxiety, inflammation, and that blissed-out euphoria scientifically defined as "being high." Cannabinoids work their magic by imitating *endocannabinoids*—chemical compounds that our bodies naturally produce. We'll explain that magical process in a minute, but first let us introduce you to three of the most popular cannabinoids found in cannabis: THCA, CBDA, CBNA.

You may be wondering what those pesky As are doing at the end of your favorite cannabinoids. They stand for "acid" and they're why, if you chowed down on a bunch of flowers, stems, and leaves, you might have found a new way to get your greens, but you wouldn't feel much of an effect. That's because when these cannabinoids are exposed to heat (a process called *decarboxylation*), they lose the A part of their compound, and it's these new compounds that generate most of the benefits of this magical plant. And what are those benefits? We're glad you asked. So glad that we wrote a whole book about them, but for now, here's your primer on the current stars of the show. But remember, despite the fact that researchers have *identified* over one hundred cannabinoids, it doesn't

1607: Colonizers write about indigenous communities using "hempe" in Powhatan village, now Richmond, VA.

1894: The British government completes a research report on cannabis in India, finding that "moderate use practically produces no ill effects."

mean they've studied them. For all we know, we'll be singing the praises of CBC in the next edition of this book.

▶ **THC**, or *tetrahydrocannabinol*, or its full name when it's in trouble, *delta-9-tetrahydrocannabinol*, is the chemical responsible for most of cannabis's psychoactive effects (elation, relaxation, laughter, slowed perception of time) and some of the less desirable effects (dry mouth, red-eye, munchies).

▶ **CBD**, or *cannabidiol*, the second most abundant cannabinoid found in cannabis, is non-psychoactive and has been shown to be useful in treating insomnia, anxiety, chronic pain, and epilepsy. But like all things cannabis, researchers are only starting to investigate the what, how, and why of CBD, so watch this space!

▶ **CBN**, or *cannabinol*, is the new kid on the block and the cannabinoid created when THC ages (so dig out that old dime bag in the back of your sock drawer). Like CBD, it won't get you high, but researchers are looking at ways it acts as an antibiotic, neuroprotectant, and anti-inflammatory.

1906: First restrictions of sale of cannabis in Washington, DC.

1930: Harry Anslinger becomes first commissioner of the Treasury Department's newly formed United States Federal Bureau of Narcotics and announces a "War on Drugs," primarily aimed at Black and brown communities.

Terpene Medical Benefits

NAME	FOUND IN	EFFECTS	AROMA	STRAINS
MYRCENE	Mangos Lemongrass Hops Basil	Anti-inflammatory Sedative Muscle relaxant Pain relief	Musky Herbal Somewhat citrusy	Chemdawg Grape Stomper Fire Alien Kush Agent Orange
A-PINENE	Pine needles Rosemary Dill Parsley	Boosts energy Improves focus Bronchodilator Improves memory	Pine Fresh mountain air Slightly woody	Vanilla Kush Cookie Cross 9lb Hammer Lavender
CARYOPHYLLENE	Clove Black pepper Cinnamon Oregano	Pain relief Anti-depressant Anti-inflammatory Anti-anxiety	Spicy Woody Pepper	Gorilla Glue #4 Tangerine Dream Sage N Sour Pineapple Express
LIMONENE	Lemons Limes Oranges Grapefruits	Improves mood Anti-anxiety Anti-depressant Relieves nausea	Citrus Lemon Orange	Girl Scout Cookies Pre-98 Bubba Kush Tangerine Dream Green Crack
HUMULENE	Hops Sage Ginger Ginseng	Anti-inflammatory Appetite suppressant Pain relief Anti-tumor	Woody Earthy Herbal Spicy	Liberty Haze Gorilla Glue #4 Green Crack Sage N Sour
LINALOOL	Coriander Jasmine Lavender Thyme	Anti-anxiety Sedative Pain relief Anti-bacterial	Floral Sugar Citrus	Bubble Gum 9lb Hammer Sour Diesel Locomotion

▶ **DELTA-8 THC**, or *Delta-8-Tetrahydrocannabinol*, is often called "cannabis light." On a molecular level, Delta-8 and Delta-9 (what most of us refer to as simply "THC") are nearly identical, but they're just different enough so that Delta-8 has a much mellower psychotropic effect. Thanks to a loophole in the 2018 farm bill, Delta-8 is unregulated at the federal level, an omission that makes it legal to ship Delta-8 across the United States.

Terpenes

Terpenes are the oils that give cannabis (and other plants) its specific smell and taste. That's why your Harlequin smells like a pine tree, your Do Si Dos like a lemon, and your Dutch Treat like pepper and cloves. But terpenes don't exist just so your mom can say, "Does anyone smell a skunk?" They protect plants against danger (Deer! Slugs! Global warming!), and they help produce the effects that, in the past, the cannabinoids have taken all the credit for. But all that's changing as researchers are finding that the terpenes are just as important for getting you the effect you're after. Meaning, if you find relaxation difficult, find a strain high

• **1936:** *Reefer Madness*, a racist anti-cannabis propaganda film with dialogue such as, "Marijuana smoking by white women makes them want to seek sexual relations with Negroes, entertainers, and others," sets the safe and legal cannabis movement back decades.

• **1937:** The Marijuana Tax Act prohibits production of hemp, in addition to cannabis, in the U.S., leading Dr. William Woodward, counsel for the American Medical Association, to announce, "That was a major mistake."

in linalool, also found in lavender, which is why those calming eye pillows smell so good. Can't focus? Limonene and its citrusy scent improve focus and decrease stress. Follow your nose to the right strain, or use our chart (and your helpful budtender, the fancy name for the cannabis expert at your local dispensary) to find the right profile for what you're after.

The Entourage Effect

In ye olden days, we thought cannabis's superpowers were fueled exclusively by the mighty cannabinoid, THC. (Raise your hand if you were today years old when you realized this wasn't true.) And although THC may be the workhorse of cannabis, it doesn't act alone. In 1998, professors Raphael Mechoulam and Shimon Ben-Shabat introduced us to the *entourage effect*—the synergy that takes place when THC, the other cannabinoids, and terpenes work together to get you both high and healthy. You may have also heard this referred to as "whole-plant medicine" or the notion that you need all the compounds in cannabis to deliver its full benefits. Sure, THC is the cannabinoid that gives us those feel-good happy times, but think of the other cannabinoids and terpenes as the folks that help

• **1943:** The U.S. government promotes production of hemp in order to produce cloth and other products for soldiers in WWII. *Hemp for Victory*, a promotional film, is released.

• **1944:** The LaGuardia Report states that contrary to earlier research and propaganda, use of cannabis does not induce violence, insanity, or sex crimes and is not a "gateway" drug that leads to addiction or other drug use.

THC be its most effective self. There's still a lot of discussion over how important the entourage effect is (which is why you shouldn't necessarily discount that pure THC edible), but it's worth keeping in mind when you're figuring out what strain or tincture works best for you.

Strains

Cannabinoids, terpenes, entourage effect. *Damn, can't I just get high?* Yes, but first answer these two questions so we can get you where you want to go: (1) What's my preferred delivery system? (2) What strains work best for my body? We'll help with the former in a moment, but for the latter, we're here to instruct. The good news is that once you find your preferred strain, you're golden. The bad news is it might take some time to get there. Remember, you don't want to walk into a dispensary and open up with, "Give me your best indica." First it's a gosh-darn mess of inbreeding out there, so who knows what you're getting. Second, you don't judge a book by its cover, so why pick a strain based on its height and leaf shape?

1948: Cheetos are invented.

1951 & 1956: The Boggs Act (1951) and President Eisenhower's Narcotics Act (1956) impose mandatory minimum sentences, making it possible for low-level drug possession, including cannabis possession, to result in prison terms of more than twenty years.

Instead, ask about strains that give you the effects you're after. If you tell your budtender you hate sativas because they make you anxious, they might hand you a high THC indica. In reality, it's the high THC that's making you think the walls have eyes, not whether it's a sativa or indica. Instead ask for something that's great for dancing but won't leave your mind racing. You might end up loving the low THC, high CBD "sativa" they suggest.

A last word on strains. The truth is, anyone can slap an OG Kush label on their product and call it a day, and while we like to think the cannabis community is here to help, the reality is that there's not a whole lot of regulation out there yet. One farm's Purple Haze may have a 15 percent THC content, while another's may have a 20 percent THC content, which is why you'll not only want to pay attention to strain but the farm it's grown on. But trust us, once you find your equivalent of our Durban Poison (preferably from UpNorth), your world will never be the same.

• **1964:** Bob Dylan introduces the Beatles to cannabis after mistaking their "I Want to Hold Your Hand" song lyrics "I can't hide" for "I get high."

• **1970:** Bill Murray, on the way back to Denver to resume his premed studies at Regis College, is busted at Chicago's O'Hare airport with two pounds of weed. He soon drops out of college and turns his attention to comedy.

HOW IT WORKS

Who's to say that cannabis isn't simply a magical enchanted plant that, upon entering the body, turns us into blissed-out beings who delight in each other and the world around us? Science, that's who. In the following six sections, we'll explain the science behind how cannabis helps us be more productive, creative, connected, and joyful. And in order to get to the specifics, we need to start at the very beginning with how and why cannabis works in our bodies. And that is due entirely to the endocannabinoid system.

The Endocannabinoid System

Get ready to have your *mind blown*. Right now, within your very body, exists a molecular system that works so perfectly with the chemical makeup of cannabis that it was named AFTER CANNABIS. In 1988, two scientists at the St. Louis University School of Medicine were researching how THC affected the brain when they discovered receptors that were activated by cannabinoids. Voilà, cannabinoid receptors were christened, specifically CB1 (cannabinoid receptor 1) and CB2 (cannabinoid receptor 2). CB1 receptors, which occur in other parts of the

1971: President Nixon signs the Controlled Substances Act into law, establishing the current U.S. federal drug policy. That same year, the first Hash Bash, a celebration of cannabis in the form of civil disobedience (that is, openly using cannabis), takes place at the University of Michigan in Ann Arbor.

1978: Cheech and Chong release *Up in Smoke*, and the cinematic cannabis canon is born.

body but are most abundant in the brain, are the lock to THC's key. When THC jiggles its way in there, we get a heavenly high. CB2 receptors are mostly found in immune cells and also have an important job to do: they help with immune system regulation.

Our cannabinoid receptors aren't just sitting around waiting until it's 4:20. It turns out that our bodies produce natural cannabinoids, called endocannabinoids ("endo" meaning "within," as in within the body), that bind to and activate cannabinoid receptors, just like cannabis. That's right, your body is producing cannabis-like compounds right at this very moment. Buuuut...they're not going to get you high, or at least not in the same way. Still, they have their own very important work to do, and they are vital to understanding the science behind the magic of cannabis. CB1 receptors, you may recall, are the lock to THC's key. Guess what other keys fit in that lock—those naturally occurring endocannabinoids. When they bind to CB1 and CB2, they help relieve pain, reduce inflammation, affect mood, shrink tumors, and more.

There are two major endocannabinoids, *anandamide* and *2-AG*, but best in show goes to anandamide. Anandamide, the name of which is derived from

1984: Ronald Reagan signs the Comprehensive Crime Control Act, which expands cannabis possession penalties and establishes federal mandatory minimum sentences.

March 29, 1992: Bill Clinton tells *Time* magazine he smoked cannabis, "but I didn't inhale."

the Sanskrit word *ananda*, which translates to "joy," is sometimes called "the bliss molecule." That's because although anandamide has many jobs (regulating ovulation, managing pain, stimulating appetite), it's best known for enhancing mood and diminishing fear and anxiety. Think of it as the neurochemical that helps keep the good vibes rolling.

But if anandamide is so good at keeping you feeling groovy, why aren't we constantly high? One reason is that although anandamide and THC both bind to CB1 receptors, they don't have the same effects. Anandamide may *help* with mood, but it's not going to get you that omgsogood feeling that THC will. Another reason has to do with the third component of the endocannabinoid system: enzymes. Enzymes break down the endocannabinoids quickly after they do their job, so there's no time for us to savor a high. On the other hand, strongman THC resists the enzymes and sticks around a lot longer.

So yes, the endocannabinoid system is there to get you feeling alright, alright, but it has an even bigger role: to keep your body in a state of homeostasis, or balance. Our bodies don't want our blood sugar to be too high or too low or our temperature to be too cold or too hot (just like suspected stoner Goldilocks). The

1993: Matthew McConaughey says his signature phrase "Alright, alright, alright" in stoner movie classic *Dazed and Confused*.

1994: The San Francisco Cannabis Buyers Club, the first legal dispensary in the United States, opens as a way to dispense cannabis to patients with HIV/AIDS.

endocannabinoid system helps regulate all this so our bodies maintain optimal performance. This is also the reason researchers are so interested in how THC, CBD, CBN, and the rest of the cannabinoids work within the endocannabinoid system. If endocannabinoids help keep our bodies healthy, it stands to reason that plant cannabinoids can do the same. And they do! We'll tell you about some of those ways in the six sections that follow, even as we're still in the early days of discovering the science behind the magic, so stay tuned.

Dopamine and Serotonin

But what about dopamine and serotonin? Doesn't cannabis trigger these feel-good hormones, thus making us...feel good? Yes. And no. For a long time, scientists thought this was the case because drugs like cocaine and amphetamines do, in fact, trigger a flood of dopamine and serotonin, but not so with cannabis. In fact, the most recent research shows that although cannabis consumption does produce an increase in dopamine and serotonin, it's not enough to get us blissed out. For that, we need the endocannabinoid system. Need more proof it's those CB1 receptors that are doing the good work? Scientists found that when

1996: California is the first U.S. state to legalize medical cannabis, defying federal law.

2001: Canada is the first country to systematically regulate medical cannabis.

cannabis was smoked by people who had their CB1 receptors blocked, those folks didn't get high. Too bad for them, but go science!

HOW YOU DO IT

Regular cannabis users reading this have probably convinced themselves they know exactly how to consume cannabis. We, dear reader, were once like you. And sure, one of us still prefers to go old school and smoke a bowl, while the other fancies an edible when given the choice. But we have learned that the cannabis world is full of wonders, and we encourage you to experiment. You might surprise yourself and find a new favorite way to imbibe.

Inhalation

Inhaling cannabis, whether through smoke or vapor, is going to be the fastest way to get you high. This is because the cannabinoids enter the body through the lungs and are passed along directly into the bloodstream, giving you almost instant effects. To smoke your cannabis, you do what comes naturally: light your flower on fire and inhale your cannabinoids. Vaporizing, or vaping, acts in a

2006: Austin-based music writer Andy Langer gets high with Willie Nelson and Snoop Dogg in the same week. See website joyofcannabis.org for the true story from Langer.

2006: Harborside Health Center, a recreational and medical cannabis dispensary, opens and serves over 50,000 registered patients in its first year.

similar way, but rather than burning your weed, you're steadily heating it to a temperature that is high enough to extract the cannabinoids via mostly odorless vapor. You can pretty much smoke and vaporize all forms of cannabis, but with all those choices out there, it can get confusing. Here's a quick primer on how to choose what you inhale and how you inhale it.

The Plant

▶ Flower is...you guessed it...the flower of the cannabis plant. If you're buying in a dispensary, it comes dried and cured and ready for incineration.

▶ Kief is an accumulation of trichomes, or resin glands, sifted from flower (and it's what makes your bud sticky). It's the most potent part of the cannabis plant with the highest amount of THC. Collect your own by using a three-chamber grinder. When you grind your flower, the kief crystals fall through a screen and collect in the bottom compartment. We recommend sprinkling

2009: Michael Phelps is suspended from all competition for three months and loses an endorsement deal from Kellogg's for a photo of him smoking from a bong.

2010: According to the United Nations' World Drug Report, cannabis is "the world's most widely produced, trafficked, and consumed drug."

it on a bowl or peppering in a joint, but use a light touch. That stuff packs a punch much stronger than the flower it came from.

Solvent-Based Extracts

▶ Concentrates or BHO (butane hash oil) are concentrates made using pressurized butane to extract THC and other cannabinoids. We like BHOs because the extraction process preserves the cannabinoids and terpenes and leaves you with a high THC product that is marketed by consistency: wax, shatter, badder, crumble, etc.

▶ CO_2 extracts use carbon dioxide to extract THC and other cannabinoids. Most vape cartridges are filled with CO_2 extracts. If you want pure THC (or CBD) without the terpenes and other plant matter, you can opt for a distillate, a form of a CO_2 extract, which is virtually tasteless and often used in edibles.

2012: Colorado and Washington legalize recreational use of cannabis, the first two American states to do so.

2013: Uruguay's president legalizes recreational cannabis and makes Uruguay the first country in the modern era to allow legal cannabis use.

LET'S GET ROLLING

Joint: Cannabis rolled up inside a rolling paper. (See "Pass the Dutchie on the Left-Hand Side" on page 149 for how to roll your own.)

Spliff: A mix of cannabis and tobacco rolled up in a rolling paper.

Blunt: Cannabis on the inside, a cigar or blunt wrapper (made of tobacco) on the outside.

Roach: The remains of a joint, spliff, or blunt after most of it has been smoked. Usually smoked with a roach clip to keep your fingers from being burned (and for maximum '70s nostalgia).

Bong: Otherwise known as a water pipe. Fire up a bowl, and then inhale the smoke that's been filtered and cooled by the water in the reservoir. The water may filter out some particulate, but don't believe the hype about it being much healthier than other smoking devices. Sorry, dudes.

Dab rig: A pipe designed for vaporizing cannabis concentrates. Similar to a bong, a dab rig filters concentrate vapor through water, but you'll need a special rig to do it because dab rigs require a "nail" (made of glass, ceramic, or titanium) to hold the dab or concentrate. You'll also need a way to heat your nail enough to vaporize your dab. A lighter won't do it, but a blow torch will. (Don't worry. They come in compact sizes, and you can also use it to brown your crème brûlée!)

Joint

Cannabis

Rolling paper

Spliff

Tobacco

Cannabis

Rolling paper

Bong

Blunt

Cannabis

Tobacco paper

Dab Rig

Roach

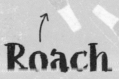

Solventless Extracts

▶ Hashish, or hash for short, is derived from kief and is harvested in one of three ways: (1) by hand (literally rubbing the kief between your hands until they're brown and sticky with resin), (2) by mechanically beating the whole plant, often in a rotating tumbler, and removing the resin, or (3) by plunging the plant into icy water and then using small sieves to remove the resin (this is often called bubble hash). Hash is then pressed into cakes using sheer force and heat. Just like kief itself, hash extracts the most potent part of the plant for some hiiiiigh THC times.

▶ Rosin combines heat and pressure to squeeze the resin from flower, hash, or kief and turn it into a sap-like consistency. Rosin is similar to BHO concentrates but without the solvents.

2014: The Justice Department announces a policy to allow Indigenous tribes to use and sell cannabis on reservations.

2016: *High Maintenance*, starring Ben Sinclair as everyone's favorite weed dealer, gets picked up by HBO.

Oral

Back in the old days, there was no dropping into a dispensary to pick up some perfectly dosed edibles. You had to make your own. Don't get us wrong, we're fans of at-home cooking with cannabis (see "Cannabis Cuisine" on page 172). It's fun. It's cheap. And you can infuse anything from the classic brownie to the ambitious lobster thermidor. But for convenience and super precise dosing, the options are abundant—gummies, popcorn, ice cream, energy drinks...pizza sauce! But before you go to your local dispensary with a grocery list, here's the rundown on how edibles work and how to use them.

There are a bunch of benefits to eating your weed: you're not inhaling anything into your lungs, you know how much THC you're consuming, it's easy and discreet, and the effects last longer. The downside is you're not always the most reliable predictor of your own high journey, so it's easy to eat just a liiiiittle more when you're not feeling the effects. And this can result in what we'll politely call "overmedicating."

When you consume an edible, THC is absorbed through the digestive system and metabolized by the liver, which converts it to *11-hydroxy-THC*. This slightly

2018: Bob Marley's son, Damian Marley, purchases a 77,000-square-foot California prison and turns it into a cannabis grow space to cultivate medical cannabis for state dispensaries.

December 3, 2020: The U.S. House of Representatives votes to decriminalize cannabis at the federal level.

different compound is particularly good at crossing the blood-brain barrier and often results in a more intense high, which may take hours to fully set in. Add in the fact that an edible high typically lasts longer than an inhaled high (four to six hours on average compared to around two hours for inhaling), and you can see why it might be easy to overconsume and then be one very unhappy camper. While overdoing it isn't usually dangerous (and has never been fatal), it can be uncomfortable, which is why you'll see this advice repeated a number of times throughout the book: start low and go slow.

The following sections provide some recommendations for easing your way into edibles, but remember everybody (and every body) interacts with cannabis a bit differently, so wait at least four hours before you eat more. You can always increase your dosage the next time. The other reason to go slow is that despite the fact that edibles are labeled with dosage information, oversight on manufacturing is still not totally reliable, so it's possible that a product has more (or less) THC than stated.

March 2021: Lawmakers in Mexico approve a bill to legalize recreational marijuana.

What's Next: Who decides the future of cannabis? Researchers, lawmakers, and you. Here's hoping and working toward a safe, legal, and equitably lit world.

KNOW YOUR DOSE

Edibles are usually packaged with information on both the total milligrams of THC per package and per serving. Make sure you read carefully so you get your dosing right.

Beginner/Low Tolerance: 1–5 mg THC

Intermediate/Mid Tolerance: 5–20 mg THC

Advanced/High Tolerance: 20+ mg THC

Topical and Transdermal

You can smoke it, you can eat it, you can...apply it? Yes! But also no. If you're looking to get high, a topical isn't going to cut it. Lotions, oils, lubes, and balms are all intended to have an effect at the application site, which makes them great for soothing skin but not the best delivery system if you're looking for full body/brain effects. This is because when THC is absorbed by the skin, cannabis molecules linger in fat cells and aren't absorbed by the bloodstream.

Transdermal products, on the other hand, are designed to penetrate the skin and work their way into your bloodstream. Transdermal patches and gels are made to release THC over time and at a controlled rate, so effects are more like those you'd get from an edible. In other words, don't go applying patches all over your body because the first one "isn't working."

GLAD YOU ASKED

There are no bad questions, said every teacher ever, and possibly Confucius. Here are some of the questions we get asked most frequently, with answers that will make for great fodder at your next dinner party.

I've never been to a dispensary, and I'm a little intimidated. Any tips?
Even seasoned cannabis users can be overwhelmed by their first trip to a dispensary, a sensation brilliantly depicted in *The Simpsons* episode in which Marge gets a job at an upscale dispensary. (Season 31, episode 17. Watch. Now.) We talked to Mimi Lam, cofounder of the Canada-based dispensary group Superette, and Steve DeAngelo, "father of the legal cannabis industry" and founder of Harborside, one of the world's largest medical cannabis dispensaries, on how to navigate your first visit like a seasoned pro.

✖ **Everyone has a first time:** "Stepping into the dispensary is most of the battle for first-timers," said Lam. "Recognize that by even getting there, you've already done a lot. Most intimidation is from the self, not the budtender." Steve DeAngelo suggests visiting a full-service dispensary that has cannabis concierges on the floor who can spend time answering all your questions. You may pay a higher price, he said, but "you can learn from them and then you can decide to go to a high-volume dispensary that will offer less personal service but cheaper prices" on subsequent visits.

✖ **Avoid bud rush hour:** "When the store opens or after office hours are going to be busiest, so a budtender will have less time," said Lam. "Go midday on a weekday for the most personalized service." That said, she recognizes that many customers prefer anonymity. If that's you, Lam recommends going during the busy hours "when it's more crowded and you can just blend in."

✖ **Leave your preconceived notions at the door:** Whether you're new to the flower or an old pro, a lot has changed in the cannabis offerings, so keep an open mind. "One size doesn't fit all," said Lam. If you haven't been a fan of flower, consider giving it another shot with a low-potency flower or vape. If you don't like the gummies or chocolate so prevalent in edibles, give a gel cap a go. If you're not an alcohol drinker but want something to hold at a party that will also bring a nice buzz, Lam recommends the fast-growing cannabis-infused beverage offerings. "That way," said Lam, "you can have a drink while others are having a drink."

✖ **The nose knows:** Steve DeAngelo encourages us to let smell guide our flower buying. "Mother Nature created layers of complexity that we don't even understand," DeAngelo said, "but our noses can identify what to put in our bodies." He recommends lining up six different strains of cannabis and giving them all a smell. The one that smells best to your nose is the one your body wants, and the one your wallet should buy.

I've noticed you almost never use the word "marijuana" in the book. What's up with that?

For thousands of years, cannabis was considered a recommended drug for both recreational and medicinal purposes. Then, in 1930, Harry Anslinger became the first commissioner of the Treasury Department's newly formed U.S. Federal Bureau of Narcotics and announced a "War on Drugs," one aimed primarily at Black and brown people. "Reefer makes darkies think they're as good as white men," he was quoted saying. "There are 100,000 total marijuana smokers in the United States, and most are Negroes, Hispanics, Filipinos, and entertainers." His racist and xenophobic beliefs also coincided with the immigration of tens of thousands of Mexicans, which escalated many Americans' anti-Mexican sentiments. Anslinger conflated the two issues and adopted the Spanish word "marijuana," rather than the already widely used "cannabis," so white Americans would associate cannabis and its purported violent side effects with Mexicans.

So on the hardworking backs of those fighting the good fight for this glorious plant, we too are weeding out the word "marijuana," with its racist origins, in favor of the scientific term, "cannabis."

Can you settle a bet with a friend? Who's the bigger weed baller, Willie Nelson or Snoop Dogg?

A question for the ages. If you need more proof that cannabis does wonders for creativity and productivity, look no further than these legends of the smoke and masters of their craft. So who is the king of cannabis? In a 2018 interview with Jimmy Kimmel, Snoop Dogg (speaking in the third person) offered the straight dope: "Willie Nelson is the only person who's ever out-smoked Snoop Dogg. I had to hit the 'time out' button."

What's the deal with "420" as shorthand for getting high? Is it Bob Marley's birthday?

Nope, not even close.

Then is it police code for a cannabis arrest?

Another urban legend.

Then is it because of Bob Dylan's legendary "Everybody must get stoned" refrain from "Rainy Day Women No. 12 & 35?" 12 multiplied by 35 does equal 420?

Uhh...no.

Fine, I give up.

4:20, as the real story goes, is the time of day when a group of friends at San Rafael High School in California would meet to hunt for a rumored abandoned stash of cannabis. The guys met at a statue of Louis Pasteur and knew it was time to meet if one called for a "4:20 Louis," which eventually became just 4:20. In a terrific recounting of this story on the podcast *Criminal* (episode 64), 4:20 posse member Dave Reddix explained that in 1971, "we'd meet at 4:20 p.m. and hop in a '66 Chevy Impala with a killer Craig 8-Track stereo, and we smoked all the way out there and started our search. It looked like a scene from one of Cheech & Chong's movies; we'd get the whole car clouded up with smoke and be listening to these eight-track tapes and talking and grooving and having a great time and excited to find this stash."

You're telling me a random treasure hunt turned into a global code for getting high?

Essentially, but there's more. This being the Bay Area, Reddix's brother was a friend of Grateful Dead drummer Phil Lesh. The Dead dug the phrase...and the rest is cannabis history.

So did the kids ever find the green treasure?

Sadly, they did not. But something even better happened. In 2017, *420* was added as an official entry in the *Oxford English Dictionary*. And while a stash of grass eventually runs out, the OED is forever.

Why won't my doctor talk to me about some of this fantastic flower's many benefits?

Lots of reasons. For over a millennium, cannabis has been shown to have huge health benefits, but the reefer madness hysteria and drug laws of the 1930s and '40s put cannabis in the proverbial corner. Even with the fast-moving legalization train and recent wokeness around its many benefits, many medical professionals still don't know much about cannabis. Blame this on lack of clinical trials and fear. Even in states where cannabis is legal, doctors risk losing their medical license if they discuss a drug that still isn't legal on the federal level.

Got it. So is this book intended as a substitute for advice from a medical professional?

No. No, it is not.

You have a lot of great ideas here. Anything I shouldn't do high?

Yes, many things. A partial list: attend a political convention (unless you're Sarah Silverman; google it); make a major purchase; skydive; enroll in a nonrefundable mime academy; light up in the parking lot of your local police station (even in

THEN	NOW
Reefer	Cannabis
7-Eleven munchies raid	Five-course farm-to-table cannabis-infused dinner
"I didn't inhale." —Bill Clinton	"I inhaled. Frequently." —Barack Obama
Pink Floyd's *The Wall*	Tycho's *Awake*
Twilight Zone on VHS	*Broad City* on Netflix
Glass water pipe	USB rechargeable vape pen with temperature-controlled battery
Pot brownies	Micro-batch salted caramels infused with hybrid terpene-enhanced distillate
Wake and bake	Wake and bake and create your own podcast
Beeping your guy	Allowing your budtender to unlock the glass display cases and offer a sniff. Take in the notes of citrus and cacao in each beautiful bouquet
Bonnaroo Festival with college buddies	Colorado Cannabis Tours weekend package: glass bong blowing demo, cannabis-infused massage, and grow house visit included
Get high and watch dumb movies	Get high and watch dumb movies

states where cannabis is legal, the open consumption laws are still pretty fuzzy); join the Merchant Marines; operate heavy machinery; drive.

So you wrote a whole book on cannabis. What's your favorite thing to do while you're high?
We're glad you asked. See any page of this book (but especially page 133).

> "We've been using the plant ever since we became human beings. This hundred-year period of history will be recognized as a bizarre aberration when we willingly divorced ourselves from this incredible plant."
>
> **STEVE DEANGELO,**
> **AKA "THE FATHER OF THE LEGAL CANNABIS INDUSTRY"**

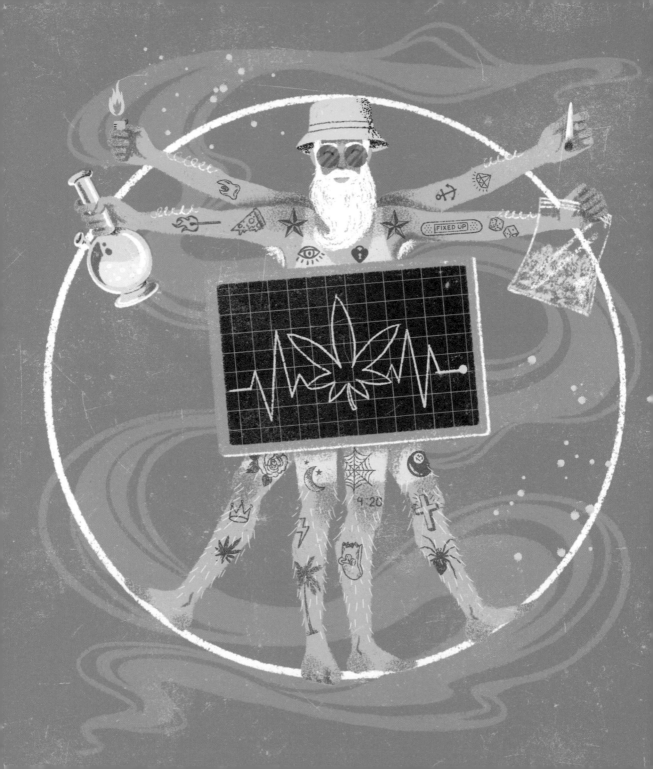

body

Cannabis is well known as a balm for the mind, but its effects on the body are just as profound. Growing research shows that cannabis acts as an anti-inflammatory, relieves chronic pain, alleviates anxiety and depression, helps with insomnia, treats chronic disease (such as epilepsy, Parkinson's disease, diabetes, and cancer), and (we swear) even helps with weight loss. And get this: cannabis may even keep you moving in the gym longer. In a study from the University of Colorado, Boulder, respondents who said they use cannabis for exercise workout forty-three minutes more per week than people surveyed who don't partake.

We could cite studies and bombard you with facts from top medical journals, but you probably didn't pick up this book to read about how a bunch of scientists discovered that cannabinol inhibits the growth of Lewis lung adenocarcinoma cells (go science!). Instead, we'll stick to broad strokes and tell you about our three favorite cannabis body benefits: increased focus and motivation, pain relief, and physical pleasure (and know we address our favorite body benefit—the joys of high sex—in "Connection" on page 133). But first a quick reminder on how the endocannabinoid system works.

The endocannabinoid system is made up of three core components: endocannabinoids, receptors, and enzymes. Endocannabinoids are neurotransmitters, or chemical messengers, that bind to the endocannabinoid receptors to help the body run smoothly by relieving pain, reducing inflammation, affecting mood, shrinking tumors, and more. The enzymes then break down the endocannabinoids once they've done their job.

Ultimately, it's the teaming up of the receptors with the endocannabinoids that makes the magic happen. Together, they have one terrific task: to bring our bodies to homeostasis, or balance. In a healthy body, they're constantly working to keep us in a place of stability. Now, add cannabis. Healthy bodies get a double dose of cannabinoids, and bodies that need a little healing get some extra TLC. Your endocannabinoid system is among the many reasons you've never lost a foot race, or a debate, to a beetle.

And since endocannabinoid receptors are found in 90 percent of our bodies, cannabis can help balance out everything from mood to inflammation and can even make exercise more effective as well as help with recovery and cool down. In one study published in the *Journal of Clinical Investigation*, researchers found that activating CB1 receptors in mice motivated them to run. There's growing evidence that CB1 receptors also play a central role in humans' motivation to seek aerobic exercise, whether it's a gentle yoga class or a hoops game with money on the line. In a moment when obesity rates are at the highest levels—nearly tripling between 1976 and 2008—we need every tool in our fitness toolbox to get our bodies moving.

Even elite athletes are finding cannabis helps with peak performance. Matt Barnes, who won an NBA championship with the Golden State Warriors, told *The Bleacher Report*, "All of my best games, I was medicated," and former Dallas Cowboy Shaun Smith said, "I smoked two blunts before every game." If the professionals are doing it, shouldn't we? The answer is yes, yes we should. But we're also going to assume you know that getting high and extreme sports probably don't mix. So maybe nix the skydiving and BMX racing when you partake.

The benefits of cannabis on the body don't just align with getting fit. Cannabis can also act like a mood enhancer, stimulating dopamine, a neurotransmitter that affects pleasure, and can even act as nature's own ADHD medicine. "Cannabis appears to treat ADD and ADHD by increasing the availability of dopamine," says cannabis researcher Dr. David Bearman, who has seen breakthroughs with his patients. "It has the same effect but is a different mechanism of action than stimulants like Ritalin and Dexedrine amphetamine, which act by binding to the dopamine and interfering with the metabolic breakdown of dopamine." That's a bona fide breakthrough if you're one of the many adults who suffer from ADHD, and it is also good news if you have a hard time rocking out repetitive tasks like push-ups and crunches. To sweeten the pot, CBD can reduce pain and inflammation and speed up the healing process, so you can go hard while minimizing the aftereffects.

Of course, no two bodies are built exactly the same, and each of our bodies will react differently to any element introduced (as your ninth-grade health teachers hopefully explained), so it's up to you to find the perfect dose and strain for your fine frame. Still, in the pages that follow, we'll offer suggestions, and, more importantly, we'll offer activities that pair perfectly with the powerful physical effects of cannabis. We hope they get you jumping for joy.

FIELD NOTES

Everything Old Is New Again: Like so many chapters in the book of cannabis, everything new is actually quite ancient. As noted in *Shen-nung Pen Ts'ao Ching*, the first book to detail Chinese medicinal practices (circa 2737 BC), hemp (the old-school name for cannabis) was recognized for its ability to treat over one hundred medical issues including gout, malaria, and rheumatism.

E is for Exercise and Edibles: Your lungs surely don't want to be inhaling combustibles pre-workout, so we recommend an edible, timed to come on at the beginning of your workout. The last thing you need is to get stuck comparing and contrasting energy bars on your way to spin class.

Ouch! One study found that cannabis helped patients with chronic pain experience a 64 percent decrease in opiate use, a decreased amount and intensity of side effects from other medications, and improved quality of life. "Using cannabis for pain can be tricky if you don't pick the right product and dosing," said Dr. Michele Ross, a neuroscientist who helps women heal chronic pain naturally with cannabis and author of five books, including *Vitamin Weed*. "While THC can reduce pain and inflammation, many patients don't know that cannabis can also make you more aware of your pain. Make sure to choose strains that are more likely to contain terpenes that dial down pain and are less likely to have terpenes that improve focus on pain." Take that, Western medicine.

ACTIVITIES

#1: RUNNER'S HIGH

We've all heard of a runner's high, but have you tried running *while* high? Running, like all cardio, triggers the production of endocannabinoids in your body, which produces that euphoria athletes can't seem to stop talking about. In other words, go out there and run that ten-minute mile (over and over), and you won't need a pre-roll!

But...what if you can't get beyond lacing up those sneakers? Rather than rewarding yourself post-run, try rewarding yourself before you've done anything. Not only will you increase motivation (as we know, there are few things weed doesn't make better), but you'll get that endocannabinoid system doubly fired up—and that runner's high just got higher.

LEVEL UP

Finding your blissed-out brain stops to inspect every friendly flower? Give it something to do and engage in a little fartlek. No, silly rabbit, we're not telling you to fart less (or more, for that matter). Fartlek stands for "speed play" in Swedish. Pick an object ahead of you and sprint toward it. Pick another object and do a slow jog until you find your next object, then sprint toward that. All that looking and choosing keeps your brain busy and entertained. Can you make it to the mailbox? Will you die trying to get to that second stoplight? Will everyone know you're high if you make that cute labradoodle a target (and possibly start chasing it)? High minds want to know.

#2: SHH, I'M DANCING

Nothing goes better with weed than music (see "Beautiful Music, Together" on page 92), and nothing goes better with music than dancing. Cannabis is a psychoacoustic enhancer, which means music literally sounds better when you're high. Add in the fact that cannabis lowers inhibitions and makes you magically in the moment, and it's clear why it's time to dance. Silently. Now hear us out. Silent discos offer countless benefits for high people. Here are our top three.

1. **Headphones.** Sure, the output from the bass of those giant speakers has its own appeal, but headphones allow you to take better advantage of cannabis's superpower as a psychoacoustic enhancer. You'll find yourself better able to select certain information and disregard other information, which can make individual sounds resonate in...well...stereo.

2. **You choose your groove.** Most silent discos have multiple DJs spinning, so your shortened attention span will thank you for giving it options.

3. **Hilarity.** Take your headphones off and observe your fellow ravers dancing to...nothing. Alternatively, you may find this a profound commentary on the state of society. Who are we to judge?

KNOW BEFORE YOU GO

Don't be the newbie who tries to talk with your headphones on. Psst...no one can hear you if they have their headphones on, and if they don't, you'll be the idiot screaming in their ear.

#3: LET'S DANCE, ECSTATICALLY

We can't certify that ecstatic dance was created by high people for high people, but...ecstatic dance *surely* was created by high people for high people. If you've never experienced the phenomenon of sweaty barefoot bodies in various states of undress abandoning themselves to house music and moving in a way that can only be described as dance-ish, have we got an activity for you. Ecstatic dance is meant to access your most primal self, so any kind of movement goes. Want to somersault across the floor? Invite someone to consensually grind against you? Channel your inner whirling dervish? All good, as long as you don't speak on the dance floor (really, it's the one rule). Most cities have their own weekly dances, so get googling.

KNOW BEFORE YOU GO

▸ Ecstatic dance is an alcohol/drug-free zone, which doesn't mean it's a sober crowd. Just plan to preparty (like many others) before you go.

▸ It's typically a shoe-free zone, unless you have a medical reason to have your tootsies covered.

▸ Yes, pajamas are acceptable (even encouraged).

#4: ZUMBA. THAT'S RIGHT, ZUMBA.

We know what you're thinking...but hold the phone. Where else can you learn a dash of salsa, a splash of flamenco, and a smidge of merengue all while getting a killer workout and not caring that you feel better than you look? Zumba's tagline is "Ditch the workout—join the party!" which we all know is code for workout and party at the same time. Add an edible before shimmying in, and your brain may relax enough to nail the choreography. Or not. Who cares when your endocannabinoid system is churning out double the endorphins?

KNOW BEFORE YOU GO

Ditch the sneakers with the thick soles. They're not made for the side-to-side movements of Zumba. Instead, go for thin soles and a simple tread. And remember to bring water and a towel. Like they say, it's a party *and* a workout.

#5: GRAVITY GAMES

The joys of jumping are timeless, ageless, and quite likely easily found in a backyard near you. Find a trampoline and catch some air. Done bouncing? Lie down. Trampolines are firmer than you remember and offer the perfect perspective to stare at the sky and space out. Bring a book and a pillow and stay awhile.

Looking for a few more ways to get high?

Pogo sticks: Yes.

Bouncy houses: Yes, please!

Bungee jumping: No.

#6: ROLL SOME GRASS

Remember how fun it was to roll down the hill? Good news: the grass hasn't changed, but you've gotten greener. Step 1: find a grassy hill on a nice day. Step 2: roll down it. Step 3: repack and repeat as necessary.

#7: BONG, BATH, AND BEYOND

Like weed, there's little that water can't make better. It's a full-service restorative system: water can both soothe and invigorate, heal the body and rejuvenate the mind. Now, combine weed and water, and you're about as close to total body bliss as you can get.

Your brain on weed is already feeling that sweet, sweet dopamine. And still, we're a greedy species, and our pleasure centers are just dying to release more of the good stuff, so swigging and soaking in this vital elixir will open the flood gates. Seventy-five percent of brain tissue is water, so drink it in (literally) to keep the good juju going. (May we suggest adding a squeeze of orange and a few crushed basil leaves?) Then when you're good and hydrated, bring on the H2Ohhhh.

TAKE A SHOWER

We're big fans of showers. Turn the pressure all the way up and you've got hundreds of tiny fingers massaging your scalp. Turn it down and it's a warm summer rain. Lather. Rinse. Try another strain on another day. Repeat.

TAKE A BATH

Savor your soak by becoming one with the water and trying (almost) total immersion. Keep the oxygen flowing, but close your eyes and get those ears underwater, and create your own sensory deprivation tank. Being in water activates your brain waves, particularly those all-important alpha waves, which help you reach a state of calm and re-alert your senses for maximum pleasure—a fancy way of saying:

taking a bath while high is incredible. But how about getting high while taking a bath? There's something blissful about stepping into a tub of steamy water stone-cold sober and stepping out flushed and faded. The environment will forgive you (this one time, and, um, when you take that way too long shower we suggest above). To fully supercharge your soak, add a bud bomb, a cannabis-infused bath bomb. See our easy DIY recipe.

PRO TIP

▸ Get that water *hot*. Hot water relaxes your pores, which helps your skin soak up the magic ingredient.

▸ Aim for at least thirty minutes of soak time for full effects.

▸ Heat + salt + weed = a perfect storm for dehydration, so keep up the hydration. (We're talking water, folks. Save the gin and tonic for another night.)

#8: BAKE IN NATURE'S WARM BATH

Nature nurtures us all, which is why it feels so good to walk in the woods. The Japanese have even perfected the experience and called it *shinrin-yoku*, or forest bathing: the practice of immersing yourself in the forest and letting your senses soak up its offerings. A decades-long study of the practice called "Shinrin-Yoku (Forest Bathing) and Nature Therapy: A State-of-the-Art Review" confirms what most of us already know about any walk in the woods: nature is a form of therapy, offering decreased stress, improved mood, more energy, less fatigue, and "feelings of awe" (the researchers' words, not ours, but we're definitely on the same page here).

BUD BOMB

There are a ton of cannabis-infused bath products out there, but it's easy to make your own, and we've got the science and the recipe to guide you there—and take you away.

Your skin may be the barrier that keeps your insides in and the outside out, but it isn't an impenetrable force field, which is good if you're trying to soak in your high. Still, you can't just dump a bunch of flower into the tub and call it a day. The body needs a carrier to deliver all that cannabis goodness, which is why you need to turn that flower into oil with this "even a high person can do it" recipe. But remember, if you're looking to get super high, this relaxing bud bomb isn't going to do it. THC is absorbed by the skin and can't cross into the bloodstream, but for on-site soothing and a warm tingly buzz, soak away!

PREP: 15 minutes • **COOK:** 1 hour 40 minutes
TOTAL TIME: 1 hour 55 minutes • **YIELD:** enough for two baths

INGREDIENTS

- 1 cup flower (ask your budtender for their favorite flower for relaxation)
- 1 cup food-grade oil (grape-seed, coconut, olive, etc.)
- 2 cups Epsom salts
- Essential oils approved for topical use (optional, but we recommend cutting the stank with some rose or eucalyptus)

SUPPLIES

- Baking sheet
- Double boiler (or make your own with a pot and metal bowl)
- Cheesecloth (or strainer)
- Molds (optional; empty plastic Easter eggs work great)

DIRECTIONS

Break your buds into smaller pieces (about ½ inch by ½ inch is good).

Spread the weed evenly onto a baking sheet and bake at 220°F for 20-ish minutes. This allows for the all-important decarboxylation, the process that activates compounds in cannabis such as THC. You'll know it's done when it turns a light brown or yellow color.

Mix baked bud with food-grade oil in the top half of a double boiler, or make your own double boiler by placing a metal bowl over a pot of gently boiling water. Watch that your oil isn't getting too hot and cooking out all that essential THC. If you want to go pro, use a cooking thermometer, and aim for 130°F to 150°F. Cook for one hour.

Let the oil cool, then strain it through cheesecloth or a strainer.

Mix the oil into the Epsom salts.

Add essential oils or—why not—rose petals for the full spa experience.

Pack mixture into molds or form into balls and allow to dry for 24 hours.

To use, drop one into a warm bath, agitate the water, and then drop your soon to be relaxed self in with it. Store in a moisture free container (a Mason jar or Tupperware work great) for up to six months.

Want to make that "awe" even more awesome? Partake of nature's candy (weed, not raisins; even if raisins get all the press), and let the power of flower slow things down and make the grass a little greener and the leaves a little leafier. For Type As like us who require a little more guidance on their nature walks, take your senses on a tour: name five things you see, four things you feel, three things you hear, two things you smell, and one thing you taste. By focusing in on the natural world, you're grounding your body while allowing your mind to fly high above the treetops.

LEVEL UP

Take your shoes and socks off and walk barefoot in the forest. This practice, also known as "earthing," has real scientific benefits. Researchers at UC Irvine have found that your feet act as a conductive system that transfer the earth's electrons from the ground into the body, promoting physiological changes like better sleep and reduced pain.

#9: TAKE THE PLUNGE

Sure, swimming is considered one of the summer sports, but there's no reason you can't compete any time of year, especially when the real prize is the plunge itself. Get suited up (or not), and enter the 420 Olympics.

BRONZE: SWIM

If Michael Phelps, arguably the best swimmer in modern history, can win eight gold medals and still enjoy a good bong hit, you too can relish a rip before taking a dip. Let's get the safety measures out of the way first: more high doesn't always equal more fun, so don't overdo it. And be sure to bring your designated sober person and keep them close. #safetyfirst

With those safety measures in place, there's no wrong way to swim high, but allow us to curate your experience. Got a pool? Add goggles and fins, and you're a marlin gliding through the water. Got an ocean? Swim out beyond the waves, starfish your body, and allow the salt water to provide total buoyancy.

SILVER: SWIM NAKED

More high may not equal more fun, but fewer clothes does. Allow your mellow to calm any qualms about modesty and strip it all off. Warmish water works best for this one (we see you, George Costanza), bringing the water and your body temperature into a groovy equilibrium that will make you—and maybe a few friends—one with the universe.

GOLD: SWIM NAKED AT NIGHT

The darkened sky, the starry night, the fact that your body is glimmering like moonlight on water—what's not to love? Diminishing one sense—in this case, sight—intensifies the others, so you'll feel the water's loving caress on all your parts. Drink it up, you water nymph, you. For Brooke Shields fans of a certain age, submerge yourself in nostalgia and try smoking the strain Blue Lagoon.

#10: BLOW SMOKE

The first thing you need to know about blowing smoke rings is you don't blow them. You let them float from your mouth like THC-infused butterflies. Follow these steps and all your friends will be aflutter, marveling at your skills.

1. Draw a thick puff of smoke into your mouth and hold it there.
2. Place your tongue on the bottom of your mouth and pull it back slightly to block your throat.
3. Open your mouth slowly (you don't want any air flow to disturb the smoke) and form it into a loose letter O. Be sure to open your mouth and jaw, not just your lips.
4. Push the smoke gently out of your mouth with your tongue using a piston-type motion—short bursts, with a slight recoil.

Step 1
Step 2
Step 3
Step 4

You'll most likely need a good smoke sesh to master these babies, but when you're ready, go to the next level and try for a heart. Here's how: Blow a ring, then snap your fingers gently above it. The slight air flow from your fingers will push the top of the smoke ring down, bending it into a heart. *Awww.*

#11: REVEL IN REFLEXOLOGY

What has twenty-six bones, thirty-three joints, forty-two muscles, more than fifty tendons and ligaments, and fifteen thousand nerve endings? Your right foot (your left one has the same, but...math). In short, it can get crowded in there. Add the capacity to handle hundreds of tons of force, and those tootsies need as much TLC as you need THC.

With this in mind, may we present reflexology, an ancient healing practice based on the principle that there are reflex points on the feet that correspond to the body's different organs and glands. (Fun fact: the first recorded history of reflexology is a pictograph on the Egyptian tomb of Ankhamor in 2330 BC.) Reflexology can energize and relax, treat the mind and the body. And if this is sounding like a recap of the benefits of cannabis, you're right. The two make perfect bedfellows. Got sinus pain? As we know, cannabis decreases inflammation; apply pressure on the base of each toe and sinus discomfort can be greatly reduced. Stomach troubles? THC can relax the GI tract, as can firm pressure on the bridge of the foot.

We picked out a few key pressure points that pair best with cannabinoids and created this handy-dandy foot diagram to help you give or get a top-shelf foot massage.

HELPFUL HINTS

▸ When massaging the foot, stick to "thumb walking" (yes, this is the technical term for using only ones' thumbs to massage) for authenticity and ideal pressure.

▶ Tenderness can indicate weakness or imbalance within a corresponding organ, so tread lightly, but don't shy away from those sensitive spots.

Reflexology Foot Chart

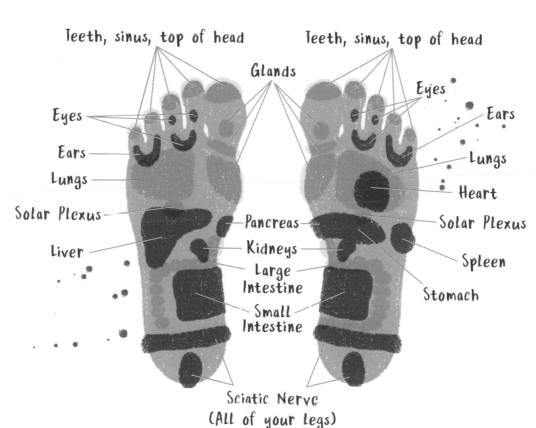

BOTTOM OF RIGHT FOOT

BOTTOM OF LEFT FOOT

Teeth, sinus, top of head

Teeth, sinus, top of head

Glands

Eyes

Ears

Lungs

Heart

Eyes

Ears

Lungs

Solar Plexus

Liver

Pancreas

Kidneys

Large Intestine

Small Intestine

Solar Plexus

Spleen

Stomach

Sciatic Nerve
(All of your legs)

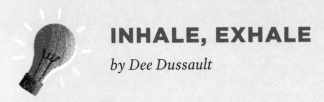

INHALE, EXHALE

by Dee Dussault

Cannabis with yoga? The plant has been imbued with a history of love and peace for decades, with practitioners finding it can deepen awareness, relaxation, connection, and even bliss, on the sticky mat and in the bedroom.

I have a deeply cool job. I'm not only the founder of Ganja Yoga and the earliest Western yoga teacher to publicly endorse plant-enhanced practice, I'm also a sexuality coach. Whether for lovemaking or yoga, I invite my clients to consider incorporating cannabis. Both THC and CBD can reduce inflammation and pain, easing bodily comfort and increasing our ability to feel pleasure. And at the right dose, these compounds also melt stress from the mind, helping us to be present and really savor what's going on. Here are some best practices to enhance your experience.

INTENTION

Make your cannabis-infused yoga practice an opportunity to practice mindfulness. Be intentional—reverent even—as you roll your joint or hit your pipe, and invite the ancient, healing plant to work its magic. Light a candle, say a short prayer, or list some things you're grateful for. Perhaps thank cannabis for being anti-inflammatory, always a happy place for a yoga body.

STRAIN AND DOSE

I love cannabis because it gets me out of my head, especially a high-CBD indica strain. Beginners to ganja should start with a low dose and develop a relationship to the plant over time. Overconsuming can feel awful, and you can always add more, but you can't add less. Once you're done imbibing, see if you can let go of expectations for the high and allow the cannabis to do its thing. The plant can enhance the sensations you feel in your body as you move, breathe, and let go of tension. Begin the first moments of your high with a basic stretch that feels good in your body. Notice the sensations as you lengthen your limbs and let out a sigh.

BE PRESENT

During your enhanced yoga or meditation, whenever you notice yourself inevitably zoning out, habitually worrying, or replaying old experiences in your mind, just come back to the present moment. How? Inhale, and return to what's happening in the now, time and time again, remembering that being mindful takes practice, so go easy on yourself (weed helps here too!).

KEEP THE POSES SIMPLE

Finally, and especially if you're new to cannabis, now is not the time to experiment with a new arm balance. In fact, cannabis can help you return to basic poses like child's pose, happy baby, and reclining twist, and feel them in a new way. Stick to whatever movements feel yummy and easy. You got this.

Dee Dussault is the internationally recognized pioneer of the Ganja Yoga movement, a sexuality coach, and the author of Ganja Yoga.

#12: ALL 4(20) SEASONS

There's more than one reason to enjoy each season, but let us direct your body to our top choices for winter, spring, summer, and fall's finest corporeal pleasures.

WINTER

It's hard to beat staring into a crackling fire for pure stoner relaxation, but going outside has its pleasures too. Mainly, snow. It's a delight for the eyes, it's refreshing for the body, and most importantly, it's nature's Play-Doh. Channel your inner Rodin, and sculpt a snowperson (add a blunt for verisimilitude); a series of perfectly round snowballs (then nail your friends); and for your *pièce de résistance*, a working snow bong.

> "If you substitute marijuana for tobacco and alcohol, you'll add eight to twenty-four years to your life."
>
> —JACK HERER, AKA THE EMPEROR OF HEMP

SNOW BONG

PREP: 5 minutes • **CREATE:** 15 minutes

TOTAL TIME: 20 minutes • **YIELD:** 5-ish ginormous bong hits

INGREDIENTS

- Snow

SUPPLIES

- A bowl (the kind you eat out of, silly)
- A dowel (for the smoking chamber)
- A skewer (for the downstem and the bowl; the kind you smoke out of, silly)

Snow

Bowl

Step 1

Dowel

Step 2

Step 3

Step 4

Skewer

Step 5

Step 6

Step 7
Pack, light up, and enjoy!

DIRECTIONS

Step 1: Pack snow into a bowl and build up until the snow bong is about one foot high.

Step 2: Insert the dowel into the top of the snow bong, leaving about two inches of snow between the dowel and the bottom of the bowl.

Step 3: Pack more snow around the dowel, sculpting up until your snow bong is as tall as you like.

Step 4: Remove the dowel to form your smoke chamber.

Step 5: Use the skewer to poke a thin downstem in the middle of your snow bong. The downstem is the smoke delivery system, so make sure you push the skewer at a downward angle and through the wall of snow until you reach the empty chamber space left by the dowel.

Step 6: At the opening of your downstem, use your skewer to carve a hole large enough to accommodate your weed.

Step 7: Pack, light up, and enjoy.

You'll probably get a good five hits off your frozen bong before snow does what snow will do when met with fire.

70

Percentage of people who said using cannabis before working out made exercising more enjoyable according to researchers at the University of Colorado Boulder.

SPRING

You can't go wrong with flowers—they're pretty, they smell good, you can smoke (some) of them. But consider wind. It tickles the skin, it provides that lovely rustling sound as it whips through the trees, and it provides a full-body workout as you become its master and get yourself and your kite high as...well...a kite. Kite flying may seem like child's play, but anyone who's tried to wrestle a single line dragon in a twenty-mile-per-hour gale will tell you different. So check out our tips for optimal high flying.

▶ **S P A C E.** Don't underestimate how much a kite needs. Find a long beach, community sports field, or even deserted parking lot to avoid losing your flying friend to high wires or hungry trees.

▶ **THE KITE.** For low wind (five to fifteen miles per hour), choose a diamond, delta, or dragon kite. For medium wind (fifteen to twenty-five miles per hour), choose a box or parafoil kite. For high wind (twenty-five miles per hour and over), sit down and give yourself a stern talking to about safety and hurricane preparedness.

▶ **THE LAUNCH.** Have the "launcher" stand approximately sixty feet away from the "flier" and keep their back to the wind with the top of the kite facing them. Wait for a gust of wind. (We repeat, wait for a gust of wind. Running will only provide too much jerky tension, keeping the kite—and possibly you—on the ground.) As the launcher releases the kite, have the flier pull the string to provide some tension. Once it catches flight, the flier can release a length of line so the kite is flying as high as any seasoned stoner.

▶ **THE DELIVERABLES.** One thing wind isn't good for? Lighting up. So bring your vape or use your friends to create a protective fortress so you don't sacrifice fire.

SUMMER

Water gets all the press at the beach, but let's give sand a second look. Sand is pure skin satisfaction. Dig your feet into the soppy sand and feel the sand crabs tickle your toes. Make drip sandcastles by picking up handfuls of super mushy sand and letting it drizzle into tall towers. Dig a human-sized hole and have a friend bury you from toes to chin; now pay attention to the sand: the steady pressure, the grainy texture, what it feels like to wiggle your fingers free.

PRO TIP

An available outdoor shower is a plus if you don't want the sensation of sand in your bikini bottoms.

FALL

Your eyes will love the colors. Your ears will appreciate the satisfying crunch under foot. But for maximum bodily pleasure, nothing beats hurling yourself into nature's own foam pit: a pile of crisp autumn leaves. Even better if you can get someone to do the raking, or get productive and pair with "Green Cleaning" (page 147) for a twofer.

#13: ZZZZZZZ

Sleep. We all want more of it, and when 30 percent of the general population complains of sleep disruptions, we're clearly not getting enough. Enter nature's own sleep aid. Whether you can't fall asleep or you can't stay asleep, cannabis is here to help. We know the research doesn't always agree, but we generally find ourselves in the camp that sativa gets you up and indica brings you down, so we recommend an indica high in the terpenes limonene and linalool. Limonene helps reduce insomnia (we like Purple Hindu Kush), and linalool increases adenosine, a sedating hormone that helps us fall asleep (try LA Confidential). The THC in cannabis can also reduce the amount of REM sleep you get, which reduces dreams (great for those who have chronic nightmares). If that's not you, stick to a lower THC content, and drift off to dreamland.

Cannabis for the Win

Need some quick stats on why weed is so much better than alcohol? This one's for you.

CANNABIS	DOES USE CONTRIBUTE TO…	ALCOHOL
NO	Overdose deaths	YES
NO	Long-term health problems	YES
NO	Violent crimes	YES
NO	Serious injuries	YES

mind

The great Bob Marley said, "When you smoke the herb, it reveals you to yourself," which attests to the power of both cannabis and the mind (not to mention Marley; have you listened to "Natural Mystic" while high?). Cannabis's greatest superpower just might be its ability to alter the mind. This is partially due to the fact that cannabis stimulates blood flow to the frontal lobe, that same area responsible for creative tasks. We'll talk more about this later (we're looking at you, "Creativity," page 189), but in short, more creativity equals a better ability to problem solve, which in turn helps us find new ways of thinking about the world. Cannabis also helps with focus by increasing the availability of our own naturally produced dopamine—the chemical responsible for activating the pleasure centers in the brain—allowing you to really dig in and explore those new ways of thinking.

If we're thinking broadly, sure it's cannabis that presents new insights and new perspectives, but it's really one very special cannabinoid, *tetrahydrocannabinol*, or THC, that makes the magic. Other cannabinoids have supporting roles, but it's mostly THC that gives weed its classification as a psychoactive—or mind-altering—drug and mild to moderate hallucinogen (at least according to the Drug Enforcement Agency). As for hallucinations, we're thinking we would have seen pink elephants by now, but what do we know?

And as a reminder, the endocannabinoid system is what allows the THC to help reveal yourself...to yourself. The THC binds to the endocannabinoid receptors in your brain to create that mind-expanding experience we know and love. This is because THC resembles another cannabinoid naturally produced in our brains, anandamide. Anandamide, the name of which is derived from the Sanskrit word for bliss (those scientists aren't as buttoned up as we thought), helps regulate mood, sleep, memory, and appetite. But if we're talking about the mind, it's mood regulation we're most interested in here.

Anandamide enhances mood and diminishes fear and anxiety, so much so that when scientists inhibited production of the enzymes that break down anandamide, they found a decrease in fear and anxiety during times of perceived threat in humans (also in mice, but we're pretty sure they're unconcerned with *why* they're less afraid of cats). Less fear and anxiety means more joy and tranquility. So anandamide and its lookalike THC can not only help you feel blissed out, but they can help with activities that help you *become* more blissed out, like mindfulness and meditation.

Of course, no introduction to cannabis and the mind would be complete without at least acknowledging that cannabis has gotten a bad rap as the wacky weed that makes you stupid. We're not going to say that we've never been high and had to reread (and reread and reread) the IKEA directions on how to assemble that Kallax bookshelf, but we've had to do that sober too. Yes, cannabis can cause mild cognitive impairment, but there's little to no research to illustrate that this is permanent (as long as you're not smoking one hundred joints a day; if you are, science wants to chat). And there are even some studies proving that THC can help improve cognitive function, at least in mice.

Still, that mild cognitive impairment can be real, but it's also what makes cannabis such a wild ride. In addition to encouraging us to find the mildly amusing hysterical (see "Laugh Your Grass Off" on page 109), it's what causes us to home in on our own inventive thinking. It keeps us fixated on one brilliant idea—until another genius thought tempts us down a different path—which is among the many reasons that when you're high, you probably don't want to engage in things that require multilateral thinking (driving, deliberating court cases, batting practice). Instead, we suggest directing that concentrated focus to the activities that follow. After all, as Jah Cure sang, "One puff, one draw, frees the mind. Mmm mmm." Mmm mmm, indeed.

FIELD NOTES

The Future Is Female: Cannabis is a dioecious plant, meaning male or female reproductive organs appear on different plants, but it's the females that do the work of making beautiful bud. The female's seedless buds (officially called *sinsemilla*) produce the THC-rich flower (officially called *the good stuff*)—and what you're buying at your local dispensary. And who is supplying you with that fine kine female bud? Women! Well, at least more than in most industries. According to *Fit Small Business*, women hold around 36 percent of executive positions as opposed to only 15 percent in other industries.

Mighty Anandamide: Anandamide—that awesome THC-like cannabinoid just discussed—is also found in truffles (the kind pigs sniff out) and cocoa beans (the kind we make into chocolate). So pop a gummy, find a movie using our handy-dandy flow chart (page 129), pass out the truffle-infused popcorn and movie theater chocolate, and let the anandamide do its job.

Laughter and Forgetting: You've probably heard that cannabis causes memory loss. But the news on this cognitive impairment is more nuanced (and good). Memory has two distinct forms: short-term and long-term. Long-term memory is where information is stored indefinitely; short-term memory is where temporary events are stored and later discarded. And why wouldn't they be? If we retained every image, sound, and situation, our brains would be silos of sensory overload. When THC binds with our endocannabinoid receptors, it kicks our brains' natural forgetting systems into gear, which does something wonderful—it puts us in the moment. In *The Botany of Desire*, Michael Pollan writes, "It is the relentless moment-by-moment forgetting...[that] helps account for the sharpening of sensory perceptions, for the aura of profundity in which cannabis bathes the most ordinary insights, and, perhaps most important of all, for the sense that time has either slowed or stopped."

ACTIVITIES

#14: MEMORY STRAIN

Weed has long been tied to short-term memory loss (think the cinematic classic *Dude, Where's My Car?*). We're not going to tell you that hundreds of peer-reviewed studies are *wrong*, but we are going to tell you that although short-term and working memory are impaired *while* you're high, there's little evidence to support the notion that memory is impaired post-high. In fact, some studies suggest that low doses of THC can actually help improve cognitive function—at least in mice, who always seem to figure things out first.

And here's even more good news: scientists are now looking into how cannabis helps make autobiographical memory more sensorial, helping you recall that time your parents surprised you with a pony (unlike *our* parents; thanks, Mom and Dad). Carl Sagan was a big fan of using cannabis to relive the past, writing in *Marihuana Reconsidered*, "When I'm high I can penetrate into the past, recall childhood memories, friends, relatives, playthings, streets, smells, sounds, and tastes from a vanished era. I can reconstruct the actual occurrences in childhood events only half understood at the time."

Be like Carl, and reconstruct memories by digging out those old baby albums or dusty yearbooks. Add your favorite strain, and you've got your own personal time machine. Page through and marvel at your (and your parents') bad fashion choices. Try to remember that little redheaded girl's name. Relive that first terrifying time on Santa's lap. Now get philosophical and ask yourself, "What would I tell my past self?"

LEVEL UP

Pair this activity with the "Letter to Yourself" activity (page 195), but instead of your future self, write a letter to thirteen-year-old you. You decide whether to warn yourself about that incident at the eighth-grade talent show.

#15: MELLOW YOUR MEDITATION

We know we *should* meditate (even a single session has been shown to significantly reduce anxiety), but actually making yourself sit, clear your mind, and do nothing else for fifteen minutes is easier said than done, which is why a hit (or two) can bring some magic to your mindfulness. Weed activates the neurotransmitters dopamine and glutamate, the same ones meditation amplifies. Dopamine helps control mood, and glutamate promotes brain health. Introduce cannabis to these two, and you'll find your brain more mellow than with just meditation (or cannabis) alone.

Still, even regular cannabis users who have been shown to have a blunted stress response (pun intended) may find it hard to overcome the existential dread of sitting all alone with themselves. To counter this, try introducing something specific for your brain (and body) to do. Break out some flower, fire, and a candle, and take a crack at the Indian practice of *trataka* or "looking intently with an unwavering gaze at a small point until tears are shed" (yes, really). Here's how:

1 Place a lit candle three feet away at eye level and keep your focus on the middle part of the flame, right above the tip of the wick.

2 Stare intently until your eyes begin to water.

3 Close your eyes and find the afterimage of the flame in your mind's eye.

4 If the image moves up and down or side to side, bring it back to the center and fix your gaze until the impression disappears and you find yourself in that floaty dissociative space that signals a good meditation (or smoke) session.

PRO TIP

Derek Beres, author of *Hero's Dose: The Case for Psychedelics in Ritual and Therapy* and the first instructor to teach cannabis-infused yoga and meditation at Equinox Fitness, said straight-up meditation may not be for everyone. If your mellow mind still needs a little distraction, try binaural beats. Binaural beats occur when your two ears hear tones with slightly different frequencies. Your brain then perceives these as a single tone, creating...get this...an auditory *illusion*, an illusion that some believe induces a mental state similar to that associated with meditation. Looking for the beats? Your favorite music streaming platform has a ton of them.

#16: CONQUER A FEAR

The worst thing about fear is that it's timeless. Your iPhone is out of date the day after you buy it, but fear keeps automatically installing its software into your psyche. Sure, you've stopped panicking that someone will put your hand in warm water at a sleepover (we hope). But spiders, public speaking, and public bathrooms are not going anywhere.

Getting high may not be your first go-to when trying to slay a fear, and make no mistake, the wrong strain at the wrong time can cause your heart to race. But hold the phone. The right strain of cannabis can decrease anxiety, which is key for what cognitive behavior therapists call exposure therapy. The idea is that the best way to overcome a fear is in small, sensible steps. Afraid of dogs? A CBT approach might suggest looking at pictures of dogs, then watching a movie with dogs. (We recommend *Air Bud*. A golden retriever with mad basketball skills? What's not to love?) Next would be going to a friend's house where a prescreened, playful puppy awaits.

As we said above, strain is everything for this one. One we recommend is the oddly named ACDC. It's CBD dominant, so your high should be mellow and your head in a good place to meet Princess.

CANNABIS AND ANXIETY

by Derek Beres

The sixteenth-century Swiss physician and alchemist Paracelsus wrote, "In all things there is a poison, and there is nothing without a poison. It depends only upon the dose whether something is poison or not."

For the anxious, cannabis can be a balm or a poison. As a longtime sufferer of an anxiety disorder, I've been hospitalized due to a panic attack after smoking too much cannabis; other incidents left me curled in a ball on the floor. To be fair, that's also happened while sober. And yet for the quarter century that I dealt with that disorder—thankfully, it's behind me—cannabis often kept me in tranquil repose. What happened? I got to know my dose.

A 2009 critical review of cannabis and anxiety discovered that cannabis can both exacerbate and precipitate existing anxiety symptoms *and* reduce anxiety. Although the researchers couldn't definitively define the relationship between anxiety and cannabis, that shouldn't surprise us: The neuroscientist Joseph Ledoux spent more than four hundred pages detailing the physiology and neurology of anxiety in his masterful book *Anxious*, and he failed to pinpoint an exact cause either. That's not Ledoux's fault—anxiety has multivariate causes. As Freud knew, anxiety is an inextricable aspect of the human condition. It's the nervous system's response to environmental, physiological, and psychological stimuli.

With so many factors to consider, evidence for the efficacy of therapeutic cannabis will likely remain anecdotal for the foreseeable future. But as science keeps homing in on the cannabis and anxiety connection, the best thing you can do is take your time and experiment—a puff or two of different strains, or, my preferred dose, a 2.5-milligram edible.

As anyone who's suffered a panic attack knows, triggers stay with you. If a 20-milligram brownie results in hours of existential dread, even the thought of a microdose down the line can cripple you. It's best to start slow and learn your dose. Be cautious and understand that cannabis's calming effect won't work for every mind and every body. But if you're struggling with anxiety, it's definitely worth exploring the power of this healing herb.

Derek Beres is the head of content marketing and community at the wellness app Centered, the author of Hero's Dose: The Case for Psychedelics in Ritual and Therapy, *and a columnist for* Big Think *and* Psychedelic Spotlight.

#17: PLAY WITH KIDS

Turning off the pressures of the day and the FOMO you get from Instagram is harder than it looks. And while we may want to "find our inner child," the part of our brains that psychologists call Sir Grumps-A-Lot (okay, it's the superego) often gets in the way. THC is here to help, offering even the most cantankerous of us access to our more playful side. So what better way to take full advantage than to round up a couple of kids and remember how important novelty, silliness, and making pipe cleaner animals just for the sake of making them is? Children + cannabis = lowered inhibitions and fun for fun's sake. While the ways to play are limitless, here are three timeless classics for you and the under-ten set.

PLAY WITH PLAY-DOH

Build a bakery complete with miniature pies, cakes, and dozens of red, yellow, and blue cookies. Channel your inner child and make the adults in the room pretend to chow down. "Mmmmm...so good!"

HAVE A WATER BALLOON FIGHT

Did you know you can now fill *twenty-five* water balloons at the same time? Neither did we, but we thank the dude that invented Bunch O Balloons. Clearly he understood that high people do not have the patience to wait for dozens of aquatic explosives. Fill a bucket with water weaponry, then destroy your miniature adversaries.

CAMP IN YOUR BACKYARD

And by "camp," we mean order takeout, utilize indoor plumbing, and sleep in your comfortable bed. But before you slumber, have fun in a tent. Disturbing flashlight faces! Spooky ghost stories! Tickle fights!

#18: MIRROR IMAGE

Cannabis increases awareness and decreases self-consciousness, so take advantage and find out what you may not be seeing sober. Before getting high, look in the mirror and draw a self-portrait. Repeat post puff. Compare, contrast, and consider your complexities. Want to level up? Wait a week and try this exercise in art and self-consciousness again, but now naked.

#19: ROLL AND READ

We know weed enhances imagination (see "Creativity" on page 189 for more mind-expanding ways to unlock your inner artist), but it can also activate the part of your brain that specializes in processing language. Pair enhanced imagination with more access to language, and reading suddenly becomes a multidimensional experience. Imagery becomes more vivid, and rather than having to focus on the words themselves, your brain is able to grasp sentences without the work of active decoding. In other words, the words aren't words; they're the building blocks of vivid worlds.

Cannabis is also great for helping with what cognitive scientists call "selective attention." If you find yourself distracted by the siren song of social media, some Sour Diesel may be just the ticket to get you immersed in a book other than this fine piece of literature you're reading right now. Not sure where to start? Here are a few we're sure were written just for high people.

Fear and Loathing in Las Vegas by Hunter S. Thompson

A classic book that starts "We were somewhere around Barstow on the edge of the desert when the drugs began to take hold" needs little introduction. Sure, your high school English teacher instructed you not to assume the intentions of an author, but we'll go out on a limb and say Hunter S. Thompson wants you to get high as he takes you on his nonstop psychedelic road trip.

Carl Sagan's essay on "Marihuana"

Originally published under the pseudonym Mr. X, the world-famous astronomer contributed an essay on the wonders of weed to the 1971 book *Marihuana Reconsidered*. It's easily found online and discusses how cannabis helped him appreciate music, sex, and even himself.

Devotions: The Selected Poems of Mary Oliver by Mary Oliver

Think you don't understand poetry? Think again. The formidable combination of cannabis and Mary Oliver will win over even the most metaphor-phobic.

Just take a look at this: "When it's over, I want to say all my life/I was a bride married to amazement./I was the bridegroom, taking the world into my arms."

The Book of Delights by Ross Gay

GQ called Gay's book "delightfully snackable." And really, what else could you want from a high read (except maybe actual snacks)? These bite-sized essays are funny, poetic, philosophical marvels—just like your brain on weed's delights.

When You Give a Mouse a Cookie by Laura Numeroff

Sure, it was written for the two-to-five-year-old set, but trust us and dust off your copy. The ramifications of giving that mouse a cookie are mind-blowing for those already well baked. (Spoiler: If you give a mouse a cookie...he'll eventually want another cookie. Just like your high self.)

LEVEL UP

Try reading something in a foreign language you're familiar with but haven't completely internalized. Weed and word translation can equal quicker pattern recognition and increased comprehension of sentences. So light up and access worlds you only peeked at before.

#20: CHANGE PERSPECTIVES

One of the reasons we love cannabis so much is that it helps us see the world anew: your cat becomes an obvious descendant of the regal lion, your drooping orchid part of the great cycle of life. This is partially due to cannabis's ability to stimulate blood flow to the frontal lobe, that same area that lights up when you do creative tasks. All that frontal lobe activity also helps us problem solve. Creativity + problem-solving = new ways of seeing and thinking about the world.

Far be it for us to say that the domesticated feline and the common houseplant don't deserve your undivided attention, but we also encourage you to expand your perspective and literally change perspectives by getting low, high, and upside down. The world looks different when your feet aren't firmly planted on the ground, and you just might find yourself gaining new insights on your place in this crazy cosmic experiment. Below you'll find perception-shifting suggestions for all levels of player.

LEVEL 1

- Lie in the grass.
- Climb a tree.
- Do a headstand (see "Inhale, Exhale" on page 60 for more yogi advice).

LEVEL 2

- Look down from a freeway overpass.
- Swim to the bottom of the pool and look up.
- Hang from your knees at a playground.

LEVEL 10

- Lie in a cemetery.
- Ride a Ferris wheel.
- Wear gravity boots.

FUN FACT

Not only can cannabis change the way you see things, it can change the way you *see* things. One study found that Moroccan fishermen experienced improved night vision when consuming *kif*, a traditional mix of tobacco and cannabis.

#21: BLOW YOUR MIND

Go down a YouTube rabbit hole of mind-blowing, mind-expanding, mind-contorting marvels. Like your first time at a bar mitzvah or Burning Man, it's better not to know too much before dropping into these singular worlds. Instead, we simply suggest typing these terms, exactly as we present them, into Google with your eyes wide open. Note: Standard data rates may apply.

- Cats AND cucumbers
- Industrial shredding machines
- Amazon salvage unboxings
- Street magic
- Lemurs getting high
- "High School" AND (insert musical of your choice)
- Strange animal friendships
- Beatboxing kids
- Bats and hummingbird feeders
- Swimming pig competition
- Kinetic sand cutting
- Cake wrecks

#22: MAKE FRIENDS WITH YOUR LOCAL BUDTENDER

William Butler Yeats wrote, "Education is not the filling of a pail, but the lighting of a fire." You've read the book (this one), you've lit the fire (metaphorically...*and* literally if you've followed our "You'll Never Forget Your First Time" tutorial on page 89), now it's time to move on to higher...higher education.

There's no one more qualified to school you than your local budtender. Many dispensaries now require their budtenders to complete a certification program, so these folks know their stuff. You probably have your own go-to questions (one of us likes to walk into a dispensary and grunt, "sex, sleep, movies" and then hand over the money), but here's a list of questions you may not have thought to ask:

▸ What's local?

▸ What's fresh?

▸ Where was it grown? (Control and consistency are often cited as benefits of a greenhouse grow.)

▸ What's the newest product you're stocking?

▸ Are your products lab tested?

▸ Can I see it/smell it?

▸ Do you have any discounts? (Our favorite dispensary provides discounts for students, teachers, and military personnel.)

EDUCATE YOURSELF

Many dispensaries are now offering community classes on all kinds of cannabis-centered topics, so ask what's on offer. Want to take it higher? There are a number of colleges and universities offering degree programs in cannabis and medicinal plant studies. And some dispensaries offer educational workshops for customers on strains, delivery systems, and more.

#23: YOU'LL NEVER FORGET YOUR FIRST TIME

William Blake (and Aldous Huxley, who borrowed the quote for his book on psychedelics) was onto something when he wrote, "If the doors of perception were cleansed, every thing would appear to man as it is: infinite." Help someone see the world as infinite, or at least as infinitely fascinating. Because what makes everything infinitely fascinating? Weed. And who has plenty of that fine, fine ganja? You.

Before lighting up, though, prepare for the possibility that your newbie friend won't feel the effects of getting high. There are two schools of thought on why this happens. One is that since weed contains cannabinoids that react with the cannabinoid receptors in your body, it may take a few smoking sessions to fully activate these receptors, since they're used to your body's naturally produced cannabinoids. The more likely scenario is that your

55

Percent of adult cannabis users who use cannabis to relax—the most frequently cited reason in the United States.

> "Marijuana, if used in moderation, plus loud, usually low-class music, make stress and boredom infinitely more bearable."
>
> **–KURT VONNEGUT**

first-timer is doing it wrong. This won't be an issue if you're taking an edible, but we recommend going old school and lighting up like thousands of years of stoners before you. To make sure your friend (a eighteen-to-twenty-one-year-old friend depending on what state you live in) doesn't make the same rookie mistake as President "I didn't inhale" Clinton, teach them how with these four easy steps.

1. Slowly draw smoke into your mouth.
2. Hold the smoke in your closed mouth.
3. Open your mouth and take a breath, inhaling the smoke along with fresh air.
4. Exhale.

"I have always loved marijuana. It has been a source of joy and comfort to me for many years. And I still think of it as a basic staple of life, along with beer and ice and grapefruits—and millions of Americans agree with me."

–HUNTER S. THOMPSON

PRO TIP:

Even experienced smokers may be under the misguided belief that you have to hold...your...smoke...as...long...as...possible. Not true. The second you inhale, the cannabinoids are absorbed by your body, so only hold it if you want to sound like the proverbial stoner when you ask your friend if they're high yet.

MUSIC

BEAUTIFUL MUSIC, TOGETHER

Music. Is. So. Good.

If you believe in the gospel of these four words, as we do, you don't need a lot of convincing that listening to music while high is even better. But how? But why? Is it all in your head?

In a way, it is. "Cannabis works like a psychoacoustic enhancer," said Dr. Jörg Fachner, a professor of music, health, and the brain at the Cambridge Institute for Music Therapy Research, which just means cannabis enhances our ability to focus on sound. In a world where most of us have too many mental (and actual) tabs open, the focus that cannabis can offer is ideal for busy brains to zero in on one thing: the music.

But before we tell you *how* to listen high, let's start with *why* to listen high. Music, like all sound, is channeled into the ear canal as sound waves, which strike the eardrum, causing vibrations and changing the acoustic energy into mechanical energy. Then things get really good. The sound waves continue their travels into the inner ear where our friends the cannabinoid receptors are found. Add cannabis, and your receptors are getting a double dose of the stuff that makes the brain's pleasure centers groove.

1976

The year Peter Tosh released the song "Legalize It," which became a lasting cult classic over the forty-year march to actual legalization.

Cannabis also helps you land deeply in the moment, and that "being in the moment" thing is one of the reasons music sounds so good. Daniel J. Levitin, a music psychologist and professor and author of *The World in Six Songs: How the Musical Brain Created Human Nature*, explains: "The disruption of short-term memory thrusts listeners into the moment of the music as it unfolds; people stoned on pot tend to hear music from note to note...completely in the moment." In other words, get ready to hear your favorite song for the first time...again...and again and again.

FIELD NOTES

Listen, Do You Want to Know a Secret? We can all probably name a bowlful of songs that are clearly about cannabis ("Roll Me Up and Smoke Me When I Die" by the iconic cannabis crooner Willie Nelson, for one). But did you know about the canon of songs you may not have realized were about your favorite herb?

1. "Brown Sugar," D'Angelo
No, D'Angelo isn't in love with a beautiful woman when he sings, "See, we be making love constantly. That's why my eyes are a shade blood burgundy." Want to know why his eyes are a shade of blood burgundy? (See "Five Dollars or Less" on page 128.)

2. "Puff the Magic Dragon," Peter, Paul, and Mary
Let's just get this out of the way: Santa Claus isn't real, you don't have to wait an hour after eating before swimming, and this song is not about a fire-breathing dragon.

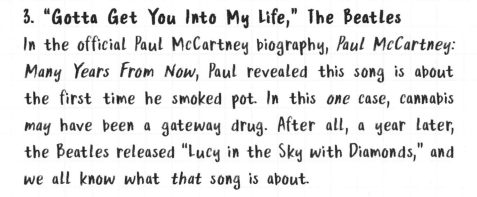

3. "Gotta Get You Into My Life," The Beatles

In the official Paul McCartney biography, *Paul McCartney: Many Years From Now*, Paul revealed this song is about the first time he smoked pot. In this *one* case, cannabis may have been a gateway drug. After all, a year later, the Beatles released "Lucy in the Sky with Diamonds," and we all know what *that* song is about.

4. "Sweet Leaf," Black Sabbath

Ozzie sings, "I love you sweet leaf, though you can't hear." Some fans think he was crooning about a famous Irish tobacco company. He was not.

5. "Mary Jane's Last Dance," Tom Petty

Yes, it's in the title, but then all that stuff about growing up in Indiana with a "good lookin' momma" might make you doubt yourself. Don't doubt yourself. "Mary Jane," not Mary Jane, is what's gonna "kill the pain."

ACTIVITIES

#24: LISTEN LIKE A MUSICIAN

Our favorite stoner scientist, Carl Sagan, knew the power cannabis had on music. Writing as "Mr. X," he discussed his views on cannabis in the 1971 book *Marihuana Reconsidered*: "For the first time I have been able to hear the separate parts of a three-part harmony and the richness of the counter-point. I have since discovered that professional musicians can quite easily keep many separate parts going simultaneously in their heads, but this was the first time for me."

We asked Rob Ahlers, drummer for 50 Foot Wave and the Kristin Hersh Electric Trio, for some tips on how to channel your inner musician and really hear each component of a song. He suggests these three activities:

▶ First, you'll want to make sure you have at least two speakers (or four if that's the kind of sound geek you are). Then, dig up some songs that were original-ly recorded in both mono and stereo. Mono is when the exact same sound comes out of both speakers (older musicians often preferred mono because it left them in charge of the listening process). Stereo is when a song has been mixed in a way that allows you to hear certain instruments from one speaker and other instruments from the other speaker. The Beatles are great for this experiment, but not *all* Beatles recordings, since some albums were only recorded in one format. We recommend one of our faves, *Rubber Soul*, for this experiment. Listen to a song first in mono, then switch over to stereo, and turn your balance all the way to the left, then all the way to the right. The instruments and vocals will isolate themselves, so you and Carl can marvel at your newfound ability to hear all the parts.

▶ Search "isolated tracks" on YouTube, and listen to each track of your favorite songs. We won't deny we favor the Beatles, so we're pushing "Here Comes the Sun" for this one. You'll get the drums, bass, guitar, moog and strings, and vocals in sequential order.

▶ Find a car that has a 5.1 surround sound system (or better yet, a 7.1 surround sound system, but those are harder to find). Most come with a CD specially made to showcase the surround sound. Park, puff, and listen to all those channels funneling sounds to your delighted ears.

#25: KIND BUD, EARBUDS, GOOD BUDDIES

Remember that simple, sexy music move you learned about in the movies and maybe even tried yourselves? You know the one: a single pair of headphones shared between you and your guy, gal, or nonbinary friend. It's a move ripe for a sequel, only now with much better headphones and artisanal Bubba Kush instead of that skunk weed you dug out of your Guess jeans. Grab some earbuds (headphones won't work for this one), cuddle up, and take turns playing DJ for each other. Enjoy the tunes, but also try pressing play on some more unusual offerings.

Try a soundscape—an "acoustic environment" that blends all kinds of far-out sounds: animal vocalizations, weather events, and cities that "speak," oh my.

#26: PLAY THE SOUNDTRACK OF YOUR LIFE GAME

A well-chosen strain of cannabis (we like Trainwreck) and a great group of friends fosters good times, connection, and giggling. Now add our Soundtrack of Your Life Game and get ready to double your fun. Here's how to play:

1 Gather a group of friends and appoint one of them the DJ.

2 Grab some note cards, yellow stickies, or bar napkins, and label with the following:

- ⚡ Middle school
- ⚡ High school
- ⚡ First or best love
- ⚡ Current or most recent relationship
- ⚡ Family (parents/kids/cousins)
- ⚡ Firsts (jobs, kisses, drugs, etc.)

3 Place them all facedown, then turn one over.

4 Have each player find a song on the streaming service of your choice that makes them think about or connects them to the time of life on the card in play. Now each player writes the title and artist of the song on a piece of paper, folds it up, and hands it back to the DJ.

5 Have the DJ add all the songs to a playlist.

6 Hit play and get your party on. Serve dinner/drinks/strains/snacks, but pay attention to the music. As each song comes on, everyone takes a turn guessing who chose it. Award one point for each correct answer, or just skip the competition and let the music and memories play.

#27: DARK SIDE OF THE RAINBOW, AKA THE WIZARD OF FLOYD

Legend has it that if you sync Pink Floyd's *Dark Side of the Moon* with *The Wizard of Oz*, you'll see the face of God. Okay, maybe not, but you'll definitely be delighted by the trippy synchronicity. Here's how to do it:

1 Queue up *The Wizard of Oz* and *Dark Side of the Moon*.

2 Get snacks.

3 Start the movie, and wait for the MGM lion as the cue. This is where experts differ, but we suggest pushing play on the album as soon as the lion finishes his third roar.

4 Turn on the subtitles, turn off the film's audio, and tune in to being one with decades of stoners before you.

connection

Buddhist writer Alan Watts said, "If you go off into a far, far forest and get very quiet, you'll come to understand that you're connected with everything." We like to think of that forest as a metaphor for the great green magic maker. Partake of the flower, and you too will come to see the vast ecosystem of connection around you. In less flowery terms (apologies), cannabis is great at helping you feel connected to the people in your life. After all, the benefits of cannabis—reducing anxiety, improving focus, activating self-awareness, and encouraging empathy—are also the keys to strong relationships. And not only *that*, cannabis is great for bonding, intimacy, and sexy times (skip to paragraph four if you're just here for the sex).

Part of the reason weed is so great at bringing us together is because it encourages bonding, and bonding triggers the neurotransmitter oxytocin (otherwise known as the cuddle chemical, the hug hormone, the mush molecule, the...oh you get it). Oxytocin is so important for bonding that when researchers sprayed monkeys with it, they became more communicative, extroverted, and social. And, it turns out, oxytocin makes these social behaviors more rewarding because it triggers the release of our favorite endocannabinoid—the one, the only, the bliss hormone, anandamide. In other words, put oxytocin, anandamide, and THC in the same room, and you've got a party to top all parties. And what makes that social event of the year even better? We're going to go with hysterical laughter and physical pleasure.

One of the main ways we humans bond is through shared joy and physical touch, and there's nothing more joyful than laughing (we promise, we'll talk about sex next). Cannabis isn't called the wacky weed for nothing. It fuels laughter by stimulating blood flow to the right frontal and left temporal lobes of the brain, which brings on the giggles. And shared laughter signals that you and your co-laugher see the world similarly, which boosts connection. And once you've boosted that connection, what do you want to do with all those warm happy feelings? Well, children, sometimes, when two people love each other very much, they want to get very close to each other. Without clothes on.

And thus we come to one of our favorite of cannabis's superpower: its ability to make sex even better. We doubt you need proof for this seemingly obvious statement, but we've got it. A study titled "The Relationship between Marijuana Use Prior to Sex and Sexual Function in Women" from the journal *Sexual Medicine* found that people who used cannabis before sex rated their pleasure higher than those who didn't. And women seem to have even more dramatic results. Most women in the study experienced an increase in sex drive and reported that they were two times more likely to have satisfying orgasms than women who did not use cannabis before sex. But it's not just good for the ladies. Research in rats suggests that stimulating the CB1 receptor delays ejaculation, and that, friends, is good for everyone.

Still, science hasn't been able to pinpoint exactly why cannabis makes sex better, not to mention more frequent. Researchers at Stanford report higher cannabis use means more sex, so get to smoking, but they think that it's partly because it reduces stress and anxiety and partly because of the large amount of endocannabinoid receptors in the areas of the brain that handle sex, like the amygdala and hypothalamus. Researchers are also discovering that the body releases naturally occurring endocannabinoids after orgasm, so cannabis is just doubling up on what's already there. Cannabis is also a vasodilator (it opens blood vessels and increases blood flow), which has a direct effect on the cannabinoid receptors in your skin and nerve pathways, making your skin even more deliciously sensitive. Add THC's ability to decrease inhibitions, diminish fear, and tamp down anxiety to your blissed-out brain, and sex suddenly goes to eleven.

So whether you plan to have a friendly hang with your favorite cats and kittens or pull a John and Yoko and spend two weeks in bed, we're going to suggest you smoke a little reefer, give the following activities a gander, and get to connecting, man.

FIELD NOTES

OK, Fumer: According to a study published in 2020 in the *Journal of the American Medical Association*, the number of Americans over age sixty-five who smoke flower or use edibles increased twofold between 2015 and 2018. Old hippies dusting off their bong? Not exactly. Older Americans are among the fastest-growing groups enjoying the fruits of this ancient flower for many of the same medicinal reasons millennials and other generations are increasingly enjoying it: anxiety, pain, and sleep. "What I'm seeing in my clinic are a lot of older adults who are very curious about cannabis to treat this or that chronic disease and symptoms," said Dr. Benjamin Han, a coauthor of the study and assistant professor of geriatric medicine and palliative care at New York University's Grossman School of Medicine. As Americans live longer, the business of bud will surely keep booming.

Gender Studies: High people are like elevated snowflakes: no two brains and bodies react the same way to cannabis, even if they're sharing the same strain, dose, and delivery system. And here's another variable to consider: your sex. A study by Washington State University looked at cannabis tolerance and found that females build a tolerance to cannabis much more easily than males. While the study was done on rats, since female rats have a menstrual cycle and experience fluctuations in hormone levels in a way that's very similar to female humans, it's likely to have the same effect on people. The one area in which males are more sensitive to THC? The munchies. A study by researchers in Washington State found that THC stimulated the appetites of male animals more than those of females. And nobody wants a bong belly.

FUN FACT

Cannabis also has a gender; it can be either male or female, but only females make buds, the part of the plant that contains the most THC.

BONUS FUN FACT

One of our all-time favorite weed podcasts, *Broccoli Talk*, is run exclusively on girl power.

Gaming with Ganja: We know, we know—that roommate who seemed to spend most of his waking life getting stoned alone and playing *Grand Theft Auto* was concerning. But maybe he was simply ahead of his time? Cannabis can increase oxygenation of tissues, improve vision, and boost concentration, which is one reason it's embraced by many extreme sports athletes and extreme gamers. With gaming's rapid evolution from solo play to multiplayer games, cannabis has become both social and a legitimate competitive sport.

ACTIVITIES

#28: WON'T YOU BE MY NEIGHBOR?

As Mr. Rogers said, "It's a beautiful day in this neighborhood, a beautiful day for a neighbor," but when's the last time you really explored your hood and got to know your neighbors? We don't (necessarily) recommend knocking on doors with packed pipe in hand, but why not smoke a little and go exploring? The THC will slow your dorsolateral prefrontal cortex and smooth over any reservations you may have about showing up unannounced. Try these activities to make new friends and see your surrounding streets through green-tinted glasses.

BAKED BAKED GOODS

Go old school and channel your inner domestic god or goddess by supplying your neighbors with "just because" sweet treats. It doesn't really matter what you bake—cookies, pie, croquembouche—but save the canna-infused sweets for those you know are 420-friendly (consent, of course, is important even outside the bedroom). If you hate baking, pick up a box of Sunday morning donuts (really, you could stick a bow on a pack of Little Debbie snack cakes and your neighbors would be just as delighted). Then go distributing. Don't forget to attach a card with contact info. Connection is, after all, the reason for the treats.

LITTLE LIBRARIES

You've seen them around town—little house-like structures that are bigger than a bird house and not made to house birds. Those little dwellings house books—*free* books. The idea is to take a book you want to read and leave a book you've read. So first go through your bookshelves (might we suggest you pair this with "Green Cleaning" on page 147?), and then set out on a quest to find your most literary neighbors. Some little libraries are part of the Little Free Library program and are mapped at littlefreelibrary.org, but there are plenty of off-brand houses about, so wander down whatever side street strikes your fancy. And if you find another copy of this compendium of pleasures you're currently reading, take a pic and send it to us. Then pass the bookie on the left-hand side.

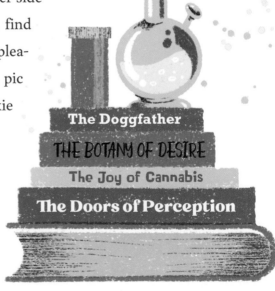

The Doggfather

THE BOTANY OF DESIRE

The Joy of Cannabis

The Doors of Perception

HIT THE OPEN HOUSES

We all love a good smoke 'n' walk, and, truthfully, it's an enjoyable experience no matter what environment you do it in, but it's ten times more enjoyable when you do it on a Sunday in the 11:00 a.m. to 3:00 p.m. window. Why? Because that's when most open houses take place. We're curious creatures, and we love snooping around other people's houses. Want to level up? Amble over to the *fancy*

94

Percent of cannabis-related arrests and summonses that involve New Yorkers of color according to a 2020 analysis by the Legal Aid Society.

side of town and see how the other half live. It's fun to dream, so let yourself wonder whether you'd have built the outdoor bed on the balcony or the deck and whether that wine cellar would have worked better as a sauna. Don't forget to help yourself to the complimentary snacks (Realtors love that stuff). Those freshly baked chocolate chip cookies aren't going to eat themselves.

#29: LAUGH YOUR GRASS OFF

The only thing more on brand than getting a case of the high munchies is getting a case of the high giggles. What's so funny? Sometimes it seems like everything. That's because cannabis stimulates blood flow to the right frontal and left temporal lobes of the brain, which stimulate laughter. So it makes sense that you're more likely to find that *Simpsons* episode *hysterical* when you're high. And if you wonder why when one person starts laughing, everyone is soon snorting away, it's because our brains contain neurotransmitters called mirror neurons. That's why you yawn when someone else yawns and laugh when there's laughter in the room. Shared laughter also signals that you and your co-laugher see the world similarly, which boosts connection. We're sure you and your baked buddies will have no trouble finding things that are *hilarious*, but in case you need a recommendation, may we suggest you fall in love with cartoons again. As a kid, who didn't love watching Wile E. Coyote getting bonked on the head with an anvil? Add cannabis, and it's still pretty damn funny. Below is a selection of some adult-friendly cartoons to check out and the strains we recommend you pair them with.

Aqua Teen Hunger Force = Laughing Buddha

Rick and Morty = Sweet Diesel

Adventure Time = Mango Kush

South Park = Gorilla Glue

Ed, Edd n Eddy = Black Diamond

Courage the Cowardly Dog = Chem Dawg

Tom and Jerry (not just for adults, but it's *Tom and Jerry*, dudes!) = Church OG

#30: PLAY NEVER HAVE I EVER, THE HIGH VERSION

This classic party game is the poster child for the joys of uninhibited hangouts. Alcohol may be the most popular social lubricant at Never Have I Ever game night, but cannabis makes a strong case to take the reins. After all, when THC binds to our endocannabinoid receptors, the brain gets the bliss signal that can decrease fear, anxiety, and any inhibitions you may have previously had about telling your friends you once got high with your second cousin and made out. Here's how to play Never Have I Ever, the High Version like never before.

1. Gather your friends and take turns sharing a statement about your cannabis use that starts with "Never have I ever." Examples include "Never have I ever bought a dime bag from a stranger." "Never have I ever got high with a family member," "Never have I ever accidentally on purpose smoked pure kief and then needed a friend to hold my hand for two hours and reassure me I was, indeed, still human." (We're not saying one of us may have done this...but one of us may have done this.)

2. Anyone who has done the "Never have I ever" action takes a hit. If the statement truthfully applies to *everyone*, then the person making the "Never have I ever" statement takes a hit.

PRO TIP

Use a low THC strain for this one, so you can play for longer. We recommend Harlequin or Sour Tsunami to avoid being *too* too high.

STONING THE ELDERS

by Alia Volz

I grew up in the cannabis underground. My mom was the driving force behind Sticky Fingers Brownies, San Francisco's first high-volume edibles business, which distributed 10,000 brownies per month in the 1970s. Later, during the HIV-AIDS crisis of the 1980s and '90s, my mom became a pioneer in the medical marijuana movement. In writing *Home Baked*, my memoir about the family business, I interviewed more than sixty elders about their involvement in the illegal weed world of yesteryear. I was nervous at first, afraid that prying would upset my interviewees. I needn't have worried.

In the United States, where we celebrate youth culture and tend to dismiss elders for being out of step with the latest trends, an attentive ear is a rare thing. Seniors might not know the difference between Tic Tacs and TikTok, but they have seen political regimes rise and fall; they've faced heartbreak, illness, global crises, and personal crises—and they have survived. We might presume that a quiet person has nothing to say. But what if they simply think no one wants to listen? Take a chance, ask a few questions, and watch eyes that have seen it all light up with story. See layers of age peel back like the petals of spring flowers.

Cannabis and storytelling go hand in hand. Stimulating the endocannabinoid system helps us slow down and unwind. It lowers our defenses and loosens our tongues. Time distends, making way for longer reminiscences. It makes us better listeners too. Thanks to the diminishing social stigma and broader knowledge about the plant's medicinal properties, senior citizens are today's fastest-growing group of cannabis enthusiasts. Some are trying cannabis for the first time, while others are returning to a pleasure of youth. This presents wonderful new opportunities for multigenerational connection. There's nothing like sharing an edible or smoking an old-fashioned "doobie" with Mom, Dad, Grandma, or a neighbor. Trust yourself (and the herb), and find out what's hiding behind the wizened faces in your life. Then kick back and let the stories swirl around you like so much smoke.

Alia Volz is a writer and author of the memoir Home Baked: My Mom, Marijuana, and the Stoning of San Francisco.

#31: ZOOM SESH

When Tim Berners-Lee created the World Wide Web in 1989, did he have any idea the Pandora's box of both horror and delight the world was about to open? We may never know, but we do know that one of the early dreams of a connected world was to bring communities together. For better or for worse, the web has done that, and when it's for better, it feels pretty darn great. That rush we get when we meet other fans of *Battlestar Galactica* comes partially from the bliss hormone, anandamide. Researchers discovered that connecting with others increased production of anandamide, which then reinforced the pleasure of connecting, which then increased anandamide—it's a circle, man. Adding actual cannabis—often called "the social plant"—into the mix kicks the pleasure of connecting into high gear.

Mingling the magic of cannabis with the timeless joy of playing games with friends is a winning combination. Now add the convenience of doing it from the comfort of your own home, and—*bam!*—total pleasure. Here are five ways to turn a Zoom room into a space of earthly delights.

STRIP TOKER

Depending on how well you know your fellow game players—or how well you *want* to know them—consider Strip Toker. It's like poker, but not like it at all! Instead of playing cards, you're all taking a hit of weed and seeing who can hold it the longest. Whoever exhales first removes a piece of clothing. Finally, it's okay to take your pants off in a Zoom room.

POWERPOINT NIGHT

Get a group of friends, and have each participant prepare a ten-minute PowerPoint on any topic of their choice. Go for the absurd (Disney Princesses I'd Smoke With), the personal (Ranking My Most Embarrassing Moments While High), or the bond making (How Each of Us Would Fare on *MasterChef: Cannabis Edition*). Go crazy with turbulent transitions, unprofessional fonts, and goofy sound effects.

SCRIBL.IO

This online drawing game will have you giggling and guessing like you used to as a kid playing Pictionary. Drawing on a laptop, phone, or tablet only makes these drawings come out sillier. You've heard of Paint & Sip. Now get ready for Doodle & Puff.

AMONG US

Any virtual game list wouldn't be complete without this viral sensation. Each player joins a game to find out who "among us" is a killer. Like Mafia but cuter and set in a command ship, this game lets you have a murder mystery night, all from the comfort of your own home. Cozy up, consume your cannabis, and find out which of your friends is the most suspicious.

PRO TIP

Whatever your Zoom pleasure, designate a Zoommaster to serve as cruise director. Your leader should be someone who stays social when stoned, can keep the game flowing, and knows how to read a Zoom room. Is it time to end the game, put on some music, and just let everyone kick back and chill? Your Zoommaster will know.

#32: GREEN GRATITUDE

Thank-you notes. Your mother told you to write them, and did you? In addition to calling your mom, we want you to write that thank-you note. But not for those decorative yoga-practicing lawn frogs Aunt Helen sent. No, we want you to write a thank-you note to someone you're grateful for. You've heard it before, but gratitude not only makes the receiver feel good, it makes the giver feel good.

1

Percent of cannabis dispensaries with Black owners, according to a 2016 *BuzzFeed* analysis.

Dr. Martin E. P. Seligman, considered the father of modern positive psychology and a professor at the University of Pennsylvania, found that people who wrote and personally delivered a letter of gratitude to someone they had never properly thanked showed a huge increase in happiness. You too can get that happiness. Use the power of the flower to decrease inhibitions and harness those big feelings hiding just under the surface. Then choose a human you're grateful for and get to writing. Stuck on who to write to? May we suggest a former teacher, a mentor, a favorite aunt or uncle, a childhood friend, or your local budtender.

HELPFUL HINTS

▸ Don't worry about length or quality of stationery. It's the sentiment that matters—we promise.

▸ If the thought of expressing yourself gives you hives, try a strain high in linalool, a calming terpene good for relaxation. We're sure your letter is the stuff of geniuses, but just to be sure, reread before sending. Sober you needs as much say in these things as high you.

THE BLACKNESS OF WEED

by Mennlay Golokeh Aggrey

Since 1998, there's been one constant in my life—weed. It certainly was not in my West African immigrant household growing up, yet the pervasive healing of cannabis entered my life at the dewy age of fourteen. Cannabis was a way to tap out of my teenage depression and tap into a secret rite of passage: a focused and mature appreciation for Black youth, a concept often uncelebrated.

It wasn't until 2005 that my portal to joy turned into a full-time career. Under California's Proposition 215, my budding career choice in the world of weed became precariously legal. On this new path, it was made clear that my involvement would be fraught with the obstacles of being Black. Black in weed. Black in a small rural hippie town. Black in the supermarket. Black in the nice neighborhood until my neighbors threatened to call the police. That naive joy of my youth hardened as I continued to clench to survive in the industry.

According to a study by *Marijuana Business Daily*, Black folks represent less than 5 percent of cannabis executives. Nevertheless, in every state, we African descendants are arrested at exorbitantly higher rates than any group for marijuana possession—including in legalized states.

What can we do to repair the wrongs for people least represented in the legal cannabis industry yet most abused by the "war on drugs"? Start by using one of these three action steps.

1. Buy Black using *InclusiveBase*, a database for conscious cannabis consumers with over 700 companies of color leading the way in the weed renaissance.

2. Support initiatives that prioritize the needs of BIPOC communities like the Floret Coalition, an antiracist cannabis collective using the giving circle model to fund equity-oriented actions via monthly donations.

3. Get active politically by voting for national and local laws that reinforce equitable industry standards.

Mennlay Golokeh Aggrey is an interdisciplinary cannabis professional, author of The Art of Weed Butter, and cofounder of the hemp brand Xula. She currently resides in Mexico City where her work explores the African diaspora via cannabis and cuisine.

THE PATH FORWARD

For a personal, historical, and political perspective on cannabis, there's perhaps no one better to turn to than **asha bandele**, an award-winning journalist, celebrated racial justice and prison abolition advocate, and bestselling writer of six books, including the memoir *The Prisoner's Wife* and Patrisse Cullors's story, *When They Call You a Terrorist: A Black Lives Matter Memoir*. Here she shares her insights into cannabis's racist past and more hopeful future.

Historically, criminalization of cannabis has disproportionately hurt Black and brown cannabis users. Can you give us a high-level overview of the problem?

The first laws criminalizing cannabis coincide with migratory patterns and economic concerns—Black people escaping white terrorism in the South, Mexicans migrating north to work the plantations, and the United States trying to pull itself out of the Great Depression. When the federal Marijuana Tax Act was passed in 1937, it effectively yanked a whole lot of Black people out of job market competition and instead returned them to a free labor system behind prison walls.

None of this could have happened without a complicit media, which continually amplified false reports (most notably pushed by Harry Anslinger, who ran the Treasury Department's Bureau of Narcotics and whose reign of terror reverberates in law enforcement today). Even with 68 percent of Americans supporting cannabis legalization, in a liberal state like New York, Black and brown people continue to comprise 90 percent of cannabis arrests—despite all the data that indicate white people use and sell it at equal or greater levels.

Legalization hasn't fixed the inequities Black and brown people face related to cannabis when it comes to the criminal legal system. What can people do to help address this?

Dr. Maya Angelou instructed that we have to have courage to do anything well, and to do this work well, we have to have the courage to reckon with the full accounting of our history, including privilege wrongfully afforded to some at the expense of others. So the first thing we need to do is ask ourselves these questions:

How do we now level-set? What are those who have benefited from others' harm willing to give up? Are we drafting and fighting for laws that undo and address the underlying and long-standing harms of criminalization? Are we considering where and with whom we ground our understanding and history? If we read about cannabis (or any drug), are we reading the leading scientists on the subjects, like Dr. Carl Hart, author of *Drug Use for Grown-Ups: Chasing Liberty in the Land of Fear*?

If you ask the wrong questions, you're bound to get the wrong answers. It's that simple. The information is there. We just need the interest, a real excavation of the query: What are our true end goals?

What organizations can people support to help make a difference in the fight for equitable drug laws and treatment?

There are many people and organizations fighting the good fight. Here are a few places to start.

The Hood Incubator (hoodincubator.org) works to help Black community members thrive as workers, owners, and investors in the growing legal cannabis economy.

Cannaclusive (cannaclusive.com) facilitates fair representation of minority cannabis consumers and provides ways for consumers to support equity in the cannabis industry.

The Harm Reduction Coalition (harmreduction.org) works to create constructive conversations with communities, legislators, and public health organizations to promote harm reduction services and change the narrative about people who use drugs.

Supernova Women (supernovawomen.com) empowers people of color to become self-sufficient shareholders in the cannabis economy.

#33: SAME THING, SAME TIME

If we told you you're about to learn how to play a collaborative word game where you and a friend try and say the same thing at the same time, you might (understandably) turn the page...but wait! Trust us when we say that this may be the most fun you can have high with another person...without spending money...or touching each other.

Here's how to play, with a real-life example to illustrate:

Get a friend (you can play with more than two, but it's a lot harder). Each of you thinks of a word and on the count of three, say the word. It doesn't matter what the word is. Sure, you can go with *snickersnee* (a large knife used to fight in the 1700s), but choosing something more commonplace will bring faster success.

> **Melanie:** circle
> **Larry:** coffee

1 Now go again, but this time try to say the same word by finding the intersection of these two words. You're looking for a word that connects the two or is something they have in common.

> **Melanie:** mug (*both mugs and circles are round*)
> **Larry:** bean (*both coffee beans and circles are round*)

2 And again. Everyone thinks differently, so it usually takes a number of rounds to get to the same word.

> **Melanie:** soup (*you put soup in a mug, soup can have beans in it*)
> **Larry:** hot (*beans are eaten/drunk hot, mugs hold hot things*)

3 And again...

> **Melanie:** chicken noodle (*whoa, mind meld*)
> **Larry:** chicken noodle (*whoa, mind meld*)

75

Percent of all employees in the cannabis industry who report that they joined this fast-growing job sector for the chance to create change.

Of course, you can play this game without the wacky weed, but cannabis is great for free association because it increases automatic semantic priming, which means when you encounter one concept, it makes related concepts more accessible. Not to mention that you'll be even more blown away by your telekinetic superpowers and be ready to take on the world like the Wonder Twins you are.

#34: HEAD TO BOLLYWOOD

What goes better with cannabis than movies? Sex (see "Get It on Ganja Style" on page 133)! Also, music ("Beautiful Music, Together" on page 92). Also, food ("Cannabis Cuisine" on page 172). But *then* it's movies. Movies *for sure*. The reason movies are so enjoyable when you're high has to do with THC's slowing effect on the amygdala. The amygdala recognizes stimuli and triggers a response. A slowed amygdala doesn't recognize stimuli as quickly, so what you're encountering (those moving images on your flat screen) seem even more fascinating and entertaining. Not to mention that when THC binds with those CB1 receptors, the effect is a blissed-out brain. Now add friends and family to the mix, and you've got the recipe for a perfect evening.

There are lots of movies that pair perfectly with our favorite herb (see our flow chart on page 129 to find your ideal match), but if you're in the mood for something a little more adventurous, take a trip east and find out why Bollywood is famous for its "masala" films. Masala is a mixture of spices and, fittingly, masala films are a spicy combination of action, comedy, romance, drama, and melodrama all tied together with fifty-seven musical numbers! To fully appreciate Bollywood's cinematic genius, we recommend preparing a bhang elixir (recipe included) and pairing it with one (or all) of our recommended technicolor masterpieces, readily available wherever you're streaming entertainment these days.

BOLLYWOOD BLOCKBUSTERS

Amar, Akbar, and Anthony

Three brothers are separated, one brought up as a Hindu, one a Muslim, and one a Christian. If it sounds like the beginning of a bad joke, you're so very wrong. This '70s epic would keep you laughing even if you weren't high.

Go Goa Gone

Friends + a rave + a remote island + an experimental drug that turns people into... zombies? This zom-com plays for laughs in this slacker comedy. We'll trust you'll ignore the "just say no to drugs" message at the end.

Delhi Belly

This funny, filthy romp is a *Hangover*-style adventure following three roommates who get mixed up with a hard-nosed gangster. Psst...if your bleary bhang eyes can't manage that subtitle-reading thing, this one is mostly in English.

Bhang Elixir

PREP: 15 minutes • **COOK:** 30 minutes

TOTAL TIME: 45 minutes • **YIELD:** 4 cups

INGREDIENTS

- 2 cups water
- ½ ounce fresh cannabis leaves, buds, and flowers
- 3 cups warm milk, divided
- ¼ teaspoon garam masala
- ¼ teaspoon ground ginger
- ½ teaspoon ground cardamom
- ½ cup sugar

DIRECTIONS

Heat the water to a rapid boil, then remove from heat and add the cannabis. Steep for about 7 minutes.

Strain the leaves and flower, squeezing all the liquid goodness out. Set the water aside.

Combine the leaves and flowers with 2 teaspoons of warm milk and grind using a mortar and pestle. Slowly add milk, and continue grinding until you've used about ½ cup of milk and formed a fine paste.

Stir the paste into the remaining milk.

Add 1 cup of steeped water to the milk/paste mixture.

Add the garam masala, ginger, cardamom, and sugar, and stir well.

Pour into mugs and serve.

THE LORD OF BHANG

Shiva, the god of destruction, is considered the lord of bhang because of his love of everything society rejects—you know, corpses, intoxicants. One of the earliest mentions of cannabis is found in the Vedas, a collection of sacred Hindu texts written around 2000 BC. According to the seventeenth-century *Raja Valabha*, the gods created cannabis because of "compassion for the human race, so they might attain delight, lose fear and have sexual desire." The gods churned the heavenly ocean so that a drop of sacred nectar fell from the sky, and from it the first cannabis plant sprouted, a plant so sacred, a guardian angel lives in its leaves (and who are we to argue?).

#35: FIVE DOLLARS OR LESS

Who says you need a lot of money for rollicking good times? After all, that edible you just ingested probably only cost you two bucks for hours of top-notch entertainment. Using the same principle, get yourself a friend or five, fix a five-dollar budget, and set yourselves loose in a big box store. Whoever finds maximum entertainment for minimum value wins. Our research shows five dollars can get you a pound of gummy bears, a five pack of silly putty, five hundred gold stars, or a deeply discounted copy of *Hocus Pocus*! With that kind of haul, everyone's a winner. Plus, collective goals are great for team building, and what are you and your friends but a super high team of flower fanatics?

PRO TIP

Bring sunglasses; it can get bright in there. Also, those shades will hide your telltale red eyes, which (fun fact) occur when THC causes the blood vessels in your eyes to dilate, creating those bloodshot eyeballs. The good news? That same dilation is treating your undiagnosed glaucoma.

WHAT MOVIE SHOULD YOU WATCH?

⟶ ARE YOU HIGH? ⟵

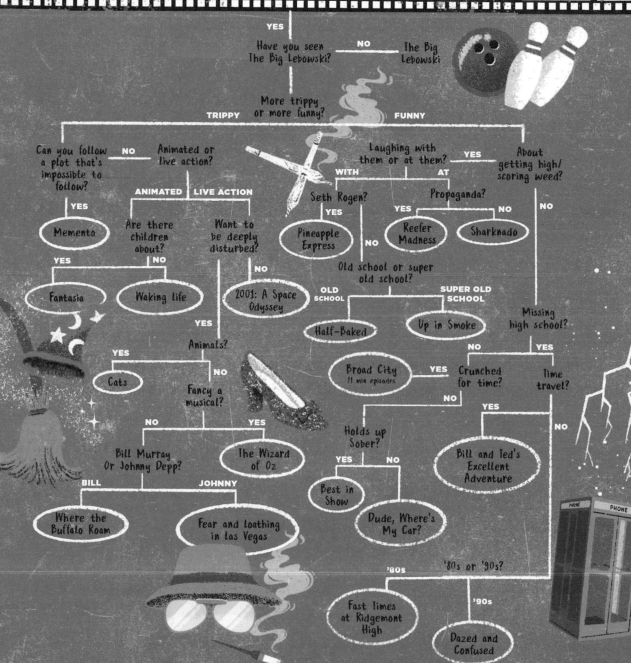

Have you seen The Big Lebowski?
- YES
- NO → The Big Lebowski

More trippy or more funny?

TRIPPY

Can you follow a plot that's impossible to follow?
- NO → **Animated or live action?**
- YES → Memento

Animated or live action?
- **ANIMATED** → **Are there children about?**
  - YES → Fantasia
  - NO → Waking Life
- **LIVE ACTION** → **Want to be deeply disturbed?**
  - NO → 2001: A Space Odyssey
  - YES → **Animals?**
    - YES → Cats
    - NO → **Fancy a musical?**
      - NO → **Bill Murray Or Johnny Depp?**
        - BILL → Where the Buffalo Roam
        - JOHNNY → Fear and loathing in Las Vegas
      - YES → The Wizard of Oz

FUNNY

Laughing with them or at them?

About getting high/ scoring weed?
- YES
- NO → **Missing high school?**
  - NO → Broad City — 11 min episodes
  - YES → **Time travel?**
    - YES → Bill and Ted's Excellent Adventure
    - NO → **'80s or '90s?**
      - '80s → Fast Times at Ridgemont High
      - '90s → Dazed and Confused

WITH

Seth Rogen?
- YES → Pineapple Express
- NO → **Old school or super old school?**
  - **OLD SCHOOL** → Half-Baked
  - **SUPER OLD SCHOOL** → Up in Smoke

AT

Propaganda?
- YES → Reefer Madness
- NO → Sharknado

Crunched for time?
- YES (Broad City)
- NO → **Holds up Sober?**
  - YES → Best in Show
  - NO → Dude, Where's My Car?

#36: THE TWENTY QUESTIONS SESSIONS

In a now-legendary *New York Times* Modern Love column, an essay titled "To Fall in Love with Anyone, Do This" captured the hearts of millions. The writer cited a study by psychologist Arthur Aron that found that intimacy between two strangers can be accelerated by having them ask each other a specific series of personal questions. Our version of these questions may not make you fall in love, but what do we know?

1. What's the first time you can remember being high? Who was there? How did it go?

2. What's one thing you love to do high?

3. Can you describe a favorite food, film, or song that you love to enjoy high?

4. If you could invite three people, living or dead, to a cannabis-themed dinner party, who would they be?

5. What's one adventure you want to have high before you die?

6. What's the strangest place you've gotten high?

7 What is the most unbelievable thing that's happened to you while stoned?

8 What do you value most in a friendship?

9 How have you become more like your mother or your father?

10 If you could experience being anyone, who would it be and why?

11 If you could turn into any animal for twenty-four hours, what animal would you be?

12 What is a memory you love to replay in your head?

13 What is the pettiest thing you've ever done, either high or sober?

14 What's the funniest text you've received from a relative?

15 Who is someone in your life you deeply admire?

16 The scholar Kylie Jenner once said, "This is the year of realizing stuff." What stuff have you realized this year or last year?

(17) Who is someone you're missing right now? (Consider writing that person a letter; see "Green Gratitude" on page 116.)

(18) If you were able to live to the age of ninety and retain either the mind or the body of a thirty-year-old for the last sixty years of your life, which would you want?

(19) What is a mundane superpower you'd want? (Not flying or reading minds but snapping your fingers and having all your laundry folded type of thing.)

(20) Okay, we'll bite: flight, invisibility, or telepathy?

> **"Is marijuana addictive? Yes, in the sense that most of the really pleasant things in life are worth endlessly repeating."**
>
> **—RICHARD NEVILLE**

SEX

GET IT ON GANJA STYLE

We contemplated leaving it at "Just Do It," but then what would you talk about at your next dinner party? Researchers are still trying to figure out exactly why cannabis makes sex better (and more frequent), but they have some ideas and think it comes down to these three things: (1) reduced anxiety and inhibitions, (2) enhanced pleasure, and (3) heightened sensation.

Alcohol, of course, can also loosen up the mind and the body, but unlike cannabis, it's a depressant, and too much can do a number on your state of being the next day (not to mention make it more difficult to...ahem...perform). To put it in layman's terms, the words "I had the best drunk sex last night" have never been spoken. Those of us who have combined the joy of sex with the joy of cannabis can promise you the reviews are five star, but don't take our word for it. Listen to the experts about how to maximize your flower powered make-out sessions.

FIELD NOTES

Is Cannabis Viagra for Women? Suzanne Mulvehill, a doctoral student at the International Institute of Clinical Sexology, was so affected by the intersection of cannabis and sex that it changed her life. "I saw four sex therapists over three decades to resolve my difficulty experiencing orgasm, and it was finally with the help of cannabis that I found relief," Mulvehill said. "I sold my business and launched the Orgasm Project, a nonprofit organization dedicated to ending female orgasmic disorder, one that affects up to 46 percent of women worldwide."

Although to date, most of the reports on the female orgasm/cannabis connection are anecdotal, Mulvehill said the clinical studies are catching up. We know that women are more affected by cannabis partly because of hormones. More estrogen means more sensitivity, both to touch and cannabis's effects, making women's high experience more relaxing and euphoric than men's. And for women who feel cultural repression or sexual inhibitions, cannabis can affect their libido even more than men. In a study of 373 women, Dr. Becky Lynn found that 34 percent were using cannabis for sex and that these women were twice as likely to orgasm as nonusers. Mulvehill also said that low libido is the number one sexual complaint among women and that cannabis can be a game changer. "As my own work and that of others continues," she said, "there's a wide-open world ahead in which cannabis can serve as a powerful, natural sexual healer."

ACTIVITIES

#37: HAVE...SEX

Believe the hype: high sex is amazing. That said, if you're new to this combination, we don't recommend taking two big bong hits and jumping into the sack. Dr. Diana Urman, a licensed clinical social worker with a doctorate in human sexuality, encourages her patients to use cannabis to create a "transformative lightness of being." As Urman said, "Relationships are so often laden with unresolved interpersonal conflict, and taking even a small amount of cannabis can lower defenses, inhibitions, and create an environment of intimacy and connection." Here are Dr. Urman's tips for high sexy times.

MASTER YOUR OWN DOMAIN FIRST

"I recommend each member of the couple try small doses of cannabis on their own time to get comfortable with it," she said. "Once each person has felt its effects, experiencing cannabis together will be a more natural feeling."

EAT IT

While everyone responds a little differently to strains and delivery systems, Urman recommends starting with edibles. "Administration of edibles is highly measurable and standardized, so you know exactly what you are taking."

TAKE IT SLOW

"The journey should be interpsychic; that's two psyches coming together, for us nonpsychology types," said Urman. "For the first forty-five to sixty minutes, engage in a solo somatic practice such as meditation, a bath, masturbation, erotic movies, or whatever else will relax and arouse each person before the delicate dance begins."

TAKE THE WEEKEND

Like many of life's pleasures, Urman prescribes taking your time. Set aside a weekend if possible, taking an edible in the morning or early afternoon with a light meal: "Peak hormonal production is around 10:00 a.m. It's ideal to ride the flow of that hormonal wave."

OPEN YOUR MIND AS WELL AS YOUR LEGS

Above all, Urman suggests keeping an open mind. "Try not to have preconceived notions or expectations. Have curiosity about what may happen, and allow your sense of adventure to lubricate your mind. Cannabis is a gift for us sexually. It would be a shame for us not to use it."

#38: PLAY TIME

Sex is supposed to be playful, so bring the games into the bedroom. You're welcome to go full-on role play (that construction worker hat you wore on Halloween pairs nicely with your birthday suit), but for something a little less prop reliant, try these two (or three?) person amusements.

420 PLAY

Before getting down and dirty, use your smoke session as a little foreplay. Try out the "shotgun kiss" where one partner takes a hit and then blows smoke into the other's mouth.

SLOW IT DOWN

Cannabis already makes time s l o w down. Take advantage of this mental phenomenon and see how long you can go before getting to second base. Now third.

Now...focus on one body part at a time. You may find that that sculpted calf is even more delicious than you thought.

PLAY 1 OR 2

THC lowers inhibitions, so bring some preference play into your sex life. You know when you get an eye exam, and the doctor asks you which one is clearer: "1 or 2?" Do this. With touch. Nibble a nipple lightly, then harder, then ask, "1 or 2?" Repeat.

#39: INFUSE YOUR LUBE

Wondering why your local dispensary or favorite online store is selling lubricants alongside the edibles, infused drinks, and flower? Topicals, like lube, won't get you super high (THC is absorbed by the skin and can't cross into the bloodstream). But since THC is a vasodilator, you increase blood flow to those sensitive spots, increasing pleasure. And you can increase your pleasure even more by extending your foreplay and getting cooking in the kitchen together. Sex educator Ashley Manta, who helms the CannaSexual brand, walked us through how to cook up some couple's lube and then gave tips for applying...in all the right places.

> **20**
>
> Percent of daily cannabis users who report having more sex than nonusers.

Infused Lube

PREP: 10 minutes • **COOK:** 4-5 hours

TOTAL TIME: 5ish hours • **YIELD:** 8 ounces

INGREDIENTS

- 8 ounces vegetable oil (Ashley likes olive oil, grape-seed oil, and MCT oil)
- ¼ ounce cannabis flower

SUPPLIES

- Baking sheet
- 2 4-ounce Mason jars or one single larger jar
- Slow cooker (or large pot)
- Funnel
- Cheesecloth
- Bottle to store the final product

DIRECTIONS

Decarboxylate your cannabis to activate the THC by breaking your cannabis into ½ inch by ½ inch pieces, spreading it on a baking sheet, and baking it at 220°F for 20-ish minutes. You'll know it's done when it turns a light brown or yellow color. Then divide evenly into your Mason jars.

Divide oil and add equal amounts to each jar. Seal the jars as tightly as possible.

Place the Mason jars in your slow cooker and cover with boiling water so that the jars are fully submerged. Set slow cooker to "warm" and let cook for four to five hours. You can also submerge jars in a pot of simmering water, but check your water levels frequently to make sure jars are covered.

Use a jar clamp or heavy oven mitts to pull the jars out every hour and give them a good shake.

After four to five hours, remove jars and place them on a cloth to cool.

Line a funnel with four layers of cheesecloth and place over a glass bowl. Slowly pour the cooled liquid through the cheesecloth, squeezing out the plant matter to get as much oil as possible. Your strained oil will be slightly green.

Transfer the oil to bottle.

MANTA'S PRO TIPS:

* Use flower that is lab tested to be sure that it's free of pesticides and so that you know the cannabinoid and terpene breakdown (everything you ever wanted to know about terpenes on page 12).

* Remember that oil products are not compatible with latex barriers, so be sure to use nitrile or polyurethane gloves and condoms for safer sex practices.

* Cannabis-infused oils can be used for full body massage but are most impactful on vulvas when given time (around fifteen to twenty-five minutes) to work their way into the tissue.

Ashley Manta is a sex educator and founder of the CannaSexual brand, a Playboy advisor writer, and author of The CBD Solution: Sex: How Cannabis, CBD, and Other Plant Allies Can Improve Your Everyday Life.

productivity

Cannabis may have earned its reputation as a fantastic mellow maker, but it's increasingly a tool the titans of tech, business, and the art world are using to kick-start ideas and find laser-sharp focus when they need it most. Just ask Stephen Kotler, who wrote nine bestsellers while stoned. Or Seth Rogen, who...well, we'll let him tell you himself (see page 170). Not to mention Willie Nelson, Maya Angelou, Alanis Morrissette, Carl Sagan, and the (probably) millions of others who have been slyly getting high and changing the world. In other words, wipe that image of the couch-locked stoner from your brain, and get ready to embrace the productive pothead.

We've known for some time that cannabis improves creativity (see "Creativity" on page 189), boosts energy (see "Body" on page 39), and decreases anxiety (See "Mind" on page 71), but studies are now showing improved performance for cognitive function, motivation, focus, and that elusive flow. You know "flow," that sought-after place where you're so absorbed by a task that everything else seems to fade away and your mental and physical performance are at optimal levels. In other words, you're flying. So it's no surprise that our favorite flower can help induce this much-desired state of being. In fact, the very same neurochemicals at work when we're in a state of flow are boosted by (you guessed it) cannabis. And what are those neurochemicals? Let us introduce you to dopamine and serotonin.

We know serotonin as the "happiness hormone," and anyone who's smoked Serious Happiness (yes, it's a strain) knows how fine it feels to activate that neurochemical, so it makes sense that dumping serotonin into your system will get you feeling good about getting shit done. Dopamine gets the same billing (happiness in a molecule!), but these two neurochemicals do more than make you blissed out. Higher serotonin levels are associated with more effective learning. Smart people found that when serotonin neurons were activated in mice, the mice were quicker to adapt their behavior to a situation that required flexibility, meaning they learned faster. And really, aren't mice and men both just reward-seeking mammals? Dopamine can also help with productivity. Often called the "motivation molecule," dopamine is what helps us focus. In fact, the ADHD drug methylphenidate (aka Ritalin) works by boosting dopamine, so more cannabis equals more dopamine equals more focus. And who doesn't want improved focus, whether you're trying to figure out the electronic structures of high-temperature superconductors or cleaning out your sock drawer?

But it's not just those neurochemicals that cannabis enhances. Weed slows the amygdala, the part of the brain that triggers fight or flight. This can be a bad thing if you're trying to figure out whether to run from or wrestle a bear, but it's a good thing if you're trying to think about a task in a new way. A slower amygdala doesn't recognize stimuli as quickly, so what you've encountered before seems new again, making boring tasks more exciting and allowing your brain more time to think about those exciting tasks in new ways. Pair this with a slowed dorsolateral prefrontal cortex (the area of the brain responsible for self-censorship and inhibition), and you've just become a noncensoring, uninhibited, innovative thinking machine!

We could also tell you that cannabis increases semantic priming (your ability to free associate more quickly) and can help you complete tasks more quickly without a loss of accuracy, but instead we'll remind you that the authors of this fine piece of literature you're currently reading have written fourteen books between them. We're not saying we wrote all those while high, but we *are* saying we're just fine with cannabis taking some of the credit.

FIELD NOTES

To Toke or Not to Toke? William Shakespeare probably answered this question with a resounding yes. Scientists discovered that 400-year-old tobacco pipes excavated from Shakespeare's garden had trace amounts of cannabis, which would explain a whole lot of *A Midsummer Night's Dream*.

Back in the Day, We Didn't Have Apps: Before there was e-commerce, there were Stanford students using the Arpanet to buy and sell weed to MIT students. Yes, the first e-commerce transaction was a drug deal.

The Hippie Speedball: Have you tapped into your "creative flow," a state of being where you are completely present and fully immersed in a task? Steven Kotler, founder of the Flow Research Collective, said that "action sport athletes for years have been combining exercise, coffee, and cannabis into a 'hippie speedball,' and they've been using it as a performance-enhancing chemical which is chemically indistinguishable from the state of flow." That's a speedball we can get behind.

ACTIVITIES

#40: GREEN CLEANING

Cannabis can make you hyperfocused—that's our increased dopamine levels talking and saying: dig in. For mucho motivation, you'll want a strain that's high energy (try Green Crack for all the reasons the name implies). Then break out your cleaning products, fire up a playlist, and scrub like you've never scrubbed before. You'll soon see why cleaning is one of the most productive and satisfying stoner tasks. Plus, weed can also help chill out your inner perfectionist, so your bathtub will end up sparkling even if those rust stains aren't going anywhere.

LEVEL DOWN

Got a case of couch lock? People-watch other people clean their homes by googling "Clean with Me" or "Extreme Cleaning" videos. Hundreds of thousands of subscribers can't be wrong.

#41: STAY LIT, SPARK JOY

With the hyperfocus that THC can provide, you're ready to Marie Kondo your space. And when your central nervous system's CB1 receptors bind with those sweet, sweet cannabinoids that produce that relaxed feeling of wellness we're all after, the answer to whether each of your sweaters "sparks joy" will be so much more obvious. Here are three tried, true, and tested high home organizational projects.

LABEL. EVERYTHING.

There are three types of people in the civilized world: (1) people who don't like to make labels, (2) people who like to make labels, and (3) people who like to get high and make labels. We cordially invite you to join us in category three. We really can't emphasize how much joy that twenty-five-dollar label maker will spark, but if you'd rather save your money for some nice Sour Tangie pre-rolls (and who doesn't love that clear-headed, euphoric high), scrap paper, a Sharpie, and some transparent tape will do the trick.

SYSTEMATIZE YOUR BOOKS

Whether your literary organizing principle takes on a straight ABC by author approach, you prefer to sort by genre, or you're into the surprisingly satisfying color-coded technique, once you're in the zone, you'll soon realize the pleasures of a lit library.

CLEAN OUT YOUR FRIDGE

Weed heightens your senses, which makes post puff an ideal time to use your super sniffing powers to suss out if that yogurt has seen better days. Go through your mainstays, but don't neglect those poor condiments. Aunt Rose's elderberry preserves aren't going to suddenly be devoured after year two.

#42: PASS THE DUTCHIE ON THE LEFT-HAND SIDE

Joints. Everyone loves them—they're easy to pack! You feel like a baller smoking one! You can sing that catchy song! But few know how to roll 'em right. And no one wants to take the time to watch a tutorial and exercise fine motor skills when they're itching to get high. But what if we told you that you could get high and *then* focus on rolling fatties? Harness the power of THC's dopamine boost and get motivated to roll the perfect joint.

Here, you'll find instructions for rolling one manageable but good-sized joint. For reference, most of the pre-rolls you buy at a dispensary are a full gram, but those fatties can be harder to get right, so start small. You'll never feel more productive than when you're making future you very thankful for past you.

Good-Sized Joint

PREP: 5 minutes · **CREATE:** 10 minutes (for a first timer, but soon you'll be rolling these bad boys in minutes)

TOTAL TIME: 15 minutes · **YIELD:** 1 good-sized joint

INGREDIENTS AND SUPPLIES

- ½ gram of cannabis
- Cannabis grinder
- Thin cardboard or thick paper for the crutch (aka filter). Many packs of rolling papers include this cardboard. If you're making your own, aim for a rectangle about 1 x 2 inches.
- Rolling papers (single or 1¼ sized)
- A pen, or a similarly shaped object to help pack the joint

DIRECTIONS

Step 1: Grind the cannabis into small pieces, commonly known as "shake." If you don't have a grinder, you can break your buds by hand or with a clean scissors.

Step 2: Create a joint crutch or filter by making a few accordion folds at one end of the cardboard. Then roll the rest of the cardboard around your folds so you end up with a cylindrical shaped filter.

Step 3: Place rolling paper on a hard surface with the glue side faceup and toward you. Lay the crutch at one end of the paper and load the paper with shake.

Step 4: Pinch the paper between your fingertips, and roll it back and forth between them to pack the cannabis down.

Step 5: For a conical roll, start rolling the paper at the crutch side of the joint, tucking the unglued side of the paper into the roll.

Step 6: Lick the glue side of the paper and tack first to the crutch side of the joint. Once the paper is tacked down on that end, work your way down the rest of the seam by tucking and sealing the joint to the end. You might need to fatten the end by adding a little weed so your joint resembles the cone pre-rolls you buy at a dispensary.

Step 7: Pack the end with your pen to ensure an even burn and close the tip with a twist.

Grinder Cannabis Thin Cardboard

Step 1 Step 2

Rolling paper

Step 3 Step 4

Step 5 Step 6 Step 7

FAQ

WHY USE A CRUTCH?

It's a mouthpiece that keeps your joint open (even when your wet-lipped friends inhale before you), blocks the shake from getting in your mouth, and keeps you from burning your pretty little mouth.

WHAT CAN I USE TO MAKE A CRUTCH?

You're looking for something thicker than printer paper but thinner than a shipping box. Possible options: an index card, a magazine subscription card, a page of this book.

WHAT ROLLING PAPERS SHOULD I USE?

Whatever you have, but if you want to be fancy, we recommend hemp paper because it's thin, strong, and burns evenly without affecting the flavor.

WHY SHOULD I PASS THE DUTCHIE ON THE LEFT-HAND SIDE?

Most of us are right-handed, so if you pass to the right, you're passing it to the next person's left hand, which forces them to either turn their body toward yours to take it or take it in their left hand. So take a puff, and then pass the dutchie on the left-hand side.

#43: HIGHER LEARNING

Fine. We can't endorse walking into a physical classroom looking like you just came from a dispensary (we're talking to you, modern-day Jeff Spicoli), but in the virtual world, the focus that cannabis offers pairs perfectly with learning from the comfort of your own desk or futon. After all, when cannabis is boosting your naturally occurring serotonin and dopamine, you're not only happier, but you're more focused and able to learn more quickly. Higher serotonin levels are associated with more effective learning, and dopamine isn't called nature's ADHD medicine for nothing.

Whether mastering a new skill, brushing up on American history, or just letting the genius of Judd Apatow's secrets of comedy writing sink in, a world of higher learning awaits you. Here are the leaders in the virtual learning space with one carefully chosen class we think will pair perfectly with your cannabis-fueled flow.

Bake San Francisco Style Sour Sourdough Bread: Udemy

Clam chowder and bread bowls, anyone? Learn to make your own sourdough starter and then bake into an artisan loaf any local San Franciscan would be proud of. It's simple: get baked and get ready to bake! Best of all, you'll end up with a delicious snack the next time the munchies hit.

Cosmology and Astronomy: Khan Academy

Getting stoned can make you think deep thoughts about life and the state of the universe. But why not actually learn something about space and time while you're flying high? This out-of-this-world course will teach you all about the scale of the universe, black holes, and life outside Earth in a way that will be sure to boggle your mind and help you think beyond "duuuude..."

Sharpened Visions: A Poetry Workshop: Coursera

Picture Jonah Hill's character in *22 Jump Street* reciting his slam poem titled "Cynthia": "Slam...poetry / YELLING! Angry??? / WAVING MY HANDS A LOT. Specific point of view on things! / Cynthia! Cyn-thi-a! / Jesus died for our sin-thi-as!" If you're interested in recreating this moment for yourself or preparing in advance to avoid embarrassment when your friends volunteer you for an open mic, take some lessons from these talented poetry professors. Get high for extra credit.

The Six Morning Habits of High Performers: LinkedIn Learning

Taking this class while high? The puns write themselves. Working on office skills and planning for your career can seem like a stressful task, but getting high will loosen you up and take off some of that pressure while you focus on your career goals. You can take LinkedIn Learning courses to gain career advice, practice graphic design, and learn how to work better with people. Leadership, management, soft skills, and customer service classes seem less daunting when you're an enhanced performer.

The Real History of Secret Societies/Forensic History: Crimes, Frauds, and Scandals: Great Courses

Going down a conspiracy theory rabbit hole when you're high is good stuff, but this time, you can actually gain some real knowledge while you're at it. Get into the nitty-gritty of the secrets of mysterious scandals that will definitely blow your mind. Learning history is like hearing a great story except it's all true, and you get extra points for remembering the facts. Absorb all the information while you're high, and when you're sober, you'll have A+ trivia to replace boring small talk whenever you need.

Judd Apatow Teaches Comedy: MasterClass

There may be little that's more fun than doubling over with a belly laugh after an edible has kicked in (see "Laugh Your Grass Off" on page 109 for why). Now you too can trigger the belly laughs. To brush up on your comedy skills, take a course from Judd Apatow, the master behind movies like *Bridesmaids* and *The 40-Year-Old-Virgin*. Learn how to write and perform stand-up, workshop comedic storylines for film and TV, and pitch your laugh-out-loud ideas to an audience. We promise you'll end up funnier, even when you're sober.

#44: MAKE A LIST

You don't need a study to tell you that cannabis is great for free association...but there's, in fact, a study to tell you that cannabis is great for free association! Some smart people at the University College London found that under the influence of cannabis, users showed increases in automatic semantic priming; that is, when you encounter one concept, it makes related concepts more easily accessible (i.e., your list making will be on point).

With that in mind, we invite you to indulge in the joys of free association while getting your life contained to a sensibly numbered (or bullet-pointed) register of things. Use our inspired list of lists (see how we did that?) for inspiration, or come up with your own:

▶ Household fix-its

▶ Christmas/birthday/420 day gifts

▶ Restaurants you want to try

▶ TV shows you want to binge

▶ Vacations you want to take

▶ Books/movies you recommend (someone is always asking)

▶ One-pot meals to cook

▶ Things you always forget at the grocery store (condiments, anyone?)

▶ Things you want to learn

▶ Podcasts you want to listen to

▶ Dog and cat names for pets of the future

▶ Reasons you rock

THAT FINE KINE MUSIC

Skip the analog on this one and go straight to whatever fine kine streaming music app you use. Make playlists for cleaning (pair with "Green Cleaning" on page 147) or sexy times (go to "Get It On, Ganja Style" on page 133).

#45: DIGITAL DECLUTTER

A messy room, home, or yard is obvious to all who enter it. The unkempt digital life is largely unseen yet can yield much more chaos in our lives. But when is a good time to declutter your digital life? How about: Right. Now. Well, right after you get really high.

We know that one of the best things about weed is that it makes almost everything more interesting (which is why we devoted a whole section to how and why cannabis makes the ordinary extraordinary—see "Joy" on page 213). One of the reasons the mundane becomes miraculous is due to cannabis's effects on the amygdala. One of the amygdala's jobs is to compare stimuli to what's come before. Cannabis makes the amygdala...well...worse at its job, which is better for boredom. A high amygdala doesn't recognize stimuli as well, so the old seems new, and the boorrrrring task of deleting apps becomes omgomgomg exciting.

Add in the fact that a study that accessed the impact of cannabis on executive function found that patients who used cannabis for three months completed tasks quicker without a loss of accuracy, and we think you'll agree that there's no better time than the high time to engage in some dope digital decluttering.

ZEN YOUR DESKTOP

This is your brain trying to make sense of dozens and dozens of docs, folders, and images piled across your desktop. Just say no. Here's how:

▶ **On a Mac**, click on any blank space, go to "View" on the menu, scroll down to "Clean Up By," and you'll see a few options to organize your files and folders. Now: decide to either move a file to a folder, tuck a folder inside another folder, or delete any files you don't need.

▶ **On a PC**: Right-click your main hard drive (usually the C: drive) and select Properties. Click the Disk Cleanup button, and you'll see a list of items that can be removed, including temporary files and more. For even more options, click Clean Up System Files. Tick the categories you want to remove, then click OK > Delete File.

Once your desktop is in order, treat yourself to a zen-like background. Lots of free options are available, and a good place to start is simpledesktops.com.

UNSUBSCRIBE WITHOUT ABANDON

We read just a fraction of the newsletters we subscribe to, not to mention the lists we've been added to without our consent. Many services will scour your email and help you shed newsletter overload, but we like Unroll.me both for its price (free) and ease of use (easy).

SCRUB YOUR SOCIAL MEDIA

Defriend, unfollow, and clean out your social newsfeeds. Move fast through your lists, unclicking feeds and unfollowing people without thinking twice—ruthless flow is your *real* friend.

OPT OUT

Finally, turn off all nonessential notifications. According to a study by the University of California, Irvine, it takes an average of twenty-three minutes and fifteen seconds to get yourself back on track after being interrupted. Every tweet or comment on an Instagram post that pops up breaks your flow for close to half an hour.

#46: THE PHOTO FINISH

You've made the memories. So why are you hiding them? We're talking about ALL. THOSE. PHOTOS. Some of us are storing them in boxes, boxes that get shuffled from house to house, from the back of one closet to the back of another. Others of us have let our pictures float invisibly in the cloud or on a hard drive. It's time to sort out this mess and unfreeze your frames.

Before we start, we should warn you that THC's ability to slow down the amygdala and make everything old feel new again means there's a real risk that you'll get lost in the rabbit hole of your life in pictures. And yet when we recall the hyperfocus cannabis offers, it's actually a perfect time to go down the long and winding road called Memory Lane (there's an activity for that; see "Memory Strain" on page 76).

GO DIGITAL

Most of our photos are safe on the cloud...where no one will ever see them. Including you. You could buy that digital frame that cycles through one hundred photos and put it on your coffee table, but if you're under eighty, you may want to find a place that allows you to store, organize, and showcase your photos. The good news is that both free and paid options are everywhere. But first, get a low-dose buzz on, invoke your Type A organizational brain, and remove as many duplicate shots as possible (there are plenty of free apps for that for both Mac and Windows users).

Now sort your images into as many clearly named folders as you can and head to the cloud, where Google Photos is the biggest (and arguably best) option for storing, organizing, and sharing pics (and your first 15GB of storage are free). Looking for other options? Old-school favorite Flickr has a solid free plan (1,000 photos), while Flickr Pro's five-dollar-a-month option offers big bang for your buck with unlimited storage and lots of perks like discounts for SmugMug (a great photo site for showcasing, and even selling, your photos). Self-publishing platform Blurb is also great for serious shutterbugs.

GO ANALOG

Bring those photos down from the ether and onto your coffee table in the form of a bound book. How to wrestle your thousands of images to the ground? Curation powered by cannabis. Sure, you could design a beautifully bound book of memories (go you!), but if you have even a modicum of perfectionism, we strongly encourage you to take the easy way out (i.e., dump all your pics in one place with the help of services like Mixbook, Shutterfly, or other easily searchable options). Let the robots organize and lay out, and then enjoy the fruits of their labor five to ten business days later.

#47: NEW HIGHS AT THE OFFICE

We know cannabis lowers inhibitions, so while we don't recommend getting high on the job (we're looking at you, air traffic controllers...okay, you too, librarians), we do recommend getting high after work. And not only do we recommend getting high after work, we recommend doing it with your coworkers. For too long, postwork happy hour has dominated colleague get-togethers. But we say, no more. Join us (and Gandhi) in saying, "Be the change you wish to see in the world," and put together your workplace's first *truly happy* happy hour.

We're sure you've sussed out your 420-friendly cohort, so enlist those folks, and use the power of many to normalize what we already know is normal. Then invite the rest of the gang, and help remove any stigma the closet cannabis users may feel. Let nonusers know they're welcome too. After all, no one ever apologized for arranging a bar hang.

BLACK BOX WARNING

Read the room. If you work with a bunch of buttoned-up nervous Nellies, inviting them to a backyard dab sesh may not be the best use of your time. Likewise, if cannabis is still (annoyingly) illegal in your state, this may be one activity to keep on the back burner.

WORKING HIGH, OR HIGHLY WORKING

Rick Doblin, founder of the Multidisciplinary Association for Psychedelic Studies (MAPS), a nonprofit research and educational organization that develops medical, legal, and cultural contexts for people to benefit from the uses of psychedelics and cannabis, practices what he preaches. Here he shares some insights about using cannabis to enhance his own work.

"One of my favorite things is getting high and editing my own writing or writing from my staff. For people who are nervous about getting high and getting work done, I want to say that for me at least, when I'm high, I see things that are missing, I see the bigger picture. I get out of the trap of thinking, *Okay, here's what I've written, and let me fine-tune it and change my perspective* and shift to *Here's a whole other argument to make or idea to bring in.* Strategizing is a great high task because it's about being imaginative and brainstorming and then fine-tuning your ideas. I've made some of the most important decisions of my life when I was blocked and got high and then was able to look at something in a new way."

#48: VISUALIZE TO ACTUALIZE

How many of you locked your teenage selves in your room with a pile of magazines, a glue stick, some posterboard, and total confidence that you could manifest those Guess jeans, dual cassette stereo, and super cool boyfriend through a vision board? Just us? Okay, fine, one of us? Sure, collaging pictures of beach houses and motivational sayings isn't going to make your wildest dreams come true, but there is something to be said for creating a physical representation of what you want in life. You can't wish a million dollars into your bank account, but you can think your way into mental and even physical transformation. One study from the Cleveland Clinic Foundation proved that visualizing exercise was almost as effective as actually doing the exercise (hands up if you too have a new exercise regime).

So visualizing the future you want can absolutely bring it into being, particularly if you're focused on how you want the future you to *feel*. And guess when your visualization powers are at their most potent? That's right, when you're high. But it's not just that your ability to imagine is increased; it's that your tendency to criticize what you've imagined is decreased. Cannabis can slow your dorsolateral prefrontal cortex (the area of the brain responsible for self-censorship and inhibition) so that you're less likely to judge yourself for needing that picture of kittens in a baby carriage. The less you judge, the more you can envision, and the more you can envision, the higher you are. We mean, the closer you are to making all your dreams come true.

GO ANALOG

Someone still gets old-school magazines, and that someone is usually having a yard sale. Get yourself a collection of magazines, newspapers, catalogs, and other paper ephemera (photo booth strips, greeting cards, your own doodles), and start snipping. Let your high brain guide you—yes, even if it wants to cut out a super burrito with green sauce (so. happy. making.).

GO DIGITAL

Every image you've ever wanted (and, frankly, didn't want) is available online, making envisioning effortless. Use Pinterest to collect, curate, and display your

243,700

The number of jobs supported by legal cannabis as of January 2020 according to Leafly's annual Cannabis Jobs Report. That's 33,700 jobs more than the previous year, a 15 percent increase, making legal cannabis the fastest-growing industry in America.

digital "pins" and create a vision board that forever lives on all your digital platforms. Want to get hyperfocused on one area of your life? FoodGawker helps all your culinary dreams come true; Hometalk will help you dream up your ideal space. No one's created an image-sharing app devoted to weed, but that doesn't mean you can't create a Pinterest board to display each and every beautiful strain you hope to smoke.

PRO TIP

Focus on tangibles like relationships, career, home, travel, and personal growth (spirituality, social life, education), or go full-on feelings and think about the emotions you want more of in your life: joy, connection, creativity, passion, and contentment.

#49: HERBS FOR HEALTH

Herb gardens are dope. And yes, we mean both kinds of herbs. Jorge Cervantes will help you nurture your little sensimilla seedlings on page 168, but we're here to get you growing the greens that are rich in antioxidants, not cannabinoids. And since we're talking about using our favorite green to promote productivity, we might as well discuss some of the less psychotropic (but no less worthy) greens that also help with getting your flow on. You can add these industrious herbs to any recipe, but why not throw a pinch into your bhang ("Head to Bollywood" on page 124) or cannabutter ("Make It Savory," on page 184) and make your edible *extra* extra.

We here at cannabis central do want to remind you that none of these claims can be confirmed by the Food and Drug Administration, but just like the legalization of weed, we're sure the FDA's endorsement can't be far behind.

YOUR HOME-GROWN PRODUCTIVITY PATCH:

▶ Ginger: for confidence

▶ Rosemary: to improve memory

▶ Peppermint: for energy

▶ Lavender: to relieve stress and anxiety

▶ Sage: for alertness and cognitive function

▶ Catnip: to stop procrastination (for you, not your cat; really, it's a thing)

GROW YOUR OWN

by Jorge Cervantes

Are you like me, a lifelong gardener enamored with cannabis? Or are you a cannabis lover who is new to gardening? Growing quality cannabis is more difficult than growing tomatoes. Start by checking out the cultivation tips below. Next, study a reputable grow guide and hit the YouTube videos. Above all, avoid advice from armchair experts, and check your state's laws about at-home growing.

1. Unpollinated female cannabis plants produce high levels of cannabinoids including mind-bending THC and no-high CBD. Undesirable male plants are culled; they pollinate females and produce minimal cannabinoids. If growing from seed, purchase "feminized" cultivars that produce no males. Grow "clones"—small female-only plants with rooted branch tips. Find seeds and clones at legal cannabis dispensaries.

2. Grow in your backyard, patio, or terrace, if possible. Mother Nature supplies all the sunlight and fresh air necessary. Soil in a garden bed is much easier to manage than plants in a pot. Sun-grown cannabis costs less time and money to cultivate than when grown indoors or in a greenhouse.

3 A greenhouse protects plants from harsh weather and extends growing seasons. A small greenhouse is economical and easy to set up.

4 Growing indoors requires a dedicated area, bright grow light, circulation and ventilation fans, store-bought growing medium, containers, clean water, a thermometer/hygrometer, timer, and scientific measuring meters. A detailed plan and budget are essential for success. Go slow and get it right: mistakes are easy to make and often difficult to correct indoors.

5 Allow yourself enough time to care for your garden. Cannabis requires regular maintenance: irrigation, fertilization, disease and pest control, and more. Missing critical events guarantees a diminished harvest.

Jorge Cervantes is a legend in the cannabis growing world and author of many books, including the Cannabis Encyclopedia *and* Marijuana Horticulture *(known as "The Bible" of cannabis growing).*

#50: THE CANNABIS CHRONICLES

You know the routine. You're at the dispensary trying to remember the strain you bought two visits ago. Was it Pineapple Express? Cherry Pie? Wedding Cake? It was some kind of dessert-themed flower. And how about that edible a friend handed you last weekend? You loved that. Was it a gummy? Or maybe some kind of lozenge? It's enough to confound even a sober person.

If the right strain of cannabis can help keep us productive (and we know it can; here's to you, Seth Rogen), it stands to reason that keeping our Bubba Kush and our OG Kush straight is important. No one wants to be couch locked when they meant to microdose. So be industrious and use our template to keep track of all your earthly delights. Copy it yourself, or download our template at joyofcannabis.org.

SETH ROGEN: "I smoke weed all day, every day of my life."

STEPHEN COLBERT: "Have you ever performed [high] ... acted?"

ROGEN: "For the last twenty years, exclusively."

COLBERT: "So any movie we see you in, there's a fairly good chance you're high."

ROGEN: "There's a 100 percent chance."

—SETH ROGEN, POSSIBLY THE MOST PRODIGIOUS HIGH ACTOR IN HISTORY, TALKING TO STEPHEN COLBERT ON *THE LATE SHOW*

DATE: 4/20/22

STRAIN: Wedding Cake

GROWER/MANUFACTURER: lolo

DISPENSARY: Harborside

CIRCLE ONE:

(Flower)   Concentrate   Tincture   Edible

CIRCLE ONE:

Sativa   Indica   (Hybrid)

THC %: 23.09%

CBD %: 0.06%

NOTES: a relaxing body high with slight euphoria. Munchies inducing. Long-lasting high (about 3 hours) that transitioned nicely into sleep.

RATING-1-5:

COOKING

CANNABIS CUISINE

You love food. You love cannabis. Now imagine a world in which cannabis could be delivered *via* food. If your head hasn't exploded, it's likely because you've visited a dispensary and seen the cornucopia of edibles available for purchase. We're fans of dispensary edibles—precise doses and shelf-stable products for the win—but think of what a productive superstar you'll be when you pull that tray of freshly baked, precisely measured, THC-rich chocolate chip cookies out of the oven?

FIELD NOTES

We asked the experts in the field to give us all the tips you need for becoming a cannabis master chef.

GO SLOW

"The best advice I can give anyone looking to cook with cannabis is to clean your bud before you start working with it, know your flower's potency, and figure out your per-serving dosing beforehand."

—JEFF DANZER has been dubbed the "Julia Child of Weed" by *The Daily Beast*, and is the author of *The 420 Gourmet: The Art of Elevated Cannabis Cuisine*

"Whether you're cooking or bartending with cannabis, I like to apply the Thai food principle: don't use too much heat, or in this case, weed."

—WARREN BOBROW, aka the Cocktail Whisperer, and the author of six books, including *Cannabis Cocktails, Mocktails, and Tonics*

"Don't overdo it. Keep doses low. Less is more; if people get too high, they may be turned off and not get the benefits of this amazing plant."

—LAURIE WOLF is the founder of Laurie + MaryJane

SUGAR AND SPICE

"I believe strongly in the creation of infused foodstuff without the use of refined sugars; if cannabis is used to lower inflammation but then combined with refined sugar, which inevitably elevates our inflammation, the net result of the cannabis is zero."

— JORDAN WAGMAN is a James Beard-nominated chef, bestselling author of three cookbooks, and cannabis visionary celebrated for his intimate cannabis-infused dinners

"One tip that has served me well is to think of cannabis as a spice: season with intention. Cannabis can be citrusy, piney, cheesy, even garlicky. Give your flower a good smell. If it smells good to you, it will very likely taste good as well. Experiment with flavors that complement and balance the cannabis profile."

— STEPHANIE HUA is the founder and chief confectioner of Mellows, cannabis-infused marshmallows handcrafted in San Francisco, and author of *Edibles: Small Bites for the Modern Cannabis Kitchen*

THERE'S AN APP(LIANCE) FOR THAT

"Building a cannabis pantry with a variety of cannabis-infused items will allow you to create many recipes with items you already have on hand. There are several counter-top devices that allow the home cook and even professional chef to infuse a range of pantry staples. Among several things that can easily be infused with full-spectrum cannabis are extra virgin olive oil, grape-seed oil, sesame seed oil, avocado oil, rice wine vinegar, red wine vinegar, cider vinegar, balsamic vinegar, vanilla extract, maple syrup, agave nectar, and honey. I've tested almost every machine on the market for infusing cannabis into products and find the MB2e botanical extractor from Magical Butter allows me to accurately infuse all the products I like."

—CHEF SEBASTIAN CAROSI is an award-winning, short-order cannabis revolutionary who has been cooking with cannabis since the early '90s

HOW TO HOST A CANNABIS DINNER PARTY

by Chef Robyn Griggs Lawrence

Hosting a cannabis dinner is a lot like teaching a yoga class. You're responsible for every person's well-being and experience—from understanding their physical limitations and apprehensions to curating a playlist that keeps them motivated, relaxed, and flowing. When you do it right, the meal is finely orchestrated to open people's minds and senses and connect them with their dinner partners, the food's tastes and aromas, and the finer notes of everything. Everyone blossoms, blissed and blessed. Below is a sample menu that will have your guests leaving happier than they came.

- Nonalcoholic Mango Mules with CBD
- Seared Crab Cakes with Golden Goat-Grilled Corn Relish
- Spinach Salad with Warm Bacon-Blue Dream Dressing
- Coq au Vin with Lamb's Bread Sourdough Toast and Mashed Potatoes
- Bread Pudding with Canna-Coconut Cream and Maple Glaze

I find it's best to infuse sauces, dressings, and sides so people can serve themselves based on their tolerance levels and experience. Full recipes available at joyofcannabis.org.

Robyn Griggs Lawrence teaches people to safely prepare and consume cannabis through her company, Cannabis Kitchen Events, and her books, including The Cannabis Kitchen Cookbook *and* Pot in Pans: A History of Eating Cannabis.

POT AND PANS
by Mollie Katzen

You may know me as a cook. Very true. I am also an aficionado of cannabis. Yet I don't like to use it as an ingredient in my recipes. Rather, from time to time, I prefer to cook under its influence. I occasionally vape it—just a touch—with my little Firefly2 and then get creative in the kitchen.

I've found that cooking on cannabis confers a sense of patience in the kitchen I might not otherwise access. When I teach a cooking class for four-year-olds, they are consistently proudest of the patience required to wait for their pizzas to bake. I realize, from observing them, that this kind of composure is key to the full enjoyment of this or any process.

My favorite interactions with cannabis are the tending and observation that come through growing. When I do grow, it's just a few cannabis plants in the outdoors: sunlight, with prayers against Berkeley's excess fog. I grow for my friends and for myself. To me, the ultimate high is the sharing.

I also grow because I love the horticulture of it. Also, the relationship with the plant. I learn from the plant itself, not from books or guidelines. I nurture the plants with all the intuitive clichés: water, light, attention. Love. These are all true and structural things, not simply filigree.

Cannabis teaches you how to manage the attachment to growing it. It has taught me to accept plant problems, pest invasion—every angle of loss—and to bless it all, even in the sad retreat that inevitably becomes part of the mix.

The blessings extend to the sticky hands that are the byproduct of discarding the rotted parts due to an overabundance of fog. I bless it too, as it is the one source of necessary moisture in times of drought. It is part of the process. The slightly rotted buds that you collect and cure anyway because no one is looking over your shoulder telling you not to is part of the process. And, best of all, the healthy plant with the full tendril-laced flowers eagerly waiting to show you worlds is part of the process.

Growing one's own is a full circle-of-life situation, replete with beautiful concentric curves. The weathering of loss is a skill, a practice. Cannabis is a teacher of that. Practice, patience, process.

Cannabis is also seasoning. A seasoning for *you*: the person, cook, eater, thinker, caregiver, mystery seeker, insight hunter. It helps you understand that mystery and insight can be jointly pursued, that they are not opposing ideologies. Oppositions shift and everything realigns.

Hold that thought. Set the table. Enjoy the meal.

Mollie Katzen has been named as one of the "Five Women Who Changed the Way We Eat" by Health Magazine *and is the author of more than a dozen cookbooks, including the Moosewood Cookbook. With four million books in print, she is one of the bestselling cookbook authors of all-time.*

ACTIVITIES

#51: LET'S BEGIN: DECARBOXYLATE TO ACTIVATE

by Pat Newton

Decarboxylation is the process of activating the cannabinoids in your cannabis, making them psychoactive and providing that happy high we're often after. It's the building block of any budding cannabis cook's education, and the two main factors are heat and time.

A raw cannabis bud that one would break up to roll and smoke is in a state of acidity. Putting fire to the joint ignites the cannabis, which then begins the conversion to activate the cannabinoids. But when we want to cook with cannabis to extract its powerful components, we need to first decarboxylate the cannabis.

The cherry of a joint burns at temperatures of up to 1,000°F. This achieves the desired results very quickly. However, cannabinoids will begin to vaporize at much lower temperatures. Using the oven to decarboxylate your cannabis is one of the more rudimentary methods of accomplishing this conversion.

There are lots of ways to decarboxylate, but the easiest one is to first grind or chop your bud into small pieces. Then spread it on a cookie sheet and cook at 220°F for about twenty minutes. You'll know it's done when the cannabis starts turning from green to light brown.

Chef Pat Newton is the founder of Munchy Brothers, a cannabis company specializing in cannabis-infused ingredients to simplify the DIY edible-making process.

#52: MAKE IT SWEET

You remember anandamide, that endocannabinoid that's similar in makeup to THC and is named for the blissful feelings it generates? Guess what else contains anandamide? Chocolate. And what better way to double your bliss than infusing some chocolatey goodness with that other bliss-producing cannabinoid, THC. Below, chef Pat Newton shares his favorite recipe for making cannabis-infused chocolates.

Cannabis Chocolate

PREP: 10 minutes-ish • **COOK:** 2 hours 30 minutes
TOTAL TIME: 2 hours 40 minutes • **YIELD:** Depends on molds, but approximately six 1-ounce squares

INGREDIENTS

- 230 grams or 1 cup cocoa butter
- 4 grams decarboxylated cannabis
- 1 teaspoon vanilla extract
- ¼ cup maple syrup or honey
- 1 cup cocoa powder
- ¼ teaspoon pink Himalayan salt

SUPPLIES

- Double boiler (or make your own with a pot and metal bowl)
- Cheesecloth or strainer
- Measuring cup with pourable spout
- Silicone spatula
- Wire whisk
- Silicone molds

DIRECTIONS

Melt the cocoa butter in the top of a double boiler. You can make your own double boiler by placing a metal bowl over a pot of gently boiling water. Make sure the water isn't touching the bowl, just the steam.

Add the decarboxylated cannabis. Steep the bud in the cocoa butter for one hour.

Strain the cocoa butter through cheesecloth or strainer into the measuring cup.

Add vanilla, maple syrup, cocoa powder, and salt to the measuring cup. Whisk well until there are no lumps. Give it a taste to make sure the mixture is to your liking. You can add more maple syrup or honey if you like it sweeter.

Pour the chocolate mixture into desired silicone molds.

Refrigerate for a few hours to harden.

#53: MAKE IT SAVORY

by Chef Harold Dieterle

It was after shoulder surgery to relieve an impingement that I first turned to THC, along with CBD. The combination of these two cannabinoids helped relieve the pain and inflammation—and also brought me a calm and focus that had eluded me most of my life.

Having used both alcohol and cannabis, I am one of many who find it simply insane and deeply hypocritical that alcohol has been an accepted part of polite society for decades while cannabis has been relegated to the black market. Once you accept cannabis as a gift from nature, the same way we accept fruits, vegetables, flowers, and other holistic medications, a whole new world of how and when to use cannabis opens up.

For me and many chefs, the vast category known as "edibles" is the most appealing means of availing ourselves of the nurturing properties of cannabis. Edibles don't just mean the gummies or chocolates you might make or buy at a dispensary; they also encompass baked goods and savory cooking. There are many ways to incorporate cannabis into cooking, but one of the easiest is infusing your butter, which can then be used in mashed potatoes, baked goods, and any other recipe in which you would use butter.

27.5

Percent increase in the edibles market from 2018 to 2019.

Cannabutter

PREP: 5 minutes · **COOK:** 3 hours

TOTAL TIME: 3 hours 5 minutes · **YIELD:** 1 cup

INGREDIENTS

- 1 cup of butter (or coconut butter)
- 1 cup (7 to 10 grams) of decarboxylated cannabis
- 1 teaspoon liquid lecithin (optional)

SUPPLIES

- Double boiler (or make your own with a pot and metal bowl)
- Cheesecloth or strainer

DIRECTIONS

Heat the butter and decarboxylated cannabis in the top of a double boiler over a very low flame for two and a half hours. You can make your own double boiler by placing a metal bowl over a pot of gently boiling water. Make sure the water isn't touching the bowl, just the steam.

Strain the flower particles from the fat infusion by pouring through the cheesecloth or strainer.

If you like, you can stir in 1 teaspoon of liquid lecithin to help the mixture emulsify. This helps avoid potency spikes and ensure even dosing across each batch.

Chef Harold Dieterle is the winner of the first season of Top Chef.
He has owned three restaurants in NYC: Perilla, Kin Shop, and The Marrow.

Does This Person Get High?

FAMOUS PERSON	GETS HIGH	DOESN'T GET HIGH	OWNS A CANNABRAND
DR. RUTH WESTHEIMER	✓		
PATRICK STEWART	✓		
ANNE HATHAWAY	✓		
STEVE JOBS	✓		
SETH ROGEN	✓		✓
OPRAH WINFREY	✓		
PINK	✓		
LEBRON JAMES	✓		
WOODY HARRELSON	✓		✓
MAYA ANGELOU	✓		
MARGARET CHO	✓		✓
MORGAN FREEMAN	✓		
RUSH LIMBAUGH	✓		
CARL SAGAN	✓		
MARTHA STEWART	✓		✓
MELISSA ETHERIDGE	✓		✓

FAMOUS PERSON	GETS HIGH	DOESN'T GET HIGH	OWNS A CANNABRAND
BILL GATES	√		
DANNY DEVITO	√		
SANJAY GUPTA	√		
PRINCE HARRY	√		
SARAH PALIN	√		
NICK JONAS	√		
KAREEM ABDUL-JABBAR	√		
CHELSEA HANDLER	√		√
BARACK OBAMA	√		
ROBERT MITCHUM	√		
THE BEATLES	√		
MARILYN MONROE	√		
WHOOPI GOLDBERG			√
YOUR GRANDMA*		√	

* We actually have no idea if your grandma gets high, but there's one way to find out. See "Stoning the Elders" on page 112.

creativity

We're of the opinion that defining creativity is kind of like the Supreme Court defining obscenity: "I know it when I see it," Justice Potter Stewart famously said when ruling on what's protected under freedom of speech (unfun fact: obscenity is *not* protected). Unlike those uptight judges, we've rarely met a creative pursuit we didn't approve of. Whether your creative self feels most at home belting out a rousing rendition of "I Will Survive" at karaoke night, composing poems on the hazards of Tinder, or just adding a well-placed sprig of parsley to your mac and cheese, we say, get down with your creative self. Creativity adds meaning and beauty to life, and we think the world's big enough for both Michelangelo's *David* and *The Real Housewives of Atlanta*. With that in mind, we ask you to not only embrace your creative self but allow cannabis to times it by ten.

What exactly is creativity? Tough question. Philosophers have been trying to define creativity for thousands of years. At its core, creativity is the ability to produce original ideas. And scientists are finally beginning to understand where those original ideas come from (shocker...it's the brain). So why is it so hard to access those ideas? Anyone who's sat down to write an intro on using cannabis for creativity will know what we're talking about. Finding and harnessing that spark of an idea doesn't come easily. But we have good news. And that news is cannabis.

It will come as a surprise to no one that many great artists love the herb and use it to get into a creative zone. You'll find a number of quotes in the following pages on the wonders of weed and creativity, but we think Kid Cudi sums it up best when he says, "Struggle is the enemy, but weed is the remedy." That's right, weed is the remedy, because it stimulates blood flow to the brain's prefrontal cortex, making this area more active and sparking creativity output in two ways.

First, the prefrontal cortex is where divergent thinking develops. Divergent thinking is that out-of-the-box, free-flowing thinking that your boss is always asking for. It helps you problem solve in original and spontaneous ways, which is really just another way of saying divergent thinking sparks creativity. One type of divergent thinking cannabis is particularly good at stoking is hyperpriming. Hyperpriming occurs when unusual connections are made between items that are only loosely related. A 2010 study revealed that levels of hyperpriming were higher in regular cannabis users even when they weren't high and were *significantly* higher when they were...high.

Second, the ancient flower also activates the *nucleus accumbens*, the area of the brain that correlates with increased creativity and an area of the brain that releases dopamine (that feel-good chemical). The prefrontal cortex regulates this release of dopamine, encouraging you to feel better about what you're creating. And when you *feel* better, you *do* better.

Cannabis is a creative maximizer because it activates areas of the prefrontal cortex, but it also brings a creative boost because it deactivates others. One of the biggest inhibitors to creative thinking is our judgment of our creative thoughts. As we know, cannabis deactivates the dorsolateral prefrontal cortex, the area of the brain that is connected to inhibition and self-censorship. In other words: Mary Jane suppresses your inner Judge Judy and lets you focus on your truly world-changing—no, universe-shifting—original ideas.

We won't say that *all* your ideas are worthy of a MacArthur genius award, but you only need one! And you don't have to be the next Langston Hughes to want your ode to OG Kush (or Purple Haze or Sour Diesel or Durban Poison) to be lit. So stoke those creative fires with a little literal fire and try out the following activities. We'll look for your magnum opus on the shelf next to ours.

FIELD ~~NOTES~~ QUOTES

See what we did there? Field *Quotes*. Why explain a bunch of stuff we learned along the way when we could let the creative geniuses speak for themselves? Take it away, high creatives!

"When I'm high...there's less of a veil, so to speak. So if ever I need some clarity...or a quantum leap in terms of writing something, it's a quick way for me to get to it."

—ALANIS MORISSETTE

"Smoking just helps to free my mind, slow my thoughts down, and think about everything not only in a more poetic way but in a more creative way in general."

—WIZ KHALIFA

"Marijuana can be like a loving partner to your creativity; a muse and inspiration and a help in many ways."

—SEBASTIÁN MARINCOLO

"Music and herb go together."

—BOB MARLEY

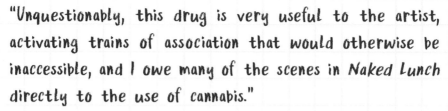

"Unquestionably, this drug is very useful to the artist, activating trains of association that would otherwise be inaccessible, and I owe many of the scenes in *Naked Lunch* directly to the use of cannabis."

–WILLIAM BURROUGHS

"Stoners usually have genius ideas; we just never do anything with them."

–SARAH SILVERMAN

"We're not sure we write our best jokes while stoned, but we enjoy the process much more. We're less rigid writers. We think more abstractly... We believe cannabis allows us to connect to our thoughts on a deeper level... Cannabis facilitates the process better than any other substance we depend on to cope with existence."

–THE LUCAS BROTHERS

ACTIVITIES

#54: DANK DREAM JOURNAL

We're speaking highly anecdotally, but we've never slept better since introducing a cannabis tincture into our bedtime routine. Sleep is the answer to so many of life's questions and is vital to a healthy, creative brain. In a study led by psychiatrist Sara Mednick, people who experience REM sleep (the time during a snooze in which dreams are most vivid) performed better on creativity-oriented word problems. Paying attention to those dreams can boost your creativity even more. Science tells us that the subconscious mind creates dreams to work out life's problems, so paying attention to your dreams can reveal where you may be stuck and ways to get unstuck. That said, there is some evidence that cannabis interferes with REM sleep, so you dream less, but there can also be a rebound effect. After not partaking for a few days, people are flooded with dreams, dreams ripe for journaling.

Here's how to give your creative flow a kick start even before your morning coffee (or cannabis) kicks in: keep a journal and pen right next to your bed so you can get to recording as soon as you wake up. Write down your dreams in as much detail as possible (the color of the socks you were wearing when you showed up naked for your high school history final might be important). Rinse, repeat, and see what patterns emerge.

MICRODOSING: GO WITH THE FLOW

Microdosing, or taking small amounts of cannabis, is an increasingly popular method of taking in the benefits of THC for focus and flow while minimizing the psychoactive effects that higher doses cause in some users. "Microdosing cannabis in doses under 5 milligrams of THC can help unlock creativity by boosting activity in an area of the brain called the frontal lobe," said Dr. Michele Ross, a neuroscientist and author of the book *Vitamin Weed*. A trusted edible or tincture brand is the best way to control the dosage (this is not the time for home-baked pot brownies). A common recommendation is to start with 2.5 milligrams, taken every few hours. Maintain that level for approximately three days and then increase as desired. "Stick to small amounts of sativa candies, gummies, or tinctures," said Dr. Ross. "The effect should be to keep your brain energized and flowing instead of relaxed and quiet." When in doubt, let these five words be your microdosing mantra: *start low and go slow*.

#55: LETTER TO YOURSELF

Your high self has some very important information it needs to convey to your sober self, not limited to but including that idea for a dope podcast on the merits of various snack foods. Cannabis can bring clarity to problems our conscious minds sometimes prefer to just ignore, so allow the THC to work its magic and see if you can do some looking inward. Cannabis is, after all, an *entheogen*—a substance that produces changes in cognition and consciousness for religious or spiritual purpose—and what's more spiritual than having a good heart-to-heart with your authentic self? If this all sounds like the far-out ramblings of a stoned person, remember that journaling keeps our thoughts organized and our heads clear, and one approach to journaling is to write a letter to your future self. That may mean your future sober self who's just a few hours away or the self that's still getting high on their eightieth birthday.

Asking yourself a series of questions about your values, relationships, hopes, and dreams is an excellent exercise in self-reflection. And getting these thoughts down and reading them later offers both a reality check and an opportunity to ask questions like: Am I becoming the person I wanted to be? Did I maintain and grow the relationships in my life that were most important? Was that snack podcast really such a good idea? Don't forget to sign and date.

#56: DOODLE A DAY

Those chicken scratches on notebooks and napkins, also known as doodles, offer more than meets the eye. Doodling can help relieve boredom (that's why it's so popular in classrooms everywhere) and decrease frustration (so don't stop your kid from scribbling because you think she's ignoring you). In a delightful TED Talk that has more than 1.5 million views, Sunni Brown, author of *The Doodle Revolution*, explains how doodling and creative thinking can improve our comprehension and problem-solving skills and help us focus on the present. It doesn't matter what you draw, but if you need inspiration, try putting two divergent things together (divergent thinking helps with divergent thinking!): a chicken and boba tea, a sock and the night sky, a sticky bud and a personal pan pizza. Now go double down on doodling by drawing with a doobie and unlock the artist within.

#57: DIY DELIVERY SYSTEM

We love maker culture because it gives your brain and body a challenge that's playful, not problematic. Why not combine your desire for DIY with an opportunity to hack your way into new smoking devices? With more blood being pumped to the prefrontal cortex, your divergent thinking will be on point so you can troubleshoot when your homemade bowl isn't perfectly symmetrical or not care because...slowed dorsolateral prefrontal cortex!

Below you'll find directions on how to turn items lying around your house into weed delivery systems (and, for goodness' sake, don't miss the snow bong on page 63).

APPLE

Granny Smith? Pink Lady? Honeycrisp? We're not gonna advise on the varietal (although there's something groovy about using a Cosmic Crisp). All you need is an apple, a knife, and a chopstick (or screwdriver). First, pull out the stem of the apple. Then, scoop out a bit at the top of the apple to make your bowl. For the mouthpiece, use your chopstick or screwdriver to push a hole, horizontally, all the way through the middle of the apple. Then, using your knife, poke a few holes through the bowl, making sure they go through to the horizontal chamber you previously made. Now you've got a bowl, a carb, and a mouthpiece! Pack it and pair with some cannabis rich in caramel notes for the perfect combo.

SODA CAN

Ah, the old soda can pipe. It's simple, it's effective, and you'll be walking in the shoes of millions of industrious stoners before you. Grab a can and press into one side to create an indent for your bowl. Poke holes into the indent with a needle or other pin-like object. To smoke, pack your cannabis into your indented bowl, bring your mouth to the can as if you were drinking out of it horizontally, light up, and inhale. Use this one in moderation, because there are minor concerns about the metal and paint on the can being harmful to ingest (unlike the cannabis, which is currently doing amazing things for your brain and body).

TWO-LITER BOTTLE

Let's make a gravity bong! Start with an empty plastic two-liter bottle. Remove the cap and cover the top with foil. Use a toothpick to poke holes into the foil to make your bowl. Next, cut the bottom of the bottle off (an X-Acto knife is great for slicing around the bottom circumference of the bottle). Congratulations, you made a bong!

Now, to use it, you'll need a waterproof container that's wider than the bottle (a dishwashing tub or even a sink with a working stopper work great). Fill the container with water until it's almost full. Next, plunge your newly constructed bong into the water. Pack a bowl, and as you light the weed, slowly lift the bottle up until it's almost out of the water. Next, remove the foil and put your mouth on the bottle. Inhale while pushing the bottle down. Rinse and repeat!

PACK OF STARBURST

It's sticky. It's messy. It's clearly invented by stoners. Unwrap all twelve Starburst and stack ten of them. Use the warmth of your hands to mold them into a pipe-like object. Stab a skewer through the stack and wiggle to create a chamber. Now lay your stacked Starburst horizontally and place the two unused Starburst on top of one end to form your bowl. Poke your skewer through the bowl to the chamber, then mold the bowl. If you're finding your medium tough to work in, heat the Starburst for a few seconds in the microwave and then shape. Now load a nug and smoke that fake fruit.

#58: SELFIE SCAVENGER HUNT

A scavenger hunt pairs perfectly with what cannabis offers your brain: increased awareness; decreased self-consciousness; a boost of creativity; and activation of the basal ganglia where motor control, executive function, and *feeeelings* happen. In other words, move your mind and move your body with this new take on an old favorite. In the good ole days, we had to walk uphill, both ways, and actually collect our assigned items, but in this world of modern miracles, we have devices in our pockets that will keep track of what we've scavenged. Let the alphabet work as an organizing principle and challenge you and your friends to go through the alphabet and take a selfie with something that corresponds with each letter. A is for apple. B is for barista. C is for cannabis.

HELPFUL HINTS

▸ Set a one-hour time limit, and then reconvene to see who made it through all twenty-six letters.

▸ Want to go analog? Polaroid cameras are fun and come with their own creative challenges (i.e., no screen to make sure everyone's in the pic).

▸ Using a X-ing sign for that intimidating X is totally allowed.

#59: ANIMAL STORIES

Interacting with animals decreases anxiety and depression. Guess what else decreases anxiety and depression? We'll give you a hint. It makes you hella creative and laugh like a hyena, which is a perfect combination for reporting on the antics of the local dog population. You've played people stories, but have you played animal stories? Grab a friend, go to the local dog park or other public dog-infested space, and narrate those canine capers. Give each of the dogs a name. Watch Gulliver sidle up to Ms. Bananas. Gossip about their illicit affair. Now channel Ilana and Abby from *Broad City* (two of our favorite stoners) and figure out what kind of dog you'd be. Abby's choice? A slim pug, and Ilana? We'll let her speak for herself: "I'd be a three-legged mutt because I'd be, like, a highly respected minority, and I'd be all the dogs' fetishes." Now it's your turn.

#60: KID KRAFTS

We've given you a host of ways to channel your inner child ("Play with Kids" on page 82; "Be a Kid Again" on page 224), but there's a special place in our hearts for kid crafts. Kids are great artists because they don't self-censor, they follow their impulses, and they have fun while they do it. But inhabiting that space for the post-ten-year-old crowd can be a bit harder, which is why you need a little help from our friend cannabis. Creativity is associated with the brain's frontal lobe, and as cannabis intake increases, so does blood flow to this area. With all those creative juices flowing, you're welcome to channel your inner Picasso and create a great masterpiece, but we're going to

100

Percent of movies Seth Rogen filmed while high.

direct you to these simple art projects we all mastered in elementary school. Just don't eat the paste.

SCRATCH ART

Completely fill a piece of paper with thick, brightly colored crayon patterns. Now color over those same designs with a black crayon. You're going to want to go hard so the primary colors aren't peeking through. Next, take a paperclip or toothpick and scratch out your design. May we suggest some psychedelic paisleys and a magic mushroom?

CHALK IT UP

The options are endless with a six-pack of sidewalk chalk: hopscotch, tic-tac-toe, inspirational sayings. We recommend lying down and having someone trace your body. Then add a fabulous outfit. Or recreate a crime scene.

SLIME TIME

What you need: 1 cup white glue, 1 teaspoon baking soda, 2 teaspoons contact lens solution, food coloring (if you want to be fancy). Put it all in a bowl. Mix. For fluffy slime, add a cup of shaving cream. Indulge your sensory-seeking self.

#61: HIGH SHARK TANK

"I have the *best* idea!" said everyone at some point while high. Now, we recognize that *maybe* 70 percent of those high ideas may not be as extraordinary when you're not under the influence, but that still leaves 30 percent that are genius (you're reading this book right now, aren't you?). And why wouldn't your ideas flow better under the creative influence of cannabis? In fact, this is the very same kind of thinking that got us thinking, and what did it get us thinking about? High Shark Tank.

Here's how it works:

1. Appoint one person as the "shark" (or judge), and have everyone else break down into groups.

2. Each group takes ten minutes to brainstorm a new product, company, or notion. To get that creative divergent thinking going, think about a need you have that isn't being met. Small annoyances always make good fodder. Stubbing your toe every night when you head to the bathroom? Headlight slippers! A delivery service that only delivers seafood caught within the last two hours? The World Is Your Oyster, Inc. Now get your two-minute pitch ready.

3. Reconvene and have each team pitch the shark.

4. Realize that at some point, one of the pitches will be an idea that already exists. So when a team comes up with, "It's a single pot where you can cook everything! We call it Big Pot," just smile. Have a heart (they're

high after all); you don't want to be the party pooper who brings everyone down by noting the Instant Pot is a two-billion-dollar business.

5. The shark declares winners in a range of categories of their creation. We suggest:

   a.   Best Idea

   b.   Worst Idea

   c.   Best Idea That Definitely Is Only Best Because We're High

PRO TIPS

▶ Have all players agree that if any of the ideas actually come to fruition, the new CEO will gift the others a $100 gift card to a local dispensary or .001 percent of the company's value (whichever is higher).

▶ Assign the person who is Most Able to Type All Ideas Into a Google Doc the job of documenting all ideas for posterity and/or future profit.

#62: THE FUNNIES

The mediums have changed, but the message stays the same: the cartoons are the best part of any newspaper. As a kid, you may have gobbled up the funny pages inside your local paper, but now the funny pages thrive online. We're not saying you need cannabis to make *Calvin and Hobbes* funny (just watch any nine-year-old transfixed by the boy and his snarky tiger). But add cannabis—which stimulates blood flow to the right frontal and left temporal lobes of the (adult!) brain, causing laughter—and what's funny just got funnier.

Since cannabis also kicks your creativity into high gear, why not really take the comics to the far side of funny and rewrite the captions? When you're ready to step it up, try your hand at the Cartoon Caption Contest in *The New Yorker*. The rules say you must be "thirteen or older," but they say nothing about disqualifying you for having an unfair advantage because you're hella high. Go to newyorker.com/humor to enter.

"Hi, I'd like to add you to my professional network on LinkedIn."

#63: THE JOY OF SIX

A six-word memoir is a story of you in exactly—you guessed it—six words. Your six-word story may be about one aspect of your life ("Clawed my way out of Tennessee."), a broader picture of who you are ("My life made my therapist laugh."), or a life motto ("If Beyoncé says it, do it!"). It's also a great way to forge a deeper—and often unexpected—connection with your friends. But if trying to condense your life into six words gives you performance anx-

iety, have we got a plant for you. As you very well know by now, cannabis decreases inhibitions, lowers anxiety, and gives your brain the signal that everything is juuuust fiiiine. Which is exactly the state you want to be in when you tell everyone, "Ex-wife and contractor now have house." Have your friends share their six-word memoirs, or level up and turn it into a fun (and informative!) game. Here's how to play:

1. Have everyone write down three six-word memoirs, fold each one up, and place them in a pile.

2 Take turns picking and reading anonymously. Whose memoir is "Superpower: big feelings. Kryptonite: big feelings." and "Big hair. Big heart. Big hurry."? (Spoiler alert...they're ours.)

The person with the most correct answers wins. Go down the six-word rabbit hole at sixwordmemoirs.com.

#64: FUN WITH ACCENTS

Dream journals, maker projects, imaginative crafts—we've offered you so many edifying ways to be creative. And when you're done with all those enriching activities, it's time to do something completely ridiculous. It's time to have an accent competition. That's right, *mon cherie*, let the power of the pot help you forget how silly you're about to sound (thanks, slowed dorsolateral prefrontal cortex!) and instead focus on the fun. After all, your mouth deserves a chance to get creative too. So choose an accent, practice your pronunciation, then tell the academy to get ready, because there's a new Meryl Streep in town.

HER ROYAL HIGHNESS

Loosen your Rs, elongate your vowels, and start saying the H in herb. Ask your partner, "How do you do?" Use some dated vocabulary ("Pip pip, cheerio!"). Refer to yourself in the singular ("One should smoke the herb now."). Perhaps (puh-haps) you can play some chess while you're at it—be sure to protect your royalty.

CROCODILE DUNDEE

While a British accent elongates vowels and drops the Rs at the ends of words, the Australian accent also warps the vowel sounds. Try saying "no" like you're trying to say "Nore" but skimp out on the R at the end. Or try saying "I"—but pronounce the long vowel as "Oi." Soon, you'll be able to say, "I know how to throw shrimp on the bahbee." But say "prawns." No *real* Australian uses the word "shrimp."

VALLEY GIRL CIRCA 1987

Okay, like, this accent is definitely, like, one of the most fun of all of them? Liberally sprinkle in the "likes" as you might salt your pasta water, and try to end all your sentences as though they're questions? Don't be afraid of words that end in -ly: totally, seriously, or literally—go big, even when you're totally not literally dying, but it seriously feels like you are. Add it all together, and you, like, definitely got it?

EPIC SCOTTISH HERO

Turn your Us into "oohs" so, "We could pull the hood off," becomes "We coohd poohl the hoohd off." Add some "ayes" and "wee bonny lassies," and you'll already be more authentic than Mel Gibson in *Braveheart*.

YODA

In English, we order sentences like subject–verb–object. You (subject) practice (verb) accents (object). In Yoda-speak, however, the object comes first, then subject, then verb. Accents, you practice, hmm? Same goes for adjectives. "Your accent is spot-on," becomes "Spot-on, your accent is." Gotten the hang of it, you have, hmm? Fear, you will not. Got this, you do. Either way: do or do not. There is no try.

> "I learned new postures and developed new dreams. From a natural stiffness, I melted into a grinning tolerance. Walking on the streets became a high adventure, eating my mother's huge dinners, and opulent entertainment, and playing with my son was side-cracking hilarity. For the first time, life amused me."
>
> —MAYA ANGELOU, ON CANNABIS

FAB 5 FREDDY TALKS CANNABIS AND CREATIVITY

by Fred Brathwaite, Fab 5 Freddy

To my knowledge, cannabis and creativity have always been synonymous. Significant artists in every genre I've encountered have felt very comfortable using the powers of the plant for the creative process. Now, it's not that cannabis itself *makes* you creative, but it can get you to the flow state—the creative flow state—that enhances creativity.

Cannabis is very personal to me. My dad was a part of the 1950s jazz scene and, like so many of his friends, was a cannabis aficionado. His friends were some of the smartest people I knew: an open and diverse group of cutting-edge jazz musicians and creatives, including my godfather, the legendary jazz musician Max Roach.

Growing up deeply embedded in this creative mix of musicians inspired me as a teen. Eventually, I became a player in the early days of hip-hop, introducing Snoop Dogg and Cypress Hill and others in the scene to a national television audience on the show I hosted, *Yo! MTV Raps*. These guys were big proponents and advocates of cannabis. And so, when I was thinking about making my film, *Grass Is Greener*, I realized a great way to tell the story about this plant in America was through its connection to America's music. From the jazz scene in the 1920s with Louis Armstrong calling cannabis "an assistant and a friend" to hip-hop acts like Snoop Dogg, who said, "It makes me feel the way

I need to feel," musicians in every genre of popular music have been cannabis aficionados.

Cannabis has been part of all my creative endeavors: making art, making and being a fan of music, and making film. The power of the cannabis plant has been integral to my mental and physical health as well as a critical assist to my creative flow state.

Fred Brathwaite, aka Fab 5 Freddy, is an American visual artist, filmmaker, and hip-hop pioneer. He was the first host of the groundbreaking hip-hop music video show, Yo! MTV Raps, and his documentary on the history of cannabis, Grass Is Greener, can be found on Netflix.

joy

Cannabis shrinks cancer cells, helps control epilepsy, reduces anxiety, and is the best anti-nausea medication on the market. But if we're honest, its number one selling point for the cannabis-curious person is that it makes you fantastically, extraordinarily, unbelievably happy. And a lot of us agree. According to a 2018 study, more than 122 million people in the United States have tried cannabis, which is almost half the adult population. The fastest-growing crop in the world is the ultimate joy maker, and you don't need a book to tell you that. Still, we were delighted to do the research on why this happy plant has you grinning like a maniacal monkey because...shhh...we also got to do the "research." And what we learned after hundreds (and hundreds) of hours of investigation was that we could have easily titled this book *Joy*...well, we guess we kind of did.

There's a reason the endocannabinoid that most closely resembles THC is called anandamide (aka "bliss"), and that reason is that cannabis makes everything blissful, even the stuff that didn't start out that way. With that in mind, we direct your attention to a host of activities designed to make the ordinary extraordinary and the mundane miraculous.

How does cannabis turn the routine remarkable, the uninspiring, well... inspiring? You may be tempted to give all the credit to that happy hormone, dopamine (we were), but the most recent research shows that although cannabis consumption *does* produce an increase in dopamine, it's nowhere near enough to get you grinning like said monkey. Same goes for serotonin, our other mood-boosting neurochemical friend. THC does produce an increase of serotonin, but it's no morphine drip. Instead, think of weed's effect on dopamine and serotonin like a 2.5-milligram THC gummy. It will get you feeling good, but not the goooood that comes from a dab of 80 percent THC live resin. For that effect, we need to look to how THC reacts when introduced to our endocannabinoid system.

As you may remember, we already have a lean, mean, happy-making machine within us, and it's called the endocannabinoid system. Both endocannabinoids (the ones made inside your body) and phytocannabinoids (the ones grown in the ground) bind to two lucky receptors (CB1 and CB2, if you want to be formal) to produce a variety of effects depending on where the receptors are located and which cannabinoid is doing the binding. If it's THC cozying up to the CB1 receptors in the brain, the effect is complete and total happiness. This is because THC resembles another cannabinoid naturally produced in our brains—the bliss neurochemical, anandamide. Anandamide's main job is to enhance your mood; thanks, anandamide! And yet it's not going to pack the euphoric punch THC does. For that, you need the one and only THC. Its chemical makeup is the reason you turn into that jubilantly joyful monkey, and it's the (main) reason for this here book.

But THC's job isn't only to bind to the CB1 receptors. It also has some pretty cool side hustles, mainly to s l o w your brain down—not so great for driving, very great for laughing. One of the parts of the brain THC targets is the amygdala. Its job? To trigger fight or flight. A slowed fight-or-flight response doesn't recognize stimuli as quickly, so what you're encountering (say, your dog cocking his head at just the right angle) suddenly seems new (and hilarious), which our brains love. Novelty is, after all, the great parent of pleasure (or so claim a bunch of memes on the internet). Add a slowed dorsolateral prefrontal cortex (the area of the brain responsible for self-censorship and inhibition), and you've suddenly got a brain that sees the world in new ways that it might not have allowed itself to see before. And that, THC-loving friends, brings joy, happiness, bliss, and maniacal monkey grins.

FIELD NOTES

Gross National Happiness: The Bhutanese government uses the Gross National Happiness index to measure the collective happiness of its people, which is why it's not surprising that cannabis grows like, well, a weed in Bhutan. In fact, cannabis is so prolific that it's fed to pigs (what better way to fatten your porkers than with some munchie-inducing flower?). But while those Bhutanese pigs are flying high, its people are not. Human consumption of cannabis is still illegal. Way to harsh your gross national mellow, Bhutan.

Smoke the Rainbow: Cannabis plants, like all plants that go through photosynthesis to produce energy, have chlorophyll, which makes them look green. As a cannabis plant matures, it produces less chlorophyll and more of a family of flavonoids called anthocyanins, which contain colorful pigments, including purples, reds, and blues. Word on the street is that the purple stuff is the kine bud, but the street is wrong. A purple-hued plant has likely

been exposed to cold temperature and is thus prone to produce less THC.

In Case of Armageddon, Weed's Got You: Imagine a secret doomsday seed vault where backup seeds for all of humanity's crops are stockpiled. No, this isn't the beginning of some apocalyptic thriller, it's the Svalbard Global Seed Vault, a seed storage facility that's designed as the ultimate insurance policy for the world's food supply. Also, its weed supply. The vault safeguards more than 21,000 cannabis seeds, so after the zombies are eradicated, you'll still be able to get your high on.

ACTIVITIES

#65: THE SECRET LIFE OF PETS

Doggies! Kitties! Red-eyed crocodile skinks! The animal kingdom is delightful, but it's even more weird and wonderful when you're high. We don't recommend going out and befriending the neighborhood squirrels (although we do recommend googling squirrel obstacle courses for some *hilarious* hijinks). Instead, we encourage you to turn on, tune in, and drop down to the level of the domesticated creatures in your life.

The THC in cannabis binds to the endocannabinoid receptors in our brains, creating that mind-expanding experience that causes us to find the things we love even more joyous and lovable. Pair this with our knowledge that petting a furry animal for even ten minutes significantly reduces cortisol levels (no research yet on caressing a skink), and it stands to reason that cannabis will help the whole animal kingdom (that includes you) reach all new levels of mellow. Now, try these two activities for more beastie fun.

CANNABIS WITH YOUR CANINE

Why not share the pleasures of cannabis with your pooch? We're not talking about passing Rover the roach but rather introducing your canine to CBD. While there are no conclusive studies that dogs get the same benefits of CBD as humans—anti-inflammatory properties, anti-nausea effects, appetite stimulation, and anxiety reduction—there's plenty of anecdotal evidence. In fact, *Dog Naturally* magazine reports that veterinarians are finding that CBD can be useful in treating acute ailments like sprains and strains, torn ligaments, and bone breaks and even reducing swelling, pain, and stiffness during postoperative care. Dr. Jerry Klein, chief veterinary officer at the American Kennel Club, agrees that CBD seems safe for canines because it doesn't contain THC, the psychoactive compound we humans love.

But be warned: if you decide to join your animal companion and imbibe your own cannabis, you might want to go with edibles if you've got a pocket-sized pet. Just like humans, the smaller the being, the more sensitive it is to cannabis, making it possible for them to get high off the secondhand smoke. Also, make sure you lock up those delicious gummies. The last thing you need is to call animal poison control and ask, hypothetically, how much THC your sixty-five-pound dog can ingest without toxicity.

SETTLE IN AT A CAT CAFÉ

Were the owners of the world's first-known cat café—the Cat Flower Garden in Taipei, Taiwan—high when they came up with the idea of a café in which cats frolic freely? We must assume so. Since its opening in 1998, many more cat cafés have opened around the world. According to Meowaround.com (yes, it's a thing), there are 117 cat cafés in the United States with names like Crumbs & Whispers (Washington, DC), Crooked Tail Café (Greensboro, North Carolina), and KitTea

(San Francisco, California). The cats provide companionship for the cat-less, and some cafés have partnerships with local animal shelters, so you can even adopt a cat you take a fancy to. And while reports are that the cats are generally well-behaved, stoners hunkering down to a piece of cake (caaaake, see "Cake and Bake" on page 229) should be warned: cats love frosting, so guard your baked goods.

#66: HOT HIGH HYGGE

You know *hygge* (pronounced *hue-guh*; see "Fun with Accents" on page 207 for more professional accent tips); it's the Danish concept of getting cozy. Think fireplaces, blankets, hot beverages, and simple pleasures. In other words, there's nothing that pairs more perfectly with the cozy hygge lifestyle than the cannabis high lifestyle. Hygge is all about relaxation. And what binds to our CB1 receptors and mimics the neurochemical 2-AG by slowing the connections between the amygdala and the frontal cortex, reducing anxiety and promoting relaxation (not to mention activating the neurotransmitter dopamine to modulate stress and control mood)? That's right, cannabis. We think you can handle the fire making (perhaps do this before you light up?) and blanket gathering, but we're here to help with the snuggly hot liquids portion of your evening.

Anyone can dump a pack of hot cocoa into a mug and call it hygge, but to appreciate the full hygge experience, you need *high* hygge, brought to you by the following cannabis-infused hot toddies. All the following beverages require can-namilk, which you can't find at your local Whole Foods (one day, Jeff Bezos?), so for now, you're going to have to make your own.

Cannamilk

PREP: 15 minutes-ish • **COOK:** 2 hours-ish
TOTAL TIME: 2½ hours-ish • **YIELD:** 2 cups

INGREDIENTS

- 4 to 7 grams decarboxylated cannabis (the more the hy[gg]ier)
- 2 cups whole milk

SUPPLIES

- Double boiler (or make your own with a pot and metal bowl)
- Cheesecloth

DIRECTIONS

Gather and tie up your decarboxylated cannabis in a piece of cheesecloth to make a bud bundle.

Heat the milk in the top of a double boiler (make your own by placing a metal bowl over a pot of gently boiling water). Be careful that the milk doesn't come to a boil. Ideally use a cooking thermometer and aim for around 150°F.

Add the bud bundle, and cook on medium heat for about one and a half hours, stirring frequently (about every 10 minutes).

Remove your bud bundle, pour cannamilk into two mugs, and don't forget to turn off the stove (we're here to help).

For each drink, stir the following ingredients into each warm mug of can-namilk. For less potency, dilute your cannamilk with regular milk.

Classic Hot Cocoa

- 1 tablespoon unsweetened cocoa
- 1 tablespoon sugar
- 2 ounces melted semisweet chocolate

Gingerbread Latte

- ½ teaspoon ground cinnamon
- ½ teaspoon ground ginger
- 1 tablespoon sugar
- 1 tablespoon molasses

Chai Latte

- 1 black tea bag
- 1 tablespoon sugar
- 1 generous pinch cinnamon
- 1 generous pinch ground ginger
- 1 generous pinch ground cardamom
- 1 pinch ground cloves

Bourbon White Hot Chocolate

- 2 ounces melted white chocolate
- 1 teaspoon vanilla
- 1 to 2 tablespoons (or more; we know our audience) bourbon

#67: BE A KID AGAIN

Kids know how to make fun anywhere, but grown-ups often need a little help recapturing their inner child. Let your weed serve as a Wayback Machine and remember the little pleasures of life's littles. After all, just like with kids, adult play (and no, we don't mean *that* kind; you'll find *that* kind on page 133) stimulates the release of endorphins. Endorphins activate the opioid receptors in your brain that generate feelings of euphoria. You know what else activates receptors in your brain that generate feelings of euphoria? See the bottom of this page for answer.

In other words, for a double dose of euphoria, try the following activities, and make the tingles of revisiting your youth even tinglier.

KID IN A CANDY STORE

Go to a fully stocked candy store and investigate the weird and wonderful evolution of confections. Give black licorice another try, figure out what an Abba-Zaba is, revisit FunDip—it's a food! It's a utensil! Fun fact: dry mouth can make fizzy candy fizzle out, so maybe skip the Zotz.

122 million

The number of people in the United States who have tried cannabis—almost half the adult population.

RAID THE ARCADE

Go to an old-timey arcade and do the rounds. The retro arcade games may be your jam, but may we direct your attention to the star of the show—skee-ball! Gold medal

Answer: THC

moment: give your winning tickets to the little kid who's come up short at the prize counter and watch a face light up.

TAKE A SWING

Your vestibular and proprioception systems (the systems that control balance and equilibrium) love to play with gravity. Visit your local park and experiment with ups and downs. Have a partner? Spider swing: face each other, one person sitting on the other's lap, and let your brain work out how to share the pumping.

HIGH FOR THE HOLIDAYS

A conversation with Rabbi Amichai Lau-Lavie

Do religion and reefer go together? Hell, yes. We're not talking about ditching Hebrew school or sneaking out during the pastor's sermon to light up with your friends. That's kid stuff. But for adults looking to rekindle or strengthen their connection to their faith, the right strain of flower can be a godsend.

Cannabis is, after all, an entheogen—a plant-based substance that produces changes in cognition and consciousness for religious or spiritual purpose. And like so much in the book of cannabis, this ancient herb's place in religion goes way back. In the Torah, there are several mentions of a substance called *kaneh bosem*, aka cannabis, referred to as among the ritual offerings Moses is instructed to give God.

We talked to Amichai Lau-Lavie, a New York City-based rabbi and founder of Storahtelling, a nonprofit organization devoted to making ancient stories and traditions accessible for new generations, about why cannabis and spirituality go together like matzah and charosets. "Cannabis was part of the ancient Hebrew 'spice set' among the other types of incense and herbs in the tabernacle," he said. "Our ancestors understood that to move from doing business, reading the news, or talking to your kid to a more spiritual mindset, we need to turn off the more linear part of our brain and turn on other nonlinear parts." There are different ways to do this. Meditation and dancing are one; using THC is another.

Lau-Lavie recalled being at a Jewish retreat back when he was a budding young scholar. Toward the end of the retreat, one of the leaders (a well-known and respected rabbi) invited the group out for a spliff. Lau-Lavie was delighted and took the opportunity to ask the rabbi where Jewish law stood on getting high. "The rabbi said something to me that I never forgot, something instructive in so many parts of life, not just the high life," Lau-Lavie recalled. "He told me that when it comes to cannabis, you need to know who's the master and who's the servant. Use it if you can handle it and feel good. If it takes over your life, it just won't work for you."

It works for Lau-Lavie, who believes in the power of cannabis to harness the divine. "I've had some very powerful and important spiritual awakenings on weed," said Lau-Lavie. "I'm grateful for when I said yes and grateful when I needed to say no." And to that, we say amen.

#68: JUST SAY YES

Our adult brains are great at saying "No!" or at least thinking, *I probably shouldn't.* Cannabis, of course, can decrease inhibition, and decreased inhibition can loosen the grip of no and turn it into yes. Take that yes and keep saying it. All day. Donuts for breakfast, lunch, and dinner? *Yes!* Eight hours of *Among Us/Animal Crossing/Candy Crush*? *Yes!* Naps after every meal? *Yes!* Meals after meals? *Yes!* We encourage you to dig into your own indulgent desires. Below are a few tips for making the best of *yes.*

▶ **Schedule smartly:** Any day you're ready to say yes works, but we recommend picking a day that's ideal for your decadent desires. National Yes Day is December 19, but we prefer to save it for a summer day when there's less going on and more chances to say yes to the great outdoors (cannabis and beaches and ice cream, anyone?).

▶ **Be safe and legal:** If you have a copilot, make sure you agree that anyone can say no to a request that doesn't feel safe personally or is, you know, against the law.

▶ **Go for broke:** Try Yes Day with a child. Division of labor: the kid picks all the things to see, do, play, and eat; you pick a day that's ideal for your schedule. Then say yes! All that affirmation has real benefits. Parents who've braved a Yes Day report a new connectedness with the small creatures who are so used to hearing "No!"

#69: WAKE AND BAKE

Some days, there's nothing joyful about waking up. For those days, there's cannabis. Your body is pretty good at manufacturing the necessary endocannabinoids (*endo* meaning within) to keep you in a state of mental homeostasis, but some mornings, you need a phytocannabinoid (*phyto* meaning plant) to help it out. After all, naturally occurring anandamide might be a THC-*like* molecule, but THC it is not. So forget all that nonsense about self-care requiring mind and body discipline, and take a day to care for yourself with repeated doses of dank weed. And if you're gonna wake and bake like a stoner, why not go full-on pothead and indulge in four pillars of stoner delight: food (page 172), movies (page 129), music (page 92), and sex (page 133).

* It should go without saying that if you're still reaching for that pipe on morning 147, there may be better mental health options than waking and baking, but for the occasional case of the blahs, we highly recommend the 420 treatment plan. May we suggest April 20 for this activity?

#70: CAKE AND BAKE

Caaaaaaaake. That's all. Just cake. Pick one (or more) of the following options.

OPTION A

Ice Cream Cake: two great foods that taste great together. Our faves in order of increasing greatness:

> Dairy Queen
>
> Baskin Robbins
>
> Carvel

OPTION B

Grocery Store Sheet Cake: possible inscriptions?

> "You're a big deal, so here's a cake."
>
> "Eat cake because it's somebody's birthday"
>
> "Happy Birthday, Marge"

OPTION C

Jeni's Splendid Ice Cream, Gooey Butter Cake

OPTION D

Wedding Cake: sure, spend a bunch of money and order one of these beauties, or just google "Wedding Cake cannabis near me" and indulge in Wedding Cake, one of our all-time favorite strains. Enjoy a side of laughter with your cake by checking out these hilariously sad attempts at cake decorating: cakewrecks.com.

#71: EXPERIENCE THE WORLD FROM YOUR COUCH

The world is full of wonders, and we want nothing more than for you to go out and experience them all. But sometimes life gets in the way—pandemics, no vacation time, the cost of an all-inclusive trip to Fiji. Fear not. The interwebs have you covered, and we don't mean watching your ex's recent trip to Tuscany on Instagram. We know the internet can be a black hole of suck, but let us (and weed) help you rethink your relationship with the World Wide Web, because when our favorite cannabinoid, THC, binds to those CB1 receptors in your brain, these virtual experiences may seem even more marvelous than the real thing. Well, at least it will feel that way for approximately 120 minutes.

VIRTUAL MUSEUMS

▸ **The Neon Museum: neonmuseum.org**

The online home of Las Vegas's legendary Neon Museum is a kaleidoscope of sites and signs from the 1930s till now. Its 360-degree virtual Neon Boneyard tour is a binge for the eyes with none of the hangover.

▸ **Mutter Museum: muttermuseum.org**

Human skull collections. Drawers and drawers of fingernails. Einstein's brain. No, you're not in a David Lynch film, you're in the Mutter Museum. No trip to Philly is complete without it, but if you can't make it to one of the nation's weirdest museums, check out its online exhibit, *Memento Mütter*, which promises to get you "uncomfortably close" to images of lobotomies, prosthetic limbs, and other things you definitely should not try at home. We're pretty sure this is close enough.

▶ **The Museum of Broken Relationships: brokenships.com**

Those feelings that can arrive after the THC hits your system can be intense. And if your high head reminds you of a broken heart, head to the Museum of Broken Relationships (which has brick-and-mortar outposts in Zagreb, Croatia, and Los Angeles). Each item in the museum's collection is memorabilia from someone's relationship, along with a story from the contributors. Go down the rabbit hole of others' love and heartbreak, and maybe even be moved to share your own. You may surprise yourself and find a little catharsis with your cannabis.

#72: ALL CREATURES GREAT AND SMALL

Need some wonder and awe in your life? Us too. And lucky for us, animals always abide. The macaw is a beautiful creature even without the mind-expanding help of THC, but add cannabis to your next trip to the Everglades, and suddenly you just can't help but smile at that crocodile. Still, you may not be making that trip anytime soon, so we're here to offer both IRL and virtual journeys into the animal kingdom. Either way, we recommend you get higher sooner rather than later, gator.

GO ANALOG

There are lots of places to see animals in a controlled environment. Zoos? A little overwhelming on 10 milligrams of THC. Animal shelters? The risk of taking home all the puppies is just too high when you're in the deeply empathetic state cannabis enables. Our surprising pick for a high animal adventure? Your local pet store. Most no longer sell dogs and cats (thanks ASPCA!), but have you tried looking into the black beady eyes of the zebra finch and having a real heart-to-heart? How about pondering whether those guppies have consciousness? Go ahead and squeeze those stuffed toys and wonder why you didn't invent Pill Pockets. Now buy some treats and make fast friends with all the clientele.

GO DIGITAL

Now *this* virtual experience might be even better than the real thing. Wild animals! Close up! Doing animal things! There are a ton of live animal cams out there, but here are our top four.

- ▶ Brooks Falls, Alaska Brown Bears Cam: grizzlies catching their salmon dinner!
- ▶ Atlanta Zoo's Panda Cam: omgomgomg, pandas!
- ▶ Warrior Canine Connection: see inside the whelping room of this non-profit that trains service dogs!
- ▶ The Monterey Aquarium's Jelly Cam: not to be missed! (but get *reeeeally* high first)

HIGH FIVE: MIND-EXPANDING OUTDOOR ADVENTURES FOR YOUR HIGH SELF

by Libby Cooper

Libby Cooper, a weed and design expert who lives in Hawaii, and spends most of her time in the ocean and immersed in nature, shares her top five outdoor adventures.

BANZAI PIPELINE, NORTH SHORE, OAHU, HAWAII, WINTER SEASON ONLY

The North Shore of Oahu is beautiful year round, but the magic of the waves turning on in the winter months creates an energetic buzz that even nonsurfers can get behind! The surf season lasts from October through April, and there's nothing better than getting high off a racy sativa and going to watch the pro surfers drop into barrels at the highest performance wave in the world. The best waves at Pipe roll through in November and December if you want to really maximize your experience.

MOUNT TAMALPAIS, MARIN COUNTY, CALIFORNIA, IN THE SPRING

It's hard to beat hiking the trails of Mount Tamalpais when the rolling hills of this Northern California gem are green and speckled with wildflowers. The best is packing a picnic with a loved one and heading to this pristine coastline with a joint in hand. Make sure to mind your ash, no matter what time of year it is, because California is prone to wildfires.

CIUTAT VELLA, THE OLD TOWN OF BARCELONA

Barcelona is incredibly liberal when it comes to cannabis, so take advantage of the culture and enjoy a relaxed afternoon immersing yourself in Gothic stone architecture while stoned. A highlight of this gorgeous part of the city is the amazing food, including organic, vegan, and gluten-free restaurants so you will have tons of things to satisfy those munchies.

CARIBBEAN SEA, WHALE SHARK DIVING, CANCUN, MEXICO

It's hard to imagine a more impressive experience than encountering a whale shark in person. The whale shark is the largest known fish, with the biggest confirmed at 18.8 meters long! To swim with these beauties, you have to boat many miles out into the Caribbean Sea. Think about it: not only does getting high enhance your dive experience, but it will also help with the sea sickness.

ROYAL BOTANIC GARDENS, KEW, LONDON, ENGLAND

Kew Gardens houses the largest and most diverse botanical and mycological collections in the world and is conveniently located off a Tube line in London. Being high is known to increase your five senses and what better way to feast your eyes and nose on flora and fauna from across the globe. My favorite is the Palm House with its humidity and multilevel viewing platforms to see the plants even from the top of the canopy.

Libby Cooper is the cofounder and CEO of the premium cannabis brand Space Coyote, based in California.

#73: TOURIST IN YOUR OWN TOWN

Sensory perceptions are heightened with cannabis thanks to the miracle of THC, that lovely chemical that also gives cannabis its classification as psychoactive (mind-altering) and hallucinogenic (we quibble with this one, DEA, but sure, there's got to be those out there who have seen the face of God). That's why a little weed can go a long way in helping you look at the world differently. We kind of hope this whole book is one long activity to help you look at the world differently, but for this one, we're encouraging you to see your literal world in a new, lit way.

There are so many roads to travel high, but we like the ones where no one high is doing the driving. So decrease the stress and double the pleasure of the place you live (or one you visit often) by hopping on one of those double decker tour buses we see so often but rarely climb aboard. You'll gain a new perspective on your own town, pick up a few fun facts, and in a wide-eyed, uninhibited state, maybe make some new friends from Peoria along the way.

FUN FACT

Cannabis-themed city bus tours featuring dance parties, cannabis cooking lessons, and stops at local dispensaries and growing facilities are popping up in states where cannabis is legal.

#74: DRIVE-IN: THE PLATINUM EXPERIENCE

Cannabis and the silver screen are old friends. And really, if you don't like to get high and go to the movies...do you really like to get high? Movies and weed go together for a host of reasons, but one such reason has to do with your slowed high brain. A slowed amygdala takes just a touch longer to process what you're seeing and hearing, which means you'll probably turn to your pals more than once during a flick to say, "Wait...what happened?" But it can also mean that what you're seeing and hearing suddenly seems altogether new, so even if this is the twelfth time you've seen *Dazed and Confused*, everything old will seem new again. And everything new will seem better, funnier, and more delightful.

It's hard to beat a midnight showing of *The Big Lebowski* for the gold medal of movies and weed, but we'd like to offer you the platinum experience: come with us to the drive-in and follow our plan for taking things a little higher.

1 The Basics

A sober driver and (ideally) a minivan. If you don't have a minivan, invite a friend who has one and buy their ticket. Or, if you must, smoosh into your Mini Cooper and imagine you and the rest of your hepcats are stuffed in a phone booth for a real cool bash, Daddy-O.

2 Pregame

▶ Get the car washed. You'll see the flick better, and if you've got pals piled into your mobile unit, you want to make it nice.

▶ Are your seats removable? If so, take them out and throw in some soft pillows and blankets for maximum coziness.

▶ Get there early and grab a good spot. As the saying goes, don't be *behind* the minivan, be *in* the minivan.

3 Deliverables

While smoking cannabis is not everyone's preferred intake system, we recommend a pipe or a travel-sized bong for this activity. Allow the delicious Forbidden Candy, a strain known for its euphoric effects, to flow through your car and create a hotbox of happiness. This would be a good time for your sober driver to investigate more snacks.

4 **Edibles (the other kind)**

The right food is vital for this magical environment you've created. Be a baller and create a snack tray for every person in your crew by doing a little recon and preparing each tray to each person's desires—Reese's Pieces for some, Skittles for others. But everyone should indulge in some truffle popcorn and Junior Mints. The truffle oil and chocolate found in these two concessions contain anandamide, the mood-enhancing bliss hormone. And you can't be in too good of a mood, can you?

5 **Postgame**

Hop to a late-night donut shop. That one spot in your town that's open late will greet you like the heroes you are.

WHAT TO EAT TO ENHANCE YOUR HIGH

- Mangoes contain myrcene terpenes, which will hitch a ride on the terpenes already in your system to make your high stronger and longer.
- Nuts are high in Omega-3 fatty acids, which bind to cannabinoids and help the THC move through the blood brain barrier faster. Especially helpful with those sometimes slow-to-set-in edibles.
- Broccoli contains high levels of the terpene beta-caryophyllene, which has been shown to help relieve anxiety, a sometimes side effect of high THC strains.

- The low-level alcohol content in beer will keep you on your feet while still widening your blood vessels, which causes THC to be absorbed faster.

#75: THE FAB FIVE

Cannabis stimulates the hunger hormone, *ghrelin*, alerting you that it's time to eat (and occasionally leading to a night arm deep in the potato chips). But it also encourages our friend THC to bind to the receptors in our brain's olfactory bulbs, making food just taste better. That's why even the Honey Nut Cheerio dust you managed to funnel into your mouth tastes like the nectar of the gods. We're sure you have your fave stoner snacks (see "Munchie Madness" on page 242 to see how your tastes line up with other cannabis connoisseurs), but why not take advantage of your uninhibited high self and explore something new? Since cannabis lowers your inhibitions and self-censorship, you may find yourself more open to that anchovy pizza.

We're betting you don't normally try to balance all five basic tastes when you're feeling munchie, which is why we've included an activity suggesting you really should. The five basic tastes—sweet, bitter, sour, salty, and umami—result from a chemical reaction that occurs when food interacts with your taste receptors, those 10,000 taste buds that line your tongue. Taste buds are sensory organs and cannabis is the queen (remember, all the best buds are female) of sensory amplification, so it makes sense that eating feels particularly orgasmic when high, providing a perfect opportunity to explore taste profiles you might not ordinarily choose.

Here you'll find our suggested tasting menu. We recommend picking one from each column and giving yourself permission to be deliciously decadent.

The Fab Five

SWEET	BITTER	SOUR	SALTY	UMAMI
Cinnamon Toast Crunch Cereal	80% Cacao Dark Chocolate	Kosher Dill Pickles	Loaded Nachos	Truffle Fries
Strawberries and Whipped Cream	Peanut Butter and Marmalade Sandwich	Warheads Extreme Sour Candy	Bake and Serve Dinner Rolls with Salted Butter	Straight up Parmesan
Ben & Jerry's Half Baked Ice Cream	Candied Lemon Peel	Hot Dog with Sauerkraut	Mozzarella Sticks	Ramen (with MSG)
Haribo Star Mix (all the gummies!)	Pulparindo Tamarind Candy	Salt and Vinegar Potato Chips	Chinese Takeout	Shrimp Chips
Trader Joe's Chocolate Babka	Matcha Horchata	Marie Callender's Frozen Key Lime Pie	Pizza (duh)	Black Olives (eaten off fingertips)

MUNCHIE MADNESS!

We've taken one for the team and tallied the results

CONFERENCE: **SWEET**   DIVISION: **CHOCOLATE**

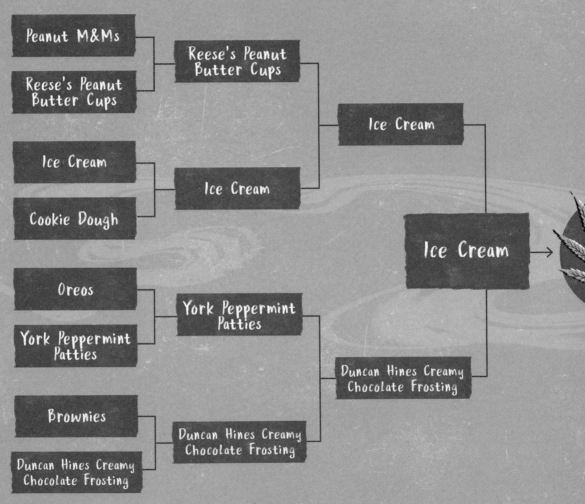

Peanut M&Ms

Reese's Peanut Butter Cups

Reese's Peanut Butter Cups

Ice Cream

Cookie Dough

Ice Cream

Ice Cream

Ice Cream

Oreos

York Peppermint Patties

York Peppermint Patties

Duncan Hines Creamy Chocolate Frosting

Brownies

Duncan Hines Creamy Chocolate Frosting

Duncan Hines Creamy Chocolate Frosting

CONFERENCE: **SWEET** DIVISION: **NOT CHOCOLATE**

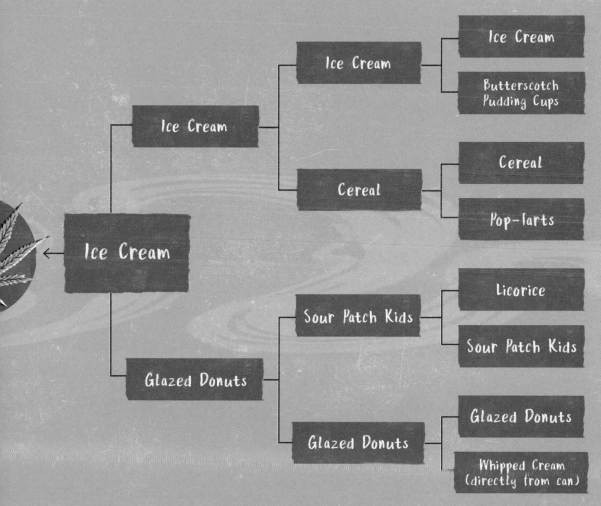

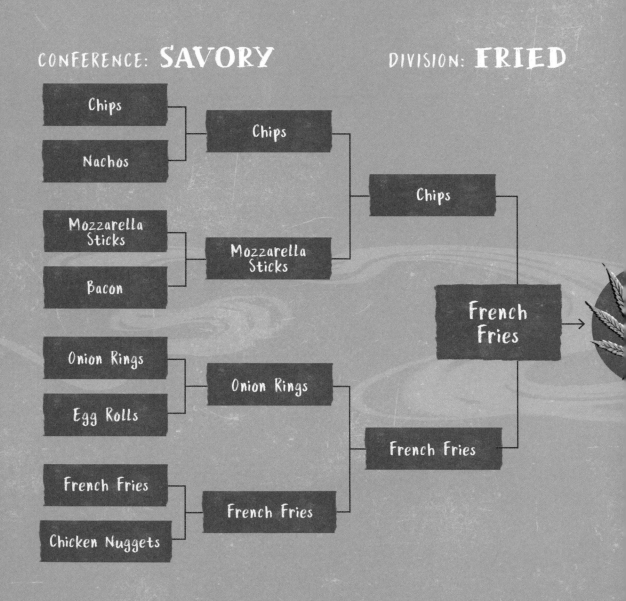

CONFERENCE: **SAVORY**   DIVISION: **FRIED**

Chips

Nachos

Chips

Mozzarella
Sticks

Bacon

Mozzarella
Sticks

Chips

Onion Rings

Egg Rolls

Onion Rings

French
Fries

French Fries

Chicken Nuggets

French Fries

French Fries

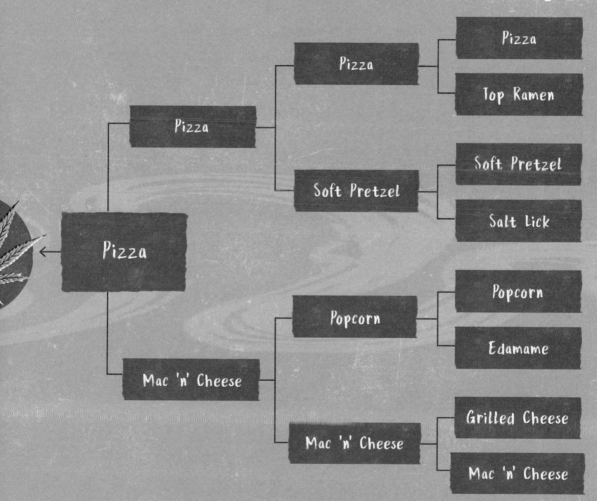

FINAL MATCH

FIRST PLACE WINNER*

Ice Cream

French Fries

Ice Cream → **??** ← French Fries

Ice Cream

Pizza

* WE HAVE A LOT OF ANSWERS, BUT THIS ONE IS PERSONAL.

Download our blank bracket form and create your own Munchie Madness challenge at joyofcannabis.org—it's the ultimate high party game.

ACKNOWLEDGMENTS

Two authors who love their topic are a great start to a book about cannabis, but we're not blowing smoke when we say we couldn't have done it without the inspiration and support of the following people, places, and things.

Thanks to team *Joy of Cannabis*: our amazing editor Erin McClary and the incredible crew at Sourcebooks including Sarah Otterness, Brittney Mmutle, Liz Kelsch, and the dynamic design and illustration team of Jillian Rahn and Camila Gray. Thank you to our indispensable and unflappable intern Aashna Avachat and to our agent and dear friend Laura Mazer, who just makes everything better.

Thanks to the many others who shared their expertise and lent support:

Elan Rae, Stacy Horne, Jake Wall, David & Daniel Sax, Anthony Giglio, Bret Kravitz, Beth Lorey, Amy & Rob Ahlers, Tara Stiles, Harrison Wise, Glenn & Sarah Abrams, Grant Faulkner, Cari Borja, Vikram Chandra, and Piper Kerman.

Thanks to the nourishing powers of: Radio Paradise, black licorice, and the fine kine strains of Red Congolese and Durban Poison.

And to the kids, Leela, Bean, and Lukas: your still-developing brains blow our minds each and every day. But until those brains are fully formed, we say: be cool, stay in school.

GLOSSARY

AMYGDALA: The almond-shaped core of the neural system that processes emotions, most notably fear. (Boo!)

ANANDAMIDE: An endocannabinoid named after the Sanskrit word for bliss, *ananda*. Anandamide closely resembles the cannabinoid THC and is best known for enhancing mood.

AUTOMATIC SEMANTIC PRIMING: A concept—kind of a heady one—that basically means that when you encounter one concept, it makes related concepts more accessible.

BASAL GANGLIA: An area of the brain that affects motor learning, executive function, and emotions.

CANNABIDIOL/CBD: Cannabidiol, or CBD, is the second most abundant cannabinoid found in cannabis. It's nonpsychoactive and has been shown to be useful in relieving stress and promoting sleep.

CANNABINOIDS: Chemical compounds found in cannabis and also produced by the human body. Both endocannabinoids (produced within the body) and phytocannbinoids (produced in cannabis) interact with the endocannabinoid system with a range of effects.

CANNABINOID RECEPTOR 1/CB1: Receptors in the endocannabinoid system, which bind with endocannabinoids and phytocannabinoids. These receptors are most abundant in the brain and are the lock to THC's key.

CANNABINOID RECEPTOR 2/CB2: Receptors in the endocannabinoid system, which bind with endocannabinoids and phytocannabinoids. These receptors are found mostly in the immune system.

CANNABINOL/CBN: The cannabinoid created when THC ages. Researchers are looking at ways it acts as an antibiotic, neuroprotectant, and anti-inflammatory. But like CBD, it won't get you high.

DAB: A powerful concentrate of THC that can have up to 80 to 90 percent THC. Proceed with caution.

DECARBOXYLATION: The process of activating the cannabinoids in your cannabis via high, fast heat (smoking and vaporizing it) or low, slow heat (baking or cooking it). THC must be decarboxylated to make it psychoactive.

DIOECIOUS: Plants that are either male or female.

DISPENSARIES: A place that sells or "dispenses" cannabis.

DOPAMINE: A neurotransmitter that is partially responsible for our ability to feel pleasure. Cannabis boosts dopamine, but not as much as previously thought.

DORSOLATERAL PREFRONTAL CORTEX: An area in the prefrontal cortex of the brain that controls executive function, including working memory and abstract reasoning.

DUTCHIE: A cannabis blunt rolled inside a Dutch Master's cigar and inspiration for the iconic cannabis party rule, "Pass the dutchie on the left-hand side."

EDIBLE: A food product that contains cannabis. Edibles can include candy, chocolate, cooking oils, and baked goods. In other words: don't leave your edibles unmarked!

ENDOCANNABINOID SYSTEM: A biological system made up of three core components—endocannabinoids, receptors, and enzymes. The ECS helps keep our bodies in a state of homeostasis, or balance. The ECS receptors also react with phytocannabinoids to get us high and happy.

ENDOCANNABINOIDS: Neurotransmitters, or chemical messengers, that occur naturally in the body and bind to endocannabinoid receptors to help the body run smoothly.

ENTHEOGEN: A psychoactive substance, often derived from plants, that is ingested to create an altered state of consciousness for religious or spiritual purposes.

GHRELIN: The "hunger hormone," or hormone in the gastrointestinal tract that increases appetite and is stimulated when you consume cannabis.

HEMP: The term used to signify cannabis that contains 0.3 percent or less THC content. Hemp can be imbibed if you're in the mood for a very (very) mellow high, but it's mostly known for being a plant material used to make paper, rope, and clothing.

HOTBOX: Smoking in an enclosed space so that the smoke from your cannabis goes into your lungs and enhances your overall experience. We're not saying you should try this at a drive-in movie, but should you want to, motor on over to "Drive-In: The Platinum Experience" (page 237).

HYPOTHALAMUS: The small region of the brain that releases hormones and helps keep your body in homeostasis, or balance.

INDICA: A stout, broad-leaf variety of cannabis, anecdotally thought to produce a relaxing full body high. Studies now reveal that effects come from the chemical profile of a strain, not whether it's an indica or sativa.

KIEF: An accumulation of trichomes, or resin glands, sifted from cannabis's flowers. It's the most potent part of the cannabis plant with the highest amount of THC.

KINE: Extra potent, premium-grade cannabis (e.g., "Can't wait to go over to Sally's for movie night; you know she's got that kine bud.").

MICRODOSE: A small amount of cannabis, typically 5 milligrams or less, in the form of an edible or tincture, often used to increase focus and flow and reduce pain and anxiety with minimized psychoactive effects. In other words: it's safe for work.

MIRROR NEURONS: Neurons that fire when you see someone act a certain way (laugh, yawn, smile). They can help with understanding and empathy.

NEUROTRANSMITTER: A chemical messenger that binds to receptors and sends signals from a neuron to other cells in the body.

NUCLEUS ACCUMBENS: A region of the brain that is in charge of pleasure and reward behavior. It releases dopamine when activated.

OXYTOCIN: A neurotransmitter, often called the "love hormone." Oxytocin triggers the release of the endocannabinoid anandamide, THC's doppelganger.

PHYTOCANNABINOIDS: Cannabinoids that are produced naturally in cannabis plants.

PREFRONTAL CORTEX: The region that covers the front part of the brain's frontal lobe and is involved in decision-making and cognitive behavior.

PSYCHOACTIVE: Any substance that affects the mind and nervous system and alters mood, perception, and behavior (i.e., cannabis).

PSYCHOTROPIC: Any drug that affects behavior, mood, thoughts, or perception. Cannabis is a psychotropic drug.

RESIN: The sticky part of the cannabis plant produced by the plant's trichomes. Resin can be turned into hash, rosin, etc. and is high in THC.

SATIVA: A tall, narrow-leaf variety of cannabis, anecdotally thought to produce an energizing and uplifting cerebral high. Studies now reveal that effects come from the chemical profile of a strain, not whether it's an indica or sativa.

SEROTONIN: A neurotransmitter that plays a role in mood, happiness, and well-being. Cannabis boosts serotonin, but not as much as previously thought.

SHAKE: Leftovers from loose cannabis that can be used in edibles and extracts (e.g., "Dude, don't toss that shake. I'm making dinner later!").

SINSEMILLA: Spanish for "without seeds." Fun fact: seedless cannabis is more potent than cannabis with seeds.

STRAIN: A particular variety, or breed, of cannabis.

TERPENES: Aromatic oils that give cannabis (and other plants) its specific smell and taste. See page 12 for a guide to the most prevalent terpenes.

TETRAHYDROCANNABINOL/THC: The main psychoactive cannabinoid in cannabis. Or...the thing that gets you high.

TINCTURE: A concentrated herbal extract that can include cannabinoids such as CBD and THC.

TRICHOMES: The tiny resinous hairs on the cannabis flower that produce the cannabinoids and terpenes. Trichomes are the reason everyone wants dank "sticky" bud.

VASODILATOR: A substance, such as THC, that widens blood vessels and increases blood flow in your body.

INDEX

BIBLIOGRAPHY

TOOLKIT

Appendino, Giovanni, Simon Gibbons, Anna Giana, Alberto Pagani, Gianpaolo Grassi, Michael Stavri, Eileen Smith, and M. Mukhlesur Rahman. "Antibacterial Cannabinoids from Cannabis sativa: A Structure-Activity Study." *Journal of Natural Products* 71, no. 8 (August 2008): 1427–30. https://doi.org/10.1021/np8002673.

Bergamaschi, Mateus M. et al. "Cannabidiol Reduces the Anxiety Induced by Simulate Public Speaking in Treatment-Naïve Social Phobia Patients." *Neuropsychopharmacology: official publication of the American College of Neuropsychopharmacology* 36, no. 6 (2011): 1219–26. https://doi.org/10.1038/npp.2011.6.

DeAngelo, Steve (founder of Harborside Health Center, author, *The Cannabis Manifesto: A New Paradigm for Wellness*). In discussion with the authors, February, 2021.

El-Talatini, Mona R., Anthony H. Taylor, and Justin C. Konje. "Fluctuation in Anandamide Levels from Ovulation to Early Pregnancy in In-Vitro Fertilization-Embryo Transfer

Women, and Its Hormonal Regulation." *Human Reproduction* 24, no. 8 (August 2009): 1989–98. https://doi.org/10.1093/humrep/dep065.

Huestis, M. A., D. A. Gorelick, S. J. Heishman, K. L. Preston, R. A. Nelson, E. T. Moolchan, and R. A. Frank. "Blockade of Effects of Smoked Marijuana by the CB1-Selective Cannabinoid Receptor Antagonist SR141716." *Archives of General Psychiatry* 58, no. 4 (April 2001): 322–28. https://doi.org/10.1001/archpsyc.58.4.322.

Kuhathasan, Nirushi, Alexander Dufort, James MacKillop, Raymond Gottschalk, Luciano Minuzzi, and Benicio N Frey. "The Use of Cannabinoids for Sleep: A Critical Review on Clinical Trials." *Exp Clin Psychopharmacol* 27, no. 4 (August 2019): 383–401. https://doi.org/10.1037/pha0000285.

Lam, Mimi (cofounder of the Canada-based dispensary group Superette). In discussion with the authors, January 2021.

Lee, Martin A. "Endocannabinoid Discovery Timeline." *Project CBD*, July 1, 2020. https://www.projectcbd.org/science/endocannabinoid-discovery-timeline.

Lord, Debbie. "What Does '420' Mean? Here Are 10 things You May Not Know about the Term." Boston 25 News, April 20, 2018. https://www.boston25news.com/news/trending-now/what-does-420-mean-here-are-10-things-you-may-not-know-about-the-term/514204460/.

McPartland, John. "Cannabis sativa and Cannabis indica versus 'Sativa' and 'Indica.'" *Botany and Biotechnology*, edited by Suman Chandra, Hemant Lata, and Mahmoud A. ElSohly, 101–21. Cham, Switzerland: Springer, 2017.

Richtel, Matt. "This Drug Gets You High, and Is Legal (Maybe) Across the Country." *New York*

Times, February 27, 2021. https://www.nytimes.com/2021/02/27/health/marijuana-hemp-delta-8-thc.html.

Russo, Ethan B. "Taming THC: Potential Cannabis Synergy and Phytocannabinoid-Terpenoid Entourage Effects." *British Journal of Pharmacology* 163, no. 7 (2011): 1344–64. https://doi.org/10.1111/j.1476-5381.2011.01238.x.

Silote, Gabriela Pandini, Ariandra Sartim, Amanda Sales, Amanda Eskelund, F. S. Guimarães, Gregers Wegener, and Samia Joca. "Emerging Evidence for the Antidepressant Effect of Cannabidiol and the Underlying Molecular Mechanisms." *Journal of Chemical Neuroanatomy* 98 (2019): 104–16. https://doi.org/10.1016/j.jchemneu.2019.04.006.

"Snoop Dogg Reveals ONLY Person to Out-Smoke Him." *Jimmy Kimmel Live.* April 10, 2018. YouTube video, 3:34. https://www.youtube.com/watch?v=jcVTImeEGqs.

Weydt, Patrick, Soyon Hong, Anke Witting, Thomas Möller, Nephi Stella, and Michel Kliot. "Cannabinol Delays Symptom Onset in SOD1 (G93A) Transgenic Mice without Affecting Survival." *Amyotrophic Lateral Sclerosis* 6, no. 3 (September 2005): 182– 84. https://doi.org/10.1080/14660820510030149.

Zurier, Robert B., and Sumner H. Burstein. "Cannabinoids, Inflammation, and Fibrosis." *FASEB Journal: official publication of the Federation of American Societies for Experimental Biology* 30, no. 11 (2016): 3682-89. https://doi.org/10.1096/fj.201600646R.

BODY

Bhaskar, Swapna, D. Hemavathy, and Shankar Prasad. "Prevalence of Chronic Insomnia in Adult Patients and Its Correlation with Medical Comorbidities." *Journal of Family Medicine and Primary Care* 5, no. 4 (2016): 780–84. https://doi.org/10.4103/2249-4863.201153.

Boehnke, Kevin F., Evangelos Litinas, and Daniel J Clauw. "Medical Cannabis Use Is Associated With Decreased Opiate Medication Use in a Retrospective Cross-Sectional Survey of Patients With Chronic Pain." *The Journal of Pain* 17, no. 6 (June 2016): 739–44. https://doi.org/10.1016/j.jpain.2016.03.002.

Chevalier, Gaétan, Stephen T Sinatra, James L Oschman, Karol Sokal, and Pawel Sokal. "Earthing: Health Implications of Reconnecting the Human Body to the Earth's Surface Electrons." *Journal of Environmental and Public Health* 2012 (January 2012): 291541. https://doi.org/10.1155/2012/291541.

Hansen, Margaret M., Reo Jones, and Kirsten Tocchini. "Shinrin-Yoku (Forest Bathing) and Nature Therapy: A State-of-the-Art Review." *International Journal of Environmental Research and Public Health* 14, no. 8 (August 2017): 851. https://doi.org/10.3390/ijerph14080851.

Muguruza, Carolina, et al. "The Motivation for Exercise over Palatable Food Is Dictated by Cannabinoid Type 1 Receptors." *JCI Insight* 4, no. 5 (March 2019): e126190. https://doi.org/10.1172/jci.insight.126190.

Munson, A. E., L. S. Harris, M. A. Friedman, W. L. Dewey, and R. A. Carchman. "Antineoplastic Activity of Cannabinoids." *Journal of the National Cancer Institute* 55, no. 3 (1975): 597–602. https://doi.org/10.1093/jnci/55.3.597.

Nguyen, Tien. "Working Out with Weed." *Nature* 572, no. 7771 (August 2019): S14–S15. https://doi.org/10.1038/d41586-019-02529-0.

Ross, Michele (neuroscientist, author of *Vitamin Weed*). In discussion with the authors, January, 2021.

Schmader, David. *Weed: The User's Guide: A 21st Century Handbook for Enjoying Marijuana.* Seattle: Sasquatch Books, 2016.

Singh, Gopal K., Mohammad Siahpush, Robert A. Hiatt, and Lava R. Timsina. "Dramatic Increases in Obesity and Overweight Prevalence and Body Mass Index Among Ethnic-Immigrant and Social Class Groups in the United States, 1976–2008." *Journal of Community Health* 163, no. 7 (2011): 94–110. https://www.ncbi.nlm.nih.gov/pmc/articles/PMC3020302/.

Tesfatsion, Master. "The World's Best Athletes Smoke Weed. Here's Proof. What Now?" *Bleacher Report*, April 20, 2018. https://bleacherreport.com/articles/2771410-the-worlds-best-athletes-smoke-weed-heres-proof-what-now.

MIND

Ahlers, Rob (drummer for Fifty Foot Wave and the Kristin Hersh Trio). In discussion with the authors, October 2020.

Andras Bilkei-Gorzo, et al., "A chronic low dose of Δ9-tetrahydrocannabinol (THC) restores cognitive function in old mice," *Nature Medicine* 23, no. 6 (2017): 782–87. https://doi.org/10.1038/nm.4311.

Beres, Derek (author, *Hero's Dose: The Case for Psychedelics in Ritual and Therapy*). In discussion with the authors, October 2020.

Christensen, Kelley. "Meditation Could Help Anxiety and Cardiovascular Health." *Michigan Tech*, April 18, 2018. https://www.mtu.edu/news/2018/04/meditation-could-help-anxiety-and-cardiovascular-health.html.

Crippa, José Alexandre, Antonio Waldo Zuardi, Rocio Martín-Santos, Sagnik Bhattacharyya,

Zerrin Atakan, Philip McGuire, and Paolo Fusar-Poli. "Cannabis and Anxiety: A Critical Review of the Evidence." *Human Psychopharmacology* 24, no. 7 (2009): 515–23. https://doi.org/10.1002/hup.1048.

Dincheva, I., et al. "FAAH genetic variation enhances fronto-amygdala function in mouse and human," *Nature Communications* 6 no. 6395 (2015).

Fachner, Jörg (professor of music, health, and the brain at the Cambridge Institute for Music Therapy Research). In conversation with the authors, December 2020.

Grinspoon, Lester. *Marihuana Reconsidered*. Cambridge, MA: Harvard University Press, 1971.

Hennings, Trevor. "How to Tell the Sex of a Marijuana Plant." Leafly. November 23, 2020. https://www.leafly.ca/news/growing/sexing-marijuana-plants?__hstc=9292970.65337744294b740e0787aea508c4a702.1559952000324.1559952000325.1559952000326.1&__hssc=9292970.1.1559952000327&__hsfp=3316667249.&jwsource=cl

Pollan, Michael. *The Botany of Desire: A Plant's Eye View of the World*. New York: Random House, 2014.

Rinzler, Carol Ann. "How Anandamide in Chocolate Affects Your Mood." Dummies.com. Accessed October 1, 2021. https://www.dummies.com/health/nutrition/anandamide-chocolate-affects-mood/.

Russo E. B., A. Merzouki, J. Molero Mesa, K. A. Frey, and P. J. Bach. "Cannabis Improves Night Vision: A Case Study of Dark Adaptometry and Scotopic Sensitivity in Kif Smokers of the Rif Mountains of Northern Morocco." *Journal of Ethnopharmacology* 93, no. 1 (2004): 99–104. https://doi.org/10.1016/j.jep.2004.03.029.

"Science Behind Cannabis and Creativity." Pilgrim Soul, October 12, 2019. https://www.pilgrimsoul.com/home/cannabisandcreativty.

Sneider, Jennifer T., Harrison G. Pope Jr, Marisa M. Silveri, Norah S. Simpson, Staci A. Gruber, and Deborah A. Yurgelun-Todd. "Altered Regional Blood Volume in Chronic Cannabis Smokers." *Experimental and Clinical Psychopharmacology* 14, no. 4 (2006): 422–28. https://doi.org/10.1037/1064-1297.14.4.422.

Strohbeck-Kühner, Peter, Gisela Skopp, and Rainer Mattern. "Cannabis Improves Symptoms of ADHD." *Cannabinoids* 3, no. 1 (2008): 1–3. https://www.researchgate.net/pub lication/237392545_Cannabis_improves_symptoms_of_ADHD.

CONNECTION

Aron, Arthur, Edward Melinat, Elaine N. Aron, Robert Darrin Vallone, and Renee J. Bator. "The Experimental Generation of Interpersonal Closeness: A Procedure and Some Preliminary Findings." *Society for Personality and Social Psychology Bulletin* 23, no. 4 (April 1997): 363–77. https://doi.org/10.1177/0146167297234003.

Craft, Rebecca M., Julie A. Marusich, and Jenny L. Wiley. "Sex Differences in Cannabinoid Pharmacology: A Reflection of Differences in the Endocannabinoid System?" *Life Sciences* 92, no. 8–9 (2013): 476– 81. https://doi.org/10.1016/j.lfs.2012.06.009.

Cuttler, Carrie, Laurie K Mischley, and Michelle Sexton. "Sex Differences in Cannabis Use and Effects: A Cross-Sectional Survey of Cannabis Users." *Cannabis and Cannabinoid Research* 1, no. 1 (2016): 166–75. https://doi.org/10.1089/can.2016.0010.

Goldman, Bruce. "Regular Marijuana Use Linked to More Sex." *Stanford Medicine*, October 27, 2017. https://med.stanford.edu/news/all-news/2017/10/regular-marijuana-use-linked -to-more-sex.html.

Gorzalka, Boris B., Anna C. Morrish, and Matthew N. Hill. "Endocannabinoid Modulation of

Male Rat Sexual Behavior." *Psychopharmacology* 198, no. 4 (2008): 479– 86. https:// doi.org/10.1007/s00213-007-0901-1.

Gratzke, Christian, George J. Christ, Christian G. Stief, Karl-Erik Andersson, and Petter Hedlund. "Localization and Function of Cannabinoid Receptors in the Corpus Cavernosum: Basis for Modulation of Nitric Oxide Synthase Nerve Activity." *European Urology Sexual Medicine* 57, no. 2 (February 2010): 342–49. https://doi.org/10.1016/j .eururo.2008.12.024.

Jenkins, Clyde. "Marijuana and Gaming." CNBS, February 24, 2019. https://www.cnbs.org /cannabis-101/cannabis-and-gaming/.

"'Love Hormone' Helps Produce 'Bliss Molecules' to Boost Pleasure of Social Interactions." *Eureka Alert*, October 26, 2015. https://www.eurekalert.org/news-releases/685230.

"Leading Reasons for Joining the Cannabis Industry among Workers in the United States in 2017." Statista and New Frontier Data, November 2017. https://www.statista.com /statistics/795052/us-cannabis-industry-work-reasons/.

Lynn, Becky K., Julia D. Lopez, Collin Miller, Judy Thompson, and E. Cristian Campian. "The Relationship between Marijuana Use Prior to Sex and Sexual Function in Women." *Sexual Medicine* 7, no. 2 (2019): 192–97. https://doi.org/10.1016/j.esxm.2019.01.003.

Miller, Michael Craig. "In Praise of Gratitude." Harvard Health Publishing, November 21, 2012. https://www.health.harvard.edu/blog/in-praise-of-gratitude-201211215561.

Morningstar, Patricia J. "Thandai and Chilam: Traditional Hindu Beliefs about the Proper Uses of Cannabis." *Journal of Psychoactive Drugs* 17, no. 3 (1985): 141–65. https://doi.org/10.1 080/02791072.1985.10472336.

Mulvehill, Suzanne (doctoral student at the International Institute of Clinical Sexology). In discussion with the authors, December 2020.

"Oxytocin Enhances Pleasure of Social Interactions by Stimulating Production of 'Bliss Molecule.'" *Neuroscience News*, October 26, 2015. https://neurosciencenews.com /oxytocin-anandamide-2926/.

"Oxytocin Promotes Social Behavior in Infant Rhesus Monkeys." NIH, April 28, 2014. https://www.nih.gov/news-events/news-releases/oxytocin-promotes-social-behavior -infant-rhesus-monkeys.

Phillips, Becky. "Females More Sensitive to Cannabis; Males Get Munchies." *WSU Insider*, September 3, 2014. https://news.wsu.edu/press-release/2014/09/03/ females-more-sensitive-to-cannabis-males-get-munchies/.

Ständer, Sonja, Martin Schmelz, Dieter Metze, Thomas Luger, and Roman Rukwied. "Distribution of Cannabinoid Receptor 1 (CB1) and 2 (CB2) on Sensory Nerve Fibers and Adnexal Structures in Human Skin." *Journal of Dermatological Science* 38, no. 3 (2005): 177–88. https://doi.org/10.1016/j.jdermsci.2005.01.007.

"Study: Marijuana Use Is Rising Sharply Among Seniors Over 65." CBS Sacramento, February 24, 2020. https://sacramento.cbslocal.com/2020/02/24/senior-study-marijuana-use -sharply-rises/.

Sun, Andrew J., and Michael L. Eisenberg. "Association between Marijuana Use and Sexual Frequency in the United States: A Population-Based Study." *J Sex Med* 14, no. 11 (November 2017): 1342–47. https://doi.org/10.1016/j.jsxm.2017.09.005.

Urman, Diana (licensed clinical social worker and sex therapist). In discussion with the authors, December 2020.

Watts, Alan. "Hermits in New York," Awakin.org. Accessed October 1, 2021. https://www
.awakin.org/read/view.php?tid=264.

Wei, Don, DaYeon Lee, Conor D. Cox, Carley A. Karsten, Olga Peñagarikano, Daniel H.
Geschwind, Christine M. Gall, and Daniele Piomelli." Endocannabinoid Signaling
Mediates Oxytocin-Driven Social Reward." *PNAS* 112, no. 45 (November 2015): 14084–
89. https://doi.org/10.1073/pnas.1509795112.

"Why Cannabis Makes You Laugh & Top Strains for a Giggle Fit." Sensi Seeds, June 10, 2020. https://
sensiseeds.com/en/blog/why-cannabis-makes-you-laugh-top-strains-for-a-giggle-fit/.

PRODUCTIVITY

Barcott, Bruce, David Downs, and Ian Chant. "2020 Cannabis Jobs Report: Legal Cannabis
Now Supports 243,700 Full-Time American Jobs." Leafly, February 7, 2020. https://
www.leafly.ca/news/industry/243700-marijuana-jobs-how-many-in-america.

Campbell, Jeremy. "How to Microdose Marijuana." CannaMD, February 23, 2020. https://
www.cannamd.com/how-to-microdose-marijuana/.

Doblin, Rick (founder and executive director of Multidisciplinary Association for Psychedelic
Studies/MAPS). In discussion with the authors, November 2020.

Erstling, Troy G. "The Neurochemistry of Flow States." TroyErstling.com, July 16, 2019, https://
medium.com/@troyerstling/the-neurochemistry-of-flow-states-6bb27e7365f3.

Gottlieb, Scott. "Methylphenidate Works by Increasing Dopamine Levels," *BMJ* (*Clinical
research ed.*) 322, no. 7281 (2001): 259. https://doi.org/10.1136/bmj.322.7281.259.

Gruber, Staci A., Kelly A. Sagar, Mary K. Dahlgren, Megan T. Racine, Rosemary T. Smith, and
Scott E. Lukas. "Splendor in the Grass? A Pilot Study Assessing the Impact of Medical

Marijuana on Executive Function." *Frontiers in Pharmacology* 38, no. 3 (2016): 177–78. https://doi.org/10.3389/fphar.2016.00355.

"How Often Is Seth Rogen High In His Movies?" *The Late Show with Stephen Colbert*. April 30, 2019. YouTube video, 8:03. https://www.youtube.com/watch?v=sWx1r9hnMgg.

Iigaya, Kiyohito, Madalena S. Fonseca, Masayoshi Murakami, Zachary F. Mainen, and Peter Dayan. "An Effect of Serotonergic Stimulation on Learning Rates for Rewards Apparent after Long Intertrial Intervals." *Nature Communications* 9, no. 2477 (2018). https://doi.org/10.1038/s41467-018-04840-2.

Malkin, Bonnie. "Cannabis Discovered in Tobacco Pipes Found in William Shakespeare's Garden." *Telegraph*, August 9, 2015. https://www.telegraph.co.uk/culture/theatre/william-shakespeare/11792533/Cannabis-discovered-in-tobacco-pipes-found-in-William-Shakespeares-garden.html.

"Marijuana Is Safer Than Alcohol: It's Time to Treat It That Way." MPP. Accessed October 1, 2021. https://www.mpp.org/marijuana-is-safer/.

Mark, Gloria, Daniela Gudith, and Ulrich Klocke. "The Cost of Interrupted Work: More Speed and Stress." In *Proceedings of the SIGCHI Conference on Human Factors in Computing Systems*, 107–110. New York: Association for Computing Machinery, 2008. https://doi.org/10.1145/1357054.1357072.

Morgan, Celia J. A., Emily Rothwell, Helen Atkinson, Oliver Mason, and H. Valerie Curran. "Hyper-Priming in Cannabis Users: A Naturalistic Study of the Effects of Cannabis on Semantic Memory Function." *Psychiatry Res.* 176, no. 2–3 (2010): 213–18. https://doi.org/10.1016/j.psychres.2008.09.002.

Phan, K. Luan, Mike Angstadt, Jamie Golden, Ikechukwu Onyewuenyi, Ana Popovska, and

Harriet de Wit. "Cannabinoid Modulation of Amygdala Reactivity to Social Signals of Threat in Humans." *Journal of Neuroscience* 28, no. 10 (March 2008): 2313–19. https://doi.org/10.1523/JNEUROSCI.5603-07.2008.

Power, Mike. "Online Highs Are Old as the Net: The First E-Commerce Was a Drugs Deal." *Guardian*, April 19, 2013. https://www.theguardian.com/science/2013/apr/19/online-high-net-drugs-deal.

Ranganathan, Vinoth K., Vlodek Siemionow, Jing Z. Liu, Vinod Sahgal, and Guang H. Yue. "From Mental Power to Muscle Power—Gaining Strength by Using the Mind." *Neuropsychologia* 42, no. 7 (2004): 944–56. https://doi.org/10.1016/j.neuropsychologia.2003.11.018.

Taylor, Chris. "How Weed, Coffee, and Exercise Can Put Your Brain in Its Most Productive Place." Mashable, November 7, 2019. https://mashable.com/article/flow-marijuana-caffeine-workout.

CREATIVITY

Kaufman, Rachel. "Dreams Make You Smarter, More Creative, Studies Suggest." *National Geographic News*, August 16, 2010. https://www.nationalgeographic.com/science/article/100813-sleep-dreams-smarter-health-science-naps-napping-rem.

O'Leary, Daniel S., Robert I. Block, Julie A. Koeppel, Michael Flaum, Susan K. Schultz, Nancy C. Andreasen, Laura Boles Ponto, G. Leonard Watkins, Richard R. Hurtig, and Richard D. Hichwa. "Effects of Smoking Marijuana on Brain Perfusion and Cognition." *Neuropsychopharmacology: official publication of the American College*

of Neuropsychopharmacology 26, no. 6 (2002): 802–16. https://doi.org/10.1016/S0893
-133X(01)00425-0.

Ricketts, Andrew. "9 Activities to Socialize Your Smoke Sesh." *High Times*, April 10, 2018.
https://hightimes.com/culture/activities-socialize-smoke-sesh/8/.

Schafer, Gráinne, Amanda Feilding, Celia J. A. Morgan, Maria Agathangelou, Tom P. Freeman,
and H. Valerie Curran. "Investigating the Interaction between Schizotopy, Divergent
Thinking and Cannabis Use." *Consciousness and Cognition* 21, no. 1 (March 2012): 292–
98. https://doi.org/10.1016/j.concog.2011.11.009.

JOY

AKC Staff. "CBD Oil for Dogs: What You Need to Know." American Kennel Club, October 29,
2020. https://www.akc.org/expert-advice/health/cbd-oil-dogs/.

Beadle, Alexander. "The Link Between Cannabis and Anxiety Has Been Found, According to
New Study." Analytical Cannabis, January 14, 2020. https://www.analyticalcannabis
.com/articles/the-link-between-cannabis-and-anxiety-has-been-found-according-to
-new-study-312187.

Henriques, Julia. "Cannabis For Your Dog: How It Can Help." *Dogs Naturally Magazine*,
October 7, 2020. https://www.dogsnaturallymagazine.com/cannabis-dog-can-help/.

King, Jason. *The Cannabible Collection: The Cannabible 1/the Cannabible 2/the Cannabible 3.*
New York: Ten Speed Press, 2007.

Lau-Lavie, Amichai (rabbi and founder of Storahtelling and Lab/Shul). In discussion with the
authors, October 2020.

Marcus, David J., et al. "Endocannabinoid Signaling Collapse Mediates Stress-Induced

Amygdalo-Cortical Strengthening." *Neuron* 105, no. 6 (March 2020): 1062–76. https://doi.org/10.1016/j.neuron.2019.12.024.

McMahon, John. "In the Land of the Thunder Dragon, Only the Pigs Get High." *Mugglehead Magazine*, January 5, 2021. https://mugglehead.com/in-the-land-of-the-thunder-dragon-only-the-pigs-get-high/.

Pendry, Patricia, and Jaymie L. Vandagriff. "Animal Visitation Program (AVP) Reduces Cortisol Levels of University Students: A Randomized Controlled Trial." *AERA Open* (April 2019). https://doi.org/10.1177/2332858419852592.

Riggs, Patricia K., Florin Vaida, Steven S. Rossi, Linda S. Sorkin, Ben Gouaux, Igor Grant, and Ronald J. Ellis. "A Pilot Study of the Effects of Cannabis on Appetite Hormones in HIV-Infected Adult Men." *Brain Research* 1431, (2012): 46–52. https://doi.org/10.1016/j.brainres.2011.11.001.

Svalbard Global Seed Vault, Nordic Genetic Resource Centre.

"2017 National Survey on Drug Use and Health: Detailed Tables." Substance Abuse and Mental Health Services Administration Center for Behavioral Health Statistics and Quality, September 7, 2018. https://www.samhsa.gov/data/sites/default/files/cbhsq-reports/NSDUHDetailedTabs2017/NSDUHDetailedTabs2017.pdf.

Watson, Josephine E., Justin S. Kim, and Aditi Das. "Class of Omega-3 Fatty Acid Endocannabinoids & Their Derivatives." *Prostaglandins & Other Lipid Mediators* 143, (2019): 106337. https://doi.org/10.1016/j.prostaglandins.2019.106337.

ABOUT THE AUTHORS

MELANIE ABRAMS is the author of the novels *Playing* and *Meadowlark*. She is a developmental editor and photographer and teaches writing at the University of California, Berkeley.

LARRY SMITH is a journalist and storytelling evangelist touted by *O: The Oprah Magazine* as "on a quest to spark the creativity in everyone." He is the founder of the Six-Word Memoir Project and book series, editor of the book *The Moment: Wild, Poignant, Life-Changing Stories from 125 Writers and Artists Famous and Obscure*, and speaks on storytelling in schools and at companies and conferences.

A LOOK AT NATURE'S CYCLES

THE NITROGEN CYCLE

BY SANTANA HUNT

Gareth Stevens
PUBLISHING

CRASHCOURSE

Please visit our website, www.garethstevens.com. For a free color catalog of all our high-quality books, call toll free 1-800-542-2595 or fax 1-877-542-2596.

Library of Congress Cataloging-in-Publication Data

Names: Hunt, Santana, author.
Title: The nitrogen cycle / Santana Hunt.
Description: New York : Gareth Stevens Publishing, [2020] | Series: A look at nature's cycles | Includes bibliographical references and index.
Identifiers: LCCN 2018047676| ISBN 9781538241141 (pbk.) | ISBN 9781538241165 (library bound) | ISBN 9781538241158 (6 pack)
Subjects: LCSH: Nitrogen cycle--Juvenile literature. | Biogeochemical cycles--Juvenile literature.
Classification: LCC QH344 .H86 2020 | DDC 577.145--dc23
LC record available at https://lccn.loc.gov/2018047676

First Edition

Published in 2020 by
Gareth Stevens Publishing
111 East 14th Street, Suite 349
New York, NY 10003

Designer: Sarah Liddell
Editor: Kristen Nelson

Photo credits: Cover, p. 1 (main) Wesley West/Shutterstock.com; cover, p. 1 (inset) Zarem/Shutterstock.com; arrow background used throughout Inka1/Shutterstock.com; p. 5 irin-k/Shutterstock.com; p. 7 Lester V. Bergman/Corbis NX/Getty Images; p. 9 John D Sirlin/Shutterstock.com; p. 11 Worachat Tokaew/Shutterstock.com; p. 13 Manbetta/Shutterstock.com; p. 15 Photoholgic/Shutterstock.com; p. 17 Oriol Domingo/Shutterstock.com; p. 19 Gabor Havasi/Shutterstock.com; p. 21 Education Images/Contributor/Universal Images Group/Getty Images; p. 23 MP_P/Shutterstock.com; p. 25 Matt Champlin/Moment/Getty Images; p. 27 Olha1981/Shutterstock.com; p. 29 Tatiana Grozetskaya/Shutterstock.com; p. 30 Designua/Shutterstock.com.

Printed in the United States of America

CPSIA compliance information: Batch #CS19GS: For further information contact Gareth Stevens, New York, New York at 1-800-542-2595.

CONTENTS

Words in the glossary appear in **bold** type the first time they are used in the text.

MEET NITROGEN

Nitrogen (N_2) is an element found in different forms in many places on Earth. It's in water and soil. It's part of **organisms**' bodies. It's also 78 percent of Earth's **atmosphere**! Nitrogen's movement through its different forms is called the nitrogen cycle.

MAKE THE GRADE

The rest of Earth's atmosphere is made up of the gases oxygen (21 percent), argon (0.9 percent), and 0.1 percent of others, including carbon dioxide, helium, and methane.

The nitrogen cycle is important for life on Earth to continue. However, plants and animals, including humans, can't use the nitrogen found in the atmosphere! They need bacteria to **convert** nitrogen from the atmosphere into a form of nitrogen they can use.

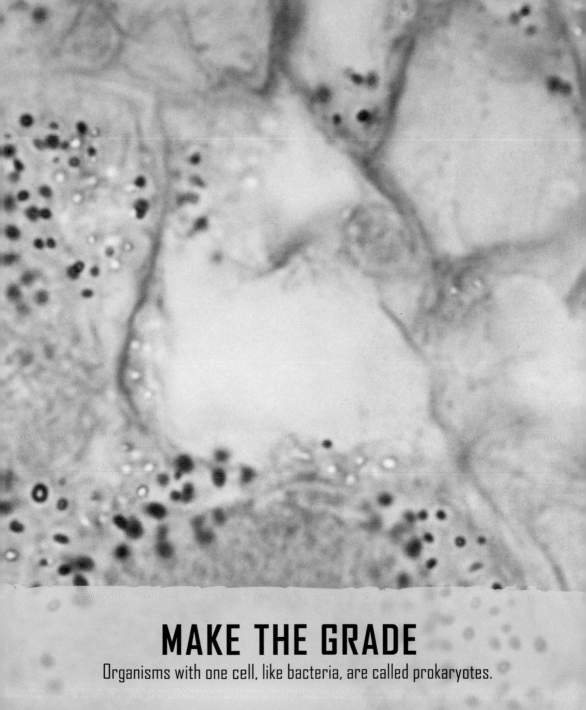

MAKE THE GRADE

Organisms with one cell, like bacteria, are called prokaryotes.

7

NITROGEN FIXATION

Certain kinds of bacteria and other prokaryotes take in nitrogen gas from the atmosphere. They convert it to ammonia, which is a **molecule** including nitrogen and hydrogen (NH_3). This part of the cycle is called nitrogen fixation.

MAKE THE GRADE

Most nitrogen fixation takes place in the soil. A small percentage occurs when lightning strikes!

AMMONIA (NH₃) MOLECULE

Plants can take in ammonia from the soil. But, some nitrogen fixation takes place inside plants' roots! Bacteria live in the root hairs of these plants, grow in number, and form root **nodules**. They convert nitrogen to forms the plant can use inside the nodules!

MAKE THE GRADE

The bacteria and the plants they live in are symbiotic. Symbiosis is a relationship between different kinds of organisms in which they each gain something.

11

NITRIFICATION

Bacteria in the soil also convert nitrogen gas to nitrates. First, the nitrogen is converted to ammonia. Then, ammonia is converted to nitrites. Finally, the nitrites become nitrates. Nitrates are another form of nitrogen plants can take in and use. This **process** is called nitrification.

MAKE THE GRADE
The bacteria and the plants they live in are symbiotic. Symbiosis is a relationship between different kinds of organisms in which they each gain something.

NITRIFICATION

Bacteria in the soil also convert nitrogen gas to nitrates. First, the nitrogen is converted to ammonia. Then, ammonia is converted to nitrites. Finally, the nitrites become nitrates. Nitrates are another form of nitrogen plants can take in and use. This **process** is called nitrification.

MAKE THE GRADE

Fungi can also carry out nitrification, but they're slower at it!

NITRITE (NO₂)

NITRATE (NO₃)

N = NITROGEN

O = OXYGEN

In denitrification, other bacteria convert nitrates in the soil to nitrogen gas. Denitrification is important because without it, nitrates from the soil would **dissolve** in Earth's oceans. Nitrogen would collect there. Nitrogen needs to be moving through its cycle!

MAKE THE GRADE

The steps of the nitrogen cycle aren't in a set order! Parts of it can happen at any time.

15

ASSIMILATION

All plants take in some form of nitrogen to live and grow. When animals eat these plants, nitrogen is passed on to them. Whenever a plant or animal takes in nitrogen and it becomes part of their **tissue**, it's called assimilation.

MAKE THE GRADE

Nitrogen naturally moves through the food chain of an
area, from animals that eat plants to the animals that eat those
animals! Nitrogen may also leave animal bodies as waste.

AMMONIFICATION

Another step in the nitrogen cycle happens when plants and animals decompose, or break down. During one part of this breakdown, ammonia is given off. This is called ammonification. This ammonia may stay in the soil and be used again by other living things.

MAKE THE GRADE

Ammonia from ammonification may also be converted into nitrogen gas.

MORE NITROGEN

In the ocean, some remains of living things fall to the ocean floor where they're **compressed**. Over time, they become rock. **Uplift** causes this rock to face weathering, which releases nitrogen from within the rock.

MAKE THE GRADE

Weathering is the wearing down of rocks by wind, water, and weather. This can occur when pieces of rock break away and move to land.

CYCLE LIMITS

In many places, parts of the nitrogen cycle are limited by the amount of nitrogen in the **environment**. Nitrogen is then considered the limiting **nutrient**, which means it's the least available needed nutrient. This limits how much plants and living things can grow.

MAKE THE GRADE

Adding more of limiting nutrients like nitrogen to an environment often causes growth to occur.

23

HUMAN EFFECTS

Because nitrogen is often a limiting nutrient, it's often part of fertilizer, or matter added to gardens and crops to help them grow. This is just one way that human activities are upsetting the natural nitrogen cycle.

MAKE THE GRADE

Runoff is the water that flows over land into bodies of water.
Fertilizer runoff causes too much nitrogen to get into some bodies of
water and plantlike organisms called algae can grow too plentifully.

Burning fossil fuels, like coal and gas, also sends more nitrogen into the atmosphere. Scientists believe too much nitrogen in the atmosphere can cause problems. It likely plays a part in acid rain, or rain that has harmful matter in it.

MAKE THE GRADE

Fossil fuels are matter that formed from ancient remains of plants and animals. They're burned for power. No wonder they give off nitrogen!

ACID RAIN HARMS THE ENVIRONMENT.

HUMANS AND INDUSTRIES BURN FOSSIL FUELS.

Increased forms of nitrogen in the atmosphere can also add to the greenhouse effect. This is the warming of Earth over time due to human activities, such as air pollution. Not only that, it changes the natural nitrogen cycle, too!

MAKE THE GRADE

The outcome of the greenhouse effect is often called global climate change or global warming.

THE NITROGEN CYCLE

NITROGEN GAS (N_2) IS
FOUND IN THE ATMOSPHERE.

BACTERIA CHANGE THIS
NITROGEN BACK TO N_2.

BACTERIA IN THE SOIL AND PLANT
ROOTS FIX N_2 INTO AMMONIA AND
NITRATES THAT PLANTS CAN USE.

PLANTS AND ANIMALS DECOMPOSE,
AND ANIMALS CREATE WASTE THAT
RETURN NITROGEN TO THE SOIL.

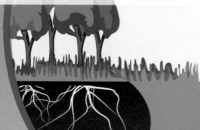

ANIMALS EAT THE PLANTS,
TAKING IN NITROGEN.

GLOSSARY

atmosphere: the mixture of gases that surround a planet

compressed: pressed or squeezed together

convert: to change into a different form

dissolve: to mix completely into a liquid

environment: the conditions that surround a living thing and affect the way it lives

fungus: a living thing that is somewhat like a plant, but doesn't make its own food, have leaves, or have a green color. Fungi include molds and mushrooms.

molecule: a group of atoms that are bonded, or connected, to one another

nodule: a small lump on the root of a plant

nutrient: something a living thing needs to grow and stay alive

organism: a living thing

process: a series of steps or actions taken to complete something

tissue: the matter that forms the parts in a plant or animal

uplift: the rising of a part of Earth's surface due to natural causes

FOR MORE INFORMATION

BOOKS

Evans, Tom. *Natural Cycles and Climate Change*. Chicago, IL: World Book, 2016.

Martin, Bobi. *The Nitrogen Cycle*. New York, NY: Britannica Educational Publishing in association with Rosen Educational Services, 2018.

WEBSITES

Cycles of the Earth System
eo.ucar.edu/kids/green/cycles1.htm
Check out simple explanations of many of Earth's cycles here.

The Nitrogen Cycle
kidsgeo.com/geography-for-kids/the-nitrogen-cycle/
Review the nitrogen cycle and other natural cycles on this website.

Publisher's note to educators and parents: Our editors have carefully reviewed this website to ensure that it is suitable for students. Many websites change frequently, however, and we cannot guarantee that a site's future contents will continue to meet our high standards of quality and educational value. Be advised that students should be closely supervised whenever they access the internet.

INDEX